T0384068

Flow Manufacturing – What Went Right, What Went Wrong

101 Mini-Case Studies that Reveal Lean's Successes and Failures

Flow Manufacturing – What Went Right, What Went Wrong

101 Mini-Case Studies that Reveal Lean's Successes and Failures

By

Richard J. Schonberger

A PRODUCTIVITY PRESS BOOK

Routledge/Productivity Press
711 Third Avenue New York, NY 10017, USA
2 Park Square, Milton Park, Abingdon, Oxon OX14 4RN, UK

© 2019 by Richard J. Schonberger
Routledge/Productivity Press is an imprint of Taylor & Francis Group, an Informa business

No claim to original U.S. Government works

Printed on acid-free paper

International Standard Book Number-13: 978-1-138-36229-1 (Hardback)
International Standard Book Number-13: 978-0-429-43217-0 (eBook)

Library of Congress Cataloging-in-Publication Data

Names: Schonberger, Richard, author.
Title: Continuous-flow manufacturing--what went right, what went wrong : 101 mini-case studies that reveal lean's successes and failures / Richard J. Schonberger.
Description: Boca Raton : Taylor & Francis, Routledge, 2019. | Includes bibliographical references and index.
Identifiers: LCCN 2018032754 (print) | LCCN 2018036990 (ebook) | ISBN 9780429432170 (e-Book) | ISBN 9781138362291 (hardback : alk. paper)
Subjects: LCSH: Just-in-time systems--Case studies. | Lean manufacturing--Case studies. | Production control--Evaluation.
Classification: LCC TS157.4 (ebook) | LCC TS157.4 .S39 2019 (print) | DDC 658.5--dc23
LC record available at https://lccn.loc.gov/2018032754

Visit the Taylor & Francis Web site at
http://www.taylorandfrancis.com

Contents

PART II   Maturing Process Improvements in the 1990s: 36 Tour Reports (30 U.S.; 5 Other Countries; and One for a Company with Plants on Both Sides of the U.S. Border)

PART III   Advances and Missteps along Process-Improvement Pathways in the 2000s

Preface

Few people read books cover-to-cover any more. In this era of communication by sound bites, a book like this one—101 mini-case studies ("caselets") may make sense. Before getting to why-the-book and what's in it, I need to explain about the book's title.

> In the title I use the term flow, with lean in parentheses, for a variety of reasons. I'll succinctly point to the degradation in usage of "lean," the term, and also "lean," the concept. Increasingly, company executives—the general and business press, too—are referring to lean in terms of reduced head counts. That is heresy to lean insiders and to most companies bent on lean implementation, who take pains to make it understood that presenting lean that way is certain to engender resistance from work forces, whose active participation is essential.
>
> As for lean concepts, they have been severely corrupted, leaving the essentials, in some companies, hard to find among all the add-ons. I am one of a growing number of lean/JIT/TPS veterans who have been gravitating toward "flow" as a worthy substitute for "lean." It makes sense: flow is a verb, an action word; it's the agenda, what organizations want to happen: we want goods, materials, and information to flow unimpeded, process to process to process. Lean is an adjective, a fixed state, common evidence of which is the lack of inventory choking flow lines.* In sum, lean has its proper uses, but flow deserves prominence, and it is mentioned that way in some of the book's 101 chapters.

The mini-case studies (for which I've coined the word "caselets") and related writings emerge from my professional life since 1981, when it got re-focused. While serving as a professor (operations management and information systems) at the University of Nebraska, I learned the what's and why's of the Japanese export juggernaut. Japan's producers were picking apart their Western competitors through application of remarkably effective improvement initiatives. Those were generally known, at first, as just-in-time production with total quality control (JIT/TQC), or Toyota production system (TPS). My 1982 book, *Japanese Manufacturing*

---

* Yes, I know: "flow" can also be stated as a noun (flow is our aim) and an adjective (flow management); also, "lean" has been reshaped as a verb form (we leaned out our plant) and a noun (lean is our aim).

Techniques: Nine Hidden Lessons in Simplicity, helped kick off JIT/TQC in the U.S. and elsewhere. I pressed on with two other 1980's-vintage books: *World Class Manufacturing: The Lessons of Simplicity Applied*, and *World Class Manufacturing Casebook: Implementing JIT and TQC*. Other authors' 1980s books and hundreds of articles on JIT or JIT/TQC followed. In 1990, the mega-selling book, *The Machine That Changed the World*, offered the term, "lean production," as a substitute for JIT.

GENESIS OF THE BOOK

From the 1980s to the present, I've been taking the message of process-improvement—pick your own term for it—far and wide. Most of these travels include brief factory tours (usually just me and company hosts) in which I take detailed notes. Then, I write them up as a brief report—my take on what they do well and what needs improvement. Then I mail, as part of a thank-you message, my *unpolished* report to the hosts of my plant tour. That is the source of the large majority this book's caselets.

> Why unpolished? For one thing, I've been too busy—preparing for next trips and writing articles and books—to spend a lot of time on the reports. Anyway, nearly all were un-asked-for and unpaid: I was invited, usually, to conduct a seminar. And to make the seminar relevant, I would arrange with my host (or they with me) for a quick plant tour. Often, that took place the day before the seminar, in late afternoon or evening after my plane had arrived. For the public seminars, I would endeavor to find out, in advance, which companies were sending attendees, then seek to get a day-early (or evening of the first day of a two-day event) tour of one or more of their nearby plants. In addition, I would sometimes do a pre-visit phone interview or email exchange with company people, plus consulting published or online information about the company and some of its competitors. That information was of use in customizing the seminar, and also in my post-visit report and thank-you note.

I can't claim to be an expert in any of the many technologies found in the plant visits. But there's no need. The emergent process-improvement practices proved to be universal, regardless of product or equipment. That became clear by the time I had visited ten or twenty improvement-oriented manufacturers and found nearly all to be pursuing, unevenly, approximately the same practices. By about 1985 I had quit referring to those practices as Japanese anything: they had simply become *good management*.

And what about Japanese terminology? In advance of my first trip to Japan in March 1982, I taught myself rudimentary Japanese—attaining partial mastery of the Hiragana form of it (enough that I could pronounce Japanese words with little accent). Then, in my seminars and other presentations in the U.S. and beyond, I would toss out Japanese words with abandon. That soon ended upon realization that use of those words got in the way of good communication. The reader will see that my caselets rarely use a Japanese word—except for "kanban," and there, too, I prefer the term, "queue limiter," because that is what kanban does.

My editing of the 101 chapters started out light: correct typos, clarify verbiage, and update to recent Microsoft Word formats (a few 1980s-vintage caselets were printed crudely on a dot-matrix-era printer). Later, I turned to more thorough editing, shortening too-long chapters, combing my rough notes for materials to add to overly short chapters, and, more generally, working on the materials to improve readability.

Commonly, the feedback report to the company did not include basic information about the company, products, plants, competitors, and so on; there was no point in including what my hosts already knew. However, my notes usually included such information, so I've often inserted a section (usually Section I) containing that information.

In some chapters I have also inserted brief explanations here and there. The purposes are to clarify points that company insiders should understand but readers of this book may not; to explain a possible point of confusion owed to changed concepts, terms, or ways of thinking from an earlier era to the present; or to inject a "teaching point" about the concept at hand.

A few of the caselets mainly point to the many excellences of the company or plant, and say little or nothing negative, i.e., weak points or opportunities for improvement. Others are the opposite: Primarily about weaknesses and improvement opportunities, and little in the way of glowing observations. Most, however, are more a mix of things done well and things needing improvement.

Lingo: In some early chapters I referred to the product line in terms of *stars* (high-volume, critical), *starlets* (moderate-volume, important), and *extras* or *others* (job-shop-like "dogs and cats"). I thought back then that these movie terms would catch on. They didn't. Too cutesy? What did catch on are *runners*, *repeaters*, and *strangers* (those excellent terms having been coined and published in 1988 by John Parnaby, a manager at Lucas Industries in the U.K., with whom I had corresponded and also with whom I shared a presentation platform at a conference in the "old days").

Is there anything special about this group of 101 caselets? Yes, there is. The large majority of these companies, business units, and plants are among best examples of flow/lean/JIT/TQC/TPS. That's because most of my hosts for the site visits steered me toward facilities that they were proud to show off. Most (all) had a good "best practices" story to tell and show.

USES OF THE BOOK

In no particular order, the book should be useful to, or for, the following:

- Students in business, economics, and engineering. Some of the caselets may bring to life the seemingly sterile process-improvement methodologies in their studies. With lots of chapters to draw from, a student may be able to find a familiar one, such as for a manufacturer in that student's local area, or some that include a focus on the student's own major area of study. For example, the caselets often include application of advanced concepts in cost management, employee training, performance management, supply chains, logistics, and other topics found in business studies. For engineering students there are plentiful applications of plant layout, quick setup, material handling, quality assurance, scheduling, ergonomics, and flow analysis. Students with some knowledge or experience in electronics, machining, sewing, warehousing, plastics, etc., will find cases in which those processes are prominent.
- Professors in business, economics, and engineering—same as for their students.
- Researchers in process improvement and economic performance. These chapters could be subject to synthesis research, such as seeking common patterns among certain industry sectors and time periods. Researchers these days have the convenience of studying what is available on the internet. But most of the lore, practices, and

tendencies from earlier periods (e.g., the early 1990s and before) are not readily (or at all) available on the internet; so, those works tend to be neglected. That neglect could be mitigated to some degree through study of goings-on in earlier times, as written up in these caselets.

- Consultants in process improvement. I believe that many of today's consultants lack grounding in important and vital concepts and methodologies that worked well and still should be in prominent use. They are in use in some quarters, but "what's new" has primarily shoved sound practices with long histories into the background.

- Manufacturers in the same industries. They may glean good ideas for their own process-improvement efforts along with competitive insights.

- The same organizations for which the caselets were written. Few—sometimes none—of the people who were employed when I visited are still employed there today. Moreover, and sadly, few companies maintain any sort of history or memory of things done in the past regarding process-improvement efforts, competitive gambits, pilot tests, and so on. I've often been astonished to read news reports that say Company X began implementing lean in 2010 or 2004 or 1997, when, in my files are news reports, published case studies, and my own plant-visit notes that detail extensive lean/JIT/flow efforts years earlier. Many of those companies retain many of the same product lines, suppliers, customers, and production processes; in their "new" initiative they are "reinventing the wheel," oftentimes with worse results than with prior, forgotten initiatives.

ALTERNATE SOURCES: PLENTIFUL ON FLOW AND QUALITY IMPLEMENTATIONS IN THE PAST, FEW TODAY

This book would have been somewhat redundant if written, say, 20 years ago. That is because, throughout the 1980s and 1990s, best-practice case reports were being published regularly in many professional/practitioner periodicals: *Target* (Association for Manufacturing Excellence), *Industrial Engineer*–renamed *ISE* (Institute of Industrial and Systems Engineers or IISE), *Quality Progress* (American Society for Quality), *Manufacturing Engineering* (Society for Manufacturing Engineers), *Journal of Supply Chain Management* (formerly, *International Journal of Purchasing and Materials*

Management, Institute for Supply Chain Management), *APICS Magazine* (American Production and Inventory Control Society), *Production and Inventory Management Journal* (also APICS), *Assembly Magazine*, *Quality Digest*, *Business Week*—renamed *Bloomberg BusinessWeek*, *The Manufacturer* (U.K. and U.S.), *Works Management* (U.K., publisher of Best Factory awards), *Management Today* (U.K.); also, more specialized publications such as *Material Handling and Logistics*, *American Machinist*, and *Cost Management* (which was the main font of papers on the cost-management impact of flow manufacturing; formerly called the *Journal of Cost Management*, it went out of business as a published periodical in 2013).

These (and a few other periodicals) have been primary sources for another large database of mine that I've called the *Honor Roll*. It is a compilation of about 1,000 brief summaries of stories from those published sources (plus a few based on my own observations from plant/company visits). In most cases, making the Honor Roll requires a few, or at least one, notable number: a percentage improvement in flow time, flow distance, number of hand-offs, number of tasks mastered or suggestions made and implemented; reductions in changeover time, inventories, number of suppliers or transactions or nonconformities; and so on. (But, in a few cases, a company gets on the Honor Roll just for impressive-sounding start-up efforts.) The Honor Roll vignettes average about five lines (as backups I retain in a file cabinet, organized by year, full hard-copy stories that came from printed periodicals). Here is one of those vignettes (the number 104 refers to the 104th entry for Michigan-Ohio—the largest region, at 128 entries, in the Honor Roll database):

> 104. Thermo Fisher Scientific, Marietta, OH (lab equipt. for medi-cal) – Employee-driven Practical Process Improvement (PPI) program, all employees trained in it; front-liners lead plant tours, 2/3 cut in WIP in welding; welding/other cells, tuggers deliver parts to cells/lines just in time: 2008 IW Best Plant [Jonathan Katz, "Empowering the Workforce: Employee Engagement Leads the Way at Thermo Fisher Scientific's Marietta, Ohio, Operations," IW, Jan. 09, p. 43].

The Honor Roll, dating back to 1981 or 1982 (I failed to date them at first), is loaded with entries from then through the early 2000s. But entries have been few and far between in more recent years. Why? Just pick up issues for, say, the past ten years of any of the publications I have just named. You will find many of them to be populated by topics of wide enough interest that they could, and do, appear in about any of those publications—as well as in general newsstand periodicals: too many articles on topics such as personal fitness, plane travel, and how the mind works. One tendency in the articles is toward general management (strategies, leadership) rather than discipline-specific applications (such as novel ways of achieving flow); the focus, instead, is more on preparation, culture, and terminology than actual improvement of processes. This is not to blame the editors or their publication boards: periodicals have been faced with change—going from print to online, or going out of business; whether wise or not, they are revising content and direction, sprucing up appearances, widening their subject matter—and hanging on.

PLAN FOR THE BOOK

The caselets are in three parts and arranged by dates: Part I is made up of 32 caselets from the 1980s; Part II, 36 from the 1990s; and Part III, 33 from the 2000s. Many employ a variation on SWOT (strengths, weaknesses, opportunities, and threats) formatting. But usually it is S-plus-WOT, meaning a section on strengths, then weaknesses/opportunities/threats as a combined grouping.

Some of the caselets are real attention-grabbers (e.g., SABMiller, III-23). At least they've grabbed mine (or re-grabbed, I should say, in view of the many intervening years). Others read, in large part, like cooking recipes: to make XXX, add two cups of L, stir in 12 oz. of C . . . . And some are loaded with factoids on inventory reductions, shortened flow paths, and the like.

Within each of the three dated parts (1980s, 1990s, and 2000s) I could see no clear value in arranging the caselets in chronological order. Rather, I mixed up the order both to provide topical variety and to ensure that certain key concepts get introduced in a timely manner.

Part I

Advanced Process Improvement Found in the 1980s

32 Tour Reports (27 U.S.; 5 Other Countries)

The 32 reports, or caselets, in Part I range from several pages to very brief, some very polished and others terse. I've selected, as the first two caselets, Apple Computer, 1988, and, Coach Leatherware, 1987. Both include a thank-you letter as well as the report, and both are well known and in pursuit of essential aspects of flow manufacturing.

CHAPTER I-1. APPLE COMPUTER, INC., FREMONT, CA, 1988

This initial caselet introduces a bulleted-points format—aimed at giving readers quick indicators of content. It also includes, at the end of this caselet, segments from my thank-you letter to an Apple vice president.	*High-Interest Topics:* • **Over-flow storage ("Don't store if you can score")** • **Useless data collection (e.g., on robots' performance)**

Positives and Negatives Noted in 1.5-hour Plant Tour June 21, 1988
In connection with a two-day world-class manufacturing seminar
at Apple, June 22–23

I. State of Apple

- *Upside*:
  - ✓ Excellent product line, R&D, and current sales trend.
  - ✓ Engineering staff, top-notch; marketing, good.
- *Downside*:
  - ✓ Inventory turnover—poor and worsening (8.2 in 1986; 5.7 in 1987).
  - ✓ Cost of purchased parts—too high (not enough supplier development and schedule evenness that would aid suppliers in lowering their overhead costs and prices). (Note: Tim Cook, CEO of Apple, globally recognized for transforming Apple's supply system into one of the world's most effective, did not join Apple until 1998.)
  - ✓ Factory overhead cost—very high (despite downsizing).
  - ✓ Employee involvement—hardly any (despite good pay).
  - ✓ Cost/price of products—high.
  - ✓ Improvement ethic—not there.
- *Elaboration on above points*: With high-volume, narrow product line, little vertical integration, rather few purchased parts and few suppliers…
  - ✓ Inventory turns should be double-digit.
  - ✓ Cost of purchased parts and factory overhead should be very low.
  - ✓ Machines should hardly ever break down.
  - ✓ Product cost should be dropping fast.
- *Evidences of lack of improvement*:
  - ✓ All finished units still go through final burn-in. (This was controversial among Apple people when I previously visited (1985), and it still is; one employee [at the seminar] stated that the retailer always repeats the burn-in after opening the box in the store.) All boards are burned in, too.
  - ✓ The tote stacker (automated inventory holder) is actually growing, and plans are in motion to add some new carousels to store stock (other computer companies have been tearing out their storage systems and carousels).

II. WCM at Apple—Miscellaneous Possibilities

- *RIP*: Combine raw material and WIP files into one RIP file.

- *Incoming parts*: Put them into empty kanban containers and send them direct to lineside; if there are no empties, only then into *overflow storage.*
- *Daily-rate schedules*: Rate-based scheduling is suitable for final assembly (in Building 1) of the MAC2, MAC-SE, MAC-Plus. Note: Some attendees say this is already the case.
- *Same daily-rate schedules*: To enable a tight kanban link between printed circuit boards (PCBs, Building 4) and assembly (Building 1). (Note: some attendees say kanban is five carts of boards *now*.)
- *Reorganization of production*: Consider locating PCB *and* final assembly of MAC-SE and MAC-Plus in Building 1; and total production (PCB and final assembly) of other products in Building 4—which would create two focused factories.
- *Overhaul management of operators*: Move to fewer temporaries and a high level of training for all operators. To make the necessary time for more and better training…
    - ✓ Under-schedule the labor force (this JIT concept enables meeting a schedule even on a bad day; on a good day, use the extra time for training and improvement activities).
    - ✓ Adopt the make-to-a-number production mode, with linearity charts (this JIT concept calls for make-to-a-number which is pre-set, then stop; don't make more just because there's extra time in the shift. Making as much as possible each shift generates variation, which ripples harmfully throughout the greater organization).
    - ✓ Use tally boards for recording all discrepancies.
    - ✓ Hold regularly-scheduled operator meetings with staff support to brain-storm discrepancy data.
    - ✓ Move toward operator-centered preventive maintenance (later known as total productive maintenance, TPM).
- *Automated storage*: Set a goal toward tearing out the tote stacker; and re-consider plans for carousels. (Another JIT concept: Automated storage automates/hides inventory retention and adds extra steps of put-away, retrieval, etc. Plus, it's ridiculous for soon-to-be-used parts to be sent into automated storage; yet the practice is commonplace; such parts should bypass storage as the norm and enter storage only as overflow.)
- *Star PC board*: Create grand cell (DIP-to-ovens) for the *star* PC board (MAC-SE board).

- *Direct-ship*: Aggressively pursue direct-ship to key customers.
- *Board burn-in*: Back away from board burn-in (aggressively push for process control and supplier quality).
- *System burn-in*: Phase down system burn-in (Building 1); use units in burn-in as a variable buffer (zero to 24 hours in burn-in).
- *Lot sizes*: Reduce lots for MAC2 and MAC2-video boards.
  - ✓ Now lots are one shift's worth; could be one burn-in-oven's worth.
  - ✓ Better: Run 1/3 of burn-in overnight (since the oven holds three carts).
- *Board-flip*: Remove the two devices that flip boards (on hand-load line); operator has the board in the air anyway and can set down the board either upside or downside. (Note: one attendee asked why operators are there at all—doing a check-fix that shouldn't be necessary.)
- *Robot metrics*: Cease collecting data on robots' performance: cycle time, utilization…
  - ✓ No use for *any* of the data.
  - ✓ Put in discrepancy tally boards instead.
- *Operator training*: Systematic training of all operators.
- *Cross-training*: Extensive, systematic cross-training.

III. Thank-you Letter

Mr. Ralph Russo, VP, Worldwide Operations, Apple Computer, Inc., Cupertino, CA.

As you may know, on June 22–23, I conducted a 2-day seminar on "world-class manufacturing" for Apple-Fremont. I had a tour of Buildings 1 and 4 the evening before. My excellent tour guides were Chuck Catania and Theresa Bond. That tour, plus discussions with people attending the seminar, form the basis for this brief letter in which I offer my "quick-and-dirty" impressions of the state of manufacturing at Apple.

It is common knowledge that Apple has been doing very well lately. However, I don't think Apple is keeping up with what's going on worldwide in manufacturing management. Here are some points that I presented to the seminar audience.

> [*Omitted here are parts of the letter discussing 2nd, 3rd, and
> 4th bulleted points, Section I*]

Part of the reason for the lack of employee involvement (and reliance on high-salaried experts to do everything) is Apple's worthy effort to never again have to lay people off. The obvious solution, use of temporary employees, would seem to make sense (the downside: a reluctance, in many companies, to spend sufficiently on training its temps). But it was clear to my seminar audience, as I guess it is now to senior company management, that the percentage of temporaries has grown far too large. (I was astounded by the percentage.) And I read in the news media about the new human-resources person that Apple brought on board to fix the many people problems.

[Next paragraph omitted as irrelevant]

Ralph, I'm forwarding these impressions to you since I am not sure who at Fremont decided to hire me for the seminar. You were my main contact in 1985.

I wish you luck in getting the improvement engine restarted—or at least speeded up.

Richard Schonberger

CHAPTER I-2. COACH LEATHERWARE, NEW YORK CITY, 1987

This caselet, on Coach Leatherware's (women's handbags) New York City facility, begins with a brief post-tour thank-you letter, which includes advice on enhancing the company's pioneering cellular/JIT manufacturing implementation. This is followed by some details extracted from rough notes.	***High-Interest Topics:*** • **Merging leather craftsmen into cells with assemblers** • **Breaking up a too-large cell** • **Reducing job descriptions and numbers of suppliers** • **Produce to a fixed daily number**

Coach: A Leader in the Fashion Industry in Striving for JIT/Flow Production
Assessment based on a plant visit, Nov. 9, 1987
In NYC that day mainly for meeting with my book publisher

I. Post-Tour Letter

- November 20, 1987, Mr. Robert Epstein, VP manufacturing Coach Leatherware Co.

Dear Robert:

The plant tour was excellent. I'm impressed by what you have accomplished with the first JIT line—and how smoothly it got launched. I have visions of the "word" about your methods leaking out to the cut-and-sew folks, and for cells and JIT lines to sweep up and down the Garment District.

The cloth apparel people have one obstacle that you don't have, however. The people I talk to in that business always raise this issue (sometimes in a defeatist manner): They have to contend with cutting many thicknesses of cloth at a time; ergo: batch manufacturing. Since in your leather-die-cutting it's just one thickness, the door is open to integrating leather cutting into the JIT lines. I understand why that step has been put on hold. The cutters are somewhat of an elite bunch—craftsmen. They have stick-together feelings. Still, that's "all" it is—an emotional issue. Good business sense—lead times, inventories, quality, scrap, etc.—says they should be members of JIT teams, not in a separate department. The *team* should have the pride of craftsmanship, rather than certain individuals.

On the other side of the JIT line is packout, with stock for packing held in a lockable cage, for the sake of security. Maybe a better way to get security is to put packers at the ends of the JIT lines. Then move packed boxes directly into shipping containers.

Robert, those are just two standout impressions that I had formed in going through the plant—for whatever they might be worth. Thanks for the tour, and congratulations on your fine progress.

Sincerely, Richard J. Schonberger

II. General information

- *Product and production*: Production of the Coach line of fine, women's handbags and belts is divided between one factory in Miami (170 employees) and this one on three floors of a building in downtown Manhattan near the garment district (300 employees, 120 of whom work in the 10th-floor factory). Pay is hourly; no piece work.
- *Competitor*: Dooney & Bourke in Connecticut is thought to have 40% higher costs than Coach.
- *Key raw material*: Products are made from natural, mostly domestically sourced unfinished leather.

    ✓ Inspecting and positioning leather pieces for die-cutting requires skilled, well-paid cutters, who are located in their own area of the same room where handbags are assembled.

    ✓ For handbags, some 58% of manufacturing cost is leather (for belts, about 15–20%).

- *Leather-cutting equipment and process*: Leather cutters work on about 30 hydraulic "clicker" presses ($6,000 each, used).

    ✓ The process includes use of paper patterns and outside die-makers (dies of heavy steel rarely wear out, can be sharpened).

    ✓ Die heights are all the same, so no setup time; about five new dies are needed every six months for new handbag styles.

    ✓ Die blocks get full of holes, so they are re-milled now and then.

- *Sewing*: The facility has about 65 sewing machines; old Singer machines costing $200 and new JUKI machines which "run too fast—run away!"
- *Bag repair*: 400 bags per week average (repairs are free to customers).
- *Sales outlets*: Coach stores, mail order (from its own catalogs), and department stores.

III. Operations

- *JIT line (cell)—for handbags*

    ✓ The cell is two 20 × 22 foot bays naturally divided by load-bearing posts; cell winds in somewhat of a serpentine configuration within that space.

    ✓ Performing 20 operations, 12 operators (most knowing all operations) produce at pace of 26 units per hour; 5-10 pieces per operation. 72 main leather piece-sets are delivered as a kit at first operation. Inventory control provides/replenishes materials (including boxes and straps) once daily.

    ✓ One operator rotates between cementing and skiving; anchor stitch to gusset. Others match for color, put in a jig with cement, and hand-paint cement; top stitch; close fronts and backs, fronts and sides; high-post binding, strap sewing, stitching, attaching straps, etc.

    ✓ Last step includes kanban, which is set at one bag, with the scheduler handling the kanban cards.

    ✓ In the packing cage, four packers wipe and wrap boxes of handbags.

✓ Lead time is 1 day—as opposed to 7 days in conventional (non-JIT) production.

✓ JIT purchasing is not in use yet, but recently the inventory of boxes has been greatly reduced.

✓ Production is to daily capacity, not to a fixed number; all is one shift with little overtime.

- *Second JIT line*: In planning, to be for briefcases.
- *11th floor*: Producing small leather belts, wallets, and key cases; also, offices for purchasing, engineering, etc.

IV. Primary Improvement Opportunities

- *Die-cutters joining assembly cell*: Suggest breaking up leather die-cutting and transitioning their presses, materials, and leather experts to positions adjacent to points of use on JIT cell lines.

  ✓ Being part of the team of stitchers, cementers, skivers, etc., will foster better awareness of how their output of cut pieces improves or detracts from quality and efficiency of downstream production of the handbags themselves.

  ✓ The difference in pay rates should not be a great obstacle (e.g., learners/new hires mix in with and are paid less than veteran employees).

  ✓ To enhance the learning advantages of mixing with others on the JIT line, leather experts may see fit to do turns in sewing, cementing, etc. In turn, some of the stitchers may aspire to become leather experts—and welcome opportunities to learn that from leather experts. See photos, Figures 2.1 and 2.2.

- *Packing cage*: Similarly, eliminate the packers' cage by making packout the final operation on the handbag line. If handbags go directly into packing cases, problems of theft should be prevented.

- *Cell team(s)*: The number of people in the JIT line, 12, stretches the advantages of a compact cell in which members feel and act like a team.

  ✓ Adding leather experts and packers probably results in too many members.

  ✓ So, it is probably best to divide the JIT line into two JIT cells, each with its own space and equipment, and each focused on its own handbag type, size, or style. Perhaps a third cell should be set up just for handbag repairs.

FIGURE 2.1
Leather die-cutting at Coach Leatherware.

- *JIT deliveries*: Begin implementing JIT deliveries from suppliers, starting with boxes, which take up excessive space; boxes are often the first item that companies put on kanban, and many box manufacturers are receptive to regular—usually daily—deliveries. This is a simple, repetitive routine that greatly reduces transactions.
- *Fixed production number*: Produce to a fixed number (latest sales/demand rate) each day and stop, rather than "see how much we can make today."
  - ✓ This routinizes and simplifies many aspects of the business, reducing many transactions.
  - ✓ On days when the number is reached early, the extra time is beneficially used for training/cross-training, certification, cleanup, problem-solving meetings, and so forth.

FIGURE 2.2
Sewing a handbag at Coach Leatherware.

CHAPTER I-3. KONE SUBSIDIARY, ROBBINS & MYERS, DAYTON, OH, 1983–85

This is one of three caselets *not* arising from my first-hand knowledge. Rather, it was extracted from a KONE document on the numerous JIT/TQC implementation efforts that were going on at Kone's Finland-based manufacturing facilities in the early 1980s. The caselet is unedited (except for added bullet formats and titles), maintaining the wording from the KONE document (even the reference to "Figure 46," though as extracted for this caselet it becomes Figure 3.1).

High-Interest Topic:
- **Diagram of many fabrication cells, plus two assembly cells**

Implementing Cell Production at Kone's Robbins & Myers Subsidiary

I. General Information

- *Information sources*:
  - ✓ A KONE document printed in 1985 was given to me later—in June 1988—while I was in Helsinki for my two-day world-class manufacturing seminar.

✓ I no longer have the complete document but retained this segment from pages 77–79.

- *Kone well-informed*: This caselet is of special interest in that it shows KONE Corp. knew all about JIT/flow manufacturing by 1983.
  - ✓ They did not learn about it from the Finnish translation of my *Japanese Manufacturing Techniques* book (*Tuotantotekniikan Japanilaiset Mallit: Yksinkertaisuus Tehokkuuden Avaimena*: Helsinki, 1984).
  - ✓ Rather, since Scandinavian companies have a long history of keeping up with developments in English-speaking countries, it is not surprising that KONE managers would have been studying and implementing JIT/TQC-focused articles and books nearly as early and avidly as in the United States.

II. From the Kone Document

- *Hoist factory*: In the summer of 1983, KONE bought Robbins & Myers' hoist factory in Dayton, OH, USA. The factory's layout was functional, and average delivery time for a hoist was 3–4 months.
  - ✓ To achieve shorter delivery times (quick ship to customers), hoists were manufactured in stock (meaning to-stock, not to-order) but with poor results.
  - ✓ Even now there is stock left over from 1982. In spite of long delivery times, delays often occurred.
- After the takeover, development of cell production began immediately in the form of training for Robbins & Myers' production and design managers in the hoist works in Hämeenlinna (Finland). During the training, the cell philosophy was studied in theory and shown in practice. After one week, the participants had become convinced that creating cells would solve such problems at Robbins & Myers as long lead times, delays, large WIP, and poor productivity.
- In October, an engineer from Hämeenlinna helped create:
  - ✓ A rough layout sketch (see Figure 46).
  - ✓ List of machines and equipment to be acquired.
  - ✓ Calculations of number of workers to be assigned to the cells.
  - ✓ Schedule for layout changes.
  - ✓ An exact layout for the rope drum and form beam cell (Figure 3.1).
- *Implementation*: Implementation started immediately, and machines were moved in the beginning of November. Because production

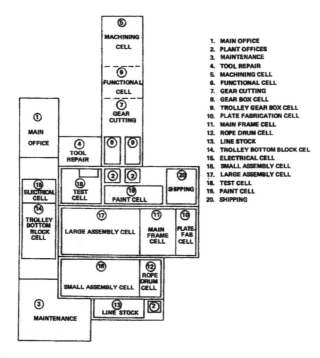

1. MAIN OFFICE
2. PLANT OFFICES
3. MAINTENANCE
4. TOOL REPAIR
5. MACHINING CELL
6. FUNCTIONAL CELL
7. GEAR CUTTING
8. GEAR BOX CELL
9. TROLLEY GEAR BOX CELL
10. PLATE FABRICATION CELL
11. MAIN FRAME CELL
12. ROPE DRUM CELL
13. LINE STOCK
14. TROLLEY BOTTOM BLOCK CEL
15. ELECTRICAL CELL
16. SMALL ASSEMBLY CELL
17. LARGE ASSEMBLY CELL
18. TEST CELL
19. PAINT CELL
20. SHIPPING

FIGURE 3.1

[Figure 46 in Kone's original]. Cell plan for KONE's Robbins & Myers hoist factory in the U.S.

never ceased, machines had to be moved (often on weekends) as rapidly as possible. The rope drum and the form beam cells were in production by middle of December.

- *Essential tasks*: Simultaneously, the following tasks essential for cell production were carried out:
  - ✓ A new production-control system was created.
  - ✓ ABC classification of inventory items was implemented.
  - ✓ Line stocks were established.
  - ✓ A new cost-accounting system was installed.
  - ✓ Capacity requirements planning was abandoned.
  - ✓ Personnel were selected for the cells.
    - Usually the employees were chosen before machines were moved so cell members would be able to assist in the planning of the layout.
    - At least one (but often several short meetings) was held before the final plan was implemented.
    - Changes in functional organization were carried out.

- *Production control*: The new production-control system was implemented at the end of January. At the same time, daily 15–20-minute production meetings were initiated in an attempt to control production with daily precision. In the same meetings, changes in routine work caused by cell production were discussed. Last cells were ready in March. Results by the summer of 1984 showed that:
  - ✓ Lean times had decreased from 3–4 months to 4–5 weeks.
  - ✓ Direct production hours had decreased 20–40%.
  - ✓ All hoist manufacturing was now based on customer orders.
- *Results*: The company, Robbins & Myers, which had shown losses for several years, is now profitable, and sales have increased almost 50%. A detail worth mentioning is that about 6,000 of the factory's 7,500 storage and transport boxes for parts and components were sold, and the number left is more than twice that required.
- *Satisfaction/enrichment*: Discussions with workers in cells indicate that job satisfaction has increased because of job enrichment.
- *Obstacles overcome*: One of the biggest problems in implementing the new system, old habits, caused some delays. After working in the new environment, however, all the employees recognized the benefits of the system and were ready to develop it further.

CHAPTER I-4. ANALOG DEVICES, INC. (ADI), WILMINGTON, MA, 1987

ADI, a high-flying producer of semiconductors, is advanced in quality and in various aspects of flow production. Though IC manufacturing has evolved greatly since then, this caselet's focus on revamping the organization for JIT/flow remains salient. The caselet is nearly verbatim from the post-tour feedback reports—with just a bit of trimming and no added remarks.

High-Interest Topics:
- **Shifts and schedules for different flow paths in wafer fabrication (Table 4.1)**
- **Surface-mount technology plant reorganized by product types (stars, starlets, and others),with accompanying before-and-after organization charts (Figures 4.1 and 4.2)**

JIT/Flow Manufacturing Inroads at a Semiconductor Manufacturer
Assessment based on a visit to ADI plants, Sept. 8, 1987
In connection with a one-day seminar, Sept. 9

I. General Information

- *The company*: ADI, which specializes in devices that convert analog signals to digital, has two plants in Massachusetts, plus other non-U.S. plants. An older "Mod B" plant in Wilmington has two wafer fabrication facilities, and a new "Mod C" plant has opened in Norwood, MA.
- *Main contact*: Arthur Schniederman, director of quality/productivity improvement. The original feedback report to the company, opening with a cover letter, is dated November 21, 1987 (an unusually long delay from when I visited company).

II. Opener to Cover Letter

Dear Art:

I found a few spare moments and used the time to type up some of my impressions from my visit to ADI in September. Mostly, these are thoughts and ideas that I had hand-scrawled on acetate sheets and used in my seminar for ADI. Since there was no chance to convey them to you, I am enclosing a copy—for what it may be worth.

1. Some Existing Manufacturing Strengths
   - *Quality improvement process*: Uses of QIP teams.
   - *Cycle-time reductions*: As one example, in wafer fab, CT has been reduced from 12 weeks to two or three.
   - *Employee certifications*: Excellent certification programs at the Norwood plant (along with operating-procedure packets).
   - *IC test*: In Wilmington, the integrated-circuit (IC) test area is being converted to cells.
   - *Plant refocus*: Few "supermachine" obstacles are in the way of plant reorganization by products/customers.
   - *Employee benefits*: Employees are on a bonus system—and have high levels of job security.
2. Miscellaneous Suggestions
   - *IC burn-in ovens*: If possible, modify the ovens (cut bolts or rivets) so that the whole rack comes out for external loading of the 64 board carriers (i.e., load a full rack into oven, then externally load a "twin rack" so it is oven-ready without setup delay).
   - *Overhead functions*: Slow down centralization of overhead functions; speed up simplification at each site—thus to reduce non-value-adding support costs at local levels.

- *Handoff from design to production*:
  - ✓ Good present plan of completing handoffs when 10 percent of revenue is in.
  - ✓ Maybe better: *when X percent process yield* is achieved.
- *Accounting cost of wafers*:
  - ✓ Present basis: wafers coming out.
  - ✓ "Simple" but needed change: *dies* coming out.
- *Labeling*: Put labels/tags/colors on "everything" for visual management.
- *Kanban*: Complete the kanban conversion, including having it run by line supervisors and leads.
- *Preventive maintenance*: Begin operator-centered P.M. (i.e., TPM, or total productive maintenance).

3. Wafer fab, Wilmington
   - *Reorganization*: Table 4.1 shows an idealized reorganization of the Mod B wafer fab area, thus to create JIT flow paths and rather complete teams—by product type, not by function. Following are features of the proposed reorganization.
     - ✓ The figure groups 114 products into seven product families, each in its own physical area with its five basic operations (steps), equipment, etchers, sets of diffusion tubes, EPI/thin film (not specified), and laser trim machines.

TABLE 4.1

JIT Organization of Mod B wafer fab area

	114 Products	5 Steps*	Etchers	44 diffusion tubes	**	20 laser trim machines	
Two Shifts	42	JCADT	E1 E2 E3	7 tubes	EPI?	3	Fully scheduled
	30	JCADT	E4 E5 E6	7 tubes		3	
	20	JCADT	E7 E8 E9	7 tubes		3	
	10	JCADT	E10 E11 E12	7 tubes		3	Make, say, every
	10	JCADT	E13 E14 E15 E16	7 tubes	Thin film?	4	two days
One Shift	585 only	JCADT	E17 E18	5 tubes		2	"Make to a
	574 only	JCADT	E19 E20	4 tubes		2'	number" (no lots; daily rate)

*JCADT: Join>Coat>Align>Develop>Test
**Not enough information (or insights) to fully consider epitaxy and thin film
Note: High-use masks are to be stored in a fixture above the aligners (third of the 5 JCADT steps).

- Top three product families—42, 30, and 20, the highest-volume "stars" of the product line—are fully scheduled for two daily shifts.
- The two "10" product families are produced on two shifts less often, perhaps every other day.
- The 585 and 574 families are produced in the "make-to-a-number" mode.

✓ Main objectives:

- Greatly reduce the frequency of equipment changeovers.
- Achieve a breakthrough regarding responsibility for results—product team having ownership; technicians and engineers becoming true support people.
- Compress flow time and WIP, and considerably improve predictability of output quantities.

4. IC test/IC assembly

- *Cells for test*: Test—currently located in Wilmington and undergoing reorganization into JIT cells by product type—will make ADI a pioneer in the IC industry because of this highly desirable and logical conversion.
- *Assembly*: Most of the assembly is currently performed very competently in the Philippines (PI).

   ✓ *Competition with PI*: Get a competition going by setting up an extended JIT cell for IC assembly/test for the 574 product (12 bit A-to-B) in Wilmington and give it half the production volume. Compete with PI on cost, cycle time, and yield.

   ✓ *Fairness*: To make competition fair, PI needs to be converted to cells for the 574 product—while also abandoning the functional organization—a serious weakness of the PI operation and an obstacle to JIT, TQC, employee involvement, team-centered accountability, and continual improvement (might as well reorganize PI into JIT cells for *all* products).

5. Surface-Mount Technology (SMT), Norwood Plant

- *Focus*: SMT needs to be divided by product volume: stars, starlets, and others.
- *SMT flow lines*:

   ✓ Figure 4.1 is an idealized schematic of SMT work centers reorganized into JIT flow lines following the product split.

   - Numbers refer to machines of a given type (the usual JIT reasons and benefits apply, prominently including

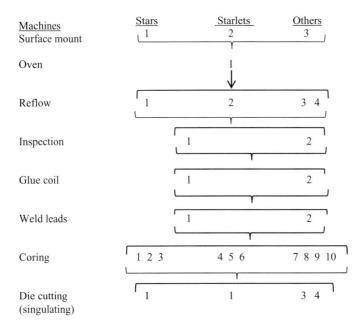

FIGURE 4.1
Reorganization of SMT into JIT flow lines.

creation of product-oriented teams with full accountability for results).

- It is common, in layouts of JIT flows, for certain machines/stations to be shared (such as the single oven and the inspection stations for glue coil and welds). Later, such sharing may be avoided by acquisition of two more ovens, and so on. In the ovens, that option could entail acquiring smaller, less expensive, ovens with better heat distribution.

- *SMT—revised organization charts*:
  - ✓ Complementary to the physical re-layout—into flow lines—Figure 4.2 shows before-and-after organization charts, showing conversion of IC test organization from department supervisors (e.g., types of test equipment) to product supervisors (Cog1, Cog2 20-pin, etc.).
  - ✓ In this, some product supervisors would become responsible for a star product, some for starlets, and some for "others."
  - ✓ Overall, the objective is to eliminate supervision by department (Old) and replace it with supervision by product type (New).

Old Human and Factory Organization

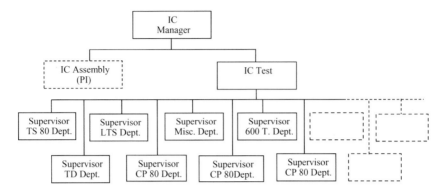

New Human and Factory Organization

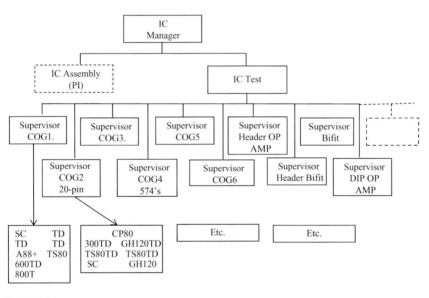

FIGURE 4.2

Old and new organization of supervision—elaborated for IC test.

CHAPTER I-5. WESTINGHOUSE, ASHEVILLE, NC, 1986

This caselet is about a major manufacturer (Westinghouse *was* that) aggressively embracing JIT production—including arranging equipment into tight flow patterns, slashing lot sizes and buffer stock, and widely employing kanban. It centers on my visit to its Asheville plant, which is one of four similar implementations of Westinghouse's Industrial Controls business unit—Asheville and Fayetteville, N.C.; Oldsmar, FL; and Coamo, Puerto Rico—and is enhanced with extra information. It was assembled from old notes, which included plentiful information on achievements but scarcely any recommendations from me.

High-Interest Topics:
- **Plants emulating other plants in the same Westinghouse division**
- **Transformation led by a no-nonsense "spark plug"**
- **Wide implementation of kanban**
- **Wipe out "mail boxes" (i.e., paperwork)**
- **Shoving buffer stock "into the corner"**

Impressive Conversions from Batch to JIT/Flow at Ashville & Three Other Factories
Observations from morning plant tour & meeting, Feb. 28, 1986

I. General Information

- *The plant visit*: This was a "last-minute" visit, fit into my scheduled afternoon plant tour and a next-day seminar for a different company in nearby Marion, NC. In visits to Westinghouse's headquarters in Pittsburgh, I had heard about JIT-oriented successes at Asheville and other sites, and those involved were eager to show off one of their most advanced factories.
- *Hosts at Asheville*: Spencer Duin, Jerry Litch, Vinod Kapoor, and John Marous.
- *Asheville plant*: Built in 1978 (400 employees), it is in the Industrial Control Business Unit (ICBU) of Westinghouse Control Division—one of four plants under Spencer Duin.
- *JIT*: Just-in-time implementation at these plants features rapid flows of orders from customers to completed production. Coamo was first to achieve this, but Fayetteville, under Kapoor, quickly

eclipsed Coamo. These same JIT methods were carried forward to Asheville.

- *Space availability*: Both Asheville and Fayetteville freed up large amounts of production space to be filled in with new products.
- *A JIT goal*: "Wipe out mail boxes"—meaning paperwork inventories.
- *Mitsubishi model*: Westinghouse's JIT concepts were patterned after Mitsubishi's "MIPS," circa-1981 (Westinghouse corporate heads had benefited from close relationships with Mitsubishi-Japan).
- *JIT conclave*: A January 1985 JIT conference had been held in Asheville for 45 Westinghouse companies. (Note: similarly, General Electric held its own 2-day JIT Workshop, in Washington, D.C., 15 months earlier. [I was there as a speaker.] There, a few dozen GE business units told about their implementations of JIT. Notably, the agenda pinpointed "flow" and "material flow" as major objectives.)

II. Random Details

- *Inventory reduction*: Inventory as a percent of sales was 26% (four month's supply) in 1981; down to 16% (one month's) in 1986.
- *On-time performance*: 60% in 1985 increased to 90% in the following year.
- *Fork trucks & racks*: 65 fork trucks 1.5 years ago, which decreased to 35—with removal of 370 racks.
- *Planned*: JIT in 1–2 years, TQC in approximately five years.
- *Progress*: For the four plants, progress along six JIT dimensions is shown below. X's mean "yes" while blanks mean planned, not done.

	Asheville	Fayetteville	Coamo	Oldsmar
1. Kanban	X	100%	X	X
2. Cells				
■ Sheet metal	X	X (4 lines)		
■ Machining	X			
■ Feeder cells			X (brazing)—kanban driven	
3. Assy.-line transporter	X	X	X	
4. 1-person "village"	X	X		
5. Pull assy.	X	X		X
6. "No touch"			X (12 wks.--> 2-3 wks.)	

III. Specifics

- *"It takes a sparkplug"*:
  - ✓ The ICBU's driving force for JIT was plant manager Vinod Kapoor.
    - ■ As an invited speaker at a 1984 Hamilton, Ontario, JIT conference sponsored by CAPICS (which I helped organize), Kapoor told of being frustrated because everyone in his plant (Fayetteville) was dubious about cutting lot sizes. So, he just "went to the data files and re-set all the lot sizes to 1."
    - ■ After much hewing and crying and complaining, Kapoor told everyone: Solve the problems; remove the obstacles.
  - ✓ In becoming plant manager at Asheville, Kapoor sent large amounts of buffer stock "into the corner" and told everyone to figure out how to get by without it.
- *Westinghouse videotape*: Westinghouse produced, in 1985, a video covering JIT happenings in multiple Westinghouse plants/divisions—including…
  - ✓ Fayetteville: Moved a product from Beaver, PA, to Fayetteville and installed a pilot JIT sheet-metal line.
    - ■ Repositioned equipment, tying locations together with a simple roller conveyor, with space for only one "structure" between each station, enabling one operator per two machines.
    - ■ Reduced floor space 20 percent, WIP 50 percent, with deep reductions in cycle times.
    - ■ 80 percent of die changes reduced to single-digit minutes.
    - ■ Implemented pull on a structures line, with work balanced between four stations.
    - ■ 1,700 items on kanban.
    - ■ Changes over a 9-month period included (1) redefining job classifications, reducing them from 51 to 3; (2) shifting from monthly to daily schedules; (3) launching a major quality-awareness campaign.
  - ✓ Asheville (older plant; a retrofit):
    - ■ 2,400 items (about half of all part numbers) on kanban; 400 items in late 1984.

- ■ Update (not in the videotape): 2,000 P/Ns (part numbers) on kanban by end of 1985. Also, in applying JIT to "front-end" offices, the customer ordering cycle was reduced from seven weeks to seven minutes.
- *Critical observation*: Too many pallets, too much conveyor; need visible measures.

CHAPTER I-6. WCM AT ASSOCIATED EQUIPMENT CO., ST. LOUIS, MO, 1988

This short caselet was included because, as with the Westinghouse caselet (I-5), the impressive conversion to flow is owed to a single person who took over operations. I had gotten to know that person, Paul Brauss, when he was with a different company bent on flow production. He sent me the information that makes up this caselet (the second of three in which I did not visit the plant—the others being Kone, Chapter I-3 and 3M Videocassettes, Chapter I-12).	*High-Interest Topics:* • **Very small manufacturer increases production ability from four products at a time to 14—in 14 cells** • **Each of 14 kanban carts holds all 50 pieces needed to make a complete product—resulting in shutting down subroutines of its MRP system**

How One Person Can Make a Big Difference in the Quest for Flow-driven Excellence
Based on information from Paul Brauss, operations manager,
Aug. 11, 1988

I. Basic Information

- *The company*: Produces commercial (not retail) battery chargers and battery testing equipment (typical battery size is 12-by-20 inches).
- *Employment*: 157 employees.

II. Conversion to Flow Manufacturing

- *Existing production mode*: When Brauss came, the plant had four conveyor-paced assembly lines 80–120 feet long. They required 8-hour changeovers and could make only four products at a time.
- *Reorganization*: Brauss reorganized plant into 14 work cells, with 25-minute changeovers, so that now they can make 14 products at a time. (In today's parlance, this capability is known as concurrent production, aka, simultaneous or parallel production.)
  - ✓ Battery chargers are produced on push roller conveyors.
  - ✓ Kanban carts are used for each of the 15 product varieties, each cart holding all 50 pieces needed for assembly. The stockroom people's job now is just to keep the carts full.
- *Subassembly to final assembly*:
  - ✓ Final assembly cells are kanban-linked to the various subassembly cells.
  - ✓ For example, one subassembly cell for 12 varieties of rectifier is run by one woman. She doesn't have a schedule but comes in the morning and produces merely to fill the standard containers of whichever of the 12 rectifiers are in need (empty kanban container) of filling.
- *Paint*: Four electrostatic powder units paint the cabinets. Formerly, eight hours were needed to change color; now 1.5 hours.
- *MRP*: A lot of the plant's MRP subroutines have been dismantled: no more pick lists, since kanban carts provide the correct parts for final assemblies and subassemblies. The old pick-ticket system often resulted in the start of an assembly—only to find an item missing.
- *Lessons from other plants*:
  - ✓ Brauss and his team were greatly enlightened by a visit to a Westinghouse Electric switch-gear plant in St. Louis, a $20 million business for Westinghouse that is *all* on kanban.
  - ✓ Now Brauss is negotiating with Westinghouse's supplier of hardware, who just comes in and fills Westinghouse's bins. The same supplier does the same for Associated Equipment, so that hardware will also be taken off MRP.

CHAPTER I-7. AHLSTROM PUMP, MANTTA, FINLAND, 1989

Ahlstrom-Mantta is a case of mastering very low-volume, high-mix machining-oriented manufacturing via simple cells, simple ordering-delivering, simple handling, simple order-promising, and simple scheduling.	*High-Interest Topics:* • **Scheduling without transactions: a 1, 2, 3 order sequence governs all 12 cells** • **"Rules of the game": Production and supply are so predictable that sales and marketing will reject disruptive orders**

Low-volume, High-mix Manufacturing: Lessons from One of the Best
Observations from a plant tour and meetings, October 4, 1989
Following a one-day in-house Schonberger seminar, October 3, 1989

I. General Information

- *Facility*: Ahlstrom Pump-Mantta produces its own brand of process-industry pumps (especially for the pulp and paper industry).
- *Product advantages*: The Ahlstar pump is ingenious in that it can pump fiber with very low water content—a big competitive advantage. The Ahlstar line has thousands of configurations, ranging from 136 kg-1040 kg.
- *From startup*: The plant started up in 1987, producing 10 pumps per week—rising to 100 per week by early 1989. The pumps-per-week target was raised eight different times, with employee incentives tied to the rate.
- *Event arrangements*: Consultant Matti Pöyhönen (who had sponsored earlier Schonberger seminars in Finland), through his relationship with Ahlstrom, arranged the details for this visit.
- *Ahlstrom contacts*: Christer Ahlstrom, president & CEO; Tuomo Rönkkö, general manager.

II. Strengths, Advantages

- *Cellular manufacturing*: Pumps are produced in 12 cells, all with different equipment making different pump components.

- ✓ The bearing-assembly cell relies on feeder cells for gearing housings, shafts, and bearing covers.
- ✓ The pump assembly cell is fed by bearing assembly, side plate, stuffing box covers, impellers, lanterns, and casings.
- ✓ In pump assembly, the unit slides 10 meters down wide rollers to testing cells, which feed the paint cell, which assembles the pump, base plate, rotor, and engine.
- *Simple schedule boards*: Every cell has, as its schedule, a large square wall board. Each has rows and columns numbered from 1 to 100, updated weekly.
- At the start of a new week, all 12 cells start work on order number 1; then 2, 3, 4… throughout the week.
- As, say, the impeller cell completes order 15 and forwards it to the pump assembly cell, the impeller cell operator "*X*'s" out number 15 and begins impeller 16. (See photo, Figure 7.1.)
- In the centrally-located final pump assembly cell, assemblers select the next job by noting the *X*'s on the boards (machinists and assemblers have a small amount of discretion to alter the sequence, e.g., group more than one similar pump). There is no other scheduling paper or computer transaction.

FIGURE 7.1
Schedule board, impeller cell, Ahlstrom Pump, Mantta, Finland.

- *"Rules"*:
  - ✓ All entities follow what they call, "rules of the game," which are made possible by highly predictable schedule completions (including supplier deliveries) achieved by close synchronization of the 12 cells. Flow time is 5 days, with little variation.
  - ✓ Special orders (outside of catalog offerings) call for a much higher price/longer delivery time—for which marketing finds suitable holes in forward schedules that can accommodate the order.
  - ✓ Also, an order is not released to the factory if, say, a purchased motor is not there.
- *The facility*:
  - ✓ The factory is equipped with sturdy, high-performance, highly flexible machines, as well as a thick concrete floor so machines can be moved.
  - ✓ Equipment capabilities overlap—for example, lanterns and volute casings. This provides insurance in cases of machine trouble.
  - ✓ The plan was to have no welding, but some welding was retained to "fill the cheese," as they put it—meaning fill holes of imperfect castings that come from the outside foundry.
  - ✓ The floor is painted off-white and machines white. No oil or grease is seen.
- *Work force*:
  - ✓ Operators are now skilled in nearly every job.
  - ✓ During training, new-hire operators are allowed to learn by error, making low-cost parts in the "sleeves/bearing covers" cell.
  - ✓ The incentive system is based on customer-serving measures: output (low cost), on-time delivery, short lead time—and, recently added, number of pumps retested (quality).
  - ✓ Fine cooperation exists with union steward, Seppo Peltola (didn't have time to meet him).
- *Strategies/planning*:
  - ✓ Special attention is given to issues of vertical integration: decisions to internally produce high-value-add, complicated, technologically sophisticated parts—and subcontract the rest.
  - ✓ An unhurried transition plan is aimed at openness and honesty:
    - ■ Employees receive extensive training, and have current opportunities to be involved in starting up a new Mantta plant.

- ■ Employees who are no longer needed in the present plant have opportunities for continued employment (in the Mantta vicinity) to work in the new Ahlstrom plant.
- ■ These kinds of efforts foster a good climate for earning support from the employees and the local community.
- *Machining-problem recovery*: Casings had been machined on a Belgian Pegard machining center, which was plagued by problems for six months. Luckily, the Mantta plant had unused space which was filled with conventional machines for making service parts. Those machines allowed the plant to be supplied with casings during problem correction.
- *Suppliers*:
  - ✓ A supplier of hardware, gaskets, etc., makes deliveries within the plant every day, and is paid once or twice monthly. Deliveries are by a (kanban) twin-bin system, or twin pegs on a pegged ("Christmas tree") rack.
  - ✓ A base-plate supplier only 10 meters away delivers just-in-time.
  - ✓ Bearing supplier SKF has its own distributors, but Ahlstrom finally convinced SKF to agree to provide the bearings through Ahlstrom's hardware distributor, simplifying logistics.
- *Supplier partnership*:
  - ✓ One aim was to develop a few nearby supplier-partners: Javasko for base plates (one-day order turnaround); Laakeri Ky distributor for bearings, keys, and other small parts (on a yearly contract, with a monthly invoice, and twice-daily deliveries); crates; and two others.
  - ✓ Purchasing is at plant- (not corporate) level, thus fostering low-level coordination with key suppliers.
  - ✓ Tool purchasing has been greatly simplified by use of a check-off form transmitted by fax, which reduces purchase time to about five minutes daily as contrasted to a few hours under the old system.
- *Design engineering*: Some efforts have been made toward standardized product designs (e.g., only five sizes of bearing units, and a 1-diameter hub on the casing cover so a single gripper can be used).
- *Material handling*:
  - ✓ No forklift trucks in use inside central cell areas.

✓ Use of visual ("kanban") gravity-feed racks (best I've seen in machining); also good use of colored labels for different kinds of parts.

- *Systems*: Ahlstrom has avoided big, complex computer systems for planning, execution, accounting, and control.
- *Performance*:
  ✓ There have been continuing, rapid rates of improvement in output, with a good return on investment.
  ✓ Good *customer-serving* measures of performance are in use at Mantta and in the pumps business unit.

III. Opportunities for Improvement

- *Pegboards*: Tools in cells hang on pegboards (good), but I noticed some tools not in their proper places. As a fix, they should paint tool silhouettes on the pegboards, so that the system is more exact (fewer search delays).
- *SPC for low volumes*: Employ the statistical process-control chart method that is designed for low-volume production (even a quantity of one); probably professors in quality control at Helsinki University know of these methods/can provide reference materials.
- *Customer deliveries*: On big, new pulp/paper plant projects, sales should attempt to forge contract agreements for delivering a few pumps per week over the customer's construction period (e.g., over two months) instead of all at once. This would cut costs for both customer and Ahlstrom (this idea was mentioned to me by Ahti).
- *P&L reports*: Look for ways to simplify accounting and improve costing/pricing in the pump business unit. Consider quarterly (or yearly) P&L reports instead of monthly (Texas Instruments changed from monthly to quarterly; U.S. laws require at least quarterly, but that's not the case in most other countries).
- *Competitive analysis*: Establish a competitive analysis "lab" at Mantta, with all employees involved, thus to avoid complacencies as well as to learn best practices from others (competitors are always in pursuit of improvements, too).

CHAPTER I-8. DAY-BRITE LIGHTING DIVISION OF EMERSON ELECTRIC, TUPELO, MS, 1986

This caselet includes a large number of detailed prescriptions for manufacturing and business improvement. It is an agenda likely to provide plenty to do over several years, with strong paybacks along the way.	*High-Interest Topics:* • **Multi-step plan for a JIT transformation of the "star" Dayliner product** • **Dedicated press-brake area with quick setup and ABC-classified dies**

Getting on Emerson Electric's "War on Inventory" Bandwagon
Summary of observations from November 6–7, 1986
In connection with two one-day Schonberger seminars

I. General

- *The company*: Day-Brite produces lighting fixtures and related components.
- *Visit & seminar*: Emerson has what it calls a "War on Inventory," featuring a just-in-time/total quality control set of concepts/practices. Day-Brite was on a circuit of promulgating the "War" through many diverse Emerson business units, and Emerson appointed Jerrard Smith as a new Day-Brite CEO, charged with carrying the agenda forward.
- *Performance*: In 1986, Day-Brite was among Emerson's poorer performers: manufacturing costs were high, and the division was having trouble holding market share.
- *Facilities*: Of five main buildings, the largest (450,000 sq. ft.) houses manufacturing and related support and division offices. Other buildings include two large leased warehouses of 125,000 and 75,000 sq. ft., an office building for marketing and engineering, and a mostly empty adjacent warehouse.

II. Strengths at Tupelo

- *Progress*: The past year has seen good progress in reducing inventories, raising productivity, cutting setup times (e.g., on the "39" press), transferring slow-moving stock and dies out of the main plant, and building a management team that works together.

- *Flow lines*: The management team is experienced in the flow-line assembly-and-pack mode of operation, with segmentation by product family.
- *Separation*: Three main businesses in the manufacturing building are mostly separate from each other—not badly comingled.

III. JIT Implementation – Things to Do

- *Sources of ideas*: Many of the following are ideas that were suggested or emerged in discussions with Day-Brite people (e.g., Dave Cornelius, Jimmy Deaton, Ken Baker, Ed Walker, Peggy Shaefer, Jerry Smith). Most ideas are in planning and not yet accomplished.
- *1st JIT project*: *"star" Dayliner*: A pilot JIT project organized for this specific product has the following newly developed features.
  - ✓ Produce daily at last month's sales rate with no scheduling paper other than the posted rate.
    - Compute the sales rate manually (no need for a computer for this).
    - Update and re-post the daily rate every 2 weeks.
  - ✓ Run the same sequence of main product variations each day so that changes are minor from variation to variation, e.g., 2-light without tubes, black; 2-light without tubes, white; light with tubes, black…
  - ✓ Ensure that daily schedules are met on the same day or early the next day, with Line 2 serving as an "overflow" line when necessary. That is, when Line 1 does not meet schedule, Line 2 runs the Dayliner first thing next morning until the day's rate is met (or run the whole shift with partial crew to meet the rate). For example: assume the daily rate (average last month) is 2,500 Dayliners.
    - Dedicate Line 1 to the Dayliner and run it one full shift with a full crew (26 people).
    - On Monday the Line 1 crew produces 1,980 fixtures (520 short of the 2,500 target). On Tuesday morning, the Line 2 crew (10 people) produces 520 fixtures, meeting Monday's rate of 2,500.
  - ✓ Have all parts lineside on "kanban squares" in standard containers with identifying kanban labels, and with containers

holding light loads, i.e., an amount light enough for movement by wheeled carts, so fork trucks are not used in this pilot project.

✓ Use standard containers to/from the paint line: as a container is emptied, take it to paint and leave it until the same part comes off the paint line (for lenses, take the container to the plastic area to be refilled); this eliminates refilling at WIP stores because no Dayliner parts are to be stored there.

✓ Each time a standard container is filled off one side of the paint line, hang the same number of the same—but unpainted—parts on the other side.

- Run each type of lens for Dayliner once a week. Put lenses into standard carts and store as near as possible to the paint line (*not* into WIP storage).

- On press 39, run Dayliner bodies every day (e.g., for 2–3 hours); put them into standard carts positioned as near as possible to the paint line.

- Run other Dayliner components in fabrication daily (if possible) and expect to paint them daily as they are used.

✓ For any component with a history of trouble (e.g., downtime on the machine or the die that produces it), keep buffer stock—in the M&H building—just in case.

✓ Receive the following purchased items dock-to-line: ballast and boxes daily; sockets weekly.

- *Next pilot JIT-line project: "starlet" products, such as strip lights.*
  - ✓ Do the same as for the Dayliner.
  - ✓ The roll-former, if its acquisition is approved and completed, will allow the strip light JIT line to use pre-painted material, and thus be nearly self-contained. Also, it will relieve severe overcapacity in the paint line.

- *Western Electric contract*:
  - ✓ Go to daily-rate assembly with a "bench assembly" crew of 2–3 people rather than the past practice of building a large quantity every 2–3 months with a large crew. Assemblers will become experts on these products, with problems of "forgetting" between production runs eliminated.
  - ✓ Change the quality assurance/inspection procedures for use by Western Electric: process control of quality rather than large-lot sampling as the preferred method so that finished goods in warehouse can be kept low and reliably stable.

- *Dedicated, quick-changeover press brakes*:
  - ✓ Move some brakes and perhaps some flat-bed presses into cells, which should be dedicated to a family of medium-volume part numbers.
  - ✓ Store dies for those parts at the cell and attack setup times aggressively with the aim to synchronize daily production with assembly.
    - Adopt die classification: slowest-moving dies already have been moved out of the main building. Next: classify all dies still in the building as A (parts used daily in assembly), B (used often but not daily), and C (lower-use parts). Store A dies at the machine or cell, B dies inside or alongside the press area while C dies stay put.
- *Bench assembly*: Expand the "bench-assembly" concept to starlet products.
- *Lens*: Develop quick-change methods on the lens extruder (e.g., pre-heated roll staged at the machine).

IV. Electro-Cable "Factory"

- *Point-of-use equipment*: Move 2–3 press brakes and dies to the electronic discharge area, i.e., at points of use beside assembly lines. Produce at the assembly rate.
- *Flex cable*: Move the two flexible cable machines from the HID area to the E/C area. Produce flex cable at the assembly rate.
- *Flex cable buffer stock*: Retain the half-day flex cable buffer stock (necessary because flex-cable machines break down a lot), but move that stock to the M&H warehouse; the stock is there when needed and can be eliminated gradually as the machines are upgraded in dependability.

V. High-Intensity Discharge (HID) "Factory"

- *HID customer*: The customer for HID products is Appleton Electric, another Emerson division, enabling a collaborative flow-manufacturing effort.

- *Flow layout*: Reorganize the HID factory with direct flow from die-casting to machining to paint to assembly-pack.
  - ✓ Move machining to other side of die-casting.
  - ✓ Move a wet paint line between machining and assembly (the present paint line or a new small-scale line).
  - ✓ Establish mini-cells of NC machines and drill presses (the suggestion of an operator who works in NC machine area).
- *Fixtures*: In HID assembly, build shelves, fixtures, etc., to hold tools and parts trays above assembly lines; then, eliminate the small lineside tables that assemblers are now using.

VI. Miscellaneous Additional Suggestions

- *Evidences of improvement*: Since a rather high rate of improvement (in WIP, lead times, flow distance, space required, scrap, rework, and setup times) should be forthcoming, put up large visible graphs showing the progress (pridefully) to everyone.
- *Product-focused leaders*: Evolve away from leadership by process and toward product managers, group leaders, and lead persons of sub-products and cells. Under the current process-oriented leaders, responsibility for whole products is fractionated and diluted.
- *TPM*: Establish total preventive maintenance. (Later, the term was standardized as total *productive* maintenance.) In part, the aim is for machine operators to feel a sense of ownership of machines, including a daily regimen of preventive maintenance.
- *Paint-line issues*: Paint is a big problem, perhaps because of lack of daily P.M.; and/or because the paint line is run too fast. Some of the above measures, including roll-former and use of pre-painted stock, should reduce pressures to run paint overly fast.
- *Inventory cleanout*: Consider an inventory cleanout plan, which requires halting fabrication for a time to lower piles of parts in WIP storage. Operant slogan: "Inventory will not go away unless production of it is halted."
- *Extra space*: Develop a longer-term plan for what to do with extra space that will be freed up by taking out WIP and racks in the center of the building.

CHAPTER I-9. APPLETON ELECTRIC DIVISION OF EMERSON ELECTRIC, NORTH CHICAGO, IL, 1986

Appleton Electric, a low-tech maker of lighting fixtures in a highly competitive market, is in the earliest stages of a transformation to JIT production. As such, the caselet is devoted to essential phased-in steps Appleton needs to take in that transformation, including overcoming inhibitors.

High-Interest Topics:
- **What to do *now*, do *soon*, phase *in* with planning**
- **Dealing with legacy obstacles (physical and system)**
- **Dealing with existing buffer stocks**

Moving toward JIT/flow in Phases
Observations from a visit, Feb. 12, 1986
In connection with same-day seminar at Appleton; feedback report dated February 13, 1986

I. General Information

- *Product line*: Electrical- and explosion-proof receptacles, fittings, connectors, lights, and unilets (shipped out in lots of 25,000)—8,000 SKUs, 5,600 being finished goods items.
- *Equipment/operations*: Among various departments are:
  - ✓ 20–30 drill presses, 10–15 indexing chuckers, several Kauman machines that make large components in one operation (indexing, milling, and threading); degrease/zinc plate (for *all* materials).
  - ✓ Also, two old die-casting machines; plating; 58 multi-spindle automatic screw machines; about eight CNC machines (three robot-loaded); two vertical Brown & Sharp mill-drills (for big parts); welders; and for plastics about 15 injection molding machines.
  - ✓ For precision operations, a portable Datamite SPC machine and a Mazak CAM (computer-aided manufacturing) system.
- *Appleton Electric's situation*:
  - ✓ Past and present profitability of Appleton is highly attributable to its still-sound product line and a well-established distribution and sales network.
  - ✓ Manufacturing is not Appleton's strong suit (probably had been for many prior years), though some elements are above average:

decent labor-management relations, some labor flexibility (operators running more than one machine, assemblers changing job assignments), a system that knows *where* the stock and the work is, and some JIT/TQC.

- *"War"*: This is another Emerson Electric division targeted in its so-named "war on inventory" (aka, JIT); see, also, Chapter I-8, Day-Brite Lighting.
- *Contacts*: Gary Karnes, president; Hank West, executive VP; Jack Marciano.

II. Obstacles, Constraints, Inhibitors

- *The building*: Too many floors, too many rooms get in the way of (a) visual flow management; (b) quick detection and response to problems; and (c) determining properly shaped space to lay-out cells, flow lines, factories-within-the-factory.
- *Screw machine/oil recovery system*: They are interlinked, making it harder to join one or more screw machines to another production stage.
- *Copper/brass process*: This process is segregated from steel processes, making it harder to merge into JIT configurations to produce a more complete fixture or module thereof.
- *MRP*: A computer-driven push system, which inserts transactions along flow paths—contrary, and an obstacle to, the simplicity of visual-pull production.
- *Consolidated finished-goods inventory (FGI)/ship*: The system of batching orders is not flexible for quick shipment out of the factory.

III. Changes: Musts and Maybe's

- *Do now*, in no particular order (and bumble through with minimal planning delays):
  - ✓ Smaller lots.
  - ✓ Pull for star products (at least through later stages, including pack and ship), bypassing WIP stockrooms.
  - ✓ Limit containers allowable at a machine.
  - ✓ Merge assembly and pack on third floor.
  - ✓ More frequent receipt of each of 300 types/mix of corrugated box (in daily incoming truck).

- *Do soon*, in no particular order (takes some planning):
  - ✓ Begin breaking up central shipping; decentralize to the OEM products plant and the special-orders plant.
  - ✓ Ship directly from the factory to large contractors.
  - ✓ Heavily emphasize training machine operators in set-up time reduction, especially on first and second floors. Arrange non-monetary reward packages (prize parking space, recognition lunch in exec. dining room, etc.) for achievements.
  - ✓ Change the computer system, making it into *two* systems:
    - ■ Present—for batch production of masses of lower-selling products.
    - ■ Visual pull with collapsed BOM's—bypassing stockrooms and cutting out WIP tracking—for star products.
- *Phase in*:
  - ✓ High operator involvement in maintenance (especially lube, other P.M.); quality control (already some of this); and setup.
  - ✓ Focused factories-within-the-factory, with dedicated receiving/shipping as the last operation.
  - ✓ Look for ways to move out of the ancient multi-story building, one floor at a time.
    - ■ Tie in with bypassing/closing down WIP stockrooms and reducing WIP in pallets by machines; much less space will be needed.
    - ■ Consider moving a major product line (e.g., with screw machine, plating, test, pack, ship) into present FGI warehouse.
    - ■ Rationale: Manufacturing effectiveness thrives in an open one-story building, especially in efforts to create flow-through production.
  - ✓ Rationalize the product line. Once there is some semblance of factory-within-a-factory for a few star products, it will be easier to determine which products are losers (e.g., Reel-Rite).

IV. Additional Comments (not mentioned during seminar)

- *Bypassing/eliminating buffer stock*: Since some products have components that have been around for 20–40 years (no significant obsolescence problems), use the "exception-based stockroom" concept. Here's how it works for a common product (e.g., fittings or unilets) while in a semi-finished state in WIP storage:

- ✓ Retain a buffer stock of the item in its present slot in the WIP stockroom. Leave it there and hope it is never needed and gathers dust.
- ✓ Normal practice: manufacture parts and feed directly to its use point (e.g., final assembly), *not* WIP storage. Buffer stock is only tapped when the producing work center cannot keep up.
- ✓ Extend this to *many* of those common parts. The result: the buffer stock protection is maintained but storage-and-pick steps are taken out of the lead time, which eliminates many transactions.
- ✓ Tell Mr. Rutledge (Emerson vice chairman and War on Inventory champion) that you didn't cut the stock in half (as he may have called for) but did cut a day out of lead time (and will save on material-handling costs).
- ✓ This bypassing of buffer stock (1) gives people time to overcome fears of a severe stockout, and (2) points to where buffer protection is and is not needed (usually we don't know). If it is never tapped, *then* abolish it from WIP storage completely.
- • *Source of recommendations*: Many of these observations/ recommendations came from or were discussed with others on the tour (Vince, Burleigh, Don, George, and the JIT team from corporate, among others).

CHAPTER I-10. GLEASON TOOL/HARBOR METAL STAMPING, ROCHESTER, NY, 1987

Gleason's Harbor Metal Stamping business unit offers an excellent platform for showing the effects of both poor and good methods of charging overhead to products made. The caselet goes into refined details on cost-allocation validity, which is a contemporary topic in management accounting.

High-Interest Topics:
- **Making more money with less costing**
- **Over-costing high-volume, under-costing low-volume products**
- **Fewer transactions, simpler costing**

Revising Overhead Charging for Improved Pricing/Bidding—and Simplified Operations
Observations in connection with a two-day on-site Schonberger seminar, July 24-25, 1987

I. Costing/Pricing Issues

- *Over-costing high-volume parts*:
  - ✓ Harbor Stamping charges overhead to products based on machine hours. A result is that high-volume parts stamped out on Harbor's 600- and 750-ton presses are over-costed and over-priced.
  - ✓ The machine-hour method heavily allocates production and inventory control (P&IC) costs to the large presses, even though their operation requires little P&IC support. (What high-volume parts do require is significant technical support, the costs of which the machine-hour method allocates rather well.)
- *Under-costing low-volume parts*: On the other hand, most low-volume parts are under-costed and underpriced.
  - ✓ They require considerable P&IC support but don't get charged for their share.
  - ✓ They are also responsible for the bulk of data entry and computer transactions, and related costs of computer hardware, software, and staff. But those costs aren't a part of the burden (overhead) cost pool at all. They are treated as sales, general, and administrative (SG&A) cost.

II. Solution

- *Revealing the money-losers*: If Harbor's costing system was modified to reflect true costs (further comments later), numerous low-volume parts and products would probably appear as money-losers. That revelation could lead to (1) weeding out losers, or (2) raising prices where it won't drive too many customers away.
- *A better way*: Better for Harbor is first to simplify the entire P&IC system, including slashing the volume of production transactions. Cutting transactions and material moving/storing actions includes:
  - ✓ Kanban—simplified through use of labeled containers (simpler than detachable cards).
  - ✓ Adopt cells for higher-volume products or standard component parts (eliminates the need for containers—until packaging).
  - ✓ Regularized, daily-rate schedules (scarcely any scheduling transactions) for star products and components.
  - ✓ Eliminating WIP stockrooms and their costs; moving materials directly from station to station.

✓ Tearing out on-line reporting stations under MAPICS (the existing IBM P&IC system). Reassigning freed-up infosystem staff people for work related directly to production, technical support, sales, supplier development, and factory renewal and reorganization.

- *Product-line rationalization*: After those (and other) simplifications, product-line "rationalization" may proceed: use a more accurate allocation of burden (see below), check costs, revise prices, and shut down money-losing products. By simplifying first, many currently unprofitable products can probably be saved.

III. Modifying the Costing System

- *Improving the not-too-bad system.*
  ✓ Current costing at Harbor is significantly more accurate than in most companies. Overhead allocation based on machine hours is, for machine-intensive companies, a modern idea. (Over 95% of industry still allocates by direct-labor hours, which, in view of the shrinking direct labor element of total product cost, can be grossly inaccurate.)
  ✓ Still, the cost system needs to be modified.
- *Overhead (burden) allocation*:
  ✓ First is to split factory overhead in two:
    1. Technical support (die design, die maintenance, machine setup, manufacturing engineering, etc.).
    2. P&IC support, which could be called "logistics" (scheduling, materials, handling, etc.).
  ✓ Next, split computer information system (IS) costs in two:
    1. Administrative support.
    2. Factory support.
  ✓ Finally, recombine as shown in Figure 10.1 under "*new*"—as compared with the existing method labeled *old* (present).
  ✓ As indicated, P&IC, in addition to factory IS, should be pulled out of SG&A and treated more accurately as factory overhead— allocated by product (or component) manufacturing lead time, aka, throughput time, flow time, cycle time).
    ■ This recommends a monthly audit of lead times (from the purchased materials stockroom to finished, packaged products) for random samples of products.

Old (present)

Factory Overhead		Sales, General, and Administrative (SG&A)
Allocated by machine hours		(Not allocated to product costs)
Technical support costs	P&IC costs	Information systems (IS), administrative & factory costs; Other costs

New (proposed)

Factory Overhead			SG&A
			(Not allocated)
Allocate by machine hours	Allocate by lead time		Information systems, admin. costs
Tech. support costs	P&IC costs	Infosys, factory costs	Other

FIGURE 10.1
Existing and improved costing system.

- At CalComp (manufacturer of electronic plotters) the method is to periodically wand a bar-code when a key component leaves the purchased-parts stockroom and again when the item becomes a finished good; the difference being lead time.

✓ Another possibility for collecting data on technical support costs is to use piece counters on all machines that have a "stroke" action. The occasional audit of piece counts (converted to machine hours) then serves as the basis for allocating periodic tech-support costs.

IV. Modifying Data Collection System

- *Data collection*: A few very broad comments—many details needing to be worked out.

✓ There is no good purpose in costing, costing, costing. The real need is to be able to occasionally and accurately cost audit selected products to find out if pricing is right, to bid on similar business, and to do feasibility studies for new equipment or new products, as well as for other major but infrequent high-cost proposals.

✓ There is no need to try to pin down all costs. It's futile and too cumbersome and costly to try to do so.

✓ An inaccurate product costing system (the kind in most companies—the cost-variance system) should not be used to appraise managerial performance or to motivate improvement.

- Instead, drive costs down and increase quality, response time, and flexibility by plotting quality, cycle time, setup time, etc., on large visible charts.

- Such visualization is the most effective way there is for upper managers and line employees alike to assess results, install fixes, and take pride in accomplishments.
- Monetizing those basics just adds a layer of indirectness to results.
- *What to do about present system*: Abandoning the present system of collecting labor and units produced for each operation (with planned upgrades) is not gutting the cost system.
   ✓ The usual cost collection by expense categories (payroll, direct materials, etc.) is still present, as are budgets and budgetary controls.
   ✓ However, operation-by-operation costing must be seen as non-value-adding duplication and waste, not as valid and necessary for control.

CHAPTER I-11. HOOVER UNIVERSAL, TILLSONBURG, ON, CANADA, 1986

A brief evening plant visit to Hoover Universal took place in preparation for my next-day seminar, which revolved around plans for converting the company's automobile seat manufacturing to JIT production. Seminar attendees included the CEO; the head engineer for seat design from the U.S.; and, from Canada, the president, treasurer, HR director, cost and IE director, accounting executive, and two hourlies from receiving inspection. For this caselet, the quite brief actual case report to the company has been supplemented using my rough notes.

High-Interest Topics:
- **Converting batched production with bulky, cumbersome foam equipment to cellular production**
- **Need to combine race-track and modular production lines**
- **Systematic training/use of SPC**
- **Extensive cross-training, job trading**
- **Product changeovers done by line employees**
- **Make-to-a-number scheduling**

Third-tier Producer of Foam for Car Seats Embraces JIT

Assessment based on a brief plant visit after arrival, evening of March 18, 1986

In connection with a one-day Schonberger seminar in London, Ontario, for the company

I. General Information

- *The Company*: Hoover Universal produces foam padding for car seats for 20 automobile assembly plants (became a subsidiary of Johnson Control in 1985).
- *Personnel & costs*: The Tillsonburg site has 390 people, 54 salaried. Product costs are 4.8% direct labor, 65–68% materials, 28–29% overhead.
- *Deliveries*:
   - ✓ Tillsonburg delivers 130 P/Ns (part numbers) to 23 customers (VW, Chrysler, Ford, G.M.), 50% exported to the U.S.; 70–80% of P/Ns are made in one day.
   - ✓ Of 128 carriers (containers) for those P/Ns, no more than four are for a given P/N; three carriers are for about six more P/Ns; and two carriers are for about 50 P/Ns.
   - ✓ A specific loading hour is set for deliveries to Chrysler's Lansing and Jefferson assembly plants. Delivery schedules for G.M. in Oshawa, ON, are computer-to-computer.
- *Customer linkages*: Customers provide overall monthly schedules (forecasts); phone weekly with updates; and call Thursday with next week's requirement. Customers send a quality surveillance person here once or twice yearly from Chrysler and G.M., once yearly from Ford, and less often from VW.
- *Competitors*: Woodbridge Foam; Lear Sigler.
- *Other Hoover Universal plants*: Three more foam plants are in Ohio, Michigan, and Jefferson City, MO. Hoover also has eight or nine seat trimming plants (putting covers on seats) operating "just in time" in the U.S.
- *Tour hosts*: Wayne Durst, plant manager; and Rick Harmon.

II. Production

- *Operational details*: See Sidebar 1, if interested in some details.
- *Production*: Employees in six labor classifications operate in three shifts, six days a week, plus four hours clean-up on Sundays.
- *SPC in use*:
   - ✓ More than 50 X-bar/R charts; four moving range charts; and many p-bar charts in incoming inspection.

SIDEBAR 1   HOOVER UNIVERSAL OPERATIONS

Equipment includes:
Two "racetrack lines" with 58 carriers each and gas heat for 54 on-line molds. A modular line with hot-water in the housing. A monorail handles frames (which have been getting larger/heavier). PLCs control it all.

Output:
Pumps 32,000 seat foams (or 6,000 or more car seat sets) per day; 1.5 days' supply in warehouse.

Processing:
Chemicals (by rail car) go into 10 tanks for compounding. Molding (over 300 molds) takes about five minutes, in the oven. About 25 seconds after molding comes de-mold, then pre-crush and full crush—using many container types. Mold changes take 15–20 seconds.

Supply:
Two types of purchased foam, one from two U.S. sources, the other from Dow in Canada. Wire is on blanket orders with phoned releases.

Shipping:
10 rail cars and 40–50 trucks ship out per day

✓ Two full-time receiving inspectors do sample inspections (e.g., sample size of 50 out of 5,000, or 1,000, or 10,000). 1.5 days' incoming raw material is on hand.
- *Metrics*: An electric display shows (at time of visit) percent utilization (94.2%), percent good (75.8%), and percent scrap (0.4%). An electric panel board shows P/Ns (part numbers) that are in repair.

III. Strengths at Tillsonburg

- *Employee exchange visits—for better communication & understanding*:
  ✓ "Olds" shop-floor people from Lansing have visited this plant.
  ✓ Some inspectors from here have visited a Ford plant.
  ✓ The Tillsonburg plant manager. and one other person had attended an employee meeting at Olds-Lansing.
- *Employee-involvement room*: Equipped with blackboards, flip charts, and growing videotape library.

- *Training*: Systematic SPC training for every employee has been partly accomplished. Recently eight managers reviewed charts with the employee who does the charting; a foreman does likewise.
- *Product changeovers*: Handled by line employees.
- *Cross-training/job trading*: On average, employees have learned 3.9 jobs—with two weeks of training on each new job.

IV. General Recommendations for Improvement

- *Technology obstacle*: From a JIT standpoint, the present foam technologies are an obstacle:
   ✓ Racetrack lines are so huge that they cannot be easily moved, and their locations are very likely to be wrong and obstructive within, say, about three years of vigorous manufacturing improvements.
   ✓ Modular lines fit the cell concept, but they create the need for a lot of bulky, costly inventory being cured for a couple of hours. Top priority is for an engineering team to seek a more compact technology that combines the best features of racetrack and modular production.
- *Smaller and in multiples*: Smaller foam lines are needed, e.g., 10 positions instead of 52, so that a *true* cell concept is possible, oriented to a customer, and with a single manager and team charged with results.
   ✓ Note: Usually a cell would be oriented to a product family, but in auto-seating, the final customer-provided shipping container and that customer's broadcast scheduling system—dictating the mix of models in the truck—make it reasonable to group by customer.
   ✓ Exception: If a single large customer uses just one seat type (e.g., Jeep seat), then best practice is to set up a dedicated foam-trim-pack line both for that product and that customer—and run it to customer's use rate.
   ✓ Note: If the industry—or several customers—could agree on a standardized *modular* container (so a seat maker could use small wheeled racks inside the plant, then stack the containers into a forklift-truck-size for the shipping dock), then it might

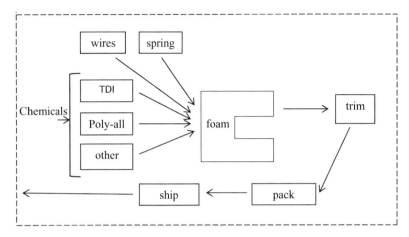

FIGURE 11.1
An example of major customers' products made in separate cells.

make sense to create cells in some other way besides by customer.
- Figure 11.1 is an example of a foam cell: incoming material (chemicals and derivatives, wires, springs) feeding foam stations, then forward to trim, pack, and ship integrated into the line—with team build.

V. Other Suggestions

- *Transport*: Make use of more trucks, fewer tank cars/box cars—thus to cut delivery lot sizes and get closer to JIT deliveries.
- *Storage*: Design and employ modular racks.
- *Prevention*: Develop and employ fail-safing devices.
- *Trouble indicators*: Adopt red and yellow trouble lights.
- *No over-production*:
  - ✓ Adopt "make-to-a-number" production (no over-production except when falling behind).
  - ✓ Under-schedule labor and production so that making the number is likely on most days.
  - ✓ Use extra time at the ends of shifts for more problem-solving and improvement projects.
- *Shifts*: Strive for two instead of three shifts.

CHAPTER I-12. 3M DATA PRODUCTS DIVISION, HUTCHINSON, MN, 1984

This caselet describes an innovative manual simulation process. It is similar to other such simulations (e.g., Legos), but it may be the most comprehensive in its involvement of the work force and its direct connection to real workplaces.

Information came from a long phone call with the production superintendent. (This is one of three caselets not involving a plant visit. I had been scheduled to visit there in May, 1985, but it did not take place.)

High-Interest Topics:
- **Pull simulation for both learning *and* execution—representing real production components**
- **Advantage: Operator participants gaining working knowledge of operational conditions**
- **Adapting to shift imbalances**

Coffee-cup Simulator Paving the Way to JIT Production
As related to Schonberger, November 21, 1984

I. General

- *Product line*: Videotape cassettes.
  - ✓ The old method was job-lot production: large stocks of materials separating one work center from another, large lots moving between them, and each machine making as much as possible and pushing it onward.
  - ✓ The new method is just-in-time (JIT) production: pull only the amount needed from the previous work center. The way JIT was planned and implemented at this plant is as notable as the results.
- *Innovative learning & implementation*:
  - ✓ Videocassettes are an obsolete product, seemingly a bit out of place for this book. However, this brief caselet does not get into details about the product or the technology.
  - ✓ Caselet is of interest because it:
    - Describes a simple, innovative table-top manual simulation method of involving the work force in implementation of kanban.
    - Infuses advanced knowledge and application of essentials of flow manufacturing.

II. Brown Paper and Coffee Cups

- *Plant & people*: The simulation began with full explanations of how it would proceed and tie in with people's actual jobs and processes. To start, JIT planners placed a large sheet of brown paper on a big table—to be marked up with process data.
- *Locations & data*: Machine locations and operating data were considered fixed, while other factors of production were deliberately altered—on paper—in order to find best ways to change from push to pull production. Pull signals (kanban) were required to make the pull approach work. Participants were advised as follows:
  - ✓ Where containers are used as kanban signals, they must be *standard* containers. Any old box, tray, or pallet *won't* do.
  - ✓ A standard container held a standard quantity, partitions often dividing the container so that over- or under-filling would be easily noticed at a glance. Also, a container needed a card or tag to identify part number, quantity, source, and destination. (Any of these could be omitted if obvious.)
  - ✓ With lean JIT inventories, you can't risk mistakes or uncertainty as to kind, quantity, or location; hence the need for rigor in container design, labeling, filling, and handling.
- *Ready for simulation*: Each coffee cup was stuffed with a card (kanban) with all the right information on it. Then the pull approach was simulated and refined with manipulations of the coffee cups.

III. Brainstorming

- *Basic question* during simulation:
  - ✓ How many coffee cups—representing standard containers of cassette components and assemblies—should go beside each machine?
  - ✓ The answer depends on many factors: reject/defect rates, machine downtime, changeover time, lot sizes, schedules, machine staffing, coffee and lunch breaks, what to do when a tool breaks or someone runs out of parts or gets sick and leaves the machine.
- *Shop-floor answers*: Planners and managers are not close enough to the work to be able to compile and expound on a full list of such factors.

✓ People on the shop floor—operators, handlers, inspectors, maintenance people, supervisors, and so forth—have much of the required knowledge in their heads.

✓ So, the simulation proceeds by bringing groups of people from all parts of cassette operations to the simulation room and getting their questions and concerns on the table—literally.

- *What-ifs*: In brainstorming sessions, simulations showed the amount of inventory in queue each simulated hour, and observers freely asked their "what-ifs." Questions without obvious answers were posted on a blackboard (100 or more problems and issues went up on the board). It took 2 months to solve them—on paper. Then the simulated plan became a reality.

IV. Implementation

- *Smoothed progress*: Implementations were done without a hitch.
  - ✓ Even the mismatch between running injection-molding on three shifts and assembly on just one shift did not become a problem.
  - ✓ Each day, assemblers watched without alarm as the pile of molded plastic components shrunk. They weren't worried about running out, because they saw it happen with coffee cups, and they knew the containers would be filled again overnight.
- *Loose but not seriously*: The Hutchinson kanban approach does not impose tight restrictions on the possibility of a maker producing more than a user can utilize in a day.
  - ✓ Actually, makers deliver parts forward instead of users fetching parts from makers—the more classical form of kanban.
  - ✓ Old habits of making and delivering too much have resurfaced from time to time, and people must be reminded about the commitment to make only what is used. This problem—one of lapses in correct execution—has not been serious.
- *Things not going wrong*: Since in manufacturing things rarely work without exasperation, struggle, and heroic measures, we tend to shake our heads in wonder or disbelief when an implementation goes smoothly. What was the secret?
- *Training & ownership*:
  - ✓ Probably there is equal value in the way the paper and coffee cups were used as a training tool and for gaining ownership from those who build the product and handle the resources.

✓ Everyone already knew how the kanban approach was supposed to work and what they were to do on the day of switching from push to pull. They all had helped design the detailed procedures and therefore were committed to seeing kanban work rather than fail.

CHAPTER I-13. 3M GRAPHIC PREPARATION SYSTEMS, WEATHERFORD, OK, AND ST. PAUL, MN, 1986

This long caselet is a highly detailed treatment of how 3M's over-arching just-in-time production initiative plays out (or should play out) with process-industry equipment (i.e., coaters) in its graphic prep factory.	**High-Interest Topics:** • **Process machines (coaters) need strong mechanical—not just chemical—engineering expertise** • **Attacking a 37-step changeover for the no. 1 coating machine** • **Idea: Can the wide coater run two different products side by side?**

Flow Management at the Plant Level Requires Corporate-level Help
Assessment from visits to the Weatherford plant and St. Paul HQ, Aug. 25-27, 1986

I. General Information

- *The agenda*:
  - ✓ These three days at 3M's Weatherford site included a half-day plant tour, a half-day seminar for all plant people, and a full day with JIT and other teams.
  - ✓ Then fly to St. Paul, 3M's headquarters, for 1-day seminar and discussion with the GPS division's corporate-level people. Many of the observations in this summary report were, in part, based on opinions and suggestions of plant-level people at Weatherford
- *Graphic Preparation Systems*: Weatherford, with some 170 employees, produces customized, high-performance colored/imaged film, which is applied by customers to surfaces large (e.g., sides of delivery vans) and small (printed brochures).
- *Processes*: Include mixing, pumping, filtering, sand milling, proofing, coating, slitting, sheeting, final converting, and packaging. Two very

large coaters are the primary equipment. Testing and lab work—e.g., to ensure color perfection—are extensive.

- *Raw materials*: 170 materials from 30 suppliers include solvents from Houston, chips from New Jersey, master rolls of polyester film from 3M in Alabama, sensitizers (Chem-I-Lite) from 3M in Minnesota, pigments from "back East," and packaging.
- *Contact persons/tour hosts in Weatherford*: Tom Hayes, production superintendent; Pat Mudd, materials and office manager; V. Synder, solution prep.

II. Strengths at Weatherford

- *Quality*: 3M's and GPS's emphasis on QITs/ZD/Crosby (quality improvement teams, zero defects, and Philip Crosby's quality-is-free message) is ingrained at Weatherford—firm ground for an improvement effort. Quality to the customer appears to be excellent.
- *Environment*: Small, focused plant, pleasant working environment, good human relationships.
- *Controls*: Production and inventory control (PP&C) and data-processing people have achieved a high degree of control of inventories and on-time completions of work orders.
- *Variability*: Quality and process engineers are aware of the need for an assault on process variability.
- *Setups*: The setup team has made some good progress (though without the benefit of training materials on setup-reduction basics):
  - ✓ Implementation of color carts that can be loaded and cleaned off-line.
  - ✓ Development and use of changeover checklists.
  - ✓ Review meetings for the changeover crew prior to start of changeover.
- *Avoiding complacency*: Years of little improvement (complacency) have ended. There is now a will to improve and stave off decline.

III. Weaknesses

- *Low emphasis on manufacturing*:
  - ✓ Process control and yields are terrible: nearly the same lack of understanding process variables exists today as 25 years ago (for

one product and for an older coater). Learning is no better on the newer coater and products. (Coaters are cantankerous—can take months to get working right; then major changes in specs can cause troubles all over again.)

✓ GPS (like most Western manufacturers) has experienced two or three decades of neglect (focusing perhaps on new products, etc., but not much on manufacturing) in which overhead costs have grown beyond reason even as problem-solving emphasis declines. Now, there are signs of improvement, but the pace of that is slow.

✓ The manufacturing process is inflexible with long lead-times, which means being out of touch with both customers and suppliers.

- *Risk*: Several potential competitors in the U.S. and Japan surely are attracted to the high profit margins of GPS's products—and are themselves likely to be involved in campaigns for process control and continual improvement. Without action, the "cash cow" at GPS is in danger of ending up in the rendering plant. Recent industrial history shows this can happen almost overnight.

IV. JIT Production at Weatherford—Scope

- *Now*: JIT teams are working at two extremities, SP&T (solutions processing and test) at the front end and converting at the tail end. But the biggest lead-time/inventory/process problems are in coating, where there is a setup team but not a full JIT campaign. Positive effects of the present emphasis on JIT are…

  ✓ JIT serving as a quality/scrap/yield improvement technique:
    - Use a solution in coating right after the solution is mixed, and use jumbo roll in converting right after it is coated—thereby exposing nonconformities before they add up to scrap.
    - Good data on these new practices are already available.

  ✓ Inducing culture change—by getting some processes close-linked in *time*, and some in geography (e.g., creation of cells for slicing jumbo rolls, packing sheets, putting into boxes, and applying labels).

  ✓ Reducing inventories and lead-time to warehouses/customers—though only minimally, because huge lots are still run through coaters.

- *Re-focus*: JIT can be expanded to place maximum focus on coating, and thereby…
  - ✓ Slash lead-times and cycle intervals (to make a particular product) as well as finished goods in the distribution system.
  - ✓ Reduce raw materials and packaging—shorter cycles result in more regular, predictable demands for them.

V. High-Impact JIT Project: Changeover on Coaters from Hours to Minutes

- *General*:
  - ✓ Figure 13.1 is a flow chart of precision roll removal, by a 2-person team from maintenance, on the 12W coater. Removal takes more than half an hour—and perhaps another half hour to install two new rolls (I did not observe the installation). Here are setup-reduction ideas for cutting that time to, say, 5 minutes:
    - Borrow people from anywhere and everywhere whenever there is to be a coater changeover. Given the cost of coaters and their very unsatisfactory performance when operating in the long production-run mode, a coater changeover should almost be treated with the urgency of a fire.
    - Develop detailed checklists, everything timed by stopwatch, floor maps diagramming where each changeover team member must be at each changeover minute.
    - Position all tools, fixtures, and materials very close to place of use (on pegboards, slings, shuttles, coil springs, glides, slides, rollers, etc.).
    - Hold a changeover meeting and get *everything* ready and into position *before* the end of the previous coating run.
  - ✓ Be sure QC is on hand at the right time, perhaps with portable test equipment.
  - ✓ Figure 13.1 is largely self-explanatory in showing lots of steps in carefully removing one wide and heavy roll of film (employing a dolly, bridge crane, forklift truck, canvas wrap) and reversing the process to install the new roll. Not shown are all the steps and adjustments to get the roll started and correctly apply the coating solutions.

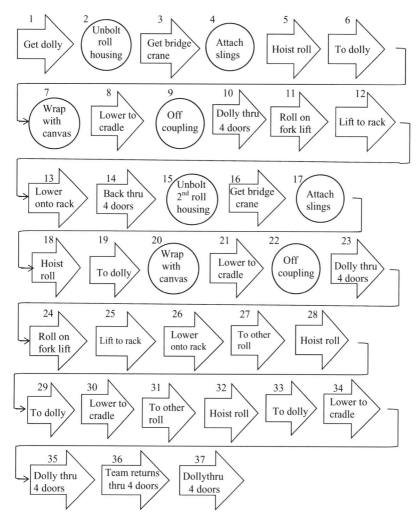

FIGURE 13.1
Changeover, precision rolls, 12W coater.

- *Specifics*
    ✓ Develop a floor or bridge crane fixture that will lift *both* rolls
      from the machine at once.
    ✓ Develop a dolly with two cradles, to receive both rolls at once,
      instead of the current single-cradle dollies.
    ✓ Have a quick-attach (maybe Velcro) protective case in the cradle.
      One person can attach the protective case while two roll-removal
      people position the crane at the next pair of rolls.

✓ Have a second two-cradle dolly on hand in advance, loaded with the next pair of rolls.

✓ Acquire extra sets of couplings so that the next pair of rolls already has couplings mounted. Then the crane can immediately hoist the next pair to the machine.

✓ Modify all fasteners (mostly bolts and screws) for very fast loosening/tightening. Basic, quick-setup fastening methods include: pear-shaped bolt holes, U-shaped washers, hinged bolts that stay at the point of use, split-thread bolts and bolt holes, spacer clamps, locator pins or tapered holes instead of threaded fasteners (where weight assists in holding top to bottom), and hydraulic clamps.*

VI. Changeover-Time Reduction: Small Lots, Regularized Scheduling

- *Eliminating large lots*: With quick-changeover techniques on each coater, the major reason for running large lots (4- to 8-week production runs) is eliminated.

- Weatherford may move with deliberate speed toward a true "JIT schedule," which, for standard products, is regular from day-to-day and repeats cyclically until clear changes in the sales mix are detected. Below is an example (for Weatherford's four major product families, labeled A, B, C, and D) of repeating 2-week cycles:

M T W T F → M T W T F → M T W T F → M T W T F
|→----------- cycle ------------- →|← ------------- cycle ----------- →|Etc.

  Or, better yet (if changeover reduction is even more successful) repeating 1-week cycles:

M T W T F → M T W T F → M T W T F
|→ ----- cycle ---- →|← ---- cycle ---- →|← ---- cycle ---- →|Etc.

- *Predictability*:
  ✓ Regular scheduling provides some certainty of need to SP&T and to suppliers of raw material and packaging items; and some certainty—and regular shipments of all products—to warehouses.

---

* See general concepts of quick setup in Shigeo Shingo, *A Revolution in Manufacturing: The SMED System* (Stamford, CT: Productivity Press, 1985.)

✓ As product mix and sales quantities change, simply adjust the number of hours of run time for each product—but not the run sequence.

- *New business*: For example, accept special high-margin orders for small volumes (as low as one jumbo). This suggestion comes from a marketing manager in St. Paul on hearing about quick changeover.

VII. Short Production Runs→Realistic Carrying Costs

- *True carrying costs*: JIT's insistence on short production runs and cycle intervals has inspired rethinking the costs of carrying large lots of inventory.
  - ✓ GPS's much-too-low 14% carrying cost rates contributes to the calculation of large lot sizes on the coaters.
  - ✓ Here is a breakdown of real carrying costs, most of which have not been previously recognized, either in practice or in textbooks:
    - ■ Lost opportunity to invest (presuming GPS's 14%).
    - ■ Cost in the materials management department to physically hold stock (space, containers, racks, stock keepers, record-keeping, counting, moving, damaging, obsolescence, aging, insurance, inventory taxes).
    - ■ Costs of the same for stock in a state of idleness on factory floor.
    - ■ Costs of lumpy workloads.
    - ■ Costs of scrap and rework present in large lots (minimal in small lots).
    - ■ Costs of cycle-interval delay introduced by large lots—which, because it results in hundreds of potential causes of bad quality, makes isolating causes difficult or not possible.
    - ■ Costs of pushing the forecast horizon so far out that the product-mix forecasting is sure to be bad (thus having wrong finished goods and raw materials in stock).
- *EOQs*: Following is an example of economic order quantity calculation, before and after:
  - ✓ Before:

$$EOQ = \sqrt{14 \div 0.14} = 10 \text{ days}.$$

where 14 is changeover (time or demand) and 0.14 is carrying-cost rate

✓ After 5-fold cut in changeover time and 5-fold increase in carrying-cost rate:

$$EOQ = \sqrt{(14/5) \div (0.14/5)} = 2\,days$$

- *Importance*: Of the many plants/companies in many industries that I have visited, none had a more pressing changeover time and lot-sizing issue than what I believed GPS had. Hence, the particular amount of space given to the topic here.

VIII. General Observations—Weatherford

- *Manufacturing support staff*:
  - ✓ Production control/data processing's very large staff has done its job of bringing wastes and delays under control. Now it's time to eliminate wastes/delays and shrink the staff.
  - ✓ The supplier-quality staff is small (a part-time committee) for such a high-impact problem area.
  - ✓ Process manufacturing and quality engineering are of respectable size, but what can they do?
    - ■ They have no confidence that raw material specs are meaningful to process control.
    - ■ Process engineers generally avoid problems of machine variability, where enormous problems have probably persisted for years. Maintenance technicians cannot bear the load of dealing with machine variability. However, it is artificial to divorce chemical variability from mechanical variability; the two come together in the machine.
    - ■ Net effects: Quality engineers deal (effectively) with *outgoing* quality; process engineers are frustrated because they are blocked from dealing effectively with much of anything.
    - ■ The process-manufacturing staff grew to its present size about six years ago, but process control hasn't noticeably improved.
    - ■ Weatherford sees the division's (St. Paul's) procedure for authorizing equipment (even a simple wheeled cart with cradles) as cumbersome.
    - ■ The division's accounting system prevents use (for other purposes) of the mostly idle 13W coater (in the "red" room),

because "it runs too slow." This type of insanity—failure to see the great value of a machine that runs slowly at a customer's use rate—surely needs to be modified by "special dispensation" policies until our accounting systems can catch-up with our growing understanding of how to make manufacturing customer-focused.

✓ The JIT team in coating/converting has come up with a plan that incorporates a particularly important JIT/TQC concept: segmenting operations by type of product/process.

- It involves treating make-to-stock (based on warehouse reorder points) as one segment and make-to-order (piece orders) as another—each to have its own equipment and be geographically apart from the other.

- This also paves the way to using two different scheduling/order tracking systems, both much simpler than the present one which requires multiple inventory transactions. (The make-to-stock segment could be put on a regular schedule, unchangeable for a few weeks at a time; make-to-order could be driven by an exploded customer order, with visual pull reaching backward to feeder materials.)

✓ The coating/converting team has an excellent plan for hands-on training using a small-scale simulator (a sort of table-top, erector-set coater). JIT/TQC requires a high degree of training, since it calls for changes, some drastic, in past practices and beliefs.

- *Miscellaneous recommendations—Weatherford*:

  ✓ Put packaging materials (from Raven) on a daily kanban delivery schedule—no inventory transactions.

  ✓ Arrange for small, frequent shipments of film from Decatur to be matched to Weatherford's ever-shorter cycle interval.

  ✓ Best sequence of codes through the coater should be one that minimizes code-to-code changes on the machine (and the same sequence prior to the coater in solution prep). For example, a B-D-C-A sequence instead of A-B-C-D might be the one with fewest changeover steps.

  ✓ Adopt TPM—in which maintenance trains operators to lube, do simple repairs, etc.

✓ 1-hour, daily planned shutdown for thorough P.M. (preventive maintenance) with regular pre-failure replacements of idler bearings, etc.

✓ Record, by frequency (tally marks on charts) the likely reason for every stoppage or slowdown. Get operators involved, in teams, to discuss and diagnose causes using collected glitch data.

✓ Decide on an exact number of material-handling carts and totes, exact quantity per cart/tote, exact location (kanban squares) of carts/totes in the converting cells.

✓ Cancel the utilization report.

- *Miscellaneous general issues*:

  ✓ Equipment policies of the past are, by hindsight, a major obstacle to quality and cost improvement. Machines are too large, rated to run too fast, run sheets that are too wide, have ovens grown larger than current needs require. What to do?

    ■ Alternative 1: Run 27-inch maximum widths on the 52-inch web—in order to get better yields, more run time per week, less scrap. Would good output per day drop severely? Maybe not. If output did drop a good deal, it might be a worthy price to pay for predictability of output—very important when you want to deliver FGI and receive raw materials just in time.

    ■ Alternative 2: Equip a coater with two side-by-side 26-inch coating heads at the feeder end. Then set up head A while head B runs product; set up head B while head A runs. (This was the thinking-out-loud suggestion of one of the Weatherford managers.)

    ■ Bypass much of the oven/oven time (since, at the slow speeds at which coaters have been forced to run, coatings tend to be dry by the time they reach the first drying stage).

    ■ For the future, never buy another coater wider than the final product. For now, perhaps invest in another coater—narrow width—at Weatherford, and dedicate it (no changeovers except for color) to the dominant-selling product family. (Narrow-width slitter, too.)

    ■ As a plant organization strategy for the future, strive for separate factories-within-factories, each dedicated to a different product family—each with its own linked set of SP&T, coater, conversion, as well as with one team and one manager in charge.

✓ Until people and machines are organized by the way work physically flows instead of by departments, employee-involvement programs will not yield much. The customer (next process) has to be next to the maker as a natural team member in order for real problem-solving to spring forth from the shop-floor level.

✓ In general, the primary obstacle to improvement seems to be failure to manage R&D as an integral part of the business. And failure to transform business objectives into supportive R&D goals. Inasmuch as business objectives—in a much more competitive world—are much more demanding, so must be R&D goals and action policies. The following might help:

- Inject a strong set of policies and performance measures that add up to *design to target yield*, *design to spec*, and *design for process control.*

- Many large industrial companies (perhaps including GPS—I did not find out) have begun using formal measures of "design for manufacturability and quality." Examples: percent of standard parts/specs used in a new product (Xerox now is *death* on the old tendency for a green-field approach to R&D); number of design-related ECO's (engineering change orders) written after design verification test (CDC likes this one).

- Tektronix (one division) has put "teeth" into its design-for-manufacturability objectives: A product development group is told, "one of you is going to follow the design into manufacturing." But the group isn't told which one.

- The latter action policy from Tek seems to have a merit for GPS. The reason: an overly large St. Paul group and a void in continuing product/process improvement at the plant level. The Tek approach is a way to implement a move toward assigning some lab people to manufacturing sites for tours of, say, two years.

─────────

CHAPTER I-14. CAMPBELL SOUP, PARIS, TX, 1985

Campbell had chosen its Paris, Texas, plant for a company initiative focused especially on just-in-time, total quality control, and total productive maintenance. The full-day plant tour yielded extensive, fairly detailed notes, selectively incorporated into this caselet. For the primary topics covered, this caselet seems almost as if it could have been written today.	*High-Interest Topics:* • **Before- and after-diagrams show a cellular-production configuration for Campbell—and a model valid for much of the packaged-food industry today** • **Producing many products to regularized repeating schedules**

**Campbell's Paris, TX, Plant Paving the Way
to JIT/TQC in Food Processing**

Observations from a one-day plant visit, Feb. 27, 1985

Followed by a one-day customized seminar, February 28

I. General Information

- *Corporate campaign*: Three years ago, Campbell mounted a major, and successful, inventory-reduction campaign, which cut corporate inventory by one-third. By extension the current campaign is represented by a set of intersecting circles labeled JIT (see image, Fig. 14.1), TQC (total quality control), and TPM (total productive maintenance).
- *Paris, TX plant*: As part of that campaign, this plant is referred to as "the guinea-pig plant."
- *Plant & products*:
  - ✓ This facility, on 1,500 acres, was opened in 1964 and is Campbell's 2nd newest and 2nd largest plant—with 600 people in soups and 600 in the can plant and warehouse. (900 acres are for treating water.) There are two manufacturing and one cleanup (high pressure, low volume) shifts daily (chemicals can't be used *during* production).

FIGURE 14.1
JIT as conceived at Campbell Soup, early 1980s.

- ✓ The plant produces canned soups, including making its own cans and cooking and filling the cans with its well-known line of soups; currently, 186 different products exist. A typical soup has 15 ingredients, plus spices. Although there is a fall-winter sales peak for these products, a current effort is being made to run level-capacity year-around.
- ✓ The can plant, second largest in the world, is highly automated, producing 200 to 700 cans per minute. 28,000 cases were produced last year.
- ✓ Among the vast amounts of purchases that are sourced worldwide (especially from the U.S. western coast) are 7-8 truckloads of poultry per week.
- *Materials*: Inventory turnover is about six per year, including 6.7 turns for red meats (including "boat time") and 2.4 turns for tomato paste.
- *Contact persons*: Leu Springer, corporate VP of manufacturing; Charles E. Miller, corporate director of procurement; Michael D. McEver, manager, logistics, Paris plant.

II. Production Processes

- *Soup production*: Soup processes are listed in Sidebar 1, in roughly chronological order.
- *Can production*: Five main processes create soup cans:
    - ✓ Tinplate arriving in coil form is cut into sheets for either bodies or ends.
    - ✓ Sheets go to two enamel ovens (depending on can class and different soup products).
    - ✓ Scroll shears form ends, which go into end presses to produce finished ends (then held for 3 days for proper curing).
    - ✓ Body sheets from ovens are cut into body blanks by slitters, then go directly into bodymakers, yielding a finished can.
    - ✓ Cans are stored in jumble bins or palletized for later use—average inventory is four hours for the No. 1 cans and varies for other sizes.
- *Can disposition*: Cans are conveyed to filling as required; can changeover time—for 28 different classes of can—is 8–10 hours.

SIDEBAR 1   SOUP PROCESS FLOW AND OPERATIONS BREAKDOWN

Ingredients: Bulk pea beans, bags of starch, tomato paste, carrots, and potatoes are received on two rail lines and three truck docks.

Prep areas: inspect, weigh, assemble (in drums)—includes broth room (uses chicken fat, bone stock, tomato paste); butcher shop for meats; blending of paste, spices, and emulsions; fresh and frozen veggie prep.

Blending/cooking: Performed in 17 600-gallon, nine 35-gallon, and four 700-gallon kettles—in one or two filling lines; change time for cookers is up to 1 or 2 hours.

Filling: Kettles pump soups to 16 fill machines.

Numerous other operations: Spaghetti/noodle extruders, frozen food dispensers, slurry blending.

Multiple sterilizer/cookers (rotary & hydrostatic), 18 labeling machines (on cans transferred from can lines), palletizers (to warehouse by "tow-veyor").

Hold areas: Full day's production must stay in its own area for 8–11 days (federal requirement) before it can be shipped.

III. Strengths or Areas of Good Progress

- *Progress*: For this visit to the "guinea-pig plant," emphasis is on what needs doing, when, and how.
  - ✓ The plant has sent 150 people to Deming (quality) training; 300 have gone through a home-grown version so far, and 1,500 more are slated to do likewise.
  - ✓ It will also send employees to University of Tennessee's excellent three-week training course in quality.
  - ✓ Buyers have been unable to find a similarly excellent training source, and so are devising their own.
  - ✓ August 1 has been set as "conversion" day.
- *Strengths*: Suffice to say that the Paris plant's own campaign is well supported locally, and especially so at corporate, including by CEO Gordon McGovern.

IV. Opportunities for Improvement

- *Focused flow lines (cells)*: Equipment is sufficient to completely deconstruct the main soup area, and re-organize a few of the highest-volume areas (and/or having most specialized processes) into tightly-linked flow lines, each with its own dedicated equipment. Figure 14.2 illustrates, for example, four "most important" products having their own flows, and the many lesser products continuing in the batch mode as at present.
- *Equipment issues*:
  - ✓ Equipment for the four proposed product-focused cells need not be very complex or costly, nor big or fast, nor needing much attention to quick changeover.
  - ✓ That is because each cell is geared to produce at the comparatively slow pace of downstream sales. Thus, the equipment would need few complex features for model-to-model switches. (Today [2018] that mode of production is referred to as concurrent [or simultaneous or parallel] production—multiple products produced at the same time, instead of one after another on complex equipment.)
- *Regularize filling schedule for "A" (most important) products*: Synchronize schedules for as many ingredients as possible.

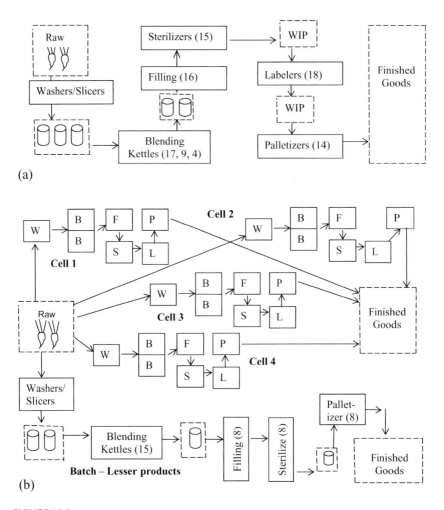

FIGURE 14.2
From present production to four flow lines focused by product family. (a) Present ("before") configuration. (b) Proposed ("after") configuration: 4 focused cells; one batch line for many fewer products.

Figure 14.3 is an example, where "x" stands for a "run" of the product on the given day. Appropriately, since (or assuming) mushroom and chicken noodle are Campbell's biggest sellers, they are shown to be scheduled every day, with other soups scheduled less often.

- *Statistical process control*:
  ✓ Cans are a top priority for SPC, with all operators involved.
  ✓ Suppliers: Reduce receiving inspections as SPC at supplier plants is phased in.

	Day											
	1	2	3	4	5	6	7	8	9	10	11	12
Mushroom	x	x	x	x	x	x	x	x	x	x	x	x
Chicken noodle	x	x	x	x	x	x	x	x	x	x	x	x
-----	x	x	x	x	x	x	x	x	x	x	x	x
-----	x		x		x		x		x		x	
-----	x		x		x		x		x		x	
-----	x		x		x		x		x		x	
*												
*												
*												

FIGURE 14.3
Regularized schedules for primary ("A") soups.

- *Total productive maintenance* (TPM):
  - ✓ Focus on the worst equipment, and Paretoize the causes.
  - ✓ Primary role of maintenance department: training operators such that most of TPM becomes part of their jobs, with maintenance continuing in its roles of equipment overhaul, installation, and so forth.
- *Critical changeover projects—those presently having long changeovers*:
  - ✓ Coil lines; ovens.
  - ✓ Palletizer/case packer/labeler.
  - ✓ Blenders/fillers/cookers/etc.
- *Buffer stock reduction*: Remove buffer stocks selectively:
  - ✓ Do so especially in cut sheet—which is the second largest unneeded stock build-up in the plant.
  - ✓ This assumes the coil-cutter is quite reliable, thus with little need for buffer stock.
- *Charts that point to key competitive targets*: Standout examples:
  - ✓ Trends in throughput time, by major product. Set up a team of supervisors over three or four consecutive processes with a mandate to cut *joint* flow time.
  - ✓ Quality: Defect awareness charts—to inspire action—photos, incidence numbers, etc.
  - ✓ Equipment *availability* rates (*not* efficiency).
- *Data media in every work center*: Flip charts, white boards, etc., where employees can record everything incorrect or going wrong.
- *Reduce suppliers*: Do so selectively, especially for cases and labels (there already is a plan for doing this), with remaining higher-volume suppliers put on contracts requiring daily deliveries (de-emphasize purchase orders, simplify ordering/receiving/paying paperwork).

- *Kanban*: Implement for delivery of cases (if not a formal kanban system, then possibly just a daily phone call to the supplier); consider trailers as warehouses.
- *Jumbo can area*: Bypass jumbo (which is can-damage prone: Plant people speak of "holes in cans" and cans that leak in filling them with soup), except for daily/Sat.-Sun. overflow needs. Bypass entirely once the can line is running right, with quick setups.
- *Forklifts*: Remove forklift trucks selectively. For example:
    - ✓ From microwave to beef cooker: use wheeled dollies with only one layer of beef boxes on each dolly. Set a goal to accomplish this within a week or two, since it is easy to do.
    - ✓ Scroll-sheared end plates: use waist-high wheeled dollies to move *one layer* of sheared end plate to end presses. (This will result in many more trips, but much less inventory/flow time).
- *Cut transit quantities*: Especially the number of layers per pallet.
- *Labor flexibility*: Mount a strong effort to reduce job classifications and to cross-train the work force.
    - ✓ There is scarcely any job rotation, partially because the plant is unionized. For example, someone in cooking is likely to stay there for life; and in cans, a body-maker cannot make can ends.
    - ✓ This limitation should be attacked by emphasizing to employees that mastering more skills is good for their career growth and job security, and for learning whole processes and contributing to their improvement.

V. Organizational & Strategic Success Factors

- *Training*: Getting the whole organization behind the improvement initiatives requires liberal amounts of training time for all.
- *Quality circles*: Existing circles need to be upgraded to action groups—taking on projects to improve up-time, lower flow time, cut setup time, etc.
- *Corporate steering committee*:
    - ✓ Impetus for the plant's improvement initiatives resides at Campbell's corporate headquarters, where Leu Springer and other executives have been the driving force.
    - ✓ By extension, corporate should join forces in some kind of multi-functional steering committee (manufacturing, marketing, engineering, planning, plant managers, et al.) with an agenda of

developing "Principles of manufacturing excellence," and heading off interference.

- *Plant steering committee*: Tasks should include prioritizing projects, hearing presentations and showering praise, and evaluating *the change process*.
- *Person of action*: Currently, the plant seems to be missing a strong champion or two, who will intervene for quick and continuing *action*.
- *Getting closer to customers/suppliers*: Do so "from top floor to shop-floor," with open channels of communication.
- *Factories-within-factories*: Included are equipment, layout, and responsibility centers: Quality improvement and flow-time reduction will bog down if responsibilities are fractionated as they are now (e.g., by product, such as mushroom, chicken noodle, frozen extract, chunky, etc.)
- *Corporate R&D*: Top priority is to spend heavily to eliminate the need for the three day cure of can ends. This is a major source of inventory, lead time, discontinuity, schedule disruption, and potential scrap.

CHAPTER I-15. MARS, VEGHEL, NETHERLANDS, 1989

My brief post-visit report to the company contained extensive, detailed hand-written tour notes. However, this caselet minimizes most of those details, centering instead on a strategic plan involving market expansion, which opens the door to equipping and operating Mars-Veghel more effectively in terms of cost, product freshness, and flexible market response. This strategy emerged from discourse with my hosts at the Mars plant and in my next-day seminar in the Mars' conference facilities. While noting the unique conditions for the facility at that time, the managers and I tossed the grand plan back and forth. What is contained in this caselet is a re-statement of the plan's main points.

High-Interest Topics
- **Transition toward additional fill-and-pack lines, each of a narrower-width and dedicated to its own product type.**
- **Issue: Can the existing wide-belt line be segmented to run two different products at the same time?**

Equipment Configurations for Better Flows in Confectionary Manufacturing

Viewpoints arising from a half-day plant tour, June 7, 1989, and one-day Schonberger seminar, June 8

I. General Information

- *Mars Veghel*: This large plant was Mars' first in Europe:
  - ✓ Produces confectionary products including Bounty (Mars Bar) and Raider (Twix) candy bars; M&Ms (plain); standard and minimal-size nougats; and chocolate and peanuts (fried) for Mars plants in Viersen, Germany, and Haguenau, France.
  - ✓ Operating four shifts, six days a week (though aiming for 7 days); the plant has 1,300 associates.
- *Company strengths* (random, incomplete):
  - ✓ Strong products.
  - ✓ Unique ability to mass-produce multi-layered candy bars.
  - ✓ Strong egalitarian culture:
    - ■ No status symbols, common parking, common toilets, open canteens, open pay, open information.
    - ■ Open office (no private ones), referred to as "office garden"— filled with plants in boxes with rollers for easy movement.
    - ■ Good pay/bonus system (got rid of output incentives 2 years ago); cross-trained versatile (including line-to-line flexibility) and technically oriented production associates.
    - ■ Everyone punches in (10% bonus for punching in early; otherwise lose 10%—no excuses).
  - ✓ Very lean corporate headquarters and hierarchy.
- *Improvement/customer focus*:
  - ✓ Methods: JIT production; cross-training; SMED (single-minute exchange of die); others.
  - ✓ Slogans:
    - ■ Don't guess, measure.
    - ■ Right the first time.
    - ■ Not me; we.
    - ■ Everybody is a customer.

II. Opportunities for Improvement

- *Market issues*: 1989 brought forth a serious problem for Mars-Veghel: lack of marketing clout and resulting insufficient demand for primary products. According to a *Fortune* article from September

26, for Mars U.S., volumes "are so huge that Mars can run, say, Milky Ways, through dedicated manufacturing machinery 24 hours a day" (Saporito p. 103). In contrast, in the immature European market, with similar "wide and fast" candy-bar equipment…

✓ Mars-Veghel must continually change from one bar type to another, requiring extensive equipment adjustments and costly, complex operations, scheduling, quality management, receiving and shipping, demand planning, and customer service.

✓ This situation entails batch production of first one product, then another, on each production line. Batches put wrong product-mixes into distribution channels, greatly increasing inventories and lead times, straining sell-by dates, and compromising product freshness.

✓ Potential quality problems are at a peak during changeovers, and batching enlarges distribution inventories, requiring extra handling (and potential handling damage).

• *What to do*: Here's a year-by-year strategic plan that couples market growth with product-dedicated production equipment—with production in close synch with real demand:

  ✓ *New-territory market growth*: One feature is a broad, planned, multi-year strategy for popularizing Mars products in southern Europe and Asia.

    ■ *Dedicated equipment*: To make better use of existing high-volume equipment, dedicate the main, existing bar-forming line to *just one primary product* (say, Bounty bars) run at the sales rate with make-to-a-number scheduling (don't strive for maximum output; stop production when "the number" is reached).

    ■ *New, smaller-scale production lines*: At same time, along with expected sales growth, add capacity in the form of new, less-complex, less-expensive, narrower-width bar-forming lines, each dedicated to its own bar-product or product family. (The front-end, bulk chocolate processor would continue to be shared by bar-forming lines. The same goes for the highly flexible array of packaging equipment that, already being on rollers, is easily moved in and out to accommodate varying package designs and specs.)

✓ *"Nutty" idea*? The present equipment builds and conveys candy bars on a wide belt—perhaps 40-units abreast—toward multiple packaging units. This proposed plan argues for simpler, narrower-belt processors. As for what to do with present wide-belt processors, an innovative idea from 3M Corp. comes to mind:

- At 3M Graphic Films in Oklahoma in 1986, coaters (special coatings applied to extruded film) were, at 52 inches, far wider than the widest film required by customers, and extra processing was required in slitting and handling prior to shipping. One solution was narrower-width coaters, which would entail a multi-year effort. For now, they might re-engineer the existing 52-inch coater so as to run—concurrently or in quick trade-offs—two different film types, with process-divider devices in the middle of the belt.

- Could Mars-Veghel similarly re-engineer its similarly wide machines to run two different candy bars side-by-side? This suggestion was debated at the post-seminar meeting on June 8.

✓ *Synchronized simplification*: In dedicated mode, production schedules may be synchronized through several stages in the customer chain:

- The production rate, for each product, more closely synchronizes with actual end-customer buying/usage—a relatively slow, steady rate on the dedicated forming lines.

- Purchase of non-strategic materials calls for ordering by rate-based contract (instead of purchase orders) with kanban signaling and receiving at that production rate.

- Delivery of finished product to Mars warehouses is at the same steady production rates, eliminating much uncertainty for merchandising people.

✓ *Simplification and overhead costs*: Although Mars is generally lean in some categories of overhead, it is plagued by complex and overhead-costly scheduling, production control, inventory management, and logistics. (No cost data are needed to see this.) Opportunities for simplification are plentiful.

✓ *Risk protection*: A given product should also have a dedicated line in at least one other plant site in this Europe-Asia region (this is already the norm for Mars U.S.).

✓ *Simplified logistics*: The Mars Europe logistics system includes a good deal of unnecessary handling.

- Seek to send purchased material directly into the plants, avoiding extra delays, costs, and damages of putting it into a warehouse, then moving it to the plant.
- Also, there should be good opportunities to direct-ship finished product to certain large customers, perhaps splitting savings with the customer.

✓ *Quick changeover*: Full-speed-ahead on quick changeover and process-control improvements on existing machines.

- Quick-changeover efforts are necessary but can only partially enable production of product line in close synch with customer demand patterns.
- The proposal for product-dedicated production equipment would avoid/reduce/eliminate changeovers.

✓ *Quality*: This multi-faceted strategic plan might be worthwhile for reasons of product freshness, safety, and shelf-life, alone. Dedicated equipment is much easier to keep clean and operate, with few things that can go wrong, and clear audit trails when they do.

- *Discrepancy charts*: Systematic, operator-centered data collection (e.g., tally marks on a discrepancy chart each time a machine jams) is needed—plus regular meetings for brainstorming, data analysis, projects, problem-solving, etc.
- *Plant maintenance*:
  ✓ Currently (and for the past 16 years), every eight weeks, production lines stop for complete PM (preventive maintenance) accomplished by both maintenance and operators.
  ✓ Now, it's time to upgrade to TPM, in which maintenance teaches and transfers to operators increasing daily responsibilities for maintaining equipment and surroundings. Visible management via 5S is part of it and involves wide use of labeling and color-coding.

CHAPTER I-16. CATERPILLAR MANUFACTURING PROGRAMS, PEORIA, IL, 1987

This caselet, centering in part on Caterpillar's much-discussed PWAF (plant with a future) program, is based on plant tours and presentations by Caterpillar managers (e.g., Ray Adams). My very brief thank-you/feedback report (with only overview items) is supplemented in this caselet by added notes from my visit.

High-Interest Topics
- **Consolidation—from 45 to 31 million square feet; with focus on plants more capable of building a whole product**
- **"Salable stock tractor" concept (base model, high volume, low cost/low price)**
- **Move toward discontinuing operation-by-operation labor reporting and material reporting**

Quick Impressions Based on a Late p.m. Visit to the Mossville Plant, Dec. 3, 1987

In connection with Schonberger's two-day seminar, Dec. 4-5

Hosted by Society of Manufacturing Engineers, Peoria, IL

I. General Information

- *Product line*: Caterpillar is the world's largest producer of earth-moving equipment. Its name, Caterpillar, has enormous market value (rather like Ditch Witch), evocative of its product line of crawling machines.
- *Competitive climate*: Japan's Komatsu, not long ago a weak player with no presence outside of Japan, had become internationally tough, with a long-term vision translated from the Japanese as "encircle Caterpillar."
- *Caterpillar response*: For its part, Caterpillar had embarked on belt-tightening that, between 1981 and 1985, cut costs by 20 percent. Strategically, it recently adopted a four-factor modernization program called "Plant With a Future."

II. Strengths or Areas of Good Progress

- *Cells/flow lines*: In progress is a reorganization of machines and people into cells and extended flow lines.

- *Suppliers*: Emphasis is on supplier certification and reduction—with daily deliveries from increasing number of its suppliers.
- *Product design*: Designs are being simplified and standardized. In wheel loaders (made in Caterpillar plants in four countries besides the U.S.), P/Ns (part numbers) for axle assemblies were reduced 35-45 percent.
- *Consolidations*: Fewer manufacturing locations for a given product are aimed at building a more complete product in a given plant. The plan for the next two years is to reduce total manufacturing space from 45 million sq. ft. to 30-32 million.
- *Capacity investments*:
  - ✓ The former justification was ROI/payback, machine by machine, project by project.
  - ✓ New is internal rate-of-return (16% rate) with "bundles of investment"—on the order of $20-40 million.
  - ✓ Aims: (1) cut product costs, (2) compare with costs of buying, (3) compare with competition.
- *Process control*: The Mossville engine plant makes good use of SPC charts.
- *Emptying of storage*: Ongoing inventory reduction has an ultimate objective of dismantling some AS/RSs (automatic storage and retrieval systems).
- *Outside "cottage-industry" suppliers*: Quite a few are delivering just in time.
- *Common-sense automation*: The aim of Cat's automation is more on value-adding processes themselves, not on wasteful storage and distance-spanning handling systems.
- *PWAF*: A "modernization" slogan and concept. (I was assured that modernization did not mean technological but referred to increased application of manufacturing-management concepts such as JIT production with total quality.)
- *Employee satisfaction program (ESP)*: The UAW represents most U.S. plant labor; ESP is meant to reduce grounds for disputes.

III. Process Details

Sidebar 1 provides summaries of certain factory processes and achievements in three of Caterpillar's plants.

SIDEBAR 1 CATERPILLAR FACTORY PROCESSES

Building LL: Results of three modular cells:

Fuel tanks/fenders/radiator guards cell: inventories cut from six to two months' worth.

Visual kanban: Applied in case-and-frame cell.

Building SS—Cat Tractors

Team-built concept: One team to build whole tractor, walking it down the line.

Salable stock tractor: Stock commodity model with good delivery, lower price!—strategic benefit made possible by focused production lines.

Tractors' throughput time: Now 3 to 5 days; formerly longer, with tractors stacked up in the yard waiting for orders for attachments.

Very large D11N tractor: Too big to ship whole, tractor goes in three pieces by truck and two by rail.

Case-and-frames inventory was one month; now two–five days.

Mossville BB Plant:

The plant: By far the largest diesel engine plant in the world.

Castings for blocks: Engine blocks poured in Mapleton plant Monday or Tuesday, received (unpainted) Thursday—six to eight truckloads per day.

Block inventory: Was two months in 1981, one month in 1983-84, and is two days, now; blocks no longer painted because they're used before they can rust!

End plates: Sub-assembled by outside minimum-wage cottage-industry supplier; delivered to nearby dock more often than daily.

Visual instructions: Plentiful charts on wall explaining how to tighten, torque, assemble, etc.

IV. Weaknesses or Opportunities

- *PWAF big-four goals*: Consolidate. Automate. Simplify. (Computer) Integrate. My opinion of the four goals:
  - ✓ *Consolidation*: Caterpillar has this right—factory focus by *product* not process.
  - ✓ *Automate and Simplify*: The concept would be better stated as, "Simplify, then Automate"—which is how *reengineering* was originally proposed.

- ✓ *Computer Integrate*: Again, it is best to simplify first, eliminating many computer transactions (e.g., via visual kanban).
- *Stack lights/line-stop*: There is an absence of and need for red/yellow lights and line-stop authority for operators and assemblers.
- *Conventional labor reporting*: Eliminate it.
  - ✓ With good progress in waste elimination and direct-labor accounting for only a small percentage of product cost, labor reporting (operation-by-operation at Cat) no longer yields useful information and is an obstacle to further simplification and team concepts.
  - ✓ Labor reporting itself wastes direct-labor time, and has high administrative, data processing, complexity costs—and is redundant since labor costs are captured in payroll records.
- *Material reporting, move by move*:
  - ✓ This reporting should be greatly reduced as the plants exploit numerous opportunities for visual kanban, e.g., recirculating containers with ID plates attached.
  - ✓ Much of the material reporting yields no useful information and is redundant since purchased material costs are a matter of record.
- *Computer system*: The need is for a *dual* manufacturing computer system:
  - ✓ One, a (complex) MRP-based system for nonstandard (irregular-use) part numbers and products.
  - ✓ Another, very simple, streamlined system that is daily-rate based, periodic (instead of episodic), and not transaction-oriented. Items accounting for high annual dollar volume ("stars") should be on the streamlined system, with its very low overhead costs.
- *Regularized schedules*: Regularized schedules make sense for "star" products and components, with a goal of linear output—hit the schedule, don't allow exceeding it. (Comment by Ray Adams: "We lack a thorough lead-time database.")
- *Successes*: My impression is that most factory employees are no more than vaguely aware of the accomplishments and the importance of the goals themselves. To correct this:
  - ✓ Major successes in time and quality improvement (lead time, setup time, flow distance, rework, inventory, defects, etc.) should be on large trend charts for all to see, pridefully.

✓ Visuals should be a main component of team spirit, reward, motivation, accountability, management intervention, communication, customer and public relations, and so forth.

V. Incidental Observations

- *Material-handling overkill*: Ray Adams: "We have god-awful material flow and layout."
- *Building BB, Mossville*:
  ✓ Tear out large portions of overhead chain, rely more on flexible handling methods, and shrink inventory in the handling system.
  ✓ There is too much use of fork trucks, pallet boxes, and large loads; increase usage of wheeled push carts with smaller, more frequent transports.
- *Large inventory reductions*: Some machining lines in Building BB have too many idle units on conveyors between machines (e.g., about a 50:1 micro-JIT ratio in some places on the machining line for cylinder liners). There are opportunities to cut throughput times and inventories by factors of 10 (at least) for those components.

CHAPTER I-17. J. I. CASE/TENNECO, EAST MOLINE, IL, 1989

Farm-equipment manufacturer, J. I. Case, has been reorganizing for JIT production. Most essential aspects center on integrating fabrication, sub-assembly, and final assembly. This caselet includes information from my rough notes in addition to what was in the feedback report to the company.

High-Interest Topics:
- **Implementing a showcase cell—as a model for further conversions**
- **Separate schedules and flows for different sized combines**
- **"Success" charts and graphs**

JIT Efforts at a Major Producer of Farm Equipment
Impressions based on a plant visit on June 22, 1989
In connection with a half-day Schonberger seminar for Case on June 23

I. General Information

- *J.I. Case, East Moline*: Produces farm equipment, specializing in large to small combines at company headquarters; also made at East Moline are planters and cotton-pickers.
  - ✓ Company sales of $563 million include $26 million in service parts and $443 million in finished machines.
  - ✓ This big plant has 1,000 suppliers (14 local, 30–35 other Case plants), 21,000 purchased P/Ns, and 15,000 WIP P/Ns.
  - ✓ A combine has 5,000 parts (the engine is one part), including 3,000 fasteners.
  - ✓ 1,700 quality checks are batched daily, with Paretoized listings of defects and repair items.
  - ✓ Two cab lines in a separate building produce 100 cabs per day, with some for other Case plants.
- *Historical information* (extracted from *Quad City Times*, Dec., 2010):
  - ✓ The East Moline site began in 1926 as a warehouse to store International Harvester's (IH's) Farmall tractors, which began production in the same year. In 1929, IH began production of combines there.
  - ✓ In 1984, IH closed its Farmall Works, selling the assets to Tenneco Inc.
  - ✓ In 1985, Case, through its parent Tenneco, acquired the assets of IH's agricultural equipment operations, including the East Moline plant. (After further ownership changes in which the plant became owned by CIH [Case International Harvester], CIH shuttered the East Moline plant and moved its production to Grand Island, Neb.)

II. Strengths—General

- *Products/markets*:
  - ✓ Strong products (innovations, good design).
  - ✓ Complementary-season products (all products are seasonal except cabs).
  - ✓ A product and market situation that allows for scheduling months out.
- *Commonalities*: Many parts are common from model to model (in combines, and perhaps in other products as well).

- *Organization*: Formerly there were six layers of management, now down to three or four. There are no general foremen anymore; 1st-line supervisors have area responsibilities.
- *Labor*: The plant population is not so large as to cause serious problems of impersonality and poor communications. Labor-management relations are relatively good (but there is minimal employee involvement in process improvement).
- *Improvements*:
  - ✓ Since 1980, defects have been reduced 80%; 95% for major defects that have field repercussions. Total number of employees has been reduced from about 4,300 to 1,525.
  - ✓ Formerly a three-shift operation, it is now mostly one—except some two-shifts in fabrication.
- *The facility*:
  - ✓ The plant has plentiful machine capacity—which leaves the door wide open for taking some sheet metal and machining equipment and moving it into a fabrication or subassembly cell.
  - ✓ Also, the plant has few physical obstacles to change (e.g., no network of overhead conveyors).
  - ✓ Good housekeeping is evident.

III. Miscellaneous—From Plant Tour

- *Final trim*: Via an indexing line, when all green lights are on, units move/are driven forward.
- *Torque inspector*: A roving inspector in a drive cart frequently checks for proper torqueing (the plant has lots of hand-torqueing, in addition to air tools).
- *Cab lines*:
  - ✓ In cabs, parts (mostly purchased) are welded, painted, then assembled on a system of low floor rollers.
  - ✓ Glass is glued in place after a robot lays adhesive onto the glass.
  - ✓ 185 people are in cabs, most having their own "maintenance cribs."
  - ✓ Recently, after a final audit raised plant's rating from excellent to superior, the crew was treated to food.

- *Cotton-pickers*: Drum assembly was formerly on a push system, to forecast; now is make-to-order.
- *Planters*: For now, all are produced to forecast.

IV. Good Progress

- *Suppliers*: 20 or so suppliers are on JIT deliveries.
- *Planned production*: In 1989 and, now, in 1st quarter, 1990, all combine scheduling is planned, right down to 40's and 60's (sizes of combine)—with those schedules passed on to suppliers.
- *Flow improvements*:
  - ✓ Good progress in (and plans for) moving subassemblies (e.g., sheet metal) to locations next to final assembly—an important configuration improvement for this (or any) producer of large-sized vehicular equipment. Multiple benefits are forthcoming.
  - ✓ Kanban and quick-change improvements include dies located by frequency of use, e.g., high-use dies close to sheet metal equipment.
  - ✓ Three SMED (single-minute exchange of die) teams include 12 hourlies!
- *Standout cell*: A start has been made in organizing machining and sheet metal cells, including painting the cell to make it stand out and look good (also, one large part-dedicated brake is due to be moved into the subassembly cell where the part is used).
- *Fabrication dept.*: Point-of-use die storage is arranged by ABC usage; nice clamp tables are adjacent to presses.
- *Salvage dept.*: Formerly, defective parts had been scrapped, now many are repaired.
- *Machine shop*: 350 machine tools have been acquired from closed plants in the area; the machine shop has 38 tool and die-makers; two senior operators are now called "co-plant managers."

V. Weaknesses or Opportunities

- *Steel shed*: Although some of the huge investment in steel may be because of a price break, there should be good opportunities to greatly reduce the investment.

- *Large combines*: By employing kanban squares, many of the parts used on the large combine line (e.g., the 50% or so common from model to model) can and should be converted to a pull system, which will slash WIP, open up congested aisles, and free floor space.
- *Model 20 combines*: A separate line probably should be set up for the model 20's, which are too different from the larger models to be merged into the same line:
  - ✓ Then, produce to a repeating, regularized schedule close to the market rate (for example, exactly one a day). Small adjustments to the market rate may be done by skipping a day, or making one on a Saturday once in a while.
  - ✓ A small team specializing on the 20 may treat it as their own business unit.
    - This would afford an opportunity for a pilot EI (employee-involvement) project, employing team training and use of process control, data collection, P.M, job switching, and process improvement.
    - The team can "flex" to a different product for, say, one or two months when demand for the 20 drops dramatically; and/or work on improvement projects if there are skip days during "the season."
  - ✓ Accounting data shows that the 20 yields very small profit margins when compared with other models.
    - But well-known research shows most companies' accounting methods under-cost lower-volume models, so the truth may be that the 20 is actually worse off—a money-loser.
    - The above-mentioned practices, aimed at smoothing and simplifying production, should raise (or solidify) profitability on the 20's.
- *40, 60, and 80 combines*: These models are well suited for production according to a repeating schedule—e.g., a weekly schedule in which all models are made each week in the same sequence. Perhaps the next phase of improvement can be a fully mixed-model schedule.
- *Off-line buffer stock*: Buffer inventories should exist only for temperamental operations or suppliers, and the product flow should normally bypass the storage locations (treat as off-line buffer stock) in order to smooth material flow.

- *Visual success indicators*:
    - ✓ Successes in waste reduction (lead time, setup time, flow distance, rework, inventory, defects, fork trucks, transactions, tearing out sections of the high-rise, etc.) should be on large trend charts for all to appreciate.
    - ✓ These visuals should be a main component of team spirit, reward, motivation, accountability, management intervention, communication, customer and public relations, etc.
- *Handling*: Fork trucks, pallet boxes, and large loads are excessive and should be replaced in favor of hand-wheeled push carts with smaller, more frequent transports and smaller load quantities (avoiding the high costs of bulk handling gear and drivers).
- *Jobs/labor*:
    - ✓ There are far too many job classifications. Keep working on cross-training, group incentives, and (if the cost/cash situation permits) pay-for-knowledge.
    - ✓ A considerable need exists for joint training and implementation that includes labor union leaders and rank-and-file [two years ago Jack Warne was hired here to explain and promote VAM (value-added manufacturing) but the union killed it]. (Warne was CEO at Omark Industries—among the first and most successful Western implementers of JIT/TPS—beginning in 1981; and active in mid-to-late 1980s helping other companies.)
- *Standard vs. actual hours incentive system*:
    - ✓ This conventional standards-based incentive system (75% of the labor force is on incentives)—with lots of industrial engineers developing MTM/standard data time standards—is cumbersome, costly, and disliked by work forces. Moreover, total cost is mostly materials, with labor costs merely a small percentage.
    - ✓ As JIT implementations take further root, tight linkages of operators, with emphasis on throughput time, should reduce the present excessive focus on labor hours—and perhaps end the standard vs. actual system.
- *Suppliers*: An excessive number of suppliers calls for reduction in number as well as certification; and suggests, in some cases, designation of a lead supplier who buys other components and delivers a complete subassembly to J. I. Case.

CHAPTER I-18. MANUFACTURING AT FORMICA, EVANDALE, OH, 1988

This caselet reports on the large-scale, much belated turn-around effort of a failing but famous manufacturing business: Formica, the well-known brand name for laminate sheeting often made into countertops, wall panels, among other items. Top management at Formica had realized the company needed total rejuvenation and sought advice and training, including from me.

High-Interest Topics:
- **Develop a dual info system—simplified for "runner" products, and with MRP only for low-volume, high-variety orders**
- **Formula for fixing a failing company—the basics of flow and total quality**

Flow/TQ: Keys to Rejuvenating a Company in Decline
Impressions from the Schonberger plant visit on January 12, 1988

I. Strengths or Areas of Good Progress

- *Coping with decline*: An experienced management group fully perceives the plant's decline in competitiveness. President Vince Langone: "The plant doesn't work."
- *Inventories & SPC*: Recent improvements have been made in inventory turns and by introducing statistical process control.
- *Suppliers*: A fairly narrow base of suppliers mostly dates back quite a few years.
- *Recent hires*: Good technical people have recently been hired (e.g., in maintenance), and are becoming productive.
- *Process engineering*: This essential facet was re-established as a department in December, 1987 (process engineering formerly had been handled by R&D).
- *Formica name*: It's a billion-dollar name that commands some attention.
- *Meetings with*: Vince Langone, president; Peter Marshall; many others.

II. Action Plans for Renewal

- *Customers*: Main action plans concern quality and service to the customer.

- *Highest priority*: Become "Number 1" in quality.
  - ✓ Statements on plant tour: Our customer requirements "exceed the capabilities of the plant," and our tests "are wrong and out of date."
  - ✓ Spend what it takes to control dust ("dust is a major problem"): air filtration; positive air flow; walls, rules, policies, and discipline to prevent dust/dirt-carriers from getting into dust-sensitive zones.
  - ✓ Revitalize lapsed P.M. efforts and begin an evolution toward employee-centered TPM and process ownership. In this, maintenance assumes the role of teacher, starting with teaching operators to do machine lubrication and simple repairs.
- *Lot sizes*:
  - ✓ Lot-size reduction is overdue and of high priority, in part because the true costs of carrying inventory are much higher than what's been presumed at Formica; and, more directly, because smaller lots provide faster information on causes of bad quality or yields.
  - ✓ Launch quick-changeover studies on all major machines (useful tool: a video camera).
    - ■ Bring operators of different machines together to become gung-ho changeover teams, who go from machine to machine developing and documenting quick-changeover procedures, with changeovers carefully pre-scheduled to the minute.
    - ■ *Slash* lot sizes as changeover times tumble.
- *Process variability*: Try to break the mind-set that segregates maintenance (mechanical) from process engineering (chemistry). It's all the same problem: process variability.
- *Manage the complexity*:
  - ✓ Identify the top 5, 10, or 20 products:
    - ■ Put them on rate-based schedules extending through all processes, if possible, with blocked-out capacity and rate changes every two weeks.
    - ■ Fit other products into blanks (non-blocked-out portions) in the schedule.
  - ✓ At the same time, revisit plans for a computer-based, transaction-driven MRP system. Then, develop a dual system:
    - ■ For "star" (high-volume) production, impose the simplicity of transaction-less kanban and "make-to-a-number" production—without the pain and cost of full MRP.
    - ■ MRP/MRPII for Formica's lower-volume products (which "quiets the chaos").

- *Closely-related items*:
  - ✓ Proceed with the excellent plans to categorize and manage all products via ABC analysis.
  - ✓ Begin revising accountability and control; emphasize, via visual data boards on factory floor, the things that *cause* cost.
- *Miscellaneous*:
  - ✓ In R&D, focus on product/process simplification and standardization (reducing numbers of product specs). In order to develop improved awareness of manufacturability, begin a progressive program to swap R&D engineers and process engineers.
  - ✓ Begin a campaign to cut job classifications.
  - ✓ Push some product testing to the shop floor. Possible examples: the magnetic thickness tester at the end of the trim-and-sand line; employ an on-line gloss tester (suggestions of Ron Keeling).
  - ✓ Work on supplier development with emphasis on supplier certification, long-term contracts (reduced use of purchase orders), small-lot deliveries, shared trucks, etc.
  - ✓ Adopt reusable plastic skids backhauled from major customers.
- *Vital long-term strategy*:
  - ✓ Since the plant is overly large with too many people, products, and processes to be manageable under one management system, begin developing factories-within-the-factory.
    - It attempts to isolate a single flow path—no choice of machines at each stage of production—at least for highest-volume products.
    - Then schedule and run those products through the flow path as if the machines along the path were just one machine.
    - While it may not be reasonable (initially, at least) to try to include all stages in a single flow path, there are large benefits when even *two* machines in two successive stages can be linked.
  - ✓ Expanding on that, look for ways to rearrange equipment and operators by flow path rather than grouping similar pieces of equipment. One option—a last resort—is to close down half of the plant and move half of the equipment to a new plant nearby or somewhere else.
  - ✓ Along with the factories-within-the-factory (or flow lines and cells) concept, support teams should be formed for a product flow (instead of by process type). The support team is to

include supervisor, R&D, process engineer, quality, buyer, and maintenance.

✓ Begin isolating small-volume products in a corner of the plant with its own small-scale equipment and its own work group, support group, and managers.

✓ Evolve to accounting *by flow line/product* with direct costing and overhead allocated by lead time (or lead time in conjunction with, say, changeover time).

CHAPTER I-19. SEALED AIR CORP. (SAC), FAIR LAWN, NJ, 1989

This caselet partly addresses SAC as a corporation but with main examples from its Hodgkins, IL plant that produces bubble packaging and foam rolls and bags. (Caselet I-20 focuses on a specific issue at the Hodgkins plant—that of employee performance metrics in the context of stock-picking, loading, and shipping.)	**High-Interest Topics:** • **More reliable and infrequent product cost audits; fixing wrong bases for allocating overhead** • **Smoothing highly-variable customer lead times in distribution channels** • **Moving toward simpler, cheaper multiples of key equipment to produce many products concurrently**

Producer of Bubble Packaging and Foam Strives to Smooth Out Manufacturing Bumps

Assessment based on a brief plant tour (Hodgkins, IL), March 12, 1989

Also, meetings with SAC people (Fair Lawn, NJ, HQ), March 14

I. General Information

- *Hodgkins plant*: Produces a high-margin product line that includes large rolls of bubble laminated rolls (used for further production elsewhere), bubble mailers (padded bags), and branded products including Jiffy bags, Mail-Lite, and Insta-Pak.
- *Material flow*: Very few raw materials (e.g., carrier-sheet from other SAC plants, polyethelene resin, blowing agent) are turned into some 1,600 SKUs.

- *Major equipment*: Co-extruder (designed in-house), bubble extruder, bubble perforator, polyethylene foam extruder, sheeter, slitter, customer wrapper, edge trimmer, regrinder.
- *Hodgkins plant configuration*: Rectangular, nearly twice as wide as it is long:
  - ✓ 102,000 sq. ft.; rail sidings on one of the long sides, 12 truck docks on the other.
  - ✓ Two large storage areas: one for foam while the other is for finished rolls and other FGI.
  - ✓ Several machine areas, with offices occupying the remainder.
- *Contact person*: Tom Haney, product manager/regional manager for foam and former plant manager at Hodgkins.

II. Strengths (Incomplete List)

- *Focused company*: "Sticks to its knitting" (no oddball businesses) with small plants disbursed to major markets; high margins and strong balance sheet.
- *Lean overhead*: Simplification and low overhead stems in part from there being no personnel manager/department at the plant sites; and there is a blending of line and corporate staff management via "wearing of more than one hat."
- *Special products*: SAC has a few dominant, innovative top-of-line products (e.g., Polycap and Instapacker).
- *Capable operators*: A few operators have stepped up to manage a small business.
- *Emoluments*: Profit-sharing; good pay, benefits, and work life.
- *Management commitments*: A strong senior and plant management commitment is evident from early WCM planning efforts and book reports.

III. Some Problems and Limitations

- *Lead times*: five-day lead times (the goal) are a big improvement over the past but still very excessive for this industry (so few product models and bill-of-material levels).
- *Technology*:
  - ✓ Especially in bubbles and foam, an evolution has occurred where most Sealed Air sites can afford only one "supermachine" of a type

which makes a large batch of only one of several models at a time. This machine is characterized by aggravatingly long setups (e.g., 10 minutes to a few hours, including getting the process stabilized).

✓ This is a long way from Al Fielding's (the co-founder) company vision: an extruder on the back of a truck that stops at a customer site, makes what is wanted, then drives on.

- *Costing/pricing*: Product pricing does not reflect real costs (e.g., low-volume products are under-costed and under-priced).
- *Comparative performance*: Site-to-site performance is highly variable because of different kinds of machines/technologies that were gained in acquisitions.
- *Capacity/equipment*: Converting is plagued by insufficient capacity.
  - ✓ Usually plentiful, converting capacity is not sufficient to respond well to normal market surges.
  - ✓ Some foam machines are temperamental, some (or most) foam sites lack enough capacity to make all products with short lead times.
- *Weak training*: Most sites recognize weaknesses in defining and specifying the process and training operators—and the need to address them.

IV. Miscellaneous Observations/Suggestions

- *Expertise & versatility*: Regarding skills training, cross-training, SPC, multi-year career-change assignments—full steam ahead.
- *Product costing/pricing components*:
  - ✓ Purchased materials (70% of cost): These are easily and accurately tied to products produced (e.g., pounds-in equals square-feet-out). Power to operate machines, if significant, should be costed the same way.
  - ✓ Direct labor (15%): In many industries, D.L. roughly matches the quantity made. But at SAC, D.L. behaves like overhead!—much higher per square foot for a production run of a low-volume product than a high-volume one.
  - ✓ Overhead (15%):
    - Generally, low-volume products require far more overhead for supervision, engineering, plant maintenance, production control, etc., per production run than "stars" (high-volume products), even though a star's usual run entails many more sq. ft.

- In this inaccurate assignment of overhead, SAC is like the large majority of manufacturers.

✓ How should the combined 30% of cost (D.L. + O.H.) be handled in a cost audit (used for pricing or go/no-go)? Here is a quick and simple approach:

- Say that 20 products are made on a certain extruder. Group them by annual sales volume into A, B, and C.
- For example, Group A consists of, say, two or three of the 20 products, each accounting for 15% or more of total sales; Group B products, each for 5% to 14% of sales; Group C, each less than 5% of sales. For SAC, the material cost rate is (about) the same for all three product types.
- Costing, then, is as follows:

	Material cost per X thousand sq. ft.	Ave. D.L. + O.H. per X thousand sq. ft.	Adjustment factor	Estimated cost per X thousand sq. ft.
Group A:	$100	+ $30	−$20	= $110
Group B:	$100	+ $30		= $130
Group C:	$100	+ $30	+$20	= $150

- Determining the plus and minus adjustment factors could involve doing a study (but that could be very complicated). Or, instead, just use some best-guess numbers.
- The takeaway is that the A Group earns a cost advantage (minus factor) while the C Group absorbs a cost penalty (plus factor). Accuracy is not so important—and may be impossible to achieve anyway.

✓ Note: This is not a cost "system." It involves no transactions. It is just a quick study (can arise from discussions by managers who *know* their processes), done once or twice a year.

✓ The purpose is to show what products to prune, *or* what products to hit with cost-cutting pressure, e.g., simplification to take out overhead cost, labor to set up, labor to regrind scrap, etc.

✓ Recommendation: Adopt this sort of costing/pricing throughout SAC quickly—for immediate positive sales/margin improvements.

- *Cost control.* At SAC there is a need for (and lack of) large, visual charts—all over plants and offices—that track progress in cutting setup times, regrind, flow distance, WIP, lead time, number of suppliers, purchase lot sizes, control charts, and cross-training.
  - ✓ SAC managers seem very interested in using this approach to control quality, cost, response time, and flexibility.
  - ✓ It is intended to replace the present cost-variance approach—as people get accustomed to and experience the value of the simple, visual method and concept.
- *Ways to chop lead times*:
  - ✓ Quick setup will help *in all cases* and will allow one-day turnaround *in a few cases* (perhaps in Dri-Loc and Jiffy products). For example, consider tandem cooling cans for quick foam changeovers.
  - ✓ Warrior already meets, with ease, the five-day goal in Jiffy bags (so I'm told); now it's time to reset to three or four days.
  - ✓ SPC will improve reliability of lead times and raise hourly output slightly *in all cases.*
  - ✓ In some products, a supermachine issue (multiple products but only one costly machine) will plague SAC for years—an open door to a competitor with a better idea. To fix the problem:
    - ■ Growth will help—over time. In the same plant locations, as sales grow, each plant adds a 2nd machine of a type (e.g., 2nd perforator or extruder). With two machines, each runs half the products and halves lead times, setup costs, startup scrap, etc.
    - ■ Growth also will allow getting rid of less efficient machines and moving to the same machine models at each site.
    - ■ Some judicious equipment acquisitions seem warranted now for quick lead time, yield, labor, and sales-growth benefits. The idea is not to acquire equipment based on hours used per week, but on attacking collective effects of long lead times and other ills.
    - ■ Best answer is innovation—simpler, slower, cheaper machines that can be installed in multiples, each dedicated to just one product family. Industry never sought such equipment in the past, and, contrarily, sought the opposite kinds of equipment.
- *Variable demand*: Actual demand for SAC products is quite smooth—at the end user level. But after going through associated

distributors who batch orders, prime distributors who batch again, and SAC plants who batch a third time, the order pattern looks like the Swiss Alps.

- ✓ At the plant level, order batching is inherent in SAC's current equipment.
- ✓ But the distribution system is causing SAC unnecessary disruption, unpredictability, unevenness, markup costs, etc. Best options to fix the problem can be found at the customer's end.

- *Distribution system*: SAC sales needs to work with distributors to smooth order patterns, move to longer-term exclusive contracts with shared forecasting information, provide advanced notice of special promotions, etc.
  - ✓ Some of the distribution system should be eliminated by seeking direct-ship opportunities. It doesn't make sense to go through distributors to reach large users in, say, a 100-mile radius of SAC plant; go to small trucks (SAC owned or not).
  - ✓ For customers who pick up at the plant—often arriving late by a half-day or more—offer discounts for picking up within a two-hour time window.

CHAPTER I-20. SEALED AIR CORP., HODGKINS, IL, 1989

This short caselet (companion to Chapter I-19) zeros in on a scenario specific to SAC's Hodgkins plant. It demonstrates effective linkage of four aspects of process improvement: visual management, operator recording of mishaps, effective performance metrics, and front-line enablement. Though not included in the report to the SAC management, this example was a key topic in end-of-tour discussions.

High-Interest Topics:
- **Big kanban square in footprint of outgoing trailer—bypassing FGI stockroom**
- **Marking pens to record all mishaps**
- **Performance-management system with fair and effective metrics**

Process Improvement Linked to Performance Management
Observations based on a brief plant tour, March 12, 1989

I. Scenario

- *Stock picker/loader*: Reggie (name changed) is a material handler whose job is to load trailers lined up at the Hodgkins plant's 12 truck docks.
    - ✓ He works from pick lists. If an item is on the list, it (supposedly) has been produced and is in the storage room area near loading docks.
    - ✓ Often, however, Reggie cannot find one or more items on the pick list: The list is wrong, the stock location or quantity in the storage rack is wrong, or the item is in the rack in the right quantity but is damaged.
    - ✓ Whatever the cause, the delay upsets the driver, but Reggie may not release the truck until every item on the pick list is in the trailer. As the wait lengthens, it's not only the driver who's angry; Reggie's supervisor and customer service are angry at him, too.
- *Reggie's work-around*:
    - ✓ Here is what Reggie sometimes did when anger and frustration levels rose high enough. He would take the problem to one of the co-extruder lines and plead for operators to halt a current job in order to run off the needed number of rolls of the missing item—an obviously costly kind of interruption that impinged on the extruder group's productivity metrics.

II. Process Improvement

- *Project solution*: At most companies an awareness that "there's a problem here" could trigger formation of a project team schooled in JIT or lean or six-sigma process improvement.
    - ✓ A satisfactory solution for the team would be that all items for a given truck go directly from production lines to a marked-off floor location: a large kanban square roughly in the footprint of a trailer right in front of the dock.
    - ✓ This eliminates two non-value-adding steps: pick lists and intermediate storage (the stockroom becomes used just for overflow storage).

- *Fix-the-processes solution*: Give Reggie some marking pens and a large white board to write on.
  - ✓ Then, throughout every day, Reggie records every mishap as a tally mark on a check sheet—with rows labeled "Bin empty," "Pick list wrong," Stock location wrong," "Rack quantity wrong," "Item damaged," etc.
  - ✓ With that kind of data—generated not only by Reggie but also, similarly, by those who prepare pick lists, set schedules for drivers, run extruders, and so on. Solutions are likely to almost fall off the pages of the accumulated mishap records. Moreover, availability of such extensive data on mishaps offers a project improvement team a wealth of pointers on what to do—including the aforementioned solution of the large kanban square fronting the truck dock.

III. Performance Management

- *Typical productivity metrics*: For years, I used this real example in audience-participation segments of my seminars. The give-and-take would usually include discussions of typical productivity metrics for someone in a job like Reggie's: number of items picked per day, number of trucks sent away on time vs. late, and so on.
- *Mishap-focused metrics*: In contrast, discussions bring in new mishap-focused metrics—not reflecting Reggie's performance but that of "the system" (Dr. Deming's well-known proviso is that 85 percent of problems are attributable to management system failures, not the employee*), which would be revealed in the tally marks under "Bin empty," "Pick list wrong," and so forth.
- *Fair and effective*: The usual productivity measures are unfair and ineffective. The tally-mark method is not only fair, but it removes primary miseries of the job and points, happily for all, to solutions—and continuous, data-driven improvement.

---

* J. Main. *Quality Wars: The Triumphs and Defeats of American Business*. New York: Free Press, 1994, p. 94.

CHAPTER I-21. RUSSELL ATHLETIC, ALEXANDER CITY, AL, 1988

My extensive notes (25 notepad pages) did not result in a post-visit written report to management at Russell. The main reason: I had, post-tour, a lively discussion session with about 15 top management people at Russell, so that there was little reason to send a report. Thus, this short, narrowly focused caselet was assembled from those notes some 30 years later.

High-Interest Topics:
- *"Need it right now"* cell for highly demanding pro basketball players
- Proposal to produce *all* apparel in the same, simple and quick fashion

Apparel Industry: in Need of Massive Conversion to Cellular Manufacturing?

Observations based on plant tour, evening of April 14, 1988

Followed by one-day Schonberger seminar, April 15

I. Basic Information

- *The company*:
    - ✓ Russell Athletic (division of Russell Corp.) is a vertically-integrated designer, producer, and marketer of active-wear apparel. It employs some 11,000 people in 26 plants in Alabama, six in Florida, and two in Georgia.
    - ✓ Of those, more than 5,000 work in 13 plants in Alexander City, AL (population 15,000), producing athletic uniforms and other garments: three plants for retail apparel and ten as a contract maker of specialty uniforms (e.g., professional, college, and high-school sports teams).
- *Headquarters environs*: In this area Russell has nine mills, a large bleachery, a knitting complex, a double-knit plant, a sewing plant, a "hi-tech" sewing plant, an in-plant printing facility, 11 warehouses, a pack-and-hold building, a large DC (distribution center), various office and maintenance buildings, and a large recreation building with a next-door day-care center.
- *Main contacts*: Dwight L. Carlisle, Jr. CEO and president; Jim Klopman, HR; Hank Spires, head of materials management; Al Berry, dyeing and finishing; Jeff Alvorson, product R&D.

II. Detailed Information

- *Points of interest*: My rough notes are mostly descriptive of processes and equipment (e.g., Bierrebi automatic cutting machine, Rosenthal sheeter, Blendomat, sleeve machine, pocket machine, Rapier loom), and mostly are not incorporated into this caselet. The following are examples of more particular interest.
- *Plant #1*: Apparel; David Booth, plant manager, 1,500 employees:
  - ✓ All production is make-to-stock, 42,000 dozens per week in 6-20 styles—with planning and control governed by RAMPS (Russell apparel manufacturing performance system).
  - ✓ There are 750 sewing machines, three clean/repair and eight pack stations (two packing and three fold-and-inspect).
  - ✓ 21 stations are in three production groups, one shift, five days per week; output is tracked in two-hour time blocks on a large display.
  - ✓ Output goes into wheeled "bundle trucks," three dozen per bundle, 60 trucks per group.
  - ✓ Groups are "teams" that perform their own inspection against the conventional approach in which output goes outside of production for inspect and pack: three packers cluster at one end of a long conveyor with 30 folders on each side.
  - ✓ Reusable totes three- or six-feet high move output to shipping docks, and on to the DC.
    - Some of the output is packed in customer-focused shipping boxes for more direct shipping to customers.
    - Specs for each customer are about the same, except different labels, packages, and "hang tags."
- *Plant #9*: A focused factory for athletic game uniforms; Billy White, plant manager.
  - ✓ One shift in sewing; two shifts in cutting; three shifts in screen printing.
  - ✓ Thousands of rolls of raw fabric are on hand; average time on the shelf is many months; 70% are items with long lead times (e.g., football jerseys).
  - ✓ 50-ply cutting is done on "flotation tables" using automated Rodway equipment.
  - ✓ WIP, from daily cutting, is 1.5 days' supply (down from 20 days').

✓ WIP in screen printing (using four ovens) has a backlog of three days (formerly 12 to 15).

✓ Numbering-machine setup: 12 minutes to load, nine minutes to take down.

III. Competitive Opportunities

- *Basketball uniform cell*: Newly formed is a sewing cell (called "sewing team")—a tight cluster of sewing operators and machines dedicated to pro-basketball uniforms.
  ✓ This is a high-margin business with flexibility to respond fast—hours, not weeks—to any order. Highly paid players want a new uniform very quickly, so Russell came up with the answer: an *immediately quick* basketball-uniform cell, a cluster of about eight sewers and machines.
  ✓ It yields excellent quality and cost performance; also, close operator-to-operator linkages quickly reveal problems and likely causes, enabling frequent in-line resolution, as well as improvement ideas from cell-team members.
- *Same cell concept for ALL production*:
  ✓ "Sewing team" was set up for and thought to be appropriate just for the special make-to-order line of pro-sports uniforms.
  ✓ But it surely is as easy and practical to effectively set up cellular hand-to-hand processing lines for standard apparel as for special uniforms.
  ✓ Thus, Russell should produce that way for virtually *all* sewn sportswear—ranging from items sold at retail to uniforms ordered seasonally by schools and other institutions.
  ✓ This would reduce production lead times from many days or weeks to hours—with large reductions in overhead costs (e.g., no department-to-department scheduling, material handling, costing, and other transactions), and far less reliance on always-wrong long-range forecasts.
- *Risk scenario*:
  ✓ In a late-afternoon wrap-up presentation to Russell top executives, I alluded glowingly to the pro-sports team uniform cell. Seeing the many benefits of sewing garments this way, the

company should quickly set forth implementing cellular sewing throughout all areas.

✓ Then I posed this "if-not" scenario (which garnered some wry smiles, but no debate):

- One of your executives decides to leave Russell, set up his (they were all men) own competing cut-and-sew business with total cellular sewing (each executive having the credentials to borrow the necessary startup funds).

- Then, this startup business begins taking away Russell's best customers via much shorter lead times, greater flexibility, lower production costs, and higher quality.

CHAPTER I-22. BIC CORP., MILFORD, CT, 1989

BIC, a well-known producer of pens, lighters, and razors, needed a total factory reorganization to link raw materials to component fabrication to assembly to packout. This caselet explores this reorganization, its greatest competitive need.	***High-Interest Topics:*** • **Two detailed flow diagrams exemplify a cellular transformation of BIC's functional layout of equipment** • **Instead of a sub-street tunnel for moving components to assembly lines, the plan calls for moving the component equipment to form product-focused flow lines**

**Factory Reorganization into Flow Lines/Cells—
for Quicker, More Flexible Production**

Viewpoints based on a visit to the main BIC plant, Sept. 15, 1989

**In connection with a two-day Schonberger
seminar for BIC executives, Sept. 16–17**

I. General information

- *The company*: BIC Corp. is headquartered in Clichy, France; BIC's North American complex is in Milford, CT.
- *U.S. product line*: Disposable razors (two types, 28 packaging configurations), lighters (about 50 SKUs), two types of writing pens (ball and marker—some 450 SKUs) in five buildings.

II. Overall Assessment

- *Strengths*:
  - ✓ Products with a global presence.
  - ✓ Scale economies through *dedicated machines*—much of it fine, "homegrown" equipment.
  - ✓ Multiple machines (not capital-intensive "supermachines").
  - ✓ Culture: a bow toward directness and simplicity.
  - ✓ Quality: emphasis on the performance dimension of quality.
- *Weaknesses*:
  - ✓ High levels of waste, delay, WIP, finished goods, raw materials; also, high overhead.
  - ✓ Lack of employee involvement, process control, and preventive maintenance.
  - ✓ Traditional cost accounting—with monthly variance reports.

III. Primary Recommendations

- *Overview*: The key recommendation concerns wholesale regrouping of equipment into cells (contrasted to the present layout done by equipment type). Although most of my feedback report to the company is missing, diagrams of a proposed re-layout into cells were found and are included at the end of this caselet. A few very incomplete remarks about the cellular plan, gleaned from raw notes, follow:
- *Present factory*: Numerous existing equipment groups and departments consist of large numbers of machines. Examples:
  - ✓ 74 injection molding machines used in producing pens and 25 for lighters; machines are multi-cavity (most 24 to 48 cavities; some up to 100 cavities). These are in Building 2, across the street from the main production center.
  - ✓ 200 Torno machines.
  - ✓ 25 extruders for tubes, five for barrels.
  - ✓ Eight machines for flint springs, six for fork springs.
  - ✓ Three pouch packers, three case packers.
  - ✓ 56 ball grinding machines, 45 peening machines.
  - ✓ Ten cartridge assembly machines and 15 walking-beam assembly machines.
- *Re-grouping into cells*: With so much equipment, mostly readily movable, the situation is ripe for moving nearly all out of the

equipment departments and into cellular groupings, with each group focused on its own product family. An example:

- ✓ One packout machine is in a location separate from the many assembly machines it serves. It runs very fast (was considered a "Cadillac" machine when originally purchased), but requires long changeovers among 36 different lower-volume ball pens and marking pens.
- ✓ As a result, it produces excessive lot sizes and inventories, and it takes many days to work through all 36 product models, which results in chronic back-order conditions.
- ✓ To cope, one manager said he would like to bring in an old packout machine and put it on wheels, so it can move across the plant from one product assembly machine to another.

- Some cell arrangements would require more equipment, either design-build (BIC has a strong belief in self-built equipment), or purchased; e.g., more units of the off-line packout equipment for the 36 pen assembly machines.
- *Sub-street tunnel?* Large amounts of equipment kept across the street (injection molding machines, etc.) make for inefficient handling and communication disconnects.
  - ✓ To cope, there was talk about tunneling under the street (as was done in a BIC plant in Europe).
  - ✓ However, cell implementation would neatly resolve that issue: move an entire product line (e.g., all pens) across the street to form its own focused factory.
- *Long implementations, immediate gains*:
  - ✓ Implementation would need to extend over many months, but multiple equipment moves could begin immediately and carry forward continually—with expectations that some equipment would move numerous times.
  - ✓ No point in delay, because payoffs of each move (sharply lowered flow times, inventories, handling costs) would be obtained right away.
- *Cellular diagrams*: Cellular plans diagrammed in Figure 22.1 are described for ball pens and lighters; markers and shavers would follow similar cellular plans. The diagrams, being rather complete and annotated, require only brief discussion. For round-ball pens:
  - ✓ Functional departments (shops), with shop-to-shop flow paths, disappear, replaced by short links that result from final assembly

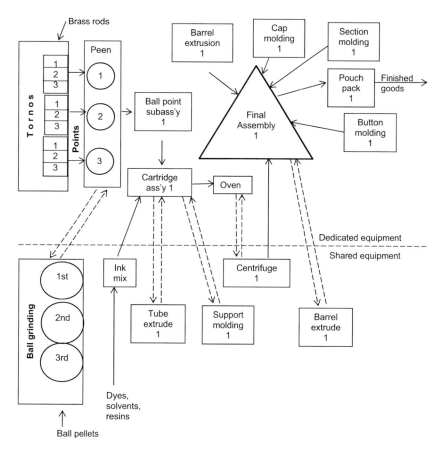

FIGURE 22.1

Organization of cells: round-ball pens. Round-Ball Pens: Cell No. 1 (of 10—because there are 10 cartridge assembly machines). Number "1" refers to the quantity of that machine needed for good balance. Pairs of dashed lines stand for kanban linkages.

being surrounded by multiple fabrication and subassembly units: barrel extrusion; cap molding; section molding; button molding; barrel extrusion; and cartridge assembly, entailing oven-bake, then centrifuge. All are synchronized via one-to-one flows.

✓ Brass rods made on nine Tornos feed (for good balance) three peen machines and balls from ball grinding to form part of a ballpoint subassembly cell.

✓ Cartridge assembly is fed in steps by dyes, solvents, and resins that form into ink, along with extruded tube and support molding.

✓ Most cell equipment is dedicated to the end product—no setup steps. However, the ball grinding, ink mixing, tube extruding, support molding, centrifuging, and barrel extruding have extra capacity so as to be shared with assembly cells for other models of the product.

✓ After pouch packaging, the completed product goes to finished-goods storage.

✓ Assembly of lighters, shown in Figure 22.2, has a similar pattern, involving many operations and mostly with synchronized flows and equipment dedicated to the given lighter model.

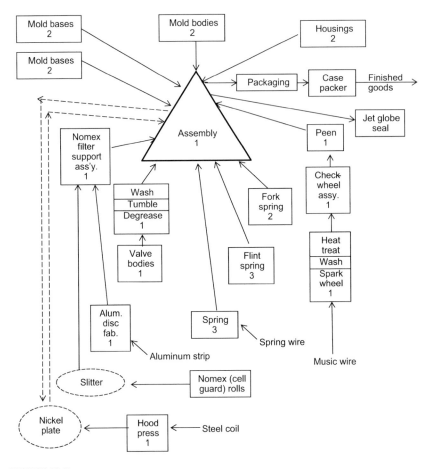

FIGURE 22.2

Organization of cells: lighters. Lighters (100,000 per day): Cell No. 1 (of 10 cells). Number "1," "2," etc. refer to the quantity of that machine needed for good balance. Pair of dashed lines stands for kanban.

- *Summary*:
  - ✓ Both lighters and pens would be produced in numerous, similar cells, each dedicated to its own model or family of models.
  - ✓ Overall, large numbers of pen and lighter models would be made concurrently, so that the factory can produce near—in quantity and time—to actual downstream usage.

CHAPTER I-23. ZANUSSI, FLORENCE, ITALY, 1989

My visit to Zanussi's refrigerator plant was arranged by RDA Consultants, sponsor of some of my seminars in Italy. RDA had been instrumental in Zanussi's early successes in adopting JIT/flow methodologies; and parent-company Electrolux, an early adopter of JIT/TPS/flow, served as a model for the Zanussi effort. The caselet is largely descriptive of Zanussi's impressive results, with a few added "opportunities/ recommendations."

High-Interest Topics:
- **1 billion lira order for more conveyors—cancelled!**
- **New management pursuing a thorough transformation of this refrigerator plant**
- **Confused flows replaced with five product-focused production lines**

Aiming for JIT/Flow at Zanussi Refrigerators, Florence

Impressions based on a plant visit, June 2, 1989

In connection with a one-day Schonberger seminar at Zanussi, hosted by Milan-based RDA Consultants

I. General information

- *Ownership*: Zanussi became a subsidiary of Sweden-based Electrolux (one of world's largest producers of major appliances) in 1984.
- *Products*: Tabletop refrigerators and freezers, which are declining products; a new side-by-side model is expected to do fairly well.
- *Competitive/business issues*: Zanussi's own assessment of its performance, prior to 1997, was: poor quality, high inventories, low delivery reliability, decreasing productivity, and negative key financials.
- *Key executives*: Mr. Andina, strong, new plant manager; his young, modern-thinking boss is Mr. Campello.

II. Strengths

- *New climate*:
  - ✓ Under the new management, operations have become more productive and efficient, with better quality and improved management-union relationships.
  - ✓ Deliberate management efforts are aimed at avoiding mistakes, complexity, inflexibility, and the former over-emphasis on direct-labor costs.
  - ✓ Good visual controls (open sight lines).
  - ✓ Inventory turns have increased to 30.
- *Eliminating paced conveyor lines*: Under Andina, paced conveyor lines were abolished. Now assemblers and welders each have their own small stock of units to work on, arranged the way units are assembled, and with time to get the quality right. (A full-time Zanussi consultant—one Mr. Billi—seen as an obstructionist, is no longer there.)
- *Moving toward integrated flows*:
  - ✓ The factory has been organized into five focused business units/plants/lines.
  - ✓ Recently, subassembly lines have been merging with final assembly lines. Further plans:
    - A new door line will allow direct hanging on paint hooks, whereas, currently, doors go to WIP (work-in-process) stores first.
    - Old machines for injection molding/thermoforming of inner liners are to be moved and dedicated (minimal changeovers) to families of sizes.
- *Multi-model lines*: In conjunction with some quick-setup gains, several lines are able to switch from model to model (one line makes both freezer and refrigerator for a side-by-side product); lot sizes are in multiples of 50.
- *Suppliers*:
  - ✓ Suppliers have been reduced from 200 in 1986 (none auto-certified), to 175 in 1987 (four certified), to 140 in 1988 (20 certified).
  - ✓ Among its certified suppliers, some are delivering in 25-piece unit loads, which is exactly half the plant's lot-size multiple.
- *Shifts/capacity*: With no capacity constraints, the plant is largely one shift, which is Andina's goal everywhere.

- *Cancelled conveyor order*: One billion liras was allocated to buy more conveyors to balance fabrication, subassembly, and final assembly—and keep WIP off the floor. Andina cancelled the conveyor order, preferring to spend on value-add equipment and fixing problems.

III. Opportunities/Recommendations

- *Further process integration*: Continue moving fabrication and subassembly to assembly lines—and isolate very low-volume units in their own area.
- *Regularize schedules*: However, Andina doubts that regularity in scheduling can be done; he thinks there are too many models. (Our limited deliberations did not include the counterpoint: segmenting the many models into runners, repeaters, and strangers, thus to simplify the regularization of schedules.)
- *Kanban*: Widely adopt formal, disciplined kanban/pull (in a few places, long setup times, an obstacle to effective kanban, need to be addressed first).
- *Operator engagement*: Record all problems by type and frequency, to be used by operator teams engaging in data analysis and brainstorming projects.
- *Quick setups*: Involve operators as leaders in setup efforts.
- *Extend visual management*: Employ visual signboard measures and controls.
- *SPC/JIT training*: All employees should receive training in statistical process control and just-in-time production.
- *Bottlenecks*:
  - ✓ Eliminate bottlenecks (which have led to, for example, 1,000 units per day "sitting on the floor getting dirty").
  - ✓ Specific example: Install a new cabinet transfer line, as planned, to alleviate the bottleneck there.
- *Cover tops*: Switch cover-top production from four to five days per week, thus to match the final assembly schedule.
- *Re-focus strategy*: Aim at quality and cost, not just higher value, more features, and more models. This requires fixing the cost system, which in its present (conventional) form distorts costs, leading to proliferation of models and features—and is an obstacle to regularizing schedules.

CHAPTER I-24. INTERCHECKS, INC., CENTRALIA, WA, 1989

Interchecks is a contract printer of bank checks/checkbooks for both individual and business customers. The caselet offers a rare example of just-in-time and flow production in the world of printing, initiated—with large-scale training of employees—by enlightened executives.	**High-Interest Topics:** • **Two examples—with diagrams—of cellular configurations for filling multi-step customer orders** • **Warehouse on wheels: delivery trucks that hold some of every item and deliver on fixed daily routes**

Paper Products Company's Moves toward JIT/Flow Production

Assessment based on a visit to Centralia plants, June 27, 1989

Slightly updated July 26, all in connection with
Schonberger's one-day seminar, July 29

I. General Information

- *The company*: Interchecks, a subsidiary of Norton Opax Commercial Printing Ltd. (U.K.), has its main base-stock plant and imprint plant in Centralia, WA. Other imprint plants are in Napa, Fresno, Santa Ana, and Irwindale in California. (Interchecks was acquired by John H. Harland of Atlanta in 1992.)
- *Product line*: Personal and business bank checkbooks.
- *Customizing checks*: Imprint plants take print paper (with scenery, etc.) from base stock plants, finish checks with customer specs, and see to their shipment to customers.
- *Competitive issues*: The nation's top check-printing companies (e.g., Deluxe) are known for very quick response to customers' orders for checkbooks.
- *Labor union*: Centralia's two plants are unionized; other Interchecks plants are not.
- *Process details*: If interested, see Sidebar 1.
- *Centralia—special note*: This smallish flood-prone town just off I-5 has surprising origins. George Washington (no, not that one),

SIDEBAR   INTERCHECKS' PROCESSES

Paper: From Simpson Paper (Northern CA)—two deliveries monthly to base stock

   Equipment: five web presses—New 6-color (1), 5-color (2), 3-color (1), 2-color (1)

   Changeovers: ten hours (ten-scene checks) to 15 mins. (for a make-ready); 2.5-hour average

   Sheet-fed: three small presses; one new, costly ($250K) 2-color Heidelberg press (to replace two of the older presses)—for adding images to sheet already through web press

   Cut-to-size: One sheeter just for this.

   "PMs": Once a month, largely by pressmen (Fred, plant mechanic, main enabler)

   Job groupings: Base stock schedules for commonality (e.g., a few 4-color jobs)

   Collating: Two ten-slot collators.

   Counting machine: Imprint plants now have their own.

   On-hand inventory: $900K finished stock (goes to imprint plants); $800K raw paper; $300K vinyl for checkbooks (from Seattle supplier to base-stock to imprint plants)

   Items handled: 2,205 finished (about 3,000 if all scenes are included)

   Personnel: Half in base stock once worked in Centralia imprint; some cross-training/job-rotation in base stock

---

son of Virginian slaves, became a successful businessman in Missouri. Tiring of racial slurs there, he journeyed to the Pacific Northwest in 1875, where he founded Centralia; prospering there, he became highly regarded by townspeople for his honorable business practices and personal attributes.

- *Contact persons*: Richard C. Lottie, CEO; Christopher J. Seung, director of marketing; Colin Aldworth, base-stock plant manager; Dan Ransdale, Napa plant manager.

II. Observations/Suggestions—Centralia Base Stock

- *Persistent backorders*: First-order task is for the base-stock plant to get out of the backorder mode, which will require some overtime or Saturday work.

- *Regularize scheduling*: For quicker, more reliable customer response, plus lower costs and better first-quality, progress to a regularized, repeating, fully-planned schedule.
  - ✓ Include, say, the top 200 products (or top 500; or top 1,000).
  - ✓ Run a planned schedule, say, four days a week, or first six hours, daily. Reserve an extra day, or two hours each day, plus overtime and Saturdays, for irregular production of the rest of the product line, plus rework, order changes from imprint plants, irregular jobs, breakdown recovery, prototyping, demand surges, and long setups.
  - ✓ Run the schedule on the same machines every time, getting the jobs down pat on those machines.
  - ✓ Run hardest-to-setup jobs, say, every week; mediums every two days; others daily (this hinges partly on successful efforts to slash setup times).
  - ✓ With very frequent runs of each product, all finished inventories— in both Centralia base stock and imprint plants—may be cut at least five-fold.
    - ■ Inventory remaining at base stock will be mostly buffer stock (today, it's mostly cycle stock, owed to big-batch production runs).
    - ■ Later (after backorders are eliminated), cut base-stock production by 25 percent or so for a few months to shrink excess inventories.
    - ■ Use that period of reduced operations for extensive training and process improvement.
- *"Warehouse on wheels"*:
  - ✓ Modify the insides of the trucks that deliver from base-stock to imprint plants:
    - ■ For regular-use items put—on shelf slots in the truck—fixed ID labels for carrying some of *every item*, *every trip*.
    - ■ Leave 30 or so unlabeled shelf slots for special-order items.
  - ✓ For delivery to Centralia Imprint, use the twin-container (kanban) system and right-sized stackable flat containers (like pizza boxes).
    - ■ Label each pair with its own P/N (part number) and stock location. Every day have the same truck deliver full containers to Imprint and bring back twin empties.
    - ■ Some containers won't come back for days because Imprint isn't using any.

- ■ This kanban system requires no scheduling/receiving transactions.
- ✓ Send a single truck every day (or every two days) on the California trip, stopping at the Napa, Fresno, Santa Ana, and Irwindale imprint plants.
  - ■ Use either standard shelved containers or the twin-cart system.
  - ■ The regularized, repeat deliveries will eliminate scheduling and receiving transactions.
- • *Ordering*: The Imprint plants cease item-by-item ordering from base-stock, except for specials; and bill monthly (transfer pricing) based on a simple checkoff of usage.
- • *Purchasing*: Offer incentives to Simpson Paper (a longer frozen schedule, better forecast information, slightly higher price) in return for running and shipping master rolls to Interchecks weekly instead of every two weeks; look for similar deals with other major suppliers.

III. Imprint Plants—Opportunities for Improvement

- • *Functional silos*: Abandon the functional arrangement of people and equipment. Break the entire operation into fairly small work-flow teams in work cells.
  - ✓ Each team handles a fixed group of products (or, in some cases, group of customers).
  - ✓ Ideally, the team includes all operations, from order processing to shipping. For processes in which there are only one or two machines, those machines will be shared among several teams (or change the processes themselves to eliminate or minimize the need for sharing).
    - ■ But, at least at Centralia Imprint, the number of machines at most processes is fairly large, which makes team/cell structure highly attractive.
    - ■ The total team, responsible for a certain group of products, would divide into perhaps three or four sub-teams, each in a different corner of the building, with shared equipment in a central area.
- • *Centralia example*: Consider a minimal example of four product teams, and a maximal example of ten teams (including one or more for business checks only).

- *If four product teams*: Team 1 should have the following sub-teams (see Figure 24.1):
  - ✓ Sub-team **1a** does order processing/creating batch-headers (three people) and data entry (three or four dedicated CRT's); shares punched-paper-tape computer with product teams 2, 3, and 4.
  - ✓ Sub-team **1b** does linotype (two dedicated linotypes), proofreading (three people), QA, linotype correction, bank cuts (two people, 1.5 dedicated racks of bank type), bank cut cleaning, lock up, letterpress (four dedicated letterpress machines), and inspection; shares bindery with other product teams.
  - ✓ Sub-team **1c** has its own boxing (three people); shares shrink wrap and mail bagging with other product teams.

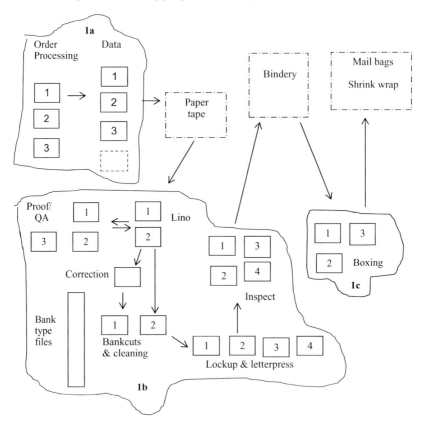

FIGURE 24.1

Centralia imprint plant—Team 1 of a four-team/cell configuration. Note: This configuration has paper tape, bindery, shrink wrap and mail bag in close proximity to the three sub-teams, as shown above. Three other sets of sub-teams (not shown) are to surround the centralized processes in the center.

- *If ten teams*: This way of organizing is even better—closer to JIT ideals; see Figure 24.2. This ten-cell full-flow version could slash turn-around time to *one day*.
  - ✓ Each of the ten teams plots all nonconformities, irregularities, delays, rework, etc., on simple check sheets, which serve as a basis for frequent brainstorming and problem-solving.
  - ✓ Team members set up a long-term cross-training schedule. As members master other jobs, they switch jobs frequently.

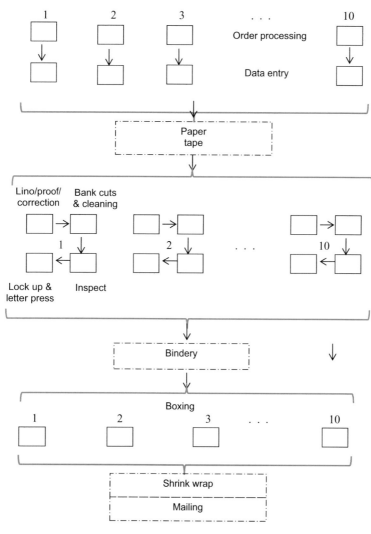

FIGURE 24.2
Centralia imprint plant—Team 1 of a ten-team/cell configuration.

Floaters—moving among processes—are common, perhaps including a floater on batch-headers and data entry in the 4 a.m.-to-noon shift.

✓ Each team/sub-team has a lead person/coordinator, rotated to give others chances to demonstrate leadership.

✓ As demand patterns change, labor is lent from team to team—with team leaders agreeing to lend *best*, most experienced people; otherwise labor lending becomes a bone of contention.

✓ Each team "owns" most of its equipment, dedicates to making it work perfectly, and keeps records on its idiosyncrasies: learning what things to replace before failure or excessive wear, learning and doing simple maintenance and repairs.

- *Implementation*: Start with a pilot team (e.g., for business checks) to prove and iron out the concept.

IV. General Opportunities for Improvement

- *Process improvement*:
  ✓ Drive total improvement with visible wall charts of all kinds.
  ✓ Keep thorough machine history records—for computer-generated predictive maintenance (replace wear-out and failed components before serious wear/failure).
  ✓ Improvements that may conflict with Interchecks' corporate performance measurement.
    - Improvements/changes at Centralia aim at deep cuts in *overall* costs; however, D.L. (direct labor) cost, the usual corporate focus, may not go down much, even could go up a bit (e.g., more setup hours, training hours) before they fall.
    - Where corporate metrics seem in conflict, and need to be changed, they should temporarily be treated with "benign neglect."
    - The recent corporate mandate to chop inventories by X percent per month *is* consistent with proposed process improvements.
- *Product costing*: Conduct a cost audit of sample products once a year—or when a new product or major sales opportunity requires it.
  ✓ The audit approach is better than job costing, which is complex and costly itself—and inaccurate. Job-by-job costing ceases to be useful because (1) product cost information is needed only about once a year for pricing or bidding, and (2) the rational approach to cost control is to directly control *causes* of cost rather than using periodic, after-the-fact cost reports as a club.

✓ Costing in much of the process industry (base stock has process-industry characteristics) has a unique feature: heavy job startup costs (e.g., scrap and changeover labor) followed by low-cost production (operators can do other beneficial things while the machine runs).

✓ The same cost pattern—high labor cost during starts/changeovers—applies to most factory overhead: scheduling, expediting, stock-picking, material handling, maintenance, supervision, and engineering.

✓ Despite the relationship between startup and cost, the cost of a product should *not* be based on number of runs per year:

 ▪ *More* runs per year (frequent, smaller-lot deliveries) is a customer-focused "just-in-time" goal.

 ▪ Instead, the many products with very low annual volume should each incur a cost/price penalty; the few with very high volume receive a cost/price reduction.

• *Product pricing*: Price to the market and price for sales growth—relying on the new cost-cutting engine to keep running, providing steadily better profit margins as prices rise or fall.

CHAPTER I-25. ZYTEC CORP., REDWOOD FALLS, MN, 1987

Zytec was fortunate to be able to hire Dave Taylor, well known for being "point man" in the widely distributed Hewlett-Packard JIT simulation video. With Taylor and other enlightened executives, this very small manufacturer went on to win a 1991 Baldrige Prize.

High-Interest Topics:
• **Partial avoidance of kitting (and its extra handling)**
• *Reduced* **product costing is part of the deal in advanced flow manufacturing**
• **Overhead allocation** *by cycle time*
• **Innovative uses of SPC in tracking variability** *in finance*

In Trouble, Zytec Brings in "Heavy Hitters" from HP in Successful Effort to Excel in JIT/TQC
Observations based on a visit to Zytec, June 2, 1987
Also, an earlier visit (Nov. 25, 1985) and JIT-focused presentation to some 450 Zytec employees
Plus ongoing communications with principal Zytec managers

I. Zytec's Transformation

- *Origins*: Zytec began in 1984 as a leveraged buyout by three Control Data Corp. (CDC) executives from what was then the CDC Magnetic Peripherals subsidiary.
- *Location*: Headquartered in Eden Prairie, MN, Zytec's 40,000 sf manufacturing plant, with 550 people, is 100 miles southwest in Redwood Falls, MN.
- *Products*: Power supplies for electronic products, including hard disk drives, telephone switching equipment, and medical equipment.
- *Competitive/business issues*: After the spin-off, sales were flat because of slow growth in computer markets and because Zytec was hardly differentiated from the 400 companies competing in the $5 billion per year power-supply business.
- *Turn-around*: Ronald Schmidt, chairman, president, and CEO, engineered a turn-around, largely by hiring some of the country's most experienced JIT experts: Floyd Burghard, VP manufacturing, who was instrumental in Northern Telecom's JIT transformation; and Gary Flack and Dave Taylor, from Hewlett-Packard Greeley, which in 1982, launched one of the western world's first and most impressive implementations of JIT/flow production.
- *Key results*: From before 1985 to after the end of 1986:
  - ✓ Total inventory fell from $17.5m to $5.1m; WIP from $6m to $0.5m; scrap from $70k/month to $7k/month; cycle time (flow time) from ten days to two.
  - ✓ Materials personnel fell from 92 to 52; warehouse personnel from 47 to 17 (the removed 30 accepted new jobs in production, though at a lower wage).
  - ✓ Schedule stability from none to four weeks; plug-and-play from 90% to 99.7%.

II. Notable Practices and Vignettes

- *JIT production*: Operations was reorganized into product flows through U-shaped cells or along straight aisles, all arranged logically to minimize motion with maximized flexibility to easily switch from one product to another.
- *Material handling*: Cells obtain their material via internally-designed kanban carts; nearly all conveyors have been removed.

- *Kitting*:
  - ✓ Undesirable under JIT/flow, in that it entails extra handling, material movement, and cycle time, kitting is avoidable by sending materials directly from the receiving dock to production stations (in suppliers' containers, when possible).
  - ✓ However, at Zytec, where a power supply requires 200 to 500 parts, direct-from-dock delivery to assembly cells would have created impossible congestion.
  - ✓ A compromise:
    - Hand-carry plastic containers, each with slots for holding the parts for a given power supply.
    - These are staged near the assembly cell, and one container is swapped by hand for another as the cell's schedule dictates— then, via visual kanban, each empty is sent back to receiving stores for refilling.
- *Cycle-time (flow time, lead time, throughput time) reduction*:
  - ✓ Total cycle time for Zytec's 250-watt Magnum switching power supply, its highest-volume product, had been averaging 80 days. Following JIT implementations (cells, kanban, scheduling weekly rather than monthly, bringing magnetic subassemblies in house) cycle time was cut to 1.15 days.
  - ✓ Cycle times are measured weekly using a cycle-time tag tracked through all operations, with the time then plotted on a trend chart.
- *Marketing & JIT*: John Steele, VP marketing & sales, had been largely indifferent to JIT—until he learned that it took longer for a salesperson to process the order than it did to manufacture the product!
- *Suppliers*:
  - ✓ The number of suppliers has been minimized to "a few good ones" that are carefully screened and that deliver frequently just-in-time and guarantee high quality of their materials.
  - ✓ Suppliers receive a rolling forecast for the next 12 months, which is instrumental in securing short lead times from suppliers.
  - ✓ Sheet metal moves in 40 circulating sheet-metal carts: two days of carts at Zytec, two days of empty carts at supplier, and one day of carts in transit.

- *Faxban*: Many purchased items are ordered via faxban, a version of kanban in which the kanban card is faxed to the supplier when the material is pulled by production.
- *SPC*: All employees were trained in SPC in 1986; CEO Schmidt says Zytec doesn't spend much time measuring productivity but does spend significant time measuring quality.
- *SPC in accounting and financial management*: Innovatively applying SPC, Zytec uses X-bar, R charts (with the usual nominal value and upper and lower control limits) in accounting—tracking (a) percentage actual revenue to forecast revenue and (b) expenses.
- *Strategy development*: Unlike just about every other company, Zytec goes beyond developing strategy via benchmarking, market research, and customer feedback.
  - ✓ Under executive guidance, it involves six cross-functional teams in developing a five-year, long-range strategic plan; then it obtains reviews and critiques from some 150 of its employees—representing all departments and shifts—even including some of its key suppliers.
  - ✓ Finally, executives translate the long-range strategy into one-year broad company objectives and help departments to develop their own quality plans.

III. Product Costs: Overhead-Allocation Issue

- *Product costing*:
  - ✓ Background:
    - While at HP (early 1980s), Taylor and Flack were involved, along with the plant's cost accountants, in grappling with JITs effects on product costing.
    - They found monthly cost reports to be useless for the usual purpose of cost control because JIT had reduced product flow times from weeks (even months) to days or hours: many shipments occurred before monthly cost/cost control reports came out.
    - Moreover, they noted that products on JIT zipped through the plant, scarcely touched by the usual manufacturing overhead

functions (storage, material handling, quality, planning and scheduling, ordering/receiving/accounting transactions, etc.). Long lead-time products, on the other hand, spent significant time collecting overhead costs.

- Among leading management accountants, this bias in assigning costs to products became a dominant rationale in favor of activity-based costing (ABC), HP being among earliest ABC adopters. So, for the sake of reliable costs, it made sense to allocate overhead by production lead time.

✓ Taylor and Flack carried this concept with them to Zytec and implemented it, including use of cycle-time tags to accumulate flow-time data in their version of ABC.

- *Dispute*:
  ✓ Case writers for a Harvard Business School study (Zytec Corp. C—1990) found problems with Zytec's use of ABC/overhead allocated by cycle time, saying, "the new system was dominated by confusion. Everybody wanted to compare the old and the new numbers …"
  ✓ The real problem, however, was that Zytec was using ABC (a mistake) for *cost management*, as in conventional cost accounting.
    - However, that use of ABC (and the confusion it entailed) was irrelevant and redundant.
    - That is because Zytec was avidly employing far more direct cost controls, namely, controlling *causes* of cost via its excellent practices in quality management, process improvement, quick response, simple flows, and so on.
  ✓ Thus, regardless of the "confusion," Zytec's use of ABC by cycle time could be used for what ABC does best—and that is to provide cost data relevant for major, *infrequent* decisions, such as evaluating a proposal for a high-cost piece of equipment, a major make-or-buy issue, or checking on whether its prices make sense. Zytec's astute managers knew better than to make use of the ABC data for overly frequent control, as most other ABC users tend to do.

CHAPTER I-26. HONEYWELL, PLYMOUTH, MN, 1989

This short caselet shows how the company keeps a famous product—the Honeywell round thermostat—viable decade after decade. It does so by continually upgrading and improving the production process—to a state of flexible (easy to modify and improve), low-cost, high-performing automation.	***High-Interest Topics:*** • **Use of standard 4-foot long assembly tables, easily swapped for upgraded assembly equipment that is constantly redesigned** • **Time to adopt "make-to-a-number" production with nearby feeder processes tightly linked by kanban**

**Continuous Improvement Driven by Modular
Equipment with Kanban Linkages**

Summary impressions from a brief plant tour, Sept. 8, 1989

**In connection with a two-day Schonberger public
seminar, September 6-7**

I. General information

- *Dominant product*: The T-87 Honeywell round thermostat—widely used in houses and commercial buildings since 1952; over three million sold with 50,000 to 75,000 produced per week. See photo, Figure 26.1.
  - ✓ Many are sold to other companies (50–70 of them), so they can put on their own bezel/logo.
  - ✓ Cost of T-87 is lower today (1989) than in 1952.
- *Markets, competition*: 75% of sales are to the after-market (main OEM customers are Carrier, York, Trane, Whirlpool, and Lennox). The main competitor is White Rogers.
- *Automation laboratory*: For this mature product (and others in various locations), Honeywell has established an automation lab of 50–60 automation specialists, computer technicians, etc. The lab employs DFA (meaning, in this case, design for automation).
- *Plymouth plant*:
  - ✓ 600 employees, two shifts; 42 salaried (two in QA, which uses SQC charts).

FIGURE 26.1
The Honeywell T87 thermostat.

AS/RS – for shipping & receiving	Chromotherm
Multi-stage	Optics
Q-Base FAS	T-87 line
Econostat	

FIGURE 26.2
Honeywell's Plymouth, MN plant configuration (rough, not at all to scale).

✓ Overtime (nine-hour days) in the peak season beginning in August.
✓ The configuration of the 208,000 sq. ft. plant is as shown in Figure 26.2.

II. Strengths

- *Good match of product & processes*:
  ✓ I rarely see a manufacturing facility that is "right" for the products made. But, in general, the T87 hard-automated line, with several feeder processes (e.g., on-line noise-baffled punch presses stamping from strip coil), looks right.

✓ A planned move of injection molding from Golden Valley will considerably enhance the operation.

- *Focused business units*: Honeywell shifted to P&Ls (profit and loss) by site about five years ago—for more focused businesses.
- *Standard machine modules*: The T87 automated line is made up of 4-foot-long machine modules, which make it quick and easy to replace given modules with improved versions—which are always under development in the lab.
  ✓ For example, say that one of the current 4-foot stations has a pick-and-place robot for fastening three components together.
  ✓ Lab engineers would be designing and testing an improved robot that is more easily programmed and has greater range of motion. When testing is complete, the present 4-foot station is unbolted overnight and the new one is bolted in its place, ready to go at start of the next morning's shift.
  ✓ This is an example of continuous improvement—in cost and quality—for a very high-volume product with long product life.
- *Q-Base FAS (flexible automation system) line*: Operational characteristics of this product include:
  ✓ Some notable quick setup processes (e.g., 30 seconds to change a trim plate).
  ✓ Use of a discrepancy board for recording any process down for five minutes or more.
  ✓ The FAS line (in its own area) is compact and team-like (only 1/5 the size of the T87 for the same potential volume) with only a 30-minute flow time.

III. Opportunities for Improvement

- *T87 thermostat line*:
  ✓ Slash flow time from 2.75 hours, to say, one hour, and OEM order-promise time from 21 to 14 days (then to 10, 7, etc.).
    ▪ The key enabler is installing limit switches on the 20-foot (roughly) conveyor lengths between processes to prevent "stuffage" of units in process; better yet, shorten conveyor lengths to 5feet, a "space-denial" action.
    ▪ A work group linked day after day by a one-hour flow time is far more cohesive (team-like) than one with a 2.75-hour flow time.

✓ Link the T87 line to nearby feeder processes via kanban (in replacement of weekly scheduling of those feeders) and include these processes in the measure of flow time. Kanban-linked feeders would include microswitch weld, bi-metal coil, heat anticipator, etc.—and, when moved (from Golden Valley), injection molding.

✓ Adopt the "make-to-a-number" discipline; e.g., in a month when average sales are 65,000 T87s per day, make exactly 65,000 each day—no more!—and synchronize all supporting processes and buying of materials to that rate.

  ▪ Part of this discipline is under-scheduling the line and its labor so that, on an average day, there is extra time for improvement activities near the shift's end (after the "number" has been met).

  ▪ On a bad day, it's overtime until the "number" is met.

✓ Keep pressing—in contract negotiations—for use of temporary employees (strive for "permanent" temps, hired back each year) in the seasonal buildup period.

• *Other*:

  ✓ Cut doors around plant walls for direct receipt of incoming materials and forwarding to each focused plant-in-a plant. Follow up by tearing out sections of the AS/RS (hold small celebrations each time).

  ✓ Disburse central factory maintenance to each plant-in-a-plant.

  ✓ Link the Q-base feeder line to other assembly lines by kanban.

  ✓ Abolish acceptance inspection (at Berkshire Storage) of materials that have been produced and are arriving from Taiwan. Replace that with guaranteed quality at the (Taiwan) source.

  ✓ Although FAS is compact with short flow time, there is still plenty of room for improvement. For example, reduce some conveyor lengths from the present 8-feet length (estimate), or install limit switches to prevent so many pallets (perhaps 350) to be in queue on those conveyors.

  ✓ "Plaster" plant walls—in each plant-in-a-plant—with large improvement charts (e.g., setup time, WIP, flow time, flow distance, and rework), cross-training charts, recognition and activity charts, etc. for enhanced visual management of the improvement process.

CHAPTER I-27. CHARLES MACHINE WORKS, PERRY, OK, 1989

This caselet doesn't dwell on "Ditch Witch's" many excellences but plunges directly into specifics on doing more and at a faster pace.	***High-Interest Topics:*** • **Cylinder barrel cell reduced through-put time from four weeks to about ten minutes.** • **Opportunity: Expansion into Europe**

This Producer of A "Ditch Witch" Equipment Excels in Multiple Ways
Assessment based on a visitation, Tuesday afternoon, July 11, 1989
In connection with a two-day Schonberger
seminar, Report Date: July 13, 1989

I. General Information

- *The company*: Charles Machine is the home of Ditch Witch trenchers and other equipment used to install materials (telephone and electrical lines, cable TV, etc.) underground. Trenchers were invented here in 1949 and have been produced here ever since.
- *Product line*: 13 basic models of trencher, from 5-HP to workhorse 100-HP tractors—with hundreds of trenching options.
- *Competitiveness*: Several strengths (aside from the wonderful Ditch Witch name) include some that are rare and unique:
  - ✓ Sticking to its "knitting" (below-ground equipment).
  - ✓ High pay with everyone on a strong bonus system and growing employee stock ownership.
  - ✓ No debt; no inspectors.
  - ✓ Everyone lives in Perry. The company provides strong support for offspring of employees when they go off to college.
  - ✓ Absence of perks and flashy spending—and others.
- *Contact persons*: Ed Malzahn, president; Barry Blades; Mike Adair; John Dolezal.

II. Strategic Issues

- *Plant & people*: Too many people (800+), too many acres (23), too many P/Ns (part numbers) to be managed as single plant.

- ✓ One option: subdivide into two or three plants-in-a-plant; perhaps one for vehicular products, one for attachments, one for non-current service parts.
- ✓ Each would have its own machines, people, tools, receiving, maintenance, etc.
- *European potential*: Ditch Witch has both the need and the means of setting up an assembly plant in Europe.
  - ✓ This strategy is partly to get more into Europe before 1992's possible "Fortress Europe" occurs.
  - ✓ A European production beachhead already exists, since German engines and components are already bought there. The cost of sending parts to Europe would be partly or wholly offset by other freight and lead time reductions within Europe.
  - ✓ A European plant would force an overdue technical change: going metric.
  - ✓ Charles Machine is debt-free, thus can stand the cost.
  - ✓ This proposal does *not* seem risky and *does* offer big growth opportunities—including much greater stock value for Ditch Witch's *very* loyal employee-owners.
  - ✓ With a plant in Europe, the Perry plant could perhaps be shrunk to a more manageable size—or at least the facility could be kept at current size even as sales grow.
- *Outside expertise*:
  - ✓ Most companies that strongly favor promotion from within are strengthened by it. However, Ditch Witch has not kept up well with the knowledge-based upheaval in manufacturing management of the 1980s.
  - ✓ Fortunately, a few outsiders are all it takes to breathe fresh life (and knowledge) into the company, which Ditch Witch is now doing.
- *Hierarchy*: As cellular manufacturing expands, a whole layer of supervision will become unnecessary. This is because cells manage themselves, to some extent, and because of employee involvement in process control/improvement. (Probably too many layers, even if nothing else changed.)

III. Other Observations

- *Cell organization*: Continue with organizing cells, but at much faster rate.

✓ Example of excellent progress and next steps:

- The cylinder barrel cell (for eight families of barrels, producing 35,000 cylinders per year, with two operators walking the cell in circular routes) cut flow time from four weeks to about ten minutes.
- The next planned step is a rod cell next to the barrel cell; then add an assembly step or cell to combine the rod with the barrel.
- Paint the cell and fully label it with big signboards proclaiming the achievements made—which will help generate enthusiasm for many other parts to go through the same transformation.

✓ Some excellent progress in organizing cells has been made in assembly as well (e.g., the 2020 U-line sets a good example).

✓ The main thrust of the cell campaign should be moving welders to subassembly and final assembly—or, sometimes, to fabrication. Also, some assembly should probably be situated near a paint line.

- *Job classifications*: Reduce the amount of job classifications—which is already being done in connection with cells (e.g., the new title, "manufacturing technician," in cylinder barrel cell; a dozen people who can work about anywhere in assembly are called "assembly technician").
- *Quick setup*: Press for more setup-reduction (like the excellent one in the cylinder barrel cell, which cut ID-machining change time from 120 to ten minutes), making full use of video cameras.
- *Supplier reduction*: Continue reducing the number of suppliers (e.g., the 30 suppliers of bar and tube stock is probably too many).
- *Welding fixtures*: Locate by frequency of use (e.g., the most frequent permanently set up in a welding booth). Place some dedicated fixtures for welding of parts on a rate-based schedule.
- *Kanban*: Implement more kanban—formal, disciplined, painted squares, etc.
- *Visual controls*: Employ large-sized visual controls all over, loaded with baseline and trend data on quality, flow distance, setup times, etc.
- *Costing*: Change the costing system, preferably with overhead allocated by lead time.

✓ Cease labor reporting.

✓ Consider costing by audit as needed (rather than job-by-job or order-by-order), as well as meeting legal requirements with a bare-bones system.

- *Regularizing & synchronizing*: Regularize schedules for final assembly of "stars" (start with the 1010). Synchronize welding and fab to the final assembly schedule.

  ✓ For example, eight per day in assembly (a *rate*, derived from a single monthly work order) and eight per day of all weldments used in the assembly (plus service parts).

  ✓ In machining, run eight a day or some reasonable multiple of that, such as 24 every three days.

- *Stockrooms only for overflow*: Run *most* parts direct from fab to weld, weld to assembly—bypassing the WIP stockroom. Tear out at least half the WIP stockroom but retain the other half for overflow and for off-line (in case of emergency) buffer stock.

- *Cross-careering*: Develop cross-career assignments for technical, indirect, and managerial employees.

CHAPTER I-28. AT&T LITTLE ROCK, LITTLE ROCK, AR, 1988

AT&T Little Rock (as with other AT&T manufacturing locations) had been aggressively implementing JIT and total quality. It was seeking outsider confirmatory and critical observations at the time of my visit and seminar.	*High-Interest Topics:* • **Impressive implementations of cells/focused factories for five of its product families—with cordoning-off of resultant saved space** • **Use of backflush costing**

AT&T's JIT Initiative Finds a Welcome Home at its Little Rock Plant

Observations from brief plant tour, afternoon of December 6, 1988

In connection with a two-day Schonberger seminar
for AT&T, December 7–8

I. General Information

- *Product line*: 5ESS digital switching system used in universities, large companies, or any large installation having its own telephone system.
  - ✓ Each 5ESS has some 500,000 parts and is sold for $3.5 to $4.0 million.
  - ✓ Output averages one unit per day.
- *Employment*: 5,900 people with union representation by International Brotherhood of Electrical Workers (IBEW).
- *Contacts*: Don Mattingly, engineering and manufacturing manager; Larry Featherstone, general manager; Jim Rush, training manager; Buzz Peters, production-control manager; Ernest Edwards, executive director; plus four others from IBEW labor union's executive board.

II. Strengths

- *Process improvement*: Contributing are SGIAs (small group improvement activities); cause-and-effect diagrams (CEDAC); and a cost-of-quality program.
- *Cells/focused factories*:
  - ✓ Labeled JIT 1, 2, 3, 4, and 5. Each cell/focused factory has its own receiving docks and PCB (printed circuit board) assembly and test.
  - ✓ Supplier deliveries are as often as twice daily—with no need for receiving inspection.
  - ✓ Very high inventory turns for JIT 1, JIT 3 (JIT 2 is moving in that direction).
  - ✓ WIP is kitted to a three-day maximum limit in JIT 1.
  - ✓ Large performance charts are in each factory area.
- *Engineering*: Located on the production floor.
- *Robots*: Simple robots are in use for switch and keytop placement—in part, as means of averting carpal tunnel syndrome (a *good* reason for robots).
- *Kanban simplicity*: Instead of cards, the plant employs the visual simplicity of kanban squares and labeled kanban containers.
- *Factory employees*: Job classifications are down to just four, with three pay steps; and with designated lead persons.

- *Empty space*: Successes create empty space, which is cordoned off so it can't be re-loaded with stock.
- *Product costing*: Employs backflush costing/inventory relief.
- *Printer paper*: Instead of an entire humidity-controlled room for printer papers, JIT-3 uses a sealed humidity-controlled cabinet, which is better for visual management as well as cost saving.
- *Invoicing*: A monthly invoice for 500 SOS items—with use of EDI/fax.

III. Miscellaneous Observations/Suggestions

- *Further cells*: Next cells should (logically) be for service parts, old products, and low-volume products.
- *Keyboard area*: In JIT 3, locate three switch machines, all fed by a common fabrication machine, each feeding one of three test machines—as in the Figure 28.1 schematic.
- *Kitting*: Phase out kitting in JIT 1 (controllers) because it adds extra steps, people, inventory, transactions, and opportunities for damage.
- *Kanban*: Drive down kanban quantities in JIT 2.
- *Incoming materials*: Develop "milk runs."
- *Factory overhead*: Apply JIT concepts in assigning overhead to products:
  - ✓ Allocate factory overhead to JIT lines *by lead time*.
  - ✓ To further improve cost accuracy: On JIT lines eliminate some categories of overhead (e.g., close down stockrooms), which

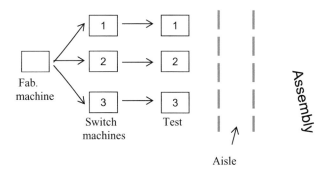

FIGURE 28.1
Linking switch machines and test machines.

loads more overhead on other, non-JIT products, thus generating financial pressure for simplification, cells, kanban, etc.

- *Training for all*: Develop a "set" training program—same for *all* line and staff—with strong SPC/JIT flavor (this may already be part of the present 40-hour training).
- *Off-line buffer stock*: For purchased parts with long lead times, place buffer stock in an off-line location. At the same time aggressively pursue direct shipment—and develop a plan with the distribution-center (Lisle, IL) to cut FGI (by half or more).
- *Linearity*: Convert to daily (instead of weekly) measurement of linearity on JIT lines.
- *Cross-training/job rotation*: Employ *planned* cross-training and job rotation for direct labor.
- *Career-change planning*: Employ a system of *planned* career-change assignments, e.g., nobody is a buyer for a whole career; business perspective is lost when someone stays in one function overly long.
- *Wall charts/graphs*: Add a few visible wall chart items, e.g., tally charts for all random mishaps, setup-time reduction charts (where appropriate), SPC control charts (should be quite a few processes where this is beneficial).
- *Visitations*: Operators and assemblers on visits to supplier plants for better, quicker coordination on company-to-company issues.
- *Excess capacity*: *Retain* (don't get rid of) some excess machines; retain for possible use as dedicated (no setup) equipment.
- *Offices*: Extend JIT, cells, SPC, and CEDAC to most offices.

IV. Obstacles to Overcome

- *Job losses*: Natural question: does continual improvement *hasten* job losses? That question and its answer(s) should be fully and frequently discussed.
- *Product line*: Products have not always been state-of-the-art, and sometimes late to market.
- *Lack of certain functions on site*: No on-site product design or marketing.
- *Policy*: Nobody may talk to suppliers except buyers (this policy is in need of amendment, or to be benignly ignored).

CHAPTER I-29. HAWORTH CORP., HOLLAND, MI, 1983 AND 1984

This caselet is heavy on process description, light on process-improvement substance (readers may want to gloss over descriptive Sections II, III, and IV). It is in the book as representative of many companies just getting started in JIT/flow/lean in the early 1980s—and includes a supplement/update from 1984.

High-Interest Topics:
- **Cross-training—with many qualified in 6 jobs**
- **Chairs needing repair go back to assembly—no more separate repair loop**
- **But need to kill the standard vs. actual variance system**
- **Panel line is *too* tightly linked, lacks configuration-improvement flexibility**

Haworth: Early-bird Efforts in Conversion to JIT/Flow:

Observations based on Schonberger's one-day JIT seminar

Plus a half-day plant visit and discussions, August 9–10, 1983

I. General

- *Scenario*: Haworth was among the earliest U.S. companies bent on implementing flow. A supplement, Sections VI and VII (much too short for its own full caselet) includes "update" information gleaned in connection with two more of my one-day seminars at Haworth in February, 1984.
- *The company*: Founded in 1948, Haworth is a privately-held manufacturer in the contract furnishings industry: office panels, chairs, and so forth.
- *Contact persons*: Dick Haworth, president; Jim Stonick, executive VP; Bill Skiiell, Sr., VP; Denny Dornbush, VP-finance; Dave McLeod, VP, R&D; Jim Meier, VP, sales.
- *Configuration*: The main plant is 20 miles away and the chair plant 12 miles away from HQ (Holland, MI).
- *"Keystone" plant*: This newer plant is 252,000 sq. ft., a small part of which is office space. Two tunnels go to the second "Center" manufacturing building, an additional 126,000 sq. ft.

- *Focused factories*: The Center building will be a focused panel plant, Keystone a components plant, and the Douglas plant for metal forming with 90 production employees—among 155 total employees.

II. Keystone Tour—File Drawers & Office Panels

- *Processes*: See more process details in Sidebar 1.
  - ✓ *Panel line*: 46 people (will go to 26), four-minute changeovers, sometimes 20 changes per day.
  - ✓ *Panels*: The coil steel machine does edge trim, slit, tension level, shear, and rotary pierce, at a rate of 300–600 panels per hour; die changes at an average of five minutes.
    - Two coil widths can become any panel width.
    - Two sheets are split off to upper and lower honeycomb insertion; then glued and pressed.
    - Coil is left "raw" until there is an actual order.
  - ✓ *Vinyl lamination*: Vinyl (a high-scrap item) requires a six-hour cure. In October, Haworth will be receiving a more scratch-resistant laminate. Laminates are 100%-inspected.
  - ✓ *Cartons*: As cartoning is switched over to discrete issue of just three pieces, racks are being emptied (no longer need a nearby rack); resulting in more care, less waste because of more careful handling.

SIDEBAR 1   KEYSTONE, FILE DRAWERS, OFFICE PANELS

Key processes: presses, roll formers, powder coating (manual line & automated line).

Handling: Mainly via 60 fork trucks

New Landbell machine: Located near unstacker, it makes fronts, backs, sides, bottoms; notcher of sheet steel corners makes sheets that are more easily bent

Paint: Includes 90-sec. wash; then post-wash with power-and-free conveyor, which allows splitting units for up to three dip or spray colors–followed by short or long bake; hanger tag directs which route

Fabric: 73 assemblers, two per table, three shifts

Wood panels: Whole pallet loads to CNC saw/router and two molders; final drill, then pack

---

- *Inventory*: Turns are up from 3.5 last year to this year projected at 6.5 turns.
  - ✓ 27% of the shop floor is taken up by storage racks, but $600,000 in inventory has eliminated (halfway to a goal of $1,200,000 for the year).
  - ✓ Screws are now weigh-counted, which revealed 900 screw shortages among 10,000 screws.
- *Distribution center*: The DC, which had been in the Center building, is now moved out.
- *Industrial engineers*: New IEs will go through two-year training including QC, production, manufacturing engineering, HR, and materials management.
- *Cross-training*: Many production people are qualified on six jobs, displayed on a cross-training reference roster.

III. Douglas (MI) Plant—Lateral Files

- *Process details*: See summary, Sidebar 2.
- *Visuals*: Walls in the work centers showing how-to diagrams and "housekeeping" graphs.
- *Quality*: 43 people are in QA, 23 of them inspectors employing p-charts, Paretos, X-bar and R (e.g., for glass), and fishbone charts.

SIDEBAR 2   DOUGLAS, MI, LATERAL FILES

Roll, punch, wash: One person to run two roll formers, two presses, and five-stage wash

   Many small parts: 16,000 sandwich-hinge pieces/week through PC press, shear, brake press, paint; go/no-go quality-check one of every 150 each 0.5 hour

   Parts: Each kit gets bar-code, picked parts held in plastic tubs on an accumulator

   Paint: Two booths saving 50 minutes on color changes (one booth for one color; other booth, two color changes)

   Supervisory skills: 14 skills-training topics

Allergan, Office Seating

The Plant: 2.5-year-old, acquired from closed-down clothing manufacturer; some sewing machines also acquired and some sewers hired

Output: 25 people on one shift produce 800–900 different chair types, many upholstery options, daily

Parts: Each kit gets bar-code, picked parts held in plastic tubs on an accumulator

Repairs: No more repair loop; rework goes back to assembly

Paint: Four-color powder-coat line being readied for use

Bases: Bought from Woodstock Co., Chicago; then to Green, MI, for polishing, Douglas for powder-coat, finally to Allegan—many bases damaged from so much handling

IV. Allegan (Mich.) Plant—Office Seating

- *Process details*: See Sidebar 2
- *Labor reports*: Reporting on labor-earned against performance is done daily by person and by work center, and accumulated weekly.
  - ✓ Just 74% of time-standard rates are current; IEs are slow to make rate changes.
  - ✓ Control by time standards won't make sense when the new integrated lines start-up—with employees evolving to become thinkers, watchers, trouble-shooters, maintainers, and NC programmers.

V. Recommendations

- *Efficiency evaluation system*: Kill it.
- *Purchasing/vendor relations/quality*: Make it a priority (currently, 21% of received materials are rejected).
- *Raw material warehouse*: Phase it out; decentralize stock to the factories.
- *Trucks*: Go to smaller trucks, three trips a day between Douglas, Allegan, Center—instead of the present one semi-load a day.
- *JIT production*: This, just beginning, centers on an evolution from separate machines and presses all the way to fully integrated machining lines.
  - ✓ That is, present machines get moved close together and merged by simple transfer devices to eliminate pallets and fork trucks.
  - ✓ In those lines, there should be minimal activity and few idle units between pieces of value-adding equipment.

- *Training materials*: Set up a training-materials library for production operatives (and supervisors). They already are primed. Exploit their eagerness and enthusiasm.
- *Accumulator*: Why the large accumulator in Allegan? Better to bypass it (not tear it out); operate it only if/when back processes are shut down.
- *Schedules*: Synchronize with customer demand; then meet those schedules.
- *Pilot tests*: Make liberal use of pilot projects/tests—for the sake of learning, participation, and pacifying doubters.
- *Goals*: Expect inventory turns to improve dramatically (example: $2 million in inventory has not moved in two years; $1 million of it is planned to be thrown out); also focus on QC and flow time.
- *Work out of a trailer*: This is Ken Hill's suggestion.
- *Parts standardization*: Continue this standardization more avidly (there were 108,000 parts, cut to 95,000 so far by eliminating obsolete stock).

FURTHER ON HAWORTH, HOLLAND, MI

In connection with two one-day Schonberger seminars—February 9–10, 1984

VI. Progress—1983 Month-by-Month Inventory Turns

- *Raw materials*: From three turns in January to nearly five in March through December.
- *WIP*: Turns up from eight to 15 from January-March, and up-up-up to 20–24 in August through December.
- *Finished goods*: Turns up from 15 in January to 30–35 in June through December.

VII. Automated Panel Line

- *Fast coil change*: Uncoil → straighten → cut (rectangle) → perforate → one sheet goes up, one down → honeycomb in between (fast change, five minutes in honeycomb) → glue applied → heat-activated bonding → top and bottom rails → turns 90 degrees & goes to another welder for side rail welding.

- *Critique*: This line is probably *too* tightly linked: (1) inflexible hard automation is a likely result; (2) there are likely to be problems in some stages of this integrated line.
  - ✓ According to new buyer from Checker Motors, Kalamazoo, the welders are sure to be down a lot, idling the whole line. He thinks these processes should be split in two and separated.
  - ✓ However, Mike, manufacturing engineer, says the line will have so much excess capacity that it won't matter if it is down quite a bit. But it *does* matter—a lot. Variability and process uncertainty are major issues—and capacity utilization is a "false god."
- *Training*. Harvey Brockheis, plant manager of the "Center" plant, says one of his supervisors (in the "components" area) has gone over the whole *Japanese Manufacturing Techniques* book, one chapter a week, with his people. They have eliminated a whole large flow-rack system so far.
- *Update (5–18-1985)*: Brockheis says they hired a consultant for re-layout.
  - ✓ Have moved some equipment, and beginning to measure lead time.
  - ✓ WIP turns were four, now eight. FGI is now 50 turns.

___

CHAPTER I-30. STEELCASE, INC., GRAND RAPIDS, MI, 1988

This is the first of two caselets on Steelcase, manufacturer of office furnishings; the second, 1989, is the next chapter. Both emphasize conversion of conventional batch-and-queue to flow manufacturing. Steelcase's efforts may be contrasted with those of its major competitors: Haworth, Ch. I-30, and Hon Industries, Ch. I-33.

High-Interest Topics:
- *Big issue*: **Internal work cells but no integration of four main departments—machining, weld, paint, and trim**
- **Example, with flow diagram, of greatly tightening flow time in an existing cell**

Fighting the Functional Silos at Steelcase
Assessments based on an August 16–17, 1988,
visit, including a 3.5 hour plant tour
Followed by two half-day Schonberger seminars
on World-Class Manufacturing,
Plus meetings/discussions with various managers and teams

I. General Information

- *Company and product line*: Privately-held, Steelcase, headquartered in Grand Rapids, is the largest U.S. manufacturer of office furnishings: desks, chairs, file cabinets, panels, and so on. Each of its plants in that area is dedicated to its own family of products.
- *Feedback report*: This caselet has been considerably reduced in length and detail from the post-visit feedback report sent to Steelcase.
- *Contact persons*: Frank Merlotti, president; Jack Stegmier, Sr. VP operations; Jerry Hecker, VP manufacturing; Rob Burch, director, manufacturing planning; Larry Barton, director, production and inventory control.

II. Strengths and Advantages

- *Major*:
  - ✓ Steelcase is admired for its good pay, excellent benefits, and caring management—which pay off in high motivation, loyalty, and very low turnover.
  - ✓ Its products are highly regarded by its commercial customers.
  - ✓ Policies on management of capacity (labor, equipment, and factories) are well conceived:
    - Like Merck and Milliken, Steelcase favors avoiding "panic mode" by having enough capacity and not overscheduling it.
    - Labor policies provide "catch-up time" on second shift, improving chances of meeting schedule commitments daily.
    - These policies avoid any tendency to "bet the company" on *unproven* advanced technology; few "supermachine" obstacles impede JIT and flexible response. (My term of the 1980s, "supermachine," has generally been superseded by "monument" machine.)
    - They also avoid excessive transfer-line tendencies (tightly linked automation in one line), which are prone to frequent shutdowns
    - Square footage and numbers of people per plant are of manageable size.
- *Other strengths (incomplete)*:
  - ✓ Good foundation of committees and task forces to guide the company's WCM (world-class manufacturing) efforts.

✓ Large number of setup-time improvements are on-going, with a good start in getting work cells organized.

✓ High production volumes and, usually, multiple machines of a type (e.g., more than one paint line or tube mill) provide an ideal setting for cells and integrated flow lines by product family.

✓ Design engineers reside in each plant.

✓ The handling of highly fluctuating item demand is well conceived in at least one area (e.g., in trim, a make-to-order policy is resulting in nearly zero inventory, along with direct-ship to the customer; however, machining, and perhaps welding, are producing to forecast demand).

✓ Several plants have an impressive record of meeting weekly, even daily, ship commitments.

✓ Overall cleanliness, orderliness, good factory appearance.

✓ Resisted info-system overkill, i.e., costly, complex systems (to track WIP, labor, scrap, etc.) and the staff empires that go with them. The door is open to easy implementation of simple methods of collecting and analyzing data by work teams in the work place.

✓ Recent, admirable record of getting PM's (preventive maintenance) done according to plan.

III. Weaknesses/Opportunities

- *Major*:
  ✓ Cells: The effort to create work cells stops at the walls of four main departments. (machining, welding, paint, trim) and lacks focus on complete product flows. *Fixing this situation is Steelcase's most important, high-benefit, improvement avenue.*

  ✓ High overhead costs: During the past six or seven years, as sales doubled, employment doubled, too. In growing companies, overhead as a percent of sales should be shrinking (especially P&IC, inspection, and middle-management overheads).

  ✓ Labor inflexibilities: Too many job classifications and lack of cross-training for *mastery*.

  ✓ Output-based wage incentives: A bulwark of competitive strength for Steelcase in the past; it now conflicts with aims and principles of WCM.

- *Others*:
  - ✓ Lack of career-development policies for salaried managers, professionals, technicians; for example, design engineers take ME assignments, buyers to line supervision.
  - ✓ Long manufacturing and order-entry lead times (roughly halved in recent years, but plenty more to do)—evidenced by high idle WIP inventories. For every part in a machine in a value-added state, there are (depending on where you look) 10, 100, 1,000, or more idle ones, extending production lead time by the same.
  - ✓ Supplier development: In this, Steelcase seems well behind other top firms.
  - ✓ Despite numerous good examples, overall employee involvement is low, mostly with processes "owned" by "experts," not operators.
  - ✓ Maintenance: Limited by lack of machine history and absence of progressive transfer of PM to machine operators.
  - ✓ Product design: Pressures to rush designs into production "before their time" and to delay redesign (e.g., using DFMA) of those rushed products.
  - ✓ Cost control and accountability: Relying on after-the-fact cost reports—outdated in light of U.S. industry–led innovations that center around controlling *causes* of cost, waste, delay.

IV. Suggestions/Comments

- *Visual evidence*: In increasing the pace of the improvement effort, take lots of photos of factory scenes; plaster factory and "war room" walls with progress charts (setup times, nonconformities, numbers of fork trucks and storage openings, flow distance, etc.), which serve as benchmarks for continuous improvement.
- *Directed improvement*: An action-oriented improvement approach with virtually no negative effects on meeting schedules is for plant managers to direct (with few exceptions) a 50 percent reduction in lot sizes for each item produced, and idle WIP in each work center. An example from the Chair I plant follows.
  - ✓ Former configuration: machines and operators were in widely separated departments, with large amounts of delay and waste in flows of work from one work center to another. Chair I machining and welding *used to be* completely organized that way.

✓ Existing configuration: Figure 30.1 is a portrayal, in flow-diagram form, of the 472 line (from rough notes, some inaccuracies). Machines and operators are excellently reorganized into cells or flow lines, although the cells retain considerable inventory.

✓ Chair I—near future. The following aim at even more considerable tightening of product flow:

■ From the diagram, by micro-JIT analysis, the ratio of idle pieces in 26 racks to busy pieces "under tool" in six work centers (three spot welds counted as one) is 2600:6, or 433:1.

■ Probably most racks of parts could be eliminated and machines moved closer together.

■ Within spot welding are 16 idle pieces to three busy ones, a 5:1 ratio. Not many pieces—yet too many.

■ After removing racks and units on conveyors, the processes are close enough together that simple automated loading/unloading options become apparent—to operators, supervisors, anyone else who watches the work flow. Simple, cheap machine-to-machine linkages will follow.

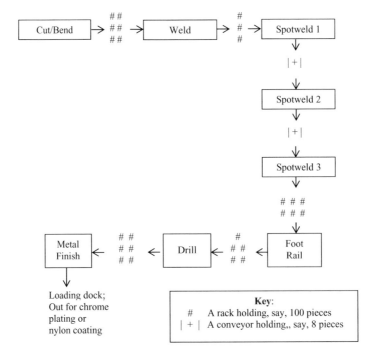

FIGURE 30.1

Elimination of delay and waste: an example from Chair I plant—the 472 line.

- Results: operators will feel and act more like a team, with flow time greatly reduced (e.g., if racks are reduced from 26 to six, flow time is cut about four-fold).

V. Further Suggestions/Comments

- *Containers*: Reduce container sizes (or put in false bottoms), so idle WIP can be reduced and held down—and so that lighter-duty handling gear is usable (simplify material handling).
- *Kanban*:
  - ✓ Launch an extensive effort to link separated processes, with operators and supervisors heavily involved in kanban containerization and trial-and-error startups of kanban usage.
  - ✓ Every kanban link eliminates one more level on the bill of materials and two or more computer transactions.
- *Part/product families*: Dedicate every paint line, tube mill, etc. to logical families of parts/products.
- *Scheduling*: Adopt scheduling to a daily rate for "star" components, considerably reducing order-processing (overhead) costs for those items; adjust the rate every two weeks as average usage changes.
- *Incentives*: Begin a diligent effort, with heavy operator involvement, to convert from individual to group incentives, in parallel with a conversion of individual job assignments to work cells and flow lines.
- *Team assembly*: Begin moving from autonomous to team assembly—with frequent job rotation and heavy involvement in process control and improvement, thus to avoid the mindless boredom that sometimes accompanies assembly work.
- *Multiple dedicated assembly lines*:
  - ✓ Final trim should consist of several assembly lines, each dedicated to a family of common products and run by a small-enough assembly team that they can get to know each other and trade jobs.
  - ✓ From the Chair I plant, examples of good/bad practices in investing in plant equipment:
    - Chair I people have long recognized the value of duplicate sizing rollers, which can be externally loaded, thereby slashing changeovers (possibly eight hours) on tube mills.
    - Steelcase's system of justifying capital expenditures usually fails to show the worth of such investments.

- ■ Chair I people have also considered investing in an automatic storage/retrieval system for cut fabric. This kind of investment was funded in the past (e.g., via a "payback" analysis), but today it is seen as automating a non-value-adding function.
- ✓ Distance-spanning conveyors (to solve problems of transport and connection among separated processes) are permanent stores of waste and delay—and divert attention to the correct solution: moving machines into compact cells and flow lines.
  - ■ The paint conveyor in System I (an artifact of long lead time batch production) needs to be progressively shrunk in length.
  - ■ Install temporary kanban links—until the ends of flow lines can be moved close to the paint booths. Load the "star" welded assemblies onto empty hooks very near to the booths.
- ✓ Expand the WCM training effort to include marketing—so marketing strategies and policies may be modified to push for the competitive advantages of DFMA, minimization of parts, care in adding product options, TQC, flexible labor/equipment, and lead-time reduction.
- ✓ The competitive advantages of lead-time reduction, diagramed in Figure 30.2, are self-explanatory/need no discussion—so as to end this caselet.

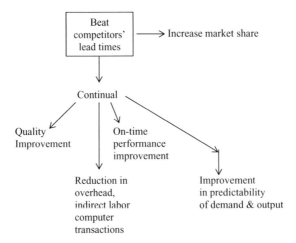

FIGURE 30.2
Importance of lead-time reduction.

CHAPTER I-31. STEELCASE, INC., GRAND RAPIDS, MI, JAN., 1989

This caselet—the second of two for Steelcase (the first, 1988, being the previous chapter), the largest U.S. manufacturer of office furnishings—is disturbing. It reports on the company's having built a talented implementation team, trained large numbers of employees, brought in consultants, developed excellent plans—but with little to show for it.

High-Interest Topics:
- **Losing the competitive edge**
- **Lending labor from one department to another: the case of trim and paint**
- **Getting plant managers into action mode—for meaningful change**
- **Kanban with labeled re-circulating pallet boxes**

JIT Bogs Down at Steelcase

Impressions from a visit to Steelcase, January 18–19, 1989

Including brief tours of File plant & Computer
Furniture and Panel Plant, Jan. 18
In connection with two half-day Schonberger seminars,
afternoon Jan. 18, and morning Jan. 19
Plus meetings/discussions with various managers/teams

I. Steelcase Manufacturing—General

- *Strengths and advantages*:
    - ✓ Core teams are well-schooled in and seemingly avid about implementation of world-class manufacturing (WCM) and have many good ideas for thorough plant renewal without costing much money.
    - ✓ Machine improvement teams are in every plant; operator-centered preventive maintenance to be started soon.
    - ✓ Also, see my August 1988 observations.
- *Competitive threats/weaknesses*:
    - ✓ Vulnerabilities:
        - ■ Fabrication areas are fat with costly parts; a slow pace of creating cells; too many labor classifications; solid "chimneys" around plant departments and office functions; costly stocks of raw material (especially steel) that nobody feels

any responsibility for; and a company seriously behind in implementing a modern program to help deal with costs, quality, and performance in its supplier base.

- At least one of Steelcase's U.S. competitors is far ahead in most of these areas.
- In short, Steelcase is losing or has lost its relative edge in cost. This isn't due to cost growth but slowness in applying the full set of mostly simple concepts for cutting plant and supplier costs.

✓ Specific examples of needed course corrections are in parts II, III, and IV for file, computer furniture, and panel plants, respectively.

- *Overall suggestions/comments*:

✓ Launch a large-scale supplier-development program, starting with training within purchasing, plus pilot projects in which purchasing partners with design, manufacturing engineering, QA, and others (must be a shared activity—purchasing doesn't the have resources or scope of responsibility to do it alone).

✓ Since paint and trim make to *the same orders* (perhaps in all plants), it is disconcerting to see them so poorly coordinated—running at different rates, with growing and falling inventories of painted parts on the trim floor, and no product-focused projects or joint projects across the two departments.

✓ In fab, it's time to break free of trying to squeeze "more, more, more" production out of a machine. Best practices require making at some close approximation of the rate of use of the "customer" at the next process—and no faster.

✓ Trim (employing largest share of direct laborers) is performed mostly in parallel at two-person benches—*autonomous assembly*—an obstacle to focus, teamwork, and operator involvement in continual improvement. To use Robert Hall's term, they are "caged" off from prior and next processes; they can't interact in a team relationship.

- Most (maybe all) Steelcase plants now have at least one *progressive assembly team* in welding (but not in trim), i.e., a cell with a few presses and welders making a complete metal component.
- For Steelcase, these cells are a breakthrough in use of the human resource; it shortcuts job-classification/incentive-pay

obstacles, showing that high labor productivity is not lost when team assembly occurs.

- For autonomous assemblers, training in problem-solving methods does little good; but for progressive assembly teams, it can create a factory floor improvement engine.

✓ As I noted in August, 1988, Steelcase has generally not fallen for costly unproven technologies (the G.M. phenomenon).

- Still there seems to be at least one "engineering toy" in each plant; they consume enormous engineering, tool department, and plant-maintenance department resources—resources which are badly needed for the many projects generated by core teams, plant managers, and involved operators.
- The "toys" tend to be placed on special platforms and consume lots of floor space, thus becoming obstacles for years to come in the way of reorganizing plants for focus.

II. File Plant

- *Strengths and advantages*:
  ✓ No WIP stockroom (that I saw).
  ✓ A few good cells (large drawer cell, conveyor-linked presses, etc.).
  ✓ Lateral case line/cell runs very lean: micro-JIT ratio of only one or two idle units on conveyor between assembly stations.
  ✓ 64 floor-roller lanes in trim offer an already-existing "platform" for focus by "star," "starlet," and "extra" model numbers.
  ✓ New hand-paint line will relieve the present paint capacity problem, which paves the way for focused alignment of paint and trim.
  ✓ Innovations include:
    - Sensor-equipped die (for quick changes, servo-adjustments, shut-off fail-safing); and specially designed die cart for heaviest dies.
    - Also, crane hooks for moving steel coil in receiving bays; and on the coil-steel truck, a "covered-wagon" retractable hood (for quick load/unload).
  ✓ Quality process improvement (QPI) groups realigned from process to a product focus.
  ✓ 24-hour response time for "perfect match" colors.

- *Suggestions/comments*:
  - ✓ Since paint is not yet in good control (not "capable"), an immediate zero-cost improvement presents itself:
    - A cadre of five or ten people from trim assist in any paint crisis. When paint quality is high, they stay in trim, keeping up with paint, with a small stock of painted parts in the staging area. During heavy repaint, trim slows its production rate and lends some labor to paint, which *still* keeps the painted stock small in staging.
    - This should allow reducing the staging area by a third or more—as one of many joint projects aimed at better coordination and product focus between paint and trim.
  - ✓ Product focus: focus trim by stars, starlets, and extras. As a pilot project, put about ten assemblers into progressive assembly teams, focused on a family of files (e.g., 36-inch, five-drawer lateral).
  - ✓ Pallet boxes on kanban: although there is no WIP stockroom between fab and weld, floor stocks of steel pallet boxes are grossly excessive. This is easily controllable:
    - Starting with highest-use (star) P/Ns (part numbers), set a maximum number of kanban-labeled boxes with a restricted quantity per box (e.g., false bottoms into pallet boxes). Then just recirculate pallet boxes on dollies between fab and weld, a la kanban.
    - The smaller loads take more handling labor, but the large cuts in costly stocks/floor space easily justify the change, especially since dollies can be pushed by hand, thus reducing costly bulk handling (by hi-lo's/forklift trucks).
  - ✓ Reorganize fab, perhaps by dedicating certain presses…
    - Say, to vertical files—providing an *end-product focus*.
    - To narrow families of parts—providing *component focus* (creating "islands of focus" that join later into grand end product-focused flows).
  - ✓ Huge steel coil stocks in receiving bays are owed to no one being accountable. So, form a project team out of Rob Burch's office to set maximums for each size. Then, buyers may exceed the max only upon signed approval by J. Hekker.
  - ✓ Sheet pieces in a hundred different sizes are (apparently) all made on *one* sheet line.

- ■ The sheet line may be a fine piece of equipment with quick-change capability, but some piece cutting should be done on other, more dedicated and lower-capacity equipment—perhaps becoming part of extended cells in welding.
- ■ This applies even if the sheet line has plentiful capacity; it is simply making too many different P/Ns now, thus cannot become part of a focused cell.
- ✓ Hand paint: When the new hand-paint line is installed, dedicate it to specials ("extras") and rework; also, its extra capacity takes the other three paint lines out of panic mode, permitting dedication to certain families of sizes/colors.
- ✓ Paint hangers: Begin design of hangers for complete knocked-down "kits" for a single file loaded on sequential hangers (as is done in another Steelcase plant, perhaps desk?). Some direct labor from paint, trim, and weld should participate in this project.

III. Computer Furniture Plant

- • *Strengths and advantages*:
  - ✓ Docks on three or four walls permit focused receiving/shipping.
  - ✓ Marker boards and flip charts in several areas provide places to document customer complaints, problems, solutions, actions taken.
  - ✓ Steel area:
    - ■ Large area holds *empty* containers, emptied because one day of lead time was recently taken out between weld and paint.
    - ■ Four NC Wiedematics are movable (because *not* in pits or special floors), thus poised for relocation into cells.
    - ■ Smallish size of presses and most other equipment allows relocation into cells at affordable cost.
    - ■ One superintendent residing over fab *and* weld.
    - ■ A cell with two, parallel three-machine lines (two brakes and one welder) produces a channel piece.
  - ✓ Wood:
    - ■ Frequent small-lot deliveries from wood suppliers.
    - ■ Good plan (or just someone's proposal?) to drill holes in wood tops back in rough wood/laminating so that the top does not have to be flipped in trim.

- *Suggestions/comments*:
  - ✓ Immediate: Eliminate the large pile of empty containers in steel fab and cordon off the space, to be used for new cells.
  - ✓ Machined parts:
    - ■ Six rows of four-high pallet racks are full of machined parts—a visible sign of unnecessary waste (including hi-lo trips and putting away/finding/picking).
    - ■ Move all high-use (star) P/Ns into a planned number of kanban containers next to the machine making them; slash or abolish the pallet-rack area.
  - ✓ Weights of wood are not enough to require hi-lo's; convert to low hand-pushed dollies.
  - ✓ Wood pieces traverse conveyor lines one piece at a time, which is ideal. But at transition points, mechanical stackers have the contrary result of merely building piles of inventory (*not* for loading onto handling containers); stackers should be removed.
  - ✓ Paint/trim run speeds: I failed to find out about paint capacity and whether paint and trim run at different speeds, but probably they could be synchronized.
  - ✓ Set up a pilot team for progressive assembly of lighting on the belt conveyor (the present assembly carousel is just an inventory holder and should be disposed of—after the pilot test).

IV. Panel Plant

- *Strengths and advantages*:
  - ✓ The 9000 line has been re-arranged (the weld and snap-on cell feeding 14 two-person "stuffing" benches), saving 70,000 sq. ft.
  - ✓ A new, more product-focused plant layout has been approved.
  - ✓ The tilted pallet boxes on wheels are an improvement over flat-on-the-floor counterparts in other Steelcase plants—but quantities per box are excessive.
- *Suggestions/comments*:
  - ✓ A severe paint/trim scheduling problem: parts are painted three days early! Two options in paint:
    - ■ Cut chain speed by, say, 40%; hang parts on about six out of ten hooks instead of every hook (I may have my number estimates wrong). Or a combination of the two.

- ■ This will allow same-day painting and a significant reduction in staging of painted parts.
- ■ A by-product is better-quality painting because of the slower speed or staggered hooks.
- ✓ The high-rise for parts from fab has to go: set a goal of emptying, say, 10% of openings per month, then remove the high-rise; allocate the floor space to something value-adding.
- ✓ Progressive assembly:
  - ■ Each pair of stuffers in the 9000 area works from a blue cart holding 18 sets of panel parts—a very large inventory (setup problems and other reasons for inventory at earlier stages of manufacturing are not present in final assembly, so there should be hardly any idle inventory).
  - ■ Solution: Pilot-test progressive assembly cells—each dedicated to a star model/family of models. For example, six people building units on flat rollers (will need some protection for the panel surface facing the rollers); besides team advantages, this will slash idle inventories.
  - ■ Probably progressive assembly should be extended to Kappa and miscellaneous panel products.
- ✓ Integrate processes.
  - ■ In the 9000 cell, seven pallets of 18 units each total 126 units on flat rollers between weld and snap-on. This serves as a buffer stock so that snap-on people can leave the area for the rest room, etc.
  - ■ But if snap-on takes one minute per unit, that is 126 minutes of buffer stock–very excessive.
  - ■ Snap-on should be fully integrated into the welding cell—one team on the same rate. Then buffer stock falls to 126 minutes' worth to zero or one.

V. K-4 Plant (in Planning Mode)

- • *Focused paint lines*:
  - ✓ K-4 is to consist of three focused plants-within-a-plant: excellent.
    - ■ But as I understand it, the three-plant plan excludes key processes—paint and fab, for example.
    - ■ Since it is normal to have multiple paint lines in a plant, paint should be focused too! Then it is easy to dedicate fab machines to paint lines for complete focus.

✓ Pollutant issue: in existing Steelcase plants, paint lines are clustered, making control of pollutants more economical.

- But from a focus standpoint, placing three paint lines in three different locations in the K-4 plant would be ideal.
- The additional costs for pollution control should be fully investigated.

- *Plants-in-a-plant.*

✓ If fab is being planned so that a single supermachine makes, say, all flat pieces, that negates focus—and needs reconsideration.

✓ When plants get as large as 500,000 sq. ft, that justifies full separation within—each focused plant-in-a-plant having its own resources—including fab.

VI. Overall Observation

- *Post-visit letter*: The cover letter accompanying my post-tour report (the body of this caselet) was addressed to my main contact at Steelcase, Rob Burch, director of manufacturing planning. Following is one paragraph from the letter:
- *Plant-manager-level commitment to act*:

"At this point in the Steelcase WCM campaign, the structure (committees, core groups, QPI, etc.) seem mostly to be in place and starting to produce results. It is time, however, for a few of the plant managers (with backing or prodding from above) to step forward and take a bold, visible action—[such as] a commitment to wipe out and dismantle a WIP stores area, or to fuse paint and trim production rates and slash staging areas between them. These are rather easy to do, have big impacts, require no investment [actually negative investment, since money tied up in inventory is immediately freed for other uses], and carry no risks; too many companies have done these things to feel that they are pioneering risky sorts of actions...."

VII. So Much Planning, So Little Action at Steelcase

- *Published article*: A lengthy article details Steelcase's efforts to "convert its 12 main North American plants to lean [which, insightfully, the article also labels as 'flow'] production."* I am providing highlights of the article in this Section VI.

- *Vignettes*: Much of article consisted of vignettes:
  - ✓ "One of the least effective leaders had to be prodded by his technical team to even put together a list of items that needed follow-up…. In the end, virtually nothing got done …."
  - ✓ When asked a standard question about his vision of a lean future, one superintendent thought a bit, then said his vision was "an area with good housekeeping and that was clean and well organized."
  - ✓ But a different superintendent said, in reply to that question, "immediately started talking about rearranging isolated pieces of equipment into cells that run to kanban production signals, dramatically reducing quantities of inventory [and] replacing a series of build-complete benches and the setup activities they require with a one-piece-flow progressive build line."
    - Much of the rest of the article focused on Steelcase's elaborate, multi-layered system of developing leaders, culture, planning, feedback, information dissemination—and readiness, in which "an organizational psychologist and a quality system assessor jointly conduct a 90-minute interview with the superintendent."
    - For all that, there were classic examples of effective implementations:
  - ✓ "Most significantly, the queue of painted parts awaiting assembly was to be cut from 36-plus hours to three hours [in an integrated process of] first in, first out (FIFO) flow through paint application and unload, and assembly." [Finally, Steelcase had, in one of its plants, broken the disconnect between the two major elements of flow: paint to final assembly—my principal recommendation as noted 12 and 13 years earlier in the reports to management that followed my plant tours of 1988 and 1989.]

---

* David W. Mann, "Leading a Lean Conversion: Lessons from Experience at Steelcase, Inc.,"*Target* magazine, 3rd Quarter 2001, pp. 28–39.

CHAPTER I-32. HON COMPANY, MUSCATINE, IA, 1987

This caselet details the advanced flow manufacturing-management practices of Hon in the mid-1980 s. Except for formatting and some re-wording, Sections II, III, and IV of this caselet are as written in my thank-you report to Hon on August 9, 1987. The added fifth section offers special perspectives on the Hon way of manufacturing.

High-Interest Topics:
- **Three different reorganiza-tion strategies—for star, star-let, and dog-and-cat products**
- **Rube Goldberg-like smallish, interconnected machines—superior in effect to any other Western factory I've visited**

Reorganizing Factories: Keys to Competitive Manufacturing at an Office Equipment Maker

Summary of observations based on a p.m. visit to Hon, Aug. 6, 1987

In connection with a one-day Schonberger seminar there on the same date

I. General Information

- *Products*: Hon's product line at its home Muscatine, IA, location is office equipment—desks, chairs, file cabinets, partitions, and so on.
- *Scope of caselet*: This is a summary of "world-class manufacturing (WCM)" opportunities at Hon, based on my visit to Geneva and Oak #1 plants in Muscatine. My remarks probably would also apply to other plants that have benefitted from being under the Hon wing for some time: the Heatilator plant in Mt. Pleasant, Iowa; and to some extent, Prime Mover in Muscatine, Firestone in Southgate, CA; and perhaps others such as Corry Hiebert.

II. Strengths

- *Extending what works well*: A WCM agenda for the two plants (and other similarly organized ones) would build on three vital already existing WCM attributes:
  - ✓ WIP is already on the floor, not in WIP stockrooms.
  - ✓ Much of subassembly and fabrication is done on main production lines, not off-line departments or shops.

✓ There are no serious equipment obstacles: hardly any "supermachines" and no investment in costly, temperamental, unproven new technologies.

■ Instead, there tend to be multiple copies of the same brand of a certain type of machine (e.g., welders and coil presses).

■ Also, existing machines have apparently received sufficient care and maintenance that they perform well and seldom suffer long-lasting breakdowns.

- *Direct labor*: Although the DL efficiency rate is very high, DL is only about 7 percent of product cost—not a factor upon which to focus quality, employee involvement, or process improvement; it is a static and independent, positive, factor.
- *Employees*: A Hon tradition is referring to all employees as *members* and having profit-sharing and other such plans. So far, that policy has helped avoid dissatisfaction—though not much for tapping employees' problem-solving capacity and hands-on experience.

III. Improvement Agenda

- *Plant configuration*: Reorganize the plants to exploit the advantages of multiple sub-factories, or factories-within-the-factory. Examples follow.
- *Geneva plant—star products.* Star products should not suffer the same intermittent delays and loose work-flow practices as lower-volume products.

✓ Therefore, reorganize with a main goal of TLC (tender loving care) for stars; also isolate the starlets from the "extras" in the product line.

■ The bad long-and-narrow shape of the Geneva building makes it natural to divide it into about five sub-factories, each in its own roughly rectangular area along the length of the building—all the better since there already are truck docks at locations along the length of the building.

■ The Anywhere Chair serves as an example (there may be another chair model or family of models that warrants the same treatment):

✓ The Anywhere, produced in volumes of 100,000 or 200,000 per year, is well suited for a sub-factory with much of its own dedicated fabric, stamping, welding, and wood back-forming processes in one zone of the plant. Probably the Chair will need to share some equipment (e.g., for plating) with one or more other sub-factories.

✓ Anywhere's final-assembly line(s) has subassembly and some fabrication equipment located at points of use alongside.

- Perhaps there should be two (or more) lines, each competing on linearity, quality, process improvement.
- Assembly can be on a slowly-moving belt conveyor, rather than at assembly benches staged along a conveyor whose only purpose is moving the chair forward. The upper limit on line speed determines how many lines to have to meet the sales rate.

✓ Linearity is the goal, not maximum output.

- The pay incentive system perhaps can be retained but modified for that goal.
- Under-capacity scheduling of direct labor should be phased in, along with line-stop authority, data collection on all disturbances, and meetings to diagnose and problems and deal with them.

✓ The sub-factory should have its own shipping and receiving, with purchased parts delivered daily direct to lineside. For some critical items, especially from a distant supplier, hold one to three days of emergency stock in another building in Muscatine.

✓ No labor or machine capacity should be lost in changeovers since machines are dedicated. Also, this sub-factory should require scarcely any support from production control, scheduling, inventory control, and data processing. WIP turns of 100 to 200 should be attainable.

✓ Product cost should quickly fall by 10 to 20 percent—and keep falling year after year:

- The dedicated, closely-coupled processes are ideal for exposing ways to reduce problems with suppliers.
- Additional pieces of enhanced-quality equipment—a steam press for chair backs, for example—should be easily accommodated.

✓ Cost and price reductions should result in sales growth—and the addition of more belt lines (*not* just running a single line faster).

- *Starlet products.*
  ✓ Next are sub-factories for starlets, with the same general approach as for stars.

✓ But the schedule, ideally, would be regularized mixed-model (make some of every model every shift with no batches), with reliance more on quick-change than dedicated equipment.
- *Staffing & costing*:
  ✓ In the Geneva plant as a whole there will be large reductions in logistics and data-processing staff, meaning that the amount of overhead to allocate to products will be slashed. And most of that will end up being charged, rightfully, to low-volume "extra" products.
  ✓ With overhead costs switching from high to low-volume products, a culling of the product line may be indicated.
- *Overall implementation*. The time sequence for reorganization should be to start with the Anywhere Chair right away. Then, the next star (if any); then the starlets.
  ✓ While that goes on, get kanban going, one pair of sequential processes after another, in the extras area. Kanban is cheap and quick and can be implemented in a "just-do-it" mode.
  ✓ Plan for many things not to work and need re-doing, and be ready to laugh at earlier mistakes.
  ✓ In fact, get used to moving equipment and lines on a regular basis, which is the nature of continual improvement.
  ✓ The whole conversion should be completed in initial form within a year.
- *Oak #1 plant*:
  ✓ By any standards of Western industry, Oak #1, making desks and file cabinets, is impressive. WCM, however, calls for continual improvement.
    - The plant's physical organization is well suited for low-grade automation, but an obstacle is increased line speeds that reduce human task times to the point of hiding process-to-process improvement opportunities from member to member.
    - Also, plant reorganization is more costly at Oak #1 than Geneva, because Oak #1 has more equipment to move and much of it is already nicely coupled and balanced.
  ✓ Still, the plant should be reorganized into more and slower production lines—say eight file cabinet and four desk lines.
    - Probably each line should specialize somewhat in a certain family of models.
    - More lines break people into small team-like groups and induce healthy line-to-line competition for linearity, quality,

and process improvement—which should be among main goals and measures of performance.

✓ The long line of 15 or 20 coil presses on the first floor offer an opportunity for further process integration—that is, move at least half to points of use on production lines and position common-use dies in die carts right at the machines.

■ This narrows the range of parts made on each one, offering many economies, and offsetting possible reductions in capacity usage. (Obstacle: getting heavy coil to the machines; ideally coil-loading would be at an outer wall.)

■ The coil-press department that remains would be for low-use parts only. For both low- and high-use parts, there is good potential for reducing setup times.

IV. Growth Strategy

- *Physical expansion*: The usual Western practice of expansion by adding onto the bldg. is usually bad. Better is to build a separate plant (this perhaps having become common in Japan simply because plants are generally so hemmed in and land costs so high as to make add-ons unattractive).
- *Best for Hon*: Keep plants small and, to meet sales growth, build another one 50 or 100 feet away; then another, if sales grow more.
  ✓ Each new plant is like the previous one, only better.
  ✓ Each may be dedicated to new family of models; or, if machine changeover times are "one-touch," the plants might build about the same models to a mixed-model schedule.

V. Special Perspectives

- *Hon's Rube Goldberg credentials*:
  ✓ Visually, the standout feature of the Hon tour was clusters of intricate linkages of one small machine to another, and another, and another, finally turning out multistep components, such as a metal desk drawer.
  ✓ Each such machine set is semi-dedicated, semi-automated, operates at a modest pace (that of final assembly of the downstream office equipment item), and tended (usually) by one operator.

- ✓ These cells conjure up memories of delightful Rube Goldberg cartoons found in newspapers years ago.
  - Now, for some 20 years there has been an annual national Rube Goldberg Machine Contest in which college or high school teams compete for the wackiest contraption that works.
  - For example, a 2002 University of Texas team's 63-step machine with a fire alarm that released a toy dog, which triggered a miniature fireman sliding down pole to get the mechanism started; then five major energy transfers that released a catapult, unlatched levelers, pulled pins, tripped phototransistors, cut strings and so on, ultimately picking up an American flag.
- ✓ The point of all this is that Rube Goldberg machines offer an excellent model for application in manufacturing companies, except aimed at rational effectiveness rather than wackiness.
- *Rubber belts*: Aside from Hon, the only manufacturer where I've encountered the same Rube Goldberg–like machine clusters was Mitsuboshi Belting Co., Kobe, Japan, in 1982.
  - ✓ That modest-sized company produces rubber belts of all kinds for customers in vehicular assembly.
  - ✓ Like Hon, Mitsubishi's products are neither large nor small; require multiple, quite different processing operations and machines; and are grouped into multiple product families.
- *Wrong way/right way*.
  - ✓ The vast majority of manufacturers of such products make them by sending batches of product from one shop to another—although some have turned to complex, highly-automated, high-speed production lines that have to switch from batches of one product to another.
  - ✓ Both those approaches are wrong. Hon's and Mitsuboshi's way is far better.

This set of caselets, pertaining to the office-furnishings sector, concludes Part I. The last two of the set sharply contrast Steelcase's failings with Hon's successes. Part II leads off with Hon again—three years later, in which things seem not to be going so well.

Part II

Maturing Process Improvements in the 1990s

36 Tour Reports (30 U.S.; 5 Other Countries; and One for a Company with Plants on Both Sides of the U.S. Border)

These Part II caselets transition from, in many cases, a surprising grasp and execution of flow manufacturing in the 1980s, to a diverse mix of faltering and forward-moving efforts in the 1990s. The first two caselets, Hon and Steelcase, are continuations (both dated 1990), of the last caselets from Part I. As in Part I, Part II caselets span a wide assortment of industrial sectors.

+ + +

CHAPTER II-33. HON COMPANY, MUSCATINE, IA, 1990

This opener to the 1990s offers an update on Hon 1987 (Chapter I-32), the final caselet of the 1980s. It presents impressive progress in "world-class manufacturing" in several Hon plants. Beyond that, it focuses on a plan to accelerate the WCM campaign through pilot projects with high involvement of all production "members."

A fifth section, added at the end, brings in follow-up information from nearly a decade later. It raises questions about whether companies—even a standout like Hon—can weather the storm of executive turnover to sustain a winning formula.

High-Interest Topics:
- **Impressive attainments in flow manufacturing—with more in the works at eight Hon plants**
- **Williamsport plant: simply moving machines close together can yield a salutary "Rube Goldberg" effect, as described in Hon, 1987**
- **At Hon, improvement teams don't go off free-form but are constrained by simple "rules of the game"**
- **Figure 33.1: 50-year up-down performance in flow manufacturing, as shown by the inventory metric**

Pilot Projects for Accelerating WCM at Hon Company

Impressions based on brief plant tours, July 31 and August 1, 1990

**In addition, dining with Hon Co. managers and
a one-day on-site seminar, July 31**

I. General

- *Pilot projects*:
  - ✓ This visit to Hon in Muscatine was set up mainly for presentation and discussion of future, present, and completed pilot projects, all aimed at accelerating use of world-class manufacturing concepts and practices.
  - ✓ Example: In most Hon plants one pilot project centers on a product-focused assembly-packout cell—with integrated or nearby synchronously scheduled subassembly and fabrication.
- *Fast-paced improvement*: Deliberations on July 31 and August 1 established "rules" for plants to follow in order to achieve uniform maximum results—summarized in Section II, with conditions for rapid improvement delineated in Section III.
- *Incentive pay*: For the pilot project, the incentive-pay system should be halted for a six-month trial period, during which wages are increased by one percent of the recent average under incentives; that later replaced by a new "pay/reward" package.
- *Progress*: Eight plants submitted written reports highlighting pilot projects in progress or completed (summaries are in Section IV).
- *Principals*: Ed Shultz, president; Tom Miller, VP sales and marketing; Jim Goughenour, VP customer service & distribution; Rennie Beltramo, VP R&D; Joe Somodi, VP HR; Bill Park, manager of manufacturing services; Cliff Brown, group VP, Seating plant; Jim Drum, group VP, Systems Furniture plant.

II. Pilot Projects: Setting "Rules of the Game"

- *Handling*:
  - ✓ Nothing to go onto the floor. No container-to-container handling, either by material handlers or assemblers.
  - ✓ Presently assemblers and welding-line operators commonly move parts from pallet boxes on the floor to shelves at work

height. Tilt top carts are to eliminate the pallet boxes and shelves and also replace handling by forklift.
  ✓ All loads to be limited to X pounds maximum.
- *WIP*: All WIP to be reduced at least 4X—with "help your neighbor" (members from team A helping team B) to cope with occasional stock run-outs arising from smaller WIP amounts.
- *Labeling*: Everything labeled—every stock location, container, utility hookup; tools on shadow boards.
- *Kanban discipline*:
  ✓ All parts flows on kanban.
  ✓ Nothing set down in a non-designated or wrong place, or other than in correct kanban locations.
- *Direct flows*: Direct "blow-by" flows from steel fabrication to pilot areas (bypass storage racks).
  ✓ For lot sizes too large, send most of the lot directly to the pilot area and only the overflow into racks. Tear out all rack storage except for overflow needs.
  ✓ Set up off-line (out-of-building) emergency stocks for potential infrequent stockouts. Purify (perfect quality) this off-line stock; rotate it as needed.
- *Make pilot area "prideful"*: Paint the pilot area in color of the team's choice.
- *Large trend charts*: All key indicators to be posted on large trend charts: flow distance, WIP, lead time, micro-response ratios, setup times, complete-and-on-time, pieces per member. Take "before" measures as baselines for observing continual improvement.
- *Training for all*: As the first step, high involvement of all hourly members in training. (At a minimum, everyone should view the Britannica video, "Just in Time, Just in Case.")

Phase III. Conditions for Continual, Fast-Paced Improvement

- *Member-centered improvements*: Members doing data collection, total quality, total P.M., setup projects, supplier/customer visits, competitive analysis, etc.
- *Time cushions*: Under-schedule labor and equipment to *make time for* improvement activities—and make it likely to meet very short lead time schedules routinely.

- *Suggestions*: Revamp/revitalize the suggestion system.
- *Support*: Assign support resources to dedicated pilot areas; look for ways to make this permanent, e.g., a manufacturing engineer physically assigned to the factory floor, dedicated full time or half time (or what makes sense) to the pilot area.
- *Decentralize steel fab*: Break up steel fabrication so that each pilot area has much of its own fab.
- *Size of pilot groups*: Subdivide large pilots (where applicable) into two-or-more smaller focused cells (linked cells/teams).
- *Minimal costing*: Adopt infrequent costing (i.e., on an as-needed audit basis), with a few simple overhead drivers. No need (no value) to know product costs every week or for every order.
- *Graphical indicators*: All pilot members involved in plotting and discussing the four long-term main competitive indicators on graphs. Costs/prices should go down (relative to competitors), sales and market share up. If not, team needs to redouble its efforts.

IV. WCM Progress at Eight Hon Plants

- *System Furniture, Muscatine*:
  - ✓ Cells are currently in progress.
  - ✓ JIT training has been plant-wide, department by department.
  - ✓ Corrective action teams (CATs) are in place on both shifts with members from all areas.
  - ✓ So far, four ten-week SPC training courses have been held, with more scheduled for 1990 for all levels.
  - ✓ Complete-and-on-time (COT) is currently at a 100% rate. Graphs and charts track COTs for all members weekly.
  - ✓ Kanban was recently installed, with plant-wide training in kanban scheduled for July.
- *Oak Street Plant No. 1, Muscatine*:
  - ✓ Several cells are up and running well: The Flex cell has three separate areas for to-order production of tables, bookcases, and unifiles.
  - ✓ Kanban is 100% on deliveries of parts to the Flex cell. At kanban's start, inventory was four weeks' supply, but now it's down to two weeks. A group is actively working on converting desks to kanban.

- ✓ Tops department is changing to a total flow layout, to be completed by September; fork trucks have already been removed.
- ✓ CITs are working with major suppliers of steel, laminate, and particle board, and they have improved first-time usability. Internally, teams are working on quick setup in File and Desk; also, various quality improvements (e.g., lateral files, paint, and warehouse) have been completed.
- ✓ Training in SPC is continuing. SPC charting is in all paint booths, drawer welders, cold headers, among others.
- *Geneva, Muscatine:*
  - ✓ Kanban.
    - In steel parts, white, green, and pink kanban tags, one per skid, impart status.
    - In veneers, white and pink laminated kanban cards go with each P/N: white attached to incoming pallets, pink sent to material control. As a part is used up, the card is matched with pink for reordering.
    - In plywood, kanban is still in planning.
  - ✓ Geneva initiated SPC in 1988. Now 90-plus parts are on SPC, with the entire quality department plus a dozen production members trained.
  - ✓ "World-class accounting": An overstated inventory shrink factor had led to overstating WIP—when, actually, shrink had been reduced through SPC, along with catching problems early in cycle instead of post-production. As a result, plant performance was not reflecting that that WIP was less than stated in accounts.
  - ✓ The first cell is for the Z series, parts of which are product-unique; the cell is now supervising itself and learning continually.
  - ✓ The G.S.A. contract afforded opportunities for several departments to collaborate on weekly schedules to be broken into daily shipments, considerably reducing warehouse congestion.
  - ✓ Supplier rejects (foam, carton, plastics) have been greatly reduced via daily schedules and quick discovery through JIT. Foam goes to production straight from trailer.
- *Williamsport, PA:*
  - ✓ In 1989, "material flow paths through our mill area were greatly reduced by simply moving machines close together and positioning them so as to keep the product moving in the correct direction." Assembly is now cellular, reducing operators and

space; rub/trim/pack are also cellular, speeding flow through the mill department.

✓ Route sheets have been cut by 23% via "communizing" parts (e.g., cleats and glide blocks), and via implementing kanban on a large number of parts (e.g., screws, cleats, beaded molding, glide blocks, partitions, and glue blocks).

✓ Formerly dependent on outside suppliers of dimensioned wood parts, we now have our own rough mills, reducing lead times, increasing flexibility, and gaining control of quality.

✓ SPC training, with a local college, now is in our second class; other training for all managers and many production members focuses on kanban and world-class manufacturing.

- *Sulphur Springs, TX*:
  ✓ Lead time for case goods has been reduced by "taking the push out of scheduling."
  ✓ In cases of major delay we don't release production members but keep them here doing other productive things (e.g., small group meetings, clean up, and basic maintenance).
  ✓ We've initiated corrective action teams (CATs), and plan to move engineering to the shop floor.

- *Southgate, CA*: (Note: In 2007, seven years after the date of this caselet, this plant was the recipient of the Shingo Prize.)
  ✓ Presses have been moved from manufacturing centers to "in-line"; selected parts are on kanban to the file line; and setup teams are in place.
  ✓ QPIP problem-solving meetings are held weekly; SPC charts are in selected locations.
  ✓ We've had reductions in WIP. Also, lead times for seating are down to less than three weeks.
  ✓ A star seating line is separately organized; also a factory-within-a-factory.

- *Cedartown, GA*: (Note: In 2003, this Hon plant was recipient of the Shingo Prize)
  ✓ COT is a basis for shipping and production schedules, yields, and defect rates; problem resolutions are posted on all lines. Hourly members do warehouse audits, and each member meeting includes product audit information.
  ✓ Kanban is in use to some extent throughout the plant, the bookcase line being totally converted to kanban.

- ✓ Plant members are going on supplier plant tours and meetings, as well as supplier meetings in our plant. Several supplier certifications are in progress.
- ✓ Inventory reduction has eliminated racks and skids.
- *Owensboro, KY plant*:
  - ✓ 600 parts are on kanban (project completed), and WIP has been reduced 60 percent in the mill.
  - ✓ Conveyorization of assembly and upholstery plants eliminated six superfluous people so far—and paves the way for spring adoption of cells.
  - ✓ Dedicated tooling for frame assembly has completely eliminated changeover time; also, quick-change fixtures (e.g., air clamps) are in use.
  - ✓ SPC is used in problem-solving; further SPC training is forthcoming.
  - ✓ Cells in frame assembly are just starting.

V. Follow Up

- *Executive turnover*: Follow-ups are often disappointing—astonishingly so.
  - ✓ A 2009 article in *Target* (flagship pub of the Association for Manufacturing Excellence) reports on an interview with Stan Askren, chair, president, and CEO of HNI Corp. (formerly named Hon Industries), parent of Hon Co.
  - ✓ Askren speaks of HNI's journey to JIT-renamed-lean as an initiative begun in 1992—and not having become a "real effort" until about seven years later.*
- *Loss of corporate memory*? This indicates Askren did not know about, or grasp the significance of, Hon's mid-1980's flow-manufacturing emphasis and prowess, and the 1990 extension of it. It also suggests that Hon may have lost some or much of its flow excellences of nearly a decade earlier.
- *Long-term inventory turnover*: Figure 33.1 shows—by the inventory turnover representation of flow—that Hon (HNI) had an impressive 4.2% per year improvement in overall turns for the 19-year period, 1981 through 2000; followed by 4.42% per year plunge from 2000 to 2016. HNI/Hon had, by that metric, lost its way.

---

* Patricia Panchak, "The Truth Behind Lean Success: It's Messy," *Target*, Fourth Issue 2009, pp. 46–47.

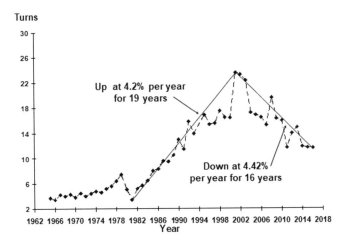

FIGURE 33.1
Inventory Turnover, Long-Term Up-Down Trend at Hon (HNI).

CHAPTER II-34. STEELCASE, INC., GRAND RAPIDS, MI, 1990

This third caselet for Steelcase (the first two are in Part I) describes the extension of its world-class excellence initiative. Included is the strategic issue of location—which plant should make which product and where plants should be located vis-à-vis customers; applying continual improvement to office areas; and observations from a quick tour of the company's proud, new factory called the Context plant.

High-Interest Topics:

- **In coping with complexities in order-consolidation, uniform lead times from each contributing factory is a potent fix**
- **The need for multiple production sites is driven by more than just the high transport costs of furniture**
- **Via *available-to-promise* ordering, marketing and the customer *schedule the factory***

Plant-location Issues

Observations based on a one-day visit to Steelcase

Including meetings, discussions, and a one-hour plant tour, September 25, 1990

I. General

- *Purpose of visit*: Reflect on corporate strategies, models for change, and dos and don'ts.
- *Main contacts*: Karan Van Gorder, training & development consultant; Jerry Hekker, VP manufacturing; Rob Burch, WCM strategy; Larry Barton, P&IC; John Gruizema, Concepts plant manager.

II. Plant Location Strategies at Steelcase

- *Focus*: More important than plant locations is getting focused plant-by-plant—already very good.
- *Freight costs*: Freight, especially for shipping bulky finished goods office equipment, necessitates some geographical dispersion of production. The long-range plan should probably include adding capacity/product breadth in Tustin, CA, and to new plants on the East Coast, as well as in the South and Europe.
- *Where*: Rather than an either/or matter (e.g., either make in Grand Rapids or Tustin), the where strategy should focus on making a given product in more than one location, as regional sales volumes justify (e.g., the Steelcase 5–10% minimum volume criterion).
- *Complexity costs*: These are costs driven not only by the extent of transcontinental shipping but just as much by numbers of parts and products in a given plant.

III. Product Sub-Assignment

- *Where to produce a product*:
  - ✓ It is generally good to produce a given product in more than one cell, production line, or plant—if there is sufficient existing or potential sales volume. Multiple production resources allow making multiple products and models *at the same time,* greatly reducing customer response time and finished inventories.
  - ✓ The economies-of-scale concept of concentrating production in *one set of resources* (and related tendencies to equip with "supermachines") often are countered by diseconomies of complexity.

- ✓ As to where to produce an item, it is hazardous to place faith in your own cost data, because conventional overhead cost allocation leads to high-volume items nearly always subsidizing low-volume ones—in both production and transportation.
- ✓ In considering, say, to produce a certain chair in Toronto or Tustin (in addition to Grand Rapids), it should be seen that a new location offers an opportunity to escape from ingrained high-cost and long lead time practices and "do it right."
- *Order consolidation*: A knotty problem in office furnishings (and various other industries) is how to consolidate orders from more than one production site.
  - ✓ It is typically handled poorly even in companies with sophisticated computer linkages among all elements, including their customers (e.g., in firms like IBM and Digital).
  - ✓ Why? Because each player has a different, partly conflicting set of expectations and hopes in regard to responsiveness.
- *Lead-time uniformity*: As plant lead times fall below two weeks, distribution/order consolidation/coordination issues become critical—calling for focus on lead time uniformity among all plants, in addition to "rules of the game."
  - ✓ Consider, for example, a proposal for seven-day fixed lead times from all plants (five days' production plus two days' shipping) and for all products except out-of-catalog, off-the-wall specials (which can be lucrative). Best ways to achieve:
    - Volume-based product scheduling and execution, e.g., two days for stars, three days for starlets, four to five days for extras.
    - Staggered shipments of large orders, e.g., 1st delivery this week, 2nd next week, 3rd the following week—sensible since customers often install new office equipment on staggered schedules. Extra benefits: reduced handling damages and fewer problems for customers in finding storage for incoming large-order shipments.
  - ✓ All sites becoming capable of *always* meeting simple, uniform, unvarying design, production, and delivery times. For example, eight days for a normal order and five days for a special—with specials constituting a fixed percent of capacity (20 percent of units, perhaps). Later, the eight and the five would be reduced, perhaps by a day each.

- *Two key actions*: In this, a given plant should (besides all the basics, such as quick setup, smaller production and handling lots, TPM, cross-training, and TQ):
  - ✓ Employ the off-line buffer-stock concept—to reduce lead times and, at the same time, ensure five-day performance:
    - Reduce active buffer stocks (in queue, in FIFO WIP racks, etc.) to where lead time for normal orders is eight days, and control that active, in-line buffer stock by the discipline of kanban.
    - For protection against infrequent emergencies, *don't* eliminate the remaining buffer stock; just relocate it to inactive, off-line storage (e.g., in low-cost storage across town). Analogy: an idle but ready personnel carrier at an army depot—with assured perfect quality.
  - ✓ A scheduling system in which short lead time star products and components, made in semi-dedicated cells or lines, are started, say, two days prior to shipment; starlets four days prior; extras six days prior. The objective is for the entire product mix for a given order to emerge from manufacturing at the same time, ready for shipment.
- *Mastery of fixed lead times*: Examples:
  - ✓ Baldor Electric (I'm familiar with just their Fort Smith, AR, "mother" plant) makes a large variety of small AC motors.
    - The fixed lead time for any motor is five days, invariable because a fixed number of cleverly designed recirculating carts keeps flow time from stage to stage (each stage color-coded differently) fixed.
    - Like Steelcase, Baldor delivers mostly to construction/renovation projects—with a narrow customer delivery window. Unlike Steelcase, Baldor usually would not need to consolidate from several plant sites, yet their uniform throughput times would make it relatively easy to do.
  - ✓ Ahlström Pump, Mänttä, Finland, produces specialty pumps for the pulp and paper industry. Again, customers are construction/renovation sites with narrow delivery windows. Ahlström-Mänttä's fixed three-day throughput time is rigidly controlled by kanban flow racks—among the most effective, simple transaction-less systems I've seen.

- *"Available-to-promise"*: Sales and marketing, both at Baldor and Ahlström, employ a simple units-available sheet for committing to delivery dates. Example: Ahlström's capacity may be 42 pumps per day.
  - ✓ If a customer wants one pump 34 days from now, sales uses up one of day 34's 42 available-to-make units (then, with production taking a fixed three days, production would start the order on day 31). If all of day 34's 42 pumps are "used up," sales looks for available capacity on day 33 or 35.
  - ✓ In this system, sales schedules the factory. (This "available-to-promise" system is not new; some of its features were described in a 1967 Plossl and Wight book.)

IV. Continual Improvement Throughout Steelcase

- *Van Gorder Group*: These consultants were hired by Steelcase to extend process improvement into non-manufacturing areas; I was asked for an opinion on topics that came up, which are as follows.
- *Continual improvement and its evolution*:
  - ✓ Defect-charts: Much more is needed than just the "defect-charts" approach that some companies (e.g., IBM) started in their offices in the late 1970s.
  - ✓ Costs: Estimating costs of slow, error-prone, variable service is an acceptable way to get attention (a la the Westinghouse OPTIM system), but trying to drive continual improvement with cost data is not advisable long term, and this approach should be phased out once continual improvement takes root.
  - ✓ Special studies: One example was to ferret out non-value-adding wastes; that can be useful in getting started, but this should generally be reserved for special project work after continual improvement becomes established.
- *All employee involvement*: The greatest need is for simple methods by which all employees and employee teams can collect data on mishaps and frustrations that plague every work place. Methods assessment:
  - ✓ Scatter diagrams, histograms, and other experimental methods are limited—mainly useful in special projects.
  - ✓ Most promising is the combination of team brainstorming, check sheets, Pareto charts, and, sometimes, fishbone charts:

- Initial brainstorming meetings held to define recurring aggravations/mishaps, which are displayed on large data boards.
- On an ongoing basis, team members simply make check (tally) marks on a data board each time an aggravation or mishap occurs—amounting to numerous tallies per day for each team.
- Periodically, summarize check marks on Pareto charts as a valuable data portrayal in team problem-solving sessions.
- As the root cause of the aggravation/mishap is corrected and eliminated from the data board, new problems will be added.
- Solved problems, plus ongoing activities and projects, get plenty of recognition and celebration.
- This procedure continues throughout everyone's employment.
- ✓ On the other hand, process control charts, widely useful in the factory (where physical dimensions/specs are keys to quality), are valuable *only selectively* in non-factory work.
- *Terminology*: It is important for process improvement to be aimed at improving everyone's work life by wiping out chronic frustrations, many from mishaps that return as bad feelings and ill will from the customer (next process) and from the supplier (prior process).

V. Tour of Context Plant

- *Overview*:
  - ✓ Some of the plant's main virtues align with WCM goals: very high paint quality, focused plants-in-a-plant, quick-change flexibility, use of pre-control charts, and advanced waste control.
  - ✓ On the other hand, some of the quick-setup capability (e.g., in the punch press) looked to be of the costly, buy-as-part-of-an-expensive-machine variety, instead of the (usually preferable) do-it-yourself kind.
- *Missing*: What I saw little of was the very low-overhead simplicity of internal and supplier kanban. Also, the degree of operator ownership—of P.M. and process improvement—looks to be low, although it appears that efforts are under way to increase it.
- *Customer impressions*: The facility seems sure to impress customers, which may itself justify much of the clearly large capital cost.

CHAPTER II-35. BALDOR ELECTRIC CO., FORT SMITH, AR, 1990

Baldor Electric is among its era's more outstanding implementers of flow manufacturing. Its advanced applications are all the more impressive in that its production—of special-purpose electric motors for industrial uses—is low-volume and high-mix.	**High-Interest Topics:** • **Special kanban carts circulate from fabrication to subassembly to final assembly—ensuring minimal WIP** • **The plant, run by "rules," achieves an *invariable* cycle time** • **No fork trucks, no internal labor reporting**

Low-volume, High-mix Production—Keeping it Simple

Observations based on a brief plant tour, evening of
January 16, 1990

Followed by a two-day Schonberger seminar co-sponsored by
Baldor and Fort Smith Manufacturer Executive Assn.

I. General Information

- *Baldor and its product line*:
  - ✓ Low-volume, high-variety producer of electric motors and bearings, largely for industrial customers, with 11 U.S. plants and one small plant in Zurich, Switzerland.
  - ✓ Fort Smith houses corporate offices, a die-casting plant, and its largest factory, which produces 1–15 HP motors with 900 employees. (See photo, Figure 35.1.)
  - ✓ Other plants: Westville, OK, the 2nd largest, for fractional (½ to ¾) HP motors, 500 employees. Columbus, MS, 3rd largest, for 15–250 HP motors. Charlotte, NC, for big (30–700 HP) DC (direct current) motors. St. Louis, die-casting and stamping. Tulsa, stamping. Fremont, CA, electric soft starters. Plymouth, MN, servo motors and drives for multi-axis machines. Charleston, capacitors (that start motors).
- *Contacts/hosts*: Quentin Ponder, president; Bob Null, group production manager.

FIGURE 35.1
A wide variety of custom-ordered industrial motors in Baldor's final assembly area.

II. Strengths

- *The product*: Rugged, durable, high-performance—esteemed by customers.
- *Most notable*: Invariable on-time production cycle (a plant run by *rules*).
- *Ingenious nesting carts*:
  - ✓ This is a key enabler of an invariable production cycle: limited numbers (kanban concept) of specially designed nesting "grocery store-like" carts for transporting fabricated and sub-assembled parts (shafts, stators, etc.) from station to station and to final assembly.
  - ✓ At a work station, if there is no empty cart (because it's full at the next station), no production.
- *Miscellaneous*:
  - ✓ "Make to a number" mode: meet schedule and stop.
  - ✓ Low WIP despite the high product mix; flow time has been cut from four weeks to five days.
  - ✓ Nearly zero fork-truck usage in production; nothing on the floor.
  - ✓ Good quick-setup achievements.

- ✓ Visual flow control, with each factory area painted a different color.
- ✓ Plant is very clean and well lit.
- ✓ No internal labor or inventory reporting.
- ✓ Good treatment of people.
- ✓ Each of Baldor's 12 plants is focused on a reasonably narrow product line.
- *Other plants on flex-flow*: Most of the above excellences were accomplished in 1987—in the Fort Smith plant. Those have largely been taken up at other Baldor sites, where, after being put onto "flex-flow," improvement has become largely a matter of fine-tuning.

III. Critical Observations

- *Excessive handling*: Lots of taking out of one container or rack and putting into another.
- *Final assembly*:
  - ✓ Unimpressive methods—much hand reorientation of the motors, for example. But automation is not among the best alternatives. Instead:
    - Focus on redesign of motors for "assembleability" (especially, layered assembly), standardizing parts, reducing parts, etc.
    - Also, teams of assemblers should work out ways to simplify, cut heavy lifting, avoiding carpal tunnel problems, and so on.

IV. Opportunities for Improvement

- *Moving toward full pull*:
  - ✓ Presently in force is a modified pull system of production cards (push) issued to three fab departments five days in advance.
  - ✓ A true pull effort needs to target star rotors, stators, and end caps, as follows:
    - Final assembly pulls one stator, rotor, etc., which empties one space in a labeled dolly or rack, which is the pull signal to make one more—this sequence extended back to the first operation after bar cutoff (optimization of bar cutoff is good reason *not* to include it in pull system).

- A mix of star products on true pull, with others driven by production cards, has an overall simplifying effect: it eliminates many transactions, along with computer use and staff support costs.

- *Production scheduling and control*: Two options for simplifying production scheduling/control are:
  - ✓ Blend star products and make-to-stock items, and separately schedule "onezy-twozies."
    - Make-to-order items are to remain scheduled as they are now.
    - Stars and make-to-stock items advance to a true pull system.
    - This split requires two physical WIP systems: the present one of unlabeled dollies/racks/lanes for to-order motors; and kanban-labeled dollies and racks for stars/to-stock motors.
  - ✓ Two plants-in-a-plant: In this scheme one plant is for make-to-order motors. The second is for a "star" family of motors in its own area ("plant") with its own equipment, team, parts, costing—perhaps even its own small bake line. (The Westville plant is said to have products that are natural for this option.)
    - Fix and regularize the schedule for two weeks, with all component suppliers (e.g., of die-castings and laminations) benefiting from the same regularized schedule.
    - Put fab and subassembly onto true pull (except for bar cutoff). The complete flow time/WIP should be reduced to one day.
    - This two-plant arrangement should include a "SWAT team" of flexible people who can move between the star plant and the other plant as demand patterns shift.

- *Shrinking distances and space*: In flex-flow lines, it should be easy to compress WIP to a four-day cycle, and eventually a three-day cycle before even lower times are achieved.
  - ✓ This involves reducing process-to-process distances and conveyor lengths, and restricting the number of units that can be on the conveyor between point A and point B, etc.
  - ✓ This is best done with involvement of the entire workforce—not just managers and staff.

- *Improvement charts*: Plaster the walls with improvement charts (particularly on WIP, flow distance, flow time, micro-response ratios, setup times—which serve to raise awareness of all employees and enhance their participation in improvement); also, check sheets, control/diagnostic charts, and recognition/celebration.
- *Job classifications*: Cut job classes and cross-train and rotate everyone—including engineers and other staff people.
- *Receiving*: Cut a receiving door into the nearest wall for daily receipts (filling kanban squares) of cardboard and wood—delivered right to the packout area—and for receipts of hardware from a single hardware supplier. With monthly invoicing.
- *Warehousing avoidance*:
  - ✓ Seek ways to provide better service to final users with less stock in the 27 distribution warehouses (e.g., shorter lead times, quick plant response, quick freight, drop ship, tapping into actual demand at final user locations).
  - ✓ Re-examine/revise the policies of paying distribution managers for warehousing. Incentives should be developed that reward distribution managers for developing direct-ship, cross-docking, etc., and thus avoid needs for warehousing.
- *Reduced, more relevant costing*:
  - ✓ Control costs by control of causes, not through cost variances, etc.
  - ✓ Adopt *contained costing* (e.g., contained within cell/product family) and costing by audit rather than through a complex, unnecessary transaction system.
- *Relocate support staff*: As WIP is reduced, use the excess space for a few desks, tables, phones, partitions to plant floor for use by engineers and others to spend most of their time on the plant floor in problem-solving teams with operators.
- *Reputation*: The 1980s apparently have preserved but not greatly improved Baldor's fine quality reputation, but it is quality narrowly defined. A total assault on variation from the design center and on all kinds of defects (even scratches, paint runs, etc.) should be undertaken. I suspect Baldor is behind its competitors in this area.
- *DFMA*: Improve the design for manufacture/assembly effort—which has far-reaching effects; certain of Baldor's competitors seem to be ahead in this area.
- *EI*: Step up the employee-involvement effort.

CHAPTER II-36. MILLER BREWING CO., TRENTON, OH, 1993

Miller Brewery-Trenton offers a rare example of high payoffs from equipping the work force with expertise usually available only to staff functionaries. The Trenton contingent did this with no help, no budget, and no coordination with corporate headquarters.

High-Interest Topics:
- **Advanced—and very successful—application of the "star-point system" of equipping production people with the skills of staff experts**
- **Paying five hours of overtime every week—to provide sufficient time for training, maintenance, shift-to-shift coordination, etc.**
- **Multiple work-arounds for coping with a plant designed for big "batch-and-queue" production**

Making the Best of Built-in Obstacles

Observations based on an evening visit, Oct. 20, 1993

Followed by Schonberger's two-day public seminar in Cincinnati, October 21–22

I. Introduction

- *Typical brewery*: Miller-Trenton is designed like many other full-sized breweries.
  - ✓ Built in 1981, it was left unopened because the flagship brand, Miller High Life, was not doing well.
  - ✓ Idle for nearly a decade, the plant finally opened in 1990, thanks to the success of a new premium beer, Miller Genuine Draft.
- *Atypical human resources*:
  - ✓ By 1993, the plant had adopted a unique set of HR practices for its 400 employees.
    - No time clocks, same color hard hats, common dress, same parking lot, no individual rewards (recognition only), social functions for all employees.
    - Moreover, the office area, built in its own corner of the large plant, was never occupied. Instead, in the same egalitarian manner, the plant manager and staff set up on the operations floor, near to those they serve.

✓ Every Wednesday, each shift (three shifts) holds a 0.5-hour meeting.

✓ This year on November 19 the plant shut down for an all-employee paid day of off-site meetings with guest speakers (this year, from Bridgestone-Firestone).

✓ Other plants have six layers; here it's four: plant manager, department managers, team managers, work teams.

✓ The can lines have teams of four to seven *technicians* (not called workers or operators); every team has an electrician and a mechanical person.

✓ Extensive training—13 weeks throughout the year—aims at 80 hours total per person. Besides direct task skills they learn and apply skills in maintenance, safety, lubrication, scheduling job orders, and coordination of production. (More on this in Section II.)

✓ All team members and technicians are multi-skilled, learning every job, rotating as often as daily. The teams also handle their own vacations, overtime, and shift-to-shift rotation.

✓ All technicians are paid the same wage, except an extra 70 cents per hour for a pre-existing skill; exceptions are worked out collaboratively with the technicians.

• *Contact persons*: Dennis Puffer, plant manager; Tim Maly, HR manager; Red Green, UAW rep.

II. Impediment: The Factory

• *Bad factory design—how to cope*:

  ✓ Puffer picked me up at the Cincinnati airport for the drive to the not-far-away plant in Trenton. On the way, he said, "You're going to hate my plant."

    ■ That's because it was the standard brewery design: just two or so long, high-speed, high-maintenance, high-cost, complex canning lines, with rattling conveyors crammed end-to-end, and side-to-side with cans in various stages of production.

    ■ Puffer said that at the speeds necessary—to meet schedules for the vast quantities that any brewery must turn out   any small glitch in the conveyor mechanism sent cans flying into air and onto the floor, stopping the line. Ever thinner, lighter cans—innovations of the aluminum industry—made such spectacles all the more common.

- That Puffer made the "hate my plant" comment is because he is the rare person in canning/bottling who understands the flow/JIT production concept of multiple, small-scale fill-and-pack lines capable of producing several types, sizes, flavors, and containers at the same time in close synch with final buyers' usage.

✓ Puffer and his team cope remarkably with this plant-design obstacle.

- They produce about same quantity of canned beer as other breweries of the same size and (dubious) design, but they do it with just 400 employees compared to the typical 800.
- The primary reason is their version of the "star-point system," in which all factory members become more than skilled in tasks of production, warehouse, etc.: they gain—and apply—the expertise of five staff functions, as shown in Figure 36.1.

✓ How it works: staff professionals—budgeting, payroll, quality, safety, maintenance, HR, etc.—instruct production technicians in each area: administration, quality, safety, productivity, and personnel.

- For example, a buyer instructs on processing orders from suppliers; a quality engineer teaches about product specs and good manufacturing practices (GMPs).
- A 6th star point (under development) is to be for product-changeover coordination.
- All production technicians are members of at least one star-point team.

FIGURE 36.1
Star-Point System at Miller-Trenton.

✓ Another key result:
- Miller-Trenton has much lower overhead costs; e.g., the maintenance department is about half its pre-star-point size.
- Many kinds of problems get resolved virtually on the spot—no delays getting engineering or purchasing to come and assess and try to understand what the factory technicians already know.

✓ How could there be time for all that learning—and time to make good use of it—in a three-shift operation? The unionized work force (United Auto Workers) and management found a way:
- All associates work nine-hour shifts; providing one hour for teaching, learning, then applying their enhanced knowledge and awareness to anticipate and forestall major and everyday problems. The extra time is useful as well for shift-to-shift coordination meetings, time being available in the ninth hour of a shift.
- The cost of overtime—five hours every week per employee, which comes out of Puffer's regular budget, not corporate's—is more than paid back.

III. Practical Opportunities for Improvement

- *Quick changeover*: These are the most important, cost-consuming events. Serial changeover (one operator going from one changeover station to another) must give way to parallel changeover, but there aren't enough people on technician teams for this.
  ✓ So, changeovers should be thoroughly documented on computer sheets with maps. At an exact, scheduled time, ten or more people (e.g., from front offices, shipping, anywhere) arrive, put on smocks, take instruction sheets, grab wrenches, cleaning materials, etc., and do a six-hour change in, say, one hour.
  ✓ This looks to be the easiest single thing that can be done to speed up the plant's multi-step changeovers. Also, it is likely to improve plant performance more than any engineering effort.
- *Visual signboards*: In conjunction with the team changeover efforts, mount, for each line, a *large* changeover-time chart for plotting times for every changeover, good product to good product.

- ✓ Many current visuals in the Trenton plant apply to what cannot be managed; instead, they are *results* of basic, manageable things done well—changeovers, PMs, training, and on-the-job coordination.
- ✓ Visually communicating results is necessary, but not about non-manageables like line and plant output. Best to convey such results, plus cost data, in plant-wide meetings.
- ✓ For high-impact actions (e.g., conveyor removal) other visuals would make sense: flow distance, in-process inventory, throughput time.
- *Check sheets*: The simplest, often most effective of SPC tools is the check sheet, especially useful in line maintenance:
  - ✓ Every time a technician finds a problem, he/she makes single tally mark on a check sheet pre-printed with common problems. Words of explanation may be written as well.
  - ✓ This yields data on incidence of various problems—powerful for later team problem-solving.

IV. Brewery redesign

For the most part, the following points are a partial recipe for advanced flow management, which describes how this brewery (or others) should be equipped and laid out. It may be seen as a long-range plan for extensive change that Puffer and his team would welcome, if institutional obstacles could be overcome.

- *Conveyors and accumulators.* As with nearly every packaging line I've seen, I believe can and bottle lines are at least two times too long, and conveyors too wide. 50 percent of conveyor and virtually all accumulators could be removed with only beneficial effects:
  - ✓ Less racket. With much less noisy apparatus, earplugs may no longer be necessary (add minor noise baffling, if necessary).
  - ✓ Less distance between technicians, who then can arrive at a problem (e.g., tipped cans) more quickly, trade jobs, and help each other more easily—generally feeling and acting more like a team.
  - ✓ Possibly no more need to equip technicians with radios—because of physical closeness, less noise.

- ✓ Less conveyor to maintain and break down, less distance over which cans can be damaged.
- ✓ Less buffer stock on conveyors, forcing attention to root causes. With lots of in-process stock, it's too easy to put off making difficult decisions to permanently fix stop-prone/jam-prone equipment.
- ✓ Quicker changeovers—because there are far fewer cans to use up to complete a run and start the next one.
- ✓ Less wear and tear on cans.

- *Palletizing*: This should be the last station on can lines, rather than, as at present, another department across a wall.
- *Plant size*: Like other plants of the big brewers, Trenton is two or three times too large.
  - ✓ The prospect of economies of scale are dubious in this one million sq. ft., 400-employee plant—over, say, a 350,000 sq. ft., 130-person plant—especially in view of the diseconomies of complexity, excessive conveyor, etc. (Not known: possible economies in *brewing*, which we did not visit or discuss.)
  - ✓ It is much easier to manage 130 people effectively—like family— than 400.
- *Layout*: The long distance from one side of the plant to other (e.g., 1,000 feet) may tend to force a generally straight-line layout. (Trenton's can lines do loop back in two or three places but are mostly linear.)
  - ✓ Layout thinking used to favor straight lines. Today, best practice is U-shaped and serpentine.
  - ✓ Without loops, continuous improvement (e.g., cut out lengths of conveyor, or put in a new multipurpose machine to replace two or three other machines) is often not feasible.
- *Cans in, cases out*: Ideally, cans would arrive empty on one wall, go out full on the same or an adjacent wall. Additional lines/can handling would be located around other walls.
- *Line speed*: As is common in packaging, line speeds are too fast.
  - ✓ No sense in striving for super-high line speeds given this one (common) result: lines are stopped for problems a large portion of the day.
  - ✓ Slower lines are cheaper to build and maintain, and (whether designed that way or simply slowed down) yield less wear and tear, stoppages and maintenance costs, and raise utilization rates appreciably.

IV. Contrasting example*

- *Eden, NC, Brewery*: "Line stops were a problem at Miller Brewing's Eden, North Carolina, facility. But the seven-hundred-foot packaging lines 'kept operators from seeing what was wrong, slowing fixes.' So, did management aim at root causes, starting with removal of six hundred feet of just-in-case conveyor on each line? They did not. They added costly technology . . . a computer on each line 'to tap data about machinery operations. Info is dashed to a server in the plant's computer room, which transforms the information into easy-to-understand diagrams. They're posted immediately on the intranet, where they can be read quickly on computer monitors by line operators.'"
- *Sequel*: MillerCoors closed its Eden plant in 2016, laying off 520 employees.

CHAPTER II-37. AMTICO CO. LTD., U.K., DIVISION OF COURTAULDS, 1991

Amtico, a division of Courtaulds, produces high-end floor tile. This short caselet was included because it represents dramatic reductions in flow times for process-industry operations and high-design, high-cost products.	***High-Interest Topics:*** • **Cross-*plant* training, and only one job Classification** • **Factory operatives on a business trip—with no managers**

Customer-focused Flow Production of Floor Tiles

Impressions based on three

one-hour plant tours of Amtico facilities, Oct. 21, 1991

A studio production facility in London plus two factories in Coventry

Followed by a two-day Schonberger seminar at
Amtico-Coventry, October 22–23

---

* Schonberger, Richard J. *Let's Fix It: Overcoming the Crisis in Manufacturing.* New York: Free Press/ Simon and Schuster, 2001, pp. 146–147.

I. General Information

- *Amtico events*:
    - ✓ Began with attendance by two Amtico directors at one of my 1989 public seminars in London.
    - ✓ CEO, John Harris, a marketing guy, became aware of my 1990 book, *Building a Chain of Customers*. Harris was interested since he was seeking ways to achieve seamless linkages from Amtico factories forward—*through advertising*—to gain new customers (e.g., department stores installing beautiful tile floors).
    - ✓ Harris may have been disappointed in my in-house seminar—which included little or nothing about advertising/marketing brochures as links between production and customers. (At the end of the seminar, Harris took the stage and addressed those matters himself.)
- *Product line*: Very high-quality floor tiles for the U.K. market—and in U.S. under different name, Azrock (because the name Amtico was already taken).
- *Production processes*: Extrude granulated PVC into rolls of material about 40 inches wide and many hundreds of feet long; the rolls are plied together with photographic film on two processing lines; then cut into smaller sizes and shapes. For intricate patterns shapes can be cut individually.
- *Contacts*: John Harris, CEO; Mary Decker, marketing.

II. Achievements and Successes

- *Cellular manufacturing*: Manufacturing cells were launched successively in 1990: a CQ cell in February, a stripwood cell in July, a black-backed cell in November, and so on.
- *Cell results—example*: The Arden cell initially achieved the following results (similar results in all the cells):
    - ✓ 4.5 mile travel reduced to yards—with lead times from a minimum of two weeks to one day.
    - ✓ Overdues were reduced from 12 weeks to zero, with a 400% increase in quality from the original 16% yield.
    - ✓ Overall inventory was cut 40%—including WIP reduction of five weeks' worth (20 yards) of backs.
    - ✓ Parquet floor team: Yields up from 16% to 85%.

- *Workforce versatility*:
  - ✓ Cross-plant training commenced in November 1990.
  - ✓ Only *one* labor classification.
- *Employee involvement*:
  - ✓ A new suggestion scheme, begun in March 1991, yielded 640 suggestions in just 20 weeks.
  - ✓ Included is a suggestion lottery; also a "fiver" (five-pound note) paid the same week to rather randomly selected, good-performing employees.
  - ✓ Example: Instead of allowing jam-ups in an annealing machine, thereby scrapping many pieces of floor covering, employees installed a window so problems in the annealing tunnel could be seen as soon as they happen, instead of waiting for the process to jam up (Figure 37.1).
- *Improvement devices*:
  - ✓ Cells include visual charts.
  - ✓ A stop button on the stripwood line is there to avoid over-processing and ensure "naturalistic quality."
  - ✓ Amtico did *not* buy a "shop-floor-control system."

FIGURE. 37.1
A seated woman is next to the window to note any problem inside the annealing machine at Amtico.

- *Commitment to customer-focused excellence*:
  - ✓ Keen sense of market opportunities.
  - ✓ Drive toward smaller self-contained "businesses."
  - ✓ Focus on *approved retailers* and *mutual gain*.
  - ✓ Delivery of "aisleway merchandising" orders *to the hour*.
- *Factory operative outreach*:
  - ✓ A PVC supplier in Calais, France (57 operators in the whole plant) had delivered PVC with black spots—*bad* since Amtico makes white tiles. At first Amtico thought the PVC contamination occurred after arrival in Coventry, but an investigation showed that not to be true.
  - ✓ So Amtico sent a team of four operators to Calais. In expectation of high-level Amtico managers, a luncheon was held in the best Calais restaurant—which the four factory operators from Amtico loved immensely!
  - ✓ The French company then was told that Amtico was considering shifting to another PVC supplier that *could* deliver PVC without black spots. The French company said *they* could do it—and did. Now factory operatives at both ends have established communications with each other.

III. Opportunities for Improvement

- *Competitive strategy*: Continuing with Amtico's excellent factory-flow practices should create some strategic opportunities, which, in turn, can help accelerate its improvement efforts in factories:
  - ✓ Cautiously examine going for a strategy of volume and market share—enabling more dedicated equipment, leading to lower costs, heat on present competition, freeze-out of new competitors, global market penetration, clout with suppliers, and so on.
  - ✓ Develop multi-functional product strategy teams, one for each product family (or customer family?)—this is already partially in force via smaller, self-contained "businesses." One purpose: to level the present highly variable production/demand patterns.
  - ✓ Develop a flex force to avoid excessive overtime and deal with summer peaks.
- *Recognition*: Implement multi-faceted reward/recognition/celebration—with *personalized* recognition (photos of worthy individuals and teams, etc.).

- *Employee development*:
  - ✓ More horizontal moves of salaried staff would be beneficial both to them and to the company.
  - ✓ Formalize cross-training—for *mastery*.
  - ✓ Develop specifications/training sheets in all areas.
  - ✓ Upgrade training rooms and resources, including train-the-trainer, videotapes, plant visits, salaried people having a strong presence in the plant, and plant people seeing/visiting customers.
- *Trend charts*: Prominently display setup time and flow-distance charts on walls within the cells; targeting dock-to-line flows; and document/paper flows—thus to keep these issues in everyone's mind.
- *SPC*: Advance to *stage 2*—continuous data-driven improvement in factory cells, especially via SPC.
- *Plant engineering*: Shift away from routine PM and a breakdown emphasis, moving toward facilitators, maintenance training for operators, and TPM.
- *Supplier development*:
  - ✓ Reach out—more "missionary" work—to/with suppliers of film, boxes/cartons, PVC, office supplies, etc.
  - ✓ Simplify low-value purchases of supplies, hardware, etc.—for example, with kanban and reduced invoicing.
- *Cutting equipment*: The London plant's color design studio project should emulate Amtico's development engineers' success in computer-aided cutting equipment.

CHAPTER II-38. ELI LILLY, INDIANAPOLIS, IN, 1996

Eli Lilly offers a platform for sharply cutting flow times and inventories in the pharmaceutical context, in which high profit margins mitigate concerns over high inventories and production costs.

Lilly's Humulin (synthetic insulin) plant presents a fascinating prospect for disentangling networks of reactors, sterilizers, pipes, valves, filters, tanks, etc., for high advantage—a prospect not only for Lilly and pharmaceuticals, but also chemicals, petroleum, and others.

High-Interest Topics:
- **Collapsing the external value chain (and its inventory overload) gets right product to right place at right time**
- **Scenario: converting complex flows in Lilly's Humulin plant to two or more simple, dedicated flow paths**

**Moving Toward Customer-focused Principles in Pharmaceutical
Manufacturing at Eli Lilly, March 11–13, 1996**

**Including a two-day Schonberger seminar, meetings with senior
staff and visits to the Humulin plant Sunday evening, March
10, and a dry products plant the evening of March 12**

I. General Information

- *Eli Lilly*: Lilly is a global pharmaceutical company with HQ and
  several plants in Indianapolis.
- *Reason for visit*: Lilly had invited me for a three-day visit that
  included a two-day seminar, partly in regard to its interest in my
  16 principles of "customer-focused, data-based, employee-driven"
  world-class excellence.
- *Consultations*: The visit included scheduled meetings with managers
  from visited plants and with other managers, including the Puerto
  Rico plant.
- *Content of caselet*: Aside from this opening Section I and an insert
  about the Humulin plant, this caselet is (with minor edits) the
  same as the summary of my visit mailed on March 16, 1996, to my
  principal contacts at Lilly.
- *Main contacts*: Mike Eagle, VP, pharmaceuticals manufacturing;
  Mark Capone, plant manager, Indy Dry Products Plant; Teresita
  Colón, plant manager, Puerto Rico 1 plant; Steve Jenison,
  manufacturing director, global business unit; Tom Wallbank, lead
  team, Park Fetcher plant; Sue Zink, QC lead person; Bob Birch,
  field executive director, biosynthetic plant; Joseph Cook, Jr., group
  VP manufacturing, engineering, and corporate quality; Stephen
  Johnson, VP manufacturing, Advanced Cardiovascular Systems;
  Dr. Frank Deane, executive director, pharmaceutical operations.

II. General Observations

- *Plant design*: Lilly's plant configurations tend to be locked in the
  plant-design stage, admitting modification only at great expense
  and delay.
  - ✓ Specifically, few process-industry companies have modified
    conventional factory design practices to permit continuous
    improvement, alternate uses, volume flexibility, and addition/

deletion of whole process steps. (Exception: Milliken's new chemical plant in Blacksburg, SC—designed with two reactor groups and equipped for quick changeover.)

✓ Two concepts that should be employed in future plant designs:

- Multiple flow lines, creating plants-in-a-plant with smaller-scale equipment, small teams, more direct one-to-one flows so as to greatly reduce machine-to-machine sources of variation.
- Deleting WIP storage tanks as processes become simplified and more dependable. WIP should always be treated as temporary, therefore readily removed; otherwise, the expectation of process failures is inherent in the design, obviating continuous improvement.

- *External customer chains*:

✓ Multi-echelon delivery chains separate Lilly from final users, each with weeks of inventories for which no group takes responsibility. This is there to ensure that Lilly and downstream entities never lose a sale; all of this seen as "good business" in view of the products' high margins.

✓ The irony is that these outsized inventories and extended lead times tend to have opposite effects: Hot-selling products often suffer stockouts, while underachievers heap up in pipelines.

✓ Very long lead times to traverse multiple delivery-chain echelons require plants to schedule to far-off forecasts, further ensuring wrong products populating distribution pipelines. The point: The old textbook wisdom that more inventory provides more protection is obsolete. Corrective actions:

- Seek to emulate the textile/apparel/department store industry and adopt Quick Response, in which a bar-coded sale of one bottle of Prozac triggers movement of one replacement bottle all along the delivery chain.
- In this pull system, formal queue limits (kanban) at every echelon act to synchronize players like members of a bucket brigade, with electronic data interchange (EDI) providing software to link the players.
- Few projects promise a higher return on investment than fixing these inventory/lead time/stockout problems. Lilly's new business-unit structure provides improved sight lines and multi-functional outlook on which these problems may be attacked.

- Remove chunks of the delivery chain. Old distribution patterns have been made partially obsolete by modern data communications and freight. The following are attractive options, depending on product volumes and customer size:
  - ➤ Shipping directly from plants to biggest accounts' DCs.
  - ➤ Shipping directly from Lilly DCs to biggest stores or medical entities.
  - ➤ Permanently eliminating distributors. (Wal-Mart is the world's driving force for this, having stated a few years ago that its intention is to deal directly with factories when possible, not with distributors)

- In the sites I visited, I saw too little evidence of employee/team recognition and celebration of gains, which is vital in closing the continual-improvement loop.

III. Humulin Biosynthetic Plant

- *Plant and product*:
  - ✓ The Humulin facility, completed in 1992, is huge, almost rivaling petrochemical and cement plants. At 87,500 sq. ft. of a long 114,000 sq. ft building, it features a network of 60 miles of piping, 1,300 miles of wiring, 315 tanks, 15,000 control instruments, and seven control rooms, and operates 24/7/365.
  - ✓ Humulin is identical to insulin made by the pancreas in the human body. This plant, dedicated to just one product, supplies insulin to millions of diabetic patients worldwide.
- *Positive observations at Humulin*:
  - ✓ Operators are becoming qualified to take first responsibility for various maintenance activities.
  - ✓ Bar-code collection of failure incidence at valves, flanges, etc., provides critical data for predictive maintenance.
  - ✓ Production offices are usually beside the processing areas.
- *Grand Strategy for Plant Segmentation*: At least two parallel pieces of equipment at each of the plant's 27 processes suggest a retrofit: segmentation of the plant into two self-contained plants-in-a-plant, each with its own equipment and team—eliminating vast amounts of piping and valves (currently needed to reroute around equipment undergoing maintenance).

✓ The current plant design—multiple feeder-to-next-process routings—makes problem trace-back grossly tangled, worsening high process variation and unpredictability.

✓ In any context, plant designs should strive for one-to-one process flows. At Humulin, this ideal—as part of a grand plan or plant segmentation—should be implemented piecemeal:

  ■ A sequence of two or more consecutive processes in which dependability is especially good becomes the first candidate for unscrambling by eliminating cross-piping and achieving "islands" of plant-in-a-plant flows.

  ■ Example: Instead of a group of six centrifuges feeding a group of two dryers, segment this pair of processes into two mini-flow lines, each with three centrifuges feeding one dryer.

- *Intermediate WIP storage tanks*:
  ✓ These storage vessels, as with cross-piping, protect against process variation—but they should be gradually bypassed by re-piping, or, if feasible, only partially filling the tanks.
  ✓ This will cut cycle times and WIP and reduce sources of in-process contamination and degradation.

IV. Dry Products—Building 100

- *Total productive maintenance*: TPM differs from conventional maintenance in that operators take on extensive maintenance roles, with the maintenance department assuming a teacher/coach role.
  ✓ During my very quick plant walk, I noticed this as the area that stuck out as a high-priority matter.
  ✓ Closely related is operators' involvement in continuing studies to cut equipment cleanout and changeover times.
- *Visual measures*: The plant's bulletin boards display mostly the "right kind" of metrics: customer-oriented (quality, cycle time, etc.) rather than inwardly-directed. Adding large, more-detailed trend charts in the work centers, owned by the operators, would provide specific visibility to vital competitive factors.
- *Positive observations*:
  ✓ Wide use of process control charts, including some advanced automated applications in use and on order.
  ✓ The new technology, vertical-drop processing from the vac-u-max to the vertical bed dryer, should improve cycle times and quality as well as cut inventories.

V. Global Business Unit

- *Product rationalization*: Mr. Jennison suspects the approximately 520 end-product SKU's include a number of money-losing low-volume "dogs and cats."
  - ✓ Best way to attack a bloated product line is through an activity-based costing (ABC) audit covering both manufacturing and marketing. Such an audit should show that low-volume products are high consumers of manufacturing overhead (a well-known phenomenon)—the same holds true in sales and marketing (less well-known).
  - ✓ This proof can help persuade business-unit managers to trim the product line and consolidate promotional efforts on the few best products and potential emergent stars. (Some losing products, though, are worth continuing for societal reasons, e.g., keeping a few patients alive or with minimal discomfort.)
- *Internal supply chain*: Cefaclor goes through two Indiana plants, then to Holland or Ireland, on to Italy or Ireland, and back to Clinton—all before distribution begins.
  - ✓ This convoluted pipeline taps tax incentives in Holland, Ireland, and Italy.
  - ✓ An ABC audit can show whether increased overhead, transportation, and lengthened cycle-time costs offset tax advantages.
  - ✓ Perhaps (Steven Jennison's thought) the European plants are worthwhile only at certain times in a product's life cycle (e.g., during peak volumes, which produce peak tax advantages).

VI. Carolina, Puerto Rico

- *Peer appraisal*: The PR 1 management team is interested in 360-degree appraisal. I am sending them reference materials on the topic.
- *Becoming Class A MRP II*: The PR 1 team questions the need for a shop-floor control system in their high-volume, single-product, straight-routed production line (Prozac)—a question that points to a serious flaw in "Class A MRP II" ratings, which are used rigidly by some consultants.
  - ✓ Queue limitation/kanban *is* a shop-floor control system (though not computer-based)—fitting for most kinds of manufacturing, including process industries. Besides shop-floor control, other

high-cost MRP II subsystems, e.g., capacity requirements planning, are even more questionable than a shop-floor control system.

✓ Therefore, PR 1—and other Lilly entities—should not treat Class A MRP II status as a worthy goal. Instead, implement only core MRP II subroutines and seek to become a "Class A Company" instead of Class A MRP II.

- *Single-digit cycle time.* Prozac's total cycle time is 11–13 days, with a goal of single digits (nine days):

  ✓ Attaining nine days could be done just by reducing lot sizes. However, Jose Fuxa's analysis indicates that that would significantly cut output, which would make no sense for this high-margin, high-demand product. Given Fuxa's point:

    ■ The better approach is to attack equipment cleanout downtimes via videotape analysis, quick couple/uncouple piping, disposable sterile liners, office people borrowed to help for any major cleanout, etc.

    ■ Some of the cleaning should take place in the 11 unused shifts (five nights in addition to six Sat.–Sun. shifts)—with careful scheduling to ensure the cycle from dispensing to packaging is complete in time for scheduled weekend (or night) cleaning.

    ■ Using off shifts will increase plant output, or, alternatively, permit cuts in lot sizes/cycle times while keeping output constant.

  ✓ A new mix method—five bins on wheels that can be picked up and shaken—is undergoing FDA-approval; when approved, it will allow each packaging line to have its own mixer, cutting cycle time and exposing machine-to-machine causes of variation.

  ✓ Actually, while cutting cycle time generally has multiple benefits, on a steady-selling, high-volume product like Prozac, benefits are somewhat less, as compared to ensuring high levels of output.

  ✓ Usually, the key benefit of cutting cycle times is to permit making a more complete mix of products on the same production lines in given time period. Not true here, as Prozac is the only product (minor exception: Prozac has multiple packaging SKUs). Still, cycle time/WIP reduction is well worth pursuing.

    ■ Total cycle from chemistry to the final user may be nearly a year, which makes accurate demand forecasting (for volume, not model mix, in this case) impossible.

■ Inaccurate forecasts result in too much or too little inventory on retailers' shelves, lost sales, overtime in supply chain to catch-up, or under-utilization in the supply chain to slow production. If PR 1 can cut its component of cycle time, demand forecasting will be that much more accurate for business as a whole.

VII. Park Fletcher Plant

• *TPM & visual measures*: Same observations as for the Dry Products plant.
• *Ergonomic handling*: Packaging operators expend significant effort "traying off," including lowering trays to floor-level pallet boxes that are then pallet-jacked to the next operations. Pallet boxes/pallet-jack handling is suitable in warehouse and dispensing. But packaging should avoid using them in favor of simple wheeled tables designed so that employees can tray off at waist height.
• *Excess capacity & inventory*: Long-lasting penicillin "contamination" in this small plant makes for utilization difficulties, e.g., a small work force that's not very busy.
  ✓ Bad habits can settle in, such as letting inventories build and allowing excessive handling (e.g., traying off).
  ✓ Staying lean and mean needs to be source of pride, reinforced by suitable recognition for inventory/waste elimination.
  ✓ To help make a case for being lean on inventories, I am sending Tom Wallbank reference materials on the high *hidden* costs of inventory.

CHAPTER II-39. JOHNSON CONTROLS, ELECTROMECHANICAL SYSTEMS UNIT (EMSU), MILWAUKEE, WI, 1990

Information for this caselet comes from a meeting in Milwaukee with a group of managers from three Johnson Controls plants in four different locales, all within its Electromechanical Systems Unit (EMSU). However, I visited only the Milwaukee, WI plant, which is the dominant topic of the caselet.	*High-Interest Topics:* • **Adopt "available-to-promise" scheduling and sales-ordering, thus to provide quicker, more reliable deliveries to customers** • **Eliminating an overhead monorail** • **Organization into cell teams—serving to combat labor-union's work rules and excessive job descriptions**

Scattered Factories Press for Flow Production

A tour of the "mother" plant, March 14, 1990, along with presentations/discussions on March 15 about other EMSU plants in Lexington, KY; Poteau, OK; and Reynosa, Mexico

I. General Information

- *Products*: Johnson Controls EMSU produces building-management equipment and controls, including heating, ventilation and air conditioning (HVAC) systems.
- *Contact persons*: James Eaton, director of manufacturing development; Michael Smith, manager, technical operations; Jim Gregg and Gregg Howard, brass valve cell; Mike Smith, Humboldt plant.

II. Strengths—General

- *EMSU's strategic plans*: First priority is getting focused plant-by-plant (e.g., dampers in Lexington), plants-within-plants (Reynosa), and cells (covering rapidly increasing percentages of employees).
    - ✓ This strategy offers wide-ranging benefits—in response time, quality, breaking down functional walls, etc.
    - ✓ Product rationalization for world production/sales of brass valves dovetails well with the plant-focused strategy.
- *Humboldt, iron valve cell (operational)*:
    - ✓ Machining of larger-sized bodies is on one horizontal machining center with smaller sizes on another (most companies seek, dubiously, one machine that can *do all sizes*).
    - ✓ Color-coded kanban locations, containers, labels, etc. (see photo, Figure 39.1).
    - ✓ Good progress and plans for completing/extending this cell.
- *Humboldt, brass valve cell (planned)*: The engineering that has gone into this cell looks to be thorough and thoughtful. This effort, involving tight synchronization of machining with assembly is ambitious, but looks feasible and would be something of a breakthrough for plants of this kind.
- *Humboldt punch presses*: Improvements include tilting up-down rollers to accommodate either coil or flat stock, cantilevered die racks near each press, a multi-spindle drill press on wheels, dies with the same shut height, a tiny degreaser in the area, and a greater attention to neatness.

FIGURE 39.1
Even the broom (even the dust) is on a kanban square at JC's Humboldt plant.

- *Humboldt screw machines*: Plans include small "clusters" and a larger cluster for plugs; use of pre-control charts; and color-coded tool pans pre-located to cabinets in the clusters.
- *Humboldt foundry*: Good progress in improving yields, reducing job classifications, cross-training, and kanban-linking with the valve plant.
- *Reynosa, Mexico plant*:
  ✓ Assembly cells are not too large (most with five or fewer people) and that do a nearly complete task (printed circuit assembly cells even have their own small-scale flow-solder equipment).
  ✓ Awards/recognition include large, nice-looking wall displays (recognition being especially important in Mexican culture).
  ✓ Kanban schedule boards and instruction displays are in use in the injection-molding area.
  ✓ Improvements are in yields, space, throughput times, etc.
- *Poteau panels plant*: Improvements include space- and throughput-time reductions, cross-training (which eases a summer crunch on electrical manpower); integration of pneumatic and electrical; and a plan for some pre-manufacturing (office) in parallel, for greatly reducing lot sizes and handling.
- *Lexington focused panels*: Good example of making the most of a "winner" of a product.

III. Opportunities for Improvement

- *Humboldt iron valve cell*:
  - ✓ Final assembly is not but should be in a central area with subassemblies feeding it from all directions. The challenge is that the cumbersome overhead monorail is an inflexible impediment. The monorail—maybe a good idea at the time—now needs to be torn out, the sooner the better.
  - ✓ Better for this type of product are several small floor-supported assembly fixtures of the type now hanging from the monorail (with easy up-down and flip-flop reorientation of assembly). Perhaps those present fixtures could be modified accordingly.
  - ✓ For subassembly and fabrication cells that are located near the final assembly, consider storing component parts in flow racks that reach from sub to final assembly (this option would cover more parts if final assembly were centrally located)—thus to avoid handling parts in and out of carts and totes.
  - ✓ Eliminate all tool boxes. Replace with tools hanging on peg boards with tool silhouettes painted behind, expansion cords, etc.
  - ✓ Sharply reduce kanban quantities (especially pieces per load), which in most cases won't stop any work.
  - ✓ Diligently seek parts for which off-line buffer stock makes sense (e.g., in processes that will "break down" no more than every two weeks on average).
  - ✓ Job classifications, though much reduced, are still excessive.
    - A subtle way to attack the issue is to create cells and tighten kanban quantities, which tends to make operators see the need for helping on jobs besides their own.
    - Some companies have found that operators may overlook contract restrictions and pitch in as a result.
  - ✓ Paint is a bottleneck even though a single color (black) operation; part of the problem is a lack of labor flexibility—the classification issue again.
    - The planning team is evaluating options, including putting color additives into castings.
    - Another, mentioned by someone, is to mask the assembled valve and paint the whole thing—probably better than the current method in every way.

✓ Increase customer-responsiveness—ideally through marketing and sales, linking the production and the customer via "available-to-promise" order scheduling.
- The rule is that sales commits only up to capacity (perhaps set at 40 valves per day), with production usually able to achieve exactly 40 valves—never more—in a given day. (Sales does not over-commit.)
- With that regularity, production learns to meet completion/delivery promises nearly 100% of the time. The graph of Figure 39.2 shows an example of an available-to-promise schedule for a given product or cell.

• *Humboldt, brass valve cell*:
✓ Keep the final-assembly conveyor and supporting machines as mobile as possible—amenable to change, improvement, relocation.
✓ Add performance measures that are cause-oriented and highly relevant to operators—such as check sheets, causes of equipment stoppages, micro-response ratios.
✓ Out of the large variety of world and cage-trim valves, are there any "stars"?
- If so, seek ways of treating them differently—e.g., dedicated equipment for certain fab or assembly operations, and with reserved slots in the schedule.
- The point: Don't try to make a huge product variety in one cell, since this usually requires fab equipment with a very large

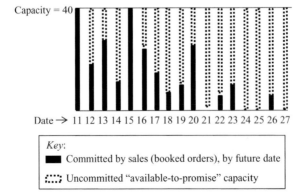

FIGURE 39.2
Committed capacity and "available-to-promise" capacity as of dates 11 through 27.

range of capabilities—meaning more costly, complex, difficult-to-maintain equipment, with more time-consuming setups.

- *Humboldt iron and brass cells*:
  ✓ I suggest a plant-visit exchange with an impressive specialty (make-to-order) pump manufacturing plant: Ahlström Pump, Mänttä, Finland. Ahlström is building an even more world-class plant in Easley, NC, which will closely integrate the iron castings foundry with fab cells as well final assembly. Construction is under way.
    ■ Mänttä uses a kind of floor-supported assembly fixture that the brass valve cell should use.
    ■ Mänttä also has a remarkably simple system of coordination from machining to final assembly, relying on flow racks extending from one cell to the next; very simple, large signboards that assembly people use as authorization to start an order; and painting linked in after the final assembly.
    ■ I have talked to my main contact at Ahlström to see if they would welcome an exchange visit; in return, they could have a tour of the iron valve cell and review plans for the brass valve cell. Contact person: Tuomo Ronkko, general manager at Easley site (formerly head of the Mäntta plant).
  ✓ Nice "alcove of excellence" but measures need updating. Safety, quality, and HR notices are fine, but no point posting production control, productivity, and expenses.
    ■ Instead, focus on on-time *customer* orders (not *internal* orders), flow time, flow distance, WIP.
    ■ There should be one "alcove" for iron valves, and one for brass—*including* foundry.
- *Humboldt screw presses*: The present three-shift operation probably strains the ability to hold to schedule commitments, or to promise short lead times (three-shift operations are chronically undependable, except in certain flow-process industries). I heard something about upcoming changes that would reduce to two shifts—highly desirable.
- *Humboldt foundry*: Set, say, three days as the next flow-time commitment; study/implement exactly what resources, run lengths, etc., will meet it consistently (e.g., some additional shift work). This will provide incentives to increase the pace of improvements that have already started.

- *Humboldt and Reynosa*:
  - ✓ The plants are too large for just one receiving/shipping zone; where feasible, cut doors around the plant walls for direct reception/shipment next to each focused plant-in-a-plant.
  - ✓ Disburse central factory maintenance to each plant-in-a-plant.
- *Reynosa*:
  - ✓ Operators need to plot *aggravations* (a.k.a., problems) throughout the day—in support of true employee involvement. Training in team building, etc., alone usually has positive effects—but takes a long time and is not very problem-directed.
  - ✓ The 16-week horizon for regularized schedules seems excessive—and greatly disconnects Reynosa from actual end-product demand.
  - ✓ Kanban boards in injection molding allow operators some freedom to line up similar jobs (good), but probably the kanban horizon should be cut from four to three weeks (later to two, and so forth) so that molding is more closely synchronized with assembly cells—creating pressure for shorter runs, quicker setups.
- *Poteau*: In panel assembly, consider moving router/glue/laminating into the empty space nearer to panel assembly (this suggestion arose during Cliff Vinson's presentation).
- *Lexington panels plant*:
  - ✓ If the main reason for charging extra cost for one-day specials is to gain new business, then this is ill-advised. It may, however, be acceptable for *good* current customers and if only a *small percentage* of orders. Otherwise, create a dedicated cell (or partial cell, e.g., assembly-only) for one-day order-filling.
  - ✓ Reassembly by two-person teams: It's usually better to create a larger cell/cell team with progressive assembly, cross-training, job switching, data collection, problem-solving.
- *All plants*: "Plaster" the walls—in each plant-in-a-plant—with large improvement charts (e.g., setup time, WIP, flow time, flow distance, rework), cross-training charts, recognition and activity charts—enhancing visual management of the improvement effort and inspiring operator involvement/ownership.
- *Overall*: EMSU appears strong on managerial and professional talent, advancing nicely in simplifying and removing waste in manufacturing, but it's not strong in employee involvement. EI is easy to initiate (hard to sustain and improve); managerial/professional people need to resist old habits of *doing it all themselves*.

CHAPTER II-40. JOHNSON CONTROLS INTERIORS, HOLLAND, MI, 1999

This JCI plant, which designs and produces automotive interiors, ranks among the globe's best, but it still has room for improvement. Its "world-class excellence" journey dates back a decade prior to this caselet.

Note: to the extent that the car industry is a haven of lean/flow manufacturing, virtually none of that is visible in a car assembly plant; nearly all is found in supplier plants, especially this one.

High-Interest Topics:
- **Seven product-focused plants, each in its own small-ish, separate building**
- **Job rotation every hour on the hour!**
- **"Build consistency"—a unique (never seen else-where) charting method— avoids tendencies to work at a slow pace early in a shift only to enter into "catch-up mode" later, when everyone would prefer to relax!**

Flow Manufacturing Done Well at JCI

Assessment based on a brief plant tour, dinner discussions, etc.

In connection with a two-day in-company seminar, February 23–24, 1999

I. General Information

- *JCI-Holland*: Formerly Prince Corp., this family-owned business grew from a machine shop some 30 years ago to a major producer of automotive interiors (except seats).
  - ✓ Prince was sold in 1996 to Johnson Controls, in part to generate more cash for Prince family members to disperse philanthropically.
  - ✓ This business is now a component, along with JCI's long-standing auto seat business, of the Automotive Systems Group, headquartered in Plymouth, MI.
- *Contact persons*: John Arnold, VP manufacturing; Joe Weber, director, manufacturing and engineering.; Bob Stander, general manager; Bob Bieri, Holland operations; Dekemer Scherighoffer, non-Holland operations; Forest Hills, director, advanced manufacturing.; Dave Kandt, director, seating, Plymouth.

- *Holland operations*: 5,000 employees in seven focused factories:
  - ✓ 1. Floor consoles.
  - ✓ 2. Arm rests—Beachwood plant, the only product with sewn fabric.
  - ✓ 3. Sun visors—16 million produced per year (about half of the nation's output), with 22 machines making visor cores; visors are not sewn but instead the fabric is edge-wrapped around two "butterfly" halves of plastic substrate that is then closed and head-bonded; produced in 25 work cells in which operators rotate jobs every hour on the hour.
  - ✓ 4. Door panels (a 350,000 sq. foot plant connected to the 300,000 sq. foot sun-visor plant).
  - ✓ 5. Map lamps and consoles.
  - ✓ 6. Overhead systems (headliners)—Maplewood plant.
  - ✓ 7. Injection molding—about 100 injection molding machines; the other half of molding is outsourced.
- *Facilities visited*:
  - ✓ Evening of Feb. 22 (tour host, Joe Weber): Plants for sun visors, door panels, and headliners; talked in some depth to several bright, well-spoken employees; also, one apprenticing but job-knowledgeable maintenance technician with a positive outlook.
  - ✓ Lunchtime, first seminar day: walked end-to-end through an impressive development/engineering center. On the second day, I walked through the People Building.
- *Facilities not visited*:
  - ✓ Cut and sew—about 75 sewers, in modular cells producing in the JIT mode (except for multi-piece fabric cutting); none of the sewing is outsourced. (Note: it is hard to find sewing facilities—anywhere in the world—that have adopted JIT/cellular sewing, which is far more effective, efficient, and employee-beneficial than individuals sewers doing one sit-down job all day every day.)
  - ✓ Cockpit, a new mega-module, complete with steering wheel, floor pedals, etc., is to be a next-generation product (not yet for sale but to be priced around $1,500, which is more than a car engine).
- *Major outsource*: Wiring harnesses (mostly from Ciudad Juárez, the "wiring harness capital of the world").

II. Strengths—General

- *World-class/lean agenda*: JCI is an early-bird adopter—over ten years ago—with extensive examples of effective implementation: cells, kanban, lot-size of one, design for assembly/modularity, training-with-a-purpose, cross-training, hourly job rotation, "water spider" kanban agents from cells, and more.
- *Avoids "programitis"*: JCI has avoided leaps onto every management bandwagon that comes along; a few terms that customers use extensively (kaizen, pokayoke, lean) have blended easily with the established JC-Interiors' improvement system.
- *Build consistency.*
    - ✓ JCI employs a locally-devised (by Dan ___), apparently unique chart that is akin to pre-control charts.
    - ✓ The charts, in each production area, have a green-shaded center zone flanked by an upper and lower yellow, and an outer upper and lower red zone. The work team updates the charts with output data every hour.
    - ✓ The aim: This effectively combats tendencies of teams to run cold (low output) early in a shift only to hurry to catch-up later—such haste leads to potential safety and quality problems. Further, this builds consistency, smooths process-to-process flows, cuts cycle times, and reduces needs for buffer stocks.
- *Product development*: State-of-the-art product development capabilities include people, facilities, multi-step processes, and budget.
- *Lean on equipment*: The lure of unnecessary automation and monumental machines has generally been rebuffed—in favor of lower-cost, simpler equipment well matched to speeds of processes and desirability to equip for cellular manufacturing.
- *Focused factories*: Each of the seven product-focused plants is in a separate building, generally of less than 300 sq. ft.—a space and number of people that maintains a manageable, "family" feeling (the door panel plant is a bit larger than this ideal).
- *Core-focused business*: JCI-Holland does not dabble in business undertakings outside of its core competency, car interiors—so far not even in the more customized interiors of the truck industry.
    - ✓ Stayed with its core while expanding in Europe through acquiring German auto interiors manufacturer, Becker, whose extensive

injection molding resources were sold so that the focus of the acquisition would be Becker's car-interiors component.

✓ Within-core targets for further growth may include airplane, boat, and passenger train interiors.

- *Physical facilities*: Nice campus, buildings, extras (e.g., the "people" building)—attractive for recruiting top-notch talent. Wide, uncluttered, safe aisles; high ceilings; utilities located aloft throughout. Shipping and receiving share the same docks (as opposed to the usually less-effective through-the-plant configuration).
- *Work force*: Youthful, above-average intelligence and conscientiousness; only one job classification for hourlies.
- *Numerous kaizens*: These are typically three-day events with a team of manufacturing engineers, other experts, and cell-team members, aimed at improving cell configurations and operation.
- *Cell audits*: Each cell is audited, by representatives of another cell, on housekeeping, quality, materials, throughput.
- *Employees/culture*: Benevolent family-owners long ago established a culture of treating people well (e.g., special attention to ergonomics and safety): giving them a voice (and part ownership); avoiding offensive behaviors (e.g., no blue language); and application of a "loose/tight" concept concerning policies and rules of behavior.

III. Opportunities for Improvement

- *TPM*: Though not highly automated, JCI-Holland has plenty of equipment, good care of which recommends TPM.
  ✓ The excellent work force has a good deal of untapped potential, especially regarding TPM, which is the most apparent deficiency/opportunity for significant improvement.
  ✓ Above all, TPM means operators own the equipment, with maintenance as facilitator—but that's not the case at JCI-Holland.
  ✓ Following are elements of TPM that should be implemented at JCI.
    - 5S, mainly focused on good housekeeping, and its close companion, visual management, are up and running, but have a way to go. Designated floor areas are well marked, but

much less so on benches, equipment, tools, fixtures, racks, etc. (e.g., labels, tool shadow boards, color-coding, cost labels on costly "hardware" parts and repair items).

■ Under TQ and TPM, all employees should be, but are not, recording every in-process hiccup. The best method for employees to collect data on glitches and annoyances on check sheets labeled with predefined, commonly-occurring problems.

■ Currently, operators do not lubricate equipment, open it for cleaning and tightening, make simple repairs, etc. Maintenance should be taking the role of teacher and facilitator, monitoring the transfer of these to operators (as with the transfer of quality from quality engineers to operators in an earlier decade).

• *Performance measurement*:

✓ An excellent trend in manufacturing management is transforming performance measurement to reflect the new era of empowerment (as opposed to command-and-control).

■ One aim is to de-emphasize aggregated measures (e.g., efficiency, utilization, lost-time accidents, inventory turns, cost per unit), which derive from so many factors that they cannot be fairly attributed to any one process team.

■ Instead, recraft measures such that they are clearly direct effects of good process management in the trenches.

✓ The seminar spent considerable time on this topic—including simulation skits and break-out teams to re-do measures in order to pinpoint natural aggravation and stimulation factors of the workplace.

✓ Following the reasoning emergent from those exercises, teams of managers, technicians, and front-line employees should join forces to develop relevant-to-the-job/relevant-to-competitiveness (customer-focused) measures.

✓ Some of the current derivative measures tracked on the shop floor (e.g., efficiency, cost off target, purchase burden of sales) may be retained in managers' offices, but they should be shared/discussed with employees only via quarterly (or special) focused-factory meetings.

- *Cell-to-cell cross-training*:
  - ✓ Cross-training is excellent within cells. However, people in feeder cells (e.g., fabric cutting or foam layup) should be cross-trained and rotated occasionally with downstream assembly cell people.
  - ✓ Extending training and rotation this way broadens whole-product awareness and generates ideas for solving problems that might not occur to people with narrower understanding.
- *Station cycle times*:
  - ✓ While the objective, according to Joe Weber, is to keep operator cycle times "long enough for people to have time to think," there are a few cases times where it is as low as 15 seconds.
  - ✓ A study by engineers at Sony's San Diego TV headquarters found that in a typical Mexico TV plant with ten-second cycle times, one second at each end of a cycle is lost to hand-offs—in other words 20% loss of productivity (in addition to problems of boredom, no time to think, etc.).
- *Operator involvement in cell design/redesign*:
  - ✓ Cell design is largely a manufacturing-engineering function, with limited involvement of cell-team members. Kaizens tap ideas of cell teams but mostly to tweak cell design and operation and not to suggest meaningful cell-design changes.
  - ✓ An overall impression is of three separate responsibility zones: one for manufacturing engineers, another for cell-team members, and a third for maintenance. These should blend and overlap extensively.
- *Competitive analysis and benchmarking*: At present, the professional staff does competitive analysis, chiefly through reverse engineering.
  - ✓ A more thorough approach focuses not just on competitors' product offerings but also employs *process* benchmarking: how they and best companies in other industries do what they do.
  - ✓ The entire work force, not just the professional staff, should be kept abreast of, and even participate in, the information gathered.
  - ✓ Observing what's happening outside, they get ideas for improvement inside and also develop healthy fears and concerns for their own work-life security.

CHAPTER II-41. SIECOR CORP., HICKORY, NC, 1990

About half of this caselet, for the Hickory, NC, facility, comes from my very brief feedback and thank-you report to my hosts. To fill out the caselet, I've drawn from my handwritten, detailed notes, which, after 17 years, were difficult for me to decipher—suggesting that inaccuracies are probable.

High-Interest Topics:
- **Peers doing interviewing and hiring to fill vacancies in production**
- **What to do when customers back-integrate into some of your finished processes: a near-future plan**
- **Two exhibits showing cell configurations**

Moving toward Cellular Production

Observations based on a brief plant tour, Feb. 14, 1990

In connection with a Schonberger seminar for Siecor and some of its suppliers, February 14–15

I. General Information

- *Company and products*:
  - ✓ This facility houses Siecor's HQ and two plants:
    - SSC (Siecor specialty cable) plant produces fiber-optic cables, primarily for indoor applications (started with copper cable in 1954, mostly switching to fiber-optic in 1966). AT&T is the biggest competitor; there are not many others.
    - TFC plant produces telephony fiber-optical cable.
  - ✓ Siecor also has a control-products plant (mainly for elevator cables) in Rocky Mount, NC; and a computer-apparatus plant (hardware for cross-connects, splicing, etc.) in Keller, TX.
- *Contact persons*: Robert Moser, cable unit general manager; Jerry Cates, SPC plant manager; Roger Cloezio, maintenance and facilities; Andy Schrall, quality manager; William McCollum, Rocky Mount plant.

II. Strengths

- *Cells*: Good start creating cells over the past several months.

- *Work force/working conditions*:
  - ✓ Lots of attention to training factory operators and other non-exempts (about 100 were sent to my seminar).
  - ✓ Good start in reducing job classifications: down from four to one in extrusions; down to one in connectorization.
  - ✓ High pay, low labor turnover for the area.
  - ✓ Good working conditions, including very clean, well-lit plants with polyurethaned floors.
- *Corrective action teams*: CATs have made good progress, especially in a few quick-changeover projects.
- *Scrap reductions, TFC plant*: Scrap reductions in the past five years are 12.8%, 11.7%, 11.1%, 10.1%, and 7.3%.
- *Inventories and kanban*:
  - ✓ Good, recent inventory turnover trend.
  - ✓ A kanban arrangement with a Siemens plant that supplies fiber has kanban set at a controlled five days' stock.
  - ✓ Good internal kanban using flow racks in the copper-cable area (a product for IBM) within the specialty cable plant.

III. Siecor Specialty Cable Plant

- *SSC plant & people*: 150,000 sq. ft. (120,000 for manufacturing); 199 permanent and five temporary employees (29 exempts; 19 administrative and technical; 151 hourly).
- *Connectorization*: Is organized into dedicated cells.
  - ✓ Includes bringing in a reel, stripping and polishing the ends, and connectorizing.
  - ✓ Though polishers are costly, plans are to buy more to accommodate more cable sizes per cell.
- *Extrusion of fibers*: Limited to a narrow range of diameters.
  - ✓ In multi-strand cables, extrusion is followed by insulation, central strengthening, and a Kevlar outer.
  - ✓ There are *no* standard lengths in this industry—can't even deviate by three inches. Fiber inventory—excelling at 20 turns per year.
- *Cable cells*: Following fiber extrusion is cable finishing—organized into eight cells, four to six people per cell. Each of the eight, in a U-shaped pattern, consists of strip and mount, epoxy base, polisher (three machines—for good balance), inspection, and inspect/pack; see Figure 41.1. Cable finishing inventory is five to six turns.

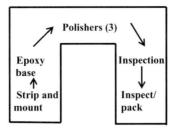

FIGURE 41.1
Cable cells' (8) configuration

- *Copper (IBM-exclusive customer)*: The process includes:
  - ✓ Wire draw-down and checks for OD, with reels then going into a 40-roll (8x5) flow rack, holding two days' stock.
  - ✓ Twisting: next, two machines can twist or quad to complete copper cores—ready for braiding.
  - ✓ Braiding setup could take a full day.
    - ▪ To greatly reduce setups, a CAT team's suggestion led to buying many low-cost, used braiding machines, each dedicated (no setup) to four, six, eight, or ten pairs (which is the way IBM orders copper wire).
    - ▪ When the number of machines was doubled, scrap was halved.
  - ✓ Of the three product-specific copper lines, four are buffer lines, four are sub-unit lines, and one is a new "cell" that includes buffer to sub-unit (buffer runs twice as fast as the sub-unit); some of the cell's output is shipped as is and some goes to multi-fibering.
  - ✓ Two optical lines feed multi-fibering.
  - ✓ Two jacketing machines achieve stranding into cable.

IV. Telephony Fiber-optical Cable (TFC) Plant

- *Orders*:
  - ✓ This is a highly-seasonal make-to-order plant with August peak demand, nevertheless operating 24/7, year-round.
  - ✓ Forecast orders, which drive MRP planning, are highly variable month to month (e.g., 177 to 135 to 184 to 144 to 125 to 161…).
- *Competition*: Pirelli, Sumitomo, and Fujicomo. Siecor's competitive edge is customer service.
- *Workforce*:

✓ Peers interview and hire permanent employees (in effect since 1989).

✓ Provisional operators and temps are brought in to handle peaks (20 or so are retirees, others are one-timers). Using temps lets TFC roughly match production to demand, even with the high seasonality.

- *Production process*:

  ✓ On the 2nd floor mezzanine are nine ink/dry/cut lines that deliver by elevator down to next processes (inking provides colors for identification).

  ✓ 13 vertical and two horizontal buffer machines extrude atop the fiber, encasing it in a double-walled tube with a jelly-like compound, with the cushioning fiber free of moisture and tension. Water-cooling solidifies the buffered fiber; and every fiber is tested.

  ✓ Tubes are bound into cores by two binders and gathered on reels of shop glass or steel.

  ✓ In several steps, plastic jackets are applied over hot glue, and after more steps and tests—plus markings with feet or meters and the company logo—they are lifted on wooden shipping reels.

- *Raw materials supplier*: JIT deliveries, five days a week, from Corning yield an excellent 60 inventory turns for Corning fiber. (One reel of this glass fiber, 16,000 meters long, is costed at $1,700.)

V. Miscellaneous Observations/Suggestions

- *Suggestion program*: Phase out "dollarizing" of suggestions—because cost-accounting numbers are untrustworthy (in nearly all companies) for such narrow purposes.

- *Visual management*: Add large wall trend charts on:

  ✓ Lead time, WIP, micro-response ratio, flow distance, setup times.

  ✓ *Total* payroll cost per linear meter/foot, normalized.

  ✓ In-progress projects, cross-training plan, suggestions.

  ✓ Unplanned machine down time.

- *Quick setup*:

  ✓ Organize setup teams with assigned operators as leaders, plus borrowed labor; use computer sheets, maps, and clockwork precision.

  ✓ Have all adjustment and setup tools on shadow boards.

- *Job classifications*: For the sake of labor flexibility, a more aggressive attack of classifications is needed.

- *Temps*: Seek more "permanent" temporaries (yearly callback employees) for the TOC plant.
- *Preventive maintenance*: Operators should take over nearly all PM.
- *Catch-up with demand*: Get capacity *ahead of* demand in SSC plant (it's been behind for several cycles, which makes demand growth seem to reflect new uses rather than exaggerated demand).
- *More cells and quicker, better customer service*: Once demand and capacity grows in TFC, organize more cells (multiple units of equipment are already available in some processes).
- *Near-future plan*: As key customers (e.g., phone companies) acquire their own capability in high-quality end-grinding/polishing, SSC should become a repetitive producer of a few "star" cable types/standard lengths and kinds. Do the same in TFC (where cable is not, if I understand correctly, sold with ends polished for immediate connection; e.g., the 25 km master length armored at 5.2 km…5.0 km…4.8 km…). Then:
    - ✓ Eliminate all work orders and transactions for those "star" items.
    - ✓ Produce to fill kanban squares ("x" number of reels allowable for each item), or make to a repetitive plan, frozen for, say, two weeks.
    - ✓ Ship in standard lengths—or, sometimes, cut to order for next-day shipment (this will waste quite a bit of cut-off material, but perhaps this will save more in overhead and inventory, also garnering a much quicker response to customers).
    - ✓ Partially break up the four main production departments—color, buffer, strand, and jacket—to form cells dedicated to narrow families of stars (especially in TFC, where there are multiple units of most machines); "extras" (low-volume products and specials) still to be processed department-to-department. As an example, see Figure 41.2.
    - ✓ This configuration calls for Cell 1, for a star product, to have all its own dedicated equipment.
        - ■ For good balance it entails two color (C)-to-buffer (B) units, feeding one strander (S) and one jacketer (J).
        - ■ Cells 2 and 3—each also having its own star or starlet product—are similar, except that they share the third jacketer (J), a likely reason being to handle one or more products that have a different jacketing specification.
    - ✓ Extras are configured as four proximate processes (C's to B's to S's to J's)—that adjacency affords fairly short flow paths but with a wide range of machine-to-machine options.

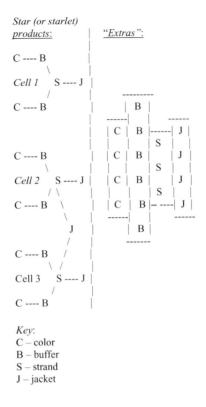

FIGURE 41.2
Dedicated cell configuration for star (or starlet) products and close (not fully dedicated) process flows for extras

CHAPTER II-42. FOUR SEASONS REMANUFACTURING DIVISION, STANDARD AUTO PARTS, COPPELL, TX, 1994

Four Seasons' big plant remanufactures automotive generators, alternators, and other products for the aftermarket. It has excelled in flow management in an environment of oily, dirty, incoming cores that go out "like new." This long and detailed caselet is the first of two dedicated to remanufacturing—the other being the next caselet, Chapter II-53.

High-Interest Topics:
- **With massive numbers and variety of parts in many stages of production—color-coding to the rescue**
- **Large array of pay/reward/recognition factors**
- **Cells, kanban, quick setup, small lots—alive and well in this remanufacture environment**

Reducing Complexity in a Remanufacturing Context

**Impressions based on a one-day of advisory services and
a one-day Schonberger seminar at the company**

Friday-Saturday, March 31-April 1, 1994

I. General

- *The Company*: Four Seasons is one of many companies that remanufacture automotive generators, alternators, etc. They buy/receive "cores" (e.g., worn-out generators) from junk yards and car parts stores; refurbish (clean and machine usable parts and supplement with new ones); assemble, pack, and ship to the aftermarket, usually with a good warranty.
- *Product line*: 5,000 SKUs, most being spare parts, not whole products. Exception: R4 compressors are about 30% of total sales at 1,000 per day.
- *Competition*: Cooper Industries of Dallas; also Everco and Murray; many more.
- *Customers*: Biggest are Pep Boys and AutoZone.
- *Contacts*: Malcolm Davidow, product development & planning manager and international manager; Stanley Davidow, VP and general manager; Ian Fisher, manufacturing director; Ron George, production manager; Shirley DeCoopring, HR; Ray Nichols, DP manager.

II. Strengths

- *Layout/organization*: Diverse mix of compressors were, about eight years ago, split into multiple focused cells/lines—an excellent foundation for improvements on many fronts. See Figure 42.1.
- *Equipment*: Few "supermachine" obstacles in the way of focused, cellular organization.
- *Transaction avoidance*: No wasteful WIP tracking or labor reporting down to the operation level.
- *Maintenance*: Good progress in:
  ✓ Transferring simple tasks from the maintenance function to operators.

FIGURE 42.1
Already cleaned parts, plus new ones at final-assembly station. Four Seasons Manufacturing Co.

- ✓ Keeping a master set of machine manuals in a locked cabinet, with a duplicate set—in three-ring binders with laminated pages—located at the machines.
- ✓ Radio contact with production lines for quick response on equipment problems.
- ✓ Calendar-based checklists for PMs (preventive maintenance)—weekly, bi-weekly, monthly, six-monthly.
- *Process quality*: X-bar and R charts are in use in piston machining.
- *Product design*: Four Seasons has its own engineering for developing improvements to OEM customers' own designs (in one case, an improved design by Four Seasons engineering resulted in one replacing three of a customer's SKUs).
- *Safety*: A Golden Broom award; and notices posted on parts to stay within a 40-lb. weight limit.
- *Job classifications*: Not many.
- *Pay, reward, recognition*: Several items make up a "basket of values": ESOP (employee stock ownership plan), 401 K, profit-sharing, dental, $100 for uniforms, free movie tickets, anniversary cards yearly.
- *Warehouse efficiencies and quick response*:

FIGURE 42.2
Finished, cartoned goods being labeled at Four Seasons Manufacturing Co.

- ✓ Pick locations are reachable with low pick vehicles; and also modern pick and high-reach vehicles.
- ✓ Cross-docking is applied in busy summer months; this follows the lead of big retailers who are widely using cross-docking in their warehouses.
- ✓ The same big retailers are forcing Four Seasons (to its benefit) toward standardized pallet sizes, advance shipping notices, and EDI (electronic data interchange) with which the retailer gains access to Four Seasons' inventory files.
- *Customer ID*: Use of customer-specific stickers and sleeves over plain boxes—for customizing finished goods to incoming orders. See Figure 42.2.

III. Opportunities for Improvement

- *Color-coding*: Presently, each production line has its own color, such as orange for R4 compressors.
  - ✓ By extension, for that product, it would make sense for all containers, fixtures, signs, documents, tools, benches, and machines to have at least an orange stripe.

✓ This will help with housekeeping, avoid errors of mis-identification, and can build pride through identification.

- *Cores to pre-wash and tear-down*: Presently, fork-trucked pallets move cores from "Up Top" (the building where incoming cores are stored; also for some WIP inventory) to pre-wash, and two-layer trollies move cores from pre-wash to tear-down. Suggestions (see also Figure 42.3 and Figure 42.4):

  ✓ Use those two-layer trollies also from Up Top to pre-wash. This eliminates the pallet-and-fork-lift method (with wasteful up-and-down handling in large, non-JIT quantities). The two-layer trollies keep work at waist-to-chest level for good ergonomics.

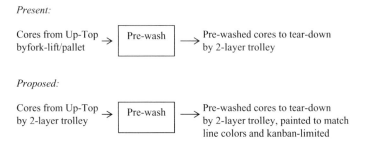

Present:

Cores from Up-Top by fork-lift/pallet → | Pre-wash | → Pre-washed cores to tear-down by 2-layer trolley

Proposed:

Cores from Up-Top by 2-layer trolley → | Pre-wash | → Pre-washed cores to tear-down by 2-layer trolley, painted to match line colors and kanban-limited

FIGURE 42.3
Present and proposed methods of handling cores before and after pre-wash.

FIGURE 42.4
Cores in 2-layer trolley at pre-wash—Four Seasons Manufacturing Co.

✓ Limit the number of trollies—one kanban set of trollies circulating between Up-Top and pre-wash; a different set between pre-wash and tear-down.

✓ Paint the pre-wash/tear-down trollies to match the colors adopted by each line, e.g., five recirculating trollies dedicated to R4 cores, painted with a stripe of R4's color. (A certain amount of color-coding might also have merit for Up Top.)

• *Kanban/buffer stock*: Currently, machined pistons go to the Up Top stockroom and later are picked for delivery to R4 assembly— presenting a good opportunity for kanban:

✓ Outfit, say, a few containers with pigeon holes, the R4 color (e.g., orange), and fixed kanban IDs. In machining, the appearance of an empty orange container with kanban authorizes production, and the full container goes back to R4 assembly.

✓ If machining has a history of significant work stoppages (or differences in hours of machining compared to hours of assembly), then off-line buffer stock of pistons in the stockroom would be okay. Then, machining maintains a record of (or kanban limits) exactly how many containers of pistons are in the stockroom.

✓ See Figure 42.5:

• *Two-hands for safety?*

✓ In hub and spoke, bench-top machines require an operator to load and then reach to hit start buttons with both hands.

✓ Better way—with even more safety, plus higher productivity: Link a pair of nearby machines electrically for the following sequence:

1. Load machine A, but don't start it. Walk to machine B.

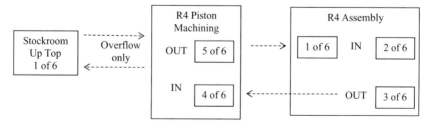

FIGURE 42.5

Five circulating kanban containers: stockroom to R4 piston-machining to R4 assembly, plus one container for off-line buffer stock.

2. Unloading machine B automatically starts A. Load B, but don't start it. Walk to A.
3. Unloading A starts B. Load A, but don't start it. Walk to B. Repeat.

- *Quick setup*: Changeover of the centerless grinder for pulleys in the hub and spoke area takes about ten minutes, involving re-fixturing positions around a large round flat plate. Suggestions:
  ✓ Have duplicate flat plates that are easily lifted on and off, each plate pre-fixtured off-line while the grinder is running. This should cut changeovers to less than a minute, justifying perhaps ten times more changes per day, cutting lot-size inventories accordingly.
  ✓ For dominant pulley models, it may be feasible to have permanently fixtured plates in a nearby rack. For lesser models, fixture a blank plate for the next job while the grinder runs the present job.
- *Lot sizes*: Lots should be reduced in many areas (not needed on R4 line, where tear down and assembly are cell-dedicated, thus absent lot-size issues). Examples:
  ✓ Presently, in HR6 assembly, an associate performs air tests, putting each tested unit into a hole in a wooden rack so it stands upright.
    ■ After filling 12 holes, the associate walks around a bench to water test each of the 12.
    ■ Suggestion: cut the 12-hole rack in half (or make even smaller), which cuts flow time and inventory by nearly half. (Also, move bench closer to the water test?)
  ✓ In several areas, metal carriers near the assembly hold parts that have come out of a wash operation, with parts dumped into plastic trays on assembly benches. Plastic trays are about half of the size of the metal carriers. Suggestions:
    ■ To avoid the extra step of dumping parts from one container to another, drill holes in the plastic trays so parts can be washed in those trays and moved directly to benches. Kanban label the trays for use between assembly and wash, and between wash and Up Top.

- If plastic trays won't tolerate the wash and earlier processes, re-design the metal carriers to hold only half (or less) of the current capacity. They are too large (and hold too much inventory) to be placed on assembly benches.
- *Information displays*: Regarding a plan (Ian Fisher's) for mounting cross-training/certification charts at the ends of each line: Add large trend charts for such metrics as flow time, flow distance, setup times, response ratio, scrap, rework.
- *Small-lot, rate-based scheduling*: Presently, each model is scheduled to run for several hours, or even a couple of days, between changeovers. Suggestion: Get supervisors, lead people, and operators to help eliminate obstacles to running small lots, with model changes, say, every hour—simple ways of restocking the line with different parts, e.g., special labeling, positioning, color-coding.
- *Layout*. A new layout for hub and pulley is in progress—along with Ian's plan for the re-layout of all tear-down, wash, and secondary operations for lines other than the R4 product and for moving the powered conveyor. Suggestion: Plan a second hub and pulley phase—dismantle the shop and integrate its equipment and people into production lines.
  - ✓ This will require extra equipment, but, as stations on assembly lines, some equipment can be dedicated, eliminating changeovers. Increased efficiencies, plus decreased inventories and handling will quickly pay for extra equipment.
  - ✓ With hub and pulley gone, move R4 tear down and assembly cells closer to packing. That makes room for other lines to also move toward packing, which, in turn, provides room to integrate hub and pulley equipment.
  - ✓ The rest of Ian's plan—clustering tear-down cells around component wash, and secondary operations around present powered conveyor—fits well with the above (and it may not be necessary to move the conveyor).
- *Job rotation*: Adopt minimum rotation frequencies in each cell (e.g., daily).
- *Suppliers*:
  - ✓ Seek to reduce the number of suppliers per part or family of parts—e.g., Lehman for boxes.

✓ At 24 bearings per R4 crankshaft, bearing usage is 24,000 per day, bought (from SKF or Timken) in lots of 500,000—a 20-day supply. Why not reduce that by getting deliveries of 125,000 weekly?

- *Purchased parts*: Selectively reduce lot sizes, arrange for kanban deliveries, and establish milk runs. Bearings from SKF may be a good candidate; also, Lehman for boxes.
- *Kanban in Coppell warehouse*: Employ kanban to link an empty pick location to high-reach reserve stocks—following Ray Nichols' ideas.

CHAPTER II-43. EAST BAY GENERATOR, NORTH OAKLAND, CA, 1990

I was escorted to this remanufacturer to see the results of a remarkable turn-around that heavily involved simple, largely visual manufacturing practices.	**High-Interest Topics:** • **Conversion to cells at a remanufacturer of electrical automotive components** • **Cutting search time for parts from six of every eight hours—to zero**

From Bottom to Top Performance in Remanufacture of Auto Parts

Observations based on a brief plant visit, Nov. 11, 1990

I. General Information

- *The company*: Reconditions generators, alternators, starters, carburetors, and other auto electrical parts for the aftermarket.
- *Tour purpose*: A "War of Waste" project, for which consultant Len Bertain had been hired, had uncovered a need to thoroughly change the production process. Len invited me there to see the results of the transformation, which focused on cells for high-volume parts and exceptional core handling for low-volume parts.
- *Contact persons*: Larry Lista, owner-manager; Len Bertain (Bertain Consulting Group), who led training classes and improvement analysis, with help from a UC-Berkeley Haas School of Business student.

II. Transformation*

- *Cell implementation*:
  - ✓ The plant was organized into 14 cells—for the 20% of major P/Ns (part numbers) that produced 80% of revenue:
    - Six cells for the highest-volume starters (e.g., for Ford, Delco, Chrysler, Toyota, among others).
    - Six alternator cells (same carmakers).
    - One carburetor cell.
    - Special cell for new business in parts for trucks, forklifts, and the like. This cell is little used, but worthwhile because it's a high-margin product line.
  - ✓ The cells were completed in two months. No employees were lost in conversion to cells.
  - ✓ Cells are set up so two assemblers can work in one cell (more than two would overcrowd)—allowing for production to react quickly to "elephant orders."
  - ✓ When there is not enough work in a cell, odd jobs serve to keep people busy.
  - ✓ Subcomponents for each type of core are torn down and cleaned up, and those cleaned parts are put into empty boxes and returned to the appropriate cell.
- *Make money on other parts*:
  - ✓ Lowest-volume parts (80% of parts yield only 20% of revenue) are managed differently—based on a realization that profit in this business element comes via optimized handling of cores (returned or failed parts). Thus, it requires bringing in (purchase) cores as cheaply as possible.
    - Great idea: An employee said if they bought parts ahead of time, they could get them for less than $10—compared to the $30 to $50 they had been paying when the customer's need was "now."
    - The revised system has two of each core. When one or two of a requested part is consumed, an empty shoe box is turned upside down, with red-tape showing—a simple, visual kanban that keeps the *right* parts on hand at low core costs.

---

* See related article: Jean V. Owen and Eugene E. Sprow, "The Power of Partnerships," *Manufacturing. Engineering*, April 1994, pp. 33–39.

- When the owner (Larry Lista) orders a large batch of high-demand cores for, say, a Ford or Delco starter or alternator, he also orders one of the low-demand parts and gets a quote; if it's too high, he goes to another supplier. Now, on-hand are over 800 parts (two of each) in a well-organized "cubby-hole" storage area.
- When one of these part orders comes from the customer, they often can get it back to the customer later the same day—and charge a premium.
- Using this strategy, East Bay became the *go-to* shop (among many competitors) for old part replacements—and, as well, the go-to place of other (competing) remanufacturers, which East Bay can supply at premium price.

- *Materials and handling*:
  - ✓ Active finished P/Ns number 500, plus 1,000 not very active ones (with close monitoring for about 800 of them).
  - ✓ Prior to reorganization (layout, materials, etc.), the work force spent six hours of every eight walking, looking for parts, tools, etc.! Now, blue parts bins for high-use parts are located within the cells for *zero search time*; red bins, for buffer overflow purposes, are stored in well-organized racks elsewhere.
  - ✓ Cores (defective units) are purchased from parts stores and repair garages, and then reconditioned. Core deposits are $20 for an "A" item, $50 for a "D" item.
  - ✓ Reconditioned parts are sold to distributors (parts stores), who sell to repair garages, who sell to car owners as part of repairs.
  - ✓ When the cells were formed, 50 loads of 28 barrels of stuff were hauled out.
  - ✓ As a visual aid in purchased stores, users turn an emptied box upside down, a la kanban.
  - ✓ Kanban is balanced to two boxes of parts equaling two weeks of projected consumption; the data comes from previous sales.
    - Cell assemblers adjust that balance as needed; for example, when they observe an increase in demand for one of the cores, they change the number of parts in inventory, up or down.
    - When one box is empty, it goes on top of the kanban rack. When two boxes are there, empty, it's time to rush and catch-up.

- ■ This kanban practice was later adapted by the cells, with the empty box placed on top of the rack in the cell.
- ■ There have been occasional personnel flare-ups in which a new person in a cell doesn't fully understand how it works, but those cases are quickly resolved.
  - ✓ *Testing*: Tests of finished alternators are simple enough that they now are done in starter cells. (Until recently, they were done off-line on expensive test equipment; less-costly equipment may be available, which is to be checked on.)
- • *Training*:
  - ✓ Classes (for the workforce, others) focus on process improvement and include identifying 30 wastes in each class.
  - ✓ Everyone receives a T-shirt for each idea. The first idea was for a wood tool caddy with holes drilled in it for holding tools.
  - ✓ After the third week of training, setup times went from 4.5 to 1.5 hours.
- • *Payoff*:
  - ✓ It takes just two months for the cost and benefit lines to cross.
  - ✓ At the end of every week, the customer is given a bill; if the customer is not satisfied, the arrangement stops.

CHAPTER II-44. ZANUSSI—SUSEGANA AND PORCIA PLANTS, ITALY, 1991

This trip to Italy included a visit to Zanussi's washing-machine plant in Portia, as well as its refrigerator plant in Susegana. Visiting Susegana permitted a comparison with Zanussi's sister refrigeration plant in Firenze (Florence), which is the subject of an earlier caselet, Chapter I-23, based on my visit there in 1989.

High-Interest Topics:
- • **In-plant logistics: three methods matched to three production situations**
- • **Production simplicity facilitating change and improvement; plant complexity and equipment rigidity stifling it**
- • **Woefully wasteful usage of an AS/RS for incoming parts**
- • **White goods industry: behind the times in 1991**

Producing Washing Machines and Refrigerators:
Steps Toward Excellence

Observations based on visits to Susegana and Porcia plants, Oct. 25, 1991

I. General Information

- *The Company*: Zanussi is the Italian arm of Electrolux Corp. of Sweden, among the world's largest major appliance (white goods) manufacturers.
- *My visits*: I had visited various Zanussi plants in three trips to Italy, in 1988, 1989, and 1991.
- *This visit*: I was led to the plant by a colleague, Carlo Baroncelli, of the Milan-based consulting firm, RDA. Our Zanussi hosts sought my/our impressions from the visit to the Porcia washing-machine plant, as well as a comparison of the refrigerator plant in Firenze (Florence) visited in 1989, and its sister plant in Susegana, visited on this 1991 trip.
- *Letter to Zanussi executive*: Following are portions of a thank-you and feedback letter to Mr. Burello, managing director.

October 30, 1991

Dear Mr. Burello:

My visits to Zanussi always seem a bit hurried. After my seminar on October 25, Carlo Baroncelli and I were able to discuss our findings at some length while driving back to Milano and at dinner that evening. I offer, in this letter, a few summary remarks and clarifications, based on those discussions plus my own further thinking.

The Porcia plant *does*, I believe, employ the pull system from fabrication to assembly, and *does* employ something like a kanban system. But there are opportunities to greatly tighten it up, reducing in-plant throughput time by half and slashing logistics costs. Specifically, instead of a single method of in-plant logistics, implement *three* methods:

[*The three methods were included in the letter—and are summarized in Section III of this caselet. After several more paragraphs, the letter continued as follows:*]

While I do not have a lot of great ideas for improving the Susegana operation, my impression is that the beginning and the end are the places where change is easiest and improvement potential greatest. At the beginning, receiving of parts, some possibilities are kanban linkages with suppliers, milk runs, and dock-to-line delivery, bypassing the AS/RS wherever possible. At the end, assembly, I think use of AGVs should be discontinued, and a more conventional tightly linked assembly method adopted. The flow distance and handling costs in assembly alone are, clearly, shockingly high.

[AGV: automatic-guided vehicle. AS/RS: automatic storage and retrieval system]

Finally, I'd like to comment further on trends in white goods over the past decade. I recall early in the 1980s hearing U.S. white-goods managers expressing the view that "white goods is Japan's next target." It didn't happen. Japanese makers were not good enough to attack Western markets. Companies like Matsushita failed to assimilate knowledge (e.g., from automotive and electronics) of how to slash non-value-adding overhead costs. Western white-goods makers, trying to emulate Matsushita, were led down the path of kitting, automatic storage and handling, etc. In contrast, a similar Western industry, office equipment (which I've worked with extensively), took the path of simplification—as well as total quality and supplier partnership.

I hope these few remarks are of some use in Zanussi's continuous-improvement effort. It was my great pleasure to have another opportunity to help fine-tune an already fine company.

II. Assessment, Porcia Washing-Machine Plant

- *Achievements/strengths*:
  - ✓ A significant achievement: Nearly total product focus at the *plant* level
  - ✓ Also, some product focus within the plant, e.g., product-focused assembly lines but with changeover flexibility to run other product models on a focused line.
  - ✓ Excellent paint quality! Impressive automation and quick setup!

✓ The pull system is in use, with periodic reductions in stocks. The plant has open sight lines with visual flows of component parts.

✓ A new self-managed team concept is in implementation.

- *Problems/opportunities/recommendations*:

  ✓ Assembly lines are too long; also, too few *in number* and therefore can make too few of the plant's many models at the same time.

  ✓ Self-managed teams are hampered by a very loose layout, requiring excessive handling, long flow paths, and excessive stock.

  ✓ Excessive within-plant throughput time (about 12 days?). Changes:

  - Put star models on daily rate-based schedules; meet the rate exactly, then stop (over-production should be disallowed, except in special cases).

  - Instead of a single method of in-plant logistics, implement *three* methods:

    1. The present high-cost method—fabrications into WIP storage, with delayed re-handling to assembly, for times when the fabrication shift is operating but assembly is idle.

    2. Direct-deliver components from fabrication to assembly (no storage) during the day shift (or whenever assembly is operating). Omit computer transactions; instead, have a small number of painted kanban containers (or pallets)—a different color for each assembly line—circulate between assembly and fab. For example, the appearance of an empty red container of tubs triggers direct delivery of a full container of tubs (with the tub model noted on a plate riveted to the container) to the red assembly line.

    3. Maintain an inactive emergency buffer of finished, ready-for-assembly components (especially dominant models) in low-cost off-line storage—to be used only for emergencies (machine breakdown, serious quality trouble, etc.) that occur, say, once or twice a month. This off-line stock is necessary, but should not be in the plant consuming throughput time, high-cost space, and administrative costs. Rotate this stock monthly (or every two months).

✓ Put parts suppliers on milk runs, delivering dock-to-line.
✓ The old Porcia plant, still in operation, offers a good place to experiment with kanban and accustom people to it.
✓ Conduct costs audits of each category of washer: high-volume, medium-volume, and low-volume models.
   ■ In these audits, employ ABC overhead allocation, thus to demonstrate the high likelihood that low-volume models cost much more than accounting data shows, and high-volume models much less.
   ■ Make use of the ABC audits for important purposes such as altered pricing, and eliminating money-losing models, or giving avid attention to process improvements that will greatly reduce their overhead costs (e.g., of inventory, handling, or quality). The watchword is *audits*; no need for, or value in, the baggage of an ABC *system*.

III. Comparison, Firenze and Susegana Refrigerator Plants

• *Significant, both sites*: They are highly product-focused at the *plant* level (operations, design, accounting, etc.). But differences between plants are considerable in other ways.
• *Focus within plants*:
   ✓ Assembly/subassembly:
      ■ Firenze has product/model-focused assembly lines, with subassemblies often built on line.
      ■ Susegana has *no* product focus *within* its plant; all resources are in process groupings—with thousands of flow paths and no clear site lines.
   ✓ Firenze's production simplicity allows freedom to pursue an improvement agenda including:
      ■ TQM/employee involvement.
      ■ Rate-based scheduling and kanban materials movement applied to "star" models.
      ■ Cutting WIP and flow distances.
      ■ Extending the product focus to more model families and to support resources.
   ✓ In contrast, Susegana's plant complexity and equipment rigidity make change and improvement costly and difficult.

✓ Firenze's costs are lower than Susegana's.

✓ Among Susegana's (few) advantages over Firenze are a nice "alcove of excellence," displaying high-interest information at the cafeteria entrance and good evidence of in-process quality monitoring.

✓ Susegana was designed according to best strategies in white-goods in 1983-1986, but now it needs extensive changes.*

- *AS/RS at Susegana*:

  ✓ The AS/RS is a huge, many-floor piece of automation to receive parts incoming from suppliers, located on an exterior wall. The plant is highly dependent on those parts to keep assembly lines running. (Susegana is not vertically integrated, so does not produce many components itself.)

  ✓ The AS/RS was obviously very expensive, and operating it is just as expensive in regards to costly idle inventory inside, plus continual handing costs of putting materials in, then taking them out and sending to lines.

  ✓ In a well-managed plant, with many suppliers delivering just-in-time with pre-ordained quality, much or most of the incoming materials should never go into the AS/RS.

    ■ Instead they should be sent directly—perhaps by kanban-limited trollies—to locations on or near the assembly lines.

    ■ Yet the Susegana system requires *all* parts to use the AS/RS, even parts needed that same day or hour. (This is not unique to Zanussi Susegana. I've seen the same at other white-goods plants, and at other companies in other industries.)

  ✓ In short, a top-most action that should be taken at Susegana is to bypass the AS/RS for incoming parts and work with suppliers to time parts arrivals so that most can be sent directly to points of use in fabrication and assembly. This should start with high-use parts and should result in dismantling portions of the AS/RS, section by section.

---

* See also: R. Panizzolo, "Cellular Manufacturing at Zanussi-Electrolux Plant, Susegana, Italy," pp. 475-490, in N.C. Suresh. 1998. *Group Technology and Cellular Manufacturing: A State-of-the-Art Synthesis of Research and Practice*. Kluwer Academic Publishers: Boston.

CHAPTER II-45. AMERICAN STEEL SERVICE CENTER (ASSC), KENT, WA, 1992

American Steel Service Center (AmSteel) is included as a caselet mainly for being a key just-in-time supplier of steel to Genie Industries, (caselet Chapter II-59).	***High-Interest Topics:*** • **Major supplier produces/delivers many steel fabrications "just in time" to top-notch assembler of heavy equipment** • **Remarkably easy "JIT-truck" access to all production/load areas**

High-level Performance of a Contract Manufacturer of Steel Products

Observations from a visit to ASSC by Schonberger, Feb. 22, 1992

Sponsored by IIE Chapter's WCM PIRG

I. General Information

- *ASSC*: A full-line steel service center, ASSC (AmSteel) is a division of American Industries, Inc., headquartered in Portland, OR.
- *Supplier to Genie*: This caselet is focused mostly on AmSteel's special contract supplying steel fabrications to Genie Industries— both located in eastern suburbs of Seattle. (My rough notes contain extensive details about AmSteel's equipment, processes, etc., which makes very dry reading and is mostly excluded from this caselet.)
- *AmSteel employment*: About 50+ employees, most cross-trained; material handlers are trained also as operators.
- *Key AmSteel customer*s: Besides Genie:
  - ✓ Extensive operations with Kenworth (Seattle-based heavy trucks).
  - ✓ Also supplies Hon Industry's Budget Panels, Inc. (BPI) division.
    - History: The old AmSteel owner, unable to handle BPI business, ended up with mountains of ornamental tubing (imported from Japan) and sold it to Hon, who chided AmSteel, saying, "We can't afford your inventory mis-management."
    - The BPI contract is working well now.
- *Contacts*: Michael Schneider, VP; Cheri Golden, quality manager.

II. Genie Contract

- *Genie and AmSteel*: Genie, producer of man-lifts (used in construction), is highly advanced in just-in-time production; and, to support ambitious growth targets, sought out AmSteel as a JIT supplier (it couldn't find others who could do JIT). By 1992, Genie had become AmSteel's largest customer, comprising 25% of its sales. Some Genie details that are relevant to AmSteel:
    - ✓ Genie could not forecast well, which made buying from its multiple suppliers a nightmare (the main issue was suppliers' large-batch delivery practices). So Genie asked if AmSteel would take charge of all Genie's subcontractors. After some hesitation, AmSteel agreed.
    - ✓ Genie did the qualifications and subcontractor selection.
    - ✓ Genie limits itself to being an assembler—but could bring back some parts for in-house fab.
    - ✓ Genie works four days a week (not Fridays); it turns its parts 12 times yearly.
- *Growth of Genie business*:
    - ✓ AmSteel began with about six Genie parts (flame cut, out for welding, back to AmSteel...JIT to Genie), which is now up to 1,200 finished parts and 2,000 unfinished parts.
    - ✓ AmSteel is almost the sole supplier to Genie, which has only one other supplier, a fabricator with only 10% of AmSteel's Genie volume.
- *AmSteel support*:
    - ✓ AmSteel has a separate Genie sales team, headed by Tom Blue, with its own PC-based system for ordering, logistics, etc.
    - ✓ AmSteel also has a focused Genie team in the plant, and focused Genie transportation, delivering daily.
    - ✓ George West, Genie VP manufacturing, went to AmSteel to train them in total quality and SPC.
- *Competition*:
    - ✓ There are many "phone booth 2%'ers" who buy, inventory, and ship (no manufacturing processes).
    - ✓ On the other hand, AmSteel is highly capital intensive (lots of processing and component assembly).

- ■ It aims for a 20% margin by adding value, including through *service*—JIT deliveries, quality, tolerances, and expertise of sales people "who understand JIT process."
- ■ Customers who want the cheapest-price-only may go elsewhere, e.g., to someone's one-man job shop.
- *Logistics*:
  - ✓ Some parts have only a one-hour window to shut down Genie.
  - ✓ Everything for Genie is kanban-packaged with shipping carts loaded for shipment.
  - ✓ AmSteel loads, by crane and forklift, eight to ten double-trailer curtain vans, and delivers daily, which Genie unloads "in parking lot in the rain by forklift only."
  - ✓ Genie is committed to take what AmSteel has in process:
    - ■ AmSteel buys for Genie based on a 90-day forecast.
    - ■ Racks of inventory for Genie hold 30 days' supply, on average.
    - ■ At one point, Genie *chose* to shut down one of its lines for 90 days, but it *did take the inventory* from AmSteel anyway.
  - ✓ Cubic space issue: Too many boxes hold too much air; AmSteel copes by maxing out *cube* before tonnage in the trailer, which is unusual in the industry.
  - ✓ Instead of the industry-typical 80% service (20% on backorder), the entire order of weldments is shipped every time; no partials.
- *For Genie*:
  - ✓ Since the Genie contract, flame cutting in AmSteel's burning department has 2% less scrap, which owed largely to the repetitiveness of the work.
  - ✓ Genie had been sending out about 18 four-inch-thick counter-weights for hole-drilling; AmSteel, however, bought a big drill press to do this for Genie.
  - ✓ At one point, 60-ft. long booms were over-forecasted by Genie, so lots of specialty-made inventory ended up on hand (about 20 booms in stock) between Genie and AmSteel.
  - ✓ AmSteel maintains many high-tensile chromium-plated pivot pins, one piece at a time—with a kit map alongside.
  - ✓ Genie wants 99.99% of ordering, etc., to be on-line.

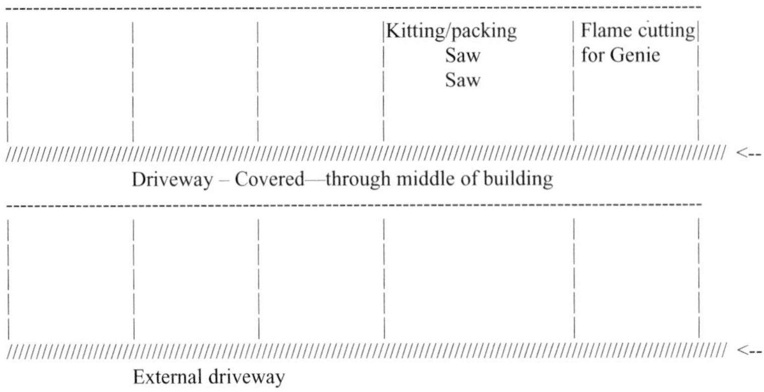

```
---------------------------------------------------------------------------
|              |              |              |Kitting/packing| Flame cutting|
|              |              |              |     Saw       | for Genie    |
|              |              |              |     Saw       |              |
|              |              |              |               |              |
|              |              |              |               |              |
///////////////////////////////////////////////////////////////////////////////  <--
         Driveway – Covered—through middle of building
---------------------------------------------------------------------------
|              |              |              |               |              |
|              |              |              |               |              |
|              |              |              |               |              |
|              |              |              |               |              |
|              |              |              |               |              |
///////////////////////////////////////////////////////////////////////////////  <--
              External driveway
```

Key:
////////// Driveways: One between production buildings,
the second just outside one of the two buildings

FIGURE 45.1
AmSteel - Rough plant layout.

- *AmSteel layout*: Figure 45.1 shows a covered driveway down the middle of the plant, with production operations (only minimally shown in a couple of the bays) on either side—providing remarkably quick and easy access (little or no waiting) for just-in-time pickups and deliveries.

III. Opportunities for Improvement

- *Inventory*: Lot sizes are too large (15% to 30% based on EOQs); the total inventory is also excessive (only about 3.5 inventory turns). To cope:
  - ✓ Put "star" component parts on regular-slot scheduling.
  - ✓ Go to Genie with a deal for them to cut finished inventories, for stars first, by one or two weeks.
  - ✓ Use the third shift as catch-up.
- *High inventory-to-people ratio*: With high inventories as a cover, employees need not be highly efficient—doing things in the right just-in-time sequence, with perfect performance. But AmSteel would benefit a good deal from various efficiency-enhancing practices. For example:
  - ✓ Along with reducing inventories, AmSteel should establish strong visual management, aimed especially at improving long, complex work flows, long and undisciplined setup times, causes of rework, etc.

✓ Visuals should include the "seven basic tools" (fishbone charts, Paretos, check sheets, etc.) and trend charts tracking setup times, cross-training matrices, and so forth.

CHAPTER II-46. MAZAK CORP., U.S., FLORENCE, KY, 1992

The Mazak plant tour was arranged on the spur of the moment and did not result in the usual plant-tour report. Rather, two days later, I sent a thank-you letter to a Mazak executive in which I expressed admiration for the company's strengths and also offered impressions of "gaps and opportunities" for improvement. That letter (slightly edited), led by an introductory section, serves as the caselet for this Mazak facility.

High-Interest Topics:
- **Cutting numbers of final assemblies in process and moving them into and out of assembly fast**
- **Reducing trips in and out of AS/RS's; a preference for simple, small, and quick**
- **An alternate way of impressing customers: press for employee involvement in the midst of CIM**

Moving toward Simpler, Quicker Flows at an Advanced Machine Tool Manufacturer

Viewpoints based on a brief plant tour, evening of Nov. 5, 1992

In connection with a Schonberger two-day public seminar in Cincinnati, Nov. 5-6, 1992

I. General Information

- *Company and products*: According to the company website, Yamazaki Mazak, producer of metalworking machine tools, had opened its Florence, KY, manufacturing facility in 1974 in order to "meet the unique requirements of the [North American] region". Its primary products are vertical and horizontal machining centers and turning centers, and the CIM (computer-integrated manufacturing) mode.
- *Processes*: The large plant includes three equipment centers, which include plentiful usages of AS/RS (automatic storage and retrieval) units:
  ✓ Sheet metal: CNC laser cutting; press-brake cells; robotic welding and grinding; eight-step paint line; subassembly; and computerized storage and handling.

✓ Metal cutting: A shaft and flange line with a gantry robot, which includes multi-process turning (with AS/RS handling), a frame line with five-face milling machines (with AS/RS handling), and ship removal.

✓ AS/RS: This builds kits for efficient assembly and delivers the kits to assembly, with computerized monitoring of inventory levels.

- *Tour arrangements*: Jack Meredith, professor, University of Cincinnati, set up the tour for six of us: five doctoral students, and me. Robert Ralston, Mazak VP manufacturing, was the local host.

II. Follow-up Letter to Robert Ralston

November 7, 1992

Dear Mr. Ralston:

Thanks very much for the plant tour Thursday evening. Since it is my habit to take notes and then summarize them, I am pleased to convey my brief summary to you, for what little it might be worth.

In general, my reaction is one of awe, mixed with excitement about what may be opportunities for further improvement, especially by adding a few "excellence" concepts to your agenda and, to some extent, shifting emphasis. I'll not elaborate on the many strengths of Mazak and your plant; you probably hear enough glowing comment to keep your egos well fed. Instead, I'll stick to my impressions of gaps and opportunities, which I presume would be more helpful (if they are at all valid).

1. Too much cash tied up in too many units in final assembly, taking too long to be completed. Too few assemblers per machine may be part of the reason.

   Makers of mainframe computers, high-end copiers, mass spectrometers, nuclear magnetic imaging machines, and the like—about as technologically complex as CNC machines—use larger assembly teams. Some associates will be doing subassemblies (modules) on kanban squares surrounding the main assembly unit. Those subs will be built, tested, and installed while assembly is also being done on the end product. One priority is getting units on and off the kanban squares with dispatch. For about the same monthly volume of units completed as Mazak-U.S., these makers will have only, say, half a dozen units in final assembly at any one time.

2. Too much multiple handling of too many parts in too many costly AS/RSs. Apple Macintosh was doing the same thing as your plant: sending all incoming parts into its tote stacker, even those to be used the same day. My proposed change in procedure (suggested to Apple a few years ago) is to adopt these priority rules:

   • All fab/machined or purchased parts try first to move directly to a value-adding destination; if none is available, detour into *overflow* storage (at Apple, this meant staging empty kanban carts in the receiving area, in position to directly intercept incoming parts, or to pull from the tote stacker).

   • If partially available, send partial load of parts to the value-adding operation and the rest into overflow storage (the AS/RS).

     Another way, related to this, is to equip all subassembly and final assembly bays with gravity flow racks, each capable of holding a small number of (e.g., one to five) units of a high-use item. This is what I expect to see, and do see, in showcase plants around the country, probably including plants of some of your best customers: simple, low-cost solutions aimed at avoiding "the seven wastes."

3. Continuous improvement in products and manufacturing technology is clearly a Mazak strong suit. But continuous improvement (a la TQM) in processes and procedures does not seem to be getting the same kind of emphasis that it gets in, say, a Baldrige award company or plant. For example, your plant seems to need a high visibility campaign, fed by large wall trend charts (not slogans) everywhere—to slash throughput times, flow distances, inventories, storages, multiple handlings—and to engage all associates in the effort. Since the emphasis on these kinds of improvements—employing visual management—is common in North American industry today (much more so than in Europe, Asia, and maybe even Japan), it would seem to make good marketing sense for Mazak-U.S. to do likewise.

4. Plant is extremely neat and clean, but seems very crowded and therefore difficult to re-configure and continuously improve: Just an observation; I haven't enough information to suggest a solution.

   Congratulations to you and your colleagues on running a class manufacturing business. I hope my comments are some way helpful. Thanks again for the excellent tour and discussion.

   Sincerely,   Richard J. Schonberger   cc. Prof. Jack Meredith

CHAPTER II-47. AMERICOLD, GULLMAN, AL, 1999

This caselet includes a large "Opportunities-for-Improvement" section made up of highly-specific suggestions. A consulting firm, RMI, Inc., had been working with Americold, and my impression is that RMI is like-minded and would welcome these suggestions and be of great help to Americold in implementing many of them.

High-Interest Topics:
- **Coping with legacies of 1950s-80s: poor plant designs and clutter**
- **Making a case—to a strongly unionized work force—for the job-saving competitive advantages of multi-skilling**
- **Multifaceted "wake-up call" for avoiding outsourcing**

Obstacles to Concurrent Production in Compressor Manufacturing

Observations based on an evening plant visit, Dec. 6, 1999

Followed by a next-day Schonberger seminar on
"World Class by Principles" in Huntsville, AL

I. General Information

- *Americold*: Subsidiary of Sweden-based Electrolux with facilities in Italy.
- *Product line*: Compressors for refrigerators in 126 models, ten accounting for 90% of volume; a compressor weighs 22 lbs., sells for about $32.
- *Gullman plant*: 500,000 sq. ft. with 750 employees, 600 of them direct labor; the plant operates three shifts, excepting some equipment that has faster output rates.
- *Sister plant*: An Athens, TN, plant produces motors that go with the compressors.
- *Workforce*: Unionized—IAM (International Association of Machinists)—with more than 100 job classifications and sometimes ten different grades within a classification.
- *Customers*: 60% to Frigidaire; other main customers include Whirlpool and G.E. (which has a refrigerator plant in nearby Decatur, AL); its minor export volume there goes mainly to South America, Middle East, and Taiwan.

- *Output and seasonality*: The plant produces about 17,000 compressors a day (four million a year). Higher refrigerator sales in the warmer construction season generate a seasonal high of 20,000 per day in March, April, and May, met by building inventory in December, January, and February via upping the daily rate from 17,000 to 20,000.
- *Main competitors*: Matsushita, in addition to Korea's Lucky Goldstar (coming on strong based on lower costs/prices). Compressors from each differ little in design, functionality, quality, and durability.
- *Machining*: Organized and laid out by component family: Crank case, shaft, piston, upper and lower shell, valve plate, bearing plate, etc. The main purchased components include lower and upper cast-metal shells and pistons made from powdered-metal blanks that require machining and fabrication (e.g., hole drilling/boring, slot cutting, milling, grinding; welded tube, bracket, and electrical jack installation).
- *Assembly*: This air-conditioned area of the plant (protection against rust) has a 30-year-old line for low-volume, high-mix models (which go into dehumidifiers, etc.), and a 15-year-old line for high-volume, low-mix models—producing 2,800 units and 3,200 units per shift respectively. High-volume models are built and shipped daily, the production cycle and station work content time being 7.5 seconds.
- *Quality*: In the field a small percentage of compressors fall to early-life failure; survivors tend to last, along with the refrigerator, many years without failure. In achieving this level of quality, fab and assembly include components being heat-treated, aligned, realigned, matched, checked for fit, cleaned, dried, purged, pressure-tested, and so on.
- *Storage*: FGI (finished-goods inventory) is about 50,000 units, rising to 120,000 in anticipation of the busy spring season. In later stages of assembly, about 3,500 parts are up the in the air on conveyor hangers.
- *Tour group*: Led by Martyn Acreman, director of manufacturing and of customer operations; George Hamilton (Hamilton and four other Americold managers attended my RMI-sponsored WCP seminar the next day); Dr. Maruf Rahman and partner George Rittenhouse of RMI, Inc., who were instrumental in arranging the visit.

II. Impressions/Comments

- *Strengths*:
  - ✓ Plant and corporate management have developed an "Americold Manufacturing Vision" featuring the fundamentals of world-class excellence, evidenced in part by a component family focus in machining and fabrication.
  - ✓ Also, in a separate building, a three-person cold-header team schedules its own production, orders its own materials, and, largely, manages itself.
- *Issues*: Plant managers (and visitors) are aware of many difficult-to-deal-with deficiencies:
  - ✓ A legacy of poor (but conventional in the 1950s–1980s era) plant design (an overly-large plant designed for non-value-adding fork trucking and powered conveying); layout (some component focus but no end-model or volume focus); equipment choices (dictated by Italy); job design (hemmed in by excessive job descriptions and boring, highly repetitive assembly tasks).
  - ✓ Retention of many models that clutter schedules without paying their way.

III. Opportunities for Improvement

- *Modular strategy*: Mr. Acreman suggested that Americold differentiate itself from competitors by the following proposal to customers: Americold take over certain value-adding operations now done by customers, thus to deliver a more complete compressor module for simple plug-in assembly in refrigerator plants.
  - ✓ This seemingly smart plan, however, would add to the plant's already excessive number of operations, employees, layout complexity, and non-value-added handling, among other areas.
  - ✓ Alternatively, Americold should do more outsourcing—get its suppliers to fabricate and deliver whole modules to Americold.
- *Complexity*: The current assembly line is a throwback to the past—far too long with excessive operations, people, flow distance, inventory, powered conveyor (holding lots of WIP, and requiring maintenance), etc. It may be feasible to shorten the assembly line by a factor of four or five:

- ✓ Re-layout portions of fab and assembly by product model and/or volume—aiming for two or more largely self-contained product-focused plants-in-a-plant.
- ✓ Push more assembly steps back into machining/fabrication cells, thus delivering more complete modules to the assembly line, further reducing the number of assembly steps.
- ✓ Relocate many steps into small cells stemming from the main line—doing this a little at a time, while maintaining output and quality and avoiding a lot of cost and retraining.
    - Each small cell then acts as small business-within-the-business, coupled to the assembly line in a pull relationship.
    - Every cell-team member ends up with at least three times the current work content (i.e., at least 3 x 7.5 seconds, or 22.5 seconds), greatly reducing extremely boring jobs prone to repetitive motion injuries.
- ✓ Remove overhead conveyor segments, while still allowing necessary time for air-drying. (If air drying is not a goal, then most conveyor should be eliminated). As one Americold person put it: move the "dungeon" in the rafters down to floor level.
- *War room*: Set total throughput time and flow distance as dominant performance measures; track these on trend charts (monthly) in management "war rooms."
- *ABC*: Have finance do careful activity-based costing audits of samples of the many low-volume models—as a lead-in to action on eliminating many money-losers (a highly likely result of the cost audits) from product line.
- *Labor force/labor union*:
    - ✓ Take union officials and opinion leaders to plants having only two or three "broad-band" job classifications—with the aim of eliminating 95% of the present classifications and paving the way for multi-skilled associates. Present this as a key to work-life security; more lines on one's resume should a resume be needed some time.
    - ✓ Propose a pilot project in a small and largely self-directed work cell, including job rotation, and with volunteers becoming multi-skilled and perhaps with pay by skill.
    - ✓ Treat the safety aspects of TPM and 5S as initial ways to get the workforce involved in process improvement.

✓ Make quick setup/changeover a part of the job of every operator, with the aid of videotape cameras for them to study and improve their own setups, and assisted by RMI kaizen events. Post setup trend charts widely and require that setups be regularly timed and charted.

✓ Assign to maintenance a responsibility for facilitating a transition of PM to the operators—perhaps proposing this to the IAM as a pilot project.

✓ Polyurethane some of the floor and have machine operators participate in eliminating oil leaks, thereby cutting places where the floor is slippery and a safety hazard.

✓ Train union officials and direct-labor leaders in JIT, kanban, cells, etc., to gain their help in launching these efforts.

✓ Find ways to gain IAM acceptance for use of temps, thus to mitigate part of the inventory build-up that occurs prior to each spring busy season (exchange inventory for labor); show that lean on inventory improves competitiveness, and thus job security.

- *Kanban*:
  ✓ Propose kanban deliveries to key accounts (Frigidaire, G.E., etc.).
  ✓ Get suppliers of shells, piston blanks, hardware, and other key items to deliver by kanban—no purchase orders.

- *Flat-rate JIT scheduling*:
  ✓ For all 7-to-10 dominant product models, adapt production scheduling to a flat rate, a smoothed representation of customers' actual jerky schedule.

  ✓ The rate stays the same every day, every shift, every hour—changeable no more often than bi-weekly (better yet, monthly)—with no work orders.

  ✓ In this, Americold would need to hold additional finished stock to handle peak weeks but with large reductions in WIP and purchased materials in return.

  ✓ (Important caveat: by the standards of 2018 [i.e., the concurrent production concept], producing to a rate with extra FGI to cover actual jerky customer usage is seen as greatly over-done because it lengthens flow times and doesn't produce in synchronization with customer needs. Concurrent production calls for many more production lines, cells, etc., so that many product models can be made simultaneously*)

---

* R.J. Schonberger and K.A. Brown, "Missing Link in Competitive Research and Practice: Customer-Responsive Concurrent Production," *Journal of Operations Management*, 49/51 (March, 2017): 83–87.

- *Avoiding outsourcing*:
  - ✓ Finally, with existing and growing global cost pressures, plus lack of distinguishing advantages of Americold compressors, it is troubling to consider the likelihood that corporate will begin shrinking the plant and moving production to Mexico— avoidable if many of the above kinds of improvements are aggressively pursued.
  - ✓ Current senior management at Americold has the experience and know-how, with wise counsel and assistance and kaizens from RMI, Inc., to lead the plant out of the danger zone.

CHAPTER II-48. SENTROL, INC., PORTLAND (TIGARD), OR, 1992

This highly detailed caselet reports on Sentrol, Inc., one of the standouts of the book. My post-tour report to the company was written up in outline form with many abbreviations. The outline form remains, but with clarified terms and wording.	*High-Interest Topics:* • **Roller-skate kanban** • **Avoidance of kitting; removal of work orders, labor reporting, robot, conveyor, AS/RS** • **Many simple warning systems (lights, time limits) for quality and stoppages**

Simplifying Flow management at a Manufacturing of Security Devices

Based on 1.75-hour plant visitation, Sept. 22, 1992

In connection with a next-day Schonberger
seminar sponsored by Portland APICS

I. General Information

- *The company*: Sentrol, in the Tigard suburb of Portland since about 1977, was bought by Berwind Industries of Nashville, a member of Berwind Group of Philadelphia. (Berwind began as a coal mining company in 1874. By the late 1950s, the owners could see little opportunity for growth in coal, and so embarked on a strategy of leasing mines to others and diversifying into other businesses, now including Sentrol.)

- *Products*: Sentrol focuses on manufacturing monitored sensor devices—for safety, health, fire (e.g., smoke detectors), emergency, security, and age.
  - ✓ Began making magnetic contactors for burglar alarms.
  - ✓ Expanded into glass-break detection, infra-red motion detection.
  - ✓ Bought ESL's smoke detector business.
- *Business units*: Sentrol, with 450 employees, is organized into four product-focused business units.
- *Customers/accounts*: Sentrol sells to national accounts and distributors, focusing on its "top 500" dealers.
- *Ratings*: Two recent industry surveys involving Sentrol and 40 competitors named Sentrol as first in customer satisfaction, value, quality, and service.
- Contacts: Cliff Licko, VP production; Mike Fossey, VP engineering.; Jim Cook, financial officer; John Hakanson, sales and marketing; Danny Charlton, psychologist/team empowerment.

II. Key Processes

- *Engineering/DFM*:
  - ✓ Engineering mirrors the business-unit structure of the division into four product-line groups (except for centralized engineering documentation).
  - ✓ DFM (design for manufacture) was launched by Mike Fossey—with early involvement of MEs (manufacturing engineers).
- *World-class manufacturing (WCM)*:
  - ✓ This initiative was begun in 1988 when Cliff Licko, formerly with Rainbird in California, came to Sentrol. According to Fossey, Licko was "a breath of fresh air."
  - ✓ (Rainbird had sent people to my Southern California and Tijuana seminars, and its managers had arranged dinners with me there, but they resisted my visiting their plants because of secretive company policies; so no Rainbird caselet in this book.)
- *WCM in operation*:
  - ✓ Shipping is in the center of the Building 2 plant, and is surrounded by 13 self-contained work cells, with about 200 products per cell/family; all cells are U-shaped or serpentine.

- ✓ Incoming orders are printed out in a U-shaped order-receive-pick-and-fill cell, using the configure-to-order method with kanban squares (associates set the kanban levels).
- ✓ Velcroed kanbans are pulled off a wall order board (no need for a shop-floor control system). Each cell has one or two orange clipboards for orders, each order color coded.
- ✓ Parts come by roller-skate kanban from the purchased-parts stock room to the cells—a roller skater being eight times faster than a walker.
- ✓ Each cell has a kanban table divided by a line down middle into an empty side (where the skater places the kanban quantity) and the full side—a two-bin twin-container kanban system with raw material quantity matched to the build quantity. See photo, Figure 48.1.
- ✓ In 1987, work orders and labor reporting were eliminated.
- *Inventory performance*:
  - ✓ Inventory turnover had been terrible at 1.78: 13 weeks of FGI, six weeks of WIP; with $28m sales volume.
  - ✓ Now (under WCM) it's three days of FGI, four hours of WIP and $65m sales.

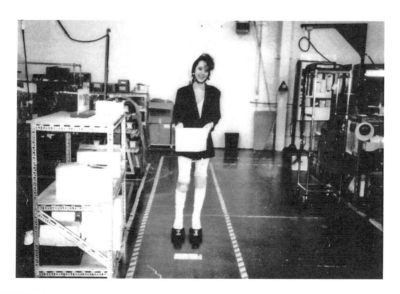

FIGURE 48.1

Roller-skate kanban: Skater is just about to deliver full container of parts from the stock room to an empty zone on the top shelf of a parts rack at Sentrol, Inc.

- *Example cell*:
  - ✓ In a cell producing magnetic contact switches, thousands are built per day by four teams. The least busy team (having the emptiest kanban area) takes the next job.
  - ✓ The 15-to-20-second cycle per unit was seen as too repetitive, so they build five at a time.
  - ✓ The cell bought 25 small marking machines, replacing one huge machine, which cut a two-minute setup to ten seconds.
  - ✓ On every table is a "reject" kanban. In case of defect problem (a unit placed in the reject kanban box), a five-step line shutdown procedure is in force (a team may be allowed five defects in a day):
    1. If reject box gets up to five, a yellow light is turned on and a record is made on a sheet; a yellow requires a team meeting.
    2. For a red light, a horn is sounded twice, MEs and the team advisor get there within one minute; purchasing and other support are summoned, too. (Each team advisor—formerly called supervisor—has 40–50 employees.) The time window to resolve a Level 2 problem is two hours. Sign off is required to re-start the line.
    3. For a Level 3 problem, call the manufacturing manager (the resolution could be, say, bring a machine in from...). Sign off to re-start the line.
    4. In a Level 4 problem, the customer can't be served in a week—a serious hit to customer service.
    5. In Level 5, something of poor quality was sent to a customer, so call the company president.

III. Performance Measurement/Management

- *Status*: 13 status boards, all alike, are at each cell/team, for use *by the associates*: They show and track:
  1. *Schedule performance*: A graph shows empty bins at the start of the day and filled bins at the end of day, both with a comfort zone and a discomfort zone; when bins get up to the discomfort zone, it may mean that "we need to work OT on Saturday," for example.
  2. *Customer service-level*: Chart showing the number of customers on backlog at the end of the day (orange clipboard); the chart shows this for total lines and kanban lines.

3. *Quality*: Number of defects (for *any* reason) daily; examples: latch, sonic weld, shorts, low (two units), dead (1447 PPM)—all set up on a Lotus spreadsheet (a production associate did the program).
4. *Weekly quality*: This is summarized weekly on an undated Pareto chart. Also weekly is a half-hour quality meeting with root cause analysis; every associate has been trained in problem-solving and corrective action; implement if acceptable.
5. *Monthly quality*, Pareto chart.
6. *Productivity*: For example, output per time unit.
7. *Scrap*, expressed as a rate or quantity per time unit.
8. *Defects*, Pareto chart and/or rate.
9. *Cross-training matrix*: Key: <u>0</u> learning, $\pm$ has experience, $\stackrel{*}{-}$ expert, <u>T</u> ability to train others. As part of a new six-step training effort, the team develops brief written descriptions of each task and time required to learn it (e.g., subassembly, 80 hours).
10. *Line shut-down*: Pareto chart.
11. *Periodic housekeeping*: Organized like a spider diagram, only in a taller form (they may cease or outgrow this chart).
12. For 12 and 13, I have no notes.

- *Other (standard) measures*: Production associates have developed units per hour as one performance measure; others are productivity, defects, scrap, PPM (parts per million defective), first-pass yield (meaning "anywhere on the line, not just at last station").

IV. Purchasing

- *Buyers*: Three are located in the security manufacturing building, one for each product line.
- *Deliveries*: 20 vendors (plating, coltage, and springs) are on dock-to-stock, or direct to the line/cell.
- *Ordering authorization*: Some associates phone the supplier.
- *Quantities*: Sentrol is trying to issue according to production in suppliers' quantities or multiples thereof.

V. Smoke Detector Building (Bldg. 1)

- *New product line/new business*: The ESL Power Supplies product line was bought in 1991 from ADT (a distribution company) and moved from the East Coast to Tigard; initial Tigard production began in Sept. 1991. As a new smoke-detector business, it is three years behind in WCM applications—but is progressing quickly.

- *Production*: 13,000 last week (2,980 in one day)—with a 445-second station cycle time (CT) for the star model.
- *Former setup*: The line was 250-feet long, with a lot size of 12,000 for 124 models, and a frozen six-week schedule.
- *First new layout*: Seven cells, each of 30–40 people:
  - ✓ 300 series, ducts, bases, board insertion, 1,400 units per day—for OEM's, national accounts, and distributors.
  - ✓ 400 series, photoelectric system detectors, 2,000 units per day—for security-equipment distributors.
  - ✓ 600 series photo/ion/thermal, interchangeable detectors, 600 units per day, European market.
  - ✓ Also: 600 series duct detectors; 600 series bases: 1,500 series control panels; and accessories.
- *Opportunities*: Five to eight people were placed in "opportunity groups" (opportunity for improvement, or OFI).
- *Kanban and kitting*: Kanban pull is quick and daily. There is no kitting. The explanation:
  - ✓ Kitting is widely used in lean/flow, but I and others—since the early 1980s—point out that it adds inventory, double handling, non-value-add people, opportunities for mistakes, and costs.
  - ✓ So it's better to send parts directly to points of use.
  - ✓ If there are too many parts for that, it suggests a need for standardization or another method to reduce parts' congestion at value-adding stations.
  - ✓ Kitting can serve as valued but *temporary* means of avoiding confusion and mistakes at points of use.
- *Kanban*: Kanban applications for production of finished goods is shown on big display boards. Indented BOMs (bills of materials) serve as natural kanban points.
- *Pull system details*:
  - ✓ Raw material: There are two kanbans per P/N. The kanban quantity equals a multiple of the supplier quantity. The target is one or two days per kanban with the kanban level set at less than $1,000.

- ✓ For cell to cell kanban, the target is less than one days' worth for a high-volume item; equal to the demand quantity for a low-volume item.
- ✓ WIP: adjust the kanban quantity to balance the line.
- ✓ Finished goods: The kanban target for high-volume items is three to four weeks; for low-volume, three months; each color, approximately three months; for make-to-order, the production quantity is the OEM's and national accounts' quantity.
- *Wave soldering*: four wave-soldering machines, each across an aisle from four customer cells.
- *Touch-up*: five associates are in touch-up (in the "gang" production mode); after three minutes there, a yellow light illuminates (but no need for help).
- *Simplifying*: Removed a robot, conveyor belt, AS/RS, and other overly complex, unneeded devices.
- *300 line*: Mixed-model on one side, dedicated on the other.
- *Special-label orders*: A kanban board has three colors, red meaning three weeks until due, yellow meaning two until due, and green meaning one until due.
- *Movability*: A staking machine is on wheels for easy moves to where needed.

VI. Miscellaneous

- *Quick-setup welder*: Setup takes one second on an ultrasonic welder, with two stop positions and a Teflon coated ramp.
- *Passive infrared cell*: With two teams/cells for three products, associates get up and move cell to cell; a circuit-board supplier delivers daily.
- *Forecast accuracy*: Improved forecasting, aimed at the four product lines, is done by item and part number. This detail is desirable for improved planning and stocking of purchased materials.
- *Mario issued edict*: Nothing higher than five feet (Mario is short, needs to see over it); one guy took a hacksaw to an eight-foot rack and cut it in half.
- *Staffing*:
  - ✓ Old: there was 86% turnover of front-line associates; now, very little. 70% of salaried staff have been at Sentrol less than two years

- ✓ Because of a lumpy order stream, the company uses 10-20% temporaries.
- ✓ Sales and marketing is organized into three geographically-focused teams.
- ✓ There are only three people in MIS, two in HR.
- *Job classes/grades*: Job classifications have been cut from 37 to 5 to 1, pay grades from 5 to 3 to 1.
- *Performance pay*:
  - ✓ Formerly, there was performance pay for individual performance; now, it is 25% for teams, 75% for team members, and a bonus paid monthly.
  - ✓ A management incentive is based on a three-year average: 70% for growth and profit, 20% for cash/assets, 10% for sales growth.
- *Rolling the dice*: Every associate—including engineering, sales, and marketing—plays Tom Billesbach's JIT-focused dice game. (Billesbach, a professor at NW Missouri University, has been a close colleague who sometimes joined me in conducting WCM seminars, or who gave the seminars, himself, upon my referral. Tom is excellent at this—with a witty repartee that engages the audience. Sentrol people probably attended a Billesbach seminar.)
- *TPM and costing transactions*: Total productive maintenance (TPM) has begun. There's been no backflush costing yet.
- *Celebration for space reduction*: The plant achieved a 35% space reduction a while back, and Cliff spent $6,000 to hire Johnny Limbo and the Lug Nuts for a dance celebration.

CHAPTER II-49. DEACERO, MONTERREY, MÉXICO, 1998

This very short caselet, concerning a company in Mexico that makes steel wire, is included in this book mainly for two standout features: kanban squares governing huge steel coils and an excellent and innovative team method for doing long changeovers.

High-Interest Topics:
- **Kanban squares trigger replenishment of huge rolls of coiled wire**
- **Frequent setups of large machines are borrow-your-neighbor efforts.**
- **Eliminated incentive pay, raised average wage, saw output go up!**

**Steel Products Manufacturer's Excellence in Quick Setup and
Use of Kanban**

Summary observations based on a plant visit, afternoon of Sept. 9, 1998

**In connection with a one-day seminar, Sept. 10, hosted by
Sintec Consultores of Monterrey**

I. General

- *Contact persons*: Raul M. Gutierrez, director general and son of the founder; Juan Carlos Alvarez Guerro, director of operations, Monterrey plant.
- *The company*: DeAcero, the largest metals company in Mexico, has plants in four cities with total employment of 2,063 people, 1,800 of them blue collar. (DeAcero means "of steel.")
  - ✓ DeAcero, now the leader in its industry, was not among the leaders 15–20 years ago.
  - ✓ DeAcero has no distribution centers but has many small distributors all over Mexico with direct local service. It has large numbers of end products (5,000 in 30 families), because it needs to be a full-line provider to those many small distributor-customers.
  - ✓ Incentive pay: Gutierrez says they axed the incentive pay plan (averaging 15% incentives) a few years ago, raising all pay 20%— and production went up!
- *Monterrey plant*:
  - ✓ The product line is wire, fences, chain, and nails.
  - ✓ DeAcero's mini-mill in Saltillo delivers large spools of raw wire (six types, two gauges) to Monterrey by kanban ("e-lote" in Spanish) squares—actually circles here; see photo, Figure 49.1. Upon delivery, an empty square is a visual signal for Saltillo to deliver more in the next truck. (Since trucks probably come every day, it may be the driver's job to see the empty kanban and convey the need to the Saltillo steel plant.)
  - ✓ Fabrication uses 35 spools per day (formerly 30 per day):
    - The cold-drawing department has five old vertical drawing machines called coilers, which run at 12 meters/sec.; and five new (five- to six-years-old) horizontal drawing machines called spoolers that run at 20 meters/sec.

FIGURE 49.1
Kanban "circles" at DeAcero—empties signaling need for the steel plant to deliver more.

- To avoid pickling, new machines called de-scalers scrape the scale. Next step are two galvanizing lines (one old, one new) with hydrochloric acid cleaning.
- Quality: After six adjustments, the coil goes to fine drawing.
✓ Final assembly: This large area is where finished wire becomes fences and related products on 70 large, wide-reach final assembly machines, which, given the many product types, are frequently undergoing changeovers.
  - The longest changeover is 14 hours the quickest is 80 minutes.
  - Changeovers are remarkable—a team effort: each of the 70 machines has an overhead light, which is turned on 30 minutes or so before the current product's run is complete. The light alerts teammates nearby that their help with the next change is soon. At changeover time two (maybe more), operators do the change as a team—thus considerably speeding up the job.
  - An accumulator allows for changing a reel while the machine is still producing. Hand-screwing unfastens the roll housing.

- On plastic protective-fence machines, setup time has been cut from 180 minutes to 20 minutes.
- Operators are given chairs to sit on. Gutierrez doesn't worry about idleness; sitting means the machine is running fine!

✓ Chain: A new chain-production building was just opened a few weeks ago:

- Three chain machines.
- The machine forms a link, welds one way, welds the other way, deburrs, and progresses to a 100% strength test.

✓ Nail department: seven machines, one operator:

- Primary customer is Senco, Cincinnati.
- Boxes of nails are on kanban; MRO (maintenance, repair, and operating supplies) too.

CHAPTER II-50. OPW FUELING COMPONENTS DIVISION OF DOVER CORP, CINCINNATI, OH, 1993

This caselet is lengthy and comprehensive because I had a full day (plus some time after my plane arrived the prior day) for the plant visit and discussions with many managers. As it is, I've omitted some of the material that was in my feedback report to management.*	**High-Interest Topics:** • **Rate-based scheduling (two examples with real numbers)—even for non-star products** • **Cells as "cost-containment centers" yield superior product cost information—for better competitive decisions** • **Elimination of time tickets, individual employee reporting, machine-utilization report, and the standard-cost/cost-variance system**

Manufacturing Excellence Limited by Inadequate Staffing at OPW

Observations based on a 1.5-day visit, November 2–3, 1993

---

* With the company's approval I also wrote up portions of my observations as a published article: R. J. Schonberger,"Rate-Based Scheduling at OPW Fueling Components," *Production and Inventory Management Journal*, 38/3,(3rd Qtr., 1997): 6-9. See, also about OPW: D. Orth, R. Hybil, D. Korzan, "Analysis of a JIT Implementation at Dover Corporation," *Production and Inventory Management Journal*, 31/3 (3rd Qtr., 1990).

I. General Information

- *The company*: OPW Fueling Components is the leading worldwide manufacturer of a line of petroleum equipment, ranging from fueling nozzles and vapor recovery devices to valves and fittings to overfill and spill containment products. Parent Dover Corp. acquired OPW in 1961.
- *Purpose of visit*: I had delivered my two-day seminar in Cincinnati the prior week, which apparently triggered or was tied to an invitation to return to Cincinnati for a visit and assessment of the OPW facility.
- *Contacts*: Fred Wilking, general manager; R.E. O'Conner; Hugh Campbell, materials manager; Any Jamieson, purchasing manager; Diane Kerrick and Kel Landers, customer service; Hal Bauer and Ron Sherder, info systems; John Young, marketing.

II. Excellent Achievements

- *Cellular manufacturing*:
  - ✓ OPW has been organized into cells since about 1984.
  - ✓ A by-product: its cells act as *cost-containment centers*, which enable precise product costing, for application at OPW in making improved product-line decisions.
- *Human resources*:
  - ✓ With just two labor classifications, the company abandoned labor incentives in the late 1980s—eliminating many HR problems (even though plant is unionized).
  - ✓ Low turnover suggests that OPW is seen as a good place to work and stay.
  - ✓ Good mix of veteran and new-blood professionals and managers.
- *Organization*: A flat structure with low-overhead administration.
- *Functional/product-line management*: OPW's two-hat structure (managers with both functional and product-line responsibilities) may lose its general appeal in time. For now, it seems beneficial in providing a degree of managerial cross-fertilization. (Sealed Air Corp., Ch. I-19, has/had a somewhat similar management structure.)

- *Dominant position*: In its industry, OPW is the only full-line producer—with high market share, margins, earnings before taxes; also, recently rated as the top producer in its sector.
- *Few machine bottlenecks*: Spending on capital equipment looks to be generally adequate (whereas many U.S. companies have under-invested) in both new technologies and sufficient capacity—for years. With insufficient capacity, many things go wrong so that no management methods can deliver good customer service.
- *Supply*:
  - ✓ The company's two buyer-planners seem to be working out well.
  - ✓ Good progress in certifying suppliers—using a "green-tag system."
  - ✓ Purchasing of MRO (maintenance, repair, and operating supplies) has been simplified: A hand-written requisition, when initialed by a supervisor, serves as the purchase order, which is simply faxed to the MRO supplier.
  - ✓ A spin-off of its foundry (in the mid-1980s) to a supplier has resulted in a natural supplier-partner.
- *ISO-9000*: Its registration to ISO-9000 is public demonstration of quality.
- *Product development*: High percentage of sales is in newest products, which is supported by acquisition of a stereo-lithography system.
- *Concept management*: In general, OPW appears to have a culture of searching out and implementing new and better ideas without waiting for a crisis.

III. Policies with Unplanned Negative Consequences

- *Labor inadequacy*:
  - ✓ Being tight on labor—for cost reasons—is having costly consequences, including constantly playing catch-up, overuse of overtime, deteriorating service, and probable lost customer allegiance.
  - ✓ This problem, festering for a long time, became severe in the past few months as sales have greatly exceeded forecasts. Insufficient labor looks to be among its most critical issues.

✓ The solution is not difficult nor especially costly because the extra expense of more production people should be offset by reductions in overtime and various, less tangible costs. The following are specific actions to alleviate the under-staffing:

- Increase the permanent work force (10 to 20 people?).
- Use temps (recent retirees, college students, second-incomers) in summer and any unexpectedly busy season.
- Contingency plan: Develop a few reliable subcontractors for working around bottleneck machines and perhaps for assembly as well.

• *Sales*: Sales-packaging ploys, such as packaging a mix of desired and less-desired products, may make next sales numbers look good but are a misuse of OPW's clout.

✓ Each product should stand on its own: prop-up packaging displeases distributors, sows mistrust. What's not good for the customer is not good for OPW.

✓ Other example: Baxter Healthcare's attempt to leverage its quick-response system to become sole supplier of widely-assorted medical devices to hospital-customers has recently backfired, as several big hospitals have cut Baxter off.

IV. Opportunities for Improvement

• *Rate-based scheduling ("levelizing")*: See Figure 50.1—for a real product, the #45 swivel (A second example—for a spill container—was in the original report, but is omitted here).

✓ This example is not for a superstar product but illustrates the concept's application; the rate might be set somewhat above actual recent sales in order to chip away at the backlog.

✓ The #45 swivel, in two sizes, has a total demand of 235 units per day. The process: receive and store castings, then machine, assemble, test, and box up the completed swivels. Production rates for the two sizes are based on last year's percentage difference in demand for the two. Finally, after a few calculations, the production rates are expressed as a weekly plan, thus to allow for long machine setup times in switching from one of the models to the other.

• *Pilot "world-class" cell*: The following is a proposed pilot-test plan for another real item, the 11A Nozzle. First comes training, in which associates view the 28-minute "JIT/JIC" video, play the JIT paper

#45 Swivel: There are two #45 models: the 5060 (3/4") and the 5075 (1")
Recent combined demand for the two is *235/day*
The model ratio last year: 78% for the 5060; 22% for the 5075
Planned rates:
* * Receive castings: *235/day*
* * Store 19:   9/day, awaiting customer order for 45B (black powder) version
             10/day, awaiting customer order for 45L (British thread) version
    235 minus 19 = 216 castings per day available for processing

* * Machine/assemble/test/box: *216/day* broken down into:
                5060: 78% or *168/day*
                5075: 22% or *48/day*
* * Because of long-machine setup time, execute as a weekly plan: *1080*/week
    - First 3+ days of the week, produce the 5060 at *168/day* to total *842* units
    - Then, 4 to 6 hours machine changeover
    - Last 1+ days of the week, produce the 5075 at *48/day* to total *238* units

FIGURE 50.1
Example of rate-based production: #45 swivel, in two models.

folding simulation game, or other similar quick-enlightenment devices. Next, they (including the union) become highly involved in planning and carrying out numerous remaining pilot-project elements (the process flow is as seen on my tour of OPW):

✓ Adopt rate-based scheduling.
✓ Establish a tight queue limit (kanban) in front of every work station:

■ Remove rotation tables and push assembly benches together; on bench tops tape off two or three kanban squares, each to hold just one nozzle.

■ Replace big wire baskets with wheeled trollies that have waste-height baskets holding 10–25% of present quantities per container, and in total. With this change, stooping is eliminated, better ergonomics are achieved, fewer back aches occur; and no fork trucks or pallet jacks for moves from trunnion machine to cell or assembly to test.

■ With no more than three units between assembly stations—as well as between test, hand insulator, and boxing—each associate must frequently help/cover for a neighbor ("help-your-neighbor" becomes necessary under tight queue limitation).

✓ Every work station has (formally or informally) a "best-qualified" associate, who documents the best method and qualifies teammates.

✓ Associates swap jobs (rotate) at least daily among the trunnion, five assembly stations, two test stations, hand insulator station, and a box station. Level 1 (senior) operators rotate through the complete cycle, and Level 2s rotate through an abbreviated but growing cycle.

✓ Note: the trunnion is poorly located, really belonging in the 11A cell; or, 11A cell belongs where trunnion is, with a door to receive castings cut into a wall adjacent to the trunnion.

✓ On the trunnion (and other equipment related to 11A), maintenance works with the "best-qualified" operator, who learns to maintain and set up the machine, which is a key element of TPM:

■ Implement lubrication checklists and diagrams, color-coded grease tanks on the production floor, as at Civacon (another Dover business unit in the Cincinnati area), and gradually add simple repairs, machine cleanouts, fluid sampling/testing/changing, spare parts responsibility, etc.

■ Have pre-printed maintenance check sheets on which operators record every machine hiccup as a tally stroke—later rearranged on a Pareto chart for use in brainstorming, problem-solving, and project teams.

✓ Customer service adopts available-to-promise (ATP) order-booking, based on known rate-driven daily additions to finished inventories.

■ This yields an accurate ship date, which can considerably improve dealings with customers.

■ Caveat: ATP won't achieve full potential until other items (as with 11A nozzles) also are on rate-based scheduling or with forward visibility (in distribution channels) of inventory status.

✓ Alternate option: Build, say, three days' worth of finished nozzles—thus allowing customer service to promise next-day shipment for all but very large orders (the same caveat still applies).

✓ Paint and brighten up the pilot cell; measure and plot "before" and "after" stats (e.g., flow time, inventory, space, response ratio, cross-training) on large (flip-chart sized) sheets.

✓ Maximize publicity for the pilot project; then, carry the same concepts to other cells.

✓ Expectation: throughput time in this pilot cell should fall to under one day, with daily output steady and predictable.

V. Further Opportunities for Improvement

- *Maintenance department*:
  - ✓ Maintenance to be upgraded: Less time on routine lubricating, etc., which will provide time for a multi-year campaign to transfer first ownership of machines to operators (operators can't have real responsibility for their processes and quality if someone else "owns" the machines).
  - ✓ TPM can't function well when shop-floor staffing is insufficient; thus, having time for TPM is another reason for hiring.
- *Tail end of the product line*: Make headway, by year's end, in carrying out OPW's plan for a plant-in-a plant in an "empty" building wing for the "dogs" of the product line.
  - ✓ Isolating these low-volume items in their own plant makes it easy to isolate their costs as well—and therefore to know their *real* costs.
  - ✓ This will do wonders for cost-sensitive decision-making on these many low-volume products—on pricing, "hold 'em or fold 'em," make or buy, quick setup, simplification/waste reduction, etc.
- *Unneeded conveyors*: Tear out conveyors in the 10R cell (apparently no one sees a reason for keeping them). With freed-up space, move feeder machines close to user machines for hand-to-hand or gravity-feed loading.
- *Verax gaging system*: A good system but should be owned by operators. Also, control charts should be on the shop floor, not in the QC dept.
- *Quick setup*: Get a highly visible quick-setup project going, the machine for #45 swivel being an obvious choice:
  - ✓ Give the Shingo book, *A Revolution in Manufacturing: The SMED System*, to operators, and suggest a book-study group. Then, give them a video camera and an appropriate challenge, and turn them loose.
  - ✓ Put up a large setup-time chart on a wall or easel in the cell; plot baseline setup time and each improvement thereafter.
  - ✓ Operators put first setup efforts on zero-cost changes: As space and tasks permit, do setups in parallel by two or more people (borrowed for the occasion) instead of serially by one person.

✓ Publicize each improvement in the company newsletter and awards ceremonies, emphasizing the competitive (and job-saving) importance of quick setup.

- *Purchasing*:
  ✓ As cells adopt rate-based scheduling, immediately pass that rate back to affected suppliers. Actually, rate-based purchasing should be obtained regardless. Giving suppliers a rate allows them to cut non-value-added costs of their overtime/undertime, simplify their own systems, and provide better service with less panic.
  ✓ Have suppliers of hardware, springs, and O-rings deliver directly to bins in the cells via kanban (take away the empty box, leave a full one)—saving significant handling labor/tasks for OPW.
    - Savvy suppliers *want* to provide this service.
    - From what I gather about positive relations with the union at OPW, this should not be a hard sell to them—all the more so since the whole plant is critically undermanned.
  ✓ Put major and secondary-operation suppliers on re-circulating kanbans: say, four or five labeled wire baskets picked up empty one day, delivered full the next. Those suppliers should include Anotex (anodizing), Poff Plastics (hand insulators), Pride Assembly (castings), Green Industries (plating), and box supplier(s).
  ✓ The current 13-week guarantee to suppliers may be a bit excessive. A possible modification (adapted from what many Hewlett-Packard divisions have been doing for seven or eight years):
    - Set a firm quantity for four weeks; plus-or-minus 10% for the next four weeks; plus-or-minus 20% (cumulative) for the following four weeks.
    - Best forecast for the rest of the year.
- *Information systems*: A project for PCs, servers, Windows, etc.:
  ✓ Top priorities should include technical data access to customer service, bar-code/EDI capability, customer-order verification, available-to-promise on-line with customer service, item (inventory) master file for use by purchasing.
  ✓ Don't buy unnecessary shop-floor control, WIP tracking, labor reporting, internal bar-coding, capacity requirements planning; simpler, more effective methods are in the offing.

- ✓ Look for software favoring rate-based (repetitive) scheduling. You may—or may not—have some remaining requirement for MRP itself (e.g., gross-to-net with back-scheduling).
- *Management accounting/new information system*:
  - ✓ Kill the daily time ticket and individual employee report, which smack of heavy-handed old-style distrustful management and provides no information that anybody uses anyway.
  - ✓ Kill the machine-utilization report, which has no value and tends to result in bad short-term decisions aimed at making the next report look good (Harley-Davidson in Milwaukee killed its machine-utilization report nearly a decade ago).
  - ✓ Convert cost management from standard-cost/cost-variance to cause-control. The rudiments are partly in place but need much more work:
    - ■ Conversion to cells do more for cost control than any other possible factory measure because cells cause a laundry list of non-value-adding (NVA) indirect, direct, and overhead costs to disappear.
    - ■ Removal of more NVAs comes from abolishing incentive payments (already done?); and avidly implementing supplier certification; SPC (good start on this); and TPM (explained above).
    - ■ Visual trend charts that track improvements and multifaceted recognition/celebration measures close the loop, keeping the removal of ever-more NVAs active and effective.
    - ■ Enough sources/causes of NVA costs have already been removed or controlled that the standard-cost/cost-variance system could be turned off now with no adverse effects.
    - ■ Budgetary controls remain—and are far more effective than cost-variance reports in controlling costs. Budgets can be managed day-to-day, but aggregated costs can only be frowned over in futile monthly post-mortems.
- *Financial accounting*: Adopt Texas Instruments' system of closing books quarterly (minimum required by law) instead of monthly. Be the lead Dover Resources division to take this admin-cost-reducing step, helping management avoid short-term thinking.
- *Anticipation*: Strategize for anticipating demand, instead of being forced into reacting to it:

256 • *Flow Manufacturing*

✓ Grow relationships with lawmakers, regulators, and oil-company customers—the aim is to have advanced knowledge and, where possible, influence in their plans.

✓ Form multi-functional product strategy teams (core members being production, finance/accounting, sales/marketing; plus as-needed members from engineering, purchasing, and human resources) for each major product line:

- When business is slack, teams meet infrequently to deliberate *jointly* on new products, markets, equipment, subcontracting, capacity, technologies, promotions, and bonus systems. These should not be independent, functional decisions, since often a "good" decision—focused on a single product or sale—can be a bad for the company.

- When business is brisk with customer service deteriorating, the team meets frequently to make joint decisions on adding capacity and/or cooling down/deferring demand for less-profitable products or less desirable customers.

- *Plant visitations*:

✓ *Highly recommended*: Miller Brewing, Trenton; see, especially, their "star-point" system of upgrading employee skills, innovative union contract with UAW, fairly good TPM (in Chapter II-36).

✓ *Also*:

- Baldor Electric's mother plant, Fort Smith, AR (fractional horsepower DC motors for specialty-industrial market); especially, queue limitation/kanban system that keeps total throughput time short and nearly invariable for effective order promising (in Chapter II-35).

- Johnson Controls, Milwaukee (foundry, sheet metal, machining, and final assembly of brass and iron valves); especially, quick changeover, kanban, exact location of everything, and (perhaps) TPM (in Chapter II-39).

- Briggs and Stratton (small gasoline engines); especially, compact and many-machine cells which—somehow— avoid excessive buildup of WIP between machines in cells. (However, all of their achievements come from professionals; no employee involvement, probably reflecting historical union-management hostilities not yet healed.)

CHAPTER II-51. WHEELABRATOR, LAGRANGE, GA, 1992–93

Wheelabrator Corp. is notable for achieving high-profit marketing, driven by product-focused cells and focused factories, and supported by advanced methods in allocating overhead costs to products. "Update" information, from a phone call in 1993, is in Section IV, which ends the caselet.	***High-Interest Topics:*** • **Sales/marketing press for orders of "golden flow" products: better for customers, designed for quick-and-easy processing** • **Weeding out a loser through ABC costing** • **Big profits on thousands of service parts** • **Component and process cells upgraded, in phases, to product cells**

Benefits of Cellular Manufacturing Extending to Sales and Financial Functions

Plant visitation – March 3, 1992

In connection with a two-day Schonberger seminar in Atlanta on March 4–5

Updated Wheelabrator information by phone, July 1, 1993

I. General Information

- *What is Wheelabrator?*
  - ✓ In 1938 the company invented the blast-wheel machine named the "wheelabrator," which launched the business.
  - ✓ Co-located engineering and manufacturing by moving engineering from Newman, GA, to LaGrange, in 1984.
- *Product line*: 350,000 part numbers (P/Ns) are capable of being made, one-third OEM and two-thirds spare parts.
- *Work force engagement*: Associates in cells perform QC, PM, and material handling. (50% of the total work force have attended a Schonberger seminar.)
- *Contacts*: R.C. Whitaker, president; Robert Anderson, director of manufacturing; Al Bennett, general manager.

II. DFM and Profit-Oriented Marketing

- *Attack on wastes*: A wide-ranging "Fastrack" initiative included reorganization of 15,196 P/Ns used in the last three years into five categories by degree of simplicity (i.e., low need for additional engineering and relatively easy to manufacture):
    1. Gold (golden-flow): 1% of items, 34% of sales—these require virtually no engineering.
    2. Silver: 1% of items, 7% of sales—require virtually no engineering.
    3. Bronze: 1% of items, 10% of sales.
    4. Lead: 84% of items, 20% of sales (non-stocked repair parts).
    5. Other: 13% of items, 29% of sales.
- *Golden-flow sales/marketing*: Targeting "golden-flow" sales influences customers to go with new, rebuilt, modern part packages.
- *Overhead cost allocation*: An initial activity-based costing (ABC) effort was aimed at allocating most overhead costs to the "lead" (not simple-to-build) P/Ns. That effort provided improved-validity cost data for use in weeding out losers/"rationalizing the product line."
- *Design for manufacture*: Under Fastrack, a one-year DFM project yielded a new modular design of a wheelabrator machine. Following that, a ten-week DFM project yielded an eight-wheel major structural machine component.

III. Other Initiatives and Results/Impacts

- *Since 1988*:
    - ✓ 80 people, including four supplier-partners, have gone through an 18-week cell-conversion workshop series.
    - ✓ Key results—in and through the workshop: Lead times were cut 30%, inventories 42%, total space 40% (from 195K to 117K sf) with 25% more output.
- *Phased improvement program*: the phases included the following:
    - ✓ Phase 1, 1990:
        - Organized three fabrication cells in machining.
        - Cut lift trucks from eight to two; material handlers/movers from eleven to four; QC inspectors from six to one; maintenance staff in half.

- Found some unused machines and increased the cell count to 21.
- ✓ Phase 2, 1991:
    - Implemented 11 assembly cells, bringing total cells to 36.
    - Eliminated 24,000 sq. ft. warehouse; merged an 80,000 sq. ft. assembly plant into an existing fab plant.
- ✓ Next phase:
    - Product-flow cells were organized by five business segments: equipment, equipment modernization, repair parts, Blastrac, and Resco.
    - Aligned sales in parallel with the alignment in manufacturing.

IV. New Information – July 1, 1993

- *Update phone call*: My call to Anderson, director of manufacturing, yielded the following new information:
- *Service parts*: The service-parts business, some 150,000 P/Ns, is highly profitable—and will *not* be eliminated through DFMA. (I am presuming that, even though activity-based costing had loaded these "lead" P/Ns with overhead costs, in the usually-lucrative service-parts context, they remain as money-makers.)
- *Further cellular development*: Production is now reorganized into five product cells + three support groups/cells:
    - ✓ Product cells, each with its own machining, welding, and assembly (equipment moved to form these cells) are for:
        - Custom equipment.
        - Distributor equipment.
        - Stock parts.
        - Non-stock parts.
        - Plate and structural preparation.
    - ✓ Support groups/cells consist of:
        - Equipment modernization program (EMP)—aimed at taking spare-parts business away from (one or more) competitors by converting parts in competitors' installed machines (e.g., a Pangborn machine) to Wheelabrator parts. Pangborn has been in this business about as long as Wheelabrator, so many Pangborn machines are out there. Badger also competes in after-market parts sales. (Another major competitor in

Wheelabrator-like equipment is Canadian company, BCP; other competitors include Blast Tech and Jet Wheel.)

- Administrative support teams (AST's).
- Waste energy cell (not active right now).

- *Planning pods, nerve centers*: Two planning "pods," sit side by side in "nerve centers," one supporting equipment cells, the other supporting after-market product cells:
  - ✓ The equipment pod consists of an accountant, buyer-planner, buyer, and projects manager.
  - ✓ An after-market pod has a master scheduler, manufacturing engineer (ME), buyer-planner, and accountant.
  - ✓ Distributors have been invited—and have attended—pod meetings on a regular basis. In conveying their needs, distributors offer comparisons of Wheelabrator with competitors—valuable competitive information.

- *Merging MEs and product designers*: Design engineering is now composed of three design engineers and three MEs.

- *Merging cross-functionally*: The existing functional organization structure was "about to collapse." So:
  - ✓ Design engineers, MEs, buyers, etc., have been relocated onto cross-functional teams (CFT's), one for each cell.
  - ✓ The smallest CFT is 12 people, largest 30 people. A CFT typically has a shop supervisor (to become a coach and facilitator), cell leader, assistant leader, buyer, ME, and production associates.

- *Peer reviews*: Wheelabrator's CFTs are about to adopt peer review.

- *Scheduling software*: Production planning and scheduling is using finite capacity software—Jobscope of Greenville, SC—with the following features:
  - ✓ Customer order-oriented—no batching of parts orders (a certain part might be scheduled again in the same day).
  - ✓ When the system determines that parts orders are piling up on a certain machine or cell—a bottleneck—it adds buffer *time* to affected upstream and downstream processes (no point in scheduling up- and downstream processes earlier than is possible, given the bottleneck).
  - ✓ For stocked parts, the system is based on reorder points. For non-stocked, it just schedules the exact quantity ordered (often just one).

  (Comment: Finite-capacity scheduling, software-driven, seems out of tune with the hands-on simplicity of Wheelabrator's dominant practices and successes.)

- *Some results*:
  - ✓ Best six months' financial performance in twelve years, with apparent significant gains in market share (over Pangborn? BCP?).
  - ✓ Quoted lead times are down to four days for stocked parts, two weeks for non-stocked parts (actual average is about 20 days); cycle time cut 50%.
  - ✓ Inventory turns are up from three (when?) to eight (shooting for ten by end of 1993).
  - ✓ On-time performance: 52% in December, 1992, 95% in March, 1992, 92% in April, 94% in May.
  - ✓ Cost of quality: 100% improvement (50% reduction).
- *Miscellaneous*:
  - ✓ "A large lot … is ten pieces"—so setup time is a large portion of cost. Thus, increased emphasis on setup time reduction.
  - ✓ A few people were unable to adapt to this new mode: two production associates and two in office support people are gone.

CHAPTER II-52. ALARIS MEDICAL SYSTEMS, SAN DIEGO, CA AND TIJUANA, MEXICO, 1999

Alaris Medical Systems is a long caselet that points to large numbers of excellent practices, as well as many detailed suggestions for improvement. For example, a sizeable block of Section III is targeted at very high employee turnover at the company's three Tijuana plants—with advice specific to the maquiladora environment along the Mexican border. The many issues included can be seen as a rather comprehensive example of "best manufacturing practices" in the context of a multi-national, multi-plant operation.

High-Interest Topics:
- **Many-factor attack on very high employee turnover**
- **Four San Diego plants competing in six performance factors**
- **In Tijuana plant, stack lights indicate status/problems—and big *K* indicates "no respect for kanban!"**
- **Why gang assembly is bad—and should be "outlawed" by "good manufacturing practices" (GMPs) in medical devices**

Medical-device Manufacture Copes with Cross-border Manufacturing Issues

Impressions from brief plant tours, August 4, 1999

(Schonberger colleague, Raúl Quiñones, also on tours of Tijuana plants)

I. General Information

- *Alaris' ownership*:
    - ✓ The company has undergone a complex series of ownership changes and name changes, and in 1999 was consolidated with IVAC Corp., which had experienced its own series of ownership/name changes.
    - ✓ Both IVAC and IMED had set up maquiladora operations in the late 1980s. IMED had 17 facilities in the San Diego/Tijuana area at the time of consolidation. Total Alaris employment is about 2,000. For further demographic information, please see Sidebar 1.
- *Hosts*: Dave Schlotterbeck, CEO; Dick Mirando, VP operations; Rob Featherstone, director, operations San Diego; José Figueroa, director, operations Tijuana; Tom Parker, director of operations, Creedmoor, NC.
- *San Diego Activity Road facility*:
    - ✓ Produces about 140,000 insulin infusion pumps and patient monitoring devices yearly in nine product families, 60% for the domestic market direct-shipped to hospitals, 40% international

---

SIDEBAR 1   ALARIS – SOME DETAILS

San Diego, Activity Road: 350
employees; 83,000 sq. ft.; warehouse/distribution building across the street
Plant presently loaded to only about 30% of capacity
Main Tijuana plant:
1,360 employees—1,183 assemblers, 120 indirect (warehouse, maintenance, etc.), 57 admin.; 95,500 sq. ft. manufacturing; 30,300 warehouse; 29,400 sq. ft. labs, offices, lunch rooms, etc.
Distribution centers (DCs): In Activity Road, Indianapolis, Reno, and two in North Carolina

---

through a distribution network. Signature models average 1,800–2,000 units per month, Genesis 1,000 per month, rectal thermometers 2,000 per month, MS3 portable units (from Siemens, 1994) 5,500 per month.

✓ A service area (for repairing field units), in its own area of the plant, requires only a few minutes' work content on simple jobs but often six to seven hours on MS3 devices.

✓ Outside service work: Physio Control (Redmond, WA), does some repairs for Alaris. Other repairs are by an Alaris technician on-site at hospitals; still others are by hospital technicians with Alaris providing training, parts, accessories.

- *Creedmoor, NC*: 186 employees produce automated disposable components, about 80% for the Tijuana plants, 20% end products.
- *Tijuana plants*
  ✓ Main plant produces 200,000 disposable IV sets daily: 425 catalog models, 35 of which cover 80% of total volume. Half of production and the work force are at the Insurgentes plant and half in the Limón plant about one mile away.

  ✓ Operates two shifts: 48 hours per week on day shift, 42 hours per week on night shift.

  ✓ Insurgentes (formerly an IMED Co. plant) still gets large amounts of direct material from Borla of Italy—but Alaris-Creedmoor, NC, is replacing Borla.

  ✓ At Insurgentes, cells/assembly lines are engineered to produce a fixed 400 units per hour, with 9.6 seconds work content per assembler.

  ✓ José Figueroa, director of operations for both Tijuana plants, has been there since early 1997; José and other function heads are located in Insurgentes but responsible for Limón, too.

  ✓ The Limón plant (formerly IVAC) receives most direct material from Alaris-Creedmoor.

  ✓ All disposables from Tijuana must go to a radiation sterilization contractor (no more ETO sterilization in use) in the San Diego area, adding about 8–12 days' lead time.

- *Corporate offices (Wateridge, North San Diego)*: This plush facility houses 200 or so employees, including executives and staff departments such as product development and purchasing.
- *Financial condition*: Alaris is deeply in debt as result of a leveraged buyout.

II. Strengths and Descriptive Observations (see, also, Sidebar 2)

- *Alaris as a whole:*
  - ✓ Current plans include aggressively removing waste (e.g., following world class by principles) and generating cash flow to pay down debt.
  - ✓ Customer-focused (and competitively-focused) manufacturing:
    - Under Schlotterbeck, the four plants compete for results in six performance areas: Cost of quality, Parts per million defectives, First-pass yield, Cycle time (throughput time), Floor space required, Inventory turns, and Schedule achievement.
    - These measures are unlike conventional manufacturing's indirect focus—on cost variance, machine utilization, direct labor productivity, and so on.
  - ✓ Company-wide measures of internal/external customer satisfaction include: Average days to close books, Quality (what measures?), Job/career rotation (?), Order-response time, Employee turnover, and Telephone response time.
  - ✓ Circuit boards: IVAC outsourced circuit boards in 1993; IMED did so in 1987. Solectron does $14 million per year circuit-board-related business with Alaris.

SIDEBAR 2   ALARIS – MORE DETAILS

Human resources

All Alaris employees are eligible for bonuses based on company earnings, plus plant performance on the six metrics

Many senior people, as well as many direct labor people at the Activity Road and North Carolina plants, have been with the company for many years

Teams/cells/lines meet daily to review customer demand, quality issues, etc.

Training features one to two hours of train-the-trainer with "just-in-time training" (train just in time to go use on job)

Operator certification has three levels for assembly, plus a 4th level for materials and other support

Supervisors: Two supervisors are for manufacturing, two for quality, one for material; also, there's one line lead for every 35 people

In San Diego (mature workforce, averaging 15 + years), operator certifications posted at work benches list 10–15 of those who are certified, certification date, their trainers' names, and other information

- ✓ Alaris has about 35–40% market share, Baxter and Abbott being main competitors.
- ✓ Purchasing at headquarters is in three commodity groups: electro-mechanical, electronic, and plastic. Buyer-planners are located in the plants.
- *All Tijuana plants*:
  - ✓ Corrugated from a U.S. producer is delivered to a Tijuana distribution center (DC); then daily to Insurgentes and Limón plants by kanban (kanban messages are sent to the DC by fax).
  - ✓ In packout areas, graphs track the top six metrics, plus skills certifications.
  - ✓ The plants are shifting their safety focus from lost-time accidents to unsafe incidents (behavior-based safety)—the emphasis on prevention.
  - ✓ Parts per million defectives are down from 15,000 in 1989 to 300 in 1999.
- *Tijuana Insurgentes*:
  - ✓ Quality hold/inspection times are recently down from 24 hours to 12 hours.
  - ✓ Incoming trucks from the U.S. turn around as outgoing (two truckloads arrive/depart daily).
  - ✓ Eight pass-through windows separate eight clean-room packaging machines from eight packout conveyor lines.
  - ✓ 5S, which began three months ago, is not yet in the audit mode. See photo in Figure 52.1.
  - ✓ JIT has reduced floor space for WIP (work-in-process inventory) from 30% to 10% (just three hours of WIP).
  - ✓ Responsibility chains:
    - Cells were formed in the past 18 months.
    - Labor in every cell/line is organized into one-to-one responsibility chains. (In sharp contrast, most maquiladora and med-device plants work in tandem ("gangs"), rather than in responsibility chains.) Alaris understands the difference.
    - (Note: Gang assembly is where two or more assemblers independently grab parts from a conveyor or fixed position, assemble them, and pass the assembly along. Later, if an assembly is defective, each can say "I didn't do it." In sequential

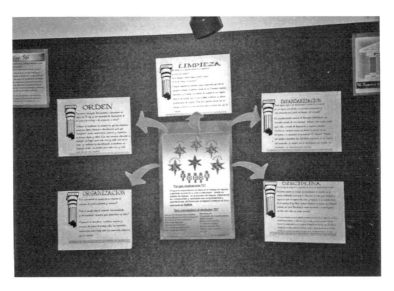

FIGURE 52.1
5S Criteria—in Spanish at the Insurgentes plant.

assembly the work is passed from assembler to assembler, each checking the work of the prior one—a responsibility chain. The regulatory agencies should upgrade regulations to *not allow* the gang method—especially in medical devices, pharma, etc.)

- Cells are dedicated to product families: Genesis 1, Genesis 2, pumping chambers, syringe sets, etc.
- Most cells have six people. Assembly lines (not yet converted to cells) have 12–13 assemblers.
- Cells are organized by three different product volumes: large, medium, and low. The "low" are short run products—e.g., made once per year, or six months, or quarterly—to which assemblers with broader skill sets are assigned.
- Dedicated support teams (manufacturing engineer, quality engineer, maintenance) are assigned to cell groups.

✓ Visual management:
- Employs colored cards displayed at stations along each cell or line.
- The cards, about 5" x 7," convey status: Green, OK; Yellow, falling behind the hourly rate; Purple, assembler in training;

Red, a quality problem; White, outside training going on; White with a big K, "no respect for kanban!"

✓ 24 cells/production lines are in groups of three, each dedicated to one of eight packaging machines (a hand-loaded disposable unit goes into blister pack, then machine heat-seal).

✓ 17 pre-assembly tubing machines serve the 24 cells.

- *Tijuana-Limón*:

  ✓ About six pass-through windows link packaging machines in the clean room with manual packout conveyor lines in the warehouse.

  ✓ Recently, cells have begun to be organized (conveyors removed), so that each is aligned with a packaging machine.

- *Activity Road, San Diego*:

  ✓ This main San Diego plant uses highly flexible Bosch work stations.

  ✓ It has numerous cells (four-person on two sides of four benches). They include:

    - Larger U-shaped cells.
    - Still larger straight flow lines with 20–25 people in three segments (product functional unit, to ESS, to final assembly and test), which are to be converted to U-cells.

  ✓ Station cycle time (work content) is around two minutes—sometimes more, sometimes less.

  ✓ Good recent progress has been made for joint scheduling between sales/marketing and operations—working toward level-loading the plant.

  ✓ 525 components (out of some 4,000) from 81 suppliers have been certified dock-to-stock.

  ✓ Two-day burn-ins have been eliminated in favor of new 45-minute environmental stress screening (ESS).

  ✓ Service technicians (in a repair area) have an electronic-technician or associate degree. Each is specialized and can do an entire repair and contact the customer (hospital) directly.

  ✓ When an existing building is leased (or bought) by Alaris, it is extensively prepared for highly flexible manufacturing: walls removed, floors surfaced with humidity conductive coating, ceilings equipped fully with power/air/data communications grid, and dock doors added all around the building.

III. Opportunities for Improvement

- *Alaris as a whole*:
  - ✓ A major effort is needed to put star products on rate-based schedules. The aim is to have one monthly work order, extending back to suppliers as a monthly purchase order, thus to make the same quantity every day and only change the rate monthly.
  - ✓ Diligent efforts are needed to keep the new SAP ERP system from making manufacturing more complex, delay-prone, inflexible, and high in overhead costs.
    - Short throughput-time products should have only two transactions: receipt at the front door and back-flush capture of material usage (plus recording of required lot-traceback data) at the back door.
    - See the July 19, 1999, issue of *Industry Week*, which reviews heavy-handed ERP systems.
  - ✓ Since the medical devices industry is not directly linked (or scarcely linked) to bar-code-based usage in hospitals, Alaris's order book, forecasts, and schedules are badly out of synch with real usage—a serious, costly problem rippling back through all stages of production and supply. As possible half measures to help with the issue:
    - Pick a few key hospitals and offer a 2% discount if they will rig their bar-code wanding so that they can electronically forward it directly to Alaris's customer service.
    - For international business, offer discounts to distributors for sending (to Alaris's customer service) their sales data at least weekly (sales will be far more timely than their orders, the aim of which is just to fill Alaris's own warehouse spaces).
- *Tijuana strategy*:
  - ✓ Move increasingly automated/semi-automated equipment to Tijuana plants.
    - Creedmoor continues as the Alaris components production center but with a new role as an automation development center.
    - Transfer equipment to Tijuana as it becomes proven (turning it over to the excellent engineers turned out yearly by numerous Mexican technológicos).

✓ Employ continuous-improvement training company-wide, linked to 5S.

✓ I detected, during the seminar, considerable opinion for reducing the catalog of old, outdated products, and a crash effort to standardize components and parts (as is feasible, given strong customer preferences); some parts' commonality exists within product families, none between families.

✓ Also, some agreement with the concept of having new-hire engineers perform a stint in manufacturing—and even offering this option to present engineers.

• *Tijuana plants—high turnover*: The greatest opportunity for improvement lies in reducing employee turnover, which is high (25% monthly) even by maquiladora standards.

✓ Following are specific means of achieving this, which...

■ Calls for check-sheet recording boards at every work station, fine-tuning of work balancing by leads and assembler teams, and enhances social aspects of the job.

■ At the same time, reduces job boredom, improves ergonomics, raises assembly productivity, and upgrades supervision.

✓ Double or triple the present 9.6-second station cycle times (station work content), which will double or triple the number of cells. Best starting point is the 12- and 14-person lines, in which tripling to a 28.8-second work cycle makes a 12-person line into three four-person cells.

✓ Enhance the present six-person cells by moving some of the 17 pre-assembly machines into the cells; the enlarged cells then might be halved to three persons, with doubled work-content cycles.

✓ Benefits of doubled/tripled work cycle:

■ Less boring jobs: A 9.6-second cycle means repeating the same task about 3,000 times per shift—which few people can long tolerate without looking for other work.

■ Reduces repetitive motion injuries.

■ Allows stand-up (no chairs) assembly with a short walk among two or three tasks. Many experts believe assemblers should not sit (some apparel industry factories have tried eliminating chairs: at first, sewers dislike it and have some leg and feet tiredness, but within a month or two never want chairs again).

- Gives operators time to think and record incidence of glitches; and for beneficial socialization, enhancing happiness, and reducing absenteeism.
- Also, it increases productivity: Sony engineers did a thorough time study to prove that their typical ten-second work cycles in Tijuana TV assembly were only 80% efficient because one second is lost to handling on both ends of the cycle; tripling the cycle raises efficiency to 93%.

✓ Use the timing designed into the cells (currently 9.6 seconds) to determine the total number of assemblers, but let the assemblers and the lead person fine-tune work assignments to the capabilities and motivations of each person in the cell.

- That can often raise productivity since cell-team members no longer need to be paced to the slowest.
- Assemblers could also interview prospective new hires who are looking for skills and social compatibility.

✓ Check sheets (e.g., using white boards):

- Every assembler should be required to check off (tally-mark) every process glitch, hiccup, slowdown, or frustration all day, every day.
- This data becomes Pareto charts that point to best opportunities for improvement; equally important, this recording serves as a relief valve and is cathartic for the work force.

✓ Upgrading supervisory training will further reduce employee turnover; Raúl Quiñones (Tijuana) offers excellent supervisory training and a Spanish-language publication for supervisors.

✓ Summary: Turnover is so serious that it might be good to set a strategy of striving to make Alaris-Tijuana plants a showcase for low turnover (e.g., nicest bathrooms, best cafeteria food and recreation programs, family activities).

✓ Note: Three (non-Alaris) Tijuana plants that I visited offer models for increased station cycle times, improved work environments, lower employee turnover:

- At Mexhon (Honeywell) nearly all stations have greater than one-minute work content (the plant includes a lot of machine assembly and test equipment).
- In the newly opened Invensys/Powerware plant (beautiful bathrooms, architecture, other amenities), station cycles are a minute or more with all assemblers in stand/walk-a-few-steps jobs.
- Plamex (Plantronics headsets) has mostly 10 second or less station times but also has a pilot program to increase times, get rid of chairs, raise assembly benches, put check sheets at every station, use 5S, track results and recognition visually, etc.

- *Tijuana plants – other issues*:
  ✓ Changeover times on packaging machines may average only about ten minutes, but the process needs to have best practices fully documented, every changeover timed and plotted on a chart.
    - Operators need brief training in quick setup, then receive a video camera to study their own motions and eliminate poor practices.
    - The main challenge should be to eliminate need for adjustment/tweaking/wasted package units after startup (I observed one rather haphazard changeover).
  ✓ If not already the practice, job rotation should include both sides of the pass-through windows and assembly cells—to encourage packout and packing machines to be viewed as part of feeder cells, not separate "departments."
  ✓ At Insurgentes, two people work in tandem on packout conveyor lines. This should be changed to sequential flow with a one-to-one responsibility chain.

- *Activity Road site*:
  ✓ The most serious issue by far appears to be quality—low first-pass yields, high repair/warranty costs. An all-out attack on this problem should free up more cash than anything else the company could do—and at same time grow market share and customer allegiance.

✓ Service (repair) department:
- Consider treating the service department as a separate entity that must pay its own way—and compete with the other four plants for results in the six performance areas.
- Space for the department could be carved out of the warehouse across the street, if no other nearby space is readily available.

✓ Kanban is needed internally between stockrooms and assembly, and externally from suppliers (e.g., start with bulky corrugated and other packaging materials).

✓ Now, on average, type A purchased materials are received weekly, B monthly, C semi-annually.
- Set new targets at, say, A twice weekly, B twice monthly, and C every three months.
- But bulk items should be daily by kanban, and some C items, e.g., from hardware and office suppliers, more than weekly (just fill trays and shelves, and bill Alaris monthly).

✓ Free up space in the plant for direct receipt of all supplier-certified items—i.e., go dock-to-line (rather than dock-to-stock—with extra handling—across the street).
- For certified items received in large lots, off-load current requirements in the production plant.
- Then send the truck across the street to put the rest of the load into "over-flow" storage.

✓ Clearing incoming materials through inspect/test takes about seven days compared to just 12 hours at the Tijuana plants.
- Perhaps partly explained by mix differences, this still should be a target for concerted time/backlog reduction—e.g., by borrowing a team of people from other functions to cut down the time it takes for inspect and test.
- After the backlog is down to a day or so, rely on cross-trained people from plant and offices for temporary duty in receiving inspection/documentation whenever a backlog threatens to grow again.

CHAPTER II-53. ROTARY LIFT, MADISON, IN, 1993

This, my first visit to Rotary Lift's plant, serves as background for the second visit, dated 1999, the chapter of which directly follows this one. My brief 1993 visit did not result in a feedback report to management; thus, this short case-let is assembled from my rough, mostly descriptive notes.

High-Interest Topics:
- **Simplification of costing and performance management as an early initiative (rather than, as is typical, a later add-on)**
- **The prod to act: precipitous emergence of many new, tough competitors**

Not Waiting for the Axe to Fall: Excellence Driven by Competitive Threats

Observations based on a mid-day plant tour, January 19, 1993

With two-day Schonberger seminar for divisions of Dover Corp., Cincinnati, January 20–21, 1993

I. Basic Information

- *Company and plant*:
  - ✓ Rotary Lift in Madison, IN, is a business unit of Dover Corp., a conglomerate.
  - ✓ The 120,000 sq. ft. plant has 400 employees.
- *Products*: Produces hydraulic lifts used in vehicle service stations to elevate cars and small trucks for oil changes and repairs. Formerly just five products, there now are 80.
- *Competition*:
  - ✓ Formerly, Rotary was #1 among five competing firms.
  - ✓ In the early 1980s, a European competitor emerged, producing two-pole surface lifts (as opposed to in-floor lifts); the number of competitors totaled 10–12.
  - ✓ Now it's about 40 competitors—"crisis mode" for Rotary.
- *Purpose of visit*: Dover Corp. had organized my visit to Rotary plus two other Dover plants in the general area, all on the same day—followed by my two-day seminar in Cincinnati for various Dover units.
- *Contact persons*: Rudy Hermann, president; Phil Wotring, plant manager.

II. Responding to Competitive Threats

- *TQM*: Total quality management, begun in 1989 with a customer focus, is now in a growth phase.
- *Customers*: Independent reps and installers are brought to Madison for training in selling and installation.
- *Reorganization initiatives*:
  - ✓ Over the period 1988–1990 the organization evolved from functionally oriented to focused.
  - ✓ The company headquarters, credit, customer service, etc., moved from Memphis to Madison and its organization levels were flattened out.
  - ✓ A re-layout of the production facilities (in the building built in 1955) was undertaken.
  - ✓ Manufacturing investments included a CNC lathe, CNC shear, turning center, machining center, among others.
- *Cost/performance reporting*:
  - ✓ The company had been using full-absorption costing. No longer.
  - ✓ In 1991, labor and overhead were combined—with no labor reporting, just bar-codes on badges for payroll reports. Inventory is material cost only, with labor and overhead no longer allocated to inventory.
  - ✓ Formerly, many financial reports; now, one management report.
  - ✓ For this SOU (small operating unit), a monthly trend report is issued covering product liability, field service, sales dollars per hour, and throughput per hour.
  - ✓ The data is collected in an AS400 relational database, as of March 1.
- *JIT features*:
  - ✓ Three focused business units are: 1. Specialty products. 2. In-ground and heavy lifts. 3. Low-volume specials with a cell in a separate building.
  - ✓ Line changeovers: Operators doing setups are videotaped—old taking 14 hours; new??
  - ✓ Materials: Ryerson delivers steel daily. Saw operators order their own materials. Some suppliers (hardware, office supplies) come on-site to restock trays and shelves. Supplier certification is ongoing.
  - ✓ Inventory turns are up from four to ten.
  - ✓ Lead times are 7.5 days for heavy products, three days for standard specialty items.

III. Improvement Advisories

- Implement kanban squares.
- Put up large wall charts tracking key trends (setup times, lead times, quality, numbers of suggestions, etc.).

CHAPTER II-54. ROTARY LIFT, MADISON, IN, 1999

This caselet emerges from my second visit here, the first being in 1993 (briefly treated in Chapter II-53). Rotary Lift may be, in 1999, the shining star of the many manufacturing business units of Dover Corp. (which include other quite outstanding units). The plant is a worthy example of multiple "best manufacturing practices."	**High-Interest Topics:** • **Which models should be eliminated: We asked shop-floor people. They knew!** • **Five cells, each with its own paint line** • **Fair-to-compare room filled with Rotary's and competitors' lifts—where installers and reps come to compare and offer tips**

Excellence in Production of Automotive Lifts—Forward to Installers and Sales Reps

Random observations based on a mid-day plant tour, Sept. 13, 1999

Followed by a two-day Schonberger seminar for
Dover Corp., Cincinnati, Sept. 14–15, 1999

I. Basic Information

- *The company*: Rotary Lift is one of numerous subsidiaries of Dover Corp. Timothy Sandker is president.
- *Product line*: Hydraulic lifts used in vehicle service stations to elevate cars and small trucks for oil changes and repairs. Peter Lunati, auto mechanic and company founder, "invented" the product in 1924 while watching a barber pump a chair up to proper cutting height.
- *Plant and offices*: Formerly a Memphis company, Rotary moved manufacturing to Madison; then, also, its administrative offices, which resolved some problems. Manufacturing went from a

single plant in 1993 to two plants, each with its own design and manufacturing engineering.

- *Four businesses*: These are: 1. Rotary U.S. 2. Rotary Canada. 3. Rotary Europe (in an embryonic state: London, sales and warehouse; Frankfurt, Germany; and Marta, Italy). 4. Forward Manufacturing, formerly a competitor in Fort Worth but acquired two weeks ago, is to be retained as a separate brand.

- *Plan (year 2001) for a fifth business*: Serval, Rotary-authorized installers, is intended as an internet service-call operation (e.g., to serve customers such as Pep Boys and Sears); and to include automated sales and service in addition to product data management (PDM). It is viewed as serving as a model for developing other auto service business opportunities.

- *Prospects*:
    - ✓ With high market share (50–55%), Rotary cannot reasonably grow except by new brands (the ALI—Automatic Lift Industry—provides market share data to member companies).
    - ✓ Its sizeable market share gives Rotary breathing room to work on innovations, thereby keeping ahead of—and keeping out—competition.
    - ✓ Rotary is in the process of responding to customers who now are interested in adding intelligence to lifts (e.g., environmental enhancement options).

- *Strategic shifts*:
    - ✓ In 1992, Rotary was producing 35 two-post units (the core product) per day with a premium-value price strategy.
        - ■ By 1993 market share losses showed that this strategy was not working, leading to a shift to a lowest-cost emphasis.
        - ■ This shift was instrumental in raising market share by 10%, and volume of two-post lifts rose to 70 per day in 1998 and 92 per day in 1999. Sales were up from $67 million in 1993 to $120 million, as the price of a two-poster fell from $3,265 to $2,299. Current production is 32,000 units per year.
    - ✓ More recently, heavy reliance on independent sales reps was abandoned—in favor of enhancing distributors with more capability to be an installer; reps were cut from 100 to 30, while regional managers were increased from four to seven to better support distributors.

✓ To upgrade the business, $6 million was invested between 1994 and 1998.

✓ The old emphasis on in-ground lifts is almost fully replaced by above-ground lifts.

✓ In 1993–94 the number of models of two-poster lifts was halved— to eliminate low-margin models.

- To find out which models to cut, "We went to the guys on the shop floor and asked them, 'which lifts are we making money on?'"
- They had good answers.

✓ Power units (tank, pump, motor) needed to be designated as a core competency—and so we brought it in-house. In support of this, a supplier will build cylinders, perhaps within Rotary-Lift space (signing an exclusive agreement).

✓ A global materials manager has been hired to qualify suppliers, enable global sourcing, drive system-wide performance metrics, and so forth.

II. Miscellaneous General Details

- *Shop administration*: Rotary has migrated from supervisors to team leaders—then back to supervisors with cell coordinators. The problem with team leaders was they "would not chastise their own."
- *Costing (notes are fuzzy—maybe wrong—here)*:

  ✓ In 1993, costing was to the business unit, but pressure to lower costs led, in 1994, to moving toward more detailed costing (e.g., down to the level of a bolt).

  ✓ By 1996, the new costing was in place and working—to where costs can be known every day if necessary.

  ✓ Though detailed, costing has also been simplified. For example, there are no more cost collection tickets, or distinction between direct and indirect labor, or labor tracking.

  - Job costing is done by clocking in and out on jobs (but is *not* done in the plastics shop).
  - Job costing for Airtomic is simply to total up the costs and divide by the number of parts made daily.

- *Supply*: Suppliers re-stock corrugated, wiring, etc., visually—hardware daily, corrugated weekly. Maintenance, repair, and operating supplies (MRO) are received directly to the building where used, rather than through central receiving.
- *Labor classes/grades*: Formerly there were 29 labor classes, now just five—85% in just two grades.
- *Gain-sharing*: Four payouts in the last 2.5 years.
- *Critical success factors*: These are displayed in a matrix, which pinpoints responsibilities.
- *Service parts*: For current models, service parts are to be in a separate cell; for discontinued models, they are contracted out (prints, tooling, etc.) to SVIC—thus to make sense out of a disruptive, often money-losing problem area.
- *Paint*: Five cells in Buildings 1 and 2 have their own paint lines, making cells fully self-contained!

III. Building 1

- *Fair-to-compare room*:
  - ✓ In this large, high-ceilinged space, Rotary positions its own lifts next to key competitors' lifts—and keeps a "book" of comparative data.
  - ✓ Reps come for three-day training on both Rotary's and competitors' lifts, ending with each rep making a presentation on what they have learned—notably, advantages of Rotary's versus competitors' lifts.
  - ✓ Rotary-authorized installers also train here, with Rotary's production operators participating in these classes to interact and learn from installers about installation problems that Rotary could address.
- *Visual factory*:
  - ✓ Performance metrics are standard—same in each area:
    - They include various production metrics relative to maintenance and tooling standards, synchronized flows, total quality (supplier oriented), and employee involvement.
    - The plant also employs 5S (using Productivity Inc.'s training package), problem-solving teams, and cross-functional first-time-quality (FTQ) teams.

- ✓ The central war room called "The Pit" (pit stop) has numerous wall charts showing performance/trends in safety, quality, delivery, cost, and inventory (16 turns yearly).
- *Uniform throughput times*: Finished stock on hand is two days or less. The reason for that much is that one order may draw from two-post, four-post, etc.; so it is desirable for all throughput times be the same (may be more important than decreasing throughput time in a given cell/product area).
- *Brief operator interviews*:
  - ✓ Al (in-ground component cell), in a pilot area for 5S, presented some 5S achievements. I asked him what he measured himself and his team on. His response: 1. Quality. 2. Neatness/cleanliness. 3. Productivity.
  - ✓ Vic (arm clevis cell) stopped and opened a CNC multi-spindle horizontal mill to demonstrate quick, hydraulic clamping via external controls. I prompted him, and he cited reduction of parts that don't match up in welding as the biggest aggravation that would be dealt with. I also asked what they measured him on. He said: 1. Safety. 2. Quality.
  - ✓ Rick (miscellaneous cell) told me about collecting data on critical-dimension non-conformities, which are entered on a form called "first-time quality tally sheet runway" (runway meaning type of process, e.g., CNC, burner, saw, press, assembly, etc.).
    - Data from the form are summarized on Pareto charts weekly, then the five biggest problems are attacked.
    - Rick noted a recent example of tracing non-conformities back to a bad die—a big aggravation resolved for Rick and his associates.
  - ✓ Lonnie (in carriage cell?) said six people rotate weekly so that everyone must do their turn on the *boring* brake press.

IV. Building 2—Specialty Products

- Building 2 (first on the tour) is 64,000 sq. ft. with 84 direct labor and 14 salaried employees; production is in seven cells, plus shipping.

- ✓ Example: The rolling bridge cell has its own paint line—integral to the cell's flame cut, punch, brake, weld, power wash/etch, powder paint, assemble, and pack operations.
- ✓ Notable in the next cell visited: a paint line with large horizontal fixtures that hold a complete set of various parts to make one unit. Because the paint booth in this line sprays from only one direction, paint fixtures are on swivels that allow the operator in the paint booth to turn the fixture 180 degrees to paint the other side.
- ✓ In shipping, outgoing boxed items pass through three separate weigh scales to ensure all parts (bolts, washers, etc.) are there—cutting missing parts from 12 to three per month.
- ✓ A centrally located, 12 x 15-foot war room (similar to the Pit in Building 1), has banners and performance trend charts on the walls.
- *PM/TPM*: Operators doing their own PM (preventive maintenance) is referred to as TPM—but here it may fall short of that.
- *Design engineering*: Most redesigns are done by MEs (manufacturing engineers), not development engineers.

V. Opportunities for Improvement

- *5S/TPM*:
  - ✓ Rotary's "TPM" appears mostly to be a conventional PM approach (i.e., regular times for PMs).
  - ✓ The good start with 5S expands rather well to embrace full TPM, in which operators gravitate toward ownership of their own equipment (instead of maintenance operating as owner).

VI. Overall Observations

- *1993 vs. 1999*: A comparison of from 1993 with 1999 observations shows major progress along world-class pathways.
- *Strategic management*: Notable is Rotary's attention to changing its strategic course. Most companies do this in "reactionary mode." Rotary's strategies for reps, certified installers, tapping internet potential, etc., are a more rational look-ahead way of thinking and planning.

CHAPTER II-55. SHADE FOODS, NEW CENTURY, KS, 1999

Shade Foods, Inc. (SFI) is the only caselet for a manufacturer of food ingredients. I was there for three days, including plant tours, presentations by Shade people and by me, discussions with staff, and—a particular reason for the visit—scoring SFI on my 16 principles of customer-centered, data-based, employee-driven world-class excellence. That scoring was an integral part of my visit and report, but discussion in this caselet omits that topic because it's peripheral to the purposes of this book.

High-Interest Topics:
- **Product pricing/costing is only about once a year or when special decisions require costs—reduces costs of costing-for-no-good-reason**
- **Multifaceted attack on high first-year quit rates**
- **Adopting continuous replenishment with/for customers**

Interest in Best-practice Principles of Manufacturing at a Food Ingredients Producer
Observations from a plant visit, Jan. 19–21, 1999

I. Descriptive Information

- *Shade Foods, Inc.*: SFI is a 50-year-old producer of food ingredients for end-product food manufacturers and, to an extent, confectionery products for retail sale. It is a wholly-owned subsidiary of Norfoods, a Canada-based, privately-held, multi-business company.
- *Competition*: Key competitors are large and tend not to be fleet-of-foot but often are able to offer low prices for high volumes, e.g., Cargill and ADM.
- *Tough customers*:
  - ✓ 1996 sales had climbed to $90 million, though suffered a $10 million loss that year—partly because customers were requiring price cuts and SFI had not reacted with cost cutting; Larry Ray took over as president and CEO.
  - ✓ SFI earned a small profit in 1997 (generally by cutting money-losing products and customers), with sales lowered to about $70 million.

- ✓ One customer had announced in 1990 that it would hold constant the cost of a 1 lb. box of its product through the decade. But (no fair!) by 1995–96 it had *cut* the cost, largely by leaning on suppliers like SFI.
- *Demographics*: SFI has about 250 employees in its 200,000 sq. ft. headquarters in Kansas—operating three shifts, seven days a week. About 200 employees are in a slightly larger building in Union City, California. A sister business, Shade Pasta, is in Fremont, Nebraska.
- *Production facilities – Kansas (partial list)*:
  - ✓ About 10–15 work centers (rooms) in the Kansas facility (nearly the same in California).
  - ✓ 16 bulk tanks for corn syrup, oils, etc.
  - ✓ Two refining rooms, one for dark chocolate and the other for colored chocolate; four chocolate lines (deposit, rake, cool tunnels, chop); and, in panning rooms, half a dozen panning machines.
  - ✓ Eight receiving docks, which use only easier-to-clean new or plastic pallets; materials arriving on old pallets are transferred.
  - ✓ Colors identify four kinds of tubs: yellow for raw material and rework, gray for trash, green for metal, red for cleaning supplies.
- *Demand patterns*:
  - ✓ Ice cream makes up about 40%; cereal, 30%; retail confections, 15%; bakery, 5%.
  - ✓ Ice cream demand surges in the summer, offset somewhat by larger sales of other products (especially candy) in winter.
- *Employment*: Some 60% of the labor force has been with SFI more than five years.
  - ✓ But keeping new hires more than one year has been a problem; temps help when needed, especially in the summer ice cream season.
  - ✓ Recently, labor shortages, especially in Kansas, have meant high overtime and employee turnover.
- *Contact persons*: Larry Ray, president & CEO; Bob Blefco, sales & marketing; Jim Cross, VP technology; Jim White, VP operations; Bill Frimel, VP purchasing; Cheryl Leweke, HR.

II. Strengths and Weaknesses

- *Unique strengths*:
    - ✓ Strong in strategic and structural linkages among sales, marketing, and customers; finance and accounting (i.e., costing and pricing); and product development.
    - ✓ Example: A several-page tract of well-considered plans and criteria for improving most areas in the company. Two specifics:
        - A 12-point plan of key criteria—notably to reduce corporate overhead by reorganizing along workflow lines rather than departments, thus to shorten response time and increase flexibility by eliminating unnecessary approvals and administrative steps.
        - A formalized program of written career paths for all employees—including desires for advancement, responsibilities, etc.
- *Weaknesses*:
    - ✓ Synchronizing to forward demands:
        - SFI is not taking advantage of a high-impact practice known variously as efficient consumer response (ECR), quick response (QR), and continuous replenishment; nor of vendor-managed inventory (VMI).
        - Continuous replenishment involves reaching out for point-of-sale data from key retail sales points—real demand information for production scheduling, in place of inaccurate forecasts and inaccurate actual orders from next-echelon customers.
        - Supplier development (a work in progress at SFI?) includes reducing to "a few good suppliers."
    - ✓ Waste: SFI's scrap and rework is about 5% (vs. 1–2% average for all competitors and 0.5% for the baking industry)—a considerable cost, mitigated a bit by sale of scrap wastes for hog feed, or OFAL.
    - ✓ People: needing more emphasis are employee empowerment, self-directed work teams, and linkages between the work force and senior management.

III. Detailed Commentary

- *Well-done*:
  - ✓ Pricing/costing: SFI does pricing/costing by product, by work center just once yearly (more often if the process changes), in contrast to many or most companies re-costing the same products and work centers every month. SFI avoids large non-value-adding overhead wastes of costing—for no good reason.
  - ✓ Tactical pricing: SFI's simple practice is just to lower the overhead rate, which lowers the price, which encourages more business to keep work centers occupied. This is in contrast to the typical company's disconnected pricing, sales, and capacity management, with rigid mark-up pricing that sometimes results in turning away a modest contract or order that holds the promise of future riches, or vice versa.
- *Needing work*:
  - ✓ It should be possible to double the 12 inventory turns in Kansas and the eight to nine turns in California. (The subject of my next visit, an American producer of a wide variety of auto interior "trim," is so well synchronized to auto assemblers that inventory turns 34 times per year.)
  - ✓ The yellow, gray, green, and red tubs should be elevated off the floor, for ergonomic reasons and to cut wasteful up-and-down load/unload motions. This could be a worthy project to tap common-sense ideas of some of the front-line associates.
  - ✓ To meet peak seasonal demands, instead of just hiring from a temp agency, establish—and re-hire year after year—a semi-permanent staff of trained casual labor; best sources: recent retirees from SFI, students, and parents who prefer to be home part-time with children and would work part days or full-time part of the year.
  - ✓ High quit rates and stated reasons—from interviews with the quitters—probably tell far less than the full story. Regardless of what they say, high stay rates depend on a host of factors:
    - People expect a food plant to be spic-and-span; it's disappointing to see powder, etc., covering equipment and floors—and a safety hazard as well.
    - People respond to an egalitarian atmosphere: The no-special-parking places practice at SFI is a worthy example. Outside

examples: At Miller Brewing, Trenton, OH, managers' offices are adjacent to the shop floor, and all managers wear the same smock as hourlies; also, an hourly (union rep) attends management staff meetings. The plant manager at Graco, Minneapolis, spends one day every week running machines, his 700–800 hourlies acting like he's one of them as he walks by (Cheryl's time spent on Shade Foods' pack line recently is the same idea).

- People who contribute ideas and track their own performance are more likely to stay.
- Opportunities to visit customers and suppliers, collect process data, and help select new equipment are meaningful to people considering a long-time or life-time job.

✓ The new, six-person internal quality/safety audit team can serve as an important counter-balance to (as I was told) overly generous external audits done by AIB (American Institute of Baking, which does food safety audits, inspection, certification, training, etc.)

✓ A sizeable, active food science staff appears to keep itself at work on product/customer projects that make good business sense—aided by cost/financial information and analysis provided by Yves Grébert's group. This appears to be a core competency and competitive advantage.

IV. Specific Comments and Suggestions

- *Customer focus*: The following are ways to energize natural inclinations of the work force to be customer-concerned:
  ✓ Customer banners with customer logos in the plant, changing as order patterns change.
  ✓ Focused customer teams of operators and technical and management staff, especially for repeat customers.
- *External awareness*: Provide healthy "competitive fear" by keeping everyone apprised of detailed competitive information.
  ✓ For operators and leads: trends in wastage, downtime, returns, physical samples, late deliveries, responses to new-product samples, time to achieve full-scale production of new items.
  ✓ For supervisors/managers: market share by product, warranty costs, unit costs, inventory turns, lead times/cycle times,

suggestions per person, training hours per person, maintenance staff per sales dollar, number of suppliers, delivery frequency, availability of slick customer-customized marketing materials in early proposal phase, etc. Sources of data: suppliers, customers, trade associations, and benchmarking.

- ✓ Plant visits:
  - Send operators to "eat-off-the-floor-clean" plants.
  - Arrange visits to plants (generally not in the food business) having "world-class" safety, TPM, self-directed work teams, single-digit changeovers, visual management/5S.

- *Quicker response*: Response times for providing customers with new-product samples and for getting up to full production on new products seem to be SFI strengths. Needed are:
  - ✓ A major effort to slash setup times and run smaller lots and a larger numbers of customer SKUs/products per time period.
  - ✓ Smaller downstream pipeline inventories should follow, eliminating various non-value-adding wastes. Upstream opportunities lie in streamlining and taking out delays with suppliers (e.g., putting cardboard suppliers on kanban).

- *Synchronizing to "drumbeat of the market"*:
  - ✓ By the time demands filter from the final consumer to SFI, they've been batched and forecast enough times as to be well out of phase with real usage. The U.S. is a crucible for treatment of this chronic, very high-cost issue, which SRI needs to address:
  - ✓ Basic to JIT are two scheduling concepts:
    - Making to a number and stopping, which allows end-of-shift time most days for operator training, data analysis, and project work—and should lead to reducing SFI's currently high use of overtime.
    - Under-scheduling the shifts, which gives enough time to meet schedules nearly all the time. Contrarily, scheduling eight hours production for an eight-hour shift means that 50% of the time—the 50% that are bad days—the schedule will not be met!

- *Coordination*: Need to address coordination and communication between the California and Kansas facilities. (Internally, some management teaming weaknesses from the past may have been shored up.)

- *Training and multi-skilling*: SFI does not have restrictive work rules or burdensome job classifications, and front-line employees can be/ are moved readily from one skill/room/product to another.
  - ✓ Missing, though, are formal skill certification and visual representations of who has attained—and has kept current on (through systematic job rotation)—what skills. Formalizing multi-skilling can help instill pride in versatility and competence among the workforce.
  - ✓ Training and wide use of problem-solving tools by the workforce also appears to be an SFI weakness.
- *Recognition and reward*: To its credit, SFI has tried many incentives (Big Bucks, President's award, etc.) and grappled with their fairness and beneficial effects. Those efforts—so far a bit frustrating and lacking in staying power—need continued emphasis.
- *Quality and visual management*:
  - ✓ Engineering, maintenance, and purchasing competently provide for delivering quality outputs, but largely through end-of-process inspections and controls. The "quality sciences" need greater emphasis, e.g., visual TQ (SPC charts, process flow charts, check sheets, etc.).
  - ✓ Process ownership of front line people is enhanced through visual devices—labeling, trend charts, process variation charts, Paretos, awards, suggestions, projects in process, cross-training matrices, etc. Little of this is evidenced at SFI.
- *Performance management*: Productivity, a dominant concern at SFI, is an internal measure. SFI should give equal/greater emphasis to externally oriented, "eyes-of-customers" measures, particularly: quality, quick response, flexibility, and value.
- *Transactions and reports*:
  - ✓ SFI is not bogged down by transactions and reports (aside from regulatory requirements for traceback, which seem thoroughly complied with). However, the new ADAGE system, in full implementation, is capable of vast overkill—so it's best to implement its subroutines selectively (i.e., the minimum you can get by with).
  - ✓ ADAGE may have valued features such as product data management, EDI, single-echelon supply-chain, kanban options, and rate-based scheduling. These tend to improve coordination and cut costs of control. If not, other means can be employed to gain the benefits (e.g., kanban on certain items) and require no computer support.

- *Facility maintenance*: SFI seems weak—relative to "best practices"—in maintaining processes to a high level of performance.
  - ✓ Bringing in equipment suppliers to help train operators is a positive step. Beyond that, total productive maintenance (TPM) should receive greater emphasis.
  - ✓ For help, two international organizations—EFESO in Milan, Italy and Proconseil in Paris, France—have strong training/advisory practices in TPM and have global clients (including North American).
- *Simple, movable, scalable, low-cost, focused or flexible equipment*:
  - ✓ While SFI equipment is not monstrous, neither is it small nor mobile. It might be possible to put some equipment (e.g., panning units) on casters, with easy coupling/uncoupling to feeder devices and utilities.
  - ✓ As process improvement begins to reduce need for storage racks, it could free up space for another production room with more equipment. More pieces of equipment, in turn, permit making more different products for more customers concurrently.
  - ✓ I did not see a sketch of the Union City plant, which has packaging lines. I would prefer to see packing at the very end of the last production process (instead of a separate packing room); also, packaging equipment on wheels can provide extra flexibility without the cost of more equipment.
- *Promoting SFI's successes/improvements*: Training and early steps to generate an improvement culture have been taken at SFI—and should pay off in future months and years, especially if each improvement is customer-focused and used in customer promotions.

CHAPTER II-56. SONIC INNOVATIONS, SALT LAKE CITY, UT, 1998

The Sonic Innovations caselet is mostly a re-formatted (in bullet points) letter to my host. Details of the production process are in my rough notes but not included (not of interest) here. Rather, the letter/caselet is organized into "very good" achievements and "high potential for improvement" items at Sonic. Sonic, in the 1990s, was fairly advanced in several aspects of flow.

High-Interest Topics:
- **Multiple cells, multiple units of equipment—replicated as sales grow**
- **Two-way kanban—with suppliers and with customers**
- **Need for "time cushions"**

**Hearing-aid Manufacturer Looks for Building on
Customer-focused Manufacturing Principles**
Impressions from a half-day Schonberger visit, Aug. 28, 1998

I. General Information

- *The company*: Sonic Innovations is a major designer and manufacturer of hearing aids.
- *Major competitors*:
  - ✓ Market leaders: Siemens, Starkey, Oticon.
  - ✓ Technology leaders: Widex, Phonak, ReSound.
- *Processes (in brief)*:
  - ✓ Sonic uses a powerful DSP chip, which is contracted out.
  - ✓ Process flow begins with receipt of a mailed order form from the audiologist (with audiogram, check-off features), which is entered into configurator software.
  - ✓ That triggers an operations sequence (highly abbreviated here): make shell, pull face plate, close, listen, finish (cut away excess and buff), ACT (auto calibration test), physical (visual), pack-out, ship.
- *Contact persons*: Andy Reguskus, president & CEO; Bob Wychoff, VP production; Jim Nee, production manager.

II. Letter to Wychoff

August 31, 1998
Mr. Bob Wychoff, VP of Production, Sonic Innovations, Salt Lake City, UT
Dear Mr. Wychoff:

I am impressed by the degree to which "world-class manufacturing" concepts are in force or in the growth plan at Sonic Innovations. In my company/plant visitations I generally take notes and write them up for my own files. For what little they may worth (considering the brevity of my visit) I am including a summary of those notes in this letter. They pertain mostly to the topics we were able to discuss during my visit (those that I can recall anyway). My most vivid impressions are the following, not in any order:

III. Very Good

- *The product itself.*
- *Kanban*: Kanban/queue limitation is in force internally and with multiple suppliers.

- *Responsiveness*: Same-day shipment via kanban; presently six-days' supply, aiming for one or two days.
- *Cells*: Production is cellular (*not* separated into functional shops) with replication as sales volumes grow.
- *Facilities*: The strategy is to have multiples of each type of equipment, facilitating cellular organization—and importantly, enabling production of multiple products at the same time.
- *On-line information*: Work instructions and specs are on-line; also bills of materials, defect photos, and barcodes.
- *Suppliers*: Careful selection of a small number of suppliers—with an outsourcing and supplier-partnership ramp-up strategy.
- *People*: Careful selection of staff; and a respect-for-people commitment (conveyed on a large wall chart).
- *Quality*: Self-inspection/quality commitment.

IV. High Potential for Improvement

- *Employee flexibility*: Embark on systematic cross-training/job rotation for the workforce and cross-careering for the support staff and technician-level people.
- *Process data recording*: Train all operators to be collectors of data (record every "hiccup"—down to root causes, where possible) all day, every day—especially using simple devices such as check sheets. Employ check-sheet, Pareto, and fishbone devices for workforce-driven continuous improvement.
- *Maintenance*: Steer the maintenance function toward a role of facilitating a transition of all routine maintenance to operators—emphasizing labeling, exact locations (e.g., shadow boards), perfect housekeeping, and zero search time.
- *Recognition/celebration*: Publicly recognize ongoing improvement activities and resulting achievements via ceremonies, prizes, visual displays (e.g., of improvement trends in changeovers, Paretos, flow charts, completed projects, etc.). Make a big deal of successes, encourage people's motivational instincts by orienting training, problem-solving, and recognition around aggravation-level company goals.
- *Suggestions*: Phase in a meaningful team/individual suggestion system.

- *Linked cells*: Tighten links between stations in the cells by moving each station/person within a hand-to-hand pass-off distance in a U-shaped (or S-shaped) configuration.
- *One-to-one flows*: Where it makes sense, strive for one-to-one flow paths within the cells. This may conflict to some extent with occasional needs to shift certain cross-trained employees from early work stations (e.g., order entry, pulling stock, starting face plates and shells) to later work stations, in order to compress cycle times.
- *Time cushions*: Build non-production time into labor plans, with extra time to be used for training, maintenance, data collection, problem-solving meetings, etc. However, on a "bad day," this time is to be used for production in order to still meet the targeted one- or two-day response time.
- *State of operations*: Implement "alcoves of excellence" in main trafficways, summarizing the state of operations (*not* the state of the business, which is beyond the manageable purview of people's jobs) on trend charts focused on quality, cycle time, flexibility, and value, as well as corrective actions on root causes (parts shortages, inconsistent training, wrong specs., undependable equipment, etc.).
- *Inventory—controlling its causes*: Rather than setting goals for inventory reduction, focus attention on causes of inventory: poor quality, long flow distances, inflexible labor, etc. As causes are reduced, lower the inventories.
- *Off-line buffer stock*: Also, for buffer inventories that are retained for infrequent emergencies, locate those buffers off-line (rather than in-line, consuming valuable cycle time and manufacturing space all year long for a rare event).
- *Audits rather than routine transactions*: Consider reducing the amount of completion reporting at each work station. To ascertain average completion times—for scheduling, staffing, and capacity planning purposes—the simpler alternative is just to do a random-sampling audit of completion times as necessary.
- *Multi-functional and multi-level coordination*: Develop strong linkages among VP-level and department or section-level managers and professionals in operations, marketing, finance—and others, as relevant. The primary aims ensure that:
  - ✓ Operations is truly customer- and real demand-oriented.
  - ✓ Sales are enabling rather than detrimental to production/capacity/supply chain limitations.

✓ Order booking and order commitment should favor the best customers and most profitable products (all customers, orders, and sales dollars are *not* equal).

- *DFMA*: Ensure that the design for manufacturing and assembly considerations are strongly supported in product and process development.

- *Staff support near at hand*: Keep support staff (manufacturing engineers, maintenance, quality, purchasing, training, budgeting, costing) close to production and sales people—for quick resolution of problems and for keeping staff's activities relevant.

- *World class by principles*: Use the WCP step-by-step continuous improvement system to drive increasing competitiveness and build a dynasty.

End of letter: Thanks for your hospitality and for the stimulating meeting with your management group.

Richard J. Schonberger

CHAPTER II-57. PRECOR, BOTHEL, WA, 1994

The Precor caselet demonstrates high commitment to best practices, including focused factories, cells, kanban, supplier involvement, cross-training, process-data-driven continuous improvement, right-sized equipment, and ergonomics. So much is right on target, with advanced thinking, that the caselet includes rather few suggestions for improvement.	***High-Interest Topics:*** • **On assembly lines, the "last one done" hits a button— noted on TV monitor above the line; if others rotated into same station are also last done, that station *needs improvement*** • **"Killing snakes" is Precor's name for fixing quality issues** • **No material handlers, no inspectors, no WIP tracking**

Multifaceted Implementation of Best Practices in Production of Fitness Equipment

Observations based on a two-hour plant visit Oct. 12, 1994

I. Setting

- *The company*:
  - ✓ Precor, a designer/producer of high-end fitness equipment, has plants in Bothel (visited) and Woodinville (not visited), both suburbs of Seattle.
  - ✓ Founded as Precision Corp. in 1980 by industrial designer David Smith, the company began with a fitness device designed by Smith in his garage in Mercer Island.
- *Parent company*: In 1989, Premark became Precor's parent company—and said to Precor, "You will have TQ." That led to Precor's hiring of Rath and Strong for managerial training (soft side of TQ).
- *Tour host and key contacts*: Bob Sepulveda, TQ manager (formerly IS manager); Bill Setter; Harlan Anderson.

II. General Information

- *Work scheduling*: Three shifts in the fall busy season make 350 treadmills/day (peak is 500 per day). In summer it's 100 or 150 per day—in a four-day week (Friday is for catch-up).
- *Work force*: Employs 300 core employees and 150 temps, and a "third/weekend shift" in the busy season. Temps get some benefits (401 K) and are eligible for profit-sharing.
- *Improvement intensity*: Precor's aim is 50% improvement per year in everything.
- Organizational focus: A business and plant focus is manifested in two businesses:
  - ✓ Commercial, $100m sales of durable fitness equipment made in Building W2 (105,000 sq. ft.) under Bill Setter. Steady demand production is 24/7, striving for 100% reliability.
  - ✓ Retail/consumer, $70m sales of consumer-grade equipment in Building W1 (55,000 sq. ft.) under Harlan Anderson. 30% of demand value occurs in the last quarter (Christmas season); striving for value, cost, and features.
- *Process focus*: The assembly plant is focused on process flow-oriented assemble-test-ship. In the fabrication plant the weld, paint, etc., processes are complicated to some extent by considerable outsourcing, e.g., of wiring harnesses and circuit boards.

- *Plants*: Formerly, there were seven buildings in Bothell, WA; now there are three newer plants, plus HQ, in Woodinville, WA, and a warehouse in Maltby, WA.

III. Product Line

- *Product*: The dominant products are treadmills and stationary bikes—both informally called "bikes."
- *Commercial*: Bikes for commercial customers cost around $5,000 and have stronger fasteners and welds, better bearings to withstand many hours per day of use—and also wheels (which retail bikes do not have).
- *Retail*: Bikes for home use look about the same and share many of the parts (e.g., frames and plastic) but require toughness to withstand only three to four hours of daily use. Retail production capacity (Building W1) is 120 bikes per day, but in the slower season output is 65 per day.

IV. Strengths

- *Manufacturing*: Precor calls it "HVM," for high velocity manufacturing (named by Yanoosh).
- *Processes*:
  - ✓ The facility has product-dedicated weld booths, its own board shop and wire harness shop, and its own tool shop.
  - ✓ Some drilling, cable making, chassis, motor, and connector processes are done on assembly lines.
- *Five assembly lines*: Four treadmill lines and one skier line. Lines move every 5, 10, 15 minutes.
- *Last one done*: On-line TV monitors high above and near the ends of the lines/cells tick down the minutes of flow time; they restart the clock when each new bike starts.
  - ✓ Each assembler has a button nearby. As each cell-team member hits the button, that member's task is noted as *done* on the monitor.
    - ■ When the last (slowest) assembler hits the button, that station is flagged as a *possible* problem.

- ■ After job rotations, if, again and again, the last one done is at that same station, it more strongly suggests problems there, revealing a target for improvement.
  - ✓ Data is also collected as to reasons for slow completions (bad part, tool, equipment, training, etc.). This mode of continuous data-driven process improvement is one of many notable reasons why Precor has halved employment even as sales have surged.
- • *Materials*:
  - ✓ Direct materials from suppliers go from dock-to-line—with backflush costing (and inventory "relief" on inventory records) by a computer transaction at the end of the assembly line.
  - ✓ Formerly under MRPII, WIP was tracked; now, there's no tracking.
  - ✓ Fasteners are replenished by line fill.
  - ✓ Kanban
    - ■ All cardboard is on kanban; also steel, shaped aluminum, and fasteners.
    - ■ All kanban IDs are riveted to containers (no designator for 1 of 5, 2 of 5, etc.).
- • *Supplier-partners*:
  - ✓ Dual suppliers get Precor feedback on each other's performance so that they can know/respond to their competition.
  - ✓ Supplier selection and certification criteria: 70 points for quality and speed, 20 for price, and ten for responsibility and cooperation.
- • *Inventory*: WIP inventory is so small that it isn't measured, and $0.5 million worth of racks have been removed. A graph shows FGI (finished-goods inventory) rather stable since 1999, but raw is falling steeply; and overall inventory turns have gone from 4.4 in 1999, to 7.3 in 2000, to 8.9 in 2001, to 10.6 in 2002.
- • *Material handling*:
  - ✓ There are no material handlers, Operators use pallet jacks (no fork trucks were in evidence) and extensive types of homemade push/pull carts—for any and every part.
  - ✓ Carts are modified repeatedly for easier load/unload, movement without strain or damage. Examples:
    - ■ Carts have bolted rather than hard-fixed wheels so that wheels are easily changed when worn, and carts are carefully padded to prevent handling damage to bikes and components.

- ■ Cart load and unload heights match what's easy for people and have handles ergonomically placed so that they're easy to pull straight without strain. (I had never before seen that kind of attention to simple, innovative ergonomic devices.)
- *Paint*: Commercial bikes go through five-stage powder paint, with gray primer and two final coats.
  - ✓ Booths on rails allow very quick color changes, two daily.
  - ✓ Unlike most plants, here there is no urge to keep paint hooks full, so painting is kanban-synchronized with assembly—85 part numbers needing to be painted.
- *Hardware department*:
  - ✓ Four hardware (fasteners) carriers are on wheels, plus two stationary ones—holding a tray full of nuts or screws.
  - ✓ For access (e.g., for a screw), the operator aligns a piece of hole-punched sheet with the placement spindle, which deposits one screw.
- *Quality*: Precor eliminated all inspectors and uses many fail-safing devices.
  - ✓ Warranty costs have fallen (since 1999?) from 2.6% to 2.2%.
  - ✓ Field failures are called "snakes" and "killing snakes" are tracked visually: snakes killed; snakes alive.
  - ✓ On-time performance basis: two days early, zero days late.
  - ✓ In the machine shop, all machines are on SPC (using pre-control charts if 2.0 CPK; otherwise they use X-bar and R charts).
- *Problem solving*: Cell teams are required to meet once monthly with a formal agenda; but they actually (I'm told) meet daily (I think I saw an ad-hoc cell meeting taking place). All employees get trained in cellular and "in-lining" concepts.
- *Workforce*:
  - ✓ To keep track of skill attainments, each person has a dossier (print-reading skill, etc.). By the end of first year, the employee is cross-trained in critical functions, able to do 80% of the stations in the cell, and can advance from Level 1 to Level 2.
  - ✓ Everyone gets profit-sharing with a "profit-plus multiplier" for quality. No suggestion system.
- *Competitive analysis*: For commercial products (Building W2), outside sales reps buy all competing products (I saw some on the factory floor). Precor MEs, quality engineers, etc., come together to analyze them.

- *Product/component design*: Precor has Boothroyd-Dewhurst DFMA software. Revenue per part number (Bill Potter's hot button) is calculated by audit once yearly by product line—currently ranging from $2,000 to $137,000 per P/N.

V. Production Processes—By Building

- *Building W1 – Retail products*:
  - ✓ Three years ago, assembly cells were long and narrow, but now they are short and wide, with the extra width used for more line-side staging of larger preassembled modules, plus subassembly and fab stations at line-side. (This configuration, allowing for module-builds at lineside, should be—but isn't—the norm for most manufacturers of medium- to large-sized products—a topic that comes up in a few other caselets.)
  - ✓ W1 is badly shaped—rather long and narrow, with welding positioned too far at one end. Bill Dixon said he wished welding had been placed 40 ft to the left so that assembly cells could be on both sides of it.
  - ✓ The stubby assembly cells are straight lines and have a glassed-in station near the end for quality checks (including someone riding the bike, running the treadmill); after that is packout.
- *Building 2 – Commercial products (heavy duty, large, tough frames)*:
  - ✓ Includes cutting, welding, grinding—with the following equipment:
    - Two waterjet cutters (they can cut three-inch thick titanium—which was needed for one order by Sargent Controls, Tucson), and a laser cutter for low-volume production.
    - Seven or eight frame welding booths.
    - Grinder (what was welded), with big belts for belt sand/grinding.
  - ✓ Scheduling is to a rate, which stays stable for a month but with model-mix changes.
  - ✓ Cells have not yet been widened and shortened much in this building, but will be. Welding robots are right beside the paint booth, with welding taking six minutes.
- *Building 3 – Components*: Three main areas:
  - ✓ These cells are generally U-shaped.

✓ Lots of dedicated milling machines (befitting an 80–20 product division).

- Emphasis is on having plenty of equipment, dedicated to avoiding setups; avoid inventories; and respond very quickly.
- Steel is delivered daily.

✓ Brake presses (five or six) are zoned off by tape, with no one allowed inside except operators. Two of the presses have red lights flashing—a safety warning that the machine is set to run and that no one may approach except the operator.

✓ Three other processes are: Shear blanks (Precor *tries* to order blanks to size); punch/deburr (five Amada punches); inspect.

VI. Observations

- *Facilities*: Plant is very clean and well lit, with what seems to be the very best equipment.
- *Space*: The plant seems a bit tight on space. Both labor-intensive and machine processes are very (excessively?) close together.
- *Size*: At the same time, the plant itself is too big. It is better to have multiple smaller buildings, each focused on its own product family.
- *Machines*: Molding machines, and other machines, too, are grouped together, with batch production. Precor should endeavor to break up the machines and move them into subassembly cells; or sub-assemble from parts conveyed off the end of the molding machine.
- *Ergonomics*: Jobs seemed quite friendly to backs, arms, etc.—except, in some places, for very short work cycles, which mean repetitive-motion problems. Each person on the assembly lines has space enough to take a few steps for each operation, and the variety of assembly operation is good for ergonomics.
- *Visualization*: Good displays of competitors' products, lots of banners extolling quality, and the 8.5 x 11 wall charts that track improvements. But dominant in these displays are efficiency and defects, with no signs regarding flow time, flow distance, inventory, etc.
- *5S*: Also, it appears that the plant is not very much involved in use of 5S (precise labeling, color-coding, etc.).

CHAPTER II-58. GOULDS PUMPS, SENECA FALLS, NY, 1993

I toured Goulds the evening before my two-day seminar. The next day, my voice gave out—and a make-up second day took place the next month, along with a second plant tour. With two tours, my feedback report to Goulds included numerous process details. Suggestions/opportunities for improvement, however, were brief, having been built into and discussed during the seminar, and debated while on the tours. Some of the process details have been pulled from the main part of this caselet and summarized in sidebars.

High-Interest Topics:
- **Extensive training in TQM, cells, etc., including wide-ranging go-see visits to other good plants and a big library of videos**
- **Lots of corrective action teams to take it from there**
- **Will the union follow through with a provisional agreement to reduce job classifications from 400 to 4?**

Emphasis on Cells, Lot Sizes, Inventories, etc., in Pump Manufacturing

Plant visitations, May 11 and June 14, 1993

In connection with two Schonberger seminar days

I. General information

- *Contacts*: John Morphey, Group VP; Jeryl Mitchell, director, learning and development; Charlie Dhalle, head of manufacturing engineering.; Ed Wollmuth; Ruth Gabak; Bob Cerza; Bob Butler; Joe Boggan, No. 2 shop.
- *The company*: Goulds Pumps has two main divisions: Water Systems Div. (WSD – small pumps, high-volume) and Engineered Products Div. (EPD – large and very large, common and highly configured pumps).
- *Seneca Falls facilities*: WSD is in Building 1, EPD in Building 2. Also, a 100,000 sq. foot distribution warehouse is in Auburn, NY, 15 miles to the north.

- ✓ Repair parts for both WSD and EPD are packed out of Building 1.
- ✓ Component parts are stocked in Building 1: 45,000 sf of WIP (work-in-process) inventory.
- *Other facilities*:
  - ✓ EPD has additional manufacturing facilities in City of Industry, CA; Baldwinsville, NY; and Huntington, WV.
  - ✓ A turbine division is in Lubbock and Slaton, TX.
  - ✓ Foreign operations: EPD–Cambridge, ON, Canada; Mexico City; Maracay, Venezuela; Ijmuiden, Netherlands; Singapore; Chung Won-Gun, Korea. WSD–Montecchio, Maggiore, Italy; Axminister, Devon, U.K.; Alzenau, Germany; Singapore; and Manila, P.I.
  - ✓ Regional distribution centers (DCs) are in Memphis; Chicago; Florida; Sacramento; and Kitchener, Ontario (which also includes assembly).
- *Employment*:
  - ✓ The workforce is represented by the United Steel Workers (about four came to the seminar, including Dick Corcoran, regional director from Buffalo).
  - ✓ Members (rank-and-file employees) are on a 50-year-old individual incentive system, with average incentive pay of 40–50% (those high payouts due to loose standards).
  - ✓ There is little staff-level turnover but quite a bit at the VP-level.
- *TQM-problem-solving focus*:
  - ✓ TQM (total quality management) training per employee averaged 28 hours in 1991. Team leaders receive 40 hours of training in problem-solving; members, 12 hours.
  - ✓ Overall, 95% of WSD employees have had this training; corporate wide, 60%. The training is now going overseas (e.g., to Venezuela).
  - ✓ There are 250 problem-solving teams. A portion of all executive bonuses is for successful support of at least one quality problem-solving team.
- *Inventory*:
  - ✓ A locked stockroom holds $44m in inventory.
  - ✓ All that inventory involves many handling transactions in and out of stockrooms—as is portrayed in Figure 58.1:

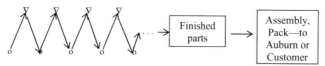

Key: ∇ Trip into/out of WIP parts stockroom
　　o Successive operations

FIGURE 58.1
Parts handling and handling transactions.

II. Water Systems Division (WSD)

- *Tour of plant*: Led by Charlie Dhalle and consultant Bob Bender. For WSD, miscellaneous process details from the tour are listed in Sidebar 1.
- *Setups*: Operators don't do much setup, in part because of dedicated equipment and pre-setting on duplicate tool sets.
- *Lot sizes*: Typical lots for component parts are 5,000 pieces; final assembly lots are six or seven pumps.
- *Manufacturing processes*: WSD is laid out into separate processes:
  - ✓ In one building, high-volume assembly of Jet pumps, effluent pumps, and light commercial pumps takes place in 13 U-shaped assemble/test lines (not cells) with a long conveyor feeding three packing lines, and finally to shipping.
  - ✓ Machine shop, paint, and sub-assembly in another building.

SIDEBAR 1   WSD PROCESS DETAILS

Product: Brass, stainless, iron, pumps

　Transfer line: Machining of motor cover done on homemade line with 11 drill and tap and facing operations—all electro-mechanical and holding 18 pallets

　Bullard: Machine with 12 chucks takes two shifts to set up

　Stampings: Formerly sub-contracted; now, a toolmaker runs it (thanks to the purchase of a massive tandem punch press), sharpening tools while machine runs itself

　Paint: A paint "superstar" manages area with everything labeled, neat, clean, and sharp

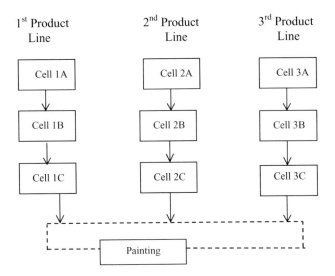

FIGURE 58.2
Linked cells for each of the three main product lines.

- *Plan for cells*: A plan calling for linked cells for each of three main product lines abutting the paint line is shown in Figure 58.2.
- *First cell*:
  - ✓ A version of this plan is to put the first linked cell—for four-inch submersible pumps—into the WIP storage area, right off the new progressive punch press, but there's insufficient space there.
  - ✓ The Bob-and-Charlie team proposed (in a recent meeting) moving some WIP to Auburn to make room for the cell but that was countered by the argument that they will lose control.
- *Kanban*:
  - ✓ 20 part sets come to final assembly on about 20 trolleys, two pumps per kanban kit.
  - ✓ A kanban rack between the hex shaft cell and assembly holds five or ten long, narrow boxes (blue plastic) of each shaft. The kanban label is on the front of the box, which is turned around to face the hex shaft cell when empty, thus authorizing more production.
  - ✓ *Extensive training*: John Morphy, group VP (was CFO before October 1992) hired Bob Bender, a consultant from California, in June 1992. Bender spends one week per month on cellular design and cell training, JIT, etc. (Bender has 25 years in the

pump industry, three years in consulting). Under the Bender influence are:

- Visitation trips taken to Stone, Gilbarco, Harley-Davison (York, PA), and Baldor Electric (Fort Smith, AR).
- Book-study groups, using JMT and WCM.
- Use of training videos: "Dwight," "JIT/JIC," John Deere, and Schonberger WCM tapes.
- Cellular training classes that include quick setup and TPM topics.

- *Improvement projects*:
  - ✓ Florida Power and Light's "7-step" SPC approach has led to seven completed 7-step projects, highlighted along one wall on a big display. (But lack of focus among project teams has caused these projects to have somewhat disappointing results.)
  - ✓ Corrective action team (CAT): CAT2 started February 15. It works great in order entry, but in manufacturing it adds paperwork and more people standing around without parts.
  - ✓ The cellular team in WSD has preliminary approval from the union to reduce job classifications from 400 to four.
- *Suppliers*: Very little supplier reduction has taken place so far—and there is still a lot of incoming inspection, involving two inspectors.
- *Product development*:
  - ✓ A new product-development process was launched in 1992; and a concurrent-engineering team in 1993.
  - ✓ WSD is presently working on improving its computer-integrated engineering.

III. Engineered Products Division

- *EPD facility*: The EPD building is about 1m sq. ft., including a foundry, producing 800–1,000 pumps per day (7,000 double-suction and 16,000 end-suction pumps per year). See Sidebar 2 for some process details.
- *Employeees*: 1,150 employees are in the division, with half on second shift for assembly. Operators do their own gauging.
- *Performance*: 65% of orders are on-time within a week (85% in end-suction pumps). Average inventory turns: 2.7. Manufacturing lead time: 6–26 weeks. Order entry (customer to release to

---

SIDEBAR 2   EPD PROCESS DETAILS

Assembly: 12 focused multi-station assembly stations—with assembly time of 30 minutes, and up to a half day for end-suction pumps. Pumps assembled at least twice because pump testing usually finds defects

Fabrication: Some "cells," e.g., mill-drill working with boring on opposite sides of an aisle; frames are done in flexible manufacturing cells (FMC)

Setup: One example has the operator set up the next job in a separate chuck while machine runs with the first chuck

Engineering: Upgrading from 2D to 3D design; also CAD/CAM & solid modeling

---

manufacturing.): 4–6 weeks. An engineered order is many pages long.

- *Quality certification*: EPD is certified to ISO-9001 (the first U.S. pump plant so certified).
- *CATs*: CAT1 teams are in reengineering, preparation of proposals, materials, and shipping. Computer systems for customer service, manufacturing, and engineering are being upgraded, replacing a not-very-effective homegrown MRP system.
- *SPC*: Statistical process control has begun in frames, casings, stuffing box covers, and shafts.
- *Transactions*: A current emphasis is on more discipline in stock records and BOMs (bills of materials), eliminating manual transactions, and trying to gain control through computer transactions in labor reporting and inventory tracking.
- *Missing*: There is no plan for reducing job classifications; and no formal, systematic preventive maintenance.

IV. Suggestions/Opportunities

- *WSD needs focus*:
  - ✓ Set up three focused factories in Building 1: 1. Jet pumps. 2. Sewage, cooling, sump pumps. 3. Commercial (e.g., pumps for Whirlpool and GE dishwashers).
  - ✓ Partially (e.g., in assembly or in fabrication, or both) subdivide commercial into a customer-dedicated cell for Whirlpool, another GE, etc.

- ✓ Re-focus/fix the 7-step SPC effort—which has not been as successful as should be, likely because project team members lack cross-functional experience/vision.
- *Product design*:
  - ✓ In collaboration with main commercial customers—such as Whirlpool and GE—try to forge agreement on common, standardized (instead of company-specific) parts or modules (Japanese competitors do this, to their mutual advantage; U.S. companies fight too much and end up with higher costs).
  - ✓ DFMA: for example, over 100 lengths of hex steel shafts need standardization.
- *Inventory*:
  - ✓ Set maximum FGI levels (increased in steps during the planned seasonal buildup period). Upon reaching a maximum, halt production and shift to another product, or stop altogether rather than just keeping capacity busy (for example, I watched a worker assembling four-inch submersibles at a furious pace, adding to already bloated inventory of that item in the Auburn warehouse.)
  - ✓ Motors from Franklin Electric come in boxes of 40, but the assembly lot is 20. Ask Franklin to pack by 20s.
  - ✓ Adopt, as standard practice, the sending of most parts from every fab and sub-assembly lot *directly* to the next operation—not to a WIP stockroom, which is best treated as overflow (then work on eliminating the need for overflow).
- *Miscellaneous*:
  - ✓ The wage structure in WSD exceeds that of competitors (because WSD wages have been made equal to EPD's, even though EPD products require higher skills). This issue could be addressed through HR and the union. (Higher wages are an insignificant reason for high costs, but higher skills in EPD deserve a higher wage.)
  - ✓ For setups in the tube mill, duplicate tooling "rafts" are anchored simply by driving wooden wedges in place to secure the "raft," but this still takes eight hours. This setup task should employ *parallel setup teams*, thus to slash lot sizes and WIP stocks.

✓ CNC lathes have quick setup but *still* produce in large lot sizes; those lots can easily be reduced with no risk, since lot size changes are reversible. Also, there are enough lathes to put two in each of the three focused factories, and thus automatically reduce setup times (in that the cells are product-focused).

✓ Paint in matched sets? Right now parts are painted in mixed sizes to avoid bunches of too-heavy parts overloading the chain, but this practice seems ripe for change.

• *EPD needs focus*: Divide EPD into two or four natural focused factories; for example, one factory for double-suction pumps and another for end-suction pumps.

• *Implementation*: Start conversion to two focused factories *now* by moving the following to the #2 plant: 1. Assembly of end-section pumps. 2. "Star" turning machines—for impellers.

V. Goulds in General

• *Incentives*:

✓ One attractive option is to shift from individual to group incentive pay. But a much better option is to work with the union to move away from labor standards and incentive pay altogether.

✓ Give supervisors the authority to do what is necessary to move people to where the work is—including making temporary pay adjustments. Example:

■ In WSD, there is a worker on a pack line who, paid a lower indirect labor rate, accumulates pumps to be packed on a long conveyor just so he can take a break or go to another area to fetch something.

■ But assemblers (higher-paid direct labor) should be able to come over to help pack a few times per day as needed.

• *Miscellaneous*:

✓ Visually enhance process management via improvement charts displaying trends in setup time, WIP, flow distance, response ratios, and so forth.

✓ Find one or more setup experts among machinists and turn them loose.

✓ In EPD and WSD, put together multifunctional kanban teams, including front-line operators. As first action, put, say, 50 parts on kanban per week in each division.

✓ Organize an order-entry team (currently a serious competitive weakness).

✓ Get all hardware, cardboard, and crating material on kanban with daily (or once every two days) deliveries, with a monthly invoice.

✓ Consider a "cold turkey" strategy for dealing with bloated inventories.

CHAPTER II-59. GENIE INDUSTRIES, REDMOND, WA, 1994

Genie Industries exemplifies one of the best, early examples of flow manufacturing in the off-road vehicles sector. The caselet does not include suggestions for improvement, mainly because I visited the company to gather information (for a formal research project) on the goings-on there, and not for give-and-take topical discussions. For further information on Genie's strong relationship with a key supplier, see caselet II-45.

High-Interest Topics:
- **Migration of flow concepts (cells, kanban, TQ, supplier partners, cross-training, etc.) from one area to another—and beyond**
- **Synchronized one-piece flows for high-mix, low-volume large vehicular lifts**

Why Genie Has Long Been a Go-to Location to See Flow Production

Impressions from a Schonberger Plant Visitation, September 29, 1994

I. General Information

- *Genie*: This privately-held company designs and manufactures industrial lifts.

- ✓ Its 12 product lines range from small, low-reach, all-aluminum lifts, to 80-foot-reach steel, extension-mast, multi-tiered vehicles with operator basket and controls at the top.
- ✓ The 12 product lines subdivide into many models, mainly relative to how high they reach: 5, 10, 15, 20, and 25 feet for aluminum; up to 80 feet for steel.
- *Customers*: Serving both end users and leasing businesses, Genie produces largely to customer orders, with a small percentage made for stock.
- *Competitors*: Pennsylvania-based JLG (which owns National Crane) and Grove Crane.
- *Plant tour*: Bob Wilkerson, president, led the tour. Bob, wearing a Genie-embroidered sport shirt, drinks diet Pepsi (no coffee). At about 6 feet, thick dark hair, well-built but not at all fat, just a bit reserved and hesitant in speech, he is friendly but not gushy. He has been with Genie since 1971. He and two partners bought the company in 1977.
- *Top-notch advice*: In 1997 Genie brought in Colin Fox of Delta Point Consulting (specializing in all aspects of JIT production). Fox's focus at Genie was on TQM (total quality management), along with JIT (just-in-time) suppliers, kanban, visual management, housekeeping, and small group improvement activities. Fox had been a principal at Omark Industries, which, along with Hewlett-Packard, was one of the first (early 1980s) non-Japanese manufacturers to deeply plunge into just-in-time production.
- *Reason for the visit*: I had invited Genie to be among the first companies to participate in my "World Class Manufacturing Benchmarking" research (later growing to more than 500 companies) that scored themselves on "16 principles of customer-focused, employee-driven, data-based improvement," which was begun in 1994 and continued until a few years ago.

II. Improving Competitiveness

- *Financial gains*: Genie, with 610 people, and $51m sales, was not making money. Now at 425 people and $95m sales, Genie is thriving financially and otherwise.

- *Suppliers*: 30 JIT suppliers deliver every day, or more often (American Steel delivers twice per day). It is common for suppliers to deliver pre-kitted parts.
- *Lead times*: Manufacturing LT formerly was 3–4 weeks, now is 3–4 days, with WIP (work in process) reduced 60%. I didn't see stockrooms for WIP, but I did see two or three small raw-material stockrooms.
- *Employees*: The workforce is all non-union, with high levels of cross-training.
- *Manufacturing configuration*: There are three manufacturing areas for three primary processes: aluminum, steel fabrication, and steel assembly.
- *Aluminum lifts*: These are produced in a separate building; the processes—all in cells—are welding-fabrication to subassembly to final assembly, with a build rate of 35 lifts per day.
  - ✓ Components must transfer to the other building for painting, then return for completion of subassembly and/or final assembly.
  - ✓ Two carousels (A and B) in the center of the building hold fabricated masts vertically—those carousels holding up to 200 units, if full. Beside each carousel is a vertical stand holding about 52 kanban disks—which serve as authority to fabricate another mast section each time that there is a carousel opening with a disk attached.
  - ✓ Carousel openings can hold singles, doubles (two sections hinged together), triples, and probably quads (this referring to the number of bends in the crane boom). Smaller lifts are made on the mezzanine.
- *Steel lifts and main offices*: The main, long building has steel fabrication in the far wing, assembly in the center wing, and offices at the street end.
  - ✓ In the fabrication wing, welding cells have large fixtures, a shot blaster, a cleaning booth, paint booths, and a paint-hook line. Welding booths are bays that build a whole mast unit, chassis, or turntable. Some masts go directly across to shot-blast/paint, others to secondary operations first.
  - ✓ Assembly wing:

- There are two focused assembly lines, one for smaller lifts, the other for larger ones. Each have five positions for progressive assembly. Tires are delivered daily at first position, so the lift can move on its own wheels through the remaining four positions.
- Assemblies move up one position about every 2.5 hours. A few extra lift baskets were sitting idle because it takes 24 hours of internal cycle time to complete one. A few other components were also idle because of changeover to a new model.
- For reasons of capacity balance, the favored assembly sequence has a large (e.g., 80-foot) lift interspersed with a few smaller lifts.
- In the center between the two lines, and adjacent to 4th position, are some electrical cells, on pull (kanban) with assembly lines. Hydraulics go into masts, etc., at earlier positions.

✓ The mezzanine, for small-lift assembly, also produces service parts, 95% of which are shipped the same day.

- *Kanban vs. work orders*: Bob says a few items are still on work orders because of long supplier lead times, the goal of full kanban not quite realized. He thinks competitors are also doing TQM, kanban, etc.

III. Update

- *Go-to location*: Genie soon became (and still is) a go-to location for "best-practice" tourism—including serving as a primary source for Boeing in its own flow-manufacturing initiatives. A current attraction is Genie's "Moose Works" (formerly the "Moonshine Shop"), where skilled associates take turns working on carts, fixtures, and other devices for tryouts in operations.
- *Terex*: Genie was acquired by Terex in 2001, and Colin Fox (who had been a consultant to Genie) became a Terex senior VP in 2004. Hall states that Genie's system became the "model to transform all of Terex" [and] thirty-eight members of the Genie leadership team have been dispersed to various Terex business units."* In the following five years (2002 through 2007) Terex's inventory turnover surged upward from a miserable 2.2 to 3.8.

---

* Robert W. Hall, "Uncorking the Genie from the Bottle," *Target* (2nd Issue, 2006): 6–14.

CHAPTER II-60. MARLOW INDUSTRIES, DALLAS, TX, 1999

The plant tour, the basis for the caselet, conveniently fit into my travel schedule, which had me in Dallas for my two-day public seminar. Part II of the caselet includes significant detail on the semiconductor-oriented production process, but also some topical discussion related to employee's jobs. Part III suggests ways for Marlow to enhance some already strong areas of performance, as well as add things that have been missing.	***High-Interest Topics:*** • **Eight mini-factories with moderate-sized cross-trained teams** • **Everyone is well-trained in TQM, on "action teams," and with representation in weekly TQM Council meetings** • **Station cycle times define bad jobs (highly repetitive, very short-cycle) and good jobs (longer-cycle)**

Marlow's Focused Plants Help Cope with Growing Sales

Observations based on a brief evening plant tour, Sept. 21, 1999

In connection with two-day Schonberger seminar, September 21–22

I. Basic Information

- *The company*: Closely-held Marlow Industries is a 1991 Baldrige award winner.
  - ✓ It processes raw materials (e.g., bismuth and tellurium) into thermoelectric (TE) semiconductors, assembles the devices into TE coolers (employing the "Peltier effect"), and integrates the coolers into heat exchangers for commercial and defense applications.
  - ✓ Marlow, with about 160 people in 1991, now has about double that number. It had one layoff a few years ago following a rapid ramp-up to meet demands of single customer, who then cancelled the contract.
  - ✓ Marlow's organization features three customer-focused business teams (CFBTs).

- *Competition*: Competitors tend to have a catalog of standard products, whereas Marlow has a common front end (ceramics and elements) but then customizes to customers' specialized needs.
  - ✓ That entails higher overhead costs (engineering) but engenders higher prices.
  - ✓ Production is back-scheduled from the customer due date.
- *Vertical integration*: Production of its own ceramics (crystal pulling, etc.) makes Marlow rather highly vertically integrated (aluminum nitride ceramics, however, are outsourced).
- *Facilities*: Four leased buildings house central offices, central production of ceramics, and focused mini-factories:
  - ✓ Each of eight mini-factories has about 15 cross-trained employees plus a supervisor, all organized by market segments. Five mini-factories are for assembly, and the following three (of the five) produce materials (each fed by centralized ceramic production):
    - ■ Defense, space, photonics (DSP, *not* meaning "digital signal processor"): applications include infra-red devices, CCDs (charge-coupled devices), and focal-point arrays.
    - ■ Laser cooling of components that go into fiber-optics networks: 50–70K units are produced per month in 30 different designs (the top five are about 80%). Customers want 20% annual cost reductions. Marlow has about 90% market share and is usually a single source (it lacks one major account, Nortel, but now has ten projects with Nortel that represent the potential to become a major account; it lost most Japanese business apparently because of insufficient presence in Japan and overall lack of resources).
    - ■ Commercial cooling is in two parts: mechanical-industrial-commercial (MIC) and large modules (LM).
- *Costing*: Marlow calculates profit monthly, by part number; controllable and uncontrollable costs are calculated in every cost center.
- *Suppliers*: After supplier-reduction activities, most of its 20 key suppliers are certified for "ship-to-stock" without inspection.
- *Continuous improvement*: From a write-up on Marlow's 1991 Baldrige National Quality Award, employee involvement is fostered by a flat organization structure and participation of all in TQM activities:

✓ 32 hours' training per year in quality methods are for all employees, including temps.

✓ Team representatives attend weekly TQM Council meetings.

✓ Nearly all employees are in "action teams" or "employee-effectiveness teams." [However, the diverse workforce, especially on 2nd shift (which is when I visited), is an obstacle to team-based activities]

• *Contact persons*: Raymond Marlow, CEO and president; Chris Witzke, senior VP, arranged this plant tour. Tour guides: Rick Flores, operations manager (attended December 1998 Dallas seminar); Dwight Johnson, VP and general manager, Laser Cooling Group.

II. Production Processes

• *Ceramic production*: Feeds the three focused factories with about 40 million dies per month out of several grades of material:

✓ With a simple bill of materials of about seven or eight components, processes are: screen print (one machine for the first screen, profiling); plate (copper, gold); send through about 16 tanks (for detergent clean, rinse, acid clean, etc.); stencil solder paste (second screen); dicing (three dicing machines).

✓ Crystals to dies—see Sidebar 1.

✓ About one of 100 ingots is tested. Typical scrap is 10–15%, 25% in the highest grade (e.g., from the lower part of tube; the top part is not as pure). Quartz and virtually all other materials are recovered and sold to recyclers (e.g., bismuth, tellurium, and selenium sludge go to a supplier for re-use).

✓ Comparison of resistivity graphs shows one operator (of 14) getting far better, more consistent results than others; so they

SIDEBAR 1   CRYSTALS-TO-DIES PROCESS

Mix raw materials (bismuth, tellurium) in a quartz tube. Seal tube. Load into crystal-growing machine (about 20 machines). Drop. Grow crystal (anywhere from one to three days). Break tube to extract ingot. Slice ingot into thin wafers, maybe of five-inch diameter (on about six slicing machines). Chemically upbraid. Break out. Wet-nickel plating. Mount (bond) on glass. Dice. Separate from glass. Inspect. Send to kitting area in warehouse.

SIDEBAR 2   LASER COOLING PROCESS

Load positive (P) and negative (N) dies into rubber matrix (molded in house). Stack (flux application). Clean. Lead attach (flux again). Clean. Thermal shock. Vacuum bake. Test. Burn in 24 hours (the typical, "historical" burn-in time). Test data. Final tin. Test. Inspect. Pack and ship.

    isolated that operator's procedures and trained the others in the same methods.

- *Building 4*: This "Miller 2" building has two mini-plants, one for laser cooling, one for DSP.
  - ✓ Laser cooling: See Sidebar 2. (Lucent also requires a vacuum-seal step.)
  - ✓ Bad and good jobs are together in one U-shaped cell:
    - The bad-jobs part of the cell has about 15 associates, all with sit-down jobs, and a four-person "gang" near the end of the cell looking through microscopes to solder two lead wires to each die, taking an estimated 15–20 seconds on each unit. Sit-down-all-day jobs and very short-cycle jobs are bad for bodies and minds.
    - The ergonomic problem of looking down through a microscope is to be dealt with by changing to magnified viewing of dies on computer screens, which should help.
    - Good jobs, all other stations in the cell, have station cycle times of 60–80 seconds.
- *Miller 1*: This is a focused factory for two kinds of commercial cooling products.
  - ✓ An LM (large-module) cell (e.g., for Raytheon-TI Systems, Cadillac) with two IBM robots doing solder reflow, 16 per matrix. The plan is to add a test machine to make the cell self-contained.
  - ✓ MIC products are high-volume (3,000 units per shift), low-margin coolers (e.g., for Russia, China), plus picnic coolers for Coleman and others (these coolers can be plugged into a car lighter for power and the polarity reversed for heat). They are made on three lines in three product families and include three Hiller reflow furnaces. MIC has its own engineering.

III. Opportunities for Improvement

- *Missing elements*: The following may be largely missing and thus potential targets for improvement: 5S/TPM (exact labeling, positioning, and visual templates can help with the issue of a diverse workforce), fail-safing, check sheets (for use by all hourly employees), formal queue limits (kanban) between processes, and setup/line-changeover time charts.
- *Flow times*:
  - ✓ To help cut flow times (and stabilize them for better predictability) consider trend charts tracking flow times and flow-time variation in each process group (the WIP chart in Miller 1 could be expanded to show WIP *trend*).
  - ✓ Also, employ formal kanban in all processes, which may stabilize flow times enough to make it attractive to schedule forward.
- *Job rotation*: Set minimum job-rotation frequency for every cell team. This would be especially attractive for very short station cycle time jobs, e.g., the four associates soldering leads to dies (rotate, say, every two hours for this tough job—unless it can be combined with one or more other short-cycle tasks).
- *Costing frequency*: Consider cutting way back on part-number costing—to events involving competitive changes (e.g., in decisions relating to product/process design, customers, materials, and prices).
- *Work orders*: Look for opportunities (e.g., for a certain regular-use product and a key customer) to produce to a daily rate—no work orders.
- *Capacity crunch*: I had an impression of Marlow being overly tight on equipment capacity, which should be dealt with (but such tightness may simply be a result of rapid sales increases).
- *Benchmarking visit*: A good company to benchmark (and potential contractor if Marlow should, sometime, want to outsource some of its crystal/slicing/etc. processes):
  - ✓ MEMC Electronic Materials, St. Peters, MO, which has more than 1,000 employees producing semiconductor wafers, with many of the same processes as Marlow. (MEMC is the following chapter in this book.)

✓ They are outstanding in employee-driven process improvement (using visual process display tools), behavior-based safety extended to behavior-based quality. Contact persons: Jim Lang, plant manager, Darrell Birks, senior TMP facilitator.

IV. Overview Observations

- *Presently*: Marlow is in an excellent, growing, high-tech business, its multiple related product lines offering protection against technology change or competitive problems in any of them. The management team seems well organized into customer-focused business teams.
- *Future prospects*: Perhaps out of concern for any (of the typical) drop-off in "excellence" in the years following the Baldrige award, there seems currently to be a healthy preoccupation over looking for new initiatives to generate enthusiasm among staff and the front-line workforce; Marlow managers are using their company's prestige advantageously, e.g., to gain access for benchmarking visits.

CHAPTER II-61. MEMC ELECTRONIC MATERIALS, ST. PETERS, MO, 1999

This caselet describes outstanding plans carried through to implementation at this manufacturer of silicon wafers that are cut into tiny dies for semiconductor customers. It begins with segments of my thank-you letter to the plant manager, which, along with glowing praise, pointedly argues for moving equipment into flow lines or cells.

High-Interest Topics:
- **Behavior-based safety (BBS), plus *behavior-based quality* (carbon-copy of BBS but applied to QA)**
- **Highly-structured and organized improvement process—with lots of facilitators, teams, controls, and displays**

Visual Management and Teaming Everywhere at MEMC

Observations based on presentations and a plant tour, May 18, 1999

In connection with a two-day Schonberger public seminar, May 19–22, 1999

I. Post-Visit Letter

May 24, 1999

Dear Mr. Lang:

I would like to thank you and your colleagues for your hospitality on May 18. The presentations by Darrell Birks and the improvement teams were excellent, and the plant visit effectively reinforced the points made.

...

There does appear to be a serious limitation, however: Since the processes are functionally separated, the improvement teams do not have the kind of whole-product visibility that would lead to the most beneficial kinds of results. In our discussions...the high cost of equipment was cited as an obstacle. I suspect that the greater reasons have to do with a broad, unfocused mix of products, customers, and demand patterns; cells work best with focused, narrow ranges of products and customers. In fact, when marketing, finance, and operations—plus best customers—get together to reduce the complex mix, cellular possibilities tend to present themselves naturally, often without need for more equipment.

...

[If my points are valid] it becomes competitively vital for MEMC to place these issues high on the company's priority list in the next round of strategic deliberations. The four MEMC people who attended my two-day seminar (including Darrell Birks) were exposed (pages 12 and 13 in their notebooks) to some rare examples of companies that had carried out the radical dismemberment of functional walls that is necessary to deal with unwieldy mixes of products, customers, and demand patterns.

Until the mix issues are addressed, your best courses of action surely revolve around what the improvement teams are presently doing so impressively. In addition, I should think that at least a few small cells (e.g., cellular islands of just two machines) could be formed, and the logical cell concept could be exploited. The main requisite for cells is multiple machines at each process, which you have.

Best wishes for maintaining—better yet, upping—the rate of improvement at MEMC, and please extend my thanks for MEMC's hospitality to your colleagues.

II. General Information

- *MEMC (Monsanto Electronic Materials Company) product/process*:
  - ✓ MEMC produces polished and epitaxial silicon wafers.
  - ✓ Sales are $500m. Wafers were selling at $200+, now down to $100. At die level, a wafer has a value of $30k to $50k.
  - ✓ Process flow (more detail given in Sidebar 1) is: poly-silicon, crystal pulling, grinding/flattening, slicing, edge grinding, lapping, etching, polishing, cleaning, slice inspection, packaging, and shipping to customer.
  - ✓ MEMC produces 4-, 5-, 6-, and 8-inch (200 mm) wafers, as well as soon-to-be-produced 12-inch wafers; 900–1,000 different ICs.
- *Employment*: 2,400 employees at the St. Peters facility a few years ago, now down to 1,800.
- *Contact persons*: Jim Lang, plant manager; Phil Glynn; Darrell Birks, Sr. TMP facilitator; Linda Hand, QA manager; Brad Eldredge, HR director; Rich Gunther; Scott Mize.

III. Specifics

- *Jim Lang presentation*:
  - ✓ Production is divided into two plants-in-a-plant: 1. Standard Products Department (4-, 5-, and 6-inch wafers). 2. Special Products Department (larger wafers).
  - ✓ MEMC's top-down "transformation process" has ten elements: the first is Purpose; then Values and Strategy; 1999 Objectives;

SIDEBAR 1   MEMC PRODUCTION PROCESS

Begins with crystal pulling (including adding impurities to improve resistivity and oxygen content). Next: 1. Cut off seed end and opposite end. 2. Round. 3. Notch or flatten. 4. Water slice into wafers, which creates damage to surfaces. 5. Edge profile (round edge). 6. Lap (very flat, very parallel). 7. Etch (etch away surface damage). 8. Polish (mirror quality): rough polish, then fine polish (flatness a key attribute—must only be a few microns peak to valley). 9. Clean (off all particles in Class 1 clean room). 40% of wafers then go through: 10. Epitaxy (deposit another silicon film on wafer, covering up any remaining damage and increasing resistivity). 10. Ship.

Goals; Functions; Plans; Programs; Methods; Measures; and Results.

■ Results are monitored via weekly staff charts and monthly performance charts.

■ The goal of improving cash flow entails: 1. Increase revenue. 2. Cut inventory. 3. Cut variable costs. 4. Increase production. 5. Cut other fixed costs.

✓ TOC vs. JIT mindsets: Jim Lang is Goldratt oriented ("make money" by increasing throughput, as opposed to reducing throughput times); Rich Gunther doesn't much like TOC (theory of constraints), preferring JIT.

• *MEMC process-improvement features*: Following are key elements of MEMC's current highly-structured and organized procedure— citing presentations by named subject-matter experts.

✓ Elements in general:

■ Purpose: "Chosen First"; and "Copy Exactly!" (the latter, borrowed from Intel, calls for standardized equipment models).

■ Reduce complexity (by June, eliminate 4- and 5-inch wafers from this plant).

■ Prioritized decision basis for everyone: 1. Speed. 2. Sacrifice yield to on-time. 3. Sacrifice delivery (on-time) to meet quality. 4. Never sacrifice the customer. 5. Never sacrifice safety.

■ MEO (Manufacturing Excellence Organization) modules: "shared learning" in which engineers from each plant meet yearly (five days?), each bringing ten slides (best practices) and returning with ten ideas.

■ Low-tech errors (e.g., documentation): These are displayed on Pareto charts showing: 1. Last three years of types-of-injuries reports. 2. "Customer advisories." 3. On-time shipments. 4. Cycle time (CT has been cut from 80 days in October, 1998 to 31 days in May, 1999).

■ Isolate what's necessary for CT reduction ("little dams"): 1. Get accurate CT data into the scheduling system. 2. Improve mainstream flow. 3. Improve local area CT (via kaizen blitzes). 4. Get "lazy lots" back into the mainstream. 5. Create visibility for CT performance throughout the organization. 6. Put a "born-on" stamp on each wafer.

- Do kaizen blitzes–Terry Barnes.
- Darrel Birks, Sr. TMP (Total Machine Performance), a facilitator who delivered one presentation in a panel of four.

✓ Behavior-based safety: Donna, OASIS system (safety).

- *Eliminate at-risk behaviors* via 320 designated trained observers using CBI (critical behavior inventory) sheets, one for each employee.
- An employee might be observed ten times per month at random. Observers' reports are submitted on the 15th and end of the month (so far, over 18,000 observations, or 700 per month).
- At first people resisted, thinking it to be a police action, but *no names are on the CBI sheets*! This behavior-based safety program was contributed by a hired safety expert from BST (Behavior Sciences Technology).
- A chart tracks feedback rates (from OASIS) against minor injuries per 200,000 hours—showing a very good negative correlation. MEMC minor injuries have fallen from 267 in 1996, to 200 in 1997, to 161 in 1998, and to 58 so far in 1999.
- OASIS facilitators rotate every two years; eight operators are on the OASIS steering committee.

✓ Behavior-based quality (one year old—again BST was hired to bring in this system): Susan Moreland, AQUA (Assurance Quality Using Awareness):

- Also employing CBI sheets, OASIS successes have led to ready acceptance and success of AQUA. So far, 51 observers have been trained, with 1,184 observations, and AQUA is now in nearly all plant areas.
- BST has also contributed the ABC (Antecedent Behaviors and Consequences) concept (apparently a feedback-to-employees feature).

✓ TMP teams: Gloria Douglas, presenter: Total Machine Performance, now nine years old, includes annual award celebrations with a paid trip for best TMP (this following Analog Devices' "QIP Fest"; Motorola's QIP teams):

- MEMC teams have also made presentations at NATPM, Missouri Quality Award, and (since 1993) the AITPM (American Institute for Total Productive Maintenance).
- TMP projects are 30-day, 60-day, 90-day, or (for new equipment) 120-day projects.

IV. Plant Tour

- *Selected details*: Following are a few improvement-oriented details for the Advance Products Division (producing larger than 5-inch wafers). (This section was much longer in the feedback report to the company.)
- *Multiple process improvement indicators*: These were demonstrated by the TMP facilitator:
    - ✓ A large wall displaying a 12 x 15-step flow-chart analysis, which shows seven value-adding (VA) operations in blue dots, 16 non-value-adding (NVA) in black dots, and the rest NV-but-currently-necessary in orange dots.
    - ✓ An *Impact on Cycle Time* chart with double green dots signifying high impact; single orange dots, medium impact; and single red dots, low impact.
    - ✓ *Ease of Implementation* chart: *A* is for "this week"; *B*, "almost this week"; and *C* connotes "long term."
    - ✓ An affinity diagram for which each person on the team receives 15 dots (pink for solutions, green for problems) to place anywhere on the big flow chart, indicating items they are most interested in.
- *Flow distance reduction*: A display shows rod travel reduction of 1,493 feet, broken into six flows that were eliminated (e.g., an HI storage step, and a move scantag step).
- *Kaizen blitz*: In the roll lab, a five-day kaizen event involved ten people, five of them operators.
    - ✓ Of 3.5 days in the rod lab, ten hours of cycle time were reduced—mainly by moving rod cuts one, two, and three from the lab to the saws immediately rather than waiting for the last cut (the fourth, which has some loss of structure) to be lab-tested. Of the entire rod area, seven days of cycle time were cut.

✓ Inventories were reduced from 4,700 to 700 inches of crystal in the storage shelves; also 400 hours of cycle time (16 days) were eliminated.

- *Preclean/Data (Sorter) area*: TMP Debby in the Sorter area explained a dot circled: "Out of control—SPC's *require* comments."
- *Customer-focus teams*: Teams meet weekly (more often for a current customer issue) and come together to make presentations quarterly.
- *Scoring of MEMC*: All eleven customers score MEMC quarterly, except two Korean customers who do it semiannually.

CHAPTER II-62. WAINWRIGHT INDUSTRIES, ST. PETERS, MO, 1999

This long caselet begins with a thank-you letter with some critical observations. Following that are plant tour details on what made Wainwright a highly admired, award-winning company, including my own critiques on good targets for improvement. Notes at the end are from a 2006 follow-on phone call to CEO Don Wainwright, which indicate that even so fine a company as Wainwright can find itself in financial trouble in times of difficult global economic conditions. Overall, it's a good caselet for showing transitions over numerous years—from bad times to great times to difficult times.

High-Interest Topics:
- **Customer-service department in middle of the plant**
- **Finding best practices from best companies—and implementing them**
- **Employees grade management, and operations grades engineering**
- **Everyone salaried, and every employee owning their own "25 sq. foot" area of influence**
- **Real kanban? or job-sheet cards referred to as kanban?**

Highly Regarded Manufacturer Experiences Challenges in a Down Market

Impressions based on a plant tour and company presentations, May 21, 1999

Following a two-day Schonberger public seminar in nearly St. Louis, May 19–20

I. Post-Visit Letter from Richard Schonberger

May 24, 1999

Dear Ms. Sanders:

I would like to thank you and your colleagues for your hospitality on Friday... You asked if I would forward a few remarks, which I am pleased to do—though, given the brevity of the visit, they won't be at all profound. I've co-addressed this letter also to David Robbins in view of his considerable participation in hosting our tour.

First of all, I was very impressed by the attention given to customer linkages, customer service, and keeping the customer base manageable. Also, by the relative simplicity of goals, which seemed to me to boil down to low costs, customer service, on-time performance, perfect quality, design excellence.

An overall impression (which I suspect others in our visit group would share): MEMC, my other visit site (on May 18) in the St. Louis area, *appears* to be superior to Wainwright in regard to employee involvement and process improvement. But the proof is in results, and your company's are far more impressive. One explanation for this inconsistency might be that your company, being small, can ill afford people on the payroll whose jobs revolve around the 5S's, TPM, and other "programs" of process improvement. Rather, to stay lean, blend the improvement activities into the jobs of folks who design, build, and sell products.

That said, I would still offer this mild criticism: I think your company could benefit from more visual representations of improvements (trend charts, projects in progress, awards won, cross-training matrices, etc.) in the work centers, kept current by the operators. The visuals need not be fancy—no need for professional sign-painters—but for proper impact they should be fairly large. A trend chart has the effect of praising past accomplishments and scolding lack of recent ones, as well as keeping what's important front and center.

The visuals that you currently have in most work centers (tracking value-added, tonnage, uptime, pieces) are important, but they are second-order results rather than relating directly to causes. In other words, I would prefer to see setup-time charts (timing and plotting every setup), check sheets (accumulating frequency and cause of every process hiccup and glitch), and so on. These comments are offered especially in light of the statement by David Robbins in our Q&A session that the whole range of metrics is currently up for reconsideration.

The plant is a good deal cleaner than is typical of machining and stamping, though not up to the standards of some facilities I've seen (e.g., in Finland and Brazil), where, for example, the floor and equipment are painted white to reveal any trace of lubricating fluid.

Small point: I noted on a flow chart of the kanban process that step 1 is "Obtain kanban cards from folders daily." That doesn't quite capture the visual simplicity of true kanban, which employs cards (or dedicated containers) that re-circulate of their own accord.

All the above comments are minor compared with the matter of strategy for future success. I think the auto industry will be moving to modular plants with some speed (I worked in a few comments on this in my own short presentation at the morning session on Friday following Mr. Simms and Mr. Robinson). This might push Wainwright Industries down a peg, from 2nd- to 3rd-tier supplier.

Whether 2nd or 3rd, your company will probably need to become more modular—what you do right now, plus a lot more welding, fastening, and assembly into larger components (perhaps sub-modules delivered to, say, a Dana plant). The complete door mechanism that was displayed in the Q&A session might be an example. Such a change would require new kinds of equipment, types of engineers, operator skills, and management techniques. Acquisitions might be required. Given the care and thoroughness with which everything gets done at your company, I have no doubt that you and the management team are fully up to the challenge. Good luck and thanks for the opportunity, at last, to pay your fine company a visit.

II. General Information

- *Tour arrangements*: This visit to Wainwright was for a select group of 12: myself, close colleagues (two from France, my textbook co-author Prof. Ed Knod, my occasional seminar partner, Prof. Tom Billesbach, three of Tom's professorial friends, and four invited senior executives from companies nearby).
  - ✓ Most also attended my two-day "World Class by Principles" seminar in St. Louis, May 19–20.
  - ✓ Wainwright was a fine choice for a plant tour, having been recipient of a 1994 Malcolm Baldrige National Quality Award and *Industry Week* magazine's 1998 Best Plant in America award.

- *Pre-tour presentation*: Plant manager Michael Simms told us:
  - ✓ He had begun as shipping clerk and was promoted five times, ultimately to plant manager; and that he has made this presentation to 70,000 people, 2,500 of whom toured the plant in one year.
  - ✓ In 1983–1987, sales, profit, etc., doubled; and in 1989–1990, market share rose while profits dropped. A search for answers revealed, Simms said, a *trust* deficiency, and a call for changes:
    - Now all employees are on salary, including salespeople.
    - One to two hours of JIT training takes place every other week.
    - Simms also told us that 50% of success comes from having every individual employee owning their "25 sq. ft" area of influence—with high recognition for successes. The other 50% comes from team-based process improvement (caution: which *could* mean mainly from teams of staff people, and not much from front-line teams).
- *Contact persons*: Don Wainwright, chairman and CEO; David Robbins, VP; Michael Simms, plant manager; Joe Sanders, customer service manager.

III. Strengths/Observations from Plant Tour

- *Suggestion system*:
  - ✓ Includes a weekly drawing based on ideas for improving one's own job: $50 awards (one reward per every 100 employees); two to three winners named weekly.
    - If two people submit, both names go into a lottery and they split the $50. The supervisor must initial the idea, signifying support.
    - This has generated 1.25 improvements per week per employee every year for years.
  - ✓ Keys to making it work:
    - A first-line manager committee developed the suggestion scheme.
    - At first, many ideas were too big for one person to carry out; it took a while for a system of "area of influence" to take hold; and then it produced suggestion overload, so it was necessary to spread the responsibility for approvals.

- Like Milliken: Respond to a suggestion within 24 hours; have an action plan within 72 hours.
- *Team-based improvement*:
  - ✓ When a single task goes through multiple improvements (e.g., ten times), it's time to form a process-improvement team.
  - ✓ Example (emulating Motorola): Finance closes books in three days compared to the former 30 days.
- *Feedback*:
  - ✓ Every six months employees grade management (managers are *suppliers* to the troops), and operations grades engineering. At first, only 5% of the grades had names on them, now it's over 90% (the grading form changes all the time).
  - ✓ Wainwright borrowed Solectron's CSI (customer satisfaction index) system for monthly feedback from customers.
- *Actual plant tour*: Began with Mark showing the impressive CAD/CAM area; then on to the following:
- *Facilities management and safety*:
  - ✓ Throughout the plant are standard checklists—usually with all or nearly all checked as having been achieved, similar to the following.

	Facilities Index				
	M	T	W	T	F
Incident free	√	√	√	√	√
Personal protection equipment	√	√	√	√	√
Safe work practices	√	√	√	√	√
Organization	√	√	√	√	√
Equipment upkeep	√	√	√	√	√

  - ✓ Other, unique signs throughout the plant tell how to distinguish between a fire alarm (a wavy sound signified by a wavy line and a red/yellow flame symbol) and a tornado (a steady sound signified by a straight line and symbol looking like a funnel cloud).
  - ✓ David Robinson said that, in four years, not a single dollar was spent for workers' compensation payments; money saved goes right to the bottom line. The company's safety record is remarkable—from 66 recordable accidents in 1990 to eight in 1998; the safety agency found their plunging accident rate off the charts.
  - ✓ Single-sheet out-of-control reaction plans are posted in every area.

- *Tool room (Don Black, Sr. operations leader):*
  - ✓ 30 people service dies and make dies. The tool room is a promotion from the shop (50% came from the shop, the rest hired in from trade schools, other companies, etc.).
  - ✓ Lots of staggered shifts—flex-time.
  - ✓ A flexible area contains a heavy-duty (15-ton) crane on floor rails, plus other fixed, smaller cranes secured to nearly every post not served by the large crane.
  - ✓ But there are few signs of visual management in the area.
- *Machining (Steve):*
  - ✓ Yellow, pink, and green cards are used to indicate where parts go next (but not with the queue-limitation discipline of kanban).
  - ✓ Setup data are kept in offices (maybe just on how long setups take; there was no talk on tour about setup *improvement*).
  - ✓ Pegboards for tools—but not on shadow boards.
- *Customer service department:*
  - ✓ This is located in middle of the plant—for quick answers and one-person contact with customers.
  - ✓ Sales people cannot make a commitment without running the request through this department, which includes a PP&C check on whether capacity and inventory are available; response is within 24 hours, making almost 100% of orders on time.
  - ✓ Lots of outreach to customers, who attend customer meetings at every stage of design.
  - ✓ David Robbins: Wainwright believes in choosing *a few good customers*!
- *Kanban*: A wall flow chart details four kanban steps, the first being "obtain kanban cards from folders daily" (a pseudo-kanban way of issuing work orders).
- Quality lab:
  - ✓ It's a standard lab with two CMMs (coordinate measuring machines) doing first-piece and (if customer requires it) mid-process checks.
  - ✓ The plant's extremely high CPKs suggest no need for inspection in some cases, but some customers may insist on it anyway.
  - ✓ Five stamping presses have stack-light indicators (white, green, yellow, red).
- *Press room (Steve Sutter):*
  - ✓ The room contains an 800-ton press, plus four to six smaller ones.

✓ Some degree of uniformity of die height (for the sake of quick setup) has been achieved:

✓ All dies are on racks against the walls of the room; however, there is no remote die storage area for low-use dies—which seems like poor use of space (or maybe it's simply a lack of available space).

✓ Each machine has SPC charts and a daily-goals chart; see below (format only; data are not shown):

	Value added	Tonnage	Up-time	Pieces (?)
Record daily				

✓ Also, a daily up-time summary chart (data not shown except for Press 22 and Average):

	M	T	W	T	F
Press 10					
12					
14					
16					
18					
20					
22	77%	70	81	74	
Ave.	53%	49	57	41	

✓ Tom Billesbach asked if they were capacity constrained; answer, no. Then why the concern over up-time, he asked (and is their measure of up-time relevant)?

✓ Like Lincoln Electric and Nucor, Wainwright seems to focus on output (tonnage) but with a much more people-oriented way of getting there.

• *EDM (electric discharge machining) area*: 67% of EDM capacity is for external customer requirements, the rest for internal purposes, such as die making.

• *Mission control room (developed by Mike Simms)*:

✓ The same five (one more recently added) measures have been on the wall since Wainwright's "epiphany": safety, employee involvement, process excellence (new), customer satisfaction, quality, business results. Red flags on the chart indicate not meeting the goal (few of these), green flags indicate meeting it.

✓ These measures are okay for a mission control room, but they are not supported by detailed, root-cause visuals around the plant.

■ It looks like conventional *management by goals* rather than by processes and their improvement.

■ [Critique: Most companies practice management-by-numeric-goals—dubious because (a) goals are little more than "hopes" pulled out of the air—like New Year's Resolutions. (b) Managers set goals, whereas more relevant goals would come from those in the affected processes. Far better is managing by visual trends (dynamic) that show progress over time rather than against single (goal) numbers (static).]

• *Self-contained production*: Few of Wainwright's products require secondary operations or fastening/assembly. The company seems to live/die on low costs, customer service, on-times, perfect quality, excellent design; generally common and simple processes but great results.

• *Training*:
  ✓ David Robbins: Up to 7% of the payroll is spent on training.
  ✓ We did not see versatility charts, but were assured they have them (should be more visible).

IV. Follow-on Phone Interview with Don Wainwright – April 6, 2006

• *Demographics*:
  ✓ Wainwright was president of the National Association of Manufacturers (he had invited me to speak at their meetings years ago). In 2005, he was appointed Chair of the U.S. Manufacturing Council, under the Department of Labor. Wainwright noted that:
    ■ Jo Sanders, former customer-service manager, took a job with GKN's automotive group.
    ■ David Robbins, Wainwright's brother-in-law, is still VP—and now also heads up a new "sequencing division."

• *Strategic matters*:
  ✓ Wainwright Industries has a much bigger presence in automotive than aerospace-defense—and with automotive in deep trouble,

the company is in survival mode: the toughest four years he can remember have forced a recent, deep layoff (30%).

✓ Seven major suppliers of Wainwright have gone bankrupt in the past five years.

✓ High prices of commodities—steel and other metals, especially—are eating them alive.

■ Since President Bush issued orders to protect the steel industry, then removed that protection a year or two later, the steel industry has changed significantly.

■ Many mergers have given steelmakers great pricing power. Less competition and high prices are killing companies like Wainwright. Oil and energy are affecting everything negatively.

✓ Toyota, a customer, sets a target price and will not budge from it for at least three years—regardless of commodity price escalation.

✓ GM is the biggest customer. Wainwright also is a tier-2 supplier to Dana and others.

✓ Wainwright has exploited a great opportunity to get into a higher-margin service business: sequencing for the auto industry. This growing business involves:

■ A warehousing operation in Texas and maybe one in the St. Louis area.

■ Receiving components from suppliers of GM/other automakers, inspecting and fixing to ensure quality, placing them into broadcast sequence, and cross-docking and shipping to GM/other automakers.

- *Operations*:

✓ Wainwright no longer counts suggestions. "It's just what we do."

✓ They have changed their mission control room to match what customers want to see—lean and six-sigma stuff, including takt-time attainments [Wainwright people—and we visitors—sneer a bit over that rather superficial and "faddish" way for customers to size up a plant].

✓ Inventory turns went to pot because of the constant scramble to find steel—all the way to/from France, and elsewhere. Now, they must buy when they can find it, not when they need steel.

✓ China suppliers (some from India, too) are never able to meet specs. So Wainwright brings in the low-cost "crap," then checks for quality and, through manufacturing and operations, brings them up to spec.

CHAPTER II-63. PROLEC/GE, MONTERREY, MÉXICO, 1998

This caselet, while very short, illustrates the unique combination of four focused product-*design* cells each linked to the plant's four product-focused *production* plants-in-a-plant.	***High-Interest Topics:*** • **Plants-in-a-plant, each focused by** *intensity of labor* • **Design engineering—a core competency for special design capabilities** • **Penalty payment for failure to record process data**

Electric Transformer Manufacturer Delivers Quick Customer Response from Design through Production

Summary of observations from a late afternoon visit, September 9, 1998

In connection with a one-day Schonberger seminar sponsored by Sintec Consultores of Monterrey

I. General

- *Prolec/GE venture*: Prolec, a Monterrey, Mexico-based manufacturer of electric transformers (and a subsidiary of Axa), established a joint venture with GE four years ago. (Axa, a $1.5 billion company, has 23,000 employees, and includes Yazaki wiring-harness plants in Saltillo and Ciudad Juárez that used to be Chrysler plants.)
- *Product line*: Small utility-pole transformers all the way up to huge power-station transformers.
- *Sales*: Business has tripled in the four years with GE; 60–70% is exported.
- *Plan*: The joint plan is for Prolec to take over GE's transformer manufacturing and for GE to close its factories.
- *Factory configuration*:
  - ✓ The facility has four focused factories—focused by lowest- to greatest-intensity of labor: tanks, least; coil, next; then, cores; and, finally, assemblies as the most labor-intensive.
  - ✓ Manufacturing flow time, 160 days a few years ago, is down to 50, now.

II. Design–Unique Advantage

- *Customized products*: Competitors produce standardized transformers. Prolec's competitive advantage is its ability to customize—its excellence in design being a core facilitating competency.
- *Product-design cells*: Design engineering, on the second floor, made up of four design cells, mirror the four focused factories in the plant downstairs! Design flow time has been reduced from 70–80 days to 42 days.
- *Visual management*: Four visual performance measures are plotted weekly: design flow time, errors, on-time (100%) completion, and output.

III. Assembly: Four Lines, Four Teams

- *Equipment*: Main equipment consists of six wrap machines numbered 6, 5, 4, 3, 2, 1; also, coil-winding equipment.
- *Kanban*: Orders are scheduled by operation, and with kanban.
- *Cells*: There are 14 cells, each with two winding machines, all in a T-configuration off a single powered conveyor used to collect the assemblies.
- *Next goal*: Via internal kanban, synchronize to the hour, rather than to the shift.
- *Recommendations*:
  - ✓ Break up the single conveyor line and form groupings of cells—for example, one cell group for three-phase transformers.
  - ✓ Adopt more visible indicators of customer focus in manufacturing, such as putting up a prominent sign in the big power transformer area stating the name of the customer for a given transformer.

IV. Tanks and Coils

- *Tanks*: It's a one-shift operation of: tank fabrication → powder coat → tank buffer.
- *Coils*: Following is the flow diagram for coils:
  Cut coil steel ↘
  CAD → EDI → Masking (3 machines) → Cut flat sheets (3 machines) → Seam weld (1 machine) → Weld (10 machines)
- *Recommendation*: Get three seam welders (instead of the current one) in order to create three separately focused production lines.

V. Training and Recording of Results

- *Improvement training*: All employees receive the following training in process improvement:
  - ✓ The seven basic tools, quality control circles for operators; TQM training for everyone else.
  - ✓ Six-sigma training and projects for specialists.
- *Recording results*: Teams are required to plot data hourly on the following kind of table—with failure to record incurring a 15-peso penalty:

	Cumulative		
Hour	Plan	Actual	Difference
1	30	30	0
2	33	63	+3
Etc.			

This recording of hourly actual-to-plan data probably is intended to prod production teams toward meeting management's productivity goals. Tacitly, though, it may have a more noble purpose, as at Johnson Controls Interiors (Chapter II-40). There, the intent of hourly plotting was to help avoid tendencies toward upping the work pace late in a shift—with increasing likelihood of mishaps.

CHAPTER II-64. DIXIE PRODUCTS, BUSINESS UNIT OF JAMES RIVER CORP, FORT SMITH, AR, 1990

This caselet is based on a brief walk-around at the Arkansas plant of Dixie Cup, the well-known brand of disposable utensils and dishes. A primary observation is that the plant is well positioned to significantly reduce flow times and inventories, along with, storage, handling, and scrap.	*High-Interest Topics:* • Multiple machines open the door to abandoning departments and converting to flowlines/cells • Coping with a badly-shaped building: eliminate WIP storage of printed rolls—so to use the space for moving machines close together • Cut a door into a wall for direct receipt/use of bulky packing boxes and cartons

How to Bring about Focused Production at a Paper-goods Producer

Observations based on a brief plant tour, January 17, 1990

In connection with a two-day Schonberger seminar hosted
by Fort Smith Manufacturer Executives Assn.

I. General Information

- *Plant and equipment*: This plant, a quarter-mile long but not very wide, has multiples of much of its equipment, most having been developed years ago by Dixie Cup engineers.
- *Output*: The plant has 1,300 SKUs and produces 4 billion items per year—on a five-day, 24-hour production schedule (with Saturday-Sunday overtime when required).
- *Primary activity*: Cup making engages 250–275 people and takes up over half the plant.
- *Contact person*: John Tripp, director of Southwest Operations

II. Strengths/Recent Improvements

- *Equipment in multiples*: Flexibility in scheduling is afforded by multiple small machines: dozens of small cup-forming presses and 21 plate presses (mostly dedicated to one of eight shapes of plate), plus several web presses and other printing machines.
- *Work in progress*: WIP (printed slit rolls) was 8–9 days, now is 4–5 days (400 to 500 rolls). Efforts are under way to stop printing whenever the WIP of printed rolls reaches a maximum number (such as 400 rolls) rather than the conventional approach favoring full-out production and maximum machine utilization.
- *Raw material*: Cardboard was 12 weeks' worth ten years ago, six weeks more recently, and down to two weeks in the last seven months.

III. Opportunities for Improvement

- *Bypass WIP storage*: As the norm, send printed rolls directly to the cup/plate department, thus avoiding extra handling and storage. Go to WIP storage only in cases of overflow (can't-use-soon) rolls.

- *Point of use deliveries*: My question: Are cardboard boxes and paper rolls received at the point of use? If not and if feasible, cut receiving-dock doors in a wall location so as to send these highly bulky materials directly to points of use in packaging—thus avoiding many extra trips to and from a stock room.
- *Moving equipment close together*: As WIP and cardboard stocks are slashed, use the extra space for moving cup-forming machines and packaging machines closer to printing.
- *Cellular manufacturing*: Consider cells (John Tripp mentioned this possibility) of one product family-dedicated web or roto-gravure press that feeds 15–20 dedicated cup-forming machines and packaging machines. Even if not dedicated, it's a worthy pursuit—to gain team benefits/team ownership of more of a complete product; also, this helps subvert the work rules and get people cross-trained and switching jobs.
- *Operator training*: The plant needs to commit heavily to operator training for greater involvement in quality improvement, quick setup, total productive maintenance, data collection, diagnosis and problem-solving. This should be nudged along by progress charts all over the plant.
- *On-line testing*: Operators should test cup diameters on line (with hand-held round metal gauges) instead of by a test person. The same goes for leak tests at a small table later in the flow.
- *Severe equipment limitations*: The capacity shortage at the conveyor lanes feeding palletizing is untenable, as is the conveyor loop that sends WIP on a long trip.
  - ✓ This deficiency can shut down a lot of costly upstream capacity. Large buffer stocks on conveyors/accumulators—there to avoid shutdown—just hide the capacity limitation.
  - ✓ The long and narrow plant seems to be part of the problem, along with lack of—and need for more—palletizing/sorting capacity.
- *Coping with the misshapen plant*: Long, narrow plants are always a problem (squarish rectangles are best). A possible ideal use of the given space is shown in Figure 64.1 (not to scale):
  - ✓ In this configuration (side-by-side along a segment of the elongated building), cells for cups are shown occupying the leftmost side and cells for plates the right side. Both sets of four

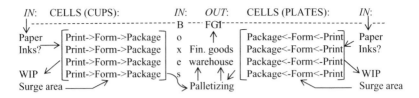

FIGURE 64.1
Side-by-side cell configuration for cups and for plates.

cells (could be more or fewer) are made up of three stations: print to form to package. The two sets of cells are fed by incoming paper and (probably) inks.

✓ Both sets have access to a WIP area for "surges." And both sets share, in between, the palletizing equipment, the finished-goods warehouse, and, finally, outgoing FGI (finished-goods inventory).

CHAPTER II-65. AMOCO POLYMERS, ALPHARETTA, GA, 1998

This caselet is in two sections (following the General Information section): the first has been resurrected (probably with some inaccuracies) from rough notes. The second is a slightly amended memo report to my tour host.

High-Interest Topics:

- **Near-miss safety, with lottery drawings for fixes**
- **Four customer/product-focused cells**
- **Cells, plus X-ray films on CD-ROM, cleared away a bottleneck that impinged on customer service**

Customer Focus, Cells, and Safety Emphasis at Thermoplastics Producer

Impressions based on an evening plant tour, April 24, 1998

In connection with a Schonberger two-day public seminar in nearby Atlanta, April 23-24

I. General Information

- *The company*: Amoco Polymers produces sulfone polymers— high-precision (cross-linked) thermoplastics used in high end- use temperature applications, such as in auto parts and hospital equipment. (This is *not* the same Amoco plant that in 2001 suffered an explosion that killed three people; that was in Augusta, GA.)
- *Precursor to caselet*: I had learned of Amoco Polymers from my colleague, Tom Billesbach, who had visited there earlier and liked what he saw, and who provided the necessary contact information for this hastily arranged tour.
- *Contacts*: Clarke McGuire, business manager; Donald Wagner, quality assurance manager; Bill Brewer.

II. Plant Tour Observations

- *Primary customers*: Chrysler and Bristol Machine.
- *Employment*: 56 employees, 44 of whom are manufacturing associates, who hire their own peers.
- *Safety*: Any near-miss is recorded (over 400 orange tags last years); the technician who fixes it turns the orange tag into a lottery drawing with AMOCO gasoline as the prize.
- *I-team*: A cross-functional team that tracks performance of cells, products, and customers on visual displays of sales, on-time, percent on-time, scrap, and percent revenues.
- *Four cells*:
  - ✓ AMOTEX (compression mold) cell:
    - Makes compression-molds for petroleum customers (Dresser Rand and Amoco Chemical). The per-unit cost of items ranges from $200 to $500.
    - The process flow is in four steps: mold (12 to 18 hours), blend (one hour), machine (one hour), and ultrasound test (one hour). Changeovers take two to three hours.
  - ✓ Job-shop cell:
    - A separate make-to-order area for processing orders of 10–10,000 pieces—equipped with three press-molds and three ovens with a six-step process flow. Production sequence is press-mold, dryer, oven, machining, inspect, and ship.

- There are frequent mold changes (since it is a job shop), with quick setup in machining employing off-line tool sets.
✓ Chrysler cell for high-volume processing:
  - The process flow is: Special blend machine (mix virgin grind and re-grind), injection molding, and oven-curing (there are 32 in total).
  - Some ovens are labeled "I-team," which refers to a cross-functional "logical cell" team. [Logical cell usually refers to a group in a flow relationship, one or more members of which are not geographically close-linked to others.]
  - Tooling, formerly centralized, is now part of the cell.
  - A cell cabinet for materials is used by both maintenance and operators; they replenish from suppliers using their "Pro-card" (e.g., MasterCard or First Chicago card); no need to go through purchasing.
  - The cell includes a "portable office" aimed at flexible and quick response.
✓ Bristol cell—produces parts for Bristol's air-conditioner compressor:
  - Two mold machines, two ovens, a tumbler, two dryers, two robot sub-cells, a test machine, a lift hoist for molds, mold supplies, and tools on peg boards.
  - Annealing is performed on kanban squares. The product moves from stage to stage in special containers.
  - Critical testing is done on a $230,000 X-ray machine: 18 times every 30 minutes the operator loads the tray, loads re-usable X-ray media, and reads the screen (looking for metal, voids, etc.).
✓ Former bottleneck: One customer required "zero flaws," so every piece had to be checked via X-ray. It ceased to be a bottleneck after the conversion to work cells, and with all X-ray films having been put on CD-ROM.

III. Thank-you Memo

May 2, 1998 Memo to Clarke McGuire:

Thank you for the excellent plant tour—and to-from transportation. I've just returned from Germany and am off to England tomorrow and haven't much time to write up my notes. So I'll just offer a few brief observations based on the visit to your plant. On the room-for-improvement side:

- *Material handling/kanban*: Though material flow is kanban-managed (kanban squares), nearly all plastic tubs for parts are on the floor. This entails extra handling and is a lifting/ergonomic problem for the work force. Wheeled carts for the tubs might be the answer.
- *Process-improvement displays*: You may have them and make vigorous use of them, but I didn't see (but there should be) visual displays of fishbone charts, Paretos, check sheets, flow charts, flow distance, cycle times, WIP.
- *Setups/changeovers*: Setup-recording and trend charts are not in evidence, and in compression (for example), setups are quite long, at about two to three hours.
  - ✓ It is easy to neglect this, since run times are long compared with setup times.
  - ✓ Still, quick setup is an important part of process improvement; setups relate to habits, discipline, and pride factors regarding housekeeping, safety, machine maintenance, and so on.
- *Boring job*: The job of the X-ray room operator repeats about 18 times every 30 minutes. Job redesign is needed, along with frequent job rotation.
- *ID labeling*: The cabinet for injection molding supplies in the Chrysler cell needs ID labels (I know, this is nitpicking).
- *Plusses*: The obvious plusses are far more numerous, and I won't try to comprehensively list them. Here are just a few off the top of my head:
  - ✓ Good cellular design, with continuing movement of more equipment (e.g., ovens) into the cells.
  - ✓ Equipment (e.g., dryers) are on wheels.
  - ✓ In the job-shop cell, quick setup employs standard tool sets kept nearby.
  - ✓ Safety: near misses are the objects of data collection, using a simple, visual, operator-driven orange-tag system.
  - ✓ Continuous reduction of process variation is achieved, for example, by moving the dryer closer to the mold press in the Chrysler cell.

- ✓ Some equipment is focused specifically on a customer or product spec (e.g., some ovens designated with customer or product labels).
- ✓ Most equipment, even an office, is movable—and often moved, adapting to customers, order patterns, and flow-distance reduction.
- ✓ Peg boards hold tools in the Bristol cell (but should have the "shadow" of the tool painted on the boards).
- ✓ Staged kanban squares are in use, e.g., for annealing.
- ✓ Intermittent has its own mold build/storage, which adds to its degree of focus.
- ✓ Large-sized visual I-Team performance charts.
- ✓ A missed delivery is called a "customer injury."
- ✓ Use of color-coding (e.g., green/red/yellow/blue WIP identification).
- Overall, I was and am impressed by your "world-class" efforts and expect that your business will grow quickly and profitably.

CHAPTER II-66. INTERMEC CO., EVERETT, WA, 1998

This caselet opens with introductory information about Intermec, which I gleaned from a visit there in 1996. Part II, is based on assessments of Intermec in 1998 by a visiting group organized by the Hong Kong Productivity Council (HKPC).

High-Interest Topics:
- **The "end-of-quarter push" conflicts with process-improvement initiatives**
- **All SMT associates are certified in all jobs, including setting up their equipment**
- **Good reasons why Intermec should adopt activity-based costing**

Plant Tours Show Keys to Excellence at Intermec:

Observations based on plant visit organized by Institute of Industrial Engineers (Puget Sound Chapter), Jan. 11, 1996. Also, presentations and plant tour, June 30, 1998, as part of a study mission in western United States for Hong-Kong-based manufacturing executives

I. About Intermec

- *Demographics*: Intermec's 321,000-sq. ft building houses its headquarters, engineering, manufacturing, and an automated warehouse in Everett, WA, a northern suburb of Seattle. It employs 800 people, 225 of whom are direct labor. Main contacts are John Niemi, director of mfg.; Jim Davidson, SMT (surface-mount technology) and process engrg. manager; and Jim VanOsdal, manager, mfg. engrg. and new products.

- *Product line*: Intermec produces the "latest" bar-code printing, scanning, and communications technology, which includes a variant of portable and stationary (on-line) devices, as well as spread spectrum radio frequency (RF) technology for real-time remote data collection with wireless networks—140 different products in 1,500 configurations, plus 625 accessories (modems, battery chargers, etc.

- *Production*: The mode is low-to-medium volume, high-mix—with four nine-hour shifts plus four hours, and with SMT production on weekends. In SMT . . .

  ✓ Cycle time is three days, one day to build the product with two days' "cushion."

  ✓ Target is 80% capacity utilization, so that the other 20% is beneficially available for repairs, prototyping, etc.

  ✓ In printed circuit assembly, lot sizes range from 360 to 30 (with 30-to-60 minute set-up times). We make "slow, little ugly boards and farm out high volumes" (10,000+ per year)—using both SMT and through-the-hole methods.

  ✓ Jim Davidson did his own activity-based costing (ABC) study (accounting hasn't engaged in ABC), which clearly showed benefits of modernized SMT equipment. Jim opines that lack of ABC has allowed sales to think they can make money next year selling five old models.

  ✓ All SMT people are certified in all jobs.

    ■ While the SMT machine runs, operators set up the next job, check the department notebook, clean the area, and walk around making sure no one needs help.

    ■ Team leaders are rotated.

- *Profit-sharing, reward, recognition*:

- ✓ Includes a Presidential award; VP's awards; Operational excellence award; "John Bucks"; photo and parking spaces; and a $500 quarterly drawing for those having suggestions approved.
- ✓ Intermec has sent people to learn from FedEx, Alaska Air, and others.
- *Problem awareness*: There are no inspectors; operators have line-stop authority, andon lights indicate problems, monthly meetings are held, at which teams present their top three Paretos.
- *Extensive training*: Employees are in training 40 hours per year (3% of payroll), coordinated by "Intermec University" and focused on:
  - ✓ Developmental training (via ZengerMiller), with emphasis on front-line leadership, team leadership, and work tasks.
  - ✓ JIT/Demand Flow Technology (DFT)
  - ✓ Quality: ISO 9001; problem-solving, SPC
  - ✓ Job skills (to certification for many): ESD (electro-static discharge), SMT soldering, Doceplex, ECNs (electronic communication networks).
  - ✓ American College of Testing's work keys: job profiling, skills assessment, etc.
  - ✓ Senior operators' use of CorelDraw to produce pictorial methods sheets (preferred over engineering drawings, which are more difficult to understand).
- *Just-in-time features*: The factory is product-family focused, including visual communications; station-to-station kanban and two-bin system; and backflush accounting (applied to nearly all parts).
- *Demand flow technology*:
  - ✓ Intermec had brought in John Costanza (one of the early-1980s JIT pioneers at Hewlett-Packard) with his trademarked DFT methods, which are oriented toward cellular manufacturing and synchronization.
  - ✓ A new DFT line (February 1996) produces five models of printer, 35,000 yearly in the mixed-model mode, with a lot size of one and bins replenished every five minutes.
  - ✓ Then (in 1997 and 1998) DFT was expanded to include Janus, networks, accessories, antennas, SMT, shipping, receiving, service, and, finally, order entry.
- *DFMA*: Intermec employs design for manufacture, design for test, and design for repairability.

- *Overall results*:
  - ✓ Lead times are down from 25 to 8 days; WIP from $2M to $1M in three years while sales are up 40%.
  - ✓ Fail-safing is estimated to have saved $2.2 million.
  - ✓ Good trends in cost-of-quality, 1st-pass failure, scrap and rework.
  - ✓ 30% labor reduction in the past three years.
  - ✓ Very low employee turnover (losing people only to Microsoft, Heart Stream, and startups).
- *"Guide to Operations Excellence"*: This guidebook, for employees and teams, is focused on JIT, total quality control, people involvement, computer-integrated enterprise, and manufacturing resource planning.
- *Critique*: Intermec's overhead costs seem extremely high.

II. HKPC Study Mission to Intermec, June 30, 1998

- *Purpose*: The tour group was in the western U.S. on a study mission co-organized by the Hong Kong Productivity Council (HKPC) and Richard Schonberger.
  - ✓ Intermec is one of several manufacturers—in California, Oregon, and Washington—visited. Numbering about 15, the visitors were business executives from Hong Kong, many or most having plants in China.
  - ✓ Note: HKPC had been sending executives on study missions to Japan; I suggested they would learn just as much—and in English—by study missions to the U.S. and other Western countries.
- *Impressions*: The group was pleased by the clarity and appropriateness of the Intermec team's presentation. The following are specific positive comments and observations of the visitors:
  - ✓ Intermec has a well-rounded recognition system.
  - ✓ Worthwhile (not force-fit) applications of Intermec's own product, barcoding, to its production, stock management, and fail-safing.
  - ✓ Good performance on cycle times and inventory turns—enabled by elimination of kitting, use of kanban squares on assembly benches, and takt-time scheduling.
  - ✓ Considerable reduction in numbers of key suppliers (targeted especially at those supplying PCBs, plastic, and sheet metal).

- ✓ Evidences of production-team "ownership" of equipment and fixtures, enabling flexibility to rebalance and redistribute test stations.
- ✓ Nice assembly diagrams prepared by three dedicated ex-assemblers (*not* by engineering).
- *Observations/room-for-improvement comments*:
  - ✓ Intermec is plagued by the much-criticized "end-of-quarter push" (to "make the numbers"), which led to:
    - Longer cycle times, higher inventories, and higher costs passed on to customers.
    - Weak strategic alignment between sales and marketing and production/supply chain.
  - ✓ Emphasis on daily production-quantity goals may divert the work force's attention from eyes-of-customer performance, operator "ownership" of processes, and process improvement.
  - ✓ Did not see much evidence of workforce use of process-improvement tools, e.g., the "seven basic tools."
  - ✓ Cell teams could be enhanced by assigning staff support (buyer-planner, manufacturing engineer, etc.) to each team.
  - ✓ We didn't ask but didn't see (may have missed) evidence of total productive maintenance (TPM).
  - ✓ Didn't ask, didn't see evidence of thoroughly using external information from benchmarking, customers, and competitive analysis to help drive improvement.
  - ✓ There may be good opportunities for standardization of components and modular design.
  - ✓ Overall comment: The study-mission participants generally considered Intermec to be an excellent tour site, providing many useful lessons.

III. Epilogue

- On November 17, 2006, Intermec, in a restructuring plan, announced it would eliminate about 9% of its work force.
- On July 11, 2008, Intermec announced the shuttering of its final-assembly plant in Everett, eliminating 260 local-area jobs—those operations to be moved to Southeast Asia and run by a contract manufacturer, Singapore-based Venture Corp. Ltd.

CHAPTER II-67. FOXBORO CORP., INTELLIGENT AUTOMATION DIVISION, INVENSYS PLC, FOXBORO, MA, 1999

The Foxboro plant produces process-control systems for customer businesses that include refineries, paper mills, power stations, cereal plants, and steel mills. Recipient of the Shingo Prize in 1995 and *Industry Week* magazine's Best Plant award in 1993 and again in 1999, this plant is a popular plant-tour site.	***High-Interest Topics:*** • **All products are made in high-mix, low-volume cells** • **Formerly, 100 people were involved in labor reporting alone; no longer** • **A supplier-alliance program has reduced suppliers from 450 to 96, 37 being "core suppliers" on JIT with "ship-to-stock"**

Award-Winning Company Attacks Delays and Complexity on Multiple Fronts: Observations Based on Presentations and Abbreviated Plant Tour, June 11, 1999

In connection with Schonberger's 2-day public seminar in Boston, June 12–13, 1999

I. General Information

- *The company*: Foxboro Co., with several plants, was acquired by Invensys plc of the U.K. in 1990. The Foxboro, MA, facility—largest, at 60,000 sq. ft, of several Foxboro Co. plants—ships 35,000 items per month.
  - ✓ Foxboro produces large systems and total automation solutions for petrochemicals, food, beverage, power, rail, buildings, utilities, other.
  - ✓ Had $400M sales and 15,000 employees in 1990. Employment fell to 11,000, then 4,500, then 1,500—but with sales up to $1.1b.
- *Contact persons*: Henry Metcalf, CEO; Dan Currie, gen. manager, systems mfg.; Marcelo Miranda, director of lean mfg.; Ray Webb.

II. Dan Currie Presentation

- *Clutter of reports—and overhead costs*:
  - ✓ "In the old days, a huge pile of reports was on supervisors' desks each morning, and every evening it all went into the waste basket."

- ✓ In 1986, we had over 100 people in labor reporting, doing "financial gymnastics."
- ✓ Now: "We do not collect costs on every order. The supervisor should know everything that happens in the work center, so why have huge stacks of reports to tell him?"
- ✓ "Manufacturing is only a small part of the reason a product is profitable or not."
- *Factory of the future*:
  - ✓ In 1986, CEO Metcalf said: Go create a factory of the future. He wanted robots, lights out.
  - ✓ Today, "We invent the factory of the future every day."
- *Taking aim at purchased components.* All plants are undergoing a transition to lean manufacturing, which is aimed in part at shrinking manufacturing costs, with a growing percentage of cost of sales from purchased components.
- *Head-count reduction?*: This became an issue when the Industrial Automation Division dropped from 22 companies to 16. As to that, Foxboro says: (a) if there are business losses, people losses are to be expected, (b) but if lean is successful, no layoffs.
- *Cells*: All products are made in high-mix, low-volume work cells.
- *Improvement projects*: Kaizen projects are three to five days (involving, e.g., customer service, purchasing, and manufacturing-floor people). 6-sigma projects are three to five months.
- *Sales orders*: 5% of sales orders are audited.
- *Foxboro's supplier alliance*:
  - ✓ Alliance is managed by a steering committee of senior managers in materials, each manufacturing division, corporate purchasing, production, and the quality organizations.
  - ✓ Number of suppliers has been reduced from 450 in 1986 to 96 in 1999. 37 are core suppliers representing 90% of value.
    - ■ Just six are alliance suppliers so far (Foxboro has 5% to 12% of these suppliers' total business).
    - ■ For those six, the alliance calls for going direct to electronic communication; no planner-buyer needed.
  - ✓ We formerly measured delivery, now we measure numbers of consignment kanbans.
  - ✓ Enclosures were our first JIT purchased part— with deliveries direct to the enclosures area, located near the shipping dock, two to three times per week as flat panels.
  - ✓ 96% of incoming orders are ship-to-stock with no inspection.

III. Tour—Production Area

- *SMT (surface-mount technology)*: SMT lines produce printed circuit boards in units of one in their own SMT area:
  - ✓ All components are pre-loaded (300–400 components) in two mirror-image SMT lines, which can make one of anything.
  - ✓ If a customer asks for a unique resistor, Foxboro knows beforehand, by working with them, to have that resistor pre-loaded on the SMT line. Foxboro and customer engineers will thereafter consider new uses for the "new" resistor.
  - ✓ *Multi-feeders ("Mu-Fu's")*: These are low, wheeled machines that plug into the back of each SMT placement machine.
- *Paperless flow control, QC, order*: There are no traveler documents— but there is paper for work instructions, training, records, spec sheets.
- *"Pizza-oven" stress testers*: These are tall, narrow testers with 32 slots; any module can be put in and taken out at any time—no lock-step testing.

IV. Systems

- *Engineering codes*: On Foxboro products, engineers wanted 1,000– 1,500 codes but we allow only 30 max.
- *3rd generation system*: This system (we've called it JIT II) is the first product able to talk to competitors' products—which is instrumental in raising our market share from 5–6% to 29%.
- *Part numbers & setups*: P/Ns are up from 186 in 1986 to 600 in 1999. Setups have been driven down from 45 min. to 3.5 min. on new P/Ns.
- *MRP/SAP*: MRP is used only for purchased material, and the SAP system dumps orders each day.
- *FoxQuote system*: This garners field sales, which go to the FoxCom order-management system, and then to the FoxCom shipping module. Demand-pull PC stations are everywhere in the plant.
- *Suppliers*: The system interfaces with suppliers through a long-term forecast, plus weekly releases, plus orders.

V. Accomplishments to Date

- *Service level*: Has been greater than 99% since the mid-1990—but service level is not a competitive differentiator any more.

- *Build cycle & inventories*: Build cycle in the plant is only two days, driving to 1. Inventory turns have risen from 2.6 to 20.5 in 5 years.
- *Clerical*: Eliminated, except for two secretaries.
- *Central warehouse*: Purchased-parts warehouse is gone; suppliers deliver at 5 a.m. daily.
- *Sales-order lead times*: Down from 16 to two to four weeks.
- *Output*: A ten-fold reduction in defectives and a 335% increase in output per person.

VI. Training

- *Getting qualified*:
  - ✓ Each of 177 employees in the factory receives over 40 hours training yearly; training topics including black belt, kaizen, Excel, Word, and PowerPoint, which are enablers of the work of 140+ teams.
  - ✓ Agency temps provide as-needed labor, usually being temps who used to work for Foxboro.
- *Multi-skilling*:
  - ✓ Employees interview for work-cell assignments, and must be trained in five different cells!
  - ✓ Office people are trained to be multifunctional.
  - ✓ The old factory had ten classifications; now it's three.

VII. Improvement Systems

- *Signs of progress*:
  - ✓ Bulletin boards throughout the plant are loaded with "green-belt" 6 sigma projects (e.g., "Staging return flow back to I/A"), 6 sigma training, 6 sigma updates, etc. The aim is for one 6-sigma black belt person for every 35 people.
  - ✓ A huge flow chart of sales-order processing occupies a hallway; also an order-processing flow chart and photos of fail-safes.
  - ✓ A big plaque-like signboard labeled "World-Class Teams" lists some 225 completed projects.
  - ✓ Another big signboard has three columns—quality, speed, cost—subdivided by performance metrics (cycle time, service level, raw-material inventory, ship-to-stock, etc.).
  - ✓ Still another big "Employee Recognition" signboard is for Outstanding Performance; Attendance; Anniversary; Special Events.

- *A main hallway's visuals are*:
  - ✓ Plant Achievements and Customer Satisfaction plaque boards.
  - ✓ Safety and Kaizens.
  - ✓ A huge banner proclaiming Shingo Prize – IW Best Plant.
  - ✓ Etc.
- *Observations*:
  - ✓ If anything, Foxboro overdoes the visual recognition.
  - ✓ The objective of continuously shrinking manufacturing so that production costs are mostly purchased materials is a unique expression of what lean is supposed to be all about. But, contrarily, some of the shrinkage in manufacturing costs could come from a shift of those costs to a growing staff of overhead people (engineers, infotech people, subject-matter experts, tacticians).
- *Missed Q&A*: Note: I had to leave and catch a plane halfway through this afternoon tour and therefore missed the Q&A session, and probably missed taking note of various opportunities for improvement.

CHAPTER II-68. PLAMEX, TIJUANA, MÉXICO – 1995, 1998

This caselet begins with a brief description of the Plamex plant in 1995; then there's a more detailed look at it in 1998; and finally some follow-up based on phone calls in 2000.	**High-Interest Topics:** • **Reluctance to adopt cells, even as a pilot test** • **The woes of 10-second cycle times** • **Finally, cellular conversion—but without fixing bad job designs and high employee turnover** • **Wooden gravity slides along assembly modules** • **In a test: manual beats automated assembly**

Good Simplification And Flow Efforts Run Into Mindset Obstacles:

Findings from plant visit, Aug. 30, 1995, in connection with
2-day Schonberger public seminar, Tijuana, Aug. 30-31; and 1.5
hour visit, plus 1-day seminar for Plamex, April 8, 1999

In connection with 2-hour talk hosted by Tijuana Industrial Relations Assn.

I. General

- *The company*: Plamex, based in the Tijuana Industrial Park (TIP), Baja Calif., México, manufactures headsets/headphones, microphones, and amplifiers for Plantronix Inc., headquartered in Santa Clara, CA. Plantronix, begun in 1961, is proud that when Neil Armstrong walked on the Moon he uttered legendary words through a Plantronix headset.
- *Contacts*: Tijuana plant: Alejandro Bustamante, president; Diana Alvarado; Jim Morris, operations director, Santa Clara HQ.

II. Plamex – Briefly in 1995*

- *Improvements under new plant manager*:
  - ✓ The old production configuration was manual assembly with assemblers lined up along lengthy powered conveyor lines.
  - ✓ Alejandro Bustamante, new plant manager, saw to the conveyors' removal, replaced by 35-ft by 5-ft bench assembly modules.
    - A long row of up to ten such modules make up one product-focused production line, with the first modules for making components and the last one for testing and packing finished product.
    - Assemblers are seated on both sides of each module.
  - ✓ Separation into modules has advantages of keeping teams small and allows problems to be localized to a given cell—with other modules capable of keeping production going down the line.
  - ✓ In the modules, much of material handling is by gravity: On finishing an operation, an assembler places the component on a simple slide made of wood, sending the unit to an assembler on the other side of the module, who, on finishing an operation, may hand it off to an assembler on the same side, or slide it back across the other side for next operations—and so on down the module's 35-foot length. See photo, Figure 68.1.
- *A test—automated vs. non-automated*: During installation of the manual wood-slide assembly modules, one conveyor-automated module remained, and its performance was directly comparable with a manual module next to it; both producing the exact same

---

* This description comes from rough notes plus excerpts from R.J. Schonberger, *World Class Manufacturing: The Next Decade* (New York: Free Press, 1996): 158.

FIGURE 68.1
Gravity handling of components from one side of progressive assembly module to the other at Plamex.

headset. The automated module required eight assemblers; the manual module had only six—and produced a larger number of components per day than the automated one!

III. Observations from 1998 Visit

- *Process details*: Additional details are summarized in Sidebar 1.
- *Receiving/shipping*:
  ✓ Plamex contracts with a third-party logistics company called Alrod, which issues and consolidates pick tickets daily—for both incoming and outgoing materials. Since outgoing shipping is five miles away, Plamex is trying to bypass Alrod for outgoing order picking and shipping.
  ✓ Incoming delivery frequency is generally good, at least for not-far-away suppliers:
    ■ Deliveries of many items are twice daily from a local supplier.
    ■ Packaging and plastics suppliers are on milk runs—trucks delivering small quantities daily, made economical by stopping at several customers, including Plamex.
    ■ 30% of P/Ns (part numbers) are dock-to-stock (none dock-to-line). Every lot is audited.

SIDEBAR 1   MISCELLANEOUS PROCESS DETAILS

Receiving/shipping
 Six docks – two receiving, three outbound, one not used
 Incoming materials in four stockrooms: 1. Raw metals from PMX
 Industries; 2. Headset components from Walker Equipt. 3. Raw for
 remanufacturing; 4. Other
Planning
 Weekly, 13 weeks; monthly, six months
 Tijuana-based master scheduler also does forecasts; head master schedule
 is in Santa Cruz
 Weekly schedule (Excel/Oracle) is printed at Tijuana plant
Human Resources
 Three gen. supervisors, nine floor supvs. over line lead persons, also
 direct "responsibles"
 1,100 direct labor, mostly one shift
 Training includes one-day orientation, quality, reading operations sheets

---

- *Inventory/purchasing/stockroom/kanban*:
  - ✓ Sustaining and day-to-day buying is (beneficially) done at the Tijuana site, and not from Santa Clara.
  - ✓ Inventory accuracy is 85% (not good at all, yet acceptable by the financial people).
  - ✓ Kanban—still a work in progress:
    - Most packing boxes are on kanban, but it's a two-step kanban system: one for incoming material, another for out to the production floor.
    - For items on kanban, the average is a very high ten weeks' inventory. As one bad example, PCBs (printed circuit boards) are on kanban, but the supplier is in central Mexico, so the kanban quantity is ten pallets (ten days' supply!) for some PCBs.
    - Subassemblies stay on the floor, but are not on kanban.
  - ✓ Total WIP: 2.5 days' sales inventory (DSI) on the floor for 20 minutes of actual work time—a nearly 8 to 1 ratio of inventory to value-add work.
  - ✓ Three ways of getting parts to the floor are:
    - Scheduled.
    - Kitted: Eight employees kit about 10% of parts. But in the Walker area ($3 million of total $70 million sales) about 90% are kitted—which incurs extra handling, inventory, chances for error, other negatives.

- Common parts that are used on high-runner items are in WIP locations near to points of use on the production floor.
  - ✓ A key performance objective is to try to stay linear with schedules. Linearity was quite good for 1.5 years, but not now: building to stock is not linear.
  - ✓ All in all: Lots of hand-offs: PC Dept. → Bin → Kit count → Store →Transaction →Move to floor.
- *Planning*:
  - ✓ Production planning is weekly for 13 weeks; monthly for six months.
  - ✓ Forecasting is by a master scheduler, now (beneficially) resident at the Tijuana plant. The forecast quantity is compromised in that it reflects financial goals.
  - ✓ Al Corso in Santa Cruz (headquarters) is head master scheduler.
  - ✓ A weekly schedule is printed in the Tijuana plant on Excel via an Oracle system and database.
- *Employee turnover*: Plamex turnover is high (but comparable with other maquilas) at 30–35% per quarter, 90% are here for fewer than nine months:
- *Assembly*:
  - ✓ The final stages are Subassembly → Decal →Final assembly →Test and packout.
  - ✓ In subassembly two people are each doing the same job in adjacent subassembly modules.
  - ✓ In final assembly, two final-assembly teams face each other across a wide workbench (which assembles the components that are made in the ten components modules), with a station cycle time (CT) of 10 seconds.
  - ✓ Cable winding is done by a gang of four (*gang*—all doing the same thing—as opposed to a bucket-brigade-like person-to-person *team*).
  - ✓ Amps (mostly sold separately) are produced by some 150 people supervised by Ernesto.
- *Cost breakdown*: Labor is no more than 10% of cost (e.g., amounting to 25 cents for one product); materials 90% ($6–$8 for one product). Implication:
  - ✓ Labor turnover as a cost is not critical, though as a key element of quality and process improvement it surely is.
  - ✓ More cost-critical by far is the large amounts of on-hand and in-process inventory—and attendant costs of storage, handling, lead times, and delayed discovery of problems.

IV. Primary Recommendation

- *Pilot test*: I suggested a pilot test of a U-cell with stand-up assembly, longer station cycle times, and so on. An ideal location was an alcove at a back wall that had work benches, etc., and was currently unused.
  - ✓ Present station cycle times—of ten seconds—are intolerably short, amounting to some 3,000 repeats of an assembler's task per shift. If the plant is to do something concrete about high employee turnover, a primary solution is, say, to triple the number of tasks per employee (e.g., to 30 seconds) and, for the same output triple the number of cells.
  - ✓ In this scenario assemblers would be on their feet walking a step or so on every cycle—instead of seated all day incurring back and body trauma.
- *Corporate reaction*: Jim Morris was strongly in favor, and said he would be back to the Tijuana plant to see that progress was being made.
- *Call to Morris*: In a phone call (in 1999 or early 2000) to Morris (at corporate headquarters in Santa Clara) Morris said they "never really got consensus and buy-in" for cellular conversion; and did not pilot-test the idea either. He did offer the following improvements:
  - ✓ In amplifiers, flow had been tightened by limiting raw material between stations, so that kanban = 1. Throughput may have increased 10%.
  - ✓ Raw materials come in quantities too large (even an hour's worth) to store on the production line. But some bulky materials (about 2 hours' worth) are delivered to a kanban area on the floor.

V. Follow-on Phone Call to Plamex

- Alejandro Bustamante, in a phone call (May 31, 2000) offered the following:
  - ✓ There are now several cells: one is S-shaped, others U-shaped—now in a second building. across the street. About half of total production is in cells now.
  - ✓ They have not gone to stand-up assembly except in packaging.
  - ✓ Station cycle times are still very short.
- WIP inventory is down from five days to 1.3 days.
- Growth has been 5% per quarter, up to 30% in a few quarters.

Part III

Advances and Missteps along Process-Improvement Pathways in the 2000s

Part III opens with the Gillette Andover Manufacturing Center, 2000, which revolves around a proposed conversion, in steps, to cellular manufacturing of a line of personal-care products. Although the local manufacturing team was strongly in favor of doing this, the plan blanked out at higher management levels—and died. Part III ends with ElectroImpact, which presents a startling alternative to the kinds of process improvement brought up in all of the other 100 caselets—a customer-focused way to excel that perhaps should be accompanied by a variation on one of those "don't try this at home" admonishments.

+ + +

CHAPTER III-69. GILLETTE ANDOVER MANUFACTURING CENTER (AMC), ANDOVER, MA, 2000

To make this caselet more understandable to those other than the Gillette people involved, I've rewritten and elaborated on parts of the original post-visit report. I was invited to this Gillette plant (AMC) on the suggestion of management-team members who had attended my two-day seminar in Chicago three months earlier.

Many High-Interest Topics:
- **Employee ownership of company stock in declining value gives impetus to an agenda for change and improvement**
- **Plan for getting closer to the customer via multiple lines/cells making multiple SKUs concurrently**
- **Pilot projects to "prove" and advance cellular manufacturing—yes, cells in consumer packaged goods, too**

The Perils of Bureaucracy: Observations Based on Management Presentations and 1-Hour Plant Tour, Sept. 26, 2000

I. Basic Information

- *Purposes of the visit*:
  - ✓ This caselet describes fairly good practices at AMC in designing and operating fill-and-pack lines for a personal-care product line and focuses on elevating "fairly good" to "much better."
  - ✓ Included is a proposal for using pilot projects in a step-by-step effort to convert production from a few multiproduct production lines to many product-family-dedicated cells; see Production Redesign in Section IV.
- *The facility*: AMC is the largest of Gillette's toiletries plants, occupying 594,000 sq. ft. of buildings, 130K being production space, and employing 600 people (200 office, 400 factory).
- *Production.* The mix-and-formulation department feeds eight medium-long, serpentine, single-channel fill-and-pack lines that turn out 428 variations (SKUs) of foam, gel, and solid shaving creams, deodorants, and antiperspirants, brand names including Foamy, Soft & Dri, and Right Guard.
- *Challenges.* So many SKUs require frequent product changeovers, which are costly and sources of control and quality issues. SKUs have proliferated mainly in labeling/packaging, and to lesser extent in formulation extensions and expansion into other countries with their different legal requirements.
- *Other Gillette toiletries plants*: Other primary plants are in Reading, U.K., and Garin, Argentina; lesser ones are in the former Soviet Union and México, as well as plants for several contract fill partners.
- *Main competitors*: Procter & Gamble, Johnson & Johnson, Mennen, Colgate.
- *Contacts*: Brian O'Neil, director of mfg.; Pat Ladd, plant manager; Gary Pincatelli, controller; Mike Butler, quality and materials; Dave Dufor, engrg., Julio Mantilla, HR.

II. Advantages/Assets

- *Work force.* AMC has very low employee turnover and no labor union. Wide ownership of Gillette stock and the sinking price of it add up to a strong climate for introducing significant improvement.

- *"Closer to the customer."* The fill-pack area has eight narrow-channel lines: good configuration to build on:
  - ✓ Production lines in many kinds of packaged goods tend to be wide-channel and few in number—maybe only two or three fill-pack lines with 10, 12, or more items abreast. It is difficult enough to make a single-channel line work well; wide-channel conveyor lines mean many more things to go wrong.
  - ✓ The eight lines at AMC allow running eight SKUs at a time, which puts eight products simultaneously into channels leading to customers. This contributes to a current Gillette corporate emphasis, transferred to AMC, on getting closer to the customer, SKU by SKU.
- *Management/professional team.* Though Gillette/AMC managers and professionals rotate a bit more often than prudent (i.e., for continuity, learning, and responsibility), that they tend to stay career-long in Gillette builds a wealth of valuable knowledge.
- *Strategic framework*: An existing structure of goals and key-result areas and plant initiatives/measures should fit well with the improved competitiveness effort.
- *Superordinate goal.* Given the above, Gillette-Andover is well positioned to become—via a plan for extensively reconstituting the production floor—a showcase of excellence for The Gillette Co., embracing improved, interlaced ways of running a mix-fill-pack operation. This offers competitive advantage over others in the industry, which, like Gillette-Andover, have many SKUs but with factories equipped for batch-and-queue production in a sequential rather than concurrent-production mode.
  - ✓ This should mostly pay for itself—little need for corporate funding (except for a small number of highly advantageous equipment improvements such as in-line blending).
  - ✓ While "showcase" status might take two years, a good deal should be achievable in one.

III. Stand-out Problems/Weaknesses

- *Scheduling.* Highly irregular patterns of scheduling and producing each SKU at AMC cause or contribute to a host of competitive weaknesses for the company and for its suppliers.
  - ✓ Such variability pushes the supply chain far out of synch with retail and consumer demand/usage, enlarging inventories and lead

times, making manufacturing and purchasing support complex and costly, and forcing a reactionary mode in most activities.

✓ The problem is self-inflicted.

- *Production lines.*
  - ✓ Stretched between each pair of work stations are segments of non-value-adding conveyor holding dozens of units.
  - ✓ Each line includes one or more accumulators—islands of just-in-case ("designed for failure") inventory on circular conveyors.
  - ✓ For gel deodorants, units face upward, exposed to possible open-air contamination, in early segments of lines—before the units are inverted and reach the cover-and-cap stations.
    - Antiperspirants are the only AMC product subject to FDA scrutiny and its GMPs (good manufacturing practices).
    - The plant does not require class 10,000 clean-room status but does need reasonably clean air.
- *Missing or minimal:*
  - ✓ There is little design commonality of product components of among the eight lines.
  - ✓ Visual management is lacking and process controls are minimal.
- *Cost focus:* A misplaced (conventional) direct-labor-cost mind-set is evident.
- *External awareness.* There appears to be an AMC-wide low awareness of competitors' competencies, and also customers' satisfaction and wants, these factors contributing to complacency and inertia in face of needs for change. (This may be the case throughout Gillette: As a *Business Week* article [Oct. 2, 2000, p. 56] put it, "virtually all of Gillette's executives have come up through the ranks.")

IV. Opportunities for Improvement

- *Production redesign:* The top-most need is conversion from the eight longish, problematic, delay-prone production lines to multiple compact product-family-dedicated cells that produce a planned quantity "every time." Space is not a problem; the production area (130K sf) appears roomy and uncluttered. O'Neil and his product team are all for the redesign, with the following features:
  - ✓ Pilot project one—to "prove" the change to cells.
    - Pick one production line. Slow the production rate and intensively attack sources of jams, stoppages, and defects.

- Remove all accumulators and incrementally remove non-value-adding conveyor between value-adding stations, with the aim of compacting this pilot line to about half its present space and one-fourth its present length.
- Run the much smaller "line" (not yet a cell) at a slower speed for more trouble-free production hours daily.
- Put up flow-distance, flow time, and other trend charts to track each phase of the changes and improvements.
- Benefits will include minimal conveyor and no accumulator—both requiring maintenance and that can be sources of defects (including scuffed cans) Further benefits: vastly reduced flow, quality problems, in-process inventory, and more—while out-producing the existing production lines. (Sell excess accumulators/conveyors, say, to competitors.)

✓ Pilot project two—"make-to-a-number" production.
  - At about the same time, pick another production line—probably the most under-utilized—for focused, make-to-a-number, daily-rate scheduling, with key suppliers on the same flat, repeating schedule.
  - The idea is to produce to a number and stop—every shift, every day, until there should be a need to change the number to match clear changes in average downstream demand. The number to produce per day (or per shift) could be a range, say, from 19,950 to 20,050 units. When "the number" has been reached with time remaining on a shift, stop and do training, projects, meetings with next shift, etc.

✓ Make a big deal out of both pilot conversions, perhaps with signs, new paint and lighting, special smocks, operator demos, etc.—making their successes stand out so other lines favor the same treatment.

✓ With viability of the pilot projects proven, next step is, one-by-one, to dismantle all the fill-and-pack lines, replacing each with two or more compact cells dedicated to its own narrow family of SKUs—so that the cells require only minor SKU-to-SKU changeovers—with make-to-a-number scheduling and output.

- *Other competitive pursuits*:
  ✓ Dominant opportunities are to produce each SKU more often in smaller quantities, ideally every product every day; reducing process and flow-time variation and cutting unit costs, pursued via the following:

- Until changeovers cease to be consequential, operators/mechanics jointly lead quick-changeover efforts, doing analysis by videotape, and documenting every step. For each changeover, they pull together a two-or-more-person changeover team. Spec sheets go to each person, specific changeover tools are on nearby shadow boards, and changeovers proceeds with stopwatch-like precision. They time and record every changeover.
- Maintain large cross-training charts in each production area. Include 5S and related displays; recognition on "wall-of-fame" displays; stack lights (red-yellow-green) on fill lines (as is presently the case in Mach 3 assembly); and track performance on trend charts in the production area and in support offices.
- Establish TPM (total productive maintenance) as a formal program, which entails maintenance/tool room mechanics transferring knowledge and first responsibility to line people—and with everything labeled, wide use of color-coding, and a strong safety component; also, include mechanics and group leaders when there is travel to check out and acquire new equipment.

✓ For most performance measures (quality, speedy response, flexibility, and value, and their derivatives), track *variability*, not just averages.

✓ Adopt personalized career-management plans for hourlies, and further develop skills certification.

✓ Train all production people in JIT, quality assurance, and process improvement—employing the just-in-time training method (train-do, train-do, etc.). Ensure that key people (e.g., opinion leaders) are involved early.

✓ Develop various approaches to raising employee awareness of competitors' product features (e.g., their products brought in periodically for all to analyze) and customers' views about Gillette products (perhaps including forms for employees to take home for friends and family assessment— which may give excellent results, because they care!).

✓ *Visitations.* Use any slowdown periods to send mixed teams on visits to suppliers, Gillette labs, the South Boston plant, and supplier plants for exchange visitations.

✓ *Capital investment.*

- Cut-and-dried corporate practices for approving capital expenditures (e.g., for in-line blending) may be ripe for modification and worth pushing by AMC.
- Senior management at Gillette may, for example, be receptive to strong arguments for acquiring simpler, more-focused cell-oriented equipment that can slash lead times and inventories and get production more closely in tune with customer demand, by SKU. The conventional hurdle-rate and the direct-labor-reduction mind-set may get loosened up.

V. Epilogue

- *Retrofit/pilot tests*: No deal: For all the plans' good sense, top-level support did not take root.
- *Resignation*: Soon Brian O'Neil left the company for a new job at Coty's Rocky Point, NC, manufacturing and distribution center.

CHAPTER III-70. MARK ANDY CO., ST. LOUIS, MO, 2001

My visit to Mark Andy was on September 10, 2001, one day before the infamous attacks upon New York's World Trade Center and other targets. I was in St. Louis as a keynote speaker on Day 1 of a September 10–11 lean manufacturing conference co-sponsored by IIE and APICS. The Mark Andy tour was that afternoon. Conference Day 2 was cancelled, and, along with all others from out of town, I was stuck in St. Louis for some days. Back home two weeks later, I completed and sent my tour report (from my notes) and thank-you letter to my tour hosts at Mark Andy.

Many High-Interest Topics:
- **A simple system lays out, in sequence, in nearby racks, the many parts and tools needed in final assembly (no computer required)**
- **Barrier-removal teams (BRTs) bring forth high levels of direct-labor involvement in process improvement**
- **Cycle time, dominant among Mark Andy goals, is a metric easy for front-line associates to relate to (unlike most companies' management metrics)**

How Mark Andy Simplifies Complexity:
Impressions from Afternoon Plant Visit, Sept. 10, 2001

I. General

- *Mark Andy.* A Dover Diversified company, it is the world's largest producer of narrow-web printing presses—with more than 400 employees and 22 CNC machines. This was my second visit there, the first being on October 23, 1997.
- *Products*: The company produces 200 flexographic printing presses yearly (almost one a day): the 4,000 (a huge press), the 2,300, and the Scout.
- *Contact people*: Paul N. Brauss, Sr. VP operations; John Eulich, president (Eulich is also president of Belvac, a packaging machine company, and GMI, a California company); John Howard, VP engrg & new product development.
- *Other Mark Andy companies.* UVT Technologies (makes an ultraviolet ink-curing module); also, a recently bought competitor, COMCO of Milford, OH, to be consolidated into the St. Louis facilities.
- *Competitors*: Rotopress, of Cincinnati, the no. 1 competitor, has filed for bankruptcy; Nilpeter A/S, a Denmark competitor, has recently bought Rotopress and is consolidating the two companies.
- *Best practices—getting it going*:
  - ✓ Mark Andy had hired the Thomas Group and implemented its TCT (total cycle time) concepts.
  - ✓ Last year Paul Brauss and his team went to Lantech in Kentucky—highly regarded for its advanced flow manufacturing. He had invited Lantech people to Mark Andy a year or two earlier for benchmarking, and at that time Lantech people had said they were way behind. But now, Wow! Lantech is impressive!
  - ✓ One or more managers went to MANTECH, a local MEP (manufacturing extension partnership) for training in lean. Also, one manager went to a lean course offered by the University of Tennessee.
  - ✓ The Brauss team developed a very formal five-year/one-year-update strategic plan with critical issues assigned to members of the steering committee.

II. Factory and Process Improvement

- *Factory tour*: Bill Thompson, plant manager and tour guide, devoted extra time explaining the factory's impressive practices in materials and handling:

✓ Suppliers, under VMI (vendor-managed inventory), come every Friday.

✓ "Material parts presenters" (stock pickers) serve module cells, which produce components for final assembly. Picking is done one module at a time (formerly six at a time), with one set of parts in progress and one on deck—an upper limit of three carts of materials.

✓ Assembly stations get their component parts and special tools—numerous given the complexity in assembly of the plant's large printing machines—in an ingeniously simple system.

■ The parts and tools are staged in several racks near to the final-assembly stations, and are laid out left-to-right, top-shelf-to-bottom *in assembly sequence!* See Figure 70.1.

■ Thus, getting the right parts and tools to final assemblers is a simple and quick picking of the items in that sequence—and as they are used throughout the hours it takes to build a machine.

■ As a result, the former labor efficiency rate of 55% (based on time standards) went up to 100%. [This way of feeding materials and tools to nearby assembly stations is among the more impressive, home-grown flow-manufacturing practices reviewed in this book.]

FIGURE 70.1
Shelves for components and tools—arranged in assembly sequence at Mark Andy Co.

✓ Ladders and pallet jacks are dispersed to each module/assembly cell area (formerly they were clustered and people were spending time fetching them).

✓ Final assembly bays run perpendicular to a main corridor astride the machining and module cells—enabling short-distance handling.

✓ A former 1,000 sq. ft. of raw-material space (for metal materials) has been converted to other uses (such as the COMCO consolidation).

✓ Painting takes place on a 3,600-sq. ft. hand-spray line.

- *Barrier-removal teams (BRTs)*:
    ✓ Three BRTs, under each of three cross-functional teams, meet one hour weekly to go over metrics and talk about "bads" (spikes in cycle times, or CTs—dominant metrics) and new ideas; and also make use of fishbone diagrams and Who What When sheets.

    ✓ Under TCT, Mark Andy was getting about 15% direct-labor involvement. Now, under chartered BRTs, it is up to about 50% involvement.

- *5S*: Begun about eight months ago.
- *PC kiosks*: Five are on the shop floor, with the intranet open to anyone.
- *Color-coding throughout*: Red is for the 2,200 press, Blue for the 4,000, and Green for the Scout.
- *Module (feeder) cells*: A print station module, an unwind module, and a die-cut module produce 26 modules per week.
- *Technical support*: Four-person teams of one electrical, one subassembly, and two with the module.

III. Best-Practice Engineering

- *Upgraded engineering*:
    ✓ John Howard, VP of engineering, went to a setup-reduction school at MANTECH—notably since Howard is a new-product engineer, not an ME (manufacturing engineer).

    ✓ He also brought in a DFMA consultant, the result being a new "2,000" version of the bread-and-butter 2,300 press, with just 15 or 20 parts vs. the former 45 to 60.

✓ It takes overly long—13 months to design and engineer a new "bare-bones" press—so instead of a new COMCO press (which was over-designed) the existing press is undergoing redesign.

- *Competitive products*: Engineering does rigorous competitive analysis—and finds competitors' claims to be exaggerated.

IV. Comments/Suggestions

- *Parts and tools*: The laying out of materials and tools in sequence, color coded, for "glitchless" assembly, is worth a visit from others in high-mix, low-volume manufacturing.
- *Performance measures*: There has been considerable improvement since 1998—and it looks as if the former emphasis on time standards-based efficiency has largely been superseded by cycle times as the dominant metric (though the old efficiency measures are still in existence).
- *Marketing/sales involvement*: Do the BRT's heavily involve marketing/sales? In most companies, various major issues usually are not dealt with because of *lack* of joint improvement efforts with marketing/sales. Examples that come to mind:
  ✓ A joint operations/marketing strategy aimed at offering a standard press at a significantly lower price. Of course, all customers want it their way, but that is costly and disruptive to Mark Andy's scheduling, capacity management, supplier responsiveness, and efforts toward lean inventories.
    - Doing a BRT properly on such a far-reaching issue should include doing an upfront ABC (activity-based costing) audit of full costs, plus a "disruption" audit of full effects on operations of offering "have it your way" instead of a relatively small set of options.
    - Boeing finally is selling passenger airplanes this way.
    - Quadrant Homes, Seattle-based subsidiary of Weyerhaeuser, is making lots of money and growing fast in home-building with much the same strategy. (They start and finish three homes every day, with 160 in process at any one time, offering more square footage but much fewer choices than the norm—and still there are hundreds or thousands of combinations customers choose from).

✓ Trimming the customer list: Aim at keeping only good, established customers who pay their bills and don't cause trouble.

  ■ Such a strategy is partly what made St. Louis metal stamper Wainwright Industries a Baldrige Prize winner. The strategy is also a dominant element of success at Nypro, the world's largest and most admired injection molder; and of Illinois Tool, which does things a bit better than similar companies, Dover and Emerson Electric.

  ■ Trimming the list must not be the purview of one department but requires true cost/revenue/profit analysis along with full analysis of disruption effects of "bad" customers.

• *Competitive analysis*: Share and involve competitive analysis with the whole work force, plus outside reps and installers; Rotary Lift's (Madison, IN) "Fair-to-Compare" room is an excellent example.

• *Supplier kanban-partnership*: I did not see or hear much about kanban with suppliers, and am guessing there should be more attention to it. The new DFMA thrust probably elevates the issue, but attention is needed to bring suppliers into a tighter loop.

• *Aggravation-based process improvement*: What little I learned about BRT sounded well conceived. However, it is best that process improvement be centered on the kinds of job-related aggravations that operators face every day. This requires operator-friendly ways of capturing and dealing with on-the-job frustrations.

  ✓ All employees experience frustrations every day, and most directly link to the essentials of competitiveness: quality, up-time on equipment, safety, response times and delays, skills, process capability, fits and finishes, instruction sets, and so on: little things, such as "I keep running out of tape," and bigger ones, such as a certain percentage of incoming wires not stripped or cut too short. Both types are good candidates for recording on check sheets (the simplest of the seven basic tools) and flip charts.

  ✓ Possibly you already have a system for tracking such things, and for BRT teams to meet regularly to go after root causes. However, I did not *see* the system, and making issues visible is one valued element of lean/world-class excellence. (At BMW in South Carolina, every team along the production line has its own alcove—just off the assembly line—equipped with chairs, table, flip charts, etc., for on-the-spot problem-solving meetings during the day. BMW was always ruled by the engineers, but has made strides in breaking the them-vs.-us barrier.)

- *Operator-relevant metrics.* In even the "leanest" companies I visit, the on-the-floor metrics seem to be too highly aggregated and remote from the work of the troops who make the product. With its CT emphasis, well known throughout, Mark Andy may do this better than most.
- *Vertical integration.* Most companies that are highly vertically integrated, as at Mark Andy, can cost-justify it.
    - ✓ However, such justifications generally presume existing, often unsatisfactory, ways of dealing with suppliers. As supplier partnerships solidify—their numbers pared to "a few good, long-term suppliers"—unsatisfactory service, with its high costs, will no longer be a rationale for bringing the work inside.
    - ✓ This said, the new world situation requiring elevated supply-chain security does tend to support more, not less, vertical integration.
- *TPM.* Total productive maintenance fits snugly with 5S and operator-centered quality, and may warrant more attention, especially in machining.

V. Post-script

- *Two years later*: I dined with Paul Brauss and John Eulich, February 11, 2003, the night before an APICS St. Louis seminar (eight Mark Andy participants). I learned the following:
- *Customer setup times*: John Howard, director of engineering, has taken quick setup to customers (users of Mark Andy printers). His engineers time-studied the way customers were setting up printers, then worked to redesign some printer features, which reduced *customer* setup 50%!
- *Re DFMA*: Howard is an advocate, but most of the design engineers would rather do it the old way: Don't bother searching for an existing part number; just design it anew.
- *Purchase of COMCO*: This was bad timing: They didn't sell a single COMCO machine for 9 months after the purchase. (COMCO's machines are much bigger, more costly).
- *Awards*: Mark Andy started offering several $1,000 awards at annual all-employee conclaves. Bill Thompson, plant manager, was against the idea; but the next day various employees were after their supervisors asking what they had to do to win the money next year, and Bill was sold!

CHAPTER III-71. MALLINCKRODT, IRVINE, CA, 2000

Mallinckrodt is a profitable, market-leading manufacturer of medical devices (syringes, etc.) that for five years aggressively implemented process improvements—and now seeks ways to accelerate the pace of that endeavor. The caselet offers extensive, positive discourse on this emphasis, and also includes highly detailed suggestions on coping with standout weaknesses.

High-Interest Topics:
- **Three product-focused factories have their own planning and scheduling—and clean rooms**
- **Large JIT assembly line in tracheostomy is split into three small lines so three products can be made simultaneously**
- **Safety: Recording "near misses" with monthly award for employee with most recorded misses**
- **Attacking SKU proliferation**

Process Improvement—Accelerating the Pace

Observations Based on Staff Presentations & Plant Tour, Oct. 10, 2000

Plus participation at two-day on-site seminar, October 11–12, 2000

I. Basic Information

- *This caselet*: Partially rewritten to be understandable to others aside from my hosts at the company.
- *Mallinckrodt*: Specialty medical-products producer in Irvine, CA, with three product lines:
  - ✓ Syringes and airway components (its syringes are no. 2 in the U.S. market with 15-20% annual growth); stopcocks; tracheostomy tubes and tracheostomy accessories.
  - ✓ Finished-goods SKUs total 1,100, with about 700 active; 20% go to distributors, 80% direct to a hospital or buying-group customers.
- *New owner*: This year (2000), Mallinckrodt was acquired by Exeter, NH-based Tyco, a $7.5b company with a lean HQ of about 100 people and many business units, including several (besides Tyco) in medical products.
- *Financials*: $100m sales with a 66% gross profit margin; 72% of sales are in the U.S.

- *Sister plant*: A Juárez, México, facility (transferred from Argyle, NY, in 1997) has 1,000 employees in two buildings and many product lines. Receives airway components from the Irvine plant.
- *Work force.* 334 full-time, 62 temps; one-third direct, one-third indirect, one-third salaried.
  - ✓ 52% of cost is wage and salary.
  - ✓ Its three-shift operations break down into six days injection molding; two to six days in assembly and packout; and two shifts in a mold-making room.
- *Key people*: Dick Nye, site manager, has a site coordination team of: Dominick Spuckes, FF1 (meaning focused-factory 1); Imelda Jasso, FF2; Samir Hijazi, FF3 (for Shiley tracheostomy devices); Bob Mitchell, QA; Ann Buckley, HR; Ed Morrissey, accounting. Each FF office has a window overlooking its assembly clean room.

II. Process Improvement Emphasis

- *Cost reduction*: Irvine plan is to drive out costs by (1) world-class manufacturing (WCM) with Juran quality management, (2) capital investment, (3) increased volumes and new products.
- *WCM*: In 1994–95 Dick Nye and John White, after reading the WCM book, began revamping the plant, organizing products into three focused factories with little inventory between production stages. Plant now has no maintenance, materials, or production-planning department; or central warehouse, and has lots of kanban devices. Current projects:
  - ✓ In FF3 (tracheostomy), one large JIT assembly line has been split into three small lines so that three products can be made simultaneously.
  - ✓ FF2 (stopcocks) is exploring reducing its customer base by requiring a minimum order or a setup fee.
  - ✓ FF1 (syringes) is studying layout of syringe assembly to eliminate non-value-added activity and reduce the total molding-through-assembly flow time.
- *Juran quality-improvement-team (QIT)*: Numerous improvements have been completed.

- *Focus*:
  - ✓ A product focus permeates flow lines, inventories, lot sizes, setup times, shipments.
  - ✓ Inventory is 55 days; flow times four to five weeks—except for stopcocks that are made to order with a flow time of three weeks, if non-sterile (which is how most are ordered; others take an extra day to go outside out for gamma sterilization).
- *Receiving/shipping*:
  - ✓ 500 shipments go out daily mostly by FedEx and RPS (and some UPS).
  - ✓ Incoming materials arrive at a single dock at the packing end of the building; bulky boxes are received nearest to packing, but resins need to traverse a long hall to the opposite end where they are stored in a hallway.
  - ✓ No items are shipped with bar-codes (an industry-wide issue).
- *FF coordination*: Each focused-factory coordinator is in charge of inventory, material handling, production planning, maintenance, engineering, tooling/molds, and quality engineering.

III. Process Descriptions (for details, see Sidebar 1)

- *FF1 – L-F syringes/airway products*: Dominick Spuckes, coordinator. These syringes are no. 2 in the U.S., with 15–20% annual growth, 52% gross profit margin.
  - ✓ When a kanban rack of 20 syringe barrels (or openings) is full, the molding machine is idled (some SKUs have one or two racks, others ten or so).
  - ✓ A 50-second run time leaves time for secondary molding-machine operations—with technicians moving to assembly of nut and cap, and on to barrels as barrels emerge from molds.
  - ✓ Attached to a wall of each machine are 6 to 8 PM (preventive maintenance) sheets plus a black trouble-call book. The book shows fairly thorough and detailed records, but I was told nobody takes time to use the book to look for patterns of root causes.
  - ✓ Behind each machine are three- or four-high stacks of plastic tubs that hold changeover clamps, hoses, etc., labeled with the relevant mold numbers.
  - ✓ Syringe barrels spend three days in WIP racks between molding and assembly.

SIDEBAR 1 PRIMARY EQUIPMENT & PROCESSES

Injection molding: 32 machines occupy 18,000 sf bldg.; 2 bridge cranes move molds in and out:

FF1, five molding machines are dedicated to L-F barrels, 2–200 ml barrels, four to airway. One week is typical flow time through assy., including SPC check for plunger depth and tilt. Steps involve plunger, cap, barrel, handifill or coil tube, and top seal.

FF2, 11 molding machines (4- to 32-cavity) dedicated to stockcocks. Finished stopcocks spend 10–15 days in gamma sterilization.

FF3, (Shiley tracheostomy), six machines (formerly nine), two are dedicated.

Production: 2 long, narrow class-100 clean rooms contain molding and assembly. Two assy. lines are fed by cylinder, print, shaft, oven time (one-hour, flash removal, at three stations per line), and a merge in a form-fill-seal machine; then by pass-through windows (for FF1, FF2, and FF3) to pack-ing. Trach & syringe/airway items go to L.A. area for sterilization taking about 9 days (except stopcocks, some out for one-day gamma sterilization), then back for a day of quarantine for bacterial culture growth, and on to customers.

FFI (syringes, airway products). Nine of the molding machines (Five for L-F barrels, two for 200 ml barrels, four for airway). When kanban rack of 20 fringe barrels is full, molding is idled. 50-second run time leaves time for technicians to move to assy. of nut and cap, and to barrels as they come out of molds.

✓ Last assembly steps are to be replaced with another form-fill-seal machine, which pays for itself quickly by avoiding a purchase of trays from outside.

✓ About seven people (all but one a temp) sit on each side of an assembly table passing units person to person, with a station cycle of less than ten seconds. They rotate jobs about every half hour.

• *FF2 – Stopcocks*: Imelda Jasso, coordinator. About 900 SKUs, 40m sold per year.

✓ Half of stopcock volume is of high-volume SKUs made in many-cavity molds; 30–40% are quick-turnaround, low-volume SKUs made in four-cavity molds and, with a typical 24-hour run, sold at a premium price.

✓ Lot sizes/production runs are one day to one month, with a four-hour interval between runs.

✓ A robot separates the stopcocks by cavity for quality traceback.

✓ Two production technicians engage in setups (they are a bit resistant to timing/charting every setup) and minor PMs, plus two counters for doing quality checks.

✓ I watched stopcocks being formed in a 16-cavity mold with a 15-second cycle, that process being dedicated to 50% of all stopcocks.

✓ Two automated assembly machines:

- One product-dedicated with 100,000-unit, 24-hour lot sizes, except for color changes that take five to ten minutes; two operators per shift do setups, repairs, packaging, maintenance, and quality. Yield and production quality charts are kept at the machine.

- Non-dedicated machine assembles one-way to four-way stopcocks with 10–15 minute to 45-minute changeovers (an obstacle to having more machines is mainly feeder bowls, which are very expensive).

- *FF3 – Shiley tracheostomy*: Samir Hijazi, coordinator. Since 1993, this area has had 50% of world market share and a 75% gross profit margin, with annual production of about 1.2 MM units. Some have a disposable inner cannula (DIC), others fixed cannula (the whole unit disposed of after use).

✓ Molding lot sizes are 5,000, 10,000, 20,000, 30,000.

- Changeovers used to take four hours, now one hour or so if urgent.
- Several associates manually cut off flash.
- Area has a nice-looking new display board.

✓ Assembly has 35 people on one line along two sides of an assembly table; 13 or fewer people are at a second line. Processes involve wash, bond head, fill gap, bond cap to head, stage for 16 hours, bag and seal 16 per plastic tray. Samir (with an IE background) intends to convert this assembly configuration into three to five cells, U-shaped, with fewer people per cell!

IV. Strengths

- *Focused factories (FFs)*:
  ✓ Each FF produces its own family of products start to finish, and has, next to production rooms, its own maintenance, scheduling,

inventory control, and sustaining engineering (FF2 also has its own customer service); but purchasing, HR, quality assurance, accounting, receiving/shipping, and facilities management are centralized.

✓ All injection molding (many machines) is in clean rooms—separate for each FF.

✓ FF structure, begun five years ago, was resisted at first but now is well accepted and valued.

✓ Resins are kanban-linked to silos that feed the molding machines.

- *Stability*: The FF structure is stable—with very low employee turnover, and most of core management at this site for 5 to 20 years. A ten-year lease was recently renewed for the Irvine location, where rents are high but labor costs moderate.

- *Improvement programs*: Twin pillars (lean basics of WCM with Juran quality management) are evident site-wide.

✓ Mostly rational applications of automation—resistance to "super-machines" with their inflexibilities and other limitations.

✓ Premium pricing on some lower-volume SKUs.

✓ QIT team displays are in hallways; kanbans are in use; plastic tubs in FF2 hold quick-changeover implements; FF3 has a fine-looking visual display board; good visual sight lines.

- *Job rotation*: From injection molding to assembly to packout—with cross-training and job rotation even between the three phases of production (but without evidence of skills qualification, and no visual skills charts on display).

- *Safety*: A form is available for employees to record "near misses;" each month a $100 gift certificate goes to the employee with the most near misses recorded.

- *Performance*:

✓ A lean overhead group has shrunk further even as sales have increased; total unit cost reductions in the past four years average 6.2% per year, with flow times and inventories shrinking 8% per year.

✓ Many U.S. shipments bypass intermediaries, going direct to a hospital or buying-group customers.

✓ Good service levels (95–100%) with most shipments going out same day as order arrives.

✓ Stopcock inventories are down from 2.5 MM to 1 or 1.5 MM units in the past 5 years, and there have been reductions in changeover times and lot sizes as well.

- *Superordinate goal.* Mallinckrodt-Irvine is well positioned for public recognition via an award such as California Quality Prize or Shingo Prize—which should be within reach after, say, a year or two of well-executed further improvements.

V. Weaknesses and Opportunities for Improvement

- *Competitiveness*: Pressing competition calls for producing each SKU more often in smaller quantities, the ideal being every product every day with reduced process and flow-time variation. Following are sub-issues, with supporting improvement initiatives/techniques:
- *SKU proliferation*: The 1,100 SKUs (700 active) are likely to be a drag that prevents much progress in further cutting of costs and becoming quicker and more flexible. The many SKUs result in numerous time-consuming changeovers.
    - ✓ SKU issue needs to be formally addressed, with careful analysis backed up by activity-based cost auditing and aimed at eliminating or up-pricing slow-moving, low-volume items.
    - ✓ A marketing specialist is to move (from the East Coast) to Irvine to engage in rationalizing the product mix.
- *Quick changeover*: Present approach to quick changeover needs an upgrade:
    - ✓ Operators and mechanics should be in the lead, working on their own changeover improvements, using product-line-specific tools at points of use on shadow boards.
    - ✓ Document every step with analysis by videotape, and time and record every changeover.
    - ✓ Bring in reinforcements for team changeovers (except where there is a lot of slack time), and use stop-watch-like precision with spec sheets handed out to each person on the changeover team.
- *Scheduling*:
    - ✓ Irregular production of some (or many) SKUs contributes to competitive weaknesses:
        - ■ Pushes the supply chain out of synch with retail and consumer demand/usage, enlarging inventories and lead times, making manufacturing and purchasing support complex and costly, and forcing a reactionary mode in most activities.

- ■ The problem is partly self/industry-inflicted—e.g., a lack, in the health-care sector, of bar-code linkages to final demand.
  - ✓ Look for products that can be produced on regular, repeating, same-quantity-every-time schedules passed back to key suppliers.
    - ■ Can be every shift, one shift per day, 4 hours per day, every second day, three staggered shifts per week, etc.
    - ■ Use production regularity as wedge to convince downstream stock locations (e.g., distribution center or hospital stock room) that they can safely cut their stocks to the bone and regularize *their* ordering, knowing more are produced regularly.
- *Visual management*: Good examples (e.g., QIT displays) are in hallways, but little elsewhere. Several forms of kanban are in use but need to be more visually exacting.
- *Maintenance*: Though operators and technicians are involved, they mostly lack sufficient training, ownership, and incentive to take over. The need is for a strong TPM (total productive maintenance)/5S initiative:
  - ✓ Everything labeled, color-coded.
  - ✓ Knowledge and first-responsibility transfer, from maintenance to line people—blending with local ownership of changeovers, housekeeping, handling, quality, safety, other aspects of process management and improvement.
  - ✓ Operators/technicians accompanying engineers on equipment buying trips.
- *Skills*: Skills certification and visual versatility displays are largely absent. Needed are standards for certifying skills and displays of every employee's skills on large versatility matrices, and personalized career management for both hourlies and salaried.
- *Process controls*:
  - ✓ Few employees have access to a means of recording process problems, except for maintenance log books in injection molding. SPC is in use in only a few areas.
  - ✓ Needed: A system wherein every associate is expected/required to record data every day on mishaps and probable causes—keys to team/individual suggestions, problem-solving, and continuous improvement. This ties in well with Juran QIT.
- *Work content*: In manual assembly, most station cycle times are very short, causing a chain of bad consequences—motivational, developmental, ergonomic, and other.

✓ Where work content per person is under ten seconds (e.g., in FF1 assembly) jobs need to be expanded by factor of three or four; and at the same time, look to elevating assembly tables/benches and eliminating chairs—in a more ergonomic standup/walk-a-few-steps production mode.

✓ The preceding points on data collection are unlikely without lengthened work content and time to think about and record mishaps.

• *Facilities costs*: These costs were fully amortized in the prior five-year lease period. Now with leases extended ten years, a shortfall of amortization costs will wrongly show profitability erosion. Since Tyco is so financial-numbers driven, this problem needs to be explicitly addressed.

• *External awareness*: Low consciousness of and emphasis on competitors' products, competencies, and customer satisfaction/wants contribute to complacency and inertia in the face of opportunities and need for change.

✓ Raise employee awareness of competitors' product features (e.g., bring in competitors' products periodically for all to analyze), also of customers' views about Irvine products (e.g., perhaps forms for employees to take home for friends and family assessment).

✓ Use any slowdown periods to send mixed teams on visits to suppliers, sister plants, customers/hospitals, etc.

CHAPTER III-72. LOZIER CORP., OMAHA, NE, 2001

Lozier, producing shelving, counters, and cabinets found in many grocery and other retail stores, employs various "best practices" in their manufacture.	*High-Interest Topics:* • **NVA conveyor seen as a disciplined scheduling sequencer** • **Quick-response painting**

Niche Business Doing Well: Observations from Plant Visit, April 18, 2001

In connection with next-day Schonberger seminar hosted by Omaha APICS chapter

I. General Information

- *Lozier Corporation*: Family-owned manufacturer of retail fixtures: Shelves, checkouts, counters, showcases, end caps, free-standing displays, and so on.
  - ✓ The company was founded by a Lozier grandfather to produce retail refrigeration. Customers asked for shelving, so Lozier got into that business. Allen Lozier (current CEO and grandson of founder) invented the self-hanging "non-tool" store fixture in 1956, which launched the business.
  - ✓ Lozier is very profitable, and first in market share with twice the share of the next closest (Maydek Co.). Among customers, no. 1 is Target; no. 2 are grocers (e.g., Albertson); no. 3 are auto parts stores; remaining customers are pharmacies and any other retail.
  - ✓ Other Lozier plants are in Scottsboro, AL, an Omaha clone with half of Omaha's volume, for the southeast market; Joplin, MO, producing tubing and garment racks; and McClure, PA, producing wire baskets and pharmacy fixtures.
- *Customer response*:
  - ✓ Short lead time is a key Lozier advantage, because customers will suddenly decide to re-shelve dozens of stores, all in a short time.
  - ✓ The busy season is late summer and fall—in advance of retailers' Christmas season.
  - ✓ Customers increasingly ask for Lozier to ship in trucks with orders staged in the sequence they plan for equipping a store (or multiple stores).
  - ✓ Right now, Giant Foods is re-shelving each store area at night, so Lozier trucks must unload and install at night within an 8-hour time slot.
- *Tour guides*/contact persons Greg Judkins, production manager; John McGovern, director of operations; also my APICS host, Janet Deane, materials management (but on leave this day).

II. Operations—General Information

- *Omaha facilities*: The Omaha complex includes the 500K-sq. ft. north plant for higher-volume shelving, etc., interconnected with the 200K-sq. ft. west plant for custom products—plus a separate

DC (distribution center). Omaha west also makes multifunction shelves; and fine-wood showcases using new CNC woodworking equipment.

- ✓ The basic product is a "gondola section" with a pegboard or slot-back wall.
- ✓ Another product is pallet racks, made mainly as a service to customers, not to make money (since the pallets industry is highly competitive).
- ✓ Eight colors of basic display racks are stocked in the warehouse for same-day shipment.

- *Maintenance management*:
  - ✓ Red electronic lights all over the plant track minutes of down time (but there are no stack lights).
  - ✓ If there are five minutes or more of down time, an operator records the reason on a maintenance form (material, equipment, etc.); then supervisors can tell at a glance if there is a problem that will require OT or other actions. Operators also record output per hour.

- *Employment*:
  - ✓ The Omaha complex is unionized but not a problem for management.
    - Lozier doesn't ever lay off people.
    - Production was three-shift three years ago; now one-shift.
  - ✓ No temps have been used in the past 8 months, but temps (e.g., college kids) are common in the summer; Lozier refers to inventory as "stored labor" (e.g., for the busy season), and relies on overtime, along with stored labor to handle the peaks.
  - ✓ Labor is in groups by degree of proficiency: Group 2 is fairly proficient, Group 3 is high skill (CNC skills, etc.).
    - Lozier believes its work force is outstanding for the Omaha area.
    - Avaya is eager to hire Lozier employees because they are diligent.
  - ✓ Job rotation is every two hours on moderate-skill jobs; on skilled jobs, rotation from machine to machine is daily. Labor versatility charts are in each area.

III. North Plant

- *Highest volume displays*: This plant, aimed at HVLC (high-volume, low cost) production, offers limited design options. It uses 20,000 tons of coil steel yearly. Cut-steel inventory is eight hours' worth.
- *Paint*: This is a critical competitive factor, requiring very high quality and quick response:
  - ✓ There are three powder paint lines: No. 2 is for the eight basic colors; no. 3 for special colors (up to about 100 colors). Two high-volume lines are dedicated to a platinum color (in the no. 1 paint line), and run to a rate; Lee: "We might over-run the rate daily, but not weekly."
  - ✓ Line 3 (two shifts) runs 38 feet/minute, 10 paint guns per booth. Booths are on rails, so it takes only a minute or two to change color. 30 minutes are required to change cartridges off-line.
    - New Allen-Bradley devices control paint thickness to 0.5 mm. 15 people are on the paint lines.
    - There are eight conveyors for the eight colors, with 48–50 minutes conveyor turn time.
    - The conveyor is against a wall, which inhibits load and "take-off," and prevents having other operations on both sides; eight to ten minutes of the cycle is NVA (non-value-adding) transport, but three to six minutes of that are needed to cool after the bake oven and before take-off.
  - ✓ Line 6 has two powder, and one liquid (polyester) paint booths; the liquid is easy to mix in-house, which offers a quick-response advantage.
- *Wood department.*
  - ✓ With a sequencing conveyor (until new conveyor loops are installed), orders got stacked up/mixed up, a headache.
    - The production cycle had taken two shifts, now down to 1¼ shifts, with the conveyors enabling schedule-by-sequence (or FIFO).
    - [Note: The case against conveyors may be mitigated here, because the conveyor serves the important purpose of maintaining schedule discipline.]
  - ✓ CNC panel saw, CNC router—each does multiple operations.

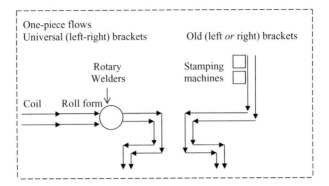

FIGURE 72.1
Two technologies for base bracket production.

- *Shelf welding:* This takes place in two focused plants-in-a-plant: Line 1 – few changes. Line 2 – quick change. Five welders produce 650 shelves/hour, 10,000 shelves/day.
- *Base brackets:* Brackets are made on two lines, one newer technology, the other old. The new produces both left and right brackets with one-piece flows. The older must be changed over from left to right brackets. See the schematic in Figure 72.1.

IV. Opportunities for Improvement

- *Root causes:* Operators record reasons for down time, though only in general categories (e.g., material, equipment), but they often know much more (e.g., what, specifically is the trouble with the material or equipment) and should be recording all they know to get closer to root causes.
- *Indicators.* Lights record minutes of down time. But stack lights, each color indicating *type* of down time, should be installed.
- *Setup-time trends.* Quick setup is a competitive advantage for Lozier. But no setup-time trend charts were in evidence on the tour. Trend charts make the importance of setup visible and prod further improvement.
- *Cut-steel inventory:* This inventory—about one day's worth—could probably be halved if the cutting were linked by kanbans to final assembly or put on the same rate-based schedules as shelf-forming.

CHAPTER III-73. OLYMPUS (SHENZHEN) INDUSTRIAL LTD., SHENZHEN, CHINA, 2003

This caselet describes extensive, highly complex production of electronic cameras outsourced to China by premier Japanese manufacturer, Olympus. The caselet ends with a thank-you letter with critical comments to the Olympus-Shenzhen plant-tour host.

High-Interest Topics:
- **Bad ergonomic effects of stand-up assemblers crowded closely together on assembly lines**
- **In other respects, excellent treatment of employees**
- **Buildings too large and unfocused**

High-End Products Massively Produced: Impressions from 2-Hour Plant Visit, Jan. 20, 2003

In connection with two-hour Schonberger talk in Shenzhen on January 20, 2003

And two-day seminar in Shenzhen, January 21–22

I. General

- *Tour group*:
  - ✓ Cao Yi Wei, vice GM, personnel and general affairs, Olympus Shenzhen.
  - ✓ From HKPC (Hong Kong Productivity Council): S.L. Law; Daniel P.M. Chan, sr. consultant; Fritz T.Y. Chan, consultant; Ms. Angel Wong, consultant for industrial technology training.
  - ✓ Bill Chan, Director; Headwin Creative Development Co., Ltd. (HKPC tech. partner).
  - ✓ Two others from Shenzhen Association of Enterprises with Foreign Investment (ZAEFI).
- *Location*: Olympus (Shenzhen) Industrial Ltd., Nantou 5th Industrial District, Nanshan, Shenzhen, PRC.
- *China operations*. Olympus Shenzhen was opened in 1994 as a 100% Japanese investment, currently with 6,100 people (30 Japanese).
  - ✓ Two years ago the Asia-Pacific headquarters of Olympus moved here—a complex of 3 million square meters (32.2 million sf) with three production buildings of 1 million square meters

(10.8 million sf) in two or three stories, and 4,000 people assembling and testing 3.5 million cameras per year.

✓ Olympus was the world's first producer of digital cameras, which this plant has been ramping up on (much construction/renovation for this production), with output last year of 10,000 digital cameras/day, the remainder being conventional cameras. China/H.K. Olympus employment is 10,000.

- *Management system.* An all-Japanese system, requiring culture-change efforts with the Chinese workforce.
- *Top management.* All Japanese executives at Olympus Hong Kong, Shenzhen, Songji, and Beijing.
- *Shenzhen plant.*
    ✓ Produces all plastic parts, and plastic and glass lenses. Components require 10,000–20,000-class clean room. Electronic cameras require a higher, 1,000-class, clean room. The plant has 200 engineers.
    ✓ Electronic components come from Japanese companies Sony and Panasonic (perhaps others). Less critical parts are contracted out.
- *Other Olympus/PRC plants*: Pongji has 4,200 people, Beijing 800 people.
- *Product line.* Cameras are dominant; also produce microscopes and ultrasonic endoscopes.
- *Equipment*:
    ✓ Dominant equipment is for injection molding—of camera frames and mechanisms, fittings, lenses (32 million pieces/year).
    ✓ The plant also has equipment for glass lenses; lead-free soldering (wave soldering and SMT); material handling and storage; surface-coating and finishing; and miscellaneous special-order sheet-metal work.
- *Distribution/customers.* About 10–16% of cameras are sold within China; the rest go to a Hong Kong DC for further distribution to New York/U.S. and other countries.

II. Production Processes

- *The tour*: Wearing booties (not hats, gloves, smocks, bunny suits, etc.), we went up and down staircases through plastic/glass components and camera assembly/test (omitting microscopes and endoscopes).

SIDEBAR 1   SOME PROCESSING DETAILS

Plastic frames and components: 24/7 operation (1st floor) includes mold design, maintenance, production, printing, assy. Very tight specs with high temp. variation (to Six Sigma quality) in mold machines. Molding in four rows of 113 mold machines.

Mold design: 20 people in room with Compaq work stations.

Mold maintenance/repair: In three rooms: One with technicians using hand tools; one with lathe, press, CNC, etc.; and one machine center for spherical lenses.

Plastic lenses: Made from transparent plastics (resin from Mitsubishi) on 49 mold machines and four vacuum coating/ plating machines; nine types of coating, all allowing 100% light to pass through.

Coatings: Color sprayed on plastic components, 90% just one coat, maximum of three.

Olympus name: Printed on camera by 44 printing machines

Glass lens department: Many small machines for raw, polish & center (about 50 machines polishing outside & finding center of lens), coat, cement two lens pieces together, paint around outside and inside. Vacuum coating, 20 minutes per tray of 100+ pieces per batch; Cement room for chemical bond with UV cure in batches.

Separate departments produce components, mostly in batch production. Some details are in Sidebar 1:

✓ Molding plastic frames and components requires high emphasis on quick mold changes; for the most difficult part, changes take just 9 minutes.

- Cycle time is 30% better here than in Japan.
- TPM (total productive maintenance) is in use, as is regenerative (remold) plastic.
- All operators are cross-trained.

✓ A critical-dimension lab is a 24-hour operation.

- *Cellular production*: As of the year prior, cells had replaced many long production lines:

✓ Cells in Micromotor PCBs have eight associates per cell, all standing up

- In all cells seen, associates were standing, and sometimes were so close together that they probably do not walk at all within or between stations. As a result, legs get tired, which calls for ten minutes rest every two hours.

- ■ Compounding the negative ergonomics, it is likely that each assembler has very short work content (e.g., estimated ten seconds).
- ✓ Cells making flex circuits are in another room.
- ✓ Lens cells (in still another room) have 20 assemblers per cell.
- *Camera assembly*: Final camera assembly and checkout (in their own room) end the tour.

III. Notable Positive (or Neutral) Observations

- *Our guide*: Head of HR, he is an engineer and could answer any and all our questions about production, engineering, etc.—unusual for an HR manager.
- *Plant and equipment*: Very clean, well-lit plant, with what seem to be the very best equipment.
- *Quality*: The responsibility of each associate.
- *TPM*: Operators are involved, and every machine's "vital signs" (like a patient in a hospital) are measured before the machine starts.
- *Kanban*: Elevated electronic kanban signboards were seen in a corridor; multiple electronic information screens (in Chinese) scroll down, some with numerical kanban information.
- *Workforce make-up*: The thousands are mostly young women of similar age and same uniform. At lunch, hordes head upstairs and down corridors to the large lunchroom. Lots of others were observed with heads down sleeping at desks/benches with overhead lights off.
- *Treatment of workforce*: Employees are treated well, to the point of buying local apartment units for some—especially the high-value technicians.
  - ✓ Such treatment yields low (for China) employee turnover: about 10% for most, only 3% for technicians.
  - ✓ Some jobs seemed friendly to backs, arms, etc.—with a major exception for those who are standing so close they cannot take steps.
  - ✓ Some of the work force receives training in quality control circles.
  - ✓ All employees wear the same special footgear: tennis shoe bottoms connected to leg sleeves that go up the calf almost to

the knee. It's a one-shift operation five days a week, 8:00 a.m. to 5:30 p.m.

- *Support staff*: At least some production control and/or engineering staff occupy desks in long, narrow open areas just on the other side of a corridor from the production area they support.
- *Visual management*: Copy-paper-sized performance charts are everywhere, as are glass cases showing sets of component parts, assemblies, etc. Also, recognition is publicly displayed.
- *Macro performance measures*: One dominant objective—from corporate HQ—was to go from loss to profitability with five years, which was achieved.

IV. Opportunities for Improvement (OFIs)

- *Micro performance measures*:
  - ✓ All employees are *individually* measured and reported on, a "blame"-oriented environment (common in developing countries).
  - ✓ The plant should gravitate toward team (not individual) performance.
- *5S*: Need be greater use of 5S (precise labeling, color-coding, etc.).
- *Further opportunities*: Following segments from an emailed letter offer additional OFI comments.

Cao Yi Wei, Vice General Manager, Olympus Shenzhen Industrial Ltd.
January 25, 2003
Dear Mr. Cao:

Thank you very much for the excellent plant tour and discussion on Monday, January 20—for me in the good company of friends from the Hong Kong Productivity Council.

. . .

May I also offer a few opinions about possible opportunities for improvement? (I had the opportunity to express some of these in our discussion directly after the plant tour.)

1. Over 15 years ago I began to see companies that had moved some of their injection molding machines to become stations on production lines or assembly cells (Allen-Bradley in Milwaukee, USA, for

example). In other companies I noticed assembly cells physically linked by short, gravity conveyors to injection molding machines (Siemens-Corning joint venture in Texas, for example). I am thinking that some of your injection molding could be linked to subassembly in some similar way.

2. Your early efforts to convert from production lines to cells are worthy. However, I noted a potential improvement in the design of the assembly cells: The assemblers are standing very close together and must have a rest every two hours to relieve tired legs. This should not happen if the average task time for each operator in the cell is longer. For example, having each stand-up assembler perform not one short task (e.g., ten seconds) but three or four. Combining three or four tasks into one job means, usually, that the assembler will have small walk time in each job cycle—possibly only one step. In that design, legs do not get tired. Rather legs become strong, because the whole body moves. More importantly, the task cycle is 30 or 40 seconds instead of only 10. Job boredom and repetitive motion problems cease to be a concern. Of course, this job design requires three or four times as many cells—a limitation if costly equipment is involved, but otherwise not.

3. The suggested cell design expands the product vision of each assembler. Thus, they are likely to have many more ideas about process improvement. You stated that only some of the work force had been trained to function in quality control circles (QCCs). QCCs are more effective when employees have enlarged product vision.

4. Your plant is highly vertically integrated—producing all plastic components and lenses inside. This is rather unusual today. For cost and competitive reasons, most companies contract out much of their injection molding. Twenty years ago there were very few excellent injection-molding firms in the world, so companies like IBM and H-P started up their own internal plastic manufacturing. By the mid-1980s, they were beginning to outsource, because outside molders were becoming excellent. Today, excellent molders are everywhere. Thus, I suspect that at some point your company will have to consider outsourcing some of your molding.

These four comments are based on a short visit in which my lack of knowledge of the Chinese language limited my understanding. Thus, no doubt, I am mistaken on some of my impressions, and I apologize for my errors. If you would like to discuss any of these or other points by email, I would be pleased to participate. Thank you again for your hospitality and the excellent visit. Best wishes for the future of your fine operation.

Richard J. Schonberger

CHAPTER III-74. WOODHEAD DE MÉXICO, CD., DE JUÁREZ, 2001

This caselet is grouped with Chapter III-7, System Sensor de México. Both are fine examples of best-practice manufacturing, featuring cellular organization and are maquiladoras with headquarters in northern U.S. states. I had visited them on the same afternoon, and both were sending people to my seminar the next day.

High-Interest Topics:
- **Five plants-in-a-plant, each with its own support staff (no departments)**
- **Employees tested for color-blindness because of color-coding throughout the plant**
- **Simple scheduling: First-order-in is first-order-processed—for average orders of six pieces**

Simplified, Focused Production: Observations Based on Quick Plant Visit, Nov. 7, 2001
In connection with a same-day evening talk sponsored by an ASQ chapter
And a Schonberger one-day public seminar on Nov. 8, 2001

I. General Information

- *The company.* Woodhead Industries, headquartered in Deerfield, IL, has 13 plants, including Woodhead de México in Cd. Juárez.
- *Contacts*: Esco Martínez, Superintendente de Planta; Lee Marsh, Director Juárez Operations
- *Products*: Plant I, 104,000 sf, produces lighting and electrical connectors in some 20,000 part numbers (Plant II, next door, 120,000 sq. ft, is soon to be occupied).
- *Big sign at entrance*: Turbo-Charged Factory: Rápido, Qualidad, Flexibilidad.

388 • *Flow Manufacturing*

- *Production system*: In 1990 Lee Marsh had been trying out various JIT tools. The company president (since terminated) told Lee, "We don't worship at the altar of JIT." Now the company has its own a version of TPS called Woodhead Production System.*

II. Manufacturing

- *Product focus*: The plant is organized as five product-focused plants-in-a-plant, or lines (they call them cells), each with self-sustaining teams. Production-line sizes are 180–200 people in the largest cell, to 100 in the smallest.
- *Organization and layout*:
  - ✓ Each focused line has its own team of ME, planner, buyer, data entry clerk. There are no departments for purchasing, HR, etc.
  - ✓ Lines are divided into multiple U-shaped cells, each with the same equipment, tooling, capacity—that high level of flexibility to shift among cells eliminating the need for line schedules.
- *Capacity*: Every line has some redundant capacity, which avoids order backups. Equipment includes a lot of refurbished rubber molding machines from the 1930s.
- *Scheduling/ordering*: The schedule is simply first order in, first processed.†
  - ✓ The average order is six pieces or less; orders arrive to the planner four times daily from Illinois.
  - ✓ Bills of materials are single-level; planning bills are used for faster materials planning.
  - ✓ For quicker response, scheduling is mixed-model.
- *Setups*: Line changeovers are less than five minutes; machine setup times less than ten minutes.
- *Visuality*: Color-coding and other visual-management elements are prominent—including kanban squares for further limiting flow time and WIP.

---

* See also Robert W. Hall, "Simplifying Administration at Daniel Woodhead de Mexico," *Target*, Second Quarter 2000, pp. 28–30.

† See also Louis & Jo Joy, "In the Job Shop, You Can't Schedule, but You Can Sequence," *APICS—The Competitive Advantage*, May 1992.

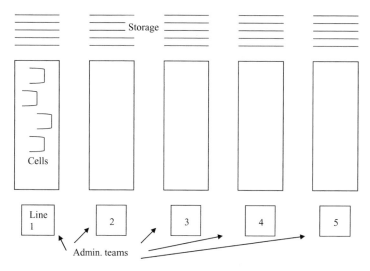

FIGURE 74.1
Five product-focused production lines—with cells and their own administrative teams.

- *Performance measures*:
  - ✓ Metrics include productivity, quality (scrap, product PPM, cell PPM, defect reduction), on time, percent certified operators, productivity, cycle count, budget goals, improvement goals.
  - ✓ Lots of before-and-after photos above every work bench (over 600 of them), are good evidence of process improvements.
  - ✓ Inspect/audit scorecards are in use, with one to five scoring.
- *Plant layout*: Figure 74.1 is a schematic of five production lines, each with several cells and each with its own administrative team fronting its line.

III. Human Resource Management

- *CI teams*: Continuous-improvement teams meet for an hour a week—all employees are encouraged to participate.
- *Suggestions*: Supervisors have up to five days to respond to suggestions.
- *Bonuses*: Monthly bonuses are paid per line.
- *Multi-skilling*: 75% to 90% of associates are skilled in at least three jobs—with pay-by-skills (written test → timed test → pay increase).
- *Color-blindness*: All employees take a color test; the 5% who fail cannot work on the lines, since there is so much color-coding; they may be put on other jobs.

IV. Potential Improvements

- *Aggravations and mishaps*: Set up check sheets for all assemblers and machine operators—to record every aggravation and mishap by a check mark on a chart; use the data for problem-solving projects.
- *Operator-relevant metrics*: Separate the higher-order management metrics (e.g., productivity) from operator-relevant metrics (e.g., flow times, flow distances, setup times.). Retain the higher-order metrics in a management room, with only operator-relevant metrics on display to all—beneficial because the operator-relative ones focus highly on quick customer response.

CHAPTER III-75. SYSTEM SENSOR DE MÉXICO, CD. JUÁREZ, 2001

This caselet is grouped with that of the preceding caselet, Ch. III-6, Woodhead de México, both located in Juárez.*	**Many High-Interest Topics:** • **How to ensure kanban discipline** • **Replacing big cutting machine with a "pizza cutter"**

Keeping It Simple: Observations from a Short Plant visit, Nov. 7, 2001
In connection with a 1-day Schonberger seminar and evening talk on November 8, 2001

I. General Information

- *The company*: Systems Sensor de México, founded in 1984, was a part of the Pittway Group until February 2000 when Pittway (and therefore System Sensor) was acquired by Honeywell—and Honeywell's six sigma methodology. The 46,000-sq. ft. plant has 450 employees.
- *Contacts*: Oscar Aguilar, quality manager; Augustin Sosa (2nd employee hired); Bob Machalak (3rd employee hired)
- *Products*:
  - ✓ Smoke detectors under many brand names (Notifier, Honeywell, Trane, ADT, Johnson Controls, etc.); also air controls for HVAC.
  - ✓ Product development and marketing are located in St. Charles, IL.

---

* See, also, Lea A.P. Tonkin, "System Sensor's Lean Journey," *Target*, 18/2 (2nd Qtr., 2002): 44–48.

✓ The plant has teamed up with St. Charles on a DFMA project. Result: a new model of smoke detector designed for layered (uni-directional) assembly.

- *Competitors*: One is Sentrol of Portland, OR; see Ch. II-16.
- *Focused organization*: There are three multifunctional teams of professionals, one for each major product line (or customer group?). Marketing in St. Charles, IL, is organized the same way!
- *Recent performance*: Inventory turns are up from 4 to 11; finished goods are one or two days' worth; throughput time is 1.5 to 3 hours. A small distribution center (15,000 sq. ft.) in El Paso holds one to two days' inventory—both incoming raw material and outgoing finished goods. Metrics on display in the hall are: quality, scrap, sales, units, inventory turns, backlog, direct/indirect labor turnover.

II. Manufacturing

- *Pull system*.
  - ✓ The organization and layout are cellular and pull driven with, in some cells, a high-mix of product colors and languages. There are no shop orders.
  - ✓ Water spiders replenish kanban locations three times daily.
  - ✓ Process time on the SMT (surface-mount technology) printed-circuit-board line was reduced by installation of 6 cooling fans after the reflow machine—which cools boards so they can be processed by hand immediately.
  - ✓ In assembly cells, kanban squares are marked off between each assembler pair. To raise kanban discipline, each square, sized to hold just one unit, is imprinted with "Grácias por poner aqui una pieza sin defector" (Thanks for putting just one piece here.). See photo, Figure 75.1.
- *Equipment*.
  - ✓ The SMT line had been equipped with a "monument"-sized brake-press machine whose only function was to split double PC boards in half. A simple, cheap, table-top local innovation replaces that machine—appropriately called a "pizza cutter"; see photo, Figure 75.2.
  - ✓ No equipment or benches are bolted to floor; comment heard on the tour: "next time we put them on wheels."

FIGURE 75.1
At System Sensor, Juarez: No putting a piece down other than on a kanban square.

FIGURE 75.2
At System Sensor, Juarez: A pizza-cutter-like board splitter replaces a big machine.

- *Security products*: Figure 75.3 sketches the layout of this area—curved arrows designating a variety of cells. The second part of the figure is a rough depiction of one of the cells—of 15–18 assemblers and testers preceded by a four-step SMT process that yields circuit boards for the assembler-testers.

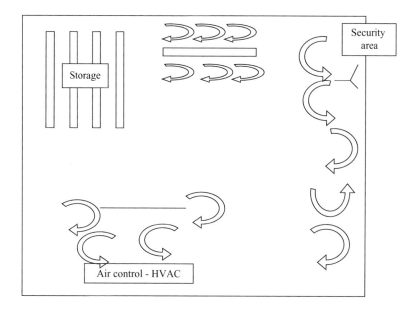

A more-detailed example of a cell for security products:

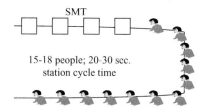

FIGURE 75.3
Layout of security products area and a typical cell.

III. Human Resource Management

- *Versatile work force*: Plant has skill-based pay with cross-training and job rotation (how frequently?); skills matrices are on display in each area.
- *Training emphasis*:
  - ✓ At any given time about 5% of the work force is in training— except on Mondays and Tuesdays, which are days of higher absenteeism.
  - ✓ Trainers (level-5 employees) wearing white smocks roam the floor, helping with production as needed.
  - ✓ When there is no production to be done, the first option is training, the second is problem-solving.

- One manager's comment: "Lean is easy. Implementation is difficult"— including convincing people, having sufficient training, achieving discipline, and getting to ownership by floor people.

IV. Notable Improvements Summarized

- *Metrics*: Fairly good (customer-centered) performance measures.
- *Responsiveness*: Quick throughput times; low inventories (including in the El Paso DC).
- *Product*: A DFMA product—was co-designed for layered assembly with engineers in Illinois.
- *Equipment*:
  ✓ "Pizza cutter" board splitter.
  ✓ Cooling fans after reflow—for quicker cool-down and shorter cycle times.
  ✓ Equipment movability—not dug in, ease of utility hookups, wheels.
- *Skills*:
  ✓ Multifunctional teams aligned with counterpart Illinois HQ teams.
  ✓ Skill-based pay and skills matrices.
  ✓ Direct-labor flexibility for both volume and mix variability.
  ✓ Job design (fairly reasonable work content).
- *Handling*: Kanban squares and "gracias" notices. Use of water spiders.

V. Potential Improvements

- *Kitting*: Eliminate kitting; place un-kitted stocks at points of use in the assembly cells—thus to cut double handling, storage locations, and flow times.
- *Cell team balance*: Allow cell teams to balance the work among themselves—so that faster, more experienced associates have more work content and slower, newer associates less. This concept is based on the view that time standards are good only for an average employee, but most are above or below average.
- *Glitches/aggravations*: Make check sheets available to all assemblers and machine operators—to record every aggravation and mishap by a check mark on a chart; use the data for problem-solving projects.

CHAPTER III-76. QUADRANT HOMES, BELLEVUE, WA, 2002

This caselet was part of a research project of Karen Brown, Tom Schmitt, and Richard Schonberger— resulting in two published articles,* the first reporting astonishing applications of JIT/lean to house building. (The second, an update over a decade later,** is not a part of in this caselet.)	***High-Interest Topics:*** • **Unique building management (JIT/lean applied to home construction)** • **Highly predictable 60-day house completions with three started, three completed daily** • **Close partnership with small number of dedicated contractors**

JIT—Even in Home-Building: Observations Based on Brief Visit to Headquarters, Showroom, and Community Site, Aug. 15, 2002

I. General Information

- *Quadrant visit*: A joint visit by Schonberger and University of Washington professors Karen Brown and Thomas Schmitt.
  - ✓ Main sources of information:
    - Headquarters: Mark Gray, VP operations. Melanie Winter, showroom mgr.
    - On-site (Snoqualmie Ridge) hosts: Wes Guyer, construction mgr.; Todd Hagstrom, superintendent; Rand Cowles, community sales mgr.
- *Quadrant Homes*: A major home builder within the Greater Seattle vicinity, Quadrant is a subsidiary of Weyerhaeuser Corp. Its headquarters and showroom are in Bellevue, WA.
- *Unique building management*: Quadrant had become renown in the home-building sector for its remarkable application of just-in-time/ lean production methods to that sector. The following are selected features:
  - ✓ Three houses are started and three are closed daily (750 built and closed in a 250-workday year). 160 houses are in process

---

* "Quadrant Homes Applies Lean Concepts in a Project Environment," *Interfaces*, 34/6, Nov.-Dec. 2004, pp. 442–450.
** "ASP, The Art and Science of Practice: Three Challenges for a Lean Enterprise in Turbulent Times." *Interfaces*, 45(3), May-June, 2015: 260–270.

at any one time, and nine or ten developments are currently (August 2002) active. Foundations are pre-built (no customer order yet).

✓ Completions take 60 working days (non-holiday Mondays through Fridays); weekends are added if needed to make up for bad weather.

✓ Total lead time varies, depending on such things as whether and when the customer can get a mortgage, if pre-qualified for a mortgage, and if the customer likes the lot and if the lot available.

- *Selling process*: This starts at the Bellevue showroom. The buyer's commitment is ten days out from lumber drop. Earnest money is required (5%) but no progress payments.

- *Available designs*: 65 floor plans are available now; to be 85–100 by end of the year. All plans have different foundations, and each has three different elevations (roof style, porch style, etc.). Choices allowed include: bedroom versus bonus room, another bathroom vs. extra closets.

- *Information.* The database (commitments, starts, finishes, etc.) is updated as often as daily.

- *Cancel rate.* The purchase and sale agreement triggers a 30% cancellation rate—high because of buyers' shifting choices, ability to sell their current home, qualifying for loan, etc.

- *Speedy closing*: The closing process is (for example): Monday house done, Tuesday finalize loan, Wednesday close. A non-work day (e.g., holiday, 8–11 per year) shoves the closing date out by one day; sometimes recouped on Saturday.

II. Contractor Partnership

- *Contractor like family*: Close partnership with a small number of contractors is a major success factor (e.g., currently there's only one roofing contractor). Contractors get paid for 15 houses at end of every week.

- *Example*: Woodinville Lumber does all framing and provides all materials. Their key managers and Quadrant managers meet monthly, including getting into pricing matters (Quadrant does ask for price cuts).

- *Autopay*: Suppliers get "autopay" every Tuesday; it's pre-set, no bill. The superintendent signs off that the work was done, and it goes to accounting, which releases the check.
- *Contractor pride*: Each contractor is diligent, not wanting to hold up others.
- *Materials*: Contractors obtains their own materials.

III. Operations

- *Working day*: 8–5 five days a week.
- *Reporting*: Every community reports to HQ, which contacts suppliers.
- *Notifications*: Suppliers are told by email every morning which three homes will start that day.
- *Aberrant situations*: Say that a roofer falls short, doing two roofs rather than three today; that means four roofs tomorrow; the plumber gets mad about this unpredictability, and may ask for new roofer. Feedback of this kind is phoned to HQ for resolution.
- *On-site management*: One to three Quadrant managers are on site, per site.
- *Delays*: A majority of delays are in the first 12 days of framing, with catch-up after the house is framed in.
- *Stringline schedule*: A large stringline schedule board (Gantt-chart-like) occupies most of a wall at HQ. A segment of it is portrayed in Figure 76.1. It shows house BG09 and NX3079 moving along well. But BG07 is delayed, which is shown on the wall chart in red. All the active houses are included in this large stringline display.

IV. Buyer (Customer) Interfacing

- *Visit appointments*: Home buyers are restricted from the home site—for safety reasons. To visit they must make appointments with the superintendent.
- *Day 58*: On this day the customer, the personal service representative (PSR), and the community sales manager (CSR) meet and review any glitches, with Quadrant having two days to fix glitches. Lots of homes have zero glitch items, the average being five or six, with some as high as 15 or 20.

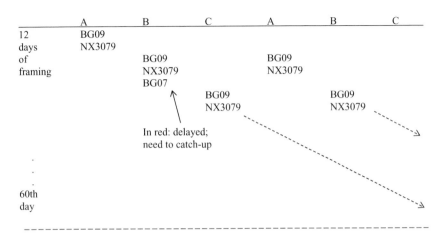

FIGURE 76.1
Example segment of Quadrant's stringline schedule.

- *Hand-off*: Upon house completion, the site superintendent hands off the house to PSR, who conducts six quality checks.
- *Corrective actions*: The PSR tracks repeat correction problems and passes them to the superintendent and into the corporate data base for analysis. A survey is done six months later. The PSR is still active for one year after move-in.

CHAPTER III-77. ULTRAFRAME, CLITHEROE, U.K., 2008

Ultraframe illustrates successful application of lean practices in production of large-sized pre-made home build units. At the end of the caselet are excerpts from my thank-you letter and observations, sent to my tour host, the company's dynamic new general manager.

High-Interest Topics:
- **Standardization through DFMA simplifies the mix of product offerings to customers**
- **A full order held in a special rack slides right into delivery trucks**

Adult-Sized Erector Sets: Impressions From a Brief Tour, March 6, 2008

In connection with one-day Schonberger workshop at Manufacturing Institute, Manchester, U.K.

I. Basic Information

- *Products*: Conservatory roofs, and elaborate, mostly custom-designed greenhouses for private homes, plus maybe 10% for commercial businesses. Ultraframe builds 80–150 roofs per day. Products are sold through distributors, architects, and construction companies.
- *The company*:
  - ✓ In its 25th year of existence, Ultraframe has 130 production people of 400 total employees; operates at 45–65% of capacity.
  - ✓ The company was doing poorly until Mike Price became GM about three years ago; now things are going very well, aided by a strong lean effort. [Note: Ultraframe was recipient, in 2009, of the Shingo Prize, bronze level.]
- *Standard metrics*: Attendance, customer complaints, productivity, safety.
- *Coping with seasonality*: Work force is on "annualized hours," which allows lots of days off when orders are low and heavy OT and extra shifts when high.
- *Equipment and processing*: Dominant processes take place on five CNC machines running three shifts. Assembly and pack operate fewer shifts and hours.
- *On the tour*: Mike Price—formerly employed at the Manufacturing Institute, Manchester (I had met him there in earlier visits); Jon Tudor of the Manufacturing Institute.

II. Details

- *Two main product lines*:
  - ✓ Pre-erect roofs are built by 17 operators with very high skill levels (lots of ex-Rolls Royce guys). Pre-erects require 10–15% "tweaking" such as extra hand-grinding, sawing to fit, and so forth.
  - ✓ Flat-Pack roofs employs 18 operators. 61 roofs were under production when I visited.
    - Flat-Packs were formerly spread out among 20 benches with lots of walking, walking, walking, It's now organized into large cells, which are to deliver to the customer a standard product-configuration package.

- Cells produce 5.5 roofs per week per person (under bench production it was 3.5 roofs). Customer complaints per week fell from 20–25 in the bench mode to two to three in cells.
- Flat-Pack includes a "Classic" product line. And now, consolidated into Flat-Pack, is the product line of an acquisition, Wendland Roofing Systems.
- A glazing-bar cell is currently present in both the Classic and the nearby Wendland cell areas. The two lines are similar enough that soon they will be integrated into the same few cells, for example, just one glazing-bar cell (the plan should do well since there are just a small number of operations per cell).
- U-Zone and Elevation processes were combined, saving 10 people (from 3 + 3 in two cells to five in one cell).
  - ✓ A simple order is five packs, 10 parts per pack; a complex order, 37 packs, 20 parts per pack. Last year there were 200–300 parts.
- *First plant area visited*:
  - ✓ 13 guys, all flexible (very few women in the work force) and mostly in a 25–45 age group.
  - ✓ The process includes cut and drill, index, and barcode. Six-foot length often cut to two- or three-foot lengths.
  - ✓ Tools are on display, shadow boards are everywhere.
- *Job rotation*: This occurs weekly; two operators had the idea for this, with an objective of allowing more difficult jobs to be rotated. The idea was tested in a six-week trial.
- *On display*: Lots of before/after photos, especially in regard to TPM and 5S.
- *Labor union*: JCC is the labor union, which is not a problem.
- *Core-competency analysis*: This analysis ended up with the outsourcing of glazing/glass.

III. My Assessment

- *Good*:
  - ✓ Striving for more Flat-Pack, fewer pre-erects (which require too much tweaking). This change is owed to a big DFMA effort that is reducing variety to a few standard modules.
  - ✓ Annualized hours providing workforce flexibility to cope with seasonal demand.

- ✓ Stillage racks (metal alternatives to pallets) go directly into truck trailers for delivery to customers, and then returning to Ultraframe.
- ✓ Maintenance breakdown sheets. Operators write down what's wrong, rather than just calling maintenance. The sheet says who fixed the problem, sometimes the operator.
- ✓ Hand-push racks of parts go from CNC onward to cells.
- ✓ Supplier day last week was attended by 80 suppliers.
- ✓ Every part is barcoded.
- ✓ A 3rd CNC machine, on order, will allow "perfect" fits.
- *Very good*:
  - ✓ Walls of the long corridor where most of work force often walk have lots of before-after photos and performance data showing improvement-project progress.
  - ✓ Only one visual has to do with labor productivity, and few contain graphs and numbers. [KPIs in numerous other companies include too many on labor productivity, OEE, etc.—which are highly aggregated and therefor pro-forma and not pointing to specifics].
- *Ugly*: The floor, but plans are afoot to renovate.
- *Issue*:
  - ✓ Parts come out of CNC machines and go into pigeon-hole slots in the racks by component type, *not* focused by roof-order type.
  - ✓ I raised the issue of restructuring to cells dedicated to whole roofs, which would require one trolley for each whole roof. Don't know if feasible—but it is an ideal to strive for.
- *Thank-you letter to Mike Price*: Dated March 16, 2008

Dear Mike,

Thank you for your hospitality on March 6 in giving Jon Tudor and me an excellent tour of your fine facilities. As is my usual practice, I took notes and later summarized them, with comments, in a computer file. Though they are rough, and no doubt wrong in some particulars, I'll share with you a few of the main points, some of which were brought up in our post-tour discussion.

. . .

One of my first impressions on entering the production floor was that the floor is ugly. I mentioned this to Jon after we left, and he informed me that plans are already afoot to fix the floor.

A topic you'll recall from our discussion is organization of the cells by component family. Usually preferred is doing so by end-product family. I don't know all that stands in the way of this, but perhaps it would make sense to work toward setting up some of the cells to handle an entire roof. (A complication—maybe excessively so—would, I suppose, be the need to load the trolleys from the CNC machines with pieces for a whole roof rather than for a narrower family of components.)

Your rotation of associates from cell to cell (if I have that correct) does ensure that they see the big picture—a whole roof—which is part of why whole-product cells are usually preferable.

Regarding job rotation, I tend to think that it should be more often than weekly. A few days ago I toured the North American packing/distribution center for Nintendo (products including the hot-selling Wii). There, all associates rotate twice per shift—or, as large signs proclaim, more often if any associate feels soreness or fatigue from doing a single job or a straining job too long.

Among next steps—to further the continuous-improvement effort—I tend to think it should be to upgrade workforce engagement. The last three years have culturally primed the work force through 1. annualized hours, 2. cells, and 3. cross-training. It may have been overload to have involved them highly in the major "vision" projects. Now might be a good time to get them involved, and annualized hours provides a lot of time-flexibility for that—including time for training them more thoroughly in lean, process improvement, and competitiveness (e.g., taking them on buses to visit other top-performing manufacturers). Training and workforce improvement projects could be fit in easily in the slower months when people might like more hours and pay anyway.

But training and workforce project involvement may not produce a whole lot of benefit without a means for associates to continuously record process data. I'm thinking of white boards, flip charts, or other places whereby each associate can record anything and everything that goes wrong during the day. Without that kind of detailed information—which easily organizes itself into Paretos, fishbone, etc.—project progress is usually much delayed.

Mike, that is about all I can make of my crude notes. Thanks again for the great tour. I'll be keen to hear what else you and your team get accomplished in upcoming months and years.

Richard J. Schonberger

CHAPTER III-78. R.W. LYALL, CORONA, CA, 2000

R.W. Lyall is a very small family-owned manufacturer with an impressive story of "world-class excellence." The caselet includes little about the production processes and lacks a section on opportunities for improvement. Rather, the discussion focuses on improvement opportunities already implemented by the time of my visit.

Winding up the caselet is Section III, a summary of a 2004 phone conversation with the chief operating officer—an update on the company 3+ years later.

High-Interest Topics:
- In re-layout projects, everyone in the area moves cut-outs on a large sheet of paper—all signing the paper when layout is finalized
- Each of 8 cells has its own document center with up-to-date specs, etc. (duplicate in engineering)
- Five good examples of operator-developed process improvements

Small Manufacturer Does Things Right: Observations from Plant Visit, Dec. 6, 2000

Followed by Schonberger two-day public seminar, San Diego, December 7–8

I. General Information

- *The company*: R.W. Lyall, a 30-year-old manufacturing company in Corona, CA, is still owned by the founding family. Robert Lyall, Sr., company founder, is retired; son Jeff Lyall and daughter Jennifer Fritchle are owner-executives.
- *Products*: Piping and distribution products for natural gas/LPG industries: meter risers, P.E. fittings and ball valves, transition fittings, steel fabrications, and LYCOFAST pre-package system.
- *Management team*:
  - ✓ Jon Slaughterback—hired, on a chance meeting, as VP and general manager in January, 1997—was from G.M.'s Allison division, Indianapolis. There he had successes in managing lean with high levels of employee empowerment, and had experience in sales, production, quality, etc. He had also worked with W. Edwards Deming for seven years.

✓ *Others on management team*:

Moises "Mo" Vasquez, plant manager

Richard McClure, engrg. manager

Samuel N. Southard, Jr., CFO

Ed Newton, quality manager

Gerry Vargas, lean mfg. coordinator

Jeffrey Sanchez, VP marketing

Paul Mawn, VP sales

Rick Rusco, supply-chain integration coordinator

- *Work force*: Total employment is about 170 people—96% Spanish-speaking, and 85% certified on multiple operations in multiple product lines.
- *Building*: 70,000 sq. ft, roughly square in shape, with two truck docks on one side of the building and two on the opposite side. Most receiving and shipping are on one side, receiving of pipes on the other side.
- *Customers*: About 165 gas-industry customers all over North America. Market share is 80% in Canada, 33% in the United States, and 70% in Mexico. There are three major customers for risers, more for other components.

II. Performance Upgrading

- *Crisis time*: Lyall was barely breaking even in 1996, on-time performance was only 74%, and employee turnover that year was 80%. Jeff Lyall, who had been in sales, put himself into the plant for six months studying the plant's problems. His decision was to hire more people in order to improve on-time delivery.
- *Lean/employee-involvement focus*: Slaughterback, hired a year later, knew that was not the right answer.
  - ✓ He instituted a one-time 42-person layoff, getting all supervisors and leads together to explain and get recommendations as to who would go—and guaranteed no more layoffs resulting from productivity improvements.
  - ✓ He raised the pay for everyone, including four pay increases the first year, and with average pay up 55% since 1997. The existing Christmas bonus system has yielded record bonuses three years in a row. Profit-sharing, in tax-deferred retirement accounts, is for all employees.

- ✓ Further to ease the pain of layoffs and build trust and credibility, Slaughterback guaranteed three kinds of improvement investments: 1. In people, via training. 2. More and better equipment. 3. New products and lower prices to increase sales.
- *Some results*:
  - ✓ Employee turnover is down from 80% to 2%, absenteeism from 13.1% to 1.7%. Overtime has been reduced 55%. Sales per direct labor is up 127%. On-times rose from 75% to 97% since 1996.
  - ✓ Lead time has been reduced from 4.5–6.5 weeks to 2.5 weeks. Inventory (not tracked before 1996) has been cut 53%, freeing up $1 million.
  - ✓ All capital investments have been paid off by cash flow, and debt paid down as well. Banks came and asked if Lyall *was needing* any more funds.
- *Rallying points*: In 1997 a main high wall and empty area just below it (in the plant near the corridor to offices) was designated a rallying place for the new environment of teamwork.
  - ✓ 22 enlarged photos of natural groups of the entire work force are on the wall along with the banner, "We Are One Team."
  - ✓ The day after the photos went up, the plant was shut down all day to explain the significance.
  - ✓ From then on, every six weeks on a Friday, groups of 20 meet below the wall for pizza and to raise issues, ask questions, and contribute ideas for improvement. Minutes are taken, with all ideas assigned to a named person with a report date posted on a bulletin board. Employees implement their own improvements if/when they can.
- *Lean training*: CMTC (California Manufacturing. Technology Center—a manufacturing extension partner or MEP) was brought in for bilingual training in getting lean.
  - ✓ Trainer Eduardo Freiwald ran weekly sessions in a conference room for 12 weeks. A roll-up-sleeves trainer, he pitched in to move machines after class—if no electrical or plumbing was required.
  - ✓ Training of people in the meter cell was first. Within three weeks, that training had paid for itself. The latest training, in 5S, in the transition cell, is slated to extend to the entire plant.
- *Cellular manufacturing*: The plant has eight cells, or departments. (Formerly, machinery had been located by product line, but the

machines were spread out and running in a batch mode, which loses most of the advantage of product focus.)

✓ Each cell has an identical grouping of trend charts and other informational aids.

- Items tracked within the cells and for the whole plant include: Document traceability; Employee turnover and absenteeism; OSHA (Occupational Safety and Health Act)-reportable items.
- Also: Cross-training matrices, including who are qualified trainers. A linearity chart. Training hours. Scrap. Control charts.

✓ Each cell has its own document center, a sturdy metal stand in the shape of a music stand.

- On the stand is a thick loose-leaf notebook with pages full of drawings, photos, and templates that give detailed product specs. See Figure 78.1.
- A duplicate of all the document centers is retained in engineering.
- The document centers solved the problem of old, outdated spec sheets squirreled away in benches around the plant, which led to making wrong parts.

✓ Meter bar (first cell to receive lean training and on to implementation) formerly had 27 people, now has 2 to 11, their being a versatile group who are trained to go to any other cell where they might be needed.

- This cell is not completely self-contained. Finished bars have to leave the cell and cross the plant for blasting on a large sand-blast machine and coating on a long coating line.
- However, quotes have already been received from equipment makers for a small rotational-indexing sand-blast machine and a small in-line coating machine.

- *Changeover times*: Longest changeover in the meter-bar cell had been 35 minutes for a bending machine. For the whole plant average changeover time was 15 minutes.

✓ Today all changeovers are five minutes or less.

✓ There are no tool boxes: tools, dies, and fixtures are on simple tilted metal racks below, above, or next to the machine they go with.

FIGURE 78.1
Loose-leaf notebook with detailed specs—one at every cell at R.W. Lyall.

- *Bench flexibility*: Throughout the plant, metal work benches have been equipped with "wings"—hinged metal bench extensions that fold down for smaller jobs or those not requiring certain steps, and up when needed for larger ones. Nearly all machines and benches are movable—some on wheels—and are moved often to accommodate improvement ideas and adjust for different orders.
- *Purchased materials*:
  - ✓ Nearly all incoming materials go right from receiving to a cell, without storage. The former two days to get parts from receiving to points of use is now just two hours.
  - ✓ Steel pipe is delivered twice weekly. Typically, only about two to three days of steel pipe are on hand.

✓ A next-year plan is to certify the top three suppliers, accounting for 80% of purchases by value.

✓ Cells have the authority to buy items costing up to $2,500 (formerly only $500) without CFO approval.

✓ Corrugated boxes for incoming purchased metal and plastic parts generally are recycled back to the supplier. Corrugated usage was cut 40%.

- *Idea generation*: Following are some of the ideas generated by operators:

  ✓ *Grit on floor*: Reusable grit, from sand blasting, was, at next processes, falling off parts onto the floor.

  - An operator suggested working on those parts on top of a bench-top grid made of expanded metal mounted on a large recovery bin with inward-slanting sides. Grit falls through and slides to a collection pan at the bottom.

  - The whole thing looks something like a barbecue—but big enough to cook a whole calf.

  ✓ *Hot parts*: Maria Ortega, leak-test operator, said parts coming out of a welder were hot to handle. Her suggestion:

  - Convert the solid metal bench top to a similar expanded-metal grid and aim a fan up through the grid to air-cool the parts.

  - A cell associate fetched petty cash from the office, went to Home Depot, bought the fan, and implemented the idea.

  ✓ *Rubber plugs*: People had been manually covering openings for T's, elbows, unions, and nipples with aluminum foil before hanging them for their trip through the coating line. This kept interior threads dry as the hangers moved to receive sprayed-on epoxy as a protective coating. New idea: standard, easily applied rubber plugs go on the top hole, and the bottom hole nests by gravity into cups permanently affixed to the hangers.

  ✓ *Coating bottleneck*: The coating line had been a bottleneck, often forced into overtime to keep up.

  - Operator Tony Salazar's simple idea, which engineering tested out as viable: Decrease distance between hangers from the former 12 inches to 6 inches.

  - That doubled line capacity, so the bottleneck was eliminated, along with the overtime.

✓ *Wrench heads*: Riveted to metal bench tops in a few cells are in-house-made wrench heads. With that, no more need to find and use a hand wrench to twist off a threaded part; instead, just lower the part into the fixed wrench head and twist half or three-quarters of a turn, and the part is off, or freed for a couple more twists by hand.

- *Improvement projects*: All these improvements are freeing up operators—who are joining Gerry's lean-manufacturing team in order to spend more time on improvement projects.
- *Kanban*: The plant employs many kinds of queue-limiting kanbans.
   ✓ For example, kanban squares, space denial (e.g., bench wings that hold no more than two pieces), and magnetic kanban plates easily slapped onto the side of a metal parts box, rack, or shelf.
   ✓ In the manifold cell, a bench-extending wing at the welder is small enough to hold only a kanban quantity; when it is full, welding stops and operators 1. clean, 2. work on a project, or 3. go help someone.
- *Frequent re-layouts*:
   ✓ Layout improvements start with an engineer preparing a preliminary layout by sticking paper cutouts on a large (about five ft by three ft) piece of light cardboard; then, operators, leads, and supervisors discuss and move the cutouts around.
   ✓ When there is agreement, everyone *signs on the cardboard*, and it is mounted in the work center while equipment gets moved into the improved layout.
- *No rework in valves cells*: Since in valves, production is in one-piece-lots, if a test reveals a problem, production stops, and the problem is fixed on the spot.
- *TPM*: Not started yet.
   ✓ But operators do their own cleaning and setups, and get involved in machine maintenance.
   ✓ If a machine is down, an operator can go directly to maintenance to get a repair part; formerly, the operator had to go through channels (e.g., to a lead, who went to a supervisor, who went to the maintenance supervisor, who went to a mechanic.).
- *Trend charts*: In the office area, trend charts track on-times and inventory in different ways, including three control charts with upper and lower limits for three different customer inventories.

- *Inventory*:
    - ✓ Lyall is managing five inventory items by fax for one customer, Supply Replenishment Services.
        - When the customer's reorder point is reached, the customer sends a fax to Lyall, and Lyall forwards a reorder to the customer.
        - A new Symix information system to be installed at Lyall will replace faxes as the communication method.
        - Another plan is for implementing customer relationship management (CRM) and an increasing emphasis on e-business.
    - ✓ Total inventory turns at Lyall are at 17, up from 4.7 four years ago.
- *Competitiveness*: Currently, Lyall has the best on-time delivery in the industry. It has a reputation for best design but needs to get cost down. To do so, emphasis will change from "selling the Lyall design" to a preference for standard designs–which would mean giving attention to design for manufacture and assembly (DFMA).
- *Fun work*: Comment by Gerry Vargas at end of Schonberger visit: "It's exciting. I like to come to work every day. My wife thinks I'm nuts."

III. Update, Three Years Later

- *Phone call*: I phoned Jon Slaughterback, Lyall's COO, in February, 2000, left a message, and he called back. The following, from my notes on the conversion, are some of what we talked about.
- *Evolving strategy*: He says things evolve slowly, but that they are aggressively going after one of 12 companies making complementary products—commissioning a search of the same SIC codes to come up with candidates for acquisition. They are currently testing the waters by starting an alliance with one (or more) of them.
- *Lyall vs. competitors*:
    - ✓ Lyall is doing great! Most competitors are "on the ropes," losing money for seven years or more. Lyall has been in contact with parent companies, but would obviously prefer to drive them out of business than to acquire them.

- ✓ A competitor shut down its Mexico plant, and "every customer in Mexico" has called to ask for Lyall's help filling orders. So far, Lyall has six new customers, and Jeff Lyall is flying to Mexico to ink a contract with a 7th one this week. Lyall expects to get all of the Mexico market.
- *Loss of key person*: "Mo" Vasquez has been hired away by a company that was at Lyall on a benchmarking visit. Mo has since turned around that company and has gone on to make his mark at still another company. Gerry Vargas has been moved into sales to broaden his experience in hopes he will remain at Lyall.
- *Retaining key people*:
  - ✓ A common topic among Slaughterback and the Lyalls centers on how to challenge top employees like Mo, so they'll not be tempted by offers from other companies to leave.
  - ✓ Although the Lyalls have been happy being small, they (and Slaughterback) are seeing how growth can provide good opportunities for valued people like Mo and Gerry to move into more responsible and more lucrative positions.
  - ✓ Growth, through buyouts of one or more of their money-losing competitors, is seen as offering those kinds of opportunities to best people.
  - ✓ Aside from growth within their own specialties, there was also talk of making one or more acquisitions of small manufacturers in other sectors—although the Lyalls do not relish taking on debt from banks to make that happen.
- *Success formula*: Success is based on "price points," meaning Lyall beats the others on pricing and gains their market share. They've had a record year in profits and revenue, and have grown as much in the past year as in the last three years.
- *Resources*: Lyall has been active in consolidating its equipment, which has freed up 40% more space, and productivity is up 32%. Inventory turns are 19.1—about same as the prior year but failed to improve only because of stocking up parts for a new product line. Plant employment is down by attrition from 169 to 162, and the plant still runs just one shift, so plenty of capacity to take on lots of new market share.

CHAPTER III-79. FENDER MUSICAL INSTRUMENTS, CORONA, CA, 2001

The Fender caselet presents a multifaceted plan, centered on operator involvement, for conversion of its long-lead-time operations to a showcase of simplicity and quick response. The plan was positively received by my hosts at Fender, with dates set. However, circumstances did not allow the plan to proceed.

Details on producing fine guitars –in Sidebar 1– may be of interest to guitar aficionados. Matters bearing on process improvement arise in Section IV at the caselet's end.

High-Interest Topics:
- **Operators estimating minimal inventories they could get by with—ushering in a "grand plan" of linking up large numbers of guitar-making steps**
- **Testing and tuning, taking place at 20 stations, is staffed with musicians**
- **Guitar making includes considerable drying time—and also steps in which correct moisture is maintained—with sprinklers going on if not**

Reluctance to Change: Assessment Based on Late P.M. Plant Visit, April 25, 2001, Plus Follow-On Deliberations

The plant tour followed Day one of a two-day Schonberger seminar for Fender and three other companies in Ontario, CA, organized by the Transformational Leadership Council

I. General Information

- *The company.* Fender, headquartered in Corona, CA, was founded by Leo Fender in 1930. In its main product line, guitars, Fender ranks 4th in market share (Yamaha is no. 1), but Fender, with 2,500 dealers, is the premier brand. Fender also makes Guild acoustic guitars in Rhode Island and licenses other companies' violins and other stringed instruments.
- *Basic data*: 700 employees, 150 on 2nd shift, occupy a 177,000-sq. ft. new (since 1998) building (formerly there were 10 buildings 2.5 miles away).
  - ✓ They produce 400 guitars, 174 amplifiers, and 40 custom guitars daily.

✓ Guitars come in 55 models, four or five colors (including two neck colors, maple and rosewood), with 300 components and 200 operations.

- *Main contacts/tour hosts*: Al Guzman, VP, mfg. operations; Frank Ku, industrial enrgr. Also (attendees at the two-day seminar), Arlene Nicholas, materials manager; Doug Mills sr. VP, U.S. operations; Jeff Schuch, plant engineer.

II. Manufacturing Guitars

- *Basic information*:
    ✓ Manufacturing lead time is 21 days, including 11 days drying time for finish and 4.5 hours assembly time. Production builds to forecast and sends finished guitars to a huge warehouse not far away.

SIDEBAR 1   SUMMARY OF FENDER PROCESS FLOW AND OPERATIONS

Flow details (21 days):

Spread fabrication, by a supplier, includes, typically, about 10 days for "dry/cure" stabilization

1 day for milling body and and neck

3 days for undercoat/seal bodies (an outside process)

1 day intermediate sand and paint

Up to 3 days dry time for urethane; or up to 10 days for lacquer

1 day for buff and polish

1 day for final assembly and packout

Operations breakdown:

Mill—about 12 body operations (ops)

Neck—about 32 ops

Undercoat—three coats

Body, intermediate sand

Paint body (color and clear)

Paint neck—two to three coats

Buff and polish body (sand and buff)

Buff and polish neck (frets and buff)

Subassembly and metal shop

Final assembly and pack

Total guitar—over 200 ops

✓ A sister Fender operation in Ensenada, Mexico, began in 1985–1986 coiling strings and now is up to 1,100 employees making 500 guitars daily (Mexico units sell for $249–$900) and 700 amplifiers daily.

✓ Custom guitars sell for $1,800 to $75,000.

✓ The Fender team at the seminar expressed frustration at higher management's insistence on large inventories (or lot sizes), and that the team is not able to convince them of manufacturing's flexibility.

- *Process flow and operations breakdowns*: See Sidebar 1.
- *Mill*: In the brightly lit mill, plus-or-minus 2% humidity and temperature are maintained; overhead sprinklers go on by automatic sensing when humidity drops.

    ✓ Material handling is done on many kinds of trolleys, dollies, Christmas trees. One holding stacks of 25 or so bodies or necks is about 3.5 feet high, two wide, and three or four long.

    ✓ In the rough mill, in an overly elongated area, most operations occupy two-thirds or more of the space leading into the finish sanding room at the far end; see Figure 79.1 (does not include the rest of building).

    ✓ Wood for bodies and necks comes in as glued rectangular blocks, just in time from a wood supplier located in a next-door building.

    ✓ Bodies are made from ash and alder from the Northwest. A body requires 25–45 minutes of labor in many separate operations; an early operation is on an 8-spindle CNC router/drill. See photo of bodies already machined in the router, Figure 79.2.

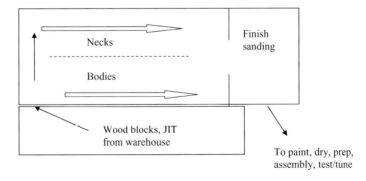

FIGURE 79.1
Rough mill.

FIGURE 79.2
Guitar bodies awaiting many machining operations at Fender Musical Instruments.

✓ Necks, made from eastern hardrock maple, require 45 minutes to 1.5 hour labor—in 45 operations:
  ■ They include planing, double-end tenoner, CNC rough-cut of the perimeter to make the neck (with a hole drilled—from the rear side of the neck—for a metal tension arm that fights the warping tendency of strings).
  ■ Many more operations follow (e.g., applying dots—white for rosewood, black for maple—and pressing them down at a later station/operation).
  ■ A traveler document accompanies all processes.

FIGURE 79.3
Machined guitar bodies awaiting many painting and finishing operations at Fender Musical Instruments.

- *Paint/finish*:
  - ✓ A $5M system (outside the building) with very strong suction and HVAC and pollution control equipment containing UV lamps sucks up and destroys fumes; California's environmental agency gives high approval.
  - ✓ It takes two airlocks to get to paint—with deionized air blowing dust off bodies and necks. See bodies ready and waiting for paint in the photo (Figure 79.3).
  - ✓ Paint is next, after which bodies go by wheeled racks into a large room for 24 hours with fresh air for paint to "gas off"; then to an oven for 48 hours' drying.
  - ✓ Necks are on Christmas-tree carts; bodies go high into the ceiling area by overhead conveyor, holding up to 5,600 bodies, for five to 10 days of ambient cure—followed by buff and polish, sand, polish.
- *Assembly*: Three sequential build areas are fed by material-handling carts holding two to four dozen neck or body pieces:
  - ✓ Prep is done at four or five stations with a 10-minute station cycle, six units per hour at each station.
  - ✓ Final assembly affixes bridge, saddles, picker, output, strings—about 16 stations.
  - ✓ Test and tune is done at about 20 stations staffed with musicians.

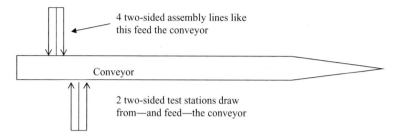

FIGURE 79.4
Amp assembly test area.

- *Machine shop*: Does stampings, cuts fret wire.
- *Receiving*: Five docks.
- *Percent value added*: VA ÷ FT [conservative assumption: 1 shift/ 8 production hours/day]
    ✓ Mill & neck: 1.23 ÷ 8 = 15%
    ✓ Undercoat (outside process): 0.15 ÷ 24 = 0.6%
    ✓ Intermediate sand and paint: 1.0 ÷ 8 = 12%
    ✓ Buff and polish: 1.41 ÷ 8 = 18%
    ✓ Final assembly and packout: 2.33 ÷ 8 = 29%

III. Manufacturing Amplifiers

- *Basic information*: Frank Ku, guide: 85 people build amps (which sell for $300–$3,000) with 1.5 hours labor and 75–100 operations.
    ✓ They do their own printed circuit boards (sequencer, auto insertion, wave solder).
    ✓ Amp assembly and test is shown roughly in Figure 79.4.
    ✓ Cabinet assembly involves flow to a pass-through window into a sound booth; flow finally is single file with relatively few units in a non-value-add (NVA) state.

IV. Opportunities for Improvement

- *Probing questions*:
    ✓ In guitars . . .
        ▪ Given the present independent mill, prep, assembly, test and tune operations, what would happen if all container sizes along the process flow were cut in half? Would anyone run out of work?

- Why are all mill operations done at separate stations? Why not link some into cells with kanban limits of only two to four necks or bodies between stations?
- Same question for all prep, assembly, and test/tune operations. Why not link some into cells with the same kanban limits between stations? Better yet, how about establishing 1-to-1 flow lines and teams throughout prep, assembly, and test-tune?

✓ In amps: How about going to 1-to-1 flows?

- *Grand plan*: Answers to those questions are addressed in a (proposed) grand plan referred to as "The Third Way."

✓ This plan aims at greatly reducing flow times and all inventories, thus quickly catching and correcting sources of defects, simplifying scheduling, reducing planning and control overheads, and so forth.

✓ The novel key to launch the plan is to engage the production employees in using their experience in designing the quick-flow system, as follows:

- Each employee counts their on-hand pieces and estimates the minimum they could get by with.
- Then production halts for the days it takes to drain the excess inventory—during which the employees train and cross-train; move stations into compact cells; and down-size (or eliminate) material-handling carriers and trolleys.
- A cross-functional team (HR, engineering, key operators) meets to redesign the performance-management (and pay) system to spur further and continuing process improvements.

✓ Al says one of the bosses is interested in going for a Baldrige award; I suggested the California State Quality Award first. Either or both are possibilities, but only if the production process is drastically simplified via cells and shrinkage of excess inventories and throughput times between processes.

- *Outcome*: The grand plan was enthusiastically received by Guzman and his team. Forms for employees to fill out with their inventory data were developed, and November 28, 2001, had been tentatively set for kickoff. But the plan never came off, the one (and only) explanation—from Guzman—being that colleagues Doug Mills and Arlene Nichols had left the company.

CHAPTER III-80. FORD STAMPING AND ASSEMBLY, HERMOSILLO, MÉXICO, 2011

In the massive MIT-organized global study of car assembly plants that was summarized in the 1990 book *The Machine That Changed the World,* this Ford plant in Hermosillo was cited as among the world's most impressive car makers. My own observations—though overly brief—tend to support that view. (This caselet applies to my second visit, in 2011, to this plant; in the first, ten years earlier, I took too few notes to enable comparisons.)

High-Interest Topics:
- **Plant has just one job description and zero fork-lift trucks**
- **All production associates participate in daily facility maintenance**
- **Kitting: viewed negatively**
- **Chunk system: viewed positively**

Do All Car Assembly Plants Look Alike? Not Quite.

Observations based on one-hour plant visit plus conference-room discussions

At Ford Hermosillo Planta de Estampedo y Ensamble (HSAP), March 14, 2011

In connection with Schonberger's keynote presentation at the Vortex 2011 Conference, Polytecnic Institute, Hermosillo, March 15, 2011

I. General

- *Note*: My notes are rough and incomplete, so some information in this caselet may be, in places, factually incorrect.
- *Products*: Currently, producing the Ford Fusion and the Lincoln MKZ series at a production rate of about 54 cars per hour.
- *Production*:
  - ✓ The plant has three assembly-trim lines with 30 stations each; and one body weld line.
  - ✓ Vehicles in three platforms and 12 body types are assembled on mixed-model lines. Production stops for lunch. Shifts are Monday 6:00 a.m. to Saturday 9:00 p.m.

✓ The current assembly line is conveyor-driven—to be replaced in the next few weeks by "skillets" (some positions have already been cleared for insertion of skillets).

✓ The pre-delivery area has spaces for 120 cars undergoing fixes, checks, and so on; the area is usually close to being filled with cars.

✓ Line-stops average 24 minutes per day, 94% scheduled (or initiated by operators).

✓ Stamping: 32 kinds of parts are made from 1.5 days' of steel coil with an average of 11-minute die changes on the large presses.

- *Demographics*: 2,666 hourlies (average age, 38), 245 salaried; 83% males overall.
- *Suppliers*: Of 346 suppliers, 54% are Mexican, 41% U.S.
- *Inventories*: The plant holds 1.6 days' supply, and 3.5 days' supply are in transit. Areas at the north and south ends of the plant hold parts for kitting to the scheduled production sequence.
- *Hosts*: Luis Chacon, plant manager; Reyna Mendoza, master black belt and FPS (Ford production system) coordinator.

II. Plant Tour – Observations

- *Overall strengths*:
  ✓ The following show up as unique strengths and advantages.
    - HSAP employs fundamentals of lean/TQ/TPM that many companies/plants strive for but few achieve.
    - HSAP appears to be advanced in these fundamentals, which would place it among the world's best auto plants (though the plant is much too big and the tour far too short for a reliable assessment).
  ✓ *Caveat*: I do not have any special depth of knowledge of the automotive industry, or any other single industry. Rather, my impressions are based on comparative studies of many industries.
- *Fork-lift trucks*. Gone (except in receiving and shipping). Tractor-trailers deliver the parts.
- *Job descriptions*: Just one—for all hourlies; not even separate job descriptions for skilled maintenance. Some production associates eventually move into maintenance.
- *Suppliers*: Five years ago key first-tier suppliers moved into a new, nearby HSAP supplier campus, which enables tight communications and logistics links.

- *TPM*:
  - ✓ All production associates participate in facility maintenance—30 minutes per shift, 1.5 hours per week!
    - ■ Operator involvement in maintenance is the primary feature of total productive maintenance. But most companies interpret TPM differently and wrongly—their maintenance departments continuing dominant with minimal workforce involvement.
    - ■ About 12,000 maintenance orders are processed per month, 65% done without stopping the lines.
  - ✓ Body weld has 321 robots, 80% of which can be bypassed for maintenance—with other robots taking over to keep the line running.
- *Special assembly features*: Car doors, 12-per-rack, arrive from a three-position door dressing line located lineside on rails. The fixed-rail locations allow moving successive racks of doors to the same lineside position every time, so door assemblers always find the door in the same assembly position.

III. Opportunities for Improvement

- *Kitting*:
  - ✓ Background: Before JIT/lean, kitting was commonplace in industry. But in the 1980s, under JIT concepts, kitting became seen as one more waste to eliminate or reduce.
    - ■ The ideal was to send parts directly from the supplier's truck, in the supplier's container, to the production cell or line—preferably color-coded, packed, or positioned so assemblers will always select the right part.
    - ■ When it is impractical to eliminate kitting, it usually is because too many product models are being produced in a single cell or line. Standardizing parts is a solution. Adding more cells or lines, each narrowly focused, is another.
  - ✓ In 2001 (my earlier visit to Ford-HSAP), incoming parts were sent directly to assembly/trim for placement in lineside flow racks, pallets, etc.
    - ■ No longer. Now kits of parts, matched to varying mixes of model configurations, go to the line from an offline kitting function.

- Although it adds extra handling, storage, and lead time, kitting has emerged at HSAP and other carmakers' plants.
- One maker did this because a growing number of configurations on a single line became confusing to assemblers, introducing search delays and errors when a wrong part is selected. Also, there can be insufficient space lineside for enlarged numbers of unkitted parts—and car assembly lines are already notoriously long.

✓ *Suggestion.* Classify assembly/trim parts in two ways: (a) kitted—for high-mix or hard-to-identify parts; and (b) sent directly to the line—for parts used in nearly every car, these parts positioned in line-side flow racks for quick and easy identification and selection.

- *Stamping capacity*:
  ✓ My impression (but lacking thorough notes):
  - Stamping of body parts is disconnected (no kanban linkages) from body weld—with too much inventory in between (I have seen this in all car assembly plants that I have visited).
  - Main reasons: (a) Setup times on presses, though improved, are still not fast enough for stamping in very small lot sizes. (b) There are not nearly enough presses for JIT stamping of the many parts needed constantly in body weld.

  ✓ *Suggestion*:
  - Have one or two contract sheet-metal manufacturers move to the supplier campus. Put them on a kanban system to stamp parts just-in-time for body weld on a large number of body parts.
  - Do the same (kanban linked to body weld) with HSAP's in-house stamping shop.
  - The aim is to be among the first car makers with most of its stamped parts kanban-synchronized with body weld, and onward (with minimal kanban quantities) to final assembly/trim in a complete pull system.

  ✓ Added stamping presses raise fixed costs. But tight synchronization has many hard-to-monetize advantages.
  - One is that with tight synchronization any system weaknesses in the system show up quickly and demand fast investigation and correction.

- As it is now, problems are buried in large inventories and lead times of stamped parts awaiting body weld, and many such problems never get identified and corrected.

✓ Initially, there will be frequent production stoppages—beneficial over time as root causes of stoppages are resolved. The best way to minimize the bad effects is to adopt the "chunk" system in final assembly and trim. (The chunk system is sensible anyway, but more so when assembly/trim is synchronized with body weld and stamping.)

- *Process data, visual management, employee engagement*: The work force is flexible and involved in daily maintenance, but its contributions to process improvement are mostly absent.

  ✓ Most important in gaining their contributions are: (a) Operators record process data as part of their job. (b) Time is made available to review data for improvement ideas. (c) Small areas near workplaces are available for idea-generation sessions. (d) A few displays prominently show improvement trends. Specifics follow:

  ✓ Close to every employee should be a flip chart, white board, or other place to record things that go wrong—which every job holder can inspect and react to on every shift.

    - Recording them yields ideal data for process improvement—whether in a project mode (e.g., kaizen projects) or by continual streams of improvement ideas from work teams.

    - Failure to record ensures process improvements will be small in number and in overall value.

    - Best way to get started is to make this *a job requirement*, and also calling it recording of *frustrations* (frustraciónes)–rather than negative words such as "mistakes," "errors," or even "problems." Anything frustrating to a production associate is likely to be a problem for the plant and the company.

  ✓ *Time*. HSAP already provides time every shift for maintenance; a few minutes may be added to that, at least on two or three days per week, so production teams and supervisors can analyze data and develop improvements.

    - Best way is by the lean method of setting a fixed production target per shift (e.g., 450 cars); when achieved, stop production for the rest of the shift and use the extra time for maintenance, training, and process-improvement deliberations.

- This requires setting the production target so it is likely to be achieved a bit early nearly every day.

✓ *Space.* Cutting back on kitting will remove a lot of inventory from the assembly/trim line, freeing space for small team areas, each with table, chairs, white board—marked off perhaps by potted plants on the area perimeter. (BMW plant in South Carolina has these areas.)

✓ *Displays.* These should mainly be trend charts showing improvements in quality (*all* employees care about and can directly affect quality), and cross-training tables showing skill attainments for all members.

  - In stamping (maybe other areas), setup/changeover times should be displayed on trend graphs—such display acting to praise the production team for each plotted improvement, scold when time passes with no improvement.

  - Best practice is to time and chart *every* setup, and plot summary average times per week, per month, etc. Timing every setup is important, because setups have high competitive impacts; also, plotting every setup reveals setup-time *variation.*

  - Setup-time variation requires buffer stock and creates unpredictability forward to next processes. Achieving consistent setup times is a key to synchronizing stamping with body weld

- *Chunk system—example*: Say that a final assembly/trim line has 20 stations, and now all 20 are staffed and busy, so that any problem is likely to stop production throughout.

  ✓ To localize such stoppages, divide the line into, for example, two "chunks" each of ten stations—with five stations between. The five stations contain five cars that have already passed through Chunk 1. Then, if a line-stop problem occurs at a station in Chunk 1, it stops assembly in Chunk 1, but Chunk 2 continues until the five cars are "used up."

  ✓ The five in-between cars are buffer stock, which lean tries to eliminate in the quest for "one-piece-flow." But when there is evidence of a need for buffer stock, it must be allowed.

- At HSAP (and I think all car assembly plants) evidence of that need is the large number of cars in the end-of-line "finish-for-delivery" area, which has room for about 120 cars.
- Some percentage is there because sometimes operators and equipment cannot finish every job perfectly.
- Solution 1 is to slow the line, which is too costly.
- Solution 2 is to catch the problem at end-of-line finishing, which is bad: Catching quality problems late always carries the risk that a whole series of cars will end up with the same defect; also that, by then, evidences of root causes are hard to find, contaminated, or lost.
- Solution 3 is the chunk system.

✓ Why the chuck system is often best:

- All assemblers have access to a line-stop button. However, in practice, they do not (are afraid to) stop the line except for very serious reasons, because everyone knows of the high costs of stopping the entire line.
- Also, they don't want to be blamed, and they know that problems can be fixed at end of the line. So total daily minutes of operator line-stop—in almost all auto assembly lines—is low.
- Assemblers *will* stop the line if they know it applies only to their own chunk.

✓ I don't know if the chunk should be ten cars or eight or six; nor how many chunks there should be; (the example of two chunks of ten cars is just for illustration). Also, if an existing line has, say, 30 stations, then perhaps line should divide into three or four chunks with idle cars between.

IV. Summary

- *Excellence in cars*: Ford Hermosillo may still (as it was designated in the MIT-organized study) rank among the best in its industry.
- *Overall excellence*: If the opportunities for improvement are also implemented, HSAP could become a showplace of excellence overall, not just in automotive.

CHAPTER III-81. VOLKSWAGEN, PUEBLA, MÉXICO, 2001

This short caselet describes aspects of VW's car assembly plant in Puebla, México. The main purpose of my visit there was to make a presentation to VW suppliers on "Supplier Day"—the tour of the plant, and related conferencing with VW staff, being secondary.	*High-Interest Topics:* • **Typical (in the industry) lack of capacity in metal stamping** • **Excellent workforce training and management**

Well-Regarded Car Plant Hemmed In by Equipment Issues:

Observations Based on 1-Hour Plant Visit, June 4, 2001

Plus conferencing with VW-México managers, June
4 and presentation at Supplier Day, June 5

I. General Information

- *Volkswagen de México*: VW began manufacturing in Puebla in 1967 (VW sales in México began in 1954).
- *Output.* The plant produces 1,500 cars/day, 80% exported (double the volume of Ford Hermosillo).
  - ✓ Models are Cabriolet (200/day or 13%); Jetta (800/day or 53%); Old Beetle (200/day or 13%); New Beetle (470 cars/day or 21%).
  - ✓ The five millionth car was produced last month.
- *Contacts*: Armando Gonzalez Rojas and Felipe Gaspariano. Others are Daniel Estrada, Antonio Martínez, Roberto Salares, Erick Noe Sánchez, Mayela Cuautle, Jose Marín, Hector Trujillo.
- *Employment*: 591 people, including 361 direct labor (70 in personnel); some specifics:
  - ✓ Formerly there were 750 job classifications, now only one—a VW technician ("technico").
  - ✓ The labor union has had one strike (for two months)—in 1992.
  - ✓ One year of OJT (on-the-job training) is received by technicos para producción (production technicians): Three months on concepts, 9 months on applications.
  - ✓ An excellent, large-scale apprentice program involves 350 maintenance apprentices, 20% classroom theory, and 80%

practice, with an early emphasis on discipline. Several dozen students were seen being trained at many work benches and equipment. A three-year program qualifies them for journeyman maintenance.

- *Plant facilities*: Puebla has two plants, one for engines (motores), which I did not tour; the other for cars (includes stamping, weld, paint, assembly).
- *Puebla's world-class manufacturing focus*: It includes 5S, visual workplace, total productive maintenance (TPM), fail-safing (mistake proofing), SMED (single-minute exchange of die)/quick changeovers, flow manufacturing, and kaizen improvement teams.

II. Plant Tour

- *Tour—in an open-top Cabriolet*: Led by Armando Gonzalez Rojas and Felipe Gaspariano, the tour also included Edwardo Garcia Marín, consellor for engrg. and planning.
  - ✓ Stamping (estampado); Gabriel Luna, guide:
    - A 600-ton eight-station tandem press line stamps out five part numbers; a 1000-ton line for five more part numbers; and other smaller stamping presses make many other parts.
    - Presses run 10–12 hours for a single part between changeovers, which (with die sets on rails) typically take 30 minutes.
    - Stamped parts are made in such large batches (unsynchronized with welding into subassemblies, or direct to final assembly) that there's no room for WIP on the main floor. Instead, stamped parts go on wheeled carriers to a basement storeroom by elevator, for later picking (we did not see the WIP in the basement but clearly it is a lot).
    - The press lines make 12 parts for the new Beetle, 20 parts for the Jetta, 26 parts for the old Beetle.
  - ✓ Body weld (robotics). 500 robots. Fernando Díaz, guide.
  - ✓ Paint. Toerro Díaz: Five paint lines in three paint buildings, operating three shifts, five days (did not see/visit).
  - ✓ Assembly line. Luis Ponóta, consellor: A car is finished every five minutes, with an eight-hour flow time. (Doors have their own line.)

- There are 175 assemblers: young people (mostly around 20 years old), including some women.
- Kanban squares are in use; floors are very clean. Takt times are posted.
- There are 27 JIT suppliers. Elfina Sánches, consellor, purchasing and logistics.

- *TPM emphasis*: A stair-step TPM attainment model displays three categories of TPM, as follows:

  3 Keeping "root" (highest level)

  2 Cleanliness (next level)

  1 Inspection (lowest level)

- *Cross-training & job rotation*: Cross-training matrices are posted on walls. Jesus Montrero, technical training:
  - ✓ Job rotation is only once monthly for the multi-skilled.
  - ✓ Every nine months supervisors measure/evaluate each mechanic on pay-for-skill attainments (indicadores de ascenso)—to see if pay will be raised.
  - ✓ Eight concepts/jobs to learn to receive more pay are: 1. Job 2. Cleanliness 3. Security 4. Absenteeism 5.? 6.? 7. Teach/train 8. One improvement idea per month.

- *Quality*: Formally evaluated for each nine cars. An andon at the end displays status. Final audit: I counted 175 cars.

III. Opportunities for Improvement

- *Stamping capacity*: As with nearly all automotive assemblers, the plant lacks sufficient stamping capacity—a testament being the large amount of stampings (WIP) in the basement:
  - ✓ The impractical (impossible) ideal is stamping in one-piece lots with direct kanban links to welding and on to final assembly. To do so would require zero changeover times on the two existing large press lines, plus the small presses. Or, having a dedicated press/press line for each of the 58 stamped parts.
  - ✓ Quick setup already gets high attention (though not nearly enough).
  - ✓ More presses *does not* get attention (this is a chronic deficiency throughout the car-making sector) but should. Many more presses will bring stamping into closer synchronization with weld and assembly, slashing WIP and throughput times, and enabling quick finding and eliminating causes of quality problems.

- ■ In acquiring more stamping presses, a few might be dedicated to just one part with zero setup time, others semi-dedicated, i.e., requiring minimal setup times within a narrow family of specs.
- ■ VW and other car companies fail to do this largely for reasons of approving capital equipment via rate-of-return, payback, and percent utilization criteria, ignoring the not-easily-monetized offsetting benefits of one-piece flow, kanban pull, synchronization, and quality assurance.
- • *Job rotation.* This should be at least daily (not once monthly as at present) for reasons of ergonomics, fairness, and insights that come with whole process familiarity.
- • *Improvement ideas.* VW already has, as a criterion for more pay, one improvement per month. As stated, frequent job rotation provides a kind of wisdom that enables high rates of the improvement ideas and raises the quality of the improvement ideas.

CHAPTER III-82. GRACO, INC., MINNEAPOLIS, 2003

This caselet includes numerous specifics. That is because, through several interactions with Graco (including my two-day seminar there in 1997), I found the company to be, at the date of the caselet, dense with impressive manufacturing and business-management practices.	**High-Interest Topics:** • **Single-minded push—in many aspects of the business—for quick customer response** • **Slashing finished-goods inventories—and branch warehouses—along value chain** • **Focused production and support** • **Trading inventory for capital investment**

Driving Flow Manufacturing Forward Through Distribution Chain:

Summarized findings (March, 2003) from written questions and answers and phone interview with Pat McHale, VP of mfg., distribution, and customer service, and Dwight Peterson, cost acctg. mgr.

I. General

- *The company*: Graco is a modest-sized, publicly traded company producing equipment systems for application of paint, sealants, adhesives, and lubricants (*not* the Graco that supplies baby products).
- *High-margin business*: It is mostly a niche business, a type that yields high margins and, for companies that are very good at it, high profits and fire-wall insulation from serious competition.
  - ✓ In the past, such businesses tended to rely on what today is unsustainable: high inventories at multiple distribution points, jerky labor practices (e.g., costly overtime), and miserly capital investment.
  - ✓ Graco rejects such practices in favor of a set better suited to the realities of: (1) global hyper-competition and (2) potent management concepts that favor flexibly quick response (e.g., same-day shipment) & outstanding quality—with little reliance on stockrooms and warehouses.
- *Long, accelerating improvement rate*: Testifying to Graco's success with its alternate approach, its inventory turnover has risen at an average annual rate of 2.6% for 32 years; moreover, its *rate* of improvement has accelerated from under 1% per year in the early years to 5.8% since 1988.

II. Specifics

- *Extensive application of "best practices"*: In achieving flexibly quick response with year-upon-year inventory reductions, Graco has applied JIT/TPS/WCM (world-class manufacturing) concepts to a degree, and over a time span (generally continuing for more than ten years), matched by few other manufacturers—in four areas. They follow, as four bulleted points, plus adding a fifth wider-ranging area.
- *Focus*: Graco's manufacturing is two-way focused:
  - ✓ Numerous product-family focused cells within five focused factories (they call them *cells*), three of which are also customer-family focused (best way!); plus two other product-focused plants (a separate Twin-Cities area Tips plant for spray tips, and a Sioux Falls, SD, plant for spray guns).
  - ✓ The cell teams include production support people (planner/buyer, engineer, manager, quality technician, maintenance), so that each functions something like a small business unit.

- *Eliminating branch warehouses*: Historically Graco had a central stand-alone finished goods distribution facility in Minneapolis from which it supplied branch warehouses scattered across the United States and Western Europe, and also finished-goods warehouses in Japan and Korea. The branch warehouses were there primarily to provide fast delivery of Graco products to its distributors and end customers. In 1998 the last two remaining North America branches were closed.
  - ✓ Today Graco distributes to all North American customers directly from two finished-goods warehouses physically co-located with its two major manufacturing operations. These warehouses also provide inventory to Graco's single European distribution center located in Belgium, as well as to its DCs in Japan, Korea, and a newly opened DC in China.
  - ✓ The beneficial effects are threefold: (1) Graco's inventories have plunged, (2) distributors have come to rely enough on Graco's quick response that they also have slashed their inventories and are ordering from Graco in closer to JIT quantities, and (3) the smaller, more frequent orders (more closely approximating actual end-customer demand) help smooth out production, purchasing, and administrative lumpiness for Graco.
- *Capital investment*: A commitment to invest considerable sums in quick (or zero) setup, high-quality performance, multifunctional CNC equipment has played a key role in Graco's customer responsiveness and inventory reduction.
  - ✓ More than other companies, inventory reduction savings are specifically sought and recognized in equipment justifications, which are initiated by cell teams.
  - ✓ For capital justification, Graco allows 100% of the inventory reduction dollars to be used as savings, plus an additional 12%.
    - ■ This allows them, in effect, to trade inventory for capital on a one-for-one basis.
    - ■ An engineer could spend $1m on a piece of equipment that would reduce inventory by $1m even if it brought no other savings to the table!
  - ✓ Newer technology almost invariably gives Graco substantial quality improvement and labor savings as well. McHale: "I believe using this approach shows the executive team is putting its money where its mouth is in terms of the desire to reduce inventories."

- *Supplier reductions*: A single-sourcing objective, dating back a decade, has been reached in some cases.
- *Other best practices*: The following are other WCM concepts in use, though less intensively or for fewer years:
  - ✓ *Kanban*: good progress with suppliers (less so for internal flows).
  - ✓ *Design for manufacture and assembly*: Graco's main application of DFMA concepts is in modular designs, which simplify customer choices and Graco's production processes as well.
  - ✓ *Enlightened cost analysis*: Graco targets the cost-containment (direct-cost) features of cells, plus assignment of staff support to the cells. One business decision that may have benefited from this kind of costing is Graco's exit from unprofitable custom orders.
  - ✓ *Setup-time and lot-size reduction*: For calculating EOQs, Graco uses 35%, which is on the high side of the textbook 25–35% (but still rather low, in that it fails to consider various "hidden" costs of inventory).
  - ✓ *Employees*:
    - ■ Reduction of job classifications.
    - ■ Good working conditions, training, and pay, which pay off in low employee turnover, no labor-union inroads, and attraction of good engineering talent.
  - ✓ *Home Depot venture*: A new, high-volume, low-mix venture with Home Depot is enabled by dedicated equipment, heavy use of kanban with suppliers, and quick customer replenishment.

III. Improvement Opportunities

- *Specifics*: There appears to be room for improvement in each of the preceding "other" areas discussed above in Section II; examples:
- *"Purify" kanban*: Use of simple, visual kanban or kanban-like internal work-flow devices.
  - ✓ In the present approach with suppliers, the kanban container has a barcode that is scanned by production associates.
  - ✓ Unfortunately, according to McHale, this does not generate any signal to the supplier. It only generates a signal to a Graco planner/buyer to release another order for a "kanban" quantity through the existing purchasing system.
  - ✓ Improving this deficiency is a 2003 active project.

- Perhaps it will involve simple, low-cost uses of internet, fax, and visual.
- In addition, shared inbound trucking can facilitate more frequent deliveries and simpler kanban.

- *Quick setup*: Setup-critical equipment warrants more intensive quick-setup efforts such that pursuing setup-reduction becomes a normal aspect of every operator's job: doing their own studies with video cameras, every setup timed and plotted on trend charts. 80–90% reductions in setup times, lot sizes, and flow times should be achievable, but do not seem that good so far.
- *Standardizing parts*: Heavy DFMA emphasis is needed in engineering, aimed especially at standardizing parts, from screws and bolts to motors. This should entail formally evaluating, recognizing, and rewarding engineers for DFMA results (including use of good, existing parts rather than designing anew just to save a few pennies in assembly).
- *ABC audits*: Further the effort to make costs reliable for better business decisions via activity-based cost audits on an as-needed basis. (Such improvements should help, especially, in providing cost rationale for intensifying DFMA and for dropping poor customers.)
- *Further reduction in job classifications*: Formalize job skill versatility via large versatility matrices on display in each cell; requirements for job rotation of a certain frequency to maintain skills; phasing in of pay-by-skills and phasing out of time-in-service; etc.
- *Better data for process improvement*: Employ more training and application of data collection (every employee recording every mishap or job-related aggravation), problem-solving, systematic team deliberation and public recognition.
- *Sharing demand data*: Develop customer (distributor) collaborations that foster frequent sharing of actual demand data. Graco's pitch to distributors may emphasize Graco price reductions in exchange for granting Graco longer contracts—with joint demand planning and perhaps Graco taking over customers' inventory management (the VMI—vendor-managed-inventory—concept).

IV. Further (General Category) Remarks

- *Cell sizes.* 30-person cells are unusually large. (See how Tennant Co. had addressed problems with a too-large cell, gaining considerable benefits when they divided it in two for two different types of sweeper or scrubber.*)

- *Management fads.* Admirably, Graco seems to have been, largely, a stay-the-course kind of company; while many others have used up enormous resources chasing management fads and spending on consultants who promote them.
  - ✓ Among those not adopted are self-directed work teams, flextime, and 360-degree appraisal—all mostly good ideas but easily done badly and not among the more proven and essential of the "best-practice" agenda items.
  - ✓ Dr. Deming's prescriptions—especially, everyone constantly collecting process data and analyzing them—on the other hand, are high on the best-practice list. The many companies that once subscribed to this message have become a small number.
  - ✓ McHale states that operatives do collect and analyze process data daily, including first-pass yield off assembly lines and SPC data in machining operations. But "We have plenty of additional opportunity to improve in this area."

CHAPTER III-83. FLUKE CORP., EVERETT, WA, 2003

This tour of Fluke Corp.—for me plus University of Washington professors Tom Schmitt and Karen Brown—was in preparation for a later-in-the-month Study Mission to the western U.S. for visiting manufacturing executives from Hong Kong. Fluke was picked for the visit because I had become familiar with the company's excellence via a visit there in 1994.

Many High-Interest Topics:
- **75 or 80 cells with packout as the final operation**
- **Adoption of the Danaher Business System—which formalized and systemized what Fluke had already been doing well**
- **Incoming raw materials are used within four hours of receipt; no need for a raw material warehouse**

Summary of Assessment Based on 1.5-Hour Plant Visit, April 3, 2003, as Part of a Tour Group from Hong Kong

---

* See R.J. Schonberger, *World Class Manufacturing Casebook: Implementing JIT and TQC* (Free Press, 1987), Tennant Co., Case: 152–164.

I. The Company

- *Changing ownership*: Originally (1953) John Fluke Manufacturing Co., it was acquired in 1998 by Danaher Corp. [In 2016 Danaher spun off Fluke and other subsidiaries to create Fortive.]
- *Product line*: Fluke's products include multimeters priced from $100 to $500; oscilloscopes around $1,700; test beds up to $40,000; network test units (low voltage—e.g., cat 5) $1,000 to $20,000; and meterman units priced at market bottom.
- *Everett-area*. Fluke's local operations are in Buildings 1 (Fluke world HQ), 3 (Evergreen Way building), and 4 (injection molding); 2 did not get built.
- *Global facilities*: Manufacturing plants are in Everett, Utah, England, Holland, Shanghai (new in 2002), Santa Cruz, and the Reno area. Distribution centers are in Everett, Eindhoven-Netherlands, Canada, Japan, Singapore, China, and Brazil.
- *Main contacts*: John Williamson, VP, operations; Jennifer Westlund, administrative asst.

II. Plant Tour – General Information

- *Purpose of tour*: The tour was undertaken as part of a study mission to the western U.S., co-sponsored by the Hong Kong Productivity Council (HKPC), for HKPC-affiliated companies.
  - ✓ I had arranged the tour agenda for the study mission (and had assisted HKPC with a similar study mission in June 1998).
  - ✓ HKPC had been sending executives on study missions to Japan but had become receptive to my contention that they could learn

---

SIDEBAR 1 DANAHER BUSINESS SYSTEM (DBS)

DBS features cells, pull system, etc. DBS-trained people populate the business units, overseeing implementation of DBS tenets—especially via week-long kaizen events.

Four Fluke people are full-time DBS implementers for four different functional areas (service, manufacturing, etc.)—positions that rotate quarterly; they spend 70% of their time in their functional area and 30% anywhere.

Also, every Fluke site has a DBS manager (not full-time).

---

as much or more about "best manufacturing practices"—and in English—by visiting top-notch U.S. manufacturers.

✓ Other Seattle/Western Washington-area companies on the agenda were Philips Ultrasound, Precor, Cutler-Hammer Sensors, Physio Control and Genie Industries.

- *Fluke's stated mission*: "To be the leader in compact, professional electronic test tools."

- *Employment*: Fluke's global workforce is 3,500 employees, 1,500 of whom are in Everett (900 in operations), the rest at scattered Fluke sites.

- *Before and since Danaher*:
  ✓ I had toured Fluke in 1994, finding the company to be advanced in cellular manufacturing and related excellences.
  ✓ Danaher—with multiple subsidiaries well-known for best manufacturing practices—may have acquired Fluke primarily because Fluke was already advanced in those practices.
  ✓ Under Danaher, Fluke has been obliged to formally adopt the "Danaher Business System," as described in Sidebar 1.

- *Training*: All cell-team members are cross-trained and can move from cell to cell (although we saw only one cross-training display—part of a large employee-developed multifaceted display board in Building 1).

- *Order processing*: The production mode is build-to-order (orders from distributor-customers), but sometimes the "order" is "to our shelf."

- *Process improvement*:
  ✓ Among improvement methods, we saw two different kaizen events taking place in conference rooms, one for a cell team, the other for the metrology lab (the latter group had cause-and-effect diagrams with Post-Its on the walls). (All senior managers/visualizers are required to spend 1 week yearly in kaizen events.)
  ✓ Value-stream mapping is in wide use.

- *Inventory reduction*: This is Danaher's dominant metric. In the past two years (since Williamson's arrival—from Danaher) inventory has plunged from $85 million to $50 million.

- *Support teams*: Formerly, each cell had a lead person, now it's one cell lead for five to eight cells. 16–20 cells also have a support team of, e.g., master scheduler, buyer-planner, team leader.

III. Evergreen Way Building

- *Building 3*: This facility, of about 160,000 sq. ft., is for assembly of low-end products, with its own raw-material receiving.
- *Products*:
  - ✓ Higher-volume, lower-cost items.
  - ✓ Also, an accessories product line (molded plugs, jacks, leads, cables, etc.) was brought in from a now-shuttered Fluke facility in Pomona, CA. (Only 12 of about 100 employees from there came to Everett with the product line, which allowed former Fluke people who had been laid off, largely for productivity-improvement reasons, to be rehired.)
- *Cells.* There are 75 or 80 cells, around 23 of them in the first room we visited.
  - ✓ Most finished-item assembly cells are U-shaped and include packout as the final operation.
    - Accessories—not cellular in Pomona—is being set up as cells in Everett.
    - To keep pace with fairly high volumes, much of the test equipment in cells is automatic.
  - ✓ Cells are easily reconfigured, with most benches, equipment, and storage racks on wheels, and facilitated by quick disconnects of utilities at ceilings. Benches and racks are made in-house from simple hole-drilled lengths of angle iron.
  - ✓ Nearby racks hold materials refilled by kanban cards—pink for internal kanban, green for external kanban. All kanban areas are marked off with tape on the floor.
- *Metric boards.* All cells have large, standardized displays, usually mounted at ends of the U-shaped cells. The main measures are 1st pass yield, on-time, and productivity. Also on the boards are four-point "issues" matrices: materials, equipment, people, processes.
- *SMT* (surface-mount technology). Not visited. Williamson commented that the main issue there is quick setup.
- *Raw-material processes*:
  - ✓ There are no raw material warehouses. All incoming materials—around 7,000 items per day—arrive at the Evergreen Way building., and within four hours have been distributed to points of use next to assembly cells, SMT lines, etc., in each of three Fluke buildings.

✓ In the receiving area there is just one job description, material handler; all can receive, drive fork trucks, move materials to cells, and so on.

✓ UPS volumes are high enough that UPS stages a semitrailer at a dock (for loading overnight? or as stockroom for incoming materials?). Cardboard packaging material is received daily by kanban from just two or three suppliers.

IV. Building 1

- *Operations*: Some of the products here are fairly large and heavy, with substantial sheet-metal skins.
- *Rotating carts*: To cope, a build-on-cart system has been adopted, with carts on wheels at bench height. Sheet-metal kits arrive on carts, which rotate among cell stations as the item is built.

V. Summary Remarks

- Because of the nature of this plant tour—three of us preparing for a later study mission—we (and I) did not do a critique on ways for Fluke to improve itself.
- Suffice to say, that we are impressed by much of what Fluke has achieved, most notably by its wide application of cellular manufacturing.

CHAPTER III-84. TVS MOTOR CO., HOSUR, TAMILNADU, INDIA, 2012

This caselet shows, for this producer of two-wheeled vehicles, superiority (over car makers) to embrace flow manufacturing. TVS employs numerous impressive practices—nearly the gamut of flow and quality methodologies.	**High-Interest Topics:** • **Half hour for employee problem-solving 4 days a week** • **Issue: converting assembly lines to dedicated cells** • **Issue: coping with three-shift machining conflicts with two-shift assembly**

TVS Does (Most) Things Right: Assessment Based on 1.5-Hour Tour of Plant 2 and 30-Minute Tour of Sundaram-Clayton Plant, Oct. 30, 2012

Tours arranged in connection with Schonberger presentation/events at 20th Anniversary CII National Quality Summit 2012, Bangalore, India

I. Basic Information

- *History*:
    - ✓ TVS is named after initials of the founder, T.V. Sundaram, who started the company in 1911 as a bus-fleet operator—with a reputation of buses "always on time." TVS today stands for Trust, Value, Service.
    - ✓ The TVS Group is the parent of TVS Motor Co., which is the subject of this caselet.
        - In addition, the TVS Group is India's leading manufacturer of automotive components.
        - Its 30-plus companies (including TVS Motor) employ a work force of 40,000.
        - Four of the companies are the first four in India to win a Deming Prize.
- *TVS Motor Co. Ltd.*:
    - ✓ Largest of the TVS companies in size and sales (US$4 billion).
    - ✓ Introduced Indian industry's first two-seater moped in 1980. Collaborative work with Suzuki in 1984 led to India's first motorcycle. Came out with a scooter for women in 1994.
    - ✓ Rank of two-wheeler producers in India: 1. Hero-Honda; 2. Bajaj; 3. TVS.
- *TVS Motor's plants*: With 2.5 million vehicles per year production capacity, its plants are the Hosur complex (1979), Chenai, Mysore (1997), Jakarta-Indonesia (2005–06); also newer plants in China and the U.K.
- *Deming Prize*: Awarded in 2002, the 1st motor-vehicle (or two-wheeler?) plant to win.
- *Basic data*: 7,000 people produce 3,000 mopeds per day (3 million per year), supported by 200 suppliers and 450 product-development engineers. With 600 "state-of-the-art" Indian dealers, the company strives for "stockless" order fulfillment.

- *Seasonality*: September–November is the busiest season because it is college entry time; Nov.–June is slow season.
- *Global*: Products are exported to 3,650 dealers in 60 countries.
- *Host and tour group*: TVS – M. Muthuraj, senior VP-operations. From CII – Tarina Basu (arrangements); Yogesh N., engineer-lean; P.M. Janagirama, senior counsellor-TPM.

II. Plant 2

- *Pre-tour meeting*: About ten managers gave presentations on their areas; then a video. Among many points made are:
  - ✓ Strong customer emphasis—in company history and today.
  - ✓ Hosur complex has four of TVS's plants: Plant 1.? Plant 2 (I toured). Plant 3, engine parts. Plant 4, three-wheelers? Also two large supplier plants are there on lease.
  - ✓ Employee engagement features world-class numbers of suggestions per employee per year (e.g., 40, 50, 60?), mostly implemented by the employee.
  - ✓ TPM and lean: Total productive maintenance began in 1999; lean two or three years ago.
  - ✓ Supply chain links: E-kanban, MRP, DOL.
- *Processes and layout*: Plant 2 (and all other assembly plants) have five basic processes: machining, fabrication, engine assembly, vehicle assembly, and quality control. Figure 84.1 highlights (bold typeface) those five (vehicle assembly is shown twice—for its two product-focused lines) in a *very* rough sketch of Plant 2.
- *Plant 2 operations*: This description ties (roughly) to Figure 84.1.
  - ✓ Machining of engine components (crankshafts, cylinder heads, etc.) takes place in three shifts, engine assembly two shifts. With that shift difference, excess machined parts from the third shift go in trolleys to a kanban area, which feeds engine assembly.
  - ✓ Engines—Machining.
    - Equipment consists of 752 machines, most in U-shaped cells, some (e.g., gear cells) with identical equipment. One machining unit, called a "kaizen corner," is useful for kaizen improvement projects. Lots of hand-push carts move materials around. Die-castings from the Sudaram plant feed the machining operations.

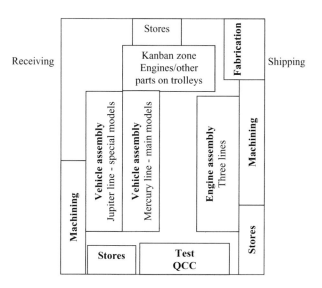

FIGURE 84.1
Sketch of TVS plant 2.

- A heavy emphasis is on standardizing all equipment: electrical units, coolant units, and so on; also new-generation fixtures, part transfer chutes (the former use of roller conveyor has given way to gravity chutes).

✓ Engine assembly:
- Three engine lines are situated along conveyors.
- The line for the four most common models has 23 stations, a batch size of 60, and takt time of 32 seconds. A second line assembles nine *strangers* (lesser models), with a takt time of 51 seconds.
- Quality is supported by large numbers of fail-safes (*pokayokes*) along the lines.
- Kits of parts come from purchased parts stores, as well as the kanban area.

✓ Vehicle assembly is made up of two lines producing 850 vehicles per shift:
- The Mercury (primary) assembly line, for higher-volume models, has an 18-second takt time.
- Jupiter (2nd) assembly line—for lower-volume models: 30-second takt time.

- ■ An automatic-guided-vehicle (AGV) system delivers parts from purchased stores to the lines.
- ✓ Pre-assembly: Feeding final assembly lines are 14 subassembly cells along a straight line separated from final assembly, which then takes a U-turn and merges with a 34-station final assembly line. An overhead conveyor brings plastic frames from where they have been painted (paint not identified on the Figure 84.1 sketch).
- ✓ Also feeding final assembly are kits of parts that load onto assembly conveyors at initial stations, with parts picked and installed at appropriate stations all along the assembly lines.
- • *Operations management and training*:
  - ✓ *Operator problem-solving*. Half an hour, four days a week, is used for operator problem-solving; on Mondays that 0.5 hour (7:00a.m.–7:30a.m.) is for audit by the plant manager.
  - ✓ *Start-of-shift meeting*. Every day.
  - ✓ *Visual management*: All areas have display boards with the same basic information on charts and graphs (e.g., shift output, schedule, "station stoppers").
  - ✓ *Training*: Two weeks of initial training, Six month' secondary— with high focus on dexterity.
  - ✓ *Cross-training/job rotation*. On assembly lines, all are cross-trained to be proficient on 3 adjacent stations.
    - ■ But job rotation is not systematic and appears infrequent.
    - ■ There seems to be little or no cross-training/job rotation *across* the 5 major processes, nor much within separate segments of each major process.
  - ✓ *Quality control circles*: These QCCs are very effective—and compete nationally and internationally.

III. Sudaram-Clayton Plant

- • *Products*: This plant (or plant complex) includes die-casting of components dating back to 1940; brake linings were added in 1968 (the Clayton plant at one time was owned by American Standard).
- • *Current facilities*: There are four plants (Hosur, Padi, plus two other plants in Chennai) and 4,000 employees (94 executives, 12 managers; and a workforce of 57% permanent, 30% apprentices, 13% temps).

- *Which plants/processes?* Die-casting is done only at Hosur and Chennai (crank cases, clutch covers, cylinder heads, etc.); brake linings at Chennai-Mahindra; and both die-castings and brake linings at another plant.
- *Markets/customers*: In this die-casting components business, TVS Motor has 60% market share. Customers include TVS, Tata, and Volvo. It competes in both national and international markets.
- *Hosur plant*: At 40,520 square meters, the plant has 177 machines, 645 employees, and three shifts, for production of high- and low-pressure die-castings.
- *Inventory*: Maximum is four hours' inventory between die-casting and the local TVS plant. Scheduling is via MRP—with a stop-signaling override when the four-hour inventory limit is reached.
- *Plant tour*: Brief comments: This looks to be an exemplary die-casting plant, with evidence of advanced TPM implementations, including monthly 5S audits, spider diagrams, fixed-point photos, and very clean machines (though the building itself not so clean and could use painting).

IV. Salutary Comments

- *Excellence*: Overall, an excellent manufacturing complex, recognized by its external awards and by positive examples cited in this caselet; while too many to restate, following are three examples:
- *TPM*: TVS plants show deep attention to TPM basics—especially for Sundaram-Clayton, because its very high-quality outputs are so dependent on high-performing equipment.
- *Quality*: Its historical and present high degree of attention to quality look to be "world class."
- *Plant meetings*: The weekly management audit and daily start-shift meetings are systematic and stabilizing.

V. Opportunities for Improvement

- *Assembly lines to cells*: The existing organization and cellular layouts indicate good progress on the lean journey—having begun only about three years ago. Much more needs doing, primarily replacing each long assembly line with several small, U-shaped cells, each dedicated to its own family of vehicle, engine, or component models.

✓ Rationale: Of all methodologies of lean manufacturing, cells usually have the greatest benefits.

- With multiple cells, each becomes its own value stream, acting like a small factory in itself, with its own team of operators and partly dedicated engineers, maintenance, customer service, etc.—each cell member with minutes instead of seconds of work content per cycle.
- All cell members learn every job to where they gain manager-like perspective. In time, a cell may achieve considerable self-management. Needs for supervisors are reduced as peer pressures among small cell teams take root in shaping up slackers.
- Product costing sharpens since cells act as *cost-containment centers*—operating with minimal, low-cost material handling, often including no conveyors. Assembly lines, on the other hand, lose out on these benefits (and others too numerous to recite here).

✓ Example: In engine assembly, lines might be broken into, say, five or six cells, each dedicated to its own engine/engine-HP family.

- This allows process simplification; perfecting the process; and raising quality, efficiency, and productivity to higher levels—with fewer needs for fail-safe devices.
- Best cell location seems to be between receiving and machining, thus to minimize distances for supplying cells with external and internal sources of parts.

- *Shift imbalances*:
  ✓ Machining and die-casting, because their operations are capital-intensive, operates three shifts versus two in assembly, which disrupts the lean ideal of continuous flow.
  ✓ It seems sensible—in selected cases—for one or more "runner" assembly cells to operate three shifts, with direct supply of machined and die-cast parts, rather than present system of having to store, then at shift startup begin picking and delivering machined or die-cast parts.
- *Rationalize kanban*:
  ✓ The present sending ALL (if notes are correct) machined parts to the kanban area, then via pull signals to final assembly, should be modified so that during day shifts, most parts flow directly

from machining to assembly, bypassing the kanban area—and its extra handling.

✓ The kanban/WIP storage area then converts to a parts overflow area, mainly for 3rd-shift machined parts. Something similar may be workable for die-castings.

- *Reliance on kitting*: Kitting is non-value-adding and un-lean.
  - ✓ *External* kitting—parts kits put together by a supplier—can be beneficial in reducing transport/handling costs, e.g., matched sets of die-cast parts from Sundaram-Clayton.
  - ✓ The same is generally not applicable to internal kitting, with their short handling distances—those who put kits together are overhead costs, and the act of kitting becomes double-handling delay and a source of errors.
  - ✓ Sometimes internal kitting is necessary simply because large numbers of product models are being made in a given production line or cell—which is a symptom either of lack of parts standardization, or lack of layouts into product-focused value streams. Then, kitting should be seen as a temporary expedient.
  - ✓ In TVS engine and vehicle assembly, conversion to cells would eliminate most reasons for kitting.
    - ■ Numbers of different parts per cell are greatly reduced.
    - ■ Then delivery of parts to a given cell becomes a simple kanban system going direct to the cell from stores (better yet, direct from supplier) or machining.
- *Systematic job rotation*:
  - ✓ I have before me a list of nine winners of awards for manufacturing excellence (*Industry Week* Best Plants awards and Shingo Prizes) and their frequencies of job rotation: Vintec, hourly; O.C. Tanner, every two hours; Sunny Fresh Foods, every 20 minutes; Tenneco Automotive, every two hours; Kodak de México, every three hours; TI Automotive, every two hours; Autoliv-Ogden, hourly; Signicast, every four hours.
  - ✓ Probably TVS lines should have job rotation at least every shift— or more often if the associates themselves should prefer it.
- *Associate engagement*: At TVS large numbers of associates' suggestions, mostly self-implemented, are impressive. But the quality of suggestions must necessarily be limited because of minimal fields of vision, just their own work station plus about two others—and without frequent job rotation.

✓ As lines convert to cells, associates will master all cell tasks/stations, with frequent job rotation offering whole-process knowledge and elevated personal motivation to "make things right." Numbers and quality of improvement ideas should considerably increase, in many cases as team rather than individual suggestions.

✓ Over time, cell members should become cross-trained and rotated among other cells, and sometimes to other processes, such as stores, machining, testing, and so on.

- The greatly expanded knowledge and awareness from such broad training and experience generates still better suggestions.
- Such rotation provides job enlargement and job enrichment—and for the more motivated a pathway to higher station and pay in the company, or elsewhere.

CHAPTER III-85. TAKATA SEAT BELTS (TSB), MONTERREY, MÉXICO, 2004

My unusually comprehensive visit to Takata centered on critiquing its efforts to implement world-class manufacturing, with hopes of receiving a Shingo Prize, as had multiple other Méxican plants—including Takata competitors (Note: Before long, four of Takata's facilities *were* awarded the prize). In this I would learn about, and offer my assessments of the company's focus on safety—in that seat belts are so safety critical. (Note: the exploding Takata air bags are *not* made here.)

Many High-Interest Topics:
- **TSB 50 product-focused assembly lines/component cells for Honda seat belts**
- **It designs/builds its own equipment**
- **Need to employ off-line buffer stock: Keep it out of the flow**
- **The plant is notable for intensive, multifaceted anti-defect practices**
- **Synchronize subassembly cells to "true" takt time**
- **Plant features stand-up, one-piece-flow sewing cells**
- **Is there *too much* fail-safing?**

Safety Above All: Observations Based on Factory Tours in Connection with one-Day Schonberger Workshop/Conferences, March 10–12, 2004

I. General

- *Takata Co.*: A family-owned, Japan-headquartered manufacturer of steering wheels, air bags, inflators, and seat belts with 4 plants in México; and other plants in the U.S. (5 states), and in Japan, Poland, Romania, and Brazil. Takata began seat-belt production in 1960, airbags in 1988. Its U.S. headquarters is in Auburn Hills, MI.
- *Visitation sites:* Apodaca (Monterrey suburb), México; San Antonio and Laredo, Texas:
  - ✓ *Takata Seat Belts (TSB), San Antonio:*
    - A center for component design for domestic products, global supplier development, and domestic purchasing, with 98 people including three executives. Japan designs the retractor but San Antonio the brackets, stays, and other seat-belt components.
    - TSB is market leader in N.A. with 2-digit growth yearly since 1990. TSB volume is 120,000 belts per day, 1 million every two weeks.
  - ✓ *Monterrey Plant 2*: This Honda-focused plant is 55-60K sf; with 600 1st-shift employees, and 400 in 2nd shift; operates 17 hours/5 days (formerly 24/6). My 2-hour visit was on March 10. [In 2005, one year after the date of this caselet, Plant 2 was recipient of the Shingo Prize]
  - ✓ *Takata Monterrey Technical Center (TMTC)*, on the other side of the city, has 140 people, plus co-op engineering students. My 2-hour visit here was on March 11.
    - With engineering in San Antonio, TMTC does prototyping, testing, machine (fixtures, fail-safing) design/build.
    - TMTC is being expanded to include a crash-sled facility for testing steering wheels, air bags, and seat belts combined.
    - A new Takata University will use Takata people as instructors and may ultimately grant a degree
- *Sites investigated without visiting*:
  - ✓ Monterrey Plant 1 with 1,200-employees makes seat belts for Toyota and Daimler-Chrysler. [In 2005, one year after the date of this caselet, Plant 1 was recipient of the Shingo Prize]
  - ✓ Agua Prieta plant (across from Douglas, AZ) has 1,800 employees making seat belts for Nissan, Ford, and Subaru. [In 2005, one year

after the date of this caselet, the Agua Prieta plant was recipient of the Shingo Prize.]

  ✓ Acuña plant (across from Del Rio, TX) makes seat belts for GM.

  ✓ U.S. warehouse is in Laredo, TX.

- *Competitors*: Delphi, TRW Auto, Autoliv, Breed Technologies (now Key Safety Systems, owned by the Carlyle Group).
- *Customers*: Automakers in the USA, Canada, and México, plus various seat makers.
- *Training*: Entrenamiento is OJT task training; capacitación is more for career development.
- *TSK goals*: Four plants winning a Shingo Prize.
- *Human resources*:
  - ✓ Assemblers' average age is 23.5 years; labor turnover is 0.85%, absenteeism 3%—extremely low for Mexico.
  - ✓ Managers, engineers, and technical support are mostly young and talented; Sergio has no managers, only asociados (advisors).
  - ✓ TMTC – Process engineers are adept at developing and mostly producing their own assembly and test fixtures and fail-safing devices.
- *Primary contact persons*: Seth Jantzen, team leader, Takata Center for Excellence, Quality Audit Office, San Antonio; Eliud Gonzalez, quality engineer, San Antonio; Sergio Valdez, plant manager, Plant 2, Podaca; Greg Willwerth, operations quality asst. manager, San Antonio.

II. Monterrey Plant 2 – General

- *Focus*: Plant 2, producing for a small number of Honda models, has about 22 final assembly and 28 subassembly lines (cells) focused by type of seat belt: driver-side, passenger-side, rear-seat.
- *Visual management*: Each cell has the same standard displays; in D-ring it is a four-box display with two boxes as updates for what's happening in production and two boxes for defect updates.
- *Alerts/alarms*:
  - ✓ All lines have stack lights: green good; orange a problem; red a line-stop, which summons roving maintenance or supervisors quickly.
  - ✓ For an A-rank customer problem, an alarm button on a wall next to offices turns on a flashing red light and loud alarm heard all over the plant and offices; staff comes pouring out of offices and plants and have 2 hours to find countermeasures.

- *Quality features on lines*:
  - ✓ Rejects go into a red bin and out to scrap.
  - ✓ Fail-safe plaques are mounted at each fail-safe location, roughly 5 fail-safe devices per line; more than 600 in total, managed by a central traceability system.
  - ✓ Calibration plaques tell what calibration is necessary, how often, and for keeping track.
  - ✓ Limit samples hang at each line and are used in verification tests of each device; results are recorded on a verification sheet.
  - ✓ 1st and last pieces are checked, and the assembler's badge is scanned to assign responsibility.
- *Defect ratings*: In 2001 Honda scored TSB 6,000 index points (for defects), putting TSB in the 50th percentile among Honda suppliers; in the last six months, points are down to 400, top 10% of suppliers. Takata rates its suppliers this same way and passes the ratings on to them.
- *Production lines*: Designed for *product safety* and *flow*.
  - ✓ Designs vary depending on the item, but nearly all are one-piece flow; and person-to person—one-to-one responsibility chains, not "gang-to-gang."
  - ✓ On Line 119, the C7 rear seatbelt black box (retractor), five assemblers on one side of the line make subassemblies and convey them by ramp to three assemblers on other side, who finish black-box assembly; gravity ramps have mechanical guides, stops, etc.
  - ✓ At places in the lines, a mechanical check will signal and stop any off-spec issue.
  - ✓ Parts feeders are mostly designed ergonomically to minimize reaching, bending, etc.
  - ✓ Photos show correct parts throughout the processes.
  - ✓ All downtimes are tracked, specific to the device, person, and time.
  - ✓ Model Line 104, C8S7 final assembly of buckles (major failure component):
    - There are about nine touch screens for nine steps, and each must turn from red to green, meaning all good quality and okay to proceed.
    - Assemblers scan their badges as they start their shift, and if one is not trained and certified, the line will not start.

✓ Sewing machines, most prone to downtime, are on wheels so another machine can be wheeled in quickly, as needed.

- Sewing is stand-up and one-piece-flow (cellular—as in the TSS/modular sewing system).
- This excellent practice is rather rare throughout the sewing world, both in apparel and in fabric for industrial uses.

✓ WIP is a lean four to six hours; no fork trucks are used except to bring parts from the warehouse to just inside Plant 2, where dollies, pallet-jacks, and hand-carry take over.

✓ No cardboard is in the plant; all plastic returnable containers.

- *Honda visit*: On Feb. 2, 20 people from Honda came for a supplier review and were favorably amazed. TSB has won a Honda Technical Merit award twice, and one of TSB's QCs (quality circles) went to Japan and competed well with Honda's and other suppliers' QCs.

III. Plant 2 – Process Flows

- *Warehouse, suppliers*: See Sidebar 1 for a few details.

  ✓ Samples for inspection are in yellow plastic trays; traceability begins with keying in data—and printing a bar-code label only if approved by receiving inspection.

  ✓ A Pansophic system keeps track of material costing, etc.

  ✓ Defect ratings: Honda rates suppliers monthly on a performance index re importance of factor X problem criticality, which has three levels: A, belt component won't function; B, bad looking; C, something minor like a scratch.

- *Models*: TSB produces belt sets for Honda Civics (selling less well than expected), Elements (selling 2.5 times better, and largely to

---

SIDEBAR 1   WAREHOUSE OPERATIONS

Inbound: Three docks, eight trucks/day (50% from Japan, 30% U.S., 20% Mexico). Laredo warehouse is trying out VMI.

Parts on hand: Eight days domestic; 13–15 days Japanese; six days finished goods.

Kitting: Everything kitted (10–40 items per kit) and bar-coded for Plant 2; bar-code wanded at start of production.

Distribution: Parts and finished belt sets go out in standard containers, blue (Canada), orange (USA), gray (Plant 1).

retirees rather than expected 20–25-year-olds), Odysseys, other. Also, three types of retractor and buckle assembly: C7, C8, and C9.

- *Changeovers*: From Civic to Element the average changeover is two hours, mostly to restock lines with alternate parts, bar-coding, first-piece testing, etc. Sometimes it is just changing a few of the many fixtures, but much of fixture/test equipment changes are by computer.
- *Plant design*: Plant 2 is as shown, roughly, in Figure 85.1—with shipping and receiving on the same wall, kanban, web-cutting, service parts, and prototyping lined up on one side and offices on the other; and the bulk of space in the middle for subassembly and final seatbelt assembly.
- *Outgoing pipeline inventory* (Monterrey-Piqua-Honda): Averages five days (73 turns/year); shipments are in car sets, with four trucks daily outbound to U.S. sites, and two per month to Brazil.
- *Line assemblers*: Cross-trained with job rotation maybe about weekly, but no policy on it.
- *Pay*: Three job classifications—assemblers are lowest paid, material handlers next, leaders highest; labor is about 2% of cost of goods sold.
- *Line balancing*: Trying to balance lines within plus-minus 10%.
- *Honda interfacing*:

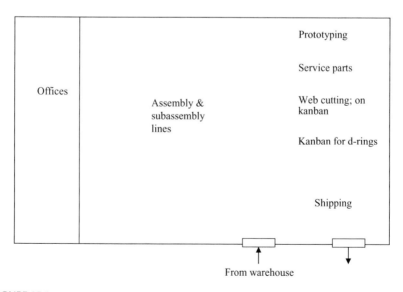

FIGURE 85.1
Rough design of Plant 2.

✓ Tom Fink heads a Honda Lean Supply Network (he was at our breakfast in the hotel) and works with the supply base in a "soft" way.

✓ A Honda SQUAD (Supplier Quality Development) program encourages suppliers (including TSB) to participate, and has the advantage of early involvement with Honda practices—before Honda makes a unilateral decision about some issue.

IV. Tech Center (TMTC)

- *Equipment*:
  ✓ Includes an impressive array of testing gear; and first in the seat-belt industry to have its own laser machine for metal cutting of prototype parts.
  ✓ Builds much of its own equipment for . . .
    ■ 1. Quick reaction; no more six-week lead times. 2. Customized to needs as they arise. 3. Fixtures, more naturally an in-house concern, as contrasted with machines, which can be more difficult for in-house design. 4. Better quality (no more soft tooling, with burrs, saving money overall).
    ■ In general, companies lacking strong in-house design are at mercy of the machine-build industry, which is less innovative when not challenged by customers who have some machine design/build capabilities themselves. (Precedent: The German machine-tool industry remained strong because, ironically, its manufacturing customers had machine design/build capability themselves and could keep machine-tool companies challenged; the opposite happened in the U.S.*)
- *Model line*: Designed for 100% inspection.
- *Machine shop*: No free ride, must do price quotes to get work from Takata plants.
- *Traceability*:
  ✓ While GM requires traceability only every two weeks, the computer-based traceability system now up and running (formerly manual documents maintained by Javier) has trace records at the ready. Excellent use of co-op students who were able to design this traceability system.

---

* See R.H. Hayes & S.C. Wheelright, *Restoring Our Competitive Edge* (New York: Wiley, 1984): 19.

✓ Data are not in a central inventory system but are separate and better protected.
- *Seat-weight sensor production:*
  ✓ This product has achieved high performance, in customer acceptance and volume, in a short time. [Three years following the data of this caselet—in 2007—the weight-sensor operation was recipient of the Shingo Prize.]
  ✓ TSB had turned away Ford as a customer because of Ford's demands, and now Ford is back more willing to accept Takata's package.
- *Continuous improvement*: Example: the newest U-shaped lines are more effective than the oldest straight lines.
- *Multiple lines producing same item*: A good lean practice (as opposed to typical engineers' preference for more resources in a single line, increasing complexity, reducing flexibility).

V. Strengths—Good Practices

- **TSB as a whole:**
  ✓ Recognition: A range of low-cost gifts for various attainments and QC's recognition.
  ✓ Challenge and retention of top people:
    - TSB staffers had been sent on eight-week assignments to transfer best practices to offshore plants—Poland, Romania, and Brazil.
    - Offers special challenges and interesting travel for good people—and is tied to the happy circumstance of good year-to-year growth in sales and market share.
  ✓ Improvement efforts: PDCA, 5S, six sigma, lean, kaizen, quality circles (QCs).
    - These blend well together (vs., in other companies, sometimes friction among various programs; few have quality circles at all).
    - QCs, rather new at TSB, are up from nine in early 2003 to 78 QCs now—with a full-time coordinator. Cross-functional teams evaluate QC analysis and recommendations. Each of six 6-sigma black belts is assigned as a facilitator for five QCs.
    - 5S is *not* owned by maintenance; facilitator Eugeño Garza does 5S scoring of all work centers daily (also safety, discipline).

- TPM has three levels of severity: (1) less than three minutes downtime are assemblers' responsibility to try to fix; assemblers also are trained for lube, adjust machine, clean machine, thread needle (2nd bobbin is always ready to go); (2) 4–30 minutes, medium issue; (3) 30+ minutes, catastrophe.
- A typical PDCA routine is gap analysis and root-cause efforts between C and A criticality.
- Daily staff meeting—12 people from all departments— review extensive process data; summary performance charts posted weekly are subject of weekly meetings; other reviews of monthly results.

- Hierarchy of problem-solving/control: (1) Eliminate the variable (DOE validation). (2) Automate the variable. (3) SPC at input end (fail-safing, go/no-go). (4) SPC at output end (measure quality). (5) Change SOP (standard operating procedure).
- *Warehouse*: Stocks are in flow racks for efficiency in picking plus FIFO traceback.
- *Process capabilities*: Very high (Seth: as high as 36 sigma); thorough lot traceability.
- *Copy exactly*: Perfecting equipment/fixtures and fail-safing at one site, then replicating at low cost at all other TSB plants is outstanding. (*Copy exactly*, developed as strategy at Intel, is now taught in universities and practiced in various industries.)
- *Line versatility*: Some (or most) lines have versatility to produce a range of models other than those normally assigned to it.

VI. Opportunities for Improvement (mostly discussed during presentations)

- *This section:* My post-visit report to my hosts at Takata Seat Belts included many pages of OFIs and recommendations that relate to the content of sections II through V of this chapter. To include them here would require more space than is fitting for this book. Instead, I am just including a few highlights from that report. The missing materials are on topics that have been fully discussed in other chapters of this book, which is all the more reason not to say much about them here. Rather, I am just summarizing, in Sidebar 2, a topical list of what they concern.

SIDEBAR 2   TOPICAL SUMMARY OF MATTERS COVERED EXTENSIVELY IN THE FULL REPORT TO TSB

Line shapes: U vs. straight

Less than 10-second cycle: intolerable for the production associate

Tandem operation of 2 machines—electrically linked to keep hands safe

Operators fetching nearby materials; material handlers more distant ones

Kitting, non-value-adding but okay if too many P/Ns or long travel distances

Raw + WIP = RIP

IE's standard times good for rough line balancing; cell teams doing fine-tuning

Quick changeovers—part of every operator's job

Graphs on the floor tracking quick changeover, flow distance, etc.—but keep second-order metrics (productivity, etc.) off the floor and in "war rooms"

Omit variance reporting, even standard costs

Off-line buffer stock

- *Fail-safing devices (aka, pokayoke):*
  - ✓ The large number and elegance of fail-safing devices on assembly lines is outstanding.
  - ✓ But could there be *too many* fail-safes at TSB (they are expensive, tend to break up teams, reduce flexibility to move and change line configurations, may add a bit of extra flow time, and perhaps send a negative signal that assemblers are unable to do the job right)? Still, given the safety required of seat belts, maybe "excess" fail-safes is correct.
- *Production-line configuration:*
  - ✓ *Takt times:*
    - Subassembly lines have station cycle times of about four, five, or six seconds, incorrectly called takt time at TSB. Takt time is the customer demand rate, which at TSB *could* be the final assembly rate, which for a typical TSB product is 26 seconds.
    - The *ideal*, then, is for all subassembly lines to match that 26 seconds by: 1. Slowing the machines. 2. Replacing too-fast with slower or speed-adjustable machines. 3. Combine jobs for each assembler, such that work content is closer to 26 seconds (not four, five, six seconds), or other means.
    - Usually it is less costly to design/build slow machines than fast ones; also, slower machines typically yield better quality, require less maintenance, and may be dedicated rather than dependent on changeovers.

- *Job design*: A nine-hour shift, less 30 minutes for breaks, is 30,600 seconds; that divided by a six-second station cycle time (assembler work content) is an intolerable 5,100 repetitions per shift. Correction: Combine jobs so each assembler can take half, one, or two steps per cycle in performing adjacent tasks. In the interim, set minimum job-rotation policies, e.g., rotate jobs at least every three hours.
  - ✓ Reduced productivity is not likely, because each assembler will have fewer non-value-adding hand-offs from/to adjacent assembler. Also, data show that assemblers who rotate frequently among a few jobs generally make fewer mistakes with fewer accidents, because variety requires higher levels of attention.
  - ✓ Both subassembly and final assembly should (ideally) produce seat belts at the 26-second rate. In this, sub lines (cells) may merge physically to points of use on the final line. Or may be somewhat physically separated, with some buffer inventory and delivery by kanban.
- *Follow-on letter*: Lastly are the following excerpts from my follow-on thank-you letter of March 16, 2004:

Seth and Sergio,

My usual practice is to get my notes and impressions into a computer file. I learn things just from going over the handwritten notes and adding what I didn't get written down. For whatever it may be worth to you, I am attaching the file called "Takata." Also attached is a photo from another company (Plamex), which is referred to among the notes.

My file is about three times longer than what is usual for me. I guess it is because TSB turned out to be such a very good case for assessing on the basis of what are global best practices. The overall excellence in what you do stands out. In addition, you have characterized, standardized, and documented processes so well that it was all the easier for me to do the assessment. Thus, my list of "opportunities for improvement" is extensive. That does not mean you have an exceptional slate of weaknesses; rather that your high state of visibility makes it easier to see what's strong or needs work.

I do not dwell at length on your strengths; not much sense in devoting a lot of space to polishing the apple. Just as in quality control, what is most valuable is to find the defects (actually, opportunities) and possible root causes.

Enough said. Thanks again. I'll be very interested in your future progress and continuing success.

Sincerely,   Richard J. Schonberger

- Note: Seth Jantzen and I communicated further by emails in April and then later in August 2004.

CHAPTER III-86. SCHWEITZER ENGINEERING LABORATORIES (SEL), PULLMAN, WA, 2003

This fairly long and detailed caselet shows SEL to be an outstanding example of managing through best practices in flow manufacturing. Part II, on the multistep production processes, is lengthy but contains examples of those best practices.	*High-Interest Topics:* • **High-flex, easy-move equipment—accommodating continuous improvement** • **Synchronizing processes and avoiding cross-flows amid complex processes** • **Sitting and/or standing jobs—a topic taken up in three places in the caselet**

SEL's Comprehensive Pursuit of Excellence: Observations from Quick Plant Visit and Short Meeting with SEL Managers/Engineers, Feb. 12, 2007

Plus one-hour Schonberger presentation to SEL suppliers (along with informative other sessions of SEL's Supplier Day), Feb. 13, 2007

I. General Information

- *SEL beginnings and contacts*:
  - ✓ SEL began in President Edmund O. Schweitzer's (Ph.D.) basement in 1982. First sale was to Otter Tail Power Co. in 1984.
  - ✓ In 1989, Ron Schwartz, senior VP, gave Schonberger's 1986 book, *World Class Manufacturing*, to Schweitzer, who read it over a holiday weekend, got copies, told company people to get it read within a week, and then immediately start implementing.
  - ✓ Other contacts: Susan Fagan, director of public affairs; Kevin Fritch, VP operations; Mike Sabo, test manager; Kelly Powell, mfg. systems analysis: Beatriz Schweitzer, director of business development; Eddie Schweitzer, mechanical engineer; Tammy Baldwin, university-relations coordinator.

- *Products*:
  - ✓ General – Devices for protection, monitoring, control, automation, and metering of electric power systems.
  - ✓ Specific – Transmission-line protection, secure communications, distribution protection, substation protection (transformers, buses, breakers, capacitors), generator and motor protection, revenue and power-quality metering, protective relays for industrial power motors, generators, transformers, feeders, integration and automation, SEL rugged computing products, precise timing devices, fiber-optic communications, SEL software solutions; software downloads, testing, SEL accessories (arc suppressors, linear power supplies, displays, UPS selector switches, panel-mount hardware, bezels, dust covers, cables, . . .)
  - ✓ A relay may cost in the range of $800 to $10,000.
- *Customers*:
  - ✓ Main: electric power and industrial companies.
  - ✓ Newer: petrochemicals, mining, pharmaceutical, government services division (in a separate building).
- *Physical plant*:
  - ✓ An inconvenient plant gave way in 1999 to a new 55,000-sq. ft. building in Pullman Industrial Park. It expanded to about 100,000 sq. ft. in 2001, and again to about 200K sf later. A nearby graveled pad is at the ready for another 45,000 expansion. 2006 brought forth a new 90,000-sq. ft. office building, and a new 18,000-sq. ft. Events Center, used by SEL 50–60 days a year and otherwise available for public uses.
  - ✓ SEL has a presence in about seven other buildings on 40 acres of an industrial park it owns.
- *Employment*:
  - ✓ In 2007 SEL had about 1,400 employees worldwide, 1,000 in Pullman. In 1999 employment was only about 350.
  - ✓ Now 350–370 employees are in the manufacturing building; 110 in the new office building; others among remaining buildings.
- *Capabilities to serve*:
  - ✓ 25 regional SEL tech service centers are in the U.S.; 17 in 9 other countries.
  - ✓ Products are sold in more than 90 countries.
  - ✓ The only non-U.S. plant is in Monterrey, México, opened in 2002 to serve the México market.

- *Awards/recognition*:
  - ✓ Many patents, many meritorious service recognitions from customer companies.
  - ✓ Newton-Evans Research rates SEL no. 1 in many categories, similar rating in prior-year surveys.
- *Main competitors*: Siemens (Germany), G.E., ABB (Swiss/Sweden), Arriva (Canada). Ametek (a lesser competitor); a Korean company. Minimal direct competition with Japanese makers (e.g., Mitsubishi Electric, Toshiba, Yokogawa Electric).
- *Suppliers, purchasing*:
  - ✓ Buyers, by commodity, purchase 3,000–4,000 part numbers—to forecast—from about 200 suppliers.
  - ✓ Primary purchases include raw boards, sheet metal, some plastic parts (no other major contract manufacturers). A Spokane supplier makes daily deliveries of sheet-metal boxes. Some materials are in bond at suppliers.
- *Production characteristics*:
  - ✓ Low-volume, high-mix production, with considerable automation (of production, not material handling), and high vertical integration, seen as helping to master best, newest technology.
  - ✓ Customer lead times are three weeks, manufacturing flow time 14–15 days.
  - ✓ Main work flow is: SMT assembly → Electronic assembly → Test → Final assembly → Mechanical assembly → Pack → Ship.
  - ✓ Other production: Harness and recloser assembly. Cable assembly. Accessories.
  - ✓ Newer ventures: Outfitting a whole "house" (e.g., a shipping container) with relays, monitors, etc., and drop it with a crane inside the fenced area of a substation, taking two weeks rather than the usual two months of installing/testing.
- *Training*:
  - ✓ SEL University trains customer technicians, etc., in advanced uses of SEL technology, plus more general topics relevant to power systems.
  - ✓ Training includes skills certification for production associates; also emphasis on closed-loop process improvement: find mishap, find why.

- *Management & engineering*:
  - ✓ Supervisory meetings are every morning, followed by 9:00 a.m. professional/manager meetings.
  - ✓ IMI teams *i*nvestigate, *m*easure, and *i*mprove.
  - ✓ Integrated product development has five MEs, five ME techs, and three manufacturing system analysts spending 90% of their time on new product introduction, yielding about 20 new products yearly.
- *Quality*:
  - ✓ About 30 DPM (defects per million). Some purchased parts are 100% inspected.
  - ✓ Quality glitches are recorded and grouped by design, process, and material defects.

II. Plant Tour

- *Main production*: Any product may be scheduled on any of three long, multistage production lines. A fourth line, forthcoming, will open the door to one or more dedicated or semi-dedicated lines.
- *Printed circuit boards*: PCBs are of several sizes (from, say, 15 inch by 7 inch to 5 inch by 5 inch) and quite complex. The first PCB line occupies about 40,000 sq. ft. of the building, the characteristics of which are summarized in Sidebar 1:
- *Mechanical assembly*: Occupies 40,000 sq. ft. in a building add-on. Here, the PC board goes into a sheet-metal box, etc.:

SIDEBAR 1   MAKEUP AND OPERATION OF PCB LINE

Auto-insert: Lots of carts pre-stocked with reels of components linked to next process via space-limit kanban

Slide lines: Seated PC board assembler with 1.5-minute cycles, that cycle maintained thru next processes—except doubled to 3 minutes in final assembly.

Displays: Plentiful, showing Paretos and CRTs for traceback recording

Further: Wave-solder, progressive tests, fixturing, 2-stage wash/coat/ UV cure; ending with 20 wheeled carts, each with 24 boards, lined up for mechanical assy.

- ✓ On a U-shaped conveyor line of about 17 stations, production steps depend on size/complexity of the relay ordered, which may have one to seven boards. Assemblers may sit or stand!
- ✓ At an early stage, kitted parts, prepared on large trays, are placed on the conveyor.
- ✓ A feeder department delivers internal cables via a cable kanban board.
- ✓ Environmental test—profile -40 to +85 degrees C without humidity; noisy from compressors, has its own room.
- ✓ In final functional test, 29 product-specific test stations, on wheels, take 5 to 50 minutes test time, some relays requiring a special test. CRT displays mounted on high show the status of testing in red or green colors.

- *Final assembly*: Each main flow line has three sub lines: Install cover, overlays, harnesses, serial number, test report, manuals (60% of outgoing orders still have paper manuals). Each sub-line is 6 stations, assemblers working standing up. CRT's show specs/metrics.
- *Packaging*: Protective wrap (Lantech wrap equipment), then foam.
- *Out-of-box audit*: Open the box, withdraw, and then 20% check against the BOM (bill of materials).
- *Other manufacturing/functions seen on tour*:
  - ✓ Relay area: 3,000–4,000 relays in their own containers for mounting high on a power pole (not in a fenced substation area).
  - ✓ Auto-cut, strip (in wiring/cables).
  - ✓ Accessories.
  - ✓ Fiber-optic cable.
  - ✓ A product "hospital": 18 engineers upgrade, repair, do warranty work—all at no charge to the customer, with fast (72–hour) turnaround (warranties are infinitely long). Engineers try to keep deficient boards for root-cause analysis.
  - ✓ Printing/multi-media: This is a large facility, printing 2 million copies per month.
- *Plant layout*: The layout is roughly as shown in a much out-of-scale (some functions/processes missing) Figure 86.1 diagram. It shows how the three lines move production forward (upward arrows) from SMT to electronic, then mechanical assembly and test—to final assembly—with accessories, cable assembly, harness and recloser assembly as feeder processes emergent from left side.

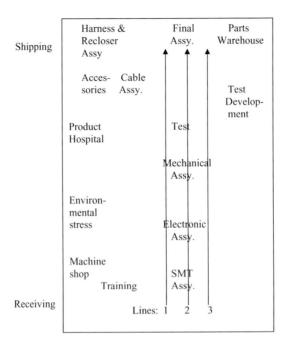

FIGURE 86.1
Schweitzer engineering labs, main factory.

III. General Comments

- *Flows*: Production along each of the three lines is impressive. Except for batching in SMT, it looks to be one-piece flow. Maintaining 1.5-minute station cycle time is a fine feat of synchronization.
- *Responsibility chain*: The long, long responsibility chains make it easy to backtrack to sources of a problem. This is a standout rarity, in that the majority of plants making complex products have criss-crossing flows so obtuse as to defy effective traceback, no matter how much flow data is in the computer.
- *Movability*: Nearly all equipment, benches, flow lines, and intermediate storage racks are easily moved—much of it being on wheels. Utilities may be (don't know) uniformly available overhead through the building—such flexibility being accommodating to process improvements, growth, and changes to the product line and technology.
- *In-house production*: The high degree of vertical integration is surprising.

✓ But the simple flow patterns act as a positive offset to concerns about in-house electronic assembly being too costly.

✓ Moreover, SEL's major competitive advantage—quick response/short customer lead times—is owed in large part to tightly linked production lines, which could be compromised if components were outsourced.

- *Job classifications*: Halved but still too many.

    ✓ But a nice offset is an 11-step career ladder for the work force.

    ✓ Progress is (should be) based on three factors: what the company needs, what the employee wants to do, and how worthy the employee is of having the company invest in necessary training and development.

- *TPM*: SEL's focus is on preventive/predictive maintenance, in which operators have maintenance duties. Maintenance is only 6 people, indicating considerable reliance on operator involvement.

- *"Manufacturing Virtual Tour"*: This refers to an SEL CD shown during the sessions:

    ✓ Employee-owners (employees have partial ownership in SEL) collect data to identify, measure, and improve processes. Use of histograms, white boards, quality records, yield charts—to track, daily, what's happening in the processes.

    ✓ Training teams recertify operators annually.

    ✓ SEL dedicates to continuous, rapid improvement of quality, lead time, value, and flexibility—all highly customer-oriented performance indicators.

IV. Likely Opportunities for Improvement (OFI)

- *OFIs*: Some of the following were suggested by SEL people:
- *White boards*: Need more white boards for the work force to record things that go wrong and need attention, and suggested changes/fixes (called for by Ed Schweitzer in his Supplier Day address).
- *Frustrations*: Each associate should record every frustration on white boards. (Calling it "frustration" [word choice makes a difference] instead of problem/mishap/error gets at what people really care about, which at the same time usually are main problems/mishaps/errors). This could be a phased-in pilot test for one well-chosen work group and group manager/supervisor.

- *Multifunction employees*: Display on large versatility matrices.
- *Quick setup*: Where setup/changeover is an important success factor (takes a lot of time, is costly, an obstacle to one-piece flow), time every setup and plot on a nearby large trend chart, with daily/weekly/monthly averages.
- *Shop-floor performance metrics*. Avoid metrics that are mostly beyond "zones of influence" of the work force. Management-by-data (white-board stuff) is powerful; management-by-management-metrics is weak.
- *Sit-down work*. People doing hand-loading on the slide lines work sitting down—a bad thing for long hours day after day.
  - ✓ If they don't rotate to other, non-slide-line jobs every couple of hours, they should.
  - ✓ Alternative: Elevate the slide lines for stand-up hand-insert. (This is not microscope work where people *must* sit). Problems of people of varying heights can be addressed in various ways.
- *Work-force training*: Increase training in quick setup, kanban, cells, other aspects of JIT/lean, conveying to employees that the purpose is quick response to the *customer*, thus to beat/stay ahead of the *competition*.
- *Synchronizing/balancing the flow*: Double the number of production lines/cells in mechanical assembly (could be practical and beneficial in electrical assembly as well), so that each associate/work station has twice as much work content. Main effect: each of the three SMT lines would end up focused on and feeding its own pair of mechanical assembly lines/cells.
- *Future expansion*: The present main building is a bit larger than 200,000 sq. ft. For further growth, begin migrating production of relatively self-contained product families to their own building—to achieve focus, isolate costs and performance, and gain social cohesion.
- *Standardization*. As Ed stated in his address, 500,000 combinations are in the model-options table but are sold to only 500 customers, indicating a great opportunity to trim, consolidate, and standardize.
  - ✓ In doing so, customers could be offered popular, higher-volume options at an attractive price with short lead time; other options at a higher price with longer lead times.
  - ✓ This tells the customer we'll still make whatever you want, but this is a sensible way to do so.

- *Inventory turnover*:
  - ✓ Present turnover, about 5.1, seems low. The fairly tight, bucket-brigade-like flow of production along the three production lines through the length of building suggests that WIP is a minor part of total inventory (I did not visit the parts warehouse). Inventory turns should be computed for all inventory, then again after subtracting lifetime/last-time buys of parts for discontinued models. The subtracted number is the relevant one.
  - ✓ Raw-material turnover is likely the main culprit. Ed's questions to the audience, asking for comparisons with ordering from SEL vs. other customers, is indicative.
    - ■ This suggests an intensive effort to collaborate with suppliers, a la Dell and Wal-Mart.
    - ■ Cost of the inventory itself is not the main concern. The long delay between when the supplier makes it and SEL uses it is a large can of worms.
- *Collaboration*: Likely major issues/opportunities with suppliers lie in the following: (1) SEL closely sharing its shipping information and forecasting intelligence (the *real* demand) with suppliers. (2) Jointly attacking proliferation of parts. (3) Logistics. (4) Metrics (e.g., joint inventory). (5) Plans for promotions, price changes, new sales channels, technology changes.

CHAPTER III-87. MILLIKEN INDUSTRIALS, WIGAN, U.K., 2002

This caselet, about Milliken's Wigan, U.K., plant is overly brief—mostly plant-specific information, with minimal plus and minus observations. Section II diverts from the Wigan situation and instead offers updated information—from the Wigan people—on Milliken Co. itself.

High-Interest Topics:
- **New-hire engineers spend two weeks running machines**
- **Milliken has long avoided chasing the latest management fads, preferring its own, stable set**

Milliken's European Outreach: Observations from P.M. Plant Visit, Oct. 24, 2002

In connection with a morning presentation at the Manufacturing Institute, Manchester

I. General Information

- *Plant visit*:
  - ✓ Following my morning presentation at Northwest Manufacturing Summit, Manufacturing Institute, Manchester, U.K., I was free to visit Millikan-Wigan, west of Manchester.
  - ✓ The attraction was related to my having come to know Milliken-the-company through several Milliken-U.S. events in the late 1980s and early 1990s. Having mostly lost contact with Milliken, this visit offered an opportunity to discuss the company with Wigan hosts—and to get somewhat of a detached view.
  - ✓ Other fine Milliken examples are not included in this book, because I've already written a lot about them in some of my earlier books.
- *Tour hosts*: Nick Bailey, plant leader; Dylan Carter, production manager; Stuart McGlasson, technology manager.

II. Update on Milliken & Co.

- *Businesses*: Milliken has about 80 plants globally, including two chemical plants. Textiles, including carpets and carpet tiles, are Milliken's primary business.
- *Carpets/carpet tiles*: Times have been tough for traditional high-end customers, so Milliken has been moving downward somewhat into lower-cost carpet.
- *Sharing*: Sharing rallies—with key customers and suppliers—are still held, every two months, but so far only in the U.S.
- *Quality meetings*: Quarterly global quality meetings are still held in Spartanburg, SC.
- *Pursuit of excellence*: The Milliken "pursuit of excellence" program has its yearly U.S. meeting at Callaway Gardens, and its Europe meeting in Manchester or elsewhere. The program's seven aims are quality, cost, delivery (lead time/on time), innovation, environment, safety, and morale.
- *PPI*: The bulk of engineering resources are in "product and process improvement" (PPI); 900 of company management people are in PPI.
- *Environmental goal*: Zero landfill by Christmas—already achieved in the U.S.

- *Programitis*: Milliken has rejected going from one management program to the next.
  - ✓ Instead, the best of each hot, new or buzzed-up initiative (one being supply-chain management) are extracted and rolled into the Milliken Performance System (MPS).
  - ✓ TPM (total productive maintenance), added about seven years ago, has become a strong initiative of Roger Milliken: 30 or 40 Milliken plants have won a JITPM award.
  - ✓ Milliken has not gone for six sigma; rather has stayed the course with SPC; all engineers are required to take an SPC course.
  - ✓ The term "lean" has not been adopted; rather Milliken stays with JIT.
- *PVC*: Milliken is getting out of PVC as the main carpet backing material, because it has a bad press in the U.S. (Ironically, PVC is actually favored in some parts of Europe.) Milliken wants to be able to say "we don't make PVC tiles."
- *Plant sizes*: Most plants are rather small (200 employees), but the LaGrange, GA, plant (destroyed by fire a few years ago) is huge—and very advanced.

III. General—Wigan Plant

- *Wigan*: This facility, acquired from Tupperware and opened as Milliken Industrials in 1984, includes an office building and a separate plant with a design center just inside the main door. It lacks a polyurethane floor, is not especially clean and well lit, but has high ceilings—needed since much equipment is huge with up-and-down rollers for threading the carpet.
  - ✓ Other U.K. plants are Berry, north of Manchester (reinforcing rubber goods, airbag fabric, door mats); and Bristol (woolens—for pool table tops).
  - ✓ Milliken has been expanding in Europe and elsewhere, with plants in Ghent, Belgium; France (cord for tires); and Spain/Portugal/Germany/Brazil (automotive).
- *Product line*:
  - ✓ Wigan produces carpet tiles and some roll carpets mainly for offices (banks, insurance companies). Since most such offices have raised floors—not amenable to roll carpets—they favor carpet tiles. Wigan is just getting into hotels, retail, airports, etc.

✓ The basic material is polypropylene, coming mostly from Milliken Chemical plants. Two main carpet tile (usually 18 inches square) product lines are:

- Hard-backed tiles (formerly/traditionally backed with PVC) in both bonded hardback and tufted hardback (cheaper, often preferred by customer).
- Cushion-backed tiles (begun in the U.S. four to five years ago, and taking off) in both bonded and tufted. Milliken is the only carpet company offering cushioned as standard.
- Material is mainly imported from the U.S., which is expensive, so nine weeks ago Wigan started making it.

- *Employment*:
  ✓ The plant has 120 non-union production associates, 50 sales/marketing, 30–40 other management associates.
  ✓ Associates are in three pay grades, one job description. Job rotation, to maintain skill levels, is left up to the associates as to how often; it appears to be monthly or less often, except within an employee's own small group.
  ✓ All new-hire engineers spend two weeks running machines.

- *Operations*:
  ✓ Colored yarn has a four-week order lead time, so the plant is going more toward importing white yarn, then coloring it, and doing the pattern ordered by customer after order booking.
    - Print-to-order promise time is ten days.
    - 10 of 160 colors are on a ten-day service promise; the rest are ordered. The plant runs two sets of 12 colors every week.
    - Most competitors (Shaw Industries; and Interface, a LaGrange, GA, competitor) use colored yarn, and so are less responsive.
  ✓ Cushion-backed tiles are run the first of the week, hard-backed in the last part—because cushion-backed require high heat, and the oven requires a 12-hour cool-down before hard-backed can be run.

- *Main equipment*: Two warping machines—creel to beam. The 160 ends have to be inserted by hand. Coloring is done on two 12-color presses—1,000 jets for each of the 16 colors. Four bonding machines.

IV. Observations

- *People gap*: There seems to be a large gap between management associates and production associates.
- *Ugly floor*: Needs to be polyurethaned.
- *Missing*: No 5S, no large signboards in "alcoves of excellence" in this plant (unlike "all" Milliken-U.S. plants, which are showcases of visuality).
- *Maintenance responsibilities*: Not much maintenance by production associates (ala TPM), except in regard to cleaning.
- *Benchmarking*: Nick says they don't do much out-of-company benchmarking—which usually is a large fault; but, it might be said, who could they benchmark that does things better than Milliken?

_____

CHAPTER III-88. LENOVO, SHANGHAI AREA, CHINA, 2008

This caselet describes production of personal computers at Lenovo—whose PCs may be or are excellent—but whose manufacturing management is largely devoid of the kinds of best practices we've come to expect of good companies—in China or elsewhere.

High-Interest Topics:
- **Each part is scanned many times—to ensure it is correct—and for data analysis**
- **Issue: Did the Lenovo management team really believe they were using cells and "best practices"?**

Oddities Observed During a Brief Group Tour of Lenovo, April 16, 2008

In connection with a Schonberger two-day WCM Workshop hosted by MenaMaxon

I. Basic Information

- *Arrangements*: MenaMaxon, a Shanghai-based consultancy, sponsored my two-day WCM workshop in Shanghai, followed by one day of my leading a panel, and then, with workshop participants, traveling to Lenovo for a plant tour and discussion.

- *Lenovo Co.*: The company has produced desktop computers since 1990, and later laptop personal computers—both commercial and consumer.
  - ✓ In 2005 Lenovo acquired IBM's Personal Computing Division to form the world's largest PC manufacturing business.
  - ✓ Three Shanghai area plants (26,000, 21,000, and 15,000 square meters, respectively) serve China and Asia-Pacific markets; also Europe and elsewhere—aiming at global expansion.
- *New plant*: This 15,000 sq. m. plant, built for $6m between May and September 2007, is located a modest distance westerly from Shanghai. It is the model plant for Lenovo.
  - ✓ The plant has nine production lines: a 1st-floor automated line for mass production (did not see); four 3rd-floor laptop lines (we saw maybe three); two 2nd-floor desktop lines; and one rework line (did not see).
  - ✓ Plant capacity, employing 1,800 people, is 6,000,000 units per year.
- *Production milestone*: Lenovo hit a milestone on Feb. 28, 2007: 100 million PCs produced.
- *Tour hosts*: Jack Zhu, plant manager; George Zhong (former boss of Jack Zhu); and three tour leaders: Steven, Edisen, and Mina (in charge of lean six sigma).

II. Pre-Tour Orientation

- *Introduction*: We viewed a film about Lenovo, and Mr. Zhu talked about the plant's origin, statistics, and organization (calling it a "lean six sigma organization" displayed as a matrix).
- *Controls*: An MAS system uses extensive bar-coding for control and traceback. Controls also include some 200 test procedures (including temperature/humidity/aging tests for every product; and a QA security/simulation test)—with purchased materials on vendor-managed inventory (VMI).
- *Personnel development*: All employees get a personalized develop-ment plan.
- *Plans and metrics*: Yearly value-stream plan; and quarterly "quality evaluation statistics" displayed on a spider chart with many rating factors around the chart's circumference, e.g., continuous flow, takt time, pull, line-stop, problem-solving, cell line, and about 15 more.
- *Product design*: Includes design for X, design for test.

III. Plant/Process Layout

- *Building configuration*: Process flow in the L-shaped building is: incoming handling → assembly → test → packing → finished goods handling. Owing to vendor-managed inventory, a modest amount of customers' finished goods is maintained in an FGI warehouse.
- *First floor*: Figure 88.1 is a rough layout of the building's first floor, about half of which is for production, including incoming raw materials and outgoing finished goods; and the other half for a large cafeteria and offices.

IV. Details

- *Third floor overview*:
  - ✓ This floor has three conventional assembly lines, each with 70, 80, and 90 people, which subdivide into three segments: (1) Many assemblers occupy 50–60% of the line's length. (2) Relatively few test people are situated at four long two-deck plug-in test stations. (3) A small number of packers are in a short pack line at end of test.
  - ✓ The schedule is an irregular mix of configurations, sequenced by customer priority.

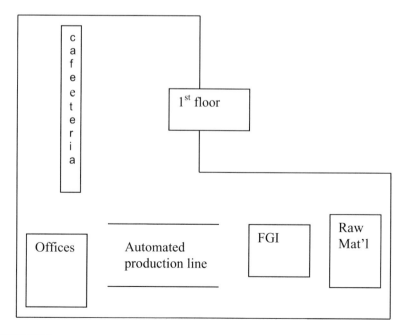

FIGURE 88.1
Lenovo plant, first floor configuration.

- ✓ Elevators at the start and end of the line bring PC bodies on two-foot-square carriers, along with main and small parts that arrive in divided, oblong, flattish boxes. Elevators take completed, boxed PCs down to the warehouse.
- ✓ Assemblers hand-scan many times for each installed part, and also scan the work order by lifting it to a mounted scanner—lots of wasted motion compared with the possibility of fixed scanners that scan as parts pass by.
- ✓ An over/under conveyor traverses the initial assembly segment, with carrier kits returned by the under-conveyor segment.
- ✓ Many stations draw parts from kits, while also getting parts from line-side flow racks (no information on how flow racks get replenished).
- ✓ Industrial engineers time everything, setting new "takt times" and rebalancing the lines weekly.
- *First line segment*: Flows are one-to-one, with station cycle times of 15 seconds, in which stand-up assemblers take maybe one step every 1.5 or 2 seconds.
- *Second line segment*:
  - ✓ The line divides and bulges out to allow for 30-second cycles on each side of the line with a feeder conveyor shoving PC carriers to whichever side first completes a unit and has space for another; about two or three carriers are buffers.
  - ✓ These assemblers look to be fairly experienced and skilled, and probably are somewhat better-paid than those on the first segment: They do about twice as many operations in their 30 second cycle—removing a panel, inserting a component or two, screwing them in place, snapping the panel back in, etc., all with several removals of gummed backing of bar-coded stickers, then quickly applying the stickers and scanning their numbers.
  - ✓ At a few stations down the line, jobs are of around 90 seconds.
- *Test segment*: After run-in tests, a small number of males install test disks for operational tests.
- *Visuals*:
  - ✓ All lines have stack lights, but most are not in use.
  - ✓ Some or all lines have an electronic display above the line with two stats: "Switch-off time" and "Line-stop time"—but none were turned on and in use.

✓ Other visual displays: a daily output record; amount of product sent to storage (goal vs. actual for days of month and total); and "Operator work life and information kanban" (here kanban being used in a generic, visual information sense).

- *Second floor*:
  ✓ On line 1, desktop PCs are produced, all with a single configuration (at least for a run of a certain lot?) on a three-minute cycle.
  ✓ Visuals display 5S; eight deadly wastes (8th is waste of ideas); lots of KPIs showing actual versus goal for output; and others.
- *Second & third floor*:
  ✓ At every line is a flip-chart-sized display on which every employee's photo-ID card is mounted, and directly adjacent is that employee's latest-shift errors made and output efficiency (maybe other factors as well, such as attendance, lateness).
  ✓ The performance chart is a schematic of a bunch of grapes, with some of large grapes colored in—which stands for a certain number/certain type of error or efficiency level.

V. Wrap-up Back in Conference Room

- Mr. Tzu answered questions (no time for previously planned presentations by me and another guy); he said:
  ✓ They are very proud of their engineers' ability to design assembly lines, fixtures, etc.
  ✓ Lenovo (this plant?) beats all other PC-makers (including Taiwan) in cost, efficiency, etc.
  ✓ Labor cost is 30-40% of total cost—about the same as competitors.
  ✓ There is very little use of TPM, given that operators have regular duties, and since equipment is relatively simple (true), but they do have some cleaning responsibilities.
- Quality-management team(s) find resources (engineers, etc.) to support ongoing six-sigma projects.
- Management does regular tours of all projects—praising, asking questions, providing support/criticism, and sometimes canceling a project.
- There is a suggestion program but very few suggestions (I think I heard this).

VI. Critical Observations and Assessments

- *Introduction*: Our tour group's surprises and disappointments.
  - ✓ My tour group and I had high expectations—retained through Mr. Zhu's opening presentation. But those were blown as we observed Lenovo's practices on the production floors.
  - ✓ I expected that in acquiring IBM's very "world-class" PC business, Lenovo would have insisted on IBM's help in adopting the same practices. Based on the tour, that did not happen.
- *PC design*: The PCs here are not designed for simple snap-together assembly (which IBM was noted for); they require a lot of screws. Also, they are not designed for quick modular assembly; they have many loose parts and components to individually install.
- *Employees*: Told to me by others on the tour: Employee turnover is 30% per year; training time is only 1 week; they get only a lunch break, no tea/coffee break; if a need to go to rest room, the line supervisor fills in.
- *Cells?* They call the 2nd and 3rd-floor lines "cells," but they are conventional, very long assembly lines.
- *Pace*: Very fast (judging by my own industrial-engineering perceptions)—maybe 100% of normal in early segments but 110, 120, and probably 130 for a couple of guys I watched.
- *Ergonomics*:
  - ✓ Jobs have to be extremely tiring. No rubber floor mats. Intolerable 15-second cycles—amounting to some 2,000 repeats per shift.
  - ✓ No walking, everyone stays at a single station, with leg movements limited to shuffling a bit from one foot to another.
  - ✓ No allowance for personal height (and quite a few on the line are tall); just one conveyor/work-station height.
  - ✓ No job rotation. However, assembly jobs do have numerous hand-arm motions/operations per cycle.
- *Visual management*:
  - ✓ No versatility charts (because no job rotation).
  - ✓ No photos of operators on improvement teams.
  - ✓ No Pareto, fishbone, or check sheets on display.
  - ✓ No media for employees to record ideas, frustrations, mishaps (except there may be a paper on which people record missing parts, etc.)—and no time for it.
  - ✓ Nothing on display of direct concern to work-force members, except aversive personal performance data.

- *Engagement*: Apparently, close to zero employee engagement.
- *Primary lean/JIT/TPS methodologies*: There is talk about lean six sigma, cells, etc.; but manifestations are not in evidence.
  - ✓ Most beneficial are VMI, bar-coding for quality/traceback, electronic kanban of parts flow, and scheduling to customer priority and timing.
  - ✓ Otherwise, in IE terms, this plant and its support seem dated (with slight exaggeration) almost to the early Ford assembly-line era.
  - ✓ Six-sigma projects appear to be traditional IE projects, mainly geared to timing jobs, balancing lines, fixturing, parts containers, conveyances.
- *Need for PC redesign*: Redesign of the PCs could open up options for jobs with fewer operations, easier to do, less waste of motion, real cells, job rotation, etc.; also allow considerable shrinkage in line length with subassembly modules stemming off main lines/cells.
- *Human accommodations*: Much could be done to improve the present lines: rubber mats, job rotation, maybe a lower-height line or line segment for shorter people.
- *Need for more lines*: The plant would greatly benefit with more lines of fewer people, better balance, more one-to-one flows, and each line dedicated to its own family of PC.
- *Assemblers per line/cell—comparison*: Regarding PC/server assembly configurations, I've seen autonomous assembly at Nokia (back when they produced PCs), two-person cells at Sun Microsystems (servers), six to seven person cells at Dell, 12-person at IBM Raleigh, 30 at HP Silicon Valley—and now 80–90 at Lenovo.

CHAPTER III-89. NINTENDO DISTRIBUTION CENTER, NORTH BEND, WA, 2008

This Nintendo DC includes a lot of manual, and some automated, assembly and packaging. Elsewhere in its building are the usual DC processes involved in shipping. (Notes for this caselet, from the confusion of a group tour, are somewhat unclear and, in part, possibly wrong.)

High-Interest Topics:
- **Direct shipment to retail stores**
- **Frequent, scheduled job rotation plus *as-needed fatigue time* in a fast-paced operation**

Production Direct to Retail Stores: Observations Based on Brief Tour, Mar. 13, 2008
Sponsored by Kent Valley Chamber of Commerce

I. Basic Information

- *The facility*
  - ✓ An assembly/packaging center with its own distribution center (DC) for Nintendo games (e.g., the Wii), with 500 active SKUs, opened September 1991: 380,000 sq. ft.; 126 acres, $60 million in sales.
  - ✓ Basic mission is direct-to-store order fulfillment, *bypassing downstream DCs*, which cuts transit time and handling costs.
  - ✓ The U.S. plan is to deliver to over 11,300 U.S. stores weekly, ordered in single units by the store.
  - ✓ Lag time from product launch to 1st sales is about six weeks. The life cycle of a typical product is five years.
- *Top 5 customers*:
  - ✓ GameStop, Wal-Mart, Target, ToysRUs, Best Buy.
  - ✓ Each store orders through its home company.
  - ✓ Nintendo entered the Canada market six to seven years ago—now delivering direct to 2,300 stores weekly.
- *Employees*:
  - ✓ 70%–80% are 15-year-or-so employees, associates, managers.
  - ✓ The facility uses lots of temps: When the planned need is for 30 people, bring in 45 just in case.
- *Returns*: North Bend does not accept returns (maybe Nintendo Redmond, WA, does).
- *Inventory performance*: 20 turns for the distribution side; 60 turns for Wii assembly.
- *Tour leaders*: Shawn Pellitier; Rick Leliu; Mark Winstead, supply-chain service.

II. Details

- *Assembly*: Manual pack lines produce five days a week, with weekends usable for surges. It's been a banner year: 40m games packaged.
  - ✓ One assembly area has Wii Line 1, Wii Line 2; Clamshell Line 1 and Line 2; and DS Line 1 and Line 2 (DS, like the Wii, is a hand-held gaming console).

- ✓ Packing employs a pull system, with scans, in FIFO (first in, first out) order.
- ✓ Buffer conveyors are 50–60 feet long, including an accumulator unit, the purpose being to keep downstream automation running when upstream production is stopped, which happens many times per day, and is displayed by stack lights each time.
- ✓ In Game Pak assembly, an in-house replenishment cycle from Asia has been reduced by 12 weeks.
- ✓ Wii assembly has been 20 hours a day in the past 18 months, producing 40,000 units per line per ship, five NOAS (notices of assessment?).
- ✓ On breaks for lunch, sometimes managers will come out of their offices to keep the lines running.
- ✓ Everything of importance is stored as both video and data, backed up on tape in a fireproof safe; video and data are separated, then merged when needed.
- *Ergonomics*: The pace is very fast—92 pieces per minute on the DS line. So:
  - ✓ Job rotation is required twice per shift.
  - ✓ More than that, a large sign over a pick area, in both English and Spanish, says: "If you are feeling soreness or fatigued, REQUEST TO ROTATE" (Pida cambiar de puesto).
- *Scheduling/shipping*: Each day, everything for Canada is picked for assembly first, thus to get it across the border or to an airport for a same-day flight to Canadian customers. Next, pick for shipments to the U.S. East Coast.
- *Incoming inventory*:
  - ✓ Inventories are bought from several suppliers (supplier selection that makes the most sense) in Japan and China, this ordering driven by months-out sales forecasts.
  - ✓ Stock-picking is full-case—and ergonomic with 26 lb. maximums.
  - ✓ Nintendo is just getting started with VMI (vendor-managed inventory) in the U.S., while it is the norm for their business with Nintendo Canada.
- *Quality*: 99.9%+ lot acceptance; QC problems are rare on the highly automated lines.
- *Distribution center (DC) technologies*:
  - ✓ Info systems include EDI, WMS, MES, barcodes, RFI scanning (but no RFI labels for outgoing, not even for Wal-Mart).

✓ 99% of customers are using EDI (electronic data interchange).

✓ Advance ship notices (ASN) employ the UCC128 label format.

✓ An IBM AS400 series is the principal computer, but with some 90% local programming on . . . user menus on their PCs, RF controller + terminals + menus. PLCs (programmable logic controllers) are employed for scans, belts, and start-stop controls; data liners.

✓ RF/WiFi devices are hand-held, truck mounted, and integrated or tethered.

- *Continuous improvement*: Employee suggestions include process upgrades on applications such as mixed-case batch picking; auto label applicators; walkie electric pallet jacks; slide shoe sorters; and ergonomic picking.

- *Performance metrics include*:

  ✓ Ship accuracy.

  ✓ Inventory accuracy—about 99.99995%.

  ✓ Units shipped per direct labor hour, currently 336 units per D.L. hour and 646,000 units per year per person.

  ✓ Total warehouse cost per unit shipped per month.

III. Impressions and Comments

- *Overall impressions*: Excellent facility, this judgment based primarily on its overriding concern for what its customers value the most, namely, quick, dependable direct shipments to retail stores and with very high product quality. Aside from that, Nintendo-North Bend could do better.

- *A few critical comments follow*:

  ✓ *Ergonomics issue—as one example*: I watched as two pickers, one a modest-sized woman, reach seemingly in some agony, across an inactive conveyor to lift from a flow rack an oblong box of 18–20 inches and maybe 26 lb., in order to set the box on an active conveyor.

  ✓ *Visual management*: I saw . . .

    ■ One 5S "Plan/Projects" display area, but the station was empty, inactive, no information displayed.

    ■ At a distance, one area with many graphs, etc., on display, but no others in active areas.

- In some areas, tape that marks zones on the floors (e.g., for safety or for denying space for excess inventory) but not rigorously used.

✓ *Lean/JIT methods*: I did not hear about or see signs of use of kanban.

✓ *Costs*: There seems to be an excessive concern over direct-labor costs—such concerns usually interfering with efforts to engage the work force, for example, in ways to smooth product flows and reduce root causes of problems (e.g., excess inventory/lead time elements).

✓ *Recording of process aggravations*: Operators should have ways to record aggravations/things gone wrong, likely causes.

CHAPTER III-90. AMERICAN SHEET METAL (ASM) AND AMERICAN INTEGRATION TECHNOLOGIES (AIT), CHANDLER, AZ, 2003

This caselet spans a wide distance between basic sheet-metal manufacturing and high-technology semiconductor processing equipment—and shows small companies ASM and AIT both doing very well.	**High-Interest Topics:** • **Drilling down to root causes & their resolution** • **Separate product-focused buildings** • **Toward a simplified alternative to heavy-handed computer-based flow management** • **Sales tuned to its capacity situation**

Odd Couple—Linking Common & Advanced Production:

Observations from Two-Hour Plant Visit, Mar. 18, 2003

I. General Information

- *American Sheet Metal*: ASM (not to be confused with dominant customer ASM International) began as a garage business in 1983 by brother-owners Gary and Brian Imdieke. Now two legal companies, AMS is a contract (make-to-print) manufacturer, and American Integration Technologies (AIT) is a design and make-to-order producer of complex equipment for the semiconductor industry.

- *Space*: Of 5 buildings totaling 75,000 sf, AMS occupies Buildings 1, 2, and 3, with recently leased Building 5 for warehousing and surge; and also extra capacity to show customers that, though small, AMS can take on larger orders. AIT is housed in a 20,000-sq. ft. building 4 across a street.
- *Capital and capacity*: With all land, buildings, and equipment fully paid for, except leased Building 5, the owners have a pay-as-you-go strategy for capacity and continue to invest in equipment even though the economy has been down.
- *Customer preferences*: The company's names are not in the phone book. The owners explain that they do not want to attract odd sheet-metal jobs; rather, they want repeat business.
- *ISO*: The company is certified to ISO 9001:2000 (which rather few companies have achieved, especially smaller ones like AMS and AIT).
- *Employment*: 78 people (including all administration, technical, and engineering) with 8 supervisors in AMS and five in AIT.
- *Training*: half-day quality training and half day safety training for every operator. Operators gain flexibility by qualifying on all items of a competency form as judged by a supervisor.
- *Tour hosts*: Sam Conti, AMS quality manager; Tim Partlowe, ERP system integrator, AIT; Mike Joseph, ASM product manager; Ted Johnson, gen. manager.

II. American Sheet Metal – Buildings 1, 2, and 3

- *Sheet-metal flow*: In general, the flow is Customer → Estimator → Prints → Pre-manufacturing → Manufacturing. The processes in the three buildings are basic and well known (to sheet-metal people), and so most of the detail (from my notes) is omitted here. So, by way of brief summarization:
  - ✓ *Building-1 production*: These processes include shear with blanks ordered to size where possible: Punch/deburr. Hardware install (screws, etc.). Brake press. Each setup is recorded digitally, so that next time the same setup procedure can be used; senior operators do the setups, not maintenance people.
  - ✓ *Building-2 production*: Waterjet cutters (for thick aluminum); laser cutters for low-volume orders. Frame welding (seven or eight weld booths). Belt sand and grind.

✓ *Building-3 production*: Cutting on table saws. Spot welding. Meticulous dimensional gauging (noting every nonconformity— in achieving very high, 98.8%, first-pass yields). Outside paint and plating (with protective packaging). Inspection and repack. Final packing and shipping.

- *Production planning/scheduling/control*:
  - ✓ A router sheet in an acetate envelope accompanies all jobs through all operations, with barcoding of each operation.
  - ✓ Along with the router, yellow, orange, and green tags are attached to the work as it progresses: Yellow, in-process. Orange, nonconforming. Green, inspected and is good.
  - ✓ Besides those manual/visual aspects of flow management, there is a computer system called RealTrac, through which, on completion of an operation, the operator wands the barcode, and keys in the employee number(s) and machine number.
  - ✓ RealTrac further displays, on scattered computer terminals, the load situation for each work station.
    - For example, it shows, in colored bar-chart form, overloads/underloads on each currently staffed welding booth; if overloaded, the needed welders will be moved to do the work on inactive weld stations, relieving the overloads. The system also shows loadings on labor-only resources, such as inspection.
    - This capacity/load system helps ensure high performance in making order promises that can be met, and then meeting them. (Did not get stats on on-time performance, etc.)
- *Costing/estimating/bidding*:
  - ✓ Operations data from keyboards and wand stations accumulates so that jobs' costs can be post-compared with estimates—thus to improve estimating/bidding.
  - ✓ Aside from that, it's a conventional standard cost system with accounting making heavy use of purchasing cost variances, which seems out of place in this small, mostly well-managed company.
- *Sales tuned to capacity*: Sales managers (Steve Hawes, regional; Jeff Wells, state) are tuned to a need to match bidding/pricing to the changing capacity-load situation (e.g., enabling ways to squeeze out profit margins when there's excess capacity, and vice versa).

- *Quality/information system:*
  - ✓ For every nonconformity, a corrective action is entered into a home-grown computer form.
    - ■ The top part records specific data all about the nonconformity.
    - ■ The lower part records the activity that caused the problem and its root cause.
  - ✓ Below that are corrective action, disposition, target date of completion, manufacturing manager's review, QA manager's review, and closed date.
  - ✓ This procedure was developed for AMS but may also be used in AIT.
- A similar form/procedure applies to discrepant material and packing-slip matters in AIT.

III. American Integrated Technologies – Building 4

- *AIT production.* AIT assembles high-tech equipment, especially for the semiconductor industry.
  - ✓ Customers include such notables as Intel and ASM International.
  - ✓ Often, orders come from another equipment manufacturer, e.g., ASM, with the completed machine to be shipped either to that customer or drop-shipped to the final using customer's customer.
  - ✓ AIT produced and shipped 65 epitaxy machines in the past two years.
- *Clean rooms.* A class-10,000 clean room is about 6,500 sq. ft. A smaller class-100 clean room is for orbital welding of stainless steel tubing and connectors for process gasses.
- *Quality assurance.* QA is responsible for purchased materials, including daily cycle counting (99.74% accuracy; sometimes outside auditors find no count/location discrepancies).
- *Part numbers.* Some 7,000 P/Ns are in the system, around 4,500 of them active (both purchased/stocked and produced).
- *Info system.* An ERP subroutine provides pick lists and kitting data, for many different-sized kitting totes that are at the ready.
- *Sourcing.* AIT uses welded sheet-metal frames from sister company, AMS. It purchases all electronic, robotic, gas delivery, etc., components.
- *Flow of purchased items.* All purchased items go through receiving, except for packing materials and (perhaps) steel, which go direct to

the production building—and hardware, which goes to receiving but with less fuss.

- *Inventory control*:
  - ✓ Purchased items are kept in a rack area with authorized access only to those needing it. Small hardware, however, is free stock and open to all.
  - ✓ Empty cardboard trays identify who, currently, has a certain tray of parts from racks.
- *ECOs.* There have been 1,200 engineering change orders from the customer on one large semiconductor product. Bob Dodge, ECO manager, keeps extensive records so disruptions and costs of ECOs can result in cost recovery from the customer.

IV. Praiseworthy Observations

- *AIT capabilities*: The capability to turn out some of the most high-tech equipment is remarkable for so small a company; and the way this ties in with sheet-metal operations (to produce frames for its products) makes good sense strategically.
- *Financial health*: No company debt. Continuous investment in good equipment.
- *Physical growth*: Expansion not by adding on to a building (usually ill-advised) but by new buildings, each of which can be focused, with short handling distances, good communication, family-like feel, etc.
- *Hardware-install equipment*: On wheels—easily moved into better flow patterns in cases of higher-volume orders.
- *Quality/nonconformity correction system.* Drilling down from direct cause to root cause, with corrective action, etc., is excellent—and would be for a G.E. or Motorola.
- *Miscellaneous*:
  - ✓ Computer displays, neatness, arrangement of fixtures, cleanliness, taped floors, colored tags, safety zones, etc.
  - ✓ ISO-9001:2000. Excellent safety (lockout zones, etc.).
  - ✓ Good job qualification system.
  - ✓ Contracting out paint—and its costs/headaches.
  - ✓ Maintaining several levels of clean room in the same AIT building is economical and effective.
  - ✓ Good systems for quality assurance/count integrity and control of purchased materials.

V. Potential Opportunities for Improvement

- *Cells*: None observed.
  - ✓ Shops should be at least partially broken up, with machines moved into cells; this could include a punch-hardware cell, install-break-drill cell, press-spot weld cell, or some lesser combination. Maybe weld and grind in a cell as well.
  - ✓ A cell team of, say, two or three cross-trained operators would rotate jobs daily; record every glitch, hiccup, and aggravation; and meet one to five times per week (without or with engineer, buyer, etc.) on problem-solving projects.
- *Employee ownership/visual management*:
  - ✓ There seem to be an overly large number of supervisors, who appear to be the responsible party, where the operator or operator team could (should) be.
  - ✓ Lacking are quick-changeover graphs, large skill matrices, etc., which would further enhance visuality and serve to drive responsibility and pride of achievement down to lowest employee levels, enhance self-management, simplify and lower costs, and accelerate rates of improvement.
  - ✓ On the corrective action form, better to use a neutral word, e.g., "mishap" instead of "error"—since most nonconformities are not "error" by the operator but of the system of providing the right resources, right time, and so forth.
- *Quick setup*: Setup analysis seems applied extensively on sheet-metal presses, but little evidence of it elsewhere. Setup improvement should be basic to every equipment operator's job—involving documenting every improvement, plotting it on graphs, and training teammates in the new procedures.
- *Simplicity and the cost system*:
  - ✓ RealTrac is an impressive tool for scheduling and control but lacks the kinds of low-cost simplicity seen at other low-volume, high-variety plants.
  - ✓ An example is that of Ahlström Pump, Mänttä, Finland, as described in Chapter I-7. It's a basic first-in-line sequencing system, with visual (kanban-like) signals to govern flow. With that in place, costing can be reduced to occasional cost audits for competitive decision purposes, still providing good data for

refined estimating/bidding—and provide impetus for weaning the company off the standard-cost/cost-variance system.
- *Growth strategy*:
  - ✓ A fine company—but sheet metal is very basic, the kind that China, México, etc., can become excellent at quickly. The old "grow-or-die" phrase did not mean much in the past. But with today's global "hyper-competition" it has new relevance.
  - ✓ A good example of how small companies should develop and execute a growth strategy is R.W. Lyall (Chapter III-78), illustrating growth especially to avoid loss of very good people.
- *Influence with customers*: You are the sheet-metal expert, and thus can be active in questioning/suggesting to customers different gauges of steel, more unitary designs that require less welding, use of pre-painted metals, etc. (You do some of this, but should do more.) This might require growing the engineering staff a bit.

CHAPTER III-91. SABMILLER, PLC, KRAKOW, POLAND, 2008

The bulk of this caselet consists of excerpts from my letter to an SABMiller executive in which I summarize my critical impressions of the company's bottling and canning processes. I had been invited to speak/participate in the company's annual Technical Conference, that year held in Poland—which included a tour of its highly regarded Tyskie Brewery. I've modestly edited the letter.	*High-Interest Topics:* • **SABMiller (and its industry)—mired in a costly mode of bottling/canning that serves customers poorly** • **Multiples of simpler, slower, more reliable equipment—for producing many SKUs simultaneously—are the key** • **What to do: Pilot projects—for proving the worth of flow (lean) production in bottling/canning**

Doing It the Way We've Always Done It: Schonberger Presentation & Other Events at SABMiller's Annual Technical Conference, Krakow, Poland, Sept. 2, 2008

Plus same-day plant tour of Tyskie Brewery in Tychy, Poland

I. Follow-on Email to Primary Host for SABMiller Conference

September 12, 2008

   From: Richard J. Schonberger, Bellevue, WA, USA

   To: Simon Wade, Director of Brewing Development, SABMiller plc, London, U.K.

   Dear Simon,

   It was a pleasure to be a part of the Technical Conference in Krakow on September 2—and to tour Tyskie Brewery. Too bad I couldn't stay through Thursday and be with the conference group on the *management* tour. I would have relished participating in discussions about that brewery's design and operations. Though my tour was just the general-public quickie, I did see enough to form some critical impressions, which is the reason for this letter.

   I am assuming that some or many of the delegates attending my presentation were not in total disagreement with my final, tossed-in comments on common weaknesses in the design of fill-and-pack plants. The scene looking down at the bottling operation at Tyskie was not all that different, except in scale, from what I recall from about age 7 in the small town where I was born. It had a soft-drink bottling plant, and operations were on display through a large window facing a public street. I was among kids who avidly watched, runny noses pressed against the window, what went on there among the clanking conveyors loaded with bottles on the march.

   Now, in the new age of lean, plant operations should be simpler, more flexible, and more reliable. By today's standards, though, the Tyskie bottling and canning operations (and perhaps those throughout most of SAB and the industry) look to be fat, not lean:

- A great many SKUs competing for production time among too few, excessively long, complex, temperamental bottling/canning lines.
- Excessive non-value-adding powered conveyors laden with thousands of in-process bottles or cans, the purpose of which is to localize trouble.
- Operators there mainly to rush to next sources of trouble for quick fixes, permanent fixes tending to be put off because they require long shutdowns and capital investment—spills and breakage, nearly always in sight, standing in mute evidence.

- High overhead costs for engineers and technicians to design, acquire, and maintain the costly, complex, high-speed equipment.
- Pressure to run the lines ever faster and with greater capacity utilization, thus to (a) justify high capital and overhead costs, (b) compensate for frequent line stoppages, and (c) offset line-change time required to accommodate all the SKUs.
- High line speeds and high utilization, in turn, being common causes of line stoppages and failures—the "vicious circle" phenomenon.

There may be no examples of lean bottling and canning anywhere in the beverage industry. That suggests the need for a pilot test. The cost of such a test should be minuscule, at least as compared with the billions that companies such as SABMiller and InBev have been spending on acquisitions and on opening new breweries and distribution throughout the world. The main purpose would be to prove the benefits of a lean beverage facility, as compared with conventional bottling/canning, namely:

- Lower costs and higher return on assets.
- Greater reliability though simplicity and prevention.
- Many more SKUs produced per week for the same overall volume.
- Greater flexibility to adjust the SKU mix.
- High operator ownership of processes.

I lack technical knowledge of bottling/canning equipment in breweries, and also of the various equipment configurations found throughout the industry. Thus my remarks on the nature of such pilot tests are surely off-base in some respects. I'll divide those remarks, which follow, into "minimal" and "full scale."

Minimal Pilot Test

The simple, quick experiment—with limited benefits—would be just to shrink an existing facility by at least 50%. That is, remove 75% or more of the conveyors, ending up with the same number of fill-and-pack lines, each in a relatively compact cluster. Initially, output will be substandard: For lack of plentiful in-process inventory, each problem will stop nearly an entire line. A tactic such as slowing line speeds may be found actually to increase daily outputs (less wear and tear on the equipment, less bottle breakage, etc.). With so much less conveyor, there are commensurately fewer root causes of stoppages. Operators and the technical staff are able to devote their time to permanent fixes of remaining equipment. In time, output will exceed best former results, and with greater reliability. Then, with equipment clustered and more reliable, a smaller team—maybe only two or three operators—can be in charge of a given line.

Full-Scale Pilot Test

A more complete pilot test would call for new production lines and different kinds of equipment. To explain: With exceptions for just a few industries, lean design of operations calls for increased numbers of productive units so that more brands, models, sizes, and SKUs may be produced simultaneously, closer to market rates. Since market rates, per SKU, are relatively slow, production rates should be similarly slow. In some cases simple, low-cost equipment of a bygone era may be seen as just right for the task. Some of the productive units—cells, assembly lines, fill-and-pack lines—are to be dedicated to high runners, others switching off among "dogs and cats"; some to large, others to small sizes of the product; or some to the commodity market, others to a special, demanding customer (e.g., a Wal-Mart or Tesco). Each line, or sometimes a group of two or more similar lines, is treated as a separate value stream, with each value stream having its own support staff, sometimes including customer service.

Consider a brewery that now has four conventional bottling lines running at very fast rates. A full-scale lean retrofit might have, say, twice as many lines—eight—occupying the same total area. Each of the eight lines is a tight cluster of equipment and runs at half the speed of the former four lines. The slower speeds allow for simpler, less costly equipment with fewer things that can go wrong. If the brewery is in a low-wage country (which is the case with most of SABMiller's breweries), older, semi-automated equipment may be the logical choice in some processes.

One or more lines are dedicated to a single size of bottle, or maybe even a single very high-volume brand and label—thus requiring regular clean-out and preventive maintenance but not much additional downtime. As few as two operators may be all that are needed to tend so compact and dedicated a line. Lines for "dogs and cats" require more frequent and more extensive changeovers, and more operators. Continually upgraded skill sets make operators the owners of their lines, to the point that their title changes from operator to technician.

Summary

The above comments draw on general lean lore and what I've seen up close in widely assorted fill-and-pack plants: food ingredients, candy bars, tea, coffee, tobacco, frozen TV dinners, soft drinks, deodorants, toothbrushes, ballpoint pens, butane lighters, greeting cards, photo film, bank checks, crayons, medical supplies and medications, and so on. (These are very high-volume types of manufacturing. The same lean-design-of-production concepts apply also to many kinds of moderate-volume production: apparel, consumer electronics, fitness equipment, furniture, hundreds of other products.)

Note: I certainly am not angling for some sort of consulting job. My company is just my wife and I and never has had other employees (except for a few part-time occasions involving one of our sons), and my business cards have never included the word, consultant. Whatever insights I might have on how to design and organize various kinds of productive resources, I prefer not to spend much time with any one company or industry.

Very sincerely,   Richard J. Schonberger

II. Epilogue

Simon Wade wrote back thanking me for my note of my "impressions from Tyskie Brewery, which is one of our better running plants!" He said he was forwarding my email to "a couple of colleagues who can best take forward your insightful comments and perhaps will result in a new challenge to our organization – we still have a long journey ahead!"

There were no further communications from Mr. Wade, his two colleagues, or others in the greater SABMiller organization.

However, I did also communicate with Dennis Puffer, Chief Operations Officer, MillerCoors, in Denver, who had also attended the Poland conference. Puffer stated that "I concur with your comments. It will take a brave individual or team to do the pilot test. I myself will look for an opportunity to do our own test in MillerCoors." Not hearing further from him, I assume that nothing came of doing the pilot test within MillerCoors.

The stark conclusion from all this—and from at least two other caselets in this book—is that professional managers, especially in large, bureaucratic organizations, are highly averse doing much of anything new and different from norms in their sector. This is hardly a case of financial risk avoidance, inasmuch as the cost of pilot tests are modest! And the benefits—and personal rewards—when the tests are successful, can be enormous.

Robert (Doc) Hall, one of the founders of the Association for Manufacturing Excellence (AME), and for many years editor-in-chief of the AME's *Target Magazine*, has said for years that any organization that preaches continuous improvement should be a process-improvement laboratory, continually testing-out, trying-out new or advanced ideas. His message needs to be become systematically integrated in the workings of every organization.

CHAPTER III-92. HOLLISTER INC., STUARTS DRAFT, VA, 2009

This caselet, for a producer of supplies for incontinence and related medical problems, describes a hard-charging advocate of flow/lean/best practices in process improvement. My notes were extensive but most of the details (of interest only to industry insiders) are not included. The high-interest segments, Sections III and IV, are followed by a segment from my thank-you letter to my hosts.

High-Interest Topics:
- **Product-wheel-driven schedules—for discipline and simplicity**
- **High operator involvement—throughout**
- **Can there be *too much* teaming, process improvement, measurement & evaluation?**

Telling the Computer When To Shut Up:
Observations from Plant Visit, Dec. 10, 2009

Linked for convenience with a presentation at the annual meeting of South Carolina Lean Alliance, Greenville, SC, December 9, 2009 – And two months later my 1.5-day presentation at Hollister's Total Process Improvement Summit, Duck Key, FL, February 9–10, 2010

I. Basic Information

- *Product line*: Medical products for ostomy and continence care, bowel management, wound care and tube fasteners. See Sidebar 1 for some details. Note: Closed (thrown away components) are common in Europe with its higher payment policies; drainable (drain pouch) is common in stingy-reimbursement U.S.
- *Hollister – Growing facilities*:
  - ✓ 1965: An innovative ostomy product introduced at the Kirksville, MO, site—a plant now doing injection molding with an 85-person plant population.
  - ✓ 1981: Expansion of Hollister, Stuarts Draft, plant in 1989; now 200,000 sq. ft., with 603,645 direct labor (D.L.) hours.
  - ✓ Other plants: 1976 Ballina, Ireland, 392 associates (ostomy, with growing incontinence business); 1989, Fredensborg, Denmark, maker of Dansac ostomy brand, 340 associates; fall 2009, Gurgaon, India, 50 associates (urine collectors, catheters).
  - ✓ 2005, acquired Apogee Medical, a contract manufacturer of medical devices, 175 associates.
  - ✓ Distribution centers: 2000, Nashville, 75 associates (DC for North America, Latin America, Asia); Etten-Leur, Netherlands, 65 associates.
- *Stuarts Draft*: 500 associates plus 68 agency temps. Key data:
  - ✓ Ostomy, with 80 million units ("eaches") produced in 1,100 finished-goods SKUs, accounts for 85% of output. Continence, 2.3 million units, 10% of output. Wound care, 1.8 million units, 5%.
  - ✓ Shifts vary a lot depending on the products/cell/capacity/demand: shifts, for example, are 6:30 a.m.–3:00 p.m. and 4:30 p.m.–1:00 a.m. But some shifts are two 12's, three shifts 24/7, four 10's, and others.
  - ✓ Cost breakdown: materials 50%; labor 35%; overhead 15%.
  - ✓ Customer-focused product aims: 1. Security 2. Comfort 3. Discretion 4. Options 5. ?
- *Contact persons/hosts*:
  - ✓ Hollister, Stuarts Draft: Bill Doran, plant manager; Steve Roeglin, master black belt; Kimberly Troyer, HR generalist.
  - ✓ Hollister, Ballina, Ireland: George McNicholas, mfg. manager; Gerry O'Mahoney, improvement champion.

SIDEBAR 1   PRODUCTS AND APPLICATIONS

Ostomist. A medical specialty.

Ileostomy: Surgically made hole (stoma) in end or loop of small intestine—mated with hole in skin through which intestinal waste passes into a bag.

Colostomy: Surgery that attaches portion of colon to abdominal wall through which waste passes into a bag through a stoma.

Urostomy: Artificial bladder formed from segment of small bowel; collects urine that drains intermittently through catheter, avoiding stoma/bag method.

Pouch components:

1-piece: Classic, Karaya (legacy), Premier, Moderna Flex.

2-piece: CPL/Tandem, New Image, Conform 2.

Moderna Flex and Conform 2 are newest, higher featured, more comfortable.

Ostomy barriers: 7 types: flat, convex (if stoma an "inny"), Karaya (gum tree from India) and five more types.

II. Thank-You Letter to Hosts

- *Content of Letter*: High points of my events at Hollister are summarized in a thank-you letter. The full letter is long and detailed; the following are a few pertinent excerpts.

  Dear Bill and Steve,

  Thanks for the excellent plant visit and evening dinner discussions. . . . For what little it may be worth, I'm including a summary, which follows. Please pardon the errors of fact and wrong-headed interpretations. My notes have rarely been so infested with gaps—since the information came at me "out of a fire hose."

- *Teams within teams within* . . . . : As I mentioned to you, Bill, my early impression—from the two-hour overview in the conference room—was that your system of teaming, process improvement, and extensive measurement and evaluation was overly elaborate. I thought it would not be workable, or if workable not sustainable. The plant tour, though, suggests you've got the system working quite well. Here are a few thoughts about why:

- *Simplicity*: One of lean's hallmarks is simplicity in all things. Yet your system is (with qualifications) not simple. On the other hand, it is a *system*, the opposite of which is something like chaos. And it's a constructive system, opposite to a destructive one. (Example of the latter: an entrenched MRP system that requires work orders, move tickets, labor and cost transactions, etc., every time a part moves somewhere. But for all its faults, the MRP era was an improvement over the prior one of expediters everywhere trying to cover for lack of systematic planning and control.)

- *Complexity*: Complex systems (dominant in most large companies) don't work well because they are mysterious and opaque, especially to production associates. Well, three cheers for your system: Your associates are *in* the system. Example: On the tour, in two cases, the tour guide or production associate explained how the associates look at the to-do list, compare with the DOH number, and spot a job for which there's excessive DOH. So they overrule the to-do list, and don't run that SKU—and, I suppose, notify SAS accordingly. Also, I saw extensive visual management at low levels, which itself is an element of simplicity that characterizes lean at its best.

III. Strong Points (some duplication with point in the letter, Part II)

- *Product*: Hollister pursues a strong focus on the product from the viewpoint of final users, and the viewpoints of nurses who care for final users.
- *Product wheel*: An excellent scheduling method for this type of manufacturing—with an emphasis on turning the wheel faster: Level flow serves as the pacemaker, the product wheel serving as a marker of responsiveness, days-on-hand (DOH)—inventory, that is—as governor.
- *DOH as dominant metric (overruling SAP)*: The tour guide/ production associate pointed out examples:
  - ✓ Associates look at the to-do list, compare it with the DOH number, and spot a job for which there's excessive DOH—and thus, overrule the SAP-driven to-do list, and do not run that job.
  - ✓ In wound care, a Jason-developed report, produced daily, showed 21 days' excess DOH for one SKU, triggering a signal to SAP that they will *not* be running that SKU.
- *Kiefel team*: A team member told of a quick-setup (less than ten-minutes) black-belt project employing quarter-turn screws and point-of-sale (POS) tooling.

- *Wound care*: In a two-day kaizen with a team of people from two shifts, a spaghetti diagram led to moving seven machines into a cellular configuration (duplicate machines where needed for line balance), cutting inventory by $21,000. Also, part numbers were reduced from 60 to 6.
- *Quality*: ISO 13485:2003; FDA registered (2006 last audit). Motto: "Attention to Detail" ..."Attention to Life."
- *Employee development*: Examples: skill-based pay with levels of attainment, multi-skilling/job rotation; in one area job rotation was said to be daily.
- *Performance boards*: Goals vs. actual are displayed on performance boards everywhere.
  - ✓ A 97% fill-rate goal is fixed by fiat.
  - ✓ Most of the other goals apparently are set by teams of associates themselves!
  - ✓ Why not set easier goals? I asked. Answers seem to be that teams are motivated, if not by pride and business success, then by gaining another level on the Hollister maturity ladder.
- *Recognition, celebration, and reward*: Includes gain-sharing, gift cards, monthly drawings, photos.
- *Shift integration and overlap*:
  - ✓ Associates in pouch, working two 12-hour shifts, manage to get together monthly.
  - ✓ In one case of 3 shifts, a night shift of less than 8 hours provides minutes that are used in the cause of shift-to-shift overlap.
- *Qualifiers for kaizen project*: Specific; Measureable; Achievable; Relevant; Time-bound.
- *Total process improvement (TPI)*: This system features training—e.g., Phase 1, 2, belts training.
- *Improvement projects*: A mix of belts (larger projects) and kaizens (smaller projects).
- *Ballina, Ireland*: Good supplier development. Examples: A year's commitment on purchase volume with supplier Dow, in exchange for more frequent deliveries and supplier kanban. Reduction from two to three monthly deliveries to lots of weekly deliveries.

IV. Company/System Issues

- *SAP*: Too complex: retards visual flow, frequent product changes, and so on. Look for ways to cut SAP's more offensive subroutines.

- *Six sigma*: Regarding commonplace tendencies and likely obstacles . . .
  - ✓ Corporate HQ is likely to see lean six sigma as something to staff off to operations; marketing is likely to be averse (or neutral at best) to lean six sigma mainly because lean favors reduction of inventories.
  - ✓ Lean six sigma needs to be redefined and re-promoted in strategic/ competitive terms; specifically, for giving customers what they value highly: flexibly quick response with excellent quality and care—quick response revolving around reducing lead times and inventories.
- *Quick setup*:
  - ✓ Needs much more attention, including timing every setup on major equipment, videotaping by operators. Debby, an operator, said, "Less changeovers, I'd like that."
  - ✓ Operators need to see setups as exciting challenges; also, with rewards and recognition for quick-setup ideas. On any critical setup, it makes sense to attack as a setup *team*.
  - ✓ Objectives are to reduce variation in setup times, not just average setup time.
- *TPM*: Total productive maintenance needs more attention, with maintenance as facilitator, enabler, trainer, and backup, so that it fosters ownership by operators. As operators gain technical expertise, maybe adopt as job titles, technician or associate technician.
- *Inventory*: There is too much inventory on the floor; kanban seems rather loose.
- *Supplier development*: Needs work.
  - ✓ Consider long-term commitments to yearly minimum quantities, so that big suppliers have reason to collaborate on inventory reduction, supplier kanban (didn't hear anything about it), supplier-managed inventory, early involvement, and so forth.
  - ✓ Need to shrink the 45-day stocks of materials in the local leased warehouse.
- *De-proliferate*: DFMA offers an excellent pathway to reducing complexities owed to Hollister's many SKUs—although Hollister may need to retain some dubious SKUs/models/old products to be a full-line brand.
- *Capital equipment*: Corporate seems very tight on capital equipment.

    ✓ The plant needs more capacity in order to reequip for doubling/tripling the number of products made simultaneously, thus to enable large reductions in inventory—with model mixes much better matched to end-user demand.

    ✓ Emphasis on turning the product wheel faster is good, but more equipment would yield "more wheels" and more frequent running of the model mix—critical in that the factory cost breakdown is *50% materials.*

- *Process problems*: There is no system of collecting/plotting things that go wrong every shift, every day, every person (frustrations).
- *Too many sit-down jobs.* Work benches are not height-adjustable for sit or stand and for taller/shorter associates; sit-down-all-day jobs are ergonomically inappropriate—and, where necessary, should involve job rotation, say, every two hours.
- *Material coordinator job*: In one area (Barbara's?), or maybe all areas, a person (a production associate or someone in planning) spends about 4 hours a day as material coordinator. Could this be taken over by production associates on rotating basis—which would give them a more whole-operation view?
- *Staggered lunches.* Why, with high focus on output, does production not continue over lunch breaks?
- *External visitations*: Maybe a need for more systematic visits by plant associates/managers to supplier and other plants.
- *Dollarizing*: I asked why put dollar signs on process improvement; it's always obvious that they are valuable.
  - ✓ Weak but usual answer: They keep requiring that we *prove* our practices.
  - ✓ Much better and more valid proofs are in natural units, such as lead-time reduction, inventory reduction, quick setup—for which competitive advantages are obvious.
  - ✓ Anyway, cost accounting has a cost validity problem (one that activity-based costing audits can help deal with).
- *Reducing kanbans*: Comment of an operator: "We haven't run out yet."
  - ✓ But one method of driving kanban/cycle-time reduction is to reduce kanbans enough that run-outs *do* (though not frequently) occur.
  - ✓ Then look for process fixes that allow lowering kanban still more.

- *Versatility matrixes*: Job rotation was said to be daily in one area, but no versatility/multi-skilling matrices are in evidence
- *Customer-focused improvement*: What would it take to achieve one-day response times?
- *Balina, Ireland issues*:
  - ✓ Could/should Ballina organize its value streams by geographic region rather than product family (as Microsoft-Dublin did in its 2nd generation of cells)? George and Gerry spoke of going opposite way—toward a technologies focus.
  - ✓ I said OEE has served its purpose, so quit measuring it. George/Gerry said they agree.
  - ✓ George and Gerry asked why/how, even in their unionized plant, you can have multi-skilling.
    - My answer was: Put up skills matrices so that multi-skilling becomes a pride factor.
    - Press upon the troops the competitive need for flexibility; and the view that multiple skills improve employability, a critical issue now in Ireland with its severe economic downturn.

CHAPTER III-93. MOTORES JOHN DEERE, S.A. DE C.V., TORREÓN, MÉXICO, 2004

This caselet, on Deere's big Mexican diesel plant, is largely descriptive of its main assembly line and a smaller one, plus machining of blocks, crankshafts, etc. Beyond that, it focuses on the plant's ponderous production configuration.	**High-Interest Topics:** • **Critique of conventional very long, complex assembly line with lots of inventory high on overhead conveyors** • **Recommending chopping and reconfiguring for simpler, quicker flows**

Physical (and Other) Obstacles to Change: Viewpoints
Based on Brief Plant Tour, Oct. 15, 2004

Linked for convenience with my two-day seminar and two-hour talk
Sponsored by Torreón Tecnologico Universidad

I. General Information

- *The facility*: Deere's Torreón diesel engine plant was opened in 1997 and expanded in January 2002—enough to double its annual capacity in production of heavy diesel engines.
- *Product line & output*:
  - ✓ Deere's new PowerTech 2.4 L and 3.0 L engines have four base models and 2,500 model variations of those four. At 65%, four-cylinder engines are the dominant model.
  - ✓ The engines are for Deere itself and other companies (Kohler, Paccar, etc.); some (perhaps most) engines are made to order.
  - ✓ Sales are hot, so the plant is running 20% over capacity, with a 4th overtime shift.
    - No stopping for lunch, just flex the line.
    - Production rose from 75,000 to 120,000 engines per year after the plant's 2002 expansion and increase in shifts.
  - ✓ Axles are to be produced in a currently empty space.
- *Employment*: About 1,000 direct labor, 200 salaried; two shifts in assembly, three in machining.
- *Tour group*: Miguel Meza Nuñez, gerente de maqinado; Rolando Treviño Cárdenas, ingeniero senior, maquinado cabeza S350; Luis G. Bárcena Alcázar, ingeniero senior, maquinado cigüeñal (crankshaft); Carlos Gerardo Echávarri Lizárraga, gerente de ensamble; Roberto Ramírez (colleague of Schonberger); Carlos García, Kaizen Institute; Mario, Universidad Autonomo de Torreón; Enrique Vega, Tecnológio Hermosillo.

II. Assembly and Related Processes

- *Progressive assembly*: Production line is an extremely long overhead chain conveyor winding, serpentine, up and down—with an 8-hour flow time.
- *Main assembly processes*: 1. Block (from machining). 2. Crankshaft install. 3. Injection pump install. 4. Head install. 5. Flywheel fixture install.
- *Tracking*: The computer tracks every step, and stations at beginning of each assembly line have an overhead CRT to provide information and take data.

      ✓ Stack lights tell where problems are; for example, blue means an empty kanban, calling for material control, which employs pick-to-light kanban replenishment.

      ✓ A register records identifiable problems as reported in March, April, May ….

- *Assembly schematic.* Figure 93.1 (inexact) depicts assembly, employing a heavy overhead conveyor carrying lots of engines up into rafters, then down for a bit of value-adding, and so on.
- *Assemblers*: Many are women. A blue shirt signifies a permanent employee; gray for temps (who make up 45–50% of direct labor— coming from tech school last semester).
- *Paint*: Five colors: black, gray, yellow, green,? in which the operator, with one paint gun, changes colors. A spray paint platform (viewable through glass) rises and falls by control of the painter.
- *Downtime*: 4–5 minutes of assembly-line downtime while we were there (noted by Roberto).
- *Small engines*: Assembled on new compact line installed in January 2004.

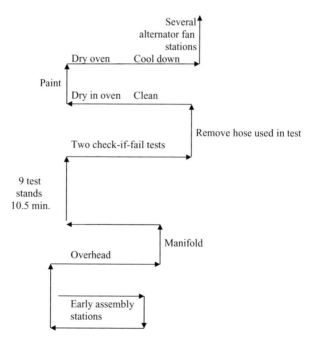

FIGURE 93.1
Schematic of key processes along the main assembly line.

- *Shipping and receiving*: 12 ship docks, with every loading square in the footprint of a trailer (one-level trailers). Castings have their own receiving docks; parts also have their own different receiving docks.
- *Maintenance*: 50–60 people (but tech support is a problem in México).
- *Visual management*: Limited and not operator-friendly.
  - ✓ 5S is in use in machining and materials, though not elsewhere.
  - ✓ An andon board tracks goals for *production* and *quality*, a bonus paid weekly for attainment of those two goals.
- *TPM*: Not implemented; to be added.
- *Competitive analysis*: Some is done by engineers at beginnings of new models.
- *Flow racks*: Many are in use.

III. Machining

- *Equipment*: Includes two machining lines for the 250 series, and three machining lines for the 350 series. There are 40 machine centers; 10 special machines.
- *Processes*: Machine head → crankshaft → block. 7 different blocks and 7 different crankshafts provide flexibility within each engine family.
- *Schematic*: Figure 93.2 is a rough schematic of machining centers for the new 250 model: Notes are unclear, but possibly a group of five machines for heads; five for crankshafts; and five for blocks. The same machines are in each group—the "copy-exactly" concept.
- *350 model*: Figure 93.3 is a schematic of machining centers for the older 350 model.
- *Crankshaft machining*:
  - ✓ Castings: Four-cylinder castings come from Brazil; six-cylinder from the U.K.
  - ✓ Tolerances very tight on seven crankshaft models.
- *Bottleneck*: Capacity is 75,000 crankshafts; 76,000 is actual production. To help cope, two people (instead of one) operate bottleneck machines.
- *Cleaning*: Crankshaft machining is very dirty. Guys have been hired just to keep cleaning the machines, especially when machines are down for PMs and tool changes at the same time.
- *Major stoppages*: Three or four times a year, typically a one- or two-day stoppage.

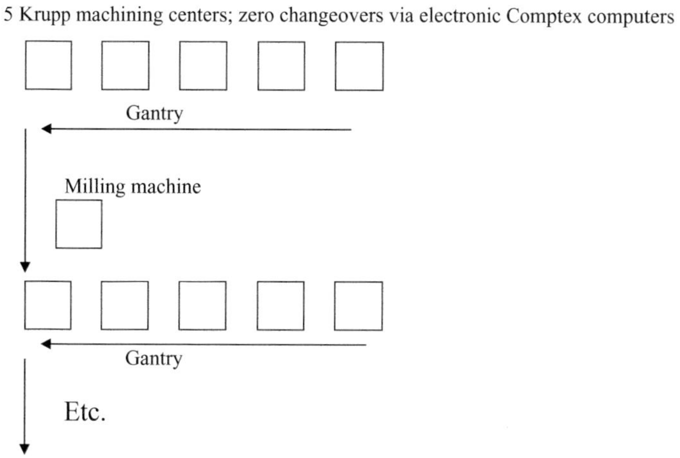

5 Krupp machining centers; zero changeovers via electronic Comptex computers
Gantry
Milling machine
Gantry
Etc.

FIGURE 93.2
Schematic of flow pattern in machining.

Makino
and
Cincy
machines
Rails

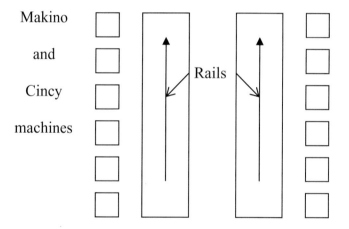

FIGURE 93.3
Schematic of flow pattern with machining centers for 350 model.

- *Changeover videos*: Some videos of changeovers have been made for ten machines; batch sizes can be two days' worth.
- *Kyosho metrics*: These metrics are in every area with the following scorecard factors:
  - ✓ Employment
  - ✓ Safety

✓ Quality   Efficiency
- ▪ —   ▪ —
- ▪ —   ▪ —
- ▪ —   ▪ —

✓ Production
- ▪ —Inventory $
- ▪ —Continuous improvement projects completed
- ▪ —Operator PMs on time (this metric for some of the lines)
- ▪ —Hours paid/unit
- ▪ —Hours worked/unit

✓ —Tool cost
✓ —% on time
✓ —Supplies cost
✓ —Scrap per piece
✓ —Production vs. goal

IV. Plant Configuration

- *Flow direction*: Flow is west → east. Assembly occupies the east half (or more) of the building.
- *Plant too large*: The plant's very large size—maybe 500,000 sq. ft.—inhibits configuration changes in the cause of product-focused improvements, which are complex and costly.
- *Assembly-line length*: The main assembly line is far too long, too linear, with too much conveyor (costly, heavy-duty necessary for heavy engines) full of inventory up in the rafters.
- *Dealing with problem engines*: The assembly conveyor is synchronous, so problem engines cannot be shunted.
- *Inventory*: Lots of inventory between machining (west end) and assembly (east end).
- *Plant environment*: Plant is clean, light, airy—and spacious, but to a fault since flow distances are very long.

V. Opportunities for Improvement

- *OFI feasibility*: Some of the following OFIs may not be feasible in the short run.
- *Primary*:
  - ✓ Chop the main assembly line into two or three short, *focused* (by engine size or type) lines—like the separate one for smaller

engines—for quick throughput, low inventory, quick discovery of problems, ease of training for good quality, and so forth.
- ✓ Cut out 30–50% of conveyor.
- ✓ For further compactness and reduction of flow distance/flow time/ inventory . . . stem subassembly stations off the main line(s). (Is this broadly or narrowly feasible?). For an excellent example—in a more complex environment—see Chapter III-98 re Boeing's 737.
- ✓ It would probably have been better to use floor (instead of overhead) conveyor—like Cat Peoria—because it would be more easily relocated, changed, compressed, expanded, etc. (but can floor conveyor be as ergonomic?).
- ✓ It is probably better to have asynchronous conveyors, with shunt capabilities for problem engines (or at least a manual/push alternative for temporary removal of a problem engine).
- ✓ Machining should go to much smaller lots, so that it becomes possible to more closely synchronize to assembly schedules, with little WIP in between.
- *Lesser OFI's*:
  - ✓ Need quick setup in crankshaft machining.
  - ✓ Probably the same in assembly (though I don't know status of current lot sizes).
  - ✓ The plant has been too busy to get around to extending 5S, installing TPM, and upgrading employee involvement—these should be full-speed-ahead *in the next slack period.*

CHAPTER III-94. FCI, CD. JUÁREZ, CHIHUAHUA, MÉXICO, 2004

FCI-Juárez has large numbers of injection molding machines and of assembly cells—the many machines and cells being necessary for coping with widely assorted customer specifications.	**High-Interest Topics:** • **Innovative, systematic attack on setup times—with "Mr. SMED"** • **Unfulfilled opportunity to merge each mold press with its own assembly cell**

Shingo Would Be Proud: Brief Plant Tour of FCI, May 10, 2004
Followed by Schonberger's two-day public seminar in Juárez, May 11–12

I. General Information

- *Ownership*: Founded in 1988, FCI was recently acquired by France-based Areva, the soon-to-be-privatized nuclear power company (owner of Cogema).
- *Product line*:
  - ✓ Electronic connectors mainly for customers in automotive and data communications.
  - ✓ Connectors for automotive airbags is a major and growing business with 30% market share.
- *Primary factory equipment*: Many injection mold press machines, which provide plastic parts to assembly stations for integration with wiring.
- *Main contacts/hosts*: Tom Borns, plant manager; Pedro García, engrg. manager.

II. Manufacturing

- Within the 230,000-sq. ft. plant are two plants-in-a-plant—one dedicated to automotive connectors, the other for consumer data communications.
- *Automotive.* 100,000 sq. ft., 600 employees, five product lines. In lean implementations, this plant is more advanced than the data-communications plant. Its five major processes are:

  No. 1 wire-cutting, five machines)

  No. 2 harnesses, pig tests (labor-intensive).

  No. 3 product, ten mold presses.

  No. 4 product:, four mold presses.

  No. 5 small harnesses.
  - ✓ TPM: 70% by operators.
  - ✓ Two methods of wiring-harness assembly:
    - Old – four assemblers, fixed (sitting) positions.
    - New – four assemblers, walking, following (or planned for) the rabbit-chase method.
  - ✓ Changeover emphasis: Figure 94.1 shows the plant's changeover expert and facilitator, known as "Mr. SMED," garbed in hard hat and appropriately labeled smock.
    - Mr. SMED is standing beside a glassed-in changeover cabinet that holds changeover tools under a large changeover clock.

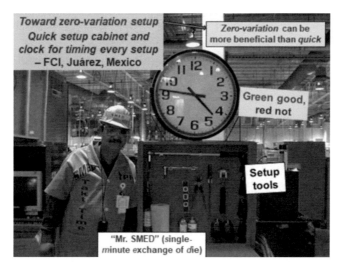

FIGURE 94.1
Mr. SMED with quick changeover apparatus at FCI.

- The clock starts at the start of a change, and, in the photo, shows a red-zone condition indicating the changeover is taking more than the set time.
- As a result of such high emphasis on it, changeover time on the mold presses has been reduced from three hours to 45 minutes, with 12–15 changeovers daily.
- *Consumer data communication (CDC)*: 130,000 sq. ft., 600 employees; processes tens of thousands of part numbers.
  - ✓ CDC operates 24/7 in injection molding; 24/6 is common for assembly.
  - ✓ Lean improvements: Last year CDC had two inventory turns (the worst of FCI's plants); now turns are up to six to seven.
  - ✓ The production area has 300 to 400 molds and four cells, each with its own dedicated supervisor, process engineer, quality engineer, and planner/buyer.
    - Cell 1: Seven mold presses in one room.
    - Cell 2: Nine presses in the next room (product families: Jumper, Dubox).
    - Cell 3: Four presses (Bergstik product family, fewer part numbers).
    - Cell 4: Seven presses (three product families or programs: Headers, Quicken II, Rib cage).

✓ One molding vault contains molds, mold maintenance, pre-install preparation, and 80 different resins.

✓ The CDC area is starting conversion to mold-to-assembly cells!

- *Other points of interest.*

    ✓ FCI uses many simple, small trollies (custom-made, in-house). They can be hooked together and pulled by tractor, though I did not see that; so simple hand-pushing is the norm.

    ✓ There is quite a bit of visual matter displayed on corridor walls; and 5 color codes (don't recall what they apply to), but colors as applied to containers, product families, etc. are not widely in evidence.

III. Problems & Opportunities for Improvement

- *Resins issue*: 80 different resins are too many; need to standardize.
- *Job design issue*: In automotive, there are large numbers of square-shaped four-person, and rectangular six-person, assembly cells with slide lines around the four sides of the cells, each side about four-feet long.

    ✓ Assemblers are sitting down, and assembly is progressive, with station cycle times of only five to ten seconds—meaning at least 3,000 repeat cycles per shift—intolerable jobs—each cell with an inspector hovering.

    ✓ There has been discussion of stand-up rabbit chase here, but still around the same too-small work tables.

- *Opportunities/recommendations.*

    ✓ Disperse higher-use molds and tools to the presses.

    ✓ See about installing gravity rollers to send plastic parts from mold presses directly into assembly machines, with shunts for overflow into boxes.

    ✓ See about marrying automotive labor-intensive assembly—now at the four to five foot tables—to the preceding operation and maybe the next operation (packing?), so that assemblers can get off the chairs and have enlarged (tolerable) work content.

    ✓ Extend uses of the changeover clock and plot times on large nearby graphs.

    ✓ Get graphs and other indicators of ongoing process data collection into the work cells.

CHAPTER III-95. GBC SCIENTIFIC INSTRUMENTS, MELBOURNE, AUSTRALIA, 2004

Of several Australian manufacturers I have visited over the years, GB Scientific is the only one included in this book.	*High-Interest Topics:* • **Labor-intensive manufacturing with high attention to multi-skilling** • **A smallish plant, which makes it easier to link the flows** • **Applying a full range of flow/lean management methodologies**

Good Now, Better Cellular: Observations Based on Brief Plant Tour, Sept. 1, 2004

In connection with one-day seminar on September 2

And two breakfast presentations on September 2 and 3, 2004

All hosted by Nestadt Consulting of Melbourne

I. General Information

- *The company*: Wholly owned GBC Scientific, with beginnings 26 years ago, has 120 non-union employees (at one time it had been 220). GBS was one of 3 plants visited on the same day, the others being Varian Spectrometers—like GBC, producer of large electronic equipment—and HM GEM Engines)—all clients of Nestadt Consulting.
- *Product line*: GBC's mass spectrometers, selling on average for around $150,000, are of various types, as follows:
  - ✓ Atomic absorption (for mining, food analysis, environmental, pathology, research). UV/Visible spectrometer. Time-of-flight mass spectrometers. Reometers. X-ray refraction. Inductively coupled (for oil, mining). Plasma optical emission spectrometer. High-performance liquid chromatography spectrometer.
  - ✓ 95% are exported to 105 countries and sold through distributors.
- *Competitors*: Perkin Elmer, Thermo Electron, and Agilent for one product.
- *Awards*: Australian Best Manufacturer Award in 1999; Clunies Ross Award in 2003. A large wall area, called Hall of Awards, displays these and other awards, flags, plaques, and so forth.

- *Contact persons*: Ron Gray, managing director; David Green, quality manager; Vonda Fenwick, operations manager. My Melbourne colleague, Kevin Nestadt, arranged for and attended the tour.

II. Specifics

- *Nature of business*: GBC is a vertically integrated, low-volume, labor-intensive, high-complexity manufacturer with a diverse supplier base (though it has been reducing its suppliers).
- *Product complexity*:
  - ✓ Many options for several different models.
  - ✓ This entails 20,000 pick part numbers: 12,000 purchased, 8,000 manufactured.
- *R&D*: The company has a full set of development engineering types.
  - ✓ All prototyping is done in production.
  - ✓ All designs are integrated, with production requirements aided by CAD/CAM.
- *Process improvement*: Four elements of systemic improvement at GBC are: leader; cross-skilling (skills matrices); training (in quality; CPI); and performance management.
- *Improvement methodologies*: Initiatives have been concentrated in layout; stores; setup; reliability; VA/VE (value analysis/value engineering) for old parts at first, now for new as well; 5S; the seven wastes; kanban (going away from MRP); DFMA ("we beat R&D over the head with it"); and significant reductions in parts. Examples noted on plant tour:
  - ✓ Lots of 5S with wide use of shadow boards.
  - ✓ Plentiful internal kanban, but zero external kanban (with suppliers and customers).
  - ✓ Within production:
    - Prominent use of color-coding (pink rework, green production, blue in-use).
    - In bench subassembly units, at least 3 people are certified for any task.
    - Overall, the plant has a very high degree of multi-skilled people (subassembly to final assembly; test to optics; etc.).
- *Machine shop*:
  - ✓ Self-managed teams have been in effect for four years.
  - ✓ Performance metrics in the machine shop are: Quality (ten years of quality emphasis—a mature effort); delivery speed

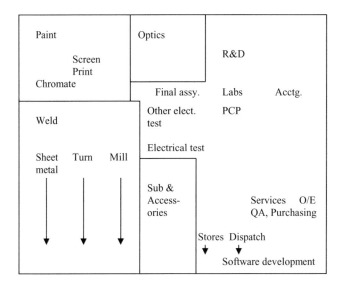

FIGURE 95.1
GBC scientific plant layout (rough).

(quick response); cost; and safety (employing behavioral safety).

- *Plant layout*: The plant, relatively small, squarish-shaped—see Figure 95.1—affords advantages in communication and knowledge transfer.

III. Observations

- *Overall*: A fine plant, much advanced in "world-class manufacturing" methodologies.
- *Primary opportunities for improvement (OFIs)*:
  - ✓ Figure 95.1 shows the plant to be laid out rather conventionally; metalworking in lower-left corner; subassembly & accessories lower-center; test & final assembly directly above; and so forth.
  - ✓ This suggests that the most far-reaching OFIs lie in breaking up those functions and reorganizing into product-family-focused cellular modules.
  - ✓ This can be done as a continuous effort, cell upon cell—as little as one process pair at a time, spread over many months.
  - ✓ Benefits of cellular manufacturing are such that this kind of transformation is likely to more than pay its way, as each increment is completed.

CHAPTER III-96. O.C. TANNER CO., SALT LAKE CITY, UT, 2003

At O.C. Tanner, long a popular plant-tour site, visitors see remarkable applications of flow in extremely low-volume, high-variety manufacturing. My notes are inadequate as to the upgrade of the work force from job-focused to the Tanner Improvement System; thus, that part of the caselet (Part III) is supplemented with information from an article by Robert Hall, along with my own phone interview.	**High-Interest Topics:** • **Conversion from depts. to cells—to achieve quick turn-around in a custom-job setting** • **Massive shipment quantities per day with two-hour order-fill times**

Global Best Model of Low-Volume, High-Mix Production

**Observations Based on Two-Hour Plant Visit,
Jan. 29, 2003**

I. General

- *Main contacts/tour hosts*: Gary Peterson, executive VP, and Mike Collins.
- *The company.* Privately held O.C. Tanner provides recognition award items ("emblems") to some 10,000 companies, reaching millions of employees in 170 countries. Its headquarters and main factory are in Salt Lake City; a second factory was opened near Toronto in the 1980s. Sales are $275 million, workforce 2,200. [Note: In 1999, four years prior to the date of this caselet, the O.C. Tanner plant was recipient of the Shingo Prize]
- *Product line*:
    - ✓ Small medallions made from gold bars, with designs stamped in and perhaps jewels set in. Most are tie-pin and lapel-pin sizes but often are mounted on pens, watches, plaques, TVs, goblets, anything. Gold is bought though price timing (not JIT) and stored in vaults. Tanner has its own facility to refine 24-carat gold to its own specs.

✓ Others: More than 4,000 "Lifestyles" awards—referring to a wide variety of products designed to fit varied preferences of customers:
  ■ These include gold and diamond rings, watches, writing instruments, necklaces, and other fine jewelry.
  ■ Also, active and sports accessories, clocks, electronics, office accessories, crystal, home accessories, and other fine gifts.
✓ An internal communications center designs and produces award brochures, posters, other printed materials for customers.
- *Customers/distribution*: Customers are mostly large companies (GE, DuPont, etc.) that do repeat business.
  ✓ Tanner has taken over employee files of many customers for the purpose of issuing longevity awards (two years, five years, etc.).
  ✓ The distribution center (not visited) has an AS/RS filled mostly with purchased watches, china, crystal, etc., on which they attach gold emblems when ordered by customers.

II. Production Processes

- *Customer orders*:
  ✓ Orders arrive in manufacturing every morning in batches and go to cells (a year or so ago it was to production lines). The plan is to release and complete orders throughout the day rather than in daily batches. A visual listing categorizes orders as Easy, Difficult, or require Setting of stones.
  ✓ Orders rotate in acetate folders with RF-scannable numbers.
    ■ A hand-held RF scanner screen displays the tool number.
    ■ Tools are two-inch cylinders with a design carved in center.
    ■ The tool goes into a kit for a given job, and the kit goes to one of the cell stations, where a design is pressed into a gold blank. 90+% of orders use existing patterns/tools.
    ■ Specs for an order can draw from hundreds of possibilities, such as stone, warp, etc.
  ✓ Ten years ago the order-fill lead time was 12 weeks; now it's down to perhaps two hours. The average order size is 2.3 pieces.
- *Cells.*
  ✓ There were 18 departments three years ago, now only three. The rest were converted to eight U-shaped, nine-person

one-piece-flow cells that process small gold blanks in 2.5-inch-square yellow plastic kanban (swap-system) trays; plus a 9th "combo cell" of 18 persons.

- ✓ Combo cell: This special cell has a 55-minute throughput time, and a 30-second station cycle time.
  - It's very long cellular flow is: Two presses → Trim → Drill stone → Wash → Sand burr → Dap (bend) → Back stamp, indicating gold quality (stamping head setup time had taken three to four minutes, now is just a spin of the head) → Solder (small vials of solder in a lazy Susan are replenished/refilled by kanban) → Bond electrically → Pickle (acid clean, formerly in separate department, now in two table-top tanks in the cell) → Sand blast or glass blast (formerly a big machine in a separate building for isolation of blast fines, but now a small home-built machine that can shift easily from sand to glass blast) → Stone set (it took two years to learn, but an easy-to-learn new table-top machine is taking over).
  - The combo team, formerly 39 operators, is now 18—with plans to further reduce to eight or nine. This is highly important in that fewer people results in expanded work content—from intolerably repetitively seconds to minutes, cutting repetitive motion injuries, and raising process ownership and awareness of opportunities for improvement.
- ✓ Job rotation in the cells is every two hours.
- ✓ People issue:
  - Management has been trying to get rid of most chairs in assembly, but many operators are elderly or handicapped, and 70% in a survey said they would have to quit if they had to stand.
  - Some had been taken to an SLC apparel plant to see modular/stand-up sewing first hand, but Tanner associates were still dubious—and the rumor mill spread the negative views.
- *Finished items*: These go to the DC where gold emblems are bonded to pins, watches, etc. (watches are popular—about 600 a day). Total volume is about 10,000 awards a day. Shipping is by UPS/FEDEX, which pick up several times daily. Return policy: Any reason.

III. Improvement System

- *Phone interview*: The following comments are partly based on my phone interview with executive VP Gary Peterson in December 2005, supplemented by information from an article by Robert Hall.*
- *TIS*. The company has fashioned for itself the Tanner Improvement System (*not* Tanner Production System), which has evolved a good deal over the years.
- *From individualistic to teams.*
  - ✓ As cells developed, it became obvious that cell members would need to be cross-trained; otherwise, in the tumult of ever-changing mixes of orders, there would be too many cases of a narrowly skilled member having nothing to do. As with many companies, pay-for-skill was introduced and was effective—but was complicated to administer.
  - ✓ Ten years ago the Tanner suggestion system included, as top prizes, sending people to Hawaii.
  - ✓ Both efforts (pay-for-skills and special suggestion prizes) soon came to be seen as too individualistic; thus, the system has shifted toward team pay, teams implementing their own suggestions, and a multifaceted system of upgrading employees from just work skills to process ownership, coaching others, special efforts, and teamwork.
- *Coaches & facilitators.* Given the huge variety of ways to build a custom emblem, innovative training and improvement practices were needed. High use of coaches date back to the 1990s, but a separate class of coaches was insufficient.
  - ✓ What evolved is a system in which everyone gets coached and everyone is expected to *be* a coach—coaching encompassing every cell and department, up to and including executive ranks.
  - ✓ Group facilitators are the main coaches, serving to guide and monitor the coaching efforts toward 16 coachable topics (e.g., solving problems, recording "close calls" in safety). Everyone meets at least every two weeks with facilitators.
- *Measures.*
  - ✓ Production boards with green (good) and red (poor) categories rate quality (internal defects and customer returns, in which the

---

* For further details, see R.W. Hall, "Creating a Culture of Expectations," *Target*, 20/6 (6th Issue, 2005): 5–12.

offending product goes back to those who built it); efficiency (pieces or awards made per hour); and delivery (meet the production rate). Red zones trigger needs for generating improvement ideas.

✓ The Canadian Tanner plant took six months to adopt the TIS; results include on-times up from 82% to 95% and customer returns cut in half.

IV. Opportunities for Improvement

- *Is it sustainable?* The TIS is very innovative (untried anywhere else?) but seems complex. Can it sustain itself over time?
- *Recording of things not right*: Members should be (but seemingly are not) engaging in a key driver of process improvement—namely, continually recording everything that isn't right or going wrong.
- *Sit versus stand*: A possibility for resolving this dilemma is to tie stand-up work to longer station cycles that *require* steps to the right and left (as is realized at Tanner, sit-down work is bad for body and mind).

CHAPTER III-97. AMOREPACIFIC, SUWON, KOREA, 2003

AmorePacific's plant is a rarity in its industry—cosmetics—having abandoned the usual long assembly line configuration in favor of numerous simple, low-cost cells, each focused on its own family of products. A long post-visit thank-you letter to company management is not included in this caselet because it covers much the same topics as the caselet.	**High-Interest Topics:** • **Adoption of cellular manufacturing slashed channel inventories and enabled simplified sales methods** • **Total elimination of sales reps and agents** • **Dubious plan to consolidate four plants into one**

Rare Example of Cellular Manufacturing in Consumer Packaged Goods:

Assessment Based on 1.5-Hour Plant Visit December 3, 2004

This following a two-hour Schonberger presentation that morning to about 60 company people

I. General

- *Tour hosts*: Yong-Nyun Kim, Sr. VP, mfg. and engrg.; Yong-Chur Hur, VP, Suwon Plant; Jae-Sung Kim, manager, production team; Yu (Doyle Yu), junior researcher, mgmt. planning div.; Kyung-Hwan Part, leader, HRD training center, KSAC.
- *AmorePacific Co.*:
  - ✓ The company, producer of cosmetics, has four factories in Korea, two in China, one in France (for perfume); also, a tea plantation in Busan to the south. Skin products are specially formulated for different regions/races.
  - ✓ Originally, just one Korean plant, executives had elected to open three more plants in Korea—mainly for the unusual purpose (so I was told) of acquiring properties at attractive real estate prices.
  - ✓ The current intent is to integrate the four plants into one large one (about 10,000 sq. meters or 100,000 sf.)—a main reason being that one or more current plants (including Suwon) are in areas zoned for family housing and so must move. The big new plant is under construction now.
- *Attainments*: AmorePacific won a Korea national quality award (a clone of the Baldrige) in November 2004; is ISO-9000 registered—all series; is 28th in sales volume globally in cosmetics (the goal is to rise to 10th by a certain date); and is #4 in perfume in France.
- *Output*. Production is about 20,000 units (a unit is 1 bottle to 1 set of bottles) daily; the plant population had been 180, now is 98.
- *Amore's factory concept*: A sign in the office says, in English, "Virtual Factory," meaning: 1. Ability to simulate the factory from mixing through shipment. 2. A vision of the perfect factory.

II. Plant Operations

- *Limited tour*: The visual part of the visit was concentrated on and limited to packing lines.
- *Schedule*: A weekly sales forecast under MRP/ERP is the basis for arranging and rearranging the schedule. A main scheduling task is to synchronize packing of different cosmetic items that make up a mixed set—each made on a different line. Raw materials are ordered D-1.

- *Batch sizes*:
  - ✓ 5000 units is a mass-production batch.
  - ✓ 2000–5000 units, medium batch.
  - ✓ < 2,000 units, small batch.
- *Production (pack-out) lines*: My tour group (three AmorePacific people and I) viewed the production lines from a walk-around mezzanine overlooking the packaging floor. My hosts explained:
  - ✓ 23 minimally automated lines (cells), with a maximum of three people for larger batch jobs, have replaced a long automated conveyor line that had 15 people working it.
  - ✓ Five or six new U-lines, cellular-like, and much more compact, for medium batches, have fewer operators in close quarters.
  - ✓ One or more cells, for very small batches, are tended by a single person.
- *Labor*: All packaging operators are multifunctional, can do any job, are moved around as schedules dictate. Mixing (not part of the tour) is entirely automated, so there's no job rotation between there and the packing lines.
- *Specs/metrics*:
  - ✓ Visual graphs, trend charts, and so on, are in wide evidence on walls, on wheeled displays, etc.
  - ✓ Each cell has specification charts and diagrams that, for easy seeing, hang on wires.
  - ✓ Efficiency and "Why-fail-to-be-efficient?" charts are updated on every line every day.
  - ✓ A "Total Cost Reduction (TCR)" program focuses on direct labor and direct materials.
- *Setups/changeovers*:
  - ✓ Setup times range from 1–80 minutes or more.
  - ✓ One setup had been reduced from 40 to 9 minutes.
  - ✓ Production associates, maintenance, and engineers work together on setups.
- *Equipment*: AmorePacific has its own engineering company, which designs equipment.
- *Improvement processes*: These include:
  - ✓ A full set of "best practice" programs: 5S, TPM, quality circles, Toyota production system (TPS). All management went to Japan to learn TPS.
  - ✓ 20 quality circles.

- ✓ Every morning before the shift begins, employees get together around a big table to discuss problems of the previous day and generate ideas for improvement.
- ✓ One day a week is for a one-day kaizen project.
- ✓ Fail-safing (they call it error-proofing).
- ✓ Dominant aims include low-cost automation and self-improvement of equipment.
- *Mixing* (discussed, not visited):
  - ✓ Big tanks (maybe three or four of them) sit on a higher mezzanine for large-volume mixing.
  - ✓ Mixing includes water and oil—a difficult mix combination.
  - ✓ 35 batches are mixed per day, where one batch = 40 tons. Mixed batches are moved to filling/packing in two ways:
    - ■ By pipes for a mass-production batch.
    - ■ Smaller tanks on wheels for smaller lots.
  - ✓ SPC system: Consists of quality assurance and inspection.
  - ✓ Control room: Like a military war room, its highly automated controls ensure exact mix amounts.
- *Delivery to customers*: With cellular production of many items concurrently, Amore is able to greatly reduce and simplify the structure of sales and distribution.
  - ✓ Sales are through AmorePacific franchises located in department stores (in Korea and elsewhere), plus a door-to-door sales force for high-end products.
  - ✓ Two distribution centers (down from eight) serve the four plants.
  - ✓ Formerly, there were many sales reps/agents; now *all have been deliberately eliminated* because they distort demand!
  - ✓ The department-store sales force and door-to-door force now are equipped with PDAs (personal data assistant devices) for sending sales data to company planners in nearly real time. So now there is scarcely any "noise" in the system of scheduling.
  - ✓ Lead time is five days for delivery to stores and also to consumers by the door-to-door sales force.

III. Faults/Improvement Opportunities at AmorePacific

- *Check sheet data collection*: I suggested to Jae-Sung Kim and Yong-Chur Hur at a post-tour tea that improvement activities should feature all employees collecting check-sheet data on things going wrong every day.

- *Plant size*: The present size, in area and number of employees, seems about ideal. Earlier I had advised, *don't consolidate* into one plant, which would be about twice as big as a recommended maximum, 50,000 sq. ft. At that, my hosts chuckled, because that topic had arisen and been discussed at my seminar earlier in the day.
- *Alternative to consolidation*: Perhaps the key (but unstated) reason for consolidating is to build all fill-and-pack lines around the costly, wholly automated mixing facilities. If the plant must be consolidated for this reason, one option would be 3 plants—2 buildings on either side of a central mixing plant.
- *Better might be*: Move automated mixing facilities into one 50,000 sq. ft. plant for large-batch orders; then, have a second 50,000-sq.-ft. mixing plant for medium- and small-batch production, with non-automated mixing.

CHAPTER III-98. BOEING 737, RENTON, WA – 2010

The Renton plant for assembly of the Boeing 737 series of aircraft exhibits a remarkable transformation from rather primitive, cumbersome, and delay-prone production to highly simplified, streamlined, and flow-focused production practices.	*High-Interest Topics:* • **Wholesale move of 2,500 support people from remote offices to spaces overlooking 737 assembly line (replacing walls of inventory)** • **"A hundred" color-coded hand-push carts holding component parts, tools, specs—adjacent to where used** • **Subassemblies stem off main assembly line at where-used points** • **Big issue: Designating each assembly line to its own customer family**

Impressive Transformation Stalls at "Next Big Step":

Impressions Based on Three-Hour Personal Tour of 737 Production, July 6, 2010

I. General Overview

- *Plant visit*: The tour focused on just the flow elements of a full lean effort, since that alone—for so large a production system as airplane manufacture—is complex enough. Thus, strategic customer roles and management of production associates and technical support, maintenance, quality, costing, etc., matters were not included.
- *Speeded-up video*: We began by viewing old versus new assembly of 737 passenger aircraft at Boeing's Renton, WA, facility (on www.newairplane.com):
  ✓ The plant opened in 1967 producing the 737-100 and 200. The 757 came in 1982, ending in 2004. The 737 Classic began in 1984—including the 737-300, 400, 500.
  ✓ The 737 Next Generation came on in 1998—a much lighter, more fuel-efficient aircraft competing with the Airbus 330 (10 years after Airbus had launched the 330)—includes the 737-600, 700, 800, and 900ER (extended range).
  ✓ Boeing Production System. The video lists Boeing's (or Boeing 737's) 9 Tactics to Lean: 1. Flow value mapping. 2. Balanced work. 3. Standard work. 4. Visual controls. 5. Point of use location. 6. Feeder lines adjacent to main assembly lines. 7. Breakthrough process/tool redesign (mostly developed in a "moonshine shop"). 8. Pulsed line movement. 9. Moving lines.
- *Old production methods, as of 1999*:
  ✓ Two stories of parts occupied both sides of the assembly lines.
  ✓ Assembly had planes in slant positions most of time. Raw and WIP materials were stored (often lost) in the "Black Hole," a 225,000 sq. ft. on-site building. The entire 3rd shift was devoted to moving aircraft from one position to next via "toe movers" and "crane moves."
- *Major developments*:
  ✓ In 1990 Boeing-Renton published a 65-page monograph, "Just-in-Time Manufacturing: Applications for the Boeing Commercial Airplane Group" (Richard Schonberger wrote the Foreword).
    ■ It included a ten-page bibliography and a vision statement citing, as benefits, reductions in lead times, inventory, WIP, setups, space, etc.

- The main author, Davis Steelquist, Total Quality Associate, expressed frustration in a handwritten note, "We are being told 'JIT' is not in this company's vocabulary or future. But I may have found a champion in the corporate headquarters."
- ✓ In 1992 a large executive team spent two years in Japan learning TPS and "world-class competitiveness." Their knowledge was shared but for some years not applied.
- ✓ 1994–96 introduced DCAC-MRM (Define and Control Aircraft Configuration/Material Requirements Management—with Baan configuration-management software), which began in Boeing's components fabrication and parts areas.
- ✓ In 1997, two major events:
  - Merger with McDonnell Douglas.
  - Sold a lot of 737s, straining capacity with dire results. In trying to ramp up from 24 to 28 planes per month, the "system broke" (as the tour guide put it). Suppliers could not ramp up, and there were up to 1,000 component-parts shortages at end of line, with 40 planes waiting for parts.
  - So Boeing shut down all 737 assembly for a full month and considered three options: 1. Move the 737 to California (former McDonnell-Douglas plant). 2. Move it to Everett, WA (the massive plant in which Boeing's biggest aircraft are assembled). 3. Adopt a moving line a la automotive.
  - Option 3 was chosen—and required, to change mind-sets and culture, (a) massive training, (b) simulation to prove it would work. In 1999 the moving line began phase-in.

II. Physical Overview

- *Tour*: Main building, in an open VIP cart:
  - ✓ Building 4–81 is the main 737 building: 750 K sf.
  - ✓ Building 4–82 is from the 1941 B-29-era: 1 million sf. The building now has "flying buttresses" all around to shore up the sides as anti-earthquake measures.
  - ✓ The rail line where the main fuselage, in green protective film, arrives from Spirit AeroSystems (Wichita, KS) and then goes onto a transporter to move it to first position in assembly.
  - ✓ Wings are assembled in one of the other Renton buildings (we did not go there).

- *Tour host*: Gordon A. Litzenberger (supply-chain management analyst in 737 materials management/supplier relations) had invited me to tour the 737 plant.
  - ✓ He had done many tours, nearly all for visiting suppliers; this tour was just me, with Litzenberger as guide.
  - ✓ He had been highly involved in teaching DCAC when it was being launched and implemented, circa 1994, and had taught other courses at Boeing and APICS since then.

III. The Flow (Lean) Mode

- *Flow and its effects*:
  - ✓ By 2002 the moving line was fully operational. By 2006 WIP was down from 30 to 11 days' worth with 60% fewer parts. Flow time fell from 22 to 10 days in 2010, and positions on the assembly line went from eight to four with one wing-join station instead of two.
  - ✓ In 1989 the number of planes in assembly was 27—now reduced to just 10 or 11.
- *Related improvements*:
  - ✓ In the "move to the Lake," 2,500 support people (QA, engineers, finance, HR, others) were moved from one or more remote office buildings into two stories of offices in the assembly building (near Lake Washington), a location where parts were previously stored.
  - ✓ Windows had been cut into outer walls to let in natural light, lots of bright colors replaced the drab.
  - ✓ 41% of total Renton land (and buildings), no longer needed, were sold off as inventories melted and support people were moved next to the action.
  - ✓ Currently, 80% of production is of the 737–800, which holds about 110 passengers, ER version 180 to 220 passengers.
  - ✓ P8A Poseidon, assembled in the 4–82 building in small quantities, is an extended-range anti-submarine warfare 737 version; the building also houses production of the BBJ business jet, a customized 737.
- *Main assembly*: two lines in Building 4–81.
  - ✓ The main assembly line is in the longer assembly bay, east of a shorter bay for the second line. Brief explanation of technical positions/flow days for the main assembly line follow:

- Days 1 and 2: Fuselage (body), from Wichita, goes through systems installation steps in three positions at the beginning (south) end of main assembly but 90 degrees off to the side of the line. The plane's body moves, by overhead crane, from a special transporter (in leather cradles, from a rail car to inside of Building 4–81) to position 2, then position 3.
- Day 3 technical position: Wings to body-join; landing gear as well. Each technical position—day 3 through day 8—has its own color, which applies to paint on the floor, fixtures, kitting carriers, etc. For example, the color for this position is blue.
- Day 4 starts the moving line—with plane, wings attached, jacked up on a wheeled transporter as long as the plane. The plane gets water and waste tanks, temporary floor, etc.
- Day 5: Rear galley, wire and plumbing connections . . .
- Day 6: Wall panels, ceiling . . .
- Day 7: Carpets, sidewalls, . . .
- Day 8: Pressure tests, seats, engines . . .
- In Day 9, the plane is toe-moved to a position 90 degrees and to the left (one's left hand if one is looking in the direction the flow line moves) of the Day-8 position, for a thorough customer examination.
- Day 10 is at an outside location, where customer issues are resolved.
- Day 11 is paint (1 of 11 planes is painted in Renton, the other 10 at Boeing field, Seattle).

✓ Further details:

- At 6:00 a.m. the moving assembly line starts at the 4th technical position. The transporter moves electronically following a narrow metallic pathway at 2 inches per minute—which moves the plane only 80 feet. The line is moving only half the time or less.
- Movement stops for morning, afternoon, and lunch breaks (by union rules).
- To make up for those stops, and for the slow movement rate, the line is "pulsed" twice per shift (at 10:00 a.m. and 2:30 p.m. for the day shift) by turning up the line speed to move the plane a half position.

✓ Future vision—now prevalent among the lean team—is:
  ▪ Go from two-per-shift pulsing to four pulses per shift—halving the "jerk" time—then eight pulses per shift, and so on—driving plane movement ever closer to continuous flow.
  ▪ Change the mostly straight assembly line to a longer, quicker, U-shaped cell-like line with fewer total flow days (e.g., eight or seven).

✓ Orders and assembly/purchasing schedule:
  ▪ The lineup sequence of planes—and orders for parts—is set (at least tentatively) years in advance, since orders for 737s are backlogged by some 5.5 years. More than half of the orders are from three big customers.
  ▪ On lines 1 and 2 the plane models/customers are sequenced irregularly from many different customers (*not* mixed-model-regularized). The main assembly line and line 2 are not dedicated to particular models/configurations or customers.
  ▪ The plane assembly is driven mainly by Wichita's delivery of fuselages, which are the largest, and (second to engines) among the most costly components of a finished plane. (Engines are about $30 million for a plane costing about $90 million.)

✓ Kitting, subassembly, and material movement:
  ▪ Nearly all small parts for all flow days are kitted in line-side material stores areas on the right side of the moving line. Some are mixes of direct materials, their required installation tools, fluids, hazardous materials, etc. Other kits are all direct materials, or all tools and other supporting items. Color indicators (wrappings, shadow boxes, containers) are blue for parts, white for tools, red for chemicals (solvents, etc.). "Water striders" (material control people), do the kitting using pick lists.
  ▪ Subassemblies, completed on the left side of the line just in time for installation in the adjacent technical position, have two advantages over old methods: They are done close to where needed rather than in an off-site location, requiring transport; and are not done within the plane itself, which would increase total flow time.

- The assembly floor is awash with small, simple, hand-push modular dollies and trolleys for moving small-lot quantities of kitted materials to the lines just in time. The plant is delightfully free of bulk handling by forklift trucks moving materials by stacked-high pallets, or tugger trains pulling materials by trailer-full.
- Small low-cost parts, such as fasteners, are received in a Renton warehouse, and then delivered to assembly via a min-max system.
- A large area (near line 2) holds buyer-furnished equipment (BFE) items, e.g., galleys and lavatories.

✓ Eight rapid-response teams (RRTs):
- Each RRT is assigned to one of the eight flow days/technical positions to fix issues there. Just to the right of each technical-position is an RRT "barge"—usually two manufacturing reps, one expediter, one pit boss, and their desks, computers, etc., marked off by a low-rail perimeter. An electronic "andon" displays the state of the technical position.
- Each RRT works with a shipside action tracker (SAT) monitoring each issue the RRT is working on. When an issue occurs, the *yellow* of a stack-light group is turned on.
- The SAT fix-time target is 15 minutes (e.g., to get the assembly problem corrected and avoid delaying the plane's move to next technical position).
- More than 15 minutes triggers a *purple* light (critical issue), referred to relevant experts in nearby offices (e.g., QA, ME, etc.), who have a two-hour fix-time target, calling for a recovery plan—agreed to by all parties.
- When a component arrives late, the plane moves continue without the component; and when it comes in, assembly associates go to where the plane has moved to install it (which could incur some difficulties, such as removing other items that are in the way).

• *Second assembly line*:
  ✓ This second line combines some of the technical positions, resulting in fewer position moves for each plane)—in a bay west of the main assembly line.

✓ Located at and maybe dedicated to the 2nd assembly line is a large kitting area, not line-side, which prepares kits (maybe; notes unclear) for the 2nd shift.
- *Point needing clarification.* What is a normal flow of parts from suppliers? Perhaps it's something like this, for, say, a typical supplier of wiring bundles:
  ✓ Truck delivers bundles to a raw materials warehouse in the vicinity of the two main assembly buildings, bundles typically residing in warehouse for, say, two days.
  ✓ In the assembly building, a kanban "disk" is hung on magnetic kanban board just behind the kitting area lineside to the given technical position; the disk is scanned by a materials person, which sends a pull signal to the warehouse.
  ✓ A warehouse attendant puts the wire bundle(s) on a carrier (tugger and trailer?) that takes the bundle(s) to assembly and off-loads it in the line-side kitting area.
  ✓ Kitting takes place in the shift just before need in assembly.

IV. Numerics

- *Parts*: 378,000 unique parts make up the 737 inventory.
- *Inventory turns*: For this plant, it had been 3 months' supply, now one week's supply.
- *Operating profit margins*: For this plant, up to double-digit.
- *Shifts/overtime*: Old was three shifts and 30–50% OT. Now two shifts, five days, and less than 5% OT.

V. Engine Build-up

- *Arrival and test*: Far left of assembly line 2 is a pulse-move, three-station engine build-up area, where, usually, an arriving Snecma-GE engine has fastening and other parts added, and then a test of the engine. But this area is seen as a "monument" obstacle:
  ✓ The engine hangs from an overhead rail, moving through each of the three positions in one day shift. The rail and other apparatus are fixed—not flexible and mobile—part of why the lean improvement group views it a "monument."
  ✓ A plan has been worked out and scheduled to eliminate the monument features—probably going to a fixture on wheels.

VI. Critique

- *Product/customer focus*: Renton 737's production design is outstanding in many respects, ranking highly among lean world's best. However, there is a missing ingredient that would beneficially combine the lean-assembly design with other aspects of the competitive whole—customers, orders, production/delivery lead times, predictability, simplicity, supplier costs and lead times, total costs, prices, profit margins, quality. I refer to lack of a hard focus (or value-stream identity) on dominant plane configurations and customers.
  - ✓ Good: The special 737 configurations/models—P8A Poseidon, and the BBJ business—are treated as separate value streams and located over in Building 4–82.
  - ✓ Need for change: The two assembly lines in Building 4–81, are *not* separately focused.
    - It would make good lean sense for the "high runners," the two or three dominant configurations—for dominant customer SW Airlines, and perhaps Ryan Air, and maybe China Air— to be assembled in one dedicated assembly line.
    - Then, assemble many low-volume configurations for many other customers, on a second, wide-mix line. That second line, given its lower volumes and much broader mix of parts and subassemblies, would operate like the present assembly line model—with eight technical stations and 11 total flow days.
- *Features of the dedicated line*:
  - ✓ The dominant configurations/dominant customers line would have a repeating mixed-model schedule, that regularity passed back to suppliers, thereby greatly simplifying and routinizing their operations with significant supplier cost reductions; also more predictable finishing and delivery regularity to airline customers.
  - ✓ Kitting would be routinized to a regular repeating takt-time-like schedule, reducing the rather chaotic scrambles to match up kitting with the irregular schedules of plane models—and reducing the present high direct and overhead costs of kitting.
  - ✓ Issues confronting the RRTs in their barges, and that enter the shipside action tracker (SAT), should be considerably reduced.

Presently, most of the issues may be related to incoming materials delays or wrong parts or defects. In the dedicated line those issues should be cut at least in half.

✓ With fewer issues, RRT teams and their technical support backup should shrink in size and budget. And with more repeatability, the line speed would be faster, reducing flow days to, say, 8 days or less instead of 11.

✓ Total production costs would be considerably lower; product costing considerably sharper.

✓ The two or three dominant customers would get price breaks, solidifying commitments to Boeing 737s versus Airbus.

✓ With lowered costs and prices of dominant models/configurations, one or two of the models might become promoted, for marketing purposes, as a high-volume, low-priced "standard model" (standard in many respects while still accommodating customer preferences regarding service facilities).

✓ The revised marketing strategy would be to get other airlines, those now in the dogs-cats ordering mode, to switch to higher-volume orders of one of the two or three Boeing Standard 737s, the main attraction: the standard model would be costed and priced at $5m, $10m, or $15m less than the airlines had been paying for low-volume, irregularly ordered configurations.

✓ Overall results would include greater sales and market share; higher margins through lowered overhead and direct costs, plus lower supplier and customer serving costs; more cash available to invest in continual upgrading of 737 aircraft design and production; and an extended life cycle for the brand.

- *Lean flow-line vision*:

✓ For reasons given above, I see the vision of the Boeing lean team, described earlier, as going backwards—from simplicity to high complexity and risk (no backup if a serious stoppage), in which the single "grand" line becomes its own "monument."

✓ The urge to compress two or more production lines into one line is widespread in industry—but it runs counter to a dominant lean concept: multiple cells or lines each dedicated to its own value-stream family of products and/or customers.

✓ In some industries—those that are more capital intensive—two or more value-stream-focused lines would be cost-prohibitive because each line would need its own costly machinery and related facilities. That is not the case here, especially since lean teams have done such great work in downsizing material handling: no overhead conveyors loaded with parts, minimal overhead crane moves, scarcely any forklift trucking, abolishment of monument machines of all kinds. Thus, compressing all assembly into a single line is not justifiable on the basis of equipment savings.

CHAPTER III-99. GLEASON CORP., ROCHESTER, NY, 2011

Gleason Corp. manufactures large, heavy-duty gear-making machine tools that are made up of several large subassemblies, each with many component parts.	*High-Interest Topics:* • **Toward reduction of machines in a state of final assembly; getting them in and out quickly** • **Big issue: Designating each assembly line to its own customer family**

Toward Moderating Confusion in Final Assembly of Large Machine Tools: Observations Based on 1.5-Hour Plant Tour, Nov. 15, 2011

In connection with Schonberger PDM (professional development meeting) presentation for APICS Rochester that evening

I. Basic Information

- *Origins*: William Gleason opened his machine shop in 1965 and moved it to its present site in 2004. James S. Gleason, grandson of founder, is chairman of the corp.
- *Facilities*: The Rochester HQ/mother plant occupies a 145-year-old, 715,000-sq. ft., very long and narrow building along University Ave., with railroad tracks behind the building. Across the street is residential plus some businesses—not at all like an industrial area.
- *Products/customers*: The sole product is machines and tooling for manufacture of bevel and cylindrical gears. Customers are machine shops of manufacturers in automotive/trucks (three-quarters of sales), aerospace, construction, farm, and marine—two-thirds of sales for which are to non-U.S. customers.

- *Other plants*: China, England, Germany, India, Switzerland, and the United States.
- *Contact persons*: Kevin Hill, director of mfg.; John Mahoney, manager, production control; Gary Figler, VP, Rochester operations; Timothy Herron, director, supply chain; also, tour arrangements by Larry Maggio, executive VP, APICS Rochester.

II. Details

- *Gleason Rochester's five businesses*: 1. Machine build. 2. Tooling. 3. Service. 4. Small lots. 5. Leasing excess space.
- *Strategic outsourcing*: Historically, Gleason was highly vertically integrated but eight years ago began an aggressive effort for strategic outsourcing; for example, it got out of sheet metal and forging while retaining core competencies.
- *Leased, in-house suppliers*: The plant is half empty, with some emptied space leased to two strategic-partner suppliers:
  ✓ 45,000 sq. ft. to Excello for electric panel boxes; the other space to Advantage Machining for sheet metal and paint.
  ✓ 50,000 sq. ft. is presently empty and available for lease. 40,000 sq. ft. is offices (or to be leased as offices).
- *Lean efforts*:
  ✓ Visual management, begun last year, now includes color-coding and hot-job IDs. And 2.5 years ago, 5S was reinvigorated.
  ✓ Eight wastes and value-add emphasis began last year, with "waste walks" done. weekly and celebrated every two weeks; 111 waste walks have taken place since then.
  ✓ "PROPEL" effort (Parts Ready . . .).
  ✓ "Chunked the machines" (presumably referring to modularized subassembly).
  ✓ Materials managed by kanban, using many pallet jacks and scarcely any forklift trucks.
- *My tour*:
  ✓ Final assembly, in a wing of the building that used to be the foundry, includes test and run off. 65% is mechanical and electrical assembly.
  ✓ Eight smaller bridge cranes extend halfway across the long bay serving a limited span along the length of the bay, and two giant

bridge cranes (on double rails, each rail supported by opposite walls).

✓ Each of 50–60 build bays assembles a customer-spec machine—about 50 bays active right now.

✓ Spindle assembly includes 20 people in a clean room subassembling spindles, a largely repetitive operation. Then, as part of final spindle assembly, spindles go out of assembly to heat treat, which is set up as a cost center, taking in work from outside manufacturers; note: grinding is high-skill, hard-to-staff.

✓ A short-run cell (where the old foundry used to be) makes parts that were obsolete years ago but are still sold.

✓ Welding was formerly ten booths, is now just one.

✓ A wear-parts cell includes turn, grind, saw, . . ., heat treat. For these wear parts, the former 16–18 week flow time has been cut to four to six weeks.

✓ Heat treat has 5 furnaces; the biggest furnace quenches (saves a lot of grinding since quenching preserves specs from distortions); also a degreaser.

III. Critical Observations

- *Machines in final assembly*:
  ✓ A large number of machines—around 60 or more—are in assembly at a given time, each requiring many weeks of assembly (my best guess; I did not ask about typical assembly throughput times).
  ✓ I have visited other manufacturers of large, complex, multi-component products. Usually, I see the same thing as at Gleason (including some years ago at Mazak in Kentucky; see Chapter II-46); also at IBM.
- *Better way*: A few manufacturers employ a better way, one that reduces throughput times manyfold, while also reducing the number of machines in final assembly by a lot—such as, perhaps at Gleason, from 60 machines to maybe 15 or 10. Examples of this reduction of machines in a state of final assembly include Boeing helicopters in Mesa, AZ, and a mainframe computer maker that I visited in Ireland years ago.

- *Better-way details*:
  - ✓ In this mode, each final-assembly station is surrounded by five, six, seven, or maybe eight or nine subassembly stations, each focused on its own family of a major module that may (or may not) be ordered by a given customer for the end-product machine. That is, each subassembly station is well equipped with common parts, hardware, fixtures, test/metrology devices, etc.
  - ✓ If a customer orders a machine requiring a certain subassembly, its station, being pre-equipped for immediate start-up, is fed component parts by kanban from purchased stores or from in-house fabrication cells. (At the end of this plant tour, I quickly drew a rough schematic of this floor configuration and briefly explained, maybe to Kevin Hill, that I think it might work well at Gleason.)
  - ✓ At start-up of a customer order, assemblers go to work on the base and frame of the end product, and at the same time subassemblers work on major modules.
  - ✓ This mode of manufacture—ideal for large, complex, multi-component products—aims at getting machines into and out of production, and onward toward the customer very quickly—and by *concurrency*: multiple subassemblies getting done concurrently and in synch with final assembly. (Mazak's production mode, when I saw it years ago, was slow, serial production instead of quick concurrent assembly.)
- *High-level synchronization/visibility*:
  - ✓ There is much more that needs doing at Gleason in regard to flow of materials; kanban linkages; flexible, multi-skilled associates who move to where the work is; and so on.
  - ✓ These steps—getting everything synchronized to what's happening on the machine and its subassembly modules—are made relatively easy and natural once the floor configuration creates its own high-level synchronization and visibility.
  - ✓ There seems to a boggling lack of such visibility as things stand today at Gleason.
- *Alternative*: An alternate for quick throughput is in place at Mark Andy, St. Louis-area producer of customer-configured flexographic printers (see Chapter III-70).
  - ✓ Those printers—though having large numbers of component parts—differ from Gleason machines, helicopters, and mainframe

computers in being at least 75% smaller. With small modules and parts, quick assembly at Mark Andy revolves around separate sequenced shelving locations for each major module rather than a floor-based configuration.

✓ This kind of focused parts sequencing may be useful at Gleason, though my short plant visit did not turn up in my notes any specific examples.

CHAPTER III-100. BMW ENGINES, STEYR, AUSTRIA, 2011

This caselet is short because its basis was a tour just for a group of us in town for an academic conference, all asking their own questions over a short tour time. It is included in this book primarily for presentation of a remarkably odd example of automation.	**High-Interest Topics:** • **Automation for automation's sake** • **Upgrading to a focus on dominant engine models**

Too Much Flexibility: Observations Based on 1.5-Hour Group Tour, May 3, 2011

In connection with International Value Chain Management Conference, May 4–5, 2011

The tour group was made up of (nearly all) professors attending the conference

I. Basic Information

- *Steyr plant*:
    - ✓ Established in 1979, the plant opened in 1982. Plant population is 3,800 in a three shift, 24/7 operation.
    - ✓ Now the largest BMW engine plant, it produces 2 out of 3 BMW engines. A recent large uptick in car sales was echoed in production here.
- *Products*: Four- and six-cylinder diesel and six-cylinder petrol engines—65% diesel, 35% petrol, in 1,000 engine variations.
    - ✓ Engines are shipped in sequence to assembly plants.
    - ✓ Maybe 60% of parts are standard, but with many wiring harnesses, 20 different turbo chargers, etc.

- *Customers*: Engines go to BMW vehicle assembly plants worldwide (i.e., Spartanburg, SC, USA; Chennai, India; Thailand; China; South Africa; Madagascar; U.K.; Kalingrad, Russia; and eight plants in Germany).
- *Simultaneous engineering*: Car and engine are designed concurrently.
- *Greenness*. This plant is the greenest in Austria, recycling water, petrol, CO_2, and others.

II. Details

- *Physical plant*: Several production "sheds" are all in a line, with supplier sheds alongside; an additional Shed 63 across rail tracks is an AS/RS (automatic storage and retrieval) warehouse.
  - ✓ *Connecting rods*: Machined as a single cylinder with a machined-in notch on either side; a sharp tool smashes the shaft at each notch so the shaft breaks into top and bottom arcs. When the crankshaft is assembled around the crank and screwed together, the top and bottom pieces fit together tighter—break to break—than if top and bottom were machined smooth.
  - ✓ *First shed for crankcase assemblies*: 9,000 sq. m., 63 employees.
    - The flow time for these major engine components is 6.5 hours, through many machining stations with high station-to-station automation and redundancy, so that if one station is down, work continues.
    - The crankshaft facility is astonishing to behold: It looks, from an upstairs mezzanine viewing platform, rather like a bowling alley of about five, six, or seven "lanes." Each lane has the automation—many machining stations in straight lines (as if toward the "pins")—and capability through programming of producing any of the multiple crankshaft models. Is there anything like it elsewhere in the world—and as complex and costly?
  - ✓ *Second shed for connecting rods*: A 500-sq.m. U-line for connecting rods, with two deburr robots.
  - ✓ *AS/RS*: The storage facility has five storage bays that hold 13,000 containers for incoming parts.
  - ✓ *Cylinder-head shed*: This 850-sq.m. facility has a flow time of 20–24 seconds for 1.3 million engines produced last year.
  - ✓ *Engine assembly*: Upstairs from the cylinder-head shed is pre-assembly of camshafts, a tall in-process AR/RS with 4 positions, and a partly or largely manual assembly line.

- *Continuous process (or product) improvement (CIP)*: Calls for two ideas per employee per year, done in groups and (in Austria) paid in groups—with a required minimum savings of 2,500 euros per idea; metrics include PPM (parts per million) defectives.
- *Quality*: Suppliers are "poor" so every part is checked.

III. Assessment

- *Overall*: The facility is impressive in size, scope, output, and product flexibility.
- *Product-focus issues*:
  - ✓ The highly automated crankshaft line comes across as automation for automation's sake—overly costly to design, build, operate, and maintain. As it stands, it *could* be simplified to good advantage by dedicating, say, one (or more) of the "lanes" to its own dominant crankshaft or family of highly similar ones—and run that lane not for 24-hour maximum output but run "to-a-number"—that number being the recent sales rate.
  - ✓ As the tour ended, I asked our tour guide about dominant engine models. He said, yes, they have that—and named one particular high-demand engine model. I suggested dedicated (no-change or little change) production lines for such models; his reply: "BMW likes to make things complicated."

CHAPTER III-101. ELECTROIMPACT, INC., MUKILTEO, WA, 2014

My notes for ElectroImpact are brief because much of the group tour I was with was just looking at massive machines that automatically rivet whole airplane wings or fuselages—one machine so perfectly balanced that a person moved it on its rail-tracks one-handed. The caselet ends with excerpts from my thank-you letter.

High-Interest Topics:
- **A product, customer, and employee focus—all at the same time!**
- **No silos, no departments**
- **Engineers who do their own ordering of materials, contracting with suppliers, building machines, and traveling with machines to global customers for installation**

Maverick Manufacturer Goes Its Own Way
Observations From an SME (Society of Mfg. Engineers) Group Plant Tour, Sept. 18, 2014

I. General Information

- *The company.* Privately held ElectroImpact produces a wide variety of automation and tooling equipment, usually of massive sizes, for aerospace manufacturers: automated drilling and fastening machines, fiber-placement machines for composite fabrication (e.g., making wings), aircraft final-assembly equipment, and robotic systems.
  - ✓ Started in 1986 by Dr. Peter Zieve, it is said to be the "ultimate engineer's company": It has no departments. Instead, each engineer has personal responsibility for designing, buying their own materials, contracting with suppliers (anyone can qualify suppliers), building, marketing, and flying to customer sites to install and staying until the customer says it's right.
  - ✓ All work is set up as dedicated-to-a-customer projects.
  - ✓ Of 677 employees, 540 are engineers, 65 are machinists, seven are in accounts payable, etc., plus five apprentices. Primary sources of engineers are Cal Poly, MIT, and Colorado School of Mines—and with 75 currently from the University of Washington. Besides the local area, it has engineers in the U.K. and a few in China, Australia, and Brazil.
  - ✓ The company has only nine patents; the owner is not inclined to try to make money on patents.
  - ✓ 10–20% of machining is in-house; outside contractors number about 12,000.
  - ✓ 40 people are currently working with Embraer to build (in Brazil) a wing-box factory with a complement of ElectroImpact machines.
  - ✓ Annual revenue is $160–200m. Projects include 25 that are up to $20m.
- *Tour host*: Ben Hempstead, chief of staff, and inventor of the electro riveter.

- *Facility*:
  - ✓ Processing includes a great deal of prototyping and testing—so that the machine will not break when used by the customer. One unusual wrinkle: instead of lab oil in testing, they use peanut butter.
  - ✓ The plant has great lighting—designed to avoid any shadows.
  - ✓ For efficiency and ergonomics, nothing (except the products themselves) is more than 52 inches tall.
  - ✓ Other than that, the plant is very messy—opposite to 5S neatness.
- *Machine in process—example*: A vertical panel assembly line—in production for Boeing's 737 plant—is 120 ft long and 40 ft tall.

II. Critical Observation

- *Thank-you letter*: The following are excerpts from my thank-you email to Mr. Hempstead (the email included other paragraphs that are not of interest here):

Dear Ben,

I am the one who shook your hand at the end of the SME tour, saying that I've toured a hundred factories in about all industries in many countries, but you were the best tour guide—and the tour was one of the best. . . .

Just one strong criticism: As you admitted, the place is a mess, which is the too-bad norm in model shops but should not be the norm in production, test, etc. (No doubt this is the subject of plentiful discussions among you and your colleagues.) Such messes are not just cosmetic, plus a possible turn-off to some prospective employees, customers, and other important visitors. They are sink holes of inefficiency, quality problems, and maintenance problems. I'm reminded of East Bay Generator Co., North Oakland, CA, which a consultant that I knew took me to see in 1990. East Bay's business was/is reconditioning auto generators, alternators, etc., and many of the parts used came in from tear-downs of incoming, nonworking units. They had been stacked and stored everywhere and anywhere, so unsystematically that, I was told, a little time-studying showed that searching for parts—assemblers walking all over the place—was consuming on average 6 hours of the 8-hour shifts. However, at the time of my visit, everything was in a labeled, easy-to-find place, within families of models of units. It was not just housekeeping, but more important was reorganization by type of product—just as you do at ElectroImpact. (Organization and layout by product/customer family is the most effective of all lean practices. You've got that very right at your company!)

+ + +

Annotated Bibliography

In the following references key topics are highlighted in bold type, and they may be roughly in order of prominence in the caselets. No doubt I've overlooked a few other key concepts, but this bibliography is peripheral to the body of the book. (Apology: Many of my most admired books and authors are not included, usually because someone else treated the topic earlier or more fully or more directly.)

N. Hyer and U. Wemmerlov. 2002. *Reorganizing the Factory: Competing through Cellular Manufacturing*. Productivity Press. – At 770 pages, this may be seen as the "bible" of **cellular manufacturing**—which, the authors aver (p. 41), is a prerequisite and core foundation for just-in-time production.

W. Skinner. 1974. "The Focused Factory," *Harvard Business Review*, (May-June): 113–121. – Skinner's important, early work, gave us the key term, **focused factory**, and led to further conceptual development, by others, of focused factory-within-the factory, plant-in-a-plant, and so on.

S. Shingo. 1985. *A Revolution in Manufacturing: The SMED System*. Productivity Press. – The leading source of detailed information on **quick setup** and **quick changeover**.

S. Nakajima. 1984. *TPM: Introduction to TPM, Total Productive Maintenance*. Productivity Press. – Source book for **total productive maintenance (TPM)**.

H. Hirano. 1994. *Five Pillars of the Visual Workplace: The Sourcebook of the 5S Implementation*. Productivity Press. – The primary book about **5S**.

P.R. Thomas. 1991. *Getting Competitive: Middle Management and the Cycle Time Ethic*. McGraw-Hill. – This book and the Thomas Group (of mostly independent, "virtual," consultants), though not (or no longer) well known, did good work in the 1990s in turning manufacturers toward a primary strategy of **reducing cycle times** (aka, flow times, throughput times, lead-times).

R. Suri. 1998. *Quick Response Manufacturing: A Companywide Approach to Reducing Lead Times*. Productivity Press. – While the Thomas book fostered cycle-time reduction, this book by Suri elevates the matter in its advocacy of **quick-response manufacturing**, which raises the stature of the concept from production to the whole company for **customer-focused manufacturing**.

H.T. Johnson and R.S. Kaplan. 1987. *Relevance Lost: The Rise and Fall of Management Accounting*. Harvard Business School Press. – This book was instrumental in launching the campaign to bury the **standard cost/cost-variance system**—ill-fitting in an era of just-in-time and flow operations (and defective for other reasons as well).

K. Ishikawa. 1985. *What Is Total Quality Control? The Japanese Way*. Prentice-Hall. – Included in this book are two important methodological contributions of Ishikawa: the **cause-and-effect diagram** (aka, Ishikawa diagram or chart); and, in Chapter XII, a listing and discussion of **the seven basic (or elementary) tools**. (The book's subtitle is an overstatement: It's not the Japanese way, it's just good quality management.) The *total quality control (TQC)* concept itself dates back to the 1961 book by that title by U.S. author, Armand Feigenbaum.

S. Shingo, 1981. *Study of Toyota Production System: from Industrial Engineering Viewpoint.* Japan Management Association. This was the first English-language book on the **Toyota production system (TPS)**, aka, **just-in-time (JIT) production** and **kanban**. The translation from the Japanese was poor, referred to in some quarters as "Janglish." Still, Omark Industries, perhaps the first Western company to plunge deeply into the methodology, bought 500 copies and put them to good use.

R.J. Schonberger. 2017. "With Machinery Purchases, Small Can Be Beautiful," *ISE Magazine*, June, pp. 40–43. – This article sets forth the rationale for equipping and operating plants with **multiple small simple, inexpensive equipment units** for producing multiple product models at the same time, in close synch with actual downstream usage. A much earlier work, from which the *ISE* article was copied, is: R.J. Schonberger. 1985. *Sizing Equipment to the Piece*, an unpublished monograph, resurrected and printed almost intact as the *ISE* 2017 article.

G. Boothroyd and P. Dewhurst. 1987. *Product Design for Assembly*. Boothroyd Dewhurst, Inc. – A precursor publication by the two originators/developers of **design for manufacture and assembly (DFMA)**.

S. Shingo. 1985. Zero Quality Control: Source Inspection and Poka-yoke system. Productivity Press. – The Japanese term, **pokayoke**, meaning something like mistake-proofing, is translated in the case-lets as **fail-safing**, a neutral word that avoids negative connotations.

R. Cooper and R.S. Kaplan. 1988. "Measure Costs Right: Make the Right Decisions," *Harvard Business Review* (Sept.-Oct.): 96–103. – While there were other publications on the innovation called **activity-based costing (ABC)**, this article prominently spread the word.

W.E. Deming. 1982. *Quality, Productivity, and Competitive Position*. MIT Center for Advance Engineering Study. – Deming's works, including this book, ardently advocate **statistical process control** (SPC).

R.J. Schonberger. 1982. *Japanese Manufacturing Technologies: Nine Hidden Lessons in Simplicity*. Free Press. – This was the first book by a non-Japanese that featured **just-in-time/total quality control (JIT/TQC)**.

R.J. Schonberger, 1990, *Building a Chain of Customers: Linking Business Functions to Create the World Class Company*. Free Press. – Chapter 8. Minimal Accounting and Noncost Cost Control, includes a section that argues (pp. 183–184) for **cost audits, as needed**, rather than uselessly costing the same products or services over and over again via extensive, ongoing cost-collection transactions.

R.J. Schonberger and K.A. Brown. 2017. "Missing Link in Competitive Manufacturing Research and Practice: Customer-Responsive Concurrent Production," *Journal of Operations Management*, 49/51: 83–87. – The rationale for multiple equipment units for producing multiple products at the same time is presented in this article under the label, **concurrent production** (aka, synchronous or parallel production).

R.J. Schonberger, 2018. "Frustration-Driven Process Improvement," *Business Horizons*, 61/2 (Mar.-Apr.): 297–307. This is the first article specific to the methodology of **every employee recording frustrations**—as grist for process improvement.

J.P. Womack, D.T. Jones, D. Roos. 1990. *The Machine That Changed the World: The Story of Lean Production: How Japan's Secret Weapon in the Global Auto Wars Will Revolutionize Western Industry*. HarperCollins. – The index to "The Machine" includes but three of the terms that are highlighted in the previous references: kanban, statistical process control, and total quality control. It does list just-in-time *inventory*, which has the unfortunate effect of down-grading flow manufacturing's primary pursuit—which is

just-in-time *production*. Just looking at the index is, of course, an inadequate portrayal of the book's content (partly because doing an index is usually rather an after-
thought by book authors). A few of the terms missing from the index can be found, at
least conceptually, within chapter discussions.

Despite its beneficial effects on industry (the book reinvigorated the flagging JIT/TPS
movement via a name change and the book's focus on the best-known industry, automotive), *The Machine* is hardly a story about *lean production* or about *Japan's secret*. Its
basis—as noted on the book's cover (my soft-cover version), is "The MIT International
Motor Vehicle Program," which exclusively researched global auto-assembly plants. If
that research and the book had also included plants making automotive components,
it would have not only included, but would have *featured* quick setup, cells, TPM, 5S,
cycle time/lead time, Ishikawa diagrams, and more.

R.J. Schonberger. 1987. "Frugal Manufacturing," *Harvard Business Review* (Sept.-Oct.):
95–100. – The article addressed most of the key topics high-lighted in the preceding
bibliography. A speculation: If "**Frugal Manufacturing**" had not been published in
HBR, perhaps that term would have been chosen instead of *lean manufacturing* in the
book, *The Machine That Changed the World*. That would have been fortuitous in that
frugal is a durable word, and the term *lean* has become problematic.

Robin Cooper and Peter B.B. Turney, Zytec Corporation (c). Harvard Business School, No.
9-190-066 (April 18, 1990).

Other key terms/concepts for which there doesn't seem to be a single,
dominant reference include: **kanban** (queue limitation), **pull system,
cross-training, job rotation, pay-for-skills, skills certification, stand-up,
walk-around jobs, flow distance, space reduction, small plant size,
"containerization"** (down-sizing and partitioning containers), **supplier
partnership, supplier reduction, supplier certification, linearity, mixed-
model production, off-line buffer stock, dock-to-stock, dock-to-line,
direct shipment, vendor** (or supplier) **managed inventory (VMI), visual
management, focused factory, six sigma, value-adding (VA), non-value
adding (NVA),**

OTHER CASES—NOT USED IN THIS BOOK

My files contain write-ups and notes about efforts of many other companies
to implement flow manufacturing. They did not make the cut for inclusion
in this book for various reasons. Many are still in the form of rough notes
taken during my plant tours and are too limited in scope or interest to
pursue further. Others are written up in computer files, but were rejected as
being insufficiently interesting or overly brief. Still others are discussed in
bits and pieces in other books of mine. Finally, twenty-six cases were ruled

out for this book because they were already published in a 1987 casebook of mine. The following summarizes the content of that casebook.

From R.J. Schonberger. 1987. *World Class Manufacturing Casebook: Implementing JIT and TQC* (New York: Free Press). The 26 full cases include a hospital and an electric-power utility, the rest being manufacturers. The 17 listed below are the cases that would have been well suited for this book and that that I had personally developed. (A few others are impressive but were borrowed, with permission, from works of other authors.) Following the identifying case number and title are, in parentheses, some of the topics making up the case (4, 5, etc., are omitted case numbers).

1. HyGain-Telex: Analysis for JIT Production – Antennas, Lincoln, NE (lead time to work content ratio, kanban, cellular manufacturing, . . .)
2. Implementing Kanban at Hewlett-Packard, Fort Collins (A) – Desktop computers, Fort Collins, CO (line storage of raw materials, kanban shelving acting as Pareto charts, . . .)
3. Hewlett-Packard, Fort Collins (B): Keeping Operators Busy—and Productive – Desktop computers, Fort Collins, CO (labor flexibility)
6. Omark Industries: Top Management-Driven JIT, Portland, OR (quick setup, machine cells, TPM, supplier reduction, finished-goods reduction, supervisory resistance, . . .)
7. JIT Beginnings at Burlington Industries, Edgeley & Oakes, NA plants, Locations disguised, later revealed as Graham and Williamsburg, NC – Custom-length draperies (JIT in spinning and yarn prep, ratio of lead time to process time, batch production and changeovers, size of equipment . . .)
8. Toyondu Company: Developing a Small Average Supplier into a Top-Notch Supplier – Panels and brackets for Nihon Trucks, Names disguised, later revealed as Nihon Chukuko supplier to Isuzu trucks – Tokyo, Japan (effects on marketing for JIT supplier . . .)
9. JIT at Intel—Penang, Malaysia – Semiconductor assembly & test, Penang (kanban, containerization, multiple pieces of equipment per process, JIT suppliers)
10. JIT at Intel—Manila, Philippines – Semiconductor assembly & test, Manila (flow lines, under-capacity scheduling of labor, length of assembly conveyor . . .)
11. Just-in-Time Production at Hewlett-Packard, Personal Computer Division – PCs, Sunnyvale, CA (parts standardization, supplier

reduction, keeping problems visible, equipment mobility, flow-line layout, intermingled desks and machines, . . .)

12. In-Line Manufacturing (Alias JIT) at Heatilator – Zero-clearance fireplaces, Mt. Pleasant, IA (post-poning MRP development; carrying-cost rate; relayout of shears, presses, brakes, backward integraton, paint conveyor; hand-push or lift truck . . .)

13. H-P—Computer Systems Division – HP 3000 minicomputer, Cupertino, CA (JIT supplier, kanban, performance data on display, disappearance of maintenance as a function . . .)

16. Getting Ready for Mixed-Model Production at Kawasaki Motors – Motorcycles, Lincoln, NE (pre-automation, mixed-model assembly sequence, . . .)

17. Ultrix Corporation – Computer printers, names disguised, later revealed as Hewlett-Packard, Vancouver, WA (from autonomous to sequential assembly, from batch to rate-based assembly, dock-to-line delivery, cross-training direct and indirect labor, backflush, . . .)

20. TQC/JIT at Tennant Company – Industrial floor sweepers/scrubbers, Minneapolis, MN (warehouse on wheels, process accounting . . .)

21. Goodstone Tire Company: Creating Responsibility Centers – Vehicle tires, Name and location disguised, later revealed as Firestone, Albany, GA (flow racks, eliminating AS/RSs, automated handling vs. cells, . . .)

22. Land and Sky Waterbed Company – Waterbeds, Lincoln, NE (make-to-order JIT, pay for knowledge/multifunctional employees . . .)

24. JIT Beginnings—Hewlett-Packard, Greeley Division – Small disc drives, Fort Collins, CO (computer-generated kanban signals, vendor day, group technology cells, . . .)

Index